Barbour's
BIBLE
Dictionary
&
Concordance

Barbour's

BIBLE

Dictionary
&
Concordance

George W. Knight
Rayburn W. Ray

BARBOUR BOOKS
An Imprint of Barbour Publishing, Inc.

Dictionary © 1998 by George W. Knight and Rayburn W. Ray
Concordance © 2002 by George W. Knight

Print ISBN 978-1-68322-298-9

Dictionary text previously published as *Layman's Bible Dictionary*,
Quicknotes Bible Dictionary, and *Pocket Bible Dictionary*. Concordance
text previously published as *Layman's Bible Concordance*, *Layman's Quick
Reference Concordance*, and *Quicknotes Bible Concordance*. All published by
Barbour Publishing, Inc.

All Scripture quotations are taken from the King James Version of the
Bible.

Published by Barbour Books, an imprint of Barbour Publishing, Inc., P.O.
Box 719, Uhrichsville, Ohio 44683, www.barbourbooks.com

*Our mission is to publish and distribute inspirational products offering
exceptional value and biblical encouragement to the masses.*

ecpa Member of the
Evangelical Christian
Publishers Association

Printed in the United States of America.

A Handy Two-in-One Book
for Effective Bible Study

This two-part book is designed to give you as a Bible student easy access to the treasures of the Word of God. The first part (pages 9–353) is a concise Bible dictionary with hundreds of brief articles on the major people, places, events, and doctrines of the Bible. The second part (pages 355–697) consists of a key-word concordance to help you find specific verses in the Bible on hundreds of important subjects. Here are some handy features of each of these two sections that should make your study of the Scriptures an exciting experience.

Bible Dictionary

The articles in this section are keyed to the familiar King James Version of the Bible. But variant words from more modern translations are cross-referenced to their King James equivalents.

For example, *Middle Wall of Partition* is the KJV term for the curtain that hung in the temple in New Testament times. When Jesus died on the cross, this curtain was split from top to bottom to symbolize that His sacrifice provided universal access to God. The term for this object is rendered as *Barrier* or *Dividing Wall* by modern translations. These variants appear in parentheses after the KJV main entry: **MIDDLE WALL OF PARTITION (BARRIER, DIVIDING WALL).** These words within the dictionary text are then cross-referenced back to this main entry in this fashion: **BARRIER.** See *Middle Wall of Partition.*

This same technique is also used for different words in the KJV Bible that refer to the same person or place. For example, the apostle Matthew was also known as *Levi.* The key word in the dictionary article on Matthew appears as **MATTHEW/LEVI**, and the word *Levi* within the running text is cross-referenced like this: **LEVI.** See *Matthew.*

Concordance

The words in this section are also based on the King James Version. But unlike exhaustive concordances such as *Strong's*, only the most important words and verses from the Bible are included in this concise collection.

Many forms of the same root word are listed under the main word in many cases. See the entry on **MOCK [ED, ETH, ING]** for a good example of this approach. In addition, many familiar biblical phrases such as **ARM OF THE LORD, ETERNAL LIFE**, and **PREACH THE GOSPEL** are included as concordance entries. And even some famous biblical truths and events such as **REMISSION OF SINS** and **PLAGUES AGAINST EGYPT** are listed as main entries. All these techniques make it possible to include more concordance entries in a concise format, thus adding to the value of this book as a Bible study tool.

I am pleased to add this book to others I have written over the years to help lay students come to a better understanding of the Bible. My prayer is that you will "study to shew thyself approved unto God, a workman that needeth not to be ashamed, rightly dividing the word of truth" (2 Timothy 2:15).

George W. Knight
Hartselle, Alabama

CONTENTS

Dictionary 9
Concordance. 355

BIBLE DICTIONARY

George W. Knight
Rayburn W. Ray

-A-

AARON. The first high priest of the Israelites (Exod. 28:1) and Moses' brother (Exod. 4:14). Designated by God as spokesman for Moses (Exod. 4:13–16), Aaron helped Moses lead the Hebrew slaves out of Egypt (Exod. 7:8–12). In the wilderness, he was consecrated by God as Israel's first high priest, and his sons inherited this position from their father (Num. 3:32). Like Moses, Aaron was not allowed to enter the Promised Land because of his act of unfaithfulness in the wilderness (Num. 20:6–12). His earthly priesthood is compared unfavorably to the eternal priesthood of Christ (Heb. 5:4; 7:11). See also *High Priest; Priest.*

AARONITES. Descendants of Aaron who were a part of the priestly tribe of Levi. A large force of Aaronites fought with David against King Saul (1 Chron. 12:27–28).

AB. The fifth month of the Jewish year, roughly equivalent to our modern August. This month is referred to, though not specifically by name, in Num. 33:38.

ABADDON/APOLLYON. A Hebrew word meaning "destruction," used to characterize the angel of the bottomless pit (Rev. 9:11; *apollyon:* Greek form).

ABANA RIVER. A river of Syria which flowed through the city of Damascus. It was mentioned by Naaman the leper as more favorable for bathing than the Jordan River (2 Kings 5:12). See also *Pharpar.*

ABARIM. A rugged mountain range east of the Jordan River in Moab from which Moses viewed the Promised Land before his death (Deut. 32:48–50).

ABBA. An Aramaic word meaning "father," used by Jesus while praying in Gethsemane (Mark 14:32, 36). It was also used by Paul to express the Christian's sonship with God the Father (Rom. 8:15).

ABDON. A minor judge of Israel who ruled for eight years (Judg. 12:13–15). See also *Judges of Israel.*

ABED-NEGO/AZARIAH. One of Daniel's three friends. Thrown into the fiery furnace by King Nebuchadnezzar of Babylonia (Dan. 3:13–27), he was later promoted by the king after his miraculous deliverance at the hand of God (Dan. 3:28–30). *Azariah:* Hebrew form (Dan. 1:7).

ABEL.

1. Second son of Adam and Eve (Gen. 4:2). Abel's animal sacrifice was pleasing to God (Gen. 4:4). Abel was then killed by his brother Cain in a jealous rage (Gen. 4:5, 8). Jesus regarded "righteous Abel" as the first martyr (Matt. 23:35). Abel's works were called "righ-teous" (1 John 3:12), and his sacrifices were commended as a testimony of faith (Heb. 11:4).

2. A fortified city in northern Israel where Sheba sought refuge during his rebellion against David. The citizens of Abel killed Sheba to end the siege by the king's army (2 Sam. 20:14–22).

ABIA. See *Abijah.*

ABIAH. A son of Samuel and corrupt judge of Israel. Abiah's dishonesty, along with that of his brother Joel, led the people to ask Samuel to appoint a king to rule the nation (1 Sam. 8:2–5). See also *Joel,* No. 2.

ABIATHAR. A high priest under David who remained faithful to the king during Absalom's rebellion (2 Sam. 15:24–35). He was later banished from the royal court by Solomon for supporting Adonijah as king (1 Kings 1:7–25; 2:22–35).

ABIB/NISAN. The first month of the Hebrew year, the time when barley opened (Exod. 13:4). Roughly equivalent to our modern April, this month was known as *Nisan* after the Babylonian Exile (Esther 3:7).

ABIGAIL. A wife of David and the mother of Chileab (2 Sam. 3:3). While married to Nabal, Abigail appeased David's anger after Nabal rejected David's servants (1 Sam. 25:14–35). She became David's wife after Nabal's death (1 Sam. 25:36 –42). See also *Nabal.*

ABIHU. One of Aaron's four sons. Abihu and his brother Nadab offered "strange fire," or a forbidden sacrifice, to God—an act for which they were destroyed by fire from God (Lev. 10:1–7). See also *Nadab,* No. 1.

ABIJAH/ABIJAM/ABIA. The son and successor of Rehoboam as king of Judah (reigned about 913–911 B.C.; 2 Chron. 11:20–22). *Abijam:* 1 Kings 14:31; *Abia:* Jesus' ancestry (Matt. 1:7).

ABILENE. A province of Syria governed by the tetrarch Lysanias during the ministry of John the Baptist (Luke 3:1–2). See also *Lysanias*.

ABIMELECH.
1. A Philistine king of Gerar in Abraham's time. He took Sarah, Abraham's wife, into his harem, then returned her to Abraham when he was informed in a dream that she was married (Gen. 20:1–8). After this incident, Abraham and Abimelech signed a treaty (Gen. 21:22–32).
2. A rebellious son of Gideon who killed all his brothers after his father's death in an attempt to become king over all Israel (Judg. 9:5–22). He was killed by his armorbearer after a woman dropped a stone on his head from a city wall (Judg. 9:50–54).

ABINADAB.
1. A man of Kirjath-jearim whose household kept the ark of the covenant for twenty years after it was returned by the Philistines (1 Sam. 7:1–2).
2. A son of King Saul killed at Gilboa, along with Jonathan (1 Chron. 10:1–6).

ABIRAM. A rebel against Moses in the wilderness who died in an earthquake because of his disobedience (Num. 16:1–33).

ABISHAG. A young woman who served as David's nurse in his old age (1 Kings 1:1–15). David's son Adonijah was killed by Solomon for desiring to marry her after David's death (1 Kings 2:13–25).

ABISHAI. The deputy commander of David's army (2 Sam. 10:9–10). Loyal to David in Absalom's rebellion (2 Sam. 16:9–12), he also saved David's life by killing a giant (2 Sam. 21:16–17).

ABISHALOM. See *Absalom*.

ABITAL. A wife of David and mother of his son Shephatiah, who was born at Hebron (2 Sam. 3:2–5).

ABLUTION. The ceremonial washing of a person's body or clothing to make them pure. Such washing was commanded in the O.T. law (Exod. 40:12 –13). True cleansing is found only in the blood of Christ (Rev. 1:5). See also *Clean*.

ABNER. The commander-in-chief of Saul's army. He introduced David to King Saul (1 Sam. 17:55–58) and established Saul's son Ish-bosheth as king after Saul's death (2 Sam. 2:8–10). Later he shifted his loyalty to David and persuaded all the tribes to follow David's leadership (2 Sam. 3:16–21). Although killed by David's commander Joab, Abner was buried with honor at David's command (2 Sam. 3:27–39).

ABOMINATION. Something considered repulsive by the Hebrews. Examples of these despised practices are heathen idolatry (Deut. 7:25–26), blemished animal sacrifices (Deut. 17:1), sexual transgressions (Lev. 18), child sacrifice (Deut. 12:31), and the practice of witchcraft, magic, and spiritism (Deut. 18:9–12). Most of these despised practices were also regarded as an abomination to God (Lev. 18:26).

ABOMINATION OF DESOLATION. The action of Antiochus Epiphanes in sacrificing a pig in the Jewish temple about 165 B.C. This despised act of the Syrian ruler is considered fulfillment of Daniel's prophecy (Dan. 9:24–27; Matt. 24:15). See also *Antiochus IV Epiphanes; Maccabees.*

ABRAHAM/ABRAM. The father of the nation of Israel (Ps. 105:6, 9). A native of Ur in southern Babylonia, he married Sarah and went to Haran (Gen. 11:28–31). Later he obeyed God's call to leave Haran for a "land that I will shew thee" (Gen. 12:1–5). God made a covenant with Abraham to bless all nations of the world through him (Gen. 12:2–3). The land of Canaan was also promised to Abraham's descendants (Gen. 12:7; 13:14–18).

Although Abraham and Sarah were childless at an advanced age, God promised Abraham a son (Gen. 15:1–21; 17:21). At Sarah's urging, Abraham fathered Ishmael by Sarah's servant Hagar (Gen. 16:1–4, 15). God changed the name of Abraham and Sarah from *Abram* and *Sarai* (Gen. 17:5–16) and established circumcision as a covenant sign (Gen. 17:6–27). The covenant was to be fulfilled through Isaac rather than Ishmael (Gen. 17:20–21; Gal. 4:22–31). Isaac was born in the couple's old age (Gen. 21:1–5).

As a test of faith, God asked Abraham to sacrifice Isaac (Gen. 22:1–13). Then God Himself intervened to save Isaac and again promised to bless Abraham for his unwavering faith (Gen. 22:16–18). Abraham died at 175 years of age and was buried beside Sarah near Hebron (Gen. 25:7–10).

The sea wall of the ancient city of Accho, located on the coast of the Mediterranean Sea. *Courtesy Israel Ministry of Tourism*

Abraham remains a model of righteousness and faith for all believers (Gen. 26:24; Ps. 47:9; Isa. 41:8). An ancestor of Christ, he is viewed as a spiritual father of all who share a like faith in Christ (Matt. 1:1; 3:9; Rom. 11:1; Gal. 3:6–9). See also *Sarah*.

ABRAHAM'S BOSOM. A symbolic expression for the blissful state after death (Luke 16:22). The Jews believed they joined their forefathers, particularly "father Abraham," upon their death (Gen. 15:15).

ABSALOM/ABISHALOM. The vain, rebellious son of David (2 Sam. 3:3). He killed his brother Amnon for molesting their sister Tamar (2 Sam. 13:22–33). Absalom conspired against David and seized Jerusalem (2 Sam. 15:1–29). Massing an army against David (2 Sam. 17:24–26), he was killed by David's commander Joab after his hair was tangled in a tree (2 Sam. 18:9–18). David mourned grievously at Absalom's death (2 Sam. 18:19–33). *Abishalom:* 1 Kings 15:2–10. See also *David*.

ABSTINENCE. To refrain from eating or drinking harmful substances or participating in sinful acts. Priests and Nazarites abstained from strong

15

drink (Lev. 10:9; Num. 6:1–4). Gentile Christians were advised to abstain from fornication and idolatry (Acts 15:20). All believers are counseled by Paul to refrain from any practices that might offend a weak brother (Rom. 14:21). See also *Moderation; Temperance.*

ABYSS/BOTTOMLESS PIT. A word translated literally as "bottomless pit" in the book of Revelation, indicating the place where Satan dwells (Rev. 9:1–2, 11).

ACACIA. See *Shittah.*

ACCAD (AKKAD). A fortified city built by Nimrod, a descendant of Noah (Gen. 10:8–10), in the land of Shinar—an ancient kingdom between the Tigris and Euphrates rivers. *Akkad:* NIV.

ACCHO/ACRE (ACCO). A coastal city near Mount Carmel in the territory of Asher (Judg. 1:31). This is the same city as N.T. *Ptolemais* (Acts 21:7). It is known today as *Acre. Acco:* NIV, NRSV.

ACCOUNTABILITY. The biblical principle that each person is answerable to God and responsible for his actions (Rom. 14:12). Accountability also involves the obligation to

act with love toward fellow believers (Rom. 14:15–19).

ACELDAMA (AKELDAMA, HAKELDAMA). A field near Jerusalem purchased with the money which Judas was paid to betray Jesus. The name means "field of blood" (Acts 1:15–19). *Akeldama:* NIV; *Hakeldama:* NRSV.

ACHAIA. A province of Greece visited by the apostle Paul (Acts 18:12). Christians at Achaia contributed to their impoverished brethren at Jerusalem (Rom. 15:26). Paul commended the Christians at Achaia (2 Cor. 11:10).

ACHAICUS. A Christian from the city of Corinth who visited Paul (1 Cor. 16:17–18).

ACHAN/ACHAR. A warrior under Joshua who was stoned to death for withholding the spoils of war (Josh. 7:16–25). *Achar:* 1 Chron. 2:7.

ACHAZ. See *Ahaz.*

ACHISH. A Philistine king of the city of Gath who provided refuge to David when he fled from King Saul (1 Sam. 21:10–15; 27:5–7).

ACHMETHA (ECBATANA). The capital city of the empire of the Medes and later one of the capitals of the Persian Empire (Ezra 6:2). *Ecbatana:* NIV, NRSV.

ACHSHAPH. A royal Canaanite city captured by Joshua (Josh. 11:1; 12:7, 20).

ACRE. See *Accho.*

ACTS OF THE APOSTLES. The one book of history in the N.T. which traces the expansion and development of the early church from the ascension of Jesus to Paul's imprisonment in Rome—a period of about thirty-five years. Written by Luke as a companion or sequel to his Gospel and addressed to Theophilus (see Luke 1:3–4; Acts 1:1–2), Acts shows clearly how the Christian witness spread in accordance with the Great Commission of Jesus (see Acts 1:8): (1) in Jerusalem (1:1–8:3), (2) throughout Judea and Samaria (8:4–12:25), and (3) to the entire world (13:1–28:31). See also *Luke.*

ADAM. The first man. Created in God's image (Gen. 1:26–27), Adam was an upright and intelligent being (Gen. 2:19–20)—the first worker (Gen. 2:8, 15) and the first husband (Gen. 2:18–25). He received God's Law (Gen. 2:16–17) and knowingly sinned, along with Eve (Gen. 3:6). Their sin resulted in broken fellowship with the Creator (Gen. 3:8) and brought God's curse (Gen. 3:14–19) and eviction from Eden (Gen. 3:22–24). Adam fathered Cain and Abel (Gen. 4:1–2), Seth (Gen. 4:25), and other children (Gen. 5:3–4). He died at age 930 (Gen. 5:5).

As head of the human race, Adam introduced sin into the world. He represents the lost and dying condition of all unrepentant sinners (Rom. 5:12–19; 1 Cor. 15:22). But Christ, referred to in the N.T. as the "Second Adam," offers deliverance from the curse of sin and death (Rom. 5:14–19; 1 Cor. 15:22). See also *Eden, Garden of; Eve; Fall of Man.*

ADAMANT. A precious stone, possibly corundum (Ezek. 3:9; Zech. 7:12).

ADAR. The twelfth month of the Jewish year, roughly equivalent to parts of our modern February and March. Haman ordered the massacre of the Jews on the thirteenth day of this month (Esther 3:13).

ADDER. See *Asp.*

17

ADMAH. One of the five cities near the Dead Sea destroyed with Sodom and Gomorrah (Gen. 10:19; Deut. 29:23). See also *Cities of the Plain.*

ADONAI. The Hebrew name for God, translated "Lord" (Ezek. 11:8). See also *God; Lord.*

ADONIJAH. David's fourth son and rival of Solomon for the throne (2 Sam. 3:4; 1 Kings 1:5, 30). Adonijah was executed by Solomon (1 Kings 2:19–25).

ADONI-ZEDEC. One of five Amorite kings who joined forces to oppose Joshua's army at Gibeon. He was defeated and killed by Joshua (Josh. 10:1–26).

ADOPTION. The legal act of giving status of a family member (Exod. 2:9–10; Esther 2:7). Paul spoke of adoption in symbolic, spiritual terms (Rom. 11:1–32; Gal. 4:4–7). Adoption as God's children is made possible by faith in Christ (Gal. 3:24–26). See also *Inheritance.*

ADORAIM. A city in southwest Judah rebuilt and fortified by King Rehoboam, son of Solomon (2 Chron. 11:5, 9). Now known as *Dura,* it is located five miles southwest of Hebron.

ADRAMMELECH. A pagan God worshiped by Assyrian colonists who settled in Samaria after the fall of the Northern Kingdom. Children were offered as sacrifices to this god (2 Kings 17:31).

ADRAMYTTIUM. An important seaport in the Roman province of Asia. Paul boarded a "ship of Adramyttium" to begin his voyage to Rome (Acts 27:2).

ADRIA/ADRIATIC SEA. A name for the central part of the Mediterranean Sea, south of modern Italy. Paul was shipwrecked here during his voyage to Rome (Acts 27:27). *Adriatic Sea:* NIV.

ADULLAM. A royal Canaanite city conquered by Joshua (Josh. 12:7, 15). In later years David sought refuge in a cave near here (1 Sam. 22:1–2).

ADULTERY. Sexual intercourse with a person other than one's husband or wife. Adultery is specifically prohibited by the seventh of the Ten Commandments (Exod. 20:14). Jesus expanded the concept to prohibit the cultivation of lust and desire which leads to adultery (Matt. 5:28). See also *Fornication.*

ADVENT OF CHRIST, THE FIRST. The birth of Jesus Christ in human form to the virgin Mary. His coming was foretold in the O.T. (Isa. 7:14; 9:6). Joseph was reassured by an angel that Mary's pregnancy was supernatural (Matt. 1:20–21). The angel Gabriel announced His coming birth to Mary (Luke 1:26–35).

Jesus was born to Mary in Bethlehem (Matt. 1:25; 2:1). His birth was revealed to shepherds (Luke 2:8–16). Wise men from the East brought gifts to the Christ child (Matt. 2:1–11). His birth was defined as a redemptive mission (Matt. 1:21–23; Luke 2:10–11). It nullified the O.T. ceremonial system (Heb. 9) and introduced the gospel age (Acts 3:20–26). See also *Incarnation of Christ; Virgin Birth.*

ADVERSARY. An active opponent; a term descriptive of Satan (1 Pet. 5:8). God's wisdom is promised to believers when they face the adversary (Luke 21:15). We are also promised that God's judgment will ultimately fall on His enemies (Heb. 10:27).

ADVERSITY. Difficult or unfavorable circumstances, perhaps caused by sin (Gen. 3:16–17) or disobedience toward God (Lev. 26:14–20). Adversity may also be used by God to test our faith (1 Pet. 1:5–8) or to chasten and correct (Heb. 12:5–11). See also *Suffering; Tribulation.*

ADVOCATE. One who pleads the cause of another (1 John 2:1). As the advocate, the Holy Spirit provides power for worldwide evangelism (Acts 1:8) and will abide with believers forever (John 14:16). See also *Comforter; Counsellor; Holy Spirit; Paraclete.*

AENEAS. A lame man healed by Peter at Lydda near Joppa. His conversion influenced many people to turn to Christ (Acts 9:32–35).

AENON. A place near Salim, exact location unknown, where John the Baptist baptized. It was probably near the Jordan River, "because there was much water there" (John 3:23).

AFFLICTION. Any condition which causes suffering or pain. Affliction may come as a result of God's judgment on sin (Rom. 2:9), or it may be an instrument of purification and perfection for believers (Rom. 5:3–5; 2 Thess. 1:4–7). See also *Anguish; Persecution; Suffering.*

AFRICA. See *Libya.*

AGABUS. A Christian prophet who warned Paul in Antioch of Syria of a worldwide famine (Acts 11:28). At Caesarea, Agabus used a symbolic demonstration to predict Paul's impending arrest (Acts 21:10–11).

AGAG.
1. A king of Amalek in Balaam's prophecy. Balaam predicted that Israel's king would be more powerful than Agag (Num. 24:7).
2. An Amalekite king spared by King Saul, in disobedience of God's command. Saul's disobedience led to his rejection as king of Israel by the Lord (1 Sam. 15:8–23). This may be the same king as Agag, No. 1.

AGAPE. A Greek word for selfless love, the type of love which characterizes God (John 15:13; 1 John 3:16). Agape is primarily an act of the will rather than the emotions (John 3:16; Rom. 5:8). Agape love for others is a badge of discipleship (John 13:34–35). This love is the greatest and most enduring of all Christian virtues (1 Cor. 13). See also *Love*.

AGAR. See *Hagar*.

AGATE. A precious stone in the breastplate of the high priest (Exod. 28:19), probably a distinct variety of quartz. See also *Chalcedony*.

AGORA. See *Marketplace*.

AGRIPPA. See *Herod*, No. 5 and 6.

AGUE. See *Burning Ague*.

AGUR. The author of Proverbs 30. Nothing else is known about Agur.

AHAB. The wicked king of Israel (reigned about 874–853 B.C.) and husband of Jezebel. Ahab was known as an aggressive builder (1 Kings 22:39). Influenced by Jezebel, he introduced Baal worship into Israel (1 Kings 16:31–33). His pagan practices were denounced by the prophet Elijah (1 Kings 17:1). Ahab waged war against King Ben-hadad of Syria (1 Kings 20:1–43) and was killed in a battle at Ramoth-gilead (1 Kings 22:34–38). See also *Jezebel*.

AHASUERUS. A king of Persia who married Esther and listened to her counsel regarding the Jewish people. He ordered his aide Haman executed—an act which saved the Jewish people from destruction (Esther

7:1–10). Most scholars agree that this Ahasuerus is the same person as King Xerxes I of Persian history (reigned 485–464 B.C.). See also *Esther; Haman.*

AHAVA/IVAH (IVVAH). A town in Babylonia where the Jewish exiles gathered after their deportation to this pagan nation. Ezra camped near a stream with this name before leading a group of exiles back to Jerusalem (Ezra 8:15–31). *Ivah:* 2 Kings 18:34; *Ivvah:* NIV, NRSV.

AHAZ/ACHAZ. A king of Judah (reigned about 742–727 B.C.) who practiced idolatry. Ahaz defended Jerusalem against Rezin of Syria and Pekah of Israel (2 Kings 16:5–6), but he was eventually defeated and many citizens of Judah were taken captive (2 Chron. 28:5–8). He foolishly paid tribute to the king of Assyria (2 Kings 16:7–9). *Achaz:* Jesus' ancestry (Matt. 1:9).

AHAZIAH.
1. A king of Israel (reigned about 853–852 B.C.) and son of Ahab. A Baal worshiper (1 Kings 22:51–53), he was seriously injured in a fall from the balcony of his palace. After consulting a pagan god for help, he died, in fulfillment of Elijah's

prophecy (2 Kings 1:2–18).
2. A king of Judah (reigned about 850 B.C.). The son of Jehoram and Athaliah, he followed in their evil ways by practicing idol worship. He was eventually assassinated by Jehu (2 Kings 9:27–28). *Jehoahaz:* 2 Chron. 21:17; *Azariah:* 2 Chron. 22:6.

AHIHUD. A leader of the tribe of Asher, appointed by Moses to help divide the land of Canaan after its occupation by the Israelites (Num. 34:27).

AHIJAH. A prophet who revealed to Jeroboam the forthcoming split of Solomon's united kingdom (1 Kings 11:29–30). Later, Ahijah foretold the death of Jeroboam's son and the elimination of his line from the kingship (1 Kings 14:1–8). See also *Jeroboam,* No. 1.

AHIKAM. An officer in King Josiah's court who protected the prophet Jeremiah from the persecution of King Jehoiakim (Jer. 26:24).

AHIMAAZ. A son of Zadok the high priest (1 Chron. 6:8–9) who warned David of Absalom's plans for rebellion. Ahimaaz also reported Absalom's defeat and death to David (2 Sam. 18:19–30).

AHIMELECH. The high priest at Nob during the reign of Saul (1 Sam. 21:1). He befriended David during his flight from Saul (1 Sam. 21:2–9). Ahimelech was killed at Saul's command (1 Sam. 22:16–19).

AHINOAM. One of David's wives (1 Sam. 25:43) and the mother of his son Amnon (2 Sam. 3:2).

AHITHOPHEL. One of David's aides who joined Absalom's rebellion (2 Sam. 15:12, 31). He committed suicide when he realized Absalom's plot was doomed (2 Sam. 17:23).

AI/AIATH/AIJA/HAI. A royal Canaanite city which first defied Joshua and then later was defeated and destroyed by the invading Israelites (Josh. 7:2–5; 8:18–21). *Aiath:* Isa. 10:28; *Aija:* Neh. 11:31; *Hai:* Gen. 12:8.

AIJALON/AJALON. A city in the territory of Dan (1 Sam. 14:31) where Joshua battled the five Amorite kings, during which the sun stood still (Josh. 10:12–13). *Ajalon:* Josh. 19:42.

AIJELETH SHAHAR. A musical term in the title of Ps. 22, probably indicating the melody to be sung.

AIN. The sixteenth letter of the Hebrew alphabet, used as a heading over Ps. 119:121–128.

AJALON. See *Aijalon.*

AKELDAMA. See *Aceldama.*

AKKAD. See *Accad.*

ALABASTER. A soft stone, similar to gypsum, which was carved into vases, boxes, jars, etc. Jesus was anointed with perfume from an alabaster box (Mark 14:3).

ALAMOTH. A musical term in the title of Ps. 46, perhaps referring to a choir of women's voices (1 Chron. 15:20).

ALEPH. The first letter of the Hebrew alphabet, used as a heading over Ps. 119:1–8.

ALEXANDER.
1. An unfaithful disciple at Ephesus condemned by Paul (1 Tim. 1:19–20).
2. Alexander the Great or Alexander III of Macedonia, Greek ruler and world conqueror. Alexander took the throne in 336 B.C. and extended his empire from Greece around the Mediterranean Sea to Egypt and then to India. He died in Babylonia at age 33. Although he is not mentioned

by name in the Bible, Alexander is perhaps the "mighty king" of Dan. 11:3–4. (See also Dan. 7:6; 8:21.)

ALEXANDRIA. A city of Egypt founded by Alexander the Great which was a cultural center and capital city of Egypt in N.T. times. Citizens of Alexandria opposed Stephen (Acts 6:9). Apollos was a native of this city (Acts 18:24). Paul left Malta for Rome on a ship from Alexandria (Acts 28:11). Jewish scholars were commissioned in this city to translate the O.T. from Hebrew into Greek—the famed version of the Bible known as the Septuagint. Alexandria was well known for its extensive library, which drew scholars from throughout the ancient world. See also *Septuagint.*

ALGUM/ALMUG. A tree imported from Lebanon (2 Chron. 2:8). Its wood was used in Solomon's temple in Jerusalem. *Almug:* 1 Kings 10:11–12.

ALIEN. A foreigner or stranger from a country other than Israel. Regarded as Gentiles, aliens did not enjoy the rights of the citizens of Israel (Deut. 14:21; Job 19:15). See also *Foreigner.*

ALLEGORY. A story which communicates an important truth in symbolic fashion. Paul spoke of the births of Ishmael and Isaac in allegorical terms (Gal. 4:22–26).

ALLELUIA. The Greek form of the Hebrew word *Hallelujah,* meaning "praise ye the Lord" (Rev. 19:1–6).

ALLIANCE. A treaty between nations or individuals. Alliances with conquered Canaanite nations were forbidden (Deut. 7:2–5; Exod. 23:32). The prophets warned Israel against forming alliances that might replace their dependence on God (Jer. 2:18). Nevertheless, alliances between O.T. characters and foreigners were common. Examples are: (1) Abraham with Abimelech of Gerar (Gen. 21:22–34); (2) King Solo-mon with Hiram of Tyre (1 Kings 5:1–12); and (3) Solomon's many marriage alliances (1 Kings 3:1; 11:1–3). See also *League.*

ALMIGHTY. A title of God which indicates His absolute power and majesty. God used this term to identify Himself as He talked to Abraham (Gen. 17:1). Ezekiel portrayed God in this light in his vision of God's glory (Ezek. 1:24; 10:5).

"Almighty" is also used of Christ (Rev. 1:8). See also *Sovereignty of God*.

ALMOND. A small tree known for its early spring blossoms. Jeremiah visualized an almond branch as a sign of God's rapidly approaching judgment against the nation of Judah (Jer. 1:11–12). See also *Hazel*.

ALMS. Voluntary gifts to the needy. The Israelites were commanded to be generous to the poor (Deut. 15:11). Jesus cautioned His disciples not to give alms for show or the praise of others (Matt. 6:2–4). See also *Poor*.

ALMUG. See *Algum*.

ALOES. A spice for embalming the dead, used by Joseph of Arimathea on the body of Jesus (John 19:38–39).

ALPHA AND OMEGA. The first and last letters of the Greek alphabet. Symbolic of the eternity of Christ, this title is applied to God the Father and God the Son (Rev. 1:8; 21:6–7). The risen Christ described Himself in this fashion, indicating He is the Creator, Redeemer, and Final Judge of all mankind (Rev. 22:13).

ALTAR. A platform, table, or elevated structure on which sacrifices were placed as offerings. Altars were originally made of earth or rocks (Exod. 20:24–25), but they evolved into more sophisticated structures after the construction of the tabernacle (Lev. 9:24). Pagan Canaanite altars were often called "high places" because they were built on hills or high platforms (Num. 33:52). See also *High Place*.

ALTASCHITH. A word of uncertain meaning in the titles of Pss. 57, 58, 59, and 75.

AMALEK. The son of Eliphaz, grandson of Esau, and ancestor of the Edomites (Gen. 36:9–12).

AMALEKITES. A tribal enemy of the Israelites. Their animosity against the Hebrews apparently began during the years of wilderness wandering with an unprovoked attack (Exod. 17:8–16). Saul battled this tribe as well (1 Sam. 14:48), and they suffered a major defeat at the hands of David (1 Sam. 30:1–31).

AMARNA TABLETS. Ancient clay tablets found in Egypt which were written by various kings shortly after the Israelites invaded Canaan under Joshua.

These tablets provided new insights into the culture and political unrest of the period. See also *Clay; Nuzi Tablets.*

AMASA. David's nephew and commander of Absalom's rebel army (2 Sam. 19:13). Later forgiven by David and appointed to command his army, Amasa was killed by Joab (2 Sam. 20:9–12).

AMAZIAH. A king of Judah (reigned about 796–767 B.C.; 2 Kings 14:1–20). He assembled an army to attack Edom and embraced the false gods of Edom (2 Chron. 25:5–15). Amaziah was assassinated by his political enemies (2 Chron. 25:25–28).

AMBASSADOR. A messenger, spokesman, or representative of a ruler or king. Paul considered himself an ambassador for Christ (Eph. 6:20) and applied this term figuratively to all believers (2 Cor. 5:20).

AMBASSAGE (DELEGATION). A group of ambassadors, or messengers (Luke 14:32). *Delegation:* NIV, NRSV.

AMBER. A gem or precious stone known for its yellowish-orange brilliance. Ezekiel compared God's glory to amber (Ezek. 1:4, 27; 8:2).

AMEN. A solemn word used to express approval (Neh. 8:6), confirm an oath (Neh. 5:13), or close a prayer (1 Cor. 14:16). Jesus is called "the Amen," meaning He is true and reliable (Rev. 3:14).

AMETHYST. A violet-colored precious stone in the breastplate of the high priest (Exod. 28:19), also used in the foundation of New Jerusalem (Rev. 21:20).

AMMIEL. One of the twelve spies who scouted the land of Canaan, representing the tribe of Dan (Num. 13:12). See also *Spies.*

AMMONITES. A race or tribe descended from Ammon who became enemies of the Israelites during the Exodus (Deut. 23:3). Their chief pagan god was Chemosh (Judg. 11:24), and the Israelites often indulged in their idolatrous practices (Ezra 9:1). Tobiah, an Ammonite, tried to prevent Nehemiah from rebuilding the walls of Jerusalem (Neh. 2:10, 19).

AMNON. A son of David. Amnon assaulted his half sister Tamar—an act avenged with his death at the hand of her brother Absalom (2 Sam. 3:2; 13:1–29). See also *Tamar,* No. 2.

AMON. An evil and idolatrous king of Judah who reigned for only two years, about 643–641 B.C. Assassinated by his own servants, he was succeeded by his son Josiah after his assassins were killed by the people of Judah (2 Kings 21:18–26). Amon is listed as an ancestor of Jesus (Matt. 1:10).

AMORITES. One of the tribal groups of Canaan defeated by the Israelites. Descendants of Ham through his son Canaan (Gen. 10:6), the Amorites were a formidable enemy, but Joshua broke their strength with victories over the armies of Sihon and Og (Josh. 12:1–6). Remnants of the Amorites were reduced to servitude under King Solomon (1 Kings 9:19–21). See also *Canaan,* No. 1.

AMOS. A herdsman from Tekoa in the Southern Kingdom (Judah) who prophesied against the Northern Kingdom (Israel) during the tenure of King Jeroboam II (Amos 1:1; 7:14–15). Known as the great "prophet of righteousness" of the O.T., he condemned the rich and indulgent for oppressing the poor (Amos 8:4–6) and foretold Israel's collapse and captivity by Assyria (Amos 7:17). A contemporary of Isaiah and Hosea, he regarded himself as a shepherd or herdsman who heeded God's call rather than a professional prophet (Amos 7:14–16).

AMOS, BOOK OF. A prophetic book of the Old Testament written by the prophet Amos about 760 B.C. to call the wayward people of the Northern Kingdom back to worship of the one true God. A short book of only nine chapters, Amos falls naturally into three major divisions: (1) Pronouncement of judgment on surrounding nations and Israel (1:3– 2:16); (2) three sermons of judgment against the idolatry, corruption, and oppression of Israel (3:1–6:14); and (3) five visions of God's approaching judgment against the nation (7:1–9:10).

Perhaps the greatest contribution of the book is the concept that religion demands righteous behavior. True religion is not a matter of observing rituals and feast days, Amos declared. It consists of following God's commands and treating others with justice: "Let judgment run down as waters, and righteousness as a mighty stream" (Amos 5:24).

AMPHIPOLIS. A city in the province of Macedonia through which Paul and Silas passed during the second missionary journey (Acts 17:1).

AMPLIAS. A fellow believer at Rome greeted and commended by Paul in his epistle to the Roman Christians (Rom. 16:8).

AMRAPHEL. A king of Shinar, or ancient Babylonia, who invaded the land of Canaan in Abraham's time (Gen. 14:1, 9).

ANAK. The son of Arba and ancestor of a tribe of giants (Deut. 9:2), or men of renown.

ANAKIMS (ANAKIM, ANAKITES). A tribe of giants, descended from Anak, who inhabited Canaan and were greatly feared in Joshua's time (Num. 13:28, 33; Deut. 9:2). The term may also refer to prominent people, or men of renown. Joshua divided their forces and captured their major walled city, Hebron, or Kirjath-arba (Josh. 14:12–15). The remnants of the Anakims may have been absorbed into the Philistine people. *Anakim:* NRSV; *Anakites:* NIV. See also *Emims*.

ANAMMELECH. A false god worshiped at Samaria by foreigners who settled the land after the defeat of the Northern Kingdom by Assyria (2 Kings 17:24, 31).

ANANIAS.
1. An early believer at Jerusalem struck dead for lying and withholding money he had pledged to the church's common treasury (Acts 5:1–11). See also *Sapphira*.
2. A believer at Damascus who befriended Paul. Ananias obeyed God's command to seek out Paul in spite of his reputation as a persecutor of Christians. He ministered to Paul as a fellow believer (Acts 9:10–18).

ANATHEMA. The transliteration of a Greek word which means "accursed" or "separated." In 1 Cor. 16:22, anathema expresses the concept of excommunication, or a cutting off of the offending party from the church.

ANATHOTH. A village about three miles north of Jerusalem and the birthplace of the prophet Jeremiah (Jer. 1:1).

ANCHOR. A heavy weight used to hold a ship steady (Acts 27:29, 40).

ANCIENT OF DAYS (ANCIENT ONE). A title for God used by the prophet Daniel to show His ruling authority over the world empires of his day (Dan. 7:9–22). *Ancient One:* NRSV.

ANDREW. One of the twelve disciples of Jesus and brother of Simon Peter. A fisherman from Bethsaida (John 1:44) on the shore of the Sea of Galilee, Andrew was a follower of John the Baptist before he became a disciple of Jesus (John 1:35–40). He was known as one who introduced others to Jesus, including his brother Simon (John 1:41–42), the boy with the loaves and fish (John 6:5–9), and certain Greek citizens who came to talk with Jesus (John 12:20–22). See also *Twelve, The.*

ANDRONICUS. A fellow believer at Rome greeted and commended by Paul in his letter to the Roman Christians (Rom. 16:7).

ANGEL. A spiritual or heavenly being whom God sends as His special messenger or helper to human beings. Angels are not to be identified with God Himself, since He created them (Ps. 148:2, 5). They serve under His direction and obey His commands (Ps. 103:20). Special functions of angels are delivering God's message to human beings (Luke 1:13), protecting God's people (Dan. 3:28), relieving human hunger and thirst (Gen. 21:17–19), and praising the name of the Lord (Ps. 103:20–21).

Before the creation of the world, certain angels revolted against God and were cast out of heaven. The ringleader of this revolt was Satan (Rev. 12: 7–9). Another of these fallen angels is Abaddon or Apollyon, "the angel of the bottomless pit" (Rev. 9:11). See also *Angel of the Lord; Gabriel; Michael,* No. 2.

ANGEL OF THE LORD. A heavenly being sent by God to human beings as His personal agent or spokesman. This messenger appeared to Hagar in the wilderness (Gen. 16:7–12), to Moses (Exod. 3:2–3), and to Gideon (Judg. 6:11–12).

ANGER. A strong feeling of displeasure. God is sometimes pictured as slow to anger (Nah. 1:3). Jesus condemned anger that was not godly anger (Matt. 5:22). See also *Wrath.*

ANGUISH. Mental or emotional stress caused by physical pain (2 Sam. 1:9), conflict of soul (Job 7:11), or physical hardships (Exod. 6:9). See also *Affliction; Suffering.*

ANISE (DILL). A common plant of little value used for seasoning food and for medicinal purposes. Jesus condemned those who tithed this insignificant plant but overlooked more important matters, such as judgment, mercy, and faith (Matt. 23:23). *Dill:* NIV, NRSV.

ANNA. An aged prophetess who praised God at Jesus' presentation as an infant in the temple at Jerusalem (Luke 2:36–38).

ANNAS. A Jewish high priest who presided at the trial of Jesus. He questioned Jesus about His disciples and His doctrine. After interrogation, Annas sent Jesus bound to Caiphas (John 18:12–24). The apostles Peter and John also appeared before Annas (Acts 4:6–7).

ANNUNCIATION. The angel Gabriel's announcement to Mary that she had been chosen to give birth to the Son of God (Luke 1:26–38). See also *Mary,* No. 1.

ANOINTED ONE. See *Jesus Christ; Messiah.*

ANOINTING. The act of setting a person apart for a specific work or task. In O.T. times kings, priests, and prophets were anointed by having oil poured on their heads (Exod. 29:7). Anointing for healing was practiced in N.T. times with the application of oil (Mark 6:13).

All Christians are anointed for service in God's kingdom (2 Cor. 1:21). See also *Oil.*

ANT. A small insect cited as an example of hard work (Prov. 6:6–8).

ANTEDILUVIANS. Persons who lived before the great flood. All except Noah were condemned for their wickedness (Gen. 6:5–8). See also *Flood, The.*

ANTHROPOMORPHISMS. Human attributes ascribed to God. For example, God is described as having an arm of deliverance (Exod. 6:6), eyes too pure to look upon evil (Hab. 1:13), and a nature that is provoked to anger and jealousy by idolatry (Ps. 78:58).

ANTICHRIST. The archenemy of Christ and all Christians who will be defeated in the end-time. Rooted in the prophecies of Daniel (Dan. 7:7–8), the Antichrist receives his authority and power from Satan (Rev. 13:4). He is lawless and deceitful (2 Thess. 2:3–12; 2 John 7). Characterized as a "beast," the Antichrist will appear before the return of Christ to wage war against Christ and His people (Rev. 13:6–8). However, he will be defeated by Christ and cast into a lake of fire (Rev. 19:20; 20:10). See also *Dragon*.

ANTINOMIANISM. The concept that grace exempts a person from the moral law. According to Paul, this idea is based on an erroneous view of grace (Rom. 6:1–2). Inconsistent with life in the spirit, antinomianism may cause a weak brother to stumble (1 Cor. 8:9). Abuse of Christian liberty violates the spirit of brotherly love (Gal. 5:13–16).

ANTIOCH OF PISIDIA. A city of Pisidia, a district in Asia Minor. Paul preached in the synagogue in this city, where resistance to the gospel caused him to redirect his ministry to the Gentiles (Acts 13:14–51). Paul later recalled his persecution at Antioch (2 Tim. 3:11). See also *Pisidia*.

ANTIOCH OF SYRIA. A city in Syria and site of the first Gentile Christian church which sent Paul on his missionary journeys (Acts 13:1–4; 15:35–41). Believers were first called Christians in this city (Acts 11:26). The church at Antioch was troubled by Judaizers who insisted that Gentile believers be circumcised (Acts 15:1–4).

ANTIOCHUS IV EPIPHANES. The cruel ruler of the Seleucid dynasty in Syria (ruled about 175–164 B.C.) whose atrocities led the Jewish people to revolt. He is not mentioned by name in the Bible, but see *Abomination of Desolation; Maccabees*.

ANTIPAS. A Christian martyr of the church at Pergamos (Rev. 2:13).

ANTIPATRIS. A city between Jerusalem and Caesarea where Paul was lodged as a prisoner while being transported to Caesarea (Acts 23:31).

ANVIL. A block of iron on which metal was shaped by a blacksmith (Isa. 41:7).

APE. A type of monkey, perhaps a baboon or chimpanzee, imported into Judah by King Solomon (1 Kings 10:22).

APELLES. A fellow believer at Rome greeted and commended by Paul in his letter to the Roman Christians (Rom. 16:10).

APHEK. A town in Jezreel where Syria's defeat was prophesied by the prophet Elisha (2 Kings 13:14–19).

APOCALYPSE. A Greek word translated "revelation" which refers to an unveiling of the hidden things known only to God (Gal. 1:12). The book of Revelation depicts the end of the present age and the coming of God's future kingdom through symbols, visions, and numbers. This imagery was probably used to hide the message in a time of persecution. Other examples of apocalyptic writing in the Bible are Dan. 7–12, Isa. 24–27, Ezek. 37–41, Zech. 9–12, Matt. 24, and Mark 13. See also *Revelation of John*.

APOCRYPHA. A group of books written about 150 B.C. to A.D. 70 and included in the Bibles of some religious groups. These books are generally not considered authoritative in the same sense as the universally recognized books of the Bible.

The books of the Apocrypha are Baruch; Bel and the Dragon; the Wisdom of Jesus, the Son of Sirach; the First and Second Books of Esdras; Additions to the Book of Esther; Epistle of Jeremiah; Judith; First and Second Maccabees; Prayer of Azariah and the Song of the Three Young Men; Prayer of Manasseh; Susanna; Tobit; and Wisdom of Solomon.

APOLLONIA. A town between Amphipolis and Thessalonica in the province of Macedonia. Paul and Silas passed through this city during the second missionary journey (Acts 17:1).

APOLLOS. A Jewish believer from Alexandria in Egypt who worked with the church at Ephesus after it was founded by Paul. Eloquent and learned, Apollos was a disciple of John the Baptist (Acts 18:24–25). Aquila and Priscilla instructed him in the true doctrines of the faith, and he became an effective church leader, preaching also in Achaia and Corinth with great success (1 Cor. 3:4–6, 22). Paul mentioned Apollos as one whom a faction of the Corinthian church favored (1 Cor. 1:12). See also *Aquila*.

APOLLYON. See *Abaddon*.

APOSTASY. A falling away from the truth or renunciation of one's faith in Christ (Heb. 3:12). Apostasy is caused by Satan (Luke 22:31–32) and influenced by false teachers (2 Tim. 4:3–4). Professed believers may fall away because of persecution (Matt. 13:21) or love of worldly things (2 Tim. 4:10). Apostasy will not occur if believers are grounded in the truth (Eph. 4:13–16) and depend on God's protective armor (Eph. 6:10–18).

APOSTLE. A person personally commissioned by Christ to represent Him (Matt. 10:1–4). The original twelve apostles or disciples were chosen by Jesus after He had prayed all night (Luke 6:12–16). Apostles are persons sent with a special message or commission (John 15:16). Jesus empowered His apostles to cast out evil spirits and to heal (Matt. 10:1).

Paul regarded himself as an apostle because of his encounter with Christ on the Damascus Road and his personal call by Jesus to missionary work (1 Cor. 15:8–10). In Paul's letters, persons who saw the risen Christ and who were specially called by Him are regarded as apostles (1 Cor. 15:5–8). See also *Disciple; Twelve, The.*

APOTHECARY (PERFUMER). A person who made perfumes, which were used in worship ceremonies or to anoint the bodies of the dead (Exod. 30:25–35) *Perfumer:* NIV, NRSV.

APPII FORUM (FORUM OF APPIUS). A station on the Roman road known as the Appian Way about forty miles south of Rome. Paul's friends traveled here to meet him as he approached the Roman Empire's capital city (Acts 28:15). *Forum of Appius:* NIV, NRSV.

AQUILA. A Christian believer who, with his wife Priscilla, worked with Paul at Corinth (Acts 18:2) and continued Paul's work at Ephesus (Acts 18:24–26). They were also associated with the church at Rome (Rom. 16:3).

ARABAH. The valley on both sides of the Jordan River which stretches for about 240 miles from Mt. Hermon in the north to the Red Sea in the south (Josh. 18:18).

ARABIA. A hot, dry, and sparsely inhabited desert area southeast of Palestine about 1,400 miles long by 800 miles wide. The queen of Sheba came from Arabia, bringing gold and precious jewels to King Solomon (1 Kings 10:2–15).

ARAD. A Canaanite city south of Hebron captured by Joshua (Josh. 12:7, 14).

ARAM.
1. A son of Shem (Gen. 10:22–23).
2. Another word for the nation of Syria (Num. 23:7). See also *Syria.*

ARARAT, MOUNT. A mountainous region where Noah's ark landed (Gen. 8:4). The location of this mountain is uncertain. Several unsuccessful expeditions to find the ark on Mount Urartu in eastern Armenia (modern Turkey) have been undertaken. See also *Ark, Noah's.*

ARAUNAH/ORNAN. A Jebusite from whom David bought a threshing floor as a place to build an altar (2 Sam. 24:16–24). This plot of ground was the site on which Solomon's temple was built in Jerusalem in later years (2 Chron. 3:1). *Ornan:* 1 Chron. 21:15; 2 Chron. 3:1.

ARBA. The father of Anak and ancestor of a tribe of giants known as the Anakims or Anakim (Josh. 14:15). See also *Anakims.*

ARCHAEOLOGY OF THE BIBLE. The study of remains of past civilizations in an attempt to understand the life and times of biblical peoples.

Archaeology involves scientific excavations, examination, and publication by museums and laboratories. Fragments of ancient writings as well as bones, metal, stone, and wood are studied. The focus area for N.T. archaeology largely coincides with the ancient Roman Empire. For the O.T. period, the focus of archaeology includes Palestine (Canaan), Syria, Egypt, the Mesopotamian Valley, and Persia (modern Iran).

Major methods of establishing dates for archaeological finds are (1) examination of the layers of soil in mounds or "tells" (stratigraphy), (2) the study of pottery materials and designs (typology), and (3) measurement of the radioactivity of an object's carbon content (radiocarbon dating).

Archaeology helps us understand the Bible better by revealing what life in biblical times was like, throwing light on obscure passages of Scripture, and helping us appreciate the historical setting of the Bible. For example, exploration of the city of Ur revealed that the home of Abraham was a thriving city of industry and idolatry in O.T. times. The Dead Sea Scrolls, the greatest manuscript discovery of modern times, includes a complete scroll of the book of Isaiah and fragments of most of the other O.T. books.

See also *Amarna Tablets; Dead Sea Scrolls; Nuzi Tablets; Ras Shamra Tablets.*

ARCHANGEL. A chief angel or perhaps a spiritual being next in rank above an angel. In the end-time Michael the archangel will contend with Satan (Jude 9) and proclaim the Lord's return (1 Thess. 4:16). See also *Angel; Michael,* No. 2.

ARCHELAUS. See *Herod,* No. 2.

ARCHER. A warrior skilled in shooting arrows with a bow (1 Sam. 31:3).

ARCHEVITES. Foreign colonists who settled in Samaria after the Northern Kingdom fell to Assyria (Ezra 4:9–16). See also *Samaritan.*

ARCHIPPUS. A fellow believer in the church at Colossae whom Paul encouraged (Col. 4:17).

ARCTURUS. A constellation of stars cited as evidence of God's sovereignty (Job 9:9).

AREOPAGUS. A council of Greek philosophers in Athens before whom Paul appeared to defend his claims about Jesus and His resurrection (Acts 17:19). The hill on which these philosophers met was apparently called *Mars' Hill* (Acts 17:22). See also *Athens.*

ARETAS. A ruler in northern Arabia whose deputy tried to capture Paul in Damascus after his conversion (2 Cor. 11:32).

ARGOB. A district of Bashan included in Solomon's kingdom. Argob contained sixty fortified cities (1 Kings 4:13).

ARIEL. A symbolic name for the city of Jerusalem, meaning "lion of God" (Isa. 29:1–2, 7). See also *Jerusalem.*

ARIMATHAEA (ARIMATHEA). A city in the Judean hills about five miles northwest of Jerusalem and home of the Joseph who buried the body of Jesus in his own tomb (John 19:38) *Arimathea:* NIV, NRSV. See also *Joseph,* No. 3.

ARISTARCHUS. A Christian who accompanied Paul on the third missionary journey (Acts 20:4). Later he traveled with Paul to Rome (Acts 27:2).

ARISTOBULUS. A fellow believer at Rome greeted and commended by Paul in his letter to the Roman Christians (Rom. 16:10).

ARK, NOAH'S. A large wooden ship in which Noah and his family and selected animals were delivered by God. The ark was necessary because God wished to preserve righteous Noah and his family while destroying the rest of mankind because of its wickedness. Noah built the ark according to God's directions (Gen. 6:14–16). Then he and his family entered the ark, along with a pair of all living creatures (Gen. 6:19–20). Rain fell for forty days (Gen. 7:17) and water covered the earth for 150 days (Gen. 7:24).

Finally, God sent a wind to restrain the water (Gen. 8:1–3) and the ark rested on a mountain in Ararat (Gen. 8:4). Noah and his passengers were delivered safely to dry land (Gen. 8:18, 19). Upon leaving the ark, Noah built an altar and offered sacrifices to God for their deliverance. God promised Noah that the earth would not be destroyed by water again (Gen. 8:20–22).

The ark is symbolic of baptism (1 Pet. 3:20–21) and God's preserving grace (Luke 17:26–27; Heb. 11:7). See also *Ararat, Mount; Noah.*

ARK OF THE COVENANT/ ARK OF THE TESTIMONY. A wooden chest containing two stone tablets on which the Ten Commandments were in-scribed. The ark symbolized God's presence to the nation of Israel (Deut. 10:3–4). It was taken into battle by the Israelites (1 Sam. 4:4–5) and captured by the Philistines (1 Sam. 4:10–11). After its return to Israel (1 Sam. 6:1–15), the ark was later placed in the temple in Jerusalem (1 Kings 8:1–11). It was probably carried away by King Nebuchadnezzar of Babylonia along with other treasures after the fall of Jerusalem (2 Chron. 36:6, 18). *Ark of the Testimony:* Exod. 25:22.

ARM OF GOD. Phrase which symbolizes God's strength and power (Ps. 89:10, 13).

ARMAGEDDON. A Greek word for the valley between Mount Carmel and the city of Jezreel. This valley was the site of many battles in Bible times due to its strategic location on two major trade routes. Because of its bloody history, this region became a symbol of the final conflict between God and the forces of evil, and of God's

35

ultimate victory (Rev. 16:16). See also *Megiddo*.

ARMENIA. A mountainous land north of Syria formerly known as Ararat (Isa. 37:38). See also *Ararat, Mount*.

ARMOR. Defensive covering used as protection during battle. The word is also symbolic of God's spiritual protection (Eph. 6:11).

ARMORBEARER. An aide or attendant who carried the armor and weapons of a military officer or warrior of high rank (Judg. 9:54).

ARNON. A swift river which runs through the mountains east of the Jordan River and into the Dead Sea (Josh. 12:1).

AROMATIC CANE. See *Calamus*.

ARPHAXAD. A son of Shem born after the great flood (Gen. 11:10–13).

ARROW. A projectile shot from a bow. This word is also used symbolically to denote a calamity inflicted by God (Job 6:4) or to signify something injurious, such as false testimony (Prov. 25:18).

ARTAXERXES I. The successor of Cyrus as king of Persia and the king in whose court Ezra and Nehemiah served (Ezra 7:1, 7). About 458 B.C. Artaxerxes authorized Ezra to lead a large group of Jews back to Jerusalem for resettlement (Ezra 7:1–28). About thirteen years later he allowed Nehemiah to return to rebuild the walls of Jerusalem (Neh. 2:1–10; 13:6). See also *Ezra; Nehemiah*.

ARTEMAS. A faithful coworker with Paul at Nicopolis (Titus 3:12).

ARTEMIS. See *Diana*.

ARTIFICER. A workman especially skilled in metalworking. Solomon hired craftsmen from Tyre with these skills to help build the temple in Jerusalem (2 Chron. 2:3, 7). See also *Smith*.

ASA. Third king of Judah (reigned about 911–869 B.C.) who led in a national religious revival. He destroyed the places of idol worship (2 Chron. 14:2–5) and fortified Judah to usher in a period of peace (2 Chron. 14:6–8). Reproved by Hanani the prophet for not relying on the Lord, he died from a foot disease (2 Chron.

16:7–14). Asa is listed as an ancestor of Jesus (Matt. 1:7).

ASAHEL. David's nephew and a captain in his army (1 Chron. 27:7). Asahel was killed by Abner, commander in Saul's army (2 Sam. 2:17–23).

ASAIAH. A Levite who helped David move the ark of the covenant to Jerusalem (1 Chron. 15:6, 11).

ASAPH. A Levite choir leader and writer of psalms mentioned in the titles of Pss. 50 and 73–83.

ASCENSION OF CHRIST. Jesus' return to His Father after His crucifixion and resurrection (Luke 24:50–51). Foretold in the O.T. (Ps. 68:18), the Ascension occurred forty days after the Resurrection (Acts 1:2–11). The event prompted great joy among early believers (Luke 24:52–53). Christ will return to earth as surely as He ascended to heaven (Acts 1:11).

ASCETICISM. Strict self-discipline and denial of bodily appetites. Asceticism was practiced by the Nazarites (Num. 6:1–21) and John the Baptist (Matt. 3:4). See also *Nazarite.*

ASENATH. The Egyptian wife of Joseph and mother of Manasseh and Ephraim (Gen. 46:20). The pharaoh of Egypt approved this union and probably arranged the marriage (Gen. 41:45). See also *Joseph,* No. 1.

ASHDOD. A major Philistine city (Josh. 13:3) and center of Dagon worship (1 Sam. 5:1–7). It was called *Azotus* in N.T. times (Acts 8:40). See also *Dagon; Philistines.*

ASHER/ASER. A son of Jacob by Zilpah (Gen. 30:12–13) and ancestor of one of the twelve tribes of Israel (Deut. 33:24). Asher's tribe settled in northern Canaan. *Aser:* Greek form (Luke 2:36). See also *Tribes of Israel.*

ASHES. Residue from burning. A symbol of mourning and repentance, ashes were also used for purification (Heb. 9:13).

ASHTAROTH/ASHTORETH. A pagan fertility goddess worshiped by the Philistines and also by the Israelites soon after the death of Joshua (Judg. 2:13). Her symbol was an evergreen tree, a pole, or a pillar near a pagan altar. *Ashtaroth, Ashtoreth:* plural forms (1 Sam. 7:4; 1 Kings 11:33).

ASHIMA. A false god worshiped by foreign colonists who settled in Samaria after the fall of the Northern Kingdom to Assyria (2 Kings 17:30).

ASHKELON/ASKELON. One of five major cities of the Philistines (Judg. 14:19) and a pagan center denounced by the prophet Amos (Amos 1:8). *Askelon:* Judg. 1:18. See also *Philistines.*

ASHKENAZ. A descendant of Noah through Japheth (Gen. 10:3).

ASIA. A Roman province in western Asia Minor which included the cities of Ephesus, Smyrna, and Pergamos —the first three cities mentioned in the book of Revelation (Rev. 1:11; 2:1–17). At first forbidden by a vision to enter Asia (Acts 16:6), Paul later did extensive evangelistic work in this province, and his message was well received (Acts 19:10).

ASKELON. See *Ashkelon.*

ASNAPPER (ASHURBANI-PAL, OSNAPPAR). The last of the great kings of Assyria (reigned about 668–626 B.C.), called the "great and noble" (Ezra 4:10). Asnapper required

King Manasseh of Judah to kiss his feet and pay tribute to him. This is probably the same king as the Ashurbanipal of Assyrian history. *Ashurbanipal:* NIV; *Osnappar:* NRSV. See also *Assyria.*

ASP. A deadly snake of the cobra variety which is symbolic of man's evil nature (Isa. 11:8). This is probably the same snake as the *adder* and *viper.*

ASS. A donkey; a common beast of burden in Bible times (Gen. 22:3). Jesus rode a young donkey rather than a prancing war horse into Jerusalem to symbolize His humble servanthood and the spiritual nature of His kingdom (Luke 19:30–38). See also *Foal.*

ASSEMBLY. A gathering or congregation of people for worship. God directed Moses to assemble the Israelites at the door of the tabernacle (Num. 10:2–3). The psalmist gathered with God's people for worship and praise (Ps. 111:1). Assembling for worship is enjoined for all Christians (Heb. 10:25). See also *Congregation; Church.*

ASSHUR. A son of Shem and ancestor of the Assyrians (Gen. 10:22). See also *Assyria.*

ASSOS. A seaport in Asia Minor through which Paul passed on the third missionary journey (Acts 20:13–14).

ASSUR. See *Assyria*.

ASSURANCE. Complete confidence in God's promises. Our spiritual security is based on our adoption as God's children (Eph. 1:4–5). Believers are secure in the grip of the Father and Son (John 10:28–30). Our love for one another as fellow believers also provides assurance of eternal life (1 John 3:14). Obedient Christians are assured of answered prayer (1 John 5:14–15) and victorious living (Rom. 8:18, 37).

ASSYRIA/ASSHUR/ASSUR. An ancient kingdom between the Tigris and Euphrates rivers which became the dominant power in the ancient world from about 900 to 700 B.C. The aggressive and war-like Assyrians were known for their cruelty in warfare, often cutting off their victims' hands or heads, and impaling them on stakes. For this cruelty and their pagan worship, they were soundly condemned by the O.T. prophets (Isa. 10:5; Ezek. 16:28; Hos. 8:9).

The region which developed into Assyria was originally settled by the hunter Nimrod, a descendant of Noah (Gen. 10:8–12). An early name for Assyria was *Asshur,* after a son of Shem who was connected with their early history (Gen. 10:11). King Sennacherib of Assyria invaded Judah (2 Kings 18:13) and exacted tribute from King Hezekiah (2 Kings 18:14–16). Later, about 722 B.C., King Shalmaneser overthrew the Northern Kingdom, enslaved many of its inhabitants, and resettled the region with foreigners (2 Kings 18:9–11). *Assur:* Ezra 4:2. See also *Asshur; Nineveh.*

ASTROLOGER. One who studied the stars in an attempt to foretell the future—a practice especially popular among the pagan Babylonians (Isa. 47:1, 13). See also *Wise Men.*

ASWAN. See *Sinim.*

ASYNCRITUS. A fellow believer at Rome greeted and commended by Paul in his letter to the Roman Christians (Rom. 16:14).

ATHALIAH. The daughter of Ahab and Jezebel who murdered all the royal heirs and claimed the throne (reigned as queen of Judah about 841–835 B.C.; 2 Kings 11).

ATHEISM. The denial of God's existence. This defiant attitude is illustrated by the Egyptian pharaoh's refusal to release the Hebrew slaves (Exod. 5:2). The psalmist declared that disbelief in God is a characteristic of the foolish (Ps. 14:1). God's clear revelation of His nature and His intent for man leaves unbelievers without excuse (Rom. 1:18–25). See also *Infidel; Unbelief.*

ATHENS. The capital city of ancient Greece where Paul debated with the philosophers about Christ and Christianity during the second missionary journey. Known as the center of Greek art, literature, and politics, Athens also struck Paul because of its idolatry, with shrines erected to numerous deities, including the "unknown god" (Acts 17:23). See also *Areopagus.*

ATONEMENT. Reconciliation of God and man through sacrifice (Rom. 5:11). In O.T. times such reconciliation was accomplished through animal sacrifices symbolic of the people's repentance. But true reconciliation is made possible by Christ's atoning death and resurrection (Rom. 5:1; Eph. 1:7). Man's justification in God's sight is made possible by repentance and faith (Eph. 2:8).

God's righteousness is imparted through Christ's sacrifice (2 Cor. 5:21). His atonement is the foundation for peace among men (Eph. 2:13–16). All who are redeemed through their acceptance by faith of the sacrifice of Christ are called as ministers of reconciliation (2 Cor. 5:18–21). See also *Atonement, Day of; Justification; Reconciliation.*

ATONEMENT, DAY OF. A Jewish holy day (Yom Kippur) on which atonement was made for all Israel (Lev. 16:29–30; 23:27). Preceded by special sabbaths (Lev. 23:24) and fasting, this event recognized man's inability to make atonement for himself (Heb. 10:1–10). On this day the Jewish high priest first made atonement for himself and then the sins of the people by sprinkling the blood of a sacrificial animal on the altar (Lev. 16:12–15), foreshadowing the once-for-all sacrifice of Christ. The scapegoat, representing the sins of the people, was released into the wilderness to symbolize pardon (Lev. 16:22–23). See also *Atonement; Scapegoat.*

The Parthenon, dedicated to the pagan goddess Athena, sits on the crest of the Acropolis in Athens.

Courtesy Rayburn W. Ray

ATTALIA. A seaport town of Pamphylia from which Paul sailed back to Antioch at the end of the first missionary journey (Acts 14:25–26).

AUGUSTUS. A title of honor, meaning "his reverence," bestowed upon the emperors of the Roman Empire (Luke 2:1). See also *Caesar; Roman Empire.*

AUL. See *Awl.*

AUTUMN RAIN. See *Former Rain.*

AVA. An Assyrian city whose citizens settled in Samaria after the Northern Kingdom fell to Assyria (2 Kings 17:24–31). This is perhaps the same place as Ahava. See also *Ahava; Samaritan.*

AVEN. See *On,* No. 2.

AVENGER OF BLOOD. The closest of kin to a slain person who was expected to kill the slayer. Cain feared the avenging relatives of his brother after he murdered Abel (Gen. 4:14). Six cities of refuge were established throughout Israel to provide a haven for those who had accidentally taken a human life (Num. 35:12). Jesus counseled against such vengeance, calling for love of one's enemies and unlimited forgiveness instead (Matt. 5:43–44). See also *Cities of Refuge; Manslayer.*

AWL/AUL. A tool used by carpenters and leather workers to punch holes. *Aul:* Exod. 21:6; Deut. 15:17.

AX. A tool for cutting wood (Deut. 19:5).

AZARIAH
1. Another name for Ahaziah, king of Judah. See *Ahaziah,* No. 2.
2. A prophet who encouraged King Asa of Judah to destroy all idols in the land (2 Chron. 15:1–8).
3. The Hebrew name of Abed-nego. See *Abed-nego.*
4. Another name for Uzziah, king of Judah. See *Uzziah.*

AZAZEL. See *Scapegoat.*

AZOTUS. See *Ashdod.*

AZZAH. See *Gaza.*

-B-

BAALAH. See *Kirjath-jearim.*

BAAL/BAALIM. The chief Canaanite god (Judg. 2:13), who, as the god of rain, was thought to provide fertility for crops and livestock. Baal worship was associated with immorality (Hos. 9:10) and child sacrifice (Jer. 19:5)—pagan rituals considered especially offensive to the one true God of the Israelites. During their history, the Hebrew people often committed idolatry by worshiping this god of their Canaanite neighbors. The prophet Elijah denounced the prophets of Baal, and the God of Israel won a decisive victory over this pagan god on Mt. Carmel (1 Kings 18:17–40). *Baalim:* plural form (1 Sam. 12:10).

BAALATH. A town built by Solomon (1 Kings 9:18) and apparently used as a storage city (2 Chron. 8:6).

BAAL-BERITH. A name under which the pagan Canaanite god Baal was worshiped at Shechem in the time of the judges (Judg. 9:4). See also *Baal.*

BAALIM. See *Baal.*

BAAL-PEOR. A local manifestation of the pagan Canaanite god Baal. Baal-peor was worshiped by the Moabites (Deut. 4:3). See also *Baal.*

BAAL-PERAZIM/PERAZIM. A place in central Palestine where David defeated the Philistines (2 Sam. 5:18–20). *Perazim:* Isa. 28:21.

BAAL-ZEBUB/BEELZEBUB. A name under which the pagan Canaanite god Baal was worshiped by the Philistines at Ekron (2 Kings 1:2). The N.T. form of this name was *Beelzebub,* used as a title for Satan, meaning "prince of devils" (Matt. 12:26–27).

BAASHA. A king of the Northern Kingdom (reigned about 909–886 B.C.) who gained the throne by killing King Jeroboam's heirs (1 Kings 15:16–30).

BABOON. See *Peacock.*

BABEL, TOWER OF. A tall structure known as a ziggurat built on the plain of Shinar in ancient Babylonia as a show of human pride and vanity. God confused the language of the builders so they could not communicate. After they abandoned the project, they were scattered abroad (Gen. 11:1–9). See also *Ziggurat.*

BABYLON. The capital city of the Babylonian Empire, built by Nimrod the hunter (Gen. 10:9–10). Site of the tower of Babel, Babylon was a magnificent city-state which attained its greatest power under Nebuchadnezzar (Dan. 4:1–3, 30). The Jewish people were taken to Babylonia as captives after the fall of Jerusalem in 587 B.C. (2 Chron. 36:5–21).

BABYLONIA/SHESHACH/ SHINAR/CHALDEA. A powerful nation in Mesopotamia which carried the Jewish people into exile about 587 B.C. Also called *Sheshach* (Jer. 25:26), *Shinar* (Isa. 11:11), and the land of the *Chaldeans* (Ezek. 12:13), Babylonia reached the zenith of its power under Nebuchadnezzar (reigned about 605–560 B.C.). The nation was a center of idolatry dominated by worship of Merodach, the Babylonian god of war (Jer. 50:2). After holding the Jewish people captive for many years, the Babylonians were defeated by the Persians about 539 B.C., fulfilling the prophecies of Isaiah and Jeremiah (Isa. 14:22; Jer. 50:9). See also *Mesopotamia; Sumer.*

BABYLONISH GARMENT. An expensive embroidered robe kept by Achan as part of the spoils of war after the battle of Jericho (Josh. 7:21).

BACKBITING. The act of reviling, slandering, or speaking spitefully of others—behavior considered unworthy of a Christian (2 Cor. 12:20).

BACKSLIDING. The act of turning from God after conversion. The causes of backsliding are spiritual blindness (2 Pet. 1:9); persecution (Matt. 13:20–21); or love of material things (1 Tim. 6:10). This sin separates the backslider from God's blessings (Isa. 59:2). But confession and repentance will bring God's forgiveness (1 John 1:9) and restoration (Ps. 51).

BADGER (GOATS' HAIR, HIDES OF SEA COWS). An animal whose skins were used as the covering for the tabernacle (Exod. 25:5). *Goats' hair:* NRSV; *Hides of sea cows:* NIV. See also *Coney*.

BAG. See *Scrip*.

BALAAM. A soothsayer or magician hired by the king of Moab to curse the Israelites to drive them out of his territory.

Prevented from doing so by an angel, Balaam blessed the Israelites instead (Num. 22:4–24:25). See also *Balak*.

BALAK/BALAC. The king of Moab who hired Balaam the soothsayer to curse the Hebrews as they crossed his territory. His scheme failed when God forced Balaam to bless them instead (Num. 22–24). *Balac:* Greek form (Rev. 2:14). See also *Balaam*.

BALANCE, BALANCES (SCALES). An instrument with matched weights, used by merchants to weigh money or food in business transactions (Prov. 11:1). *Scales:* NIV.

BALM OF GILEAD. An aromatic gum or resin exported from Gilead in Arabia. It apparently was used as an incense and for medicinal purposes (Jer. 8:22).

BALSAM. See *Mulberry*.

BANNER. See *Standard*.

BANQUET. An elaborate and sumptuous meal, usually served on a special occasion. Esther exposed the plot of Haman to destroy the Jews during a banquet (Esther 7:1).

BAPTISM. An observance signifying a believer's cleansing from sin through Christ's atoning death. John the Baptist baptized converts to signify their repentance (Matt. 3:6–8). Jesus was baptized by John in the Jordan River to fulfill all righteousness and to set an example for us (Matt. 3:15). The Father's approval of Jesus' baptism was expressed by the descent of the Holy Spirit and a voice from heaven (Mark 1:10–11).

In the N.T. church, Gentiles who received the Holy Spirit were promptly baptized (Acts 10:44–48). Christian baptism memorializes the death, burial, and resurrection of Christ (Rom. 6:3–5). For the believer, baptism is a testimony of faith and a pledge to "walk in newness of life" with Jesus Christ (Rom. 6:4–14).

BARABBAS. A notorious prisoner, guilty of murder and insurrection, at the time when Jesus appeared before Pilate (John 18:40). Incited by Jewish leaders, the mob demanded that Barabbas be released instead of Jesus (Mark 15:9–11).

BARAK. A general under Deborah and judge of Israel. He and Deborah were victorious against the Canaanites (Judg. 4:1–24). See also *Deborah.*

BARBARIAN. A word meaning "uncivilized" and a title used by the Greeks to designate foreigners, or citizens of other nations besides Greece (Rom. 1:14).

BAR-JESUS/ELYMAS. A sorcerer and false prophet who opposed Paul and Silas at Paphos during the first missionary journey (Acts 13:6–12). Also called *Elymas.*

BAR-JONA. The surname of the apostle Peter, meaning "son of Jonah" (Matt. 16:17). See *Simon,* No. 1.

BARLEY. A grain similar to oats, used as food for livestock (1 Kings 4:28) and also ground into meal for bread by poor people (John 6:5, 13).

BARNABAS/JOSES. A Jewish Christian who befriended Paul after Paul's conversion, introduced the apostle to the Jerusalem church (Acts 9:27), and traveled with Paul during the first missionary journey (Acts 11:25–26). *Joses:* Acts 4:36.

BARRACKS. See *Castle.*

BARREN. Unable to bear children. In the O.T., barrenness was seen as a sign of God's judgment (1 Sam. 1:5–7). See also *Children; Womb.*

BARRIER. See *Middle Wall of Partition.*

BARTHOLOMEW. One of the twelve apostles of Jesus (Mark 3:18). Some scholars believe he is the same person as *Nathanael* (John 1:45–49). According to tradition, Bartholomew became a missionary to Armenia and India and was flayed and crucified for his faith. See also *Twelve, The.*

BARTIMAEUS. A blind beggar healed by Jesus on the road to Jericho (Mark 10:46–52).

BARUCH. The friend and scribe of the prophet Jeremiah. Baruch faithfully recorded Jeremiah's messages warning of the impending defeat of the nation of Judah (Jer. 36:4–32). Like Jeremiah, he fled to Egypt after the fall of Jerusalem (Jer. 43:1–7). See also *Jeremiah.*

BARZILLAI. An aged friend of David who helped the king during his flight from Absalom (2 Sam. 17:27–29).

BASHAN. A fertile plain east of the Jordan River conquered by the Israelites (Num. 21:33) and allotted to the half-tribe of Manasseh (Josh. 13:29–30).

BASON (BASIN, BOWL). A container used in the home (2 Sam. 17:28) and as a ceremonial vessel in the temple or tabernacle (Exod. 24:6). *Basin:* NRSV; *Bowl:* NIV. See also *Bowl; Laver.*

BAT. A nocturnal flying mammal, considered unclean by the Hebrews (Lev. 11:19).

BATH. Standard Hebrew measure for liquids, equivalent to about six gallons (1 Kings 7:26).

BATHING. A washing of the body to make it ceremonially clean and pure (Lev. 15:5, 16). See also *Clean; Wash.*

BATH-SHEBA/BATH-SHUA. The wife of Uriah who committed adultery with David and became his wife (2 Sam. 11:6–27). Because of their sin, Bath-sheba's first child died. She later gave birth to four sons, including Solomon, who succeeded David as king. *Bathshua:* 1 Chron. 3:5. See also *David; Solomon.*

BATTLEMENT (PARAPET). A railing around the roof of a house, required by law to prevent falls (Deut. 22:8) *Parapet:* NIV, NRSV.

BDELLIUM. A word which probably refers to a fragrant gum resin (Num. 11:7) as well as a precious stone (Gen. 2:12).

BEAR. A large animal similar to our brown bear which was common in Palestine in Bible times. David killed a bear to protect his father's sheep (1 Sam. 17:34–37).

BEARD. Trimmed and groomed facial hair—a mark of pride among Jewish men. To shave one's beard or pull out the hair was a gesture of anguish and grief (Jer. 48:37–38).

BEATITUDES. Pronouncements of blessing at the beginning of Jesus' Sermon on the Mount. God's special reward is promised to those who recognize their spiritual need (Matt. 5:3); those who mourn (5:4); those who are humble (5:5); obedient (5:6); merciful (5:7); pure in heart (5:8); those who practice peacemaking (5:9); and those who are persecuted for Jesus' sake (5:10–11). See also *Sermon on the Mount.*

BEAUTIFUL GATE. A gate which served as one of the main entrances into the temple area in Jerusalem in N.T. times (Acts 3:2).

BEDAN. A minor judge of Israel who served after Gideon and before Jephthah. His name is not recorded in the book of Judges (1 Sam. 12:11). See also *Judges of Israel.*

BEDCHAMBER (BEDROOM). The sleeping room in houses of Bible times (2 Sam. 4:7–11). *Bedroom:* NIV.

BEELIADA/ELIADA. A son of David, born at Jerusalem (1 Chron. 14:7). *Eliada:* 2 Sam. 5:16; 1 Chron. 3:8.

BEELZEBUB (BEELZEBUL). *Beelzebul:* NRSV; See *Baal-zebub.*

BEER.
1. A place in Moab where the Israelites camped during their wilderness wanderings (Num. 21:16–18). Possibly the same place as Beer Elim (Isa. 15:8).
2. A town in Judah where Jotham sought refuge from his brother Abimelech (Judg. 9:21).

BEER-SHEBA. The name of a well in southern Judah which

Abraham and Abimelech dug to seal their covenant of friendship (Gen. 21:31). The name was also applied to the surrounding wilderness (Gen. 21:14) and an important city which grew up around the well (Gen. 26:32–33; Judg. 20:1). See also *Well*.

BEGGAR. One who lives by handouts (Luke 16:3). The Israelites were commanded by God to care for the poor (Deut. 15:7–10). See also *Alms; Poor*.

BEGOTTEN. A word which describes Christ as the only and unique Son of His heavenly Father (John 3:16–18).

BEGUILE. To deceive, cheat, or defraud—actions characteristic of Satan. Eve was beguiled by the serpent in the Garden of Eden (Gen. 3:13).

BEHEADING. To cut off a person's head; a form of execution or capital punishment. John the Baptist was put to death in this manner (Matt. 14:10).

BEHEMOTH. A large beast mentioned by Job (Job 40:15–24), probably referring to the elephant or the hippopotamus.

BEKAH. A Hebrew weight equal to one-half shekel, or about one-quarter ounce (Exod. 38:26).

BELA. See *Zoar*.

BELIAL. A word for wickedness or wicked people (1 Kings 21:10). The word also means wickedness personified—a reference to Satan (2 Cor. 6:15). See also *Satan*.

BELIEVE. To accept or trust fully. Belief or trust in Christ is necessary for salvation (Acts 16:31) and essential to righteousness (Gal. 3:6). See also *Faith; Trust*.

BELIEVERS. A term for Christian converts (Acts 5:14). The believers at Pentecost enjoyed fellowship and shared property according to need (Acts 2:44–45). Paul encouraged Timothy to serve as an example for other believers (1 Tim. 4:12). See also *Brother*.

BELLOWS. A blacksmith's tool, used to force air onto a fire to make it hot enough to work metal (Jer. 6:29). See also *Smith*.

BELSHAZZAR. The son or grandson of Nebuchadnezzar and the last king of the Babylonian Empire (Dan. 5:1–2). Daniel interpreted a mysterious handwriting on the wall for Belshazzar as a prediction of doom for the Babylonians (Dan. 5:17). That night, Belshazzar was killed when the Persians captured Babylonia (Dan. 5:30–31). See also *Babylonia*.

BELT. See Girdle.

BELTESHAZZAR. See *Daniel*, No. 1.

BENAIAH. A loyal supporter of David and Solomon. A commander of David's bodyguard (2 Sam. 20:23), he later became commander-in-chief of Solomon's army (1 Kings 2:35).

BEN-AMMI. Lot's son by his youngest daughter. Born in a cave near Zoar (Gen. 19:30–38), he was the ancestor of the Ammonites. See also *Ammonites; Lot*.

BENEDICTION. A prayer for God's blessings upon His people. The benediction which priests were to use was spoken by God to Aaron through Moses (Num. 6:22–26). See also *Blessing*.

BENEVOLENCE. Generosity toward others. Paul commended generosity toward the needy (Gal. 2:10). Christian benevolence should be shown toward God's servants (Phil.

4:14–17) and even our enemies (Prov. 25:21).

BEN-HADAD. A general title for the kings of Damascus, Syria. Three separate Ben-hadads are mentioned in the Bible:

1. Ben-hadad I (reigned about 950 B.C.). In league with Asa, king of Judah, he invaded the Northern Kingdom (1 Kings 15:18–21).

2. Ben-hadad II (reigned about 900 B.C.). He waged war against King Ahab of Israel. This Ben-hadad is probably the unnamed "king of Syria" whose officer Naaman was healed of leprosy by the prophet Elisha (2 Kings 5:1–19).

3. Ben-hadad III (reigned about 750 B.C.). He was defeated by the Assyrian army, as the prophet Amos predicted (Amos 1:4).

BENJAMIN. The youngest of Jacob's twelve sons and ancestor of the tribe of Benjamin. His mother Rachel died at his birth (Gen. 35:16–20). Benjamin was greatly loved by his father Jacob (Gen. 42:2–4) and by his brother Joseph (Gen. 43:29–34). See also *Tribes of Israel*.

BEREA (BEROEA). A city in southern Macedonia visited by

Paul. The Bereans searched the Scriptures eagerly, and many became believers (Acts 17:10–15). *Beroea:* NRSV.

BERNICE. The sister of Herod Agrippa II, Roman governor of Palestine before whom Paul appeared. She was present when Paul made his defense (Acts 26:1–32).

BERODACH-BALADAN/ MERODACH-BALADAN. A king of Babylonia (reigned about 721–704 B.C.) who sent ambassadors to visit King Hezekiah of Judah. Hezekiah showed them his vast wealth—an act condemned by the prophet Isaiah (2 Kings 20:12–19). *Merodach-baladan:* Isa. 39:1. See also *Babylonia.*

BEROEA. See *Berea.*

BEROTHAI (BEROTHAH). A city of Syria taken by David (2 Sam. 8:8). *Berothah:* Ezek. 47:16.

BERYL (CHRYSOLITE). A precious stone, probably similar to emerald, used in the breastplate of the high priest (Exod. 28:20), and in the foundation of New Jerusalem (Rev. 21:20). *Chrysolite:* NIV. See also *Carbuncle; Chrysolite.*

BESEECH. To request or ask earnestly (Rom. 12:1).

BESIEGE. To surround with armed forces (Deut. 20:12). This battle tactic was used against walled cities of Bible times to starve the inhabitants into submission. See also *Fenced City; Wall.*

BESOR. A brook south of Ziklag crossed by David's army in pursuit of the Amalekites (1 Sam. 30:9–21).

BESTIALITY. Sex relations with an animal. The death penalty was imposed on those who were guilty of this offense (Exod. 22:19).

BETH. The second letter of the Hebrew alphabet, used as a heading over Ps. 119:9–16.

BETHABARA. A place on the Jordan River where John the Baptist baptized believers (John 1:28). Jesus was also apparently baptized at this place (John 1:29–34).

BETHANY. A village near the Mount of Olives outside Jerusalem (Mark 11:1) and home of Lazarus, Mary, and Martha—friends of Jesus (John 11:1). Jesus ascended to heaven from Bethany (Luke 24:50).

Modern Bethlehem, a village six miles south of Jerusalem, where Jesus was born. *Courtesy Israel Ministry of Tourism*

BETHEL/LUZ/EL-BETHEL. A city north of Jerusalem where Jacob had a life-changing vision of angels going up and down a staircase (Gen. 28:10–19). Before it was renamed by Jacob, Bethel was known by its Canaanite name, *Luz* (Gen. 28:19). *El-bethel:* Gen. 35:7.

BETHESDA (BETH-ZATHA). The name of a pool in Jerusalem believed to have miraculous healing powers. Jesus healed a lame man at this pool (John 5:2–8). *Beth-zatha:* NRSV. See also *Pool.*

BETH-HORON. Upper and Lower Beth-horon were twin towns in the territory of Ephraim which served as important military outposts in Bible times. They stood on the main pass through the mountains between the Mediterranean Sea and Jerusalem. Solomon fortified the cities to protect Jerusalem from invading armies (2 Chron. 8:5).

BETHLEHEM/ BETH-LEHEM-JUDAH/ EPHRATH/EPHRATAH. A town in southern Palestine near Jerusalem, also called *Beth-lehem-judah* (Judg. 19:18), where Jesus was born in fulfillment of prophecy (Mic. 5:2; Luke 2:4–7). It was called the

"City of David" because King David grew up there centuries before (1 Sam. 16:1–13). David's ancestor Ruth gleaned grain in the fields of Boaz nearby (Ruth 2:4–8). Bethlehem was known in O.T. times as *Ephrath* (Gen. 35:16–19) and *Ephratah* (Ruth 4:11). See also *City of David*.

BETH-MILLO. See *Millo*, No. 1.

BETH-PEOR. A town of Moab east of the Jordan River in the territory where Moses was buried (Deut. 34:6).

BETHPHAGE. A village near Bethany and the Mount of Olives just outside Jerusalem mentioned in connection with Jesus' triumphant entry into the city (Matt. 21:1).

BETHSAIDA. A fishing village on the Sea of Galilee; the home of Andrew, Peter, and Philip—apostles of Jesus (John 1:44). Some scholars believe the Bethsaida where the 5,000 were fed (Luke 9:10–17) was a different city with the same name.

BETH-SHAN/BETH-SHEAN. A Philistine city where King Saul's corpse was displayed (1 Sam. 31:10–13). In later years, Solomon stationed troops in this city (1 Kings 4:12). *Beth-shean:* Josh. 17:11.

BETH-SHEMESH/ IR-SHEMESH. A border town between the territories of Judah and Dan taken by the Philistines. Later the ark of the covenant was kept here (1 Sam. 6:10–7:2). *Ir-shemesh:* Josh. 19:41.

BETH-ZATHA. See *Bethesda*.

BETH-ZUR. A city in the mountains of Judah fortified by King Rehoboam as a defensive outpost along the road leading to Jerusalem (2 Chron. 11:7).

BETROTHAL. A marriage agreement, usually made by the groom with the parents of the bride. A betrothed woman was regarded as the lawful wife of her spouse. Joseph and Mary were betrothed before the birth of Jesus (Matt. 1:18–19; *espoused:* KJV). See also *Dowry; Marriage*.

BEULAH. A name for Israel after the Babylonian Exile when the nation would be in a fruitful relationship with God (Isa. 62:4).

BEZER. A fortified city in the territory of Reuben designated as one of the six cities of

Excavated ruins of the ancient city of Beth-shan.
Courtesy Israel Ministry of Tourism

refuge (Josh. 20:8). See also *Cities of Refuge*.

BIBLE. God's written record of His revelation which is accepted by Christians as uniquely inspired and authoritative for faith and practice. The Bible's O.T. books chronicle the expectation of a Messiah, while the N.T. books reveal the fulfillment of God's redemptive purpose through Jesus Christ and the church.

The Bible was written under God's inspiration during a period of more than 1,000 years from the time of Moses through the first century A.D. The N.T. was completed within about sixty years of Jesus' resurrection. Much of the N.T., including the Gospels, was recorded by eyewitnesses of the events about which they wrote. The O.T. was written originally in Hebrew and Aramaic, while the N.T. was recorded in the Greek language.

All copies of the Scripture were written by hand until the invention of printing in the fifteenth century A.D. The original writings have been translated into hundreds of languages and dialects to make the Bible the world's best loved and most accessible book. The Geneva Bible, published in 1560, was the first complete English Bible translated from the original languages. The popular King James Version appeared in 1611, and numerous English versions and revisions have followed.

Although written by many people over a long period, the Bible has a remarkable unity, explained only by the inspiration and oversight of the Holy Spirit to bring God's redemptive message to mankind.

BIER. A portable frame for carrying a body to its burial place (2 Sam. 3:31).

BILDAD. One of the three friends who comforted the sorrowing Job (Job 2:11). His speeches expressed the conviction that all suffering is the direct result of sin (Job 8:1–22; 18:1–21; 25:1–6). See also *Job, Book of*.

BILHAH. Rachel's maid and a wife of Jacob. She bore two of Jacob's twelve sons, Dan and Naphtali (Gen. 30:1–8). See also *Jacob*.

BIRD OF PREY. See *Speckled Bird*.

BIRTHRIGHT. The inheritance rights of the firstborn son, who received a double portion of his father's assets

(Deut. 21:17) plus the father's blessing and responsibility for family leadership. These inheritance rights could be taken away and conferred on another because of immoral acts or irresponsible behavior by the oldest son (Gen. 25:29–34). See also *Firstborn; Inheritance.*

BISHOP. An overseer, pastor, or elder who served as leader of a local church in N.T. times (Titus 1:5–8). See also *Elder; Pastor.*

BITHYNIA. A Roman province of Asia Minor which Paul was prevented from entering, through the intervention of the Holy Spirit (Acts 16:7). The gospel did enter this province later (1 Pet. 1:1).

BITTER HERBS. Herbs eaten by the Hebrew people during their celebration of the Passover to help them remember their bitter affliction during their enslavement in Egypt (Exod. 12:8). See also *Passover.*

BITTER WATER. A test or trial to which a woman was subjected when her husband suspected her of being unfaithful (Num. 5:11–31). See also *Water of Jealousy; Water of Separation.*

BITTERN (SCREECH OWL). A bird noted for its melancholy cries and thus symbolic of the loneliness and despair which follows God's judgment (Zeph. 2:14). *Screech owl:* NIV, NRSV. See also *Screech Owl.*

BITUMEN. See *Slime.*

BLACK VULTURE. See *Ospray.*

BLAINS (BOILS). Infectious boils on the skin; one of the plagues brought upon the Egyptians for their refusal to release the Hebrew slaves (Exod. 9:8 –11). *Boils:* NIV, NRSV.

BLASPHEMY. The act of reviling, cursing, or showing contempt toward God. This was considered a capital offense by the Jewish people, punishable by death. Jesus was accused of blasphemy by the Jewish leaders. They considered Him only a man, while He claimed to be God's Son (Matt. 9:3).

BLASPHEMY AGAINST THE HOLY SPIRIT. A sin which consists of attributing Christ's miracles to the work of Satan (Matt. 12:31–32). Jesus declared such contempt for the work of God was an unforgivable sin (Mark 3:28 –30). Paul regarded a person's bitter opposition to the gospel as a form of blasphemy against God (Rom. 2:24). See also *Unpardonable Sin.*

BLESSING. The act of invoking or declaring God's goodness and favor upon others, as Jacob did with his twelve sons (Gen. 49:1–28). God also blesses His people by giving life (Gen. 1:22) and forgiving our sins (Rom. 4:7–8). See also *Benediction.*

BLIND. Unable to see, in either a physical (Matt. 9:27) or spiritual (Eph. 4:18) sense. The Hebrews were enjoined to show compassion toward the blind (Deut. 27:18).

BLOOD. Life-sustaining fluid of the body. In the O.T., the blood of a sacrificial animal represented the essence of life and symbolized repentance and atonement for sin (Lev. 17:11). In the N.T., the phrase "the blood of Christ" refers to the sacrificial death of Jesus on the cross (Heb. 9:12–14). Jesus' sacrificial blood is the agent of redemption for believers (Heb. 9:12). Christ's shed blood is memorialized in the Lord's Supper (1 Cor. 10:16). Nothing perishable or material can save; only Christ's precious blood has the power to redeem

(1 Pet. 1:18–19). See also *Atonement; Redeem.*

BOANERGES. A name, meaning "sons of thunder," given by Jesus to James and John, the sons of Zebedee (Mark 3:17). This was a reference to their fiery zeal. See also *James,* No. 1; *John the Apostle.*

BOAR. A male wild hog, noted for its vicious nature (Ps. 80:13).

BOASTING. To brag or to speak of one's accomplishments with pride and haughtiness (2 Chron. 25:19).

BOAZ/BOOZ. The husband of Ruth and an ancestor of Christ. Boaz granted Ruth the right to gather leftover grain in his fields (Ruth 2:8–9). He married Ruth, who gave birth to Obed, grandfather of David (Ruth 4:17). *Booz:* Jesus' ancestry (Matt. 1:5). See also *Ruth.*

BODY OF CHRIST. A symbolic expression for the church. Paul identified the church as Christ's body (Col. 1:24). The risen Christ dwells in His body and presides over the church (Eph. 1:19–23). Christ assigns spiritual gifts to His body to accomplish His work and bring believers to maturity (Eph. 4:7–13). Members of the body are to care for one another (1 Cor. 12:25–27). See also *Church*.

BODY, SPIRITUAL. The glorified or redeemed body of believers. Our hope of a glorified body is based on Christ's victory over the grave (Rom. 6:6). Believers will receive a glorified body, free of sin and death, at the return of Christ (1 Cor. 15:50–57). The redeemed body of a believer will be like that of Christ's glorified body (Phil. 3:21), immortal and incorruptible (1 Cor. 15:53–54). Christians need not fear death because we are provided a new spiritual body "eternal in the heavens" (2 Cor. 5:1–6).

BOILS. See *Blains*.

BOLDNESS. Courage and confidence. Boldness which honors God is aided by earnest prayer (Eph. 6:18–19).

BONDAGE. To be held against one's will by an oppressor. The Israelites were enslaved by the Egyptians for more than 400 years. Sin also holds a person in spiritual bondage (Rom. 8:15). See also *Slave*.

BONDSERVANT. A slave; a person who serves another against his will and without wages (1 Kings 9:21). See also *Slave*.

BONE. The skeletal framework of humans. The phrase "bone of my bones" uttered by Adam (Gen. 2:23) showed that he was united to woman in the closest possible relationship.

BOOK. Pieces of animal skin or papyrus written on and then bound together (Job 19:23). See also *Roll; Scroll*.

BOOK OF JASHER. A lost book which apparently described great events in the life of Israel (Josh. 10:13).

BOOK OF LIFE. God's record of the names of the saved (Mal. 3:16–18). This book will be used as the basis for God's final judgment (Rev. 20:12–15). Inclusion in the book of life by virtue of one's salvation by God's grace provides reason for joy (Luke 10:20) and hope of heaven (Rev. 21:27).

BOOK OF THE LAW. A term for the Law of Moses or the Pentateuch, the first five books of the O.T. After receiving and recording these instructions from God, Moses delivered the law to the priests for public reading (Deut. 31:9–11). In later years, the Book of the

Law became the basis for King Josiah's religious reforms (2 Kings 23:1–28).

BOOK OF THE WARS OF THE LORD. A lost book which may have celebrated Israel's victories in battle under Moses (Num. 21:14).

BOOTH. A temporary shelter made of tree branches. During the Feast of Tabernacles, also called the Feast of Booths, the Israelites lived in such shelters as a reminder of their harsh life in the wilderness after their deliverance from Egyptian slavery (Neh. 8:13–18).

BOOTHS, FEAST OF. See *Tabernacles, Feast of.*

BOOTY. Anything of value taken in war, including livestock, slaves, gold and silver, clothing, and tools (Zeph. 1:13). See also *Spoil.*

BOOZ. See *Boaz.*

BORN AGAIN. See *New Birth.*

BOSOM. Another word for the human chest, or breast, used symbolically to imply closeness or intimacy (Isa. 40:11). See also *Abraham's Bosom; Breast.*

BOTTLE (WINESKIN). A vessel made of animal skins (Josh. 9:4). Old wineskins became brittle and unable to hold new wine during the fermentation process. Thus, Jesus declared, "No man putteth new wine into old bottles; else the new wine will burst the bottles, and be spilled" (Luke 5:37). *Wineskin:* NIV, NRSV.

BOTTOMLESS PIT. See *Abyss.*

BOUNDARY MARKER, BOUNDARY STONE. See *Landmark.*

BOW. A weapon used in war and for hunting (Gen. 48:22). Soldiers of the tribe of Benjamin were especially skilled with the bow (1 Chron. 12:2).

BOWELS (INWARD PARTS). The internal digestive system of the human body. The bowels were considered the center of a person's feelings and emotions, expressive of compassion and tenderness (Job 30:27–28). *Inward parts:* NRSV.

BOWING. An act of reverence or submission, performed by kneeling on one knee and bending the head forward. Bowing is considered appropriate for prayer and worship (Ps. 95:6).

Jesus knelt or bowed to pray in Gethsemane (Matt. 26:36–39). See also *Kneel.*

BOWL. A vessel for holding food or liquids. Bowls were made of wood, clay, or silver. Large bowls were used by priests in sacrificial rituals (Zech. 9:15). See also *Bason.*

BOX TREE (CYPRESS, PINE). An evergreen which produces a wood ideal for carving. Boxwood was used in the temple in Jerusalem (Isa. 60:13) *Cypress:* NIV; *Pine:* NRSV.

BOZRAH. The ancient capital city of Edom. Isaiah spoke of this city in figurative terms to describe the Messiah's victory over the pagan nations (Isa. 63:1). See also *Edom, No. 2.*

BRACELET. A piece of jewelry worn on the wrist (Isa. 3:19). The bracelet of King Saul (2 Sam. 1:10) was probably a military armband.

BRAMBLE (THORNBUSH). A bush of thistles. In Jotham's parable, the bramble bush, representing Abimelech, ruled over the trees of the forest, in spite of its lowly position (Judg. 9:7–15). *Thornbush:* NIV. See also *Brier.*

BRASEN SEA (BRONZE SEA). A large brass basin in the temple court which held water for purification rituals (2 Kings 25:13). *Bronze sea:* NIV, NRSV. See also *Molten Sea.*

BRASS. An alloy of copper with some other metal, perhaps zinc or tin (Num. 21:9). The word is also used as a symbol of stubbornness, insensibility, and rebellion toward God (Isa. 48:4).

BRASS SERPENT (BRONZE SNAKE). A serpent cast from metal and raised up by Moses in the wilderness on a pole as an instrument of healing for those who had been bitten by poisonous snakes (Num. 21:9). Jesus referred to this incident to illustrate the healing from sin made possible by His crucifixion (John 3:14). *Bronze snake:* NIV. See also *Fiery Serpents.*

BREAD. A word often used for food in general. True bread was made from flour or meal and baked in loaves. Jesus described Himself as the Bread of Life (John 6:35). See also *Corn; Wheat.*

BREAD OF THE PRESENCE. See *Shewbread.*

BREAST. The chest of the human body. To strike or beat

one's chest was to signify extreme sorrow (Luke 23:48).

BREASTPLATE (BREAST-PIECE). The vestment worn by the Jewish high priest, containing twelve precious stones and engraved with the names of the tribes of Israel (Exod. 28:15–30) *Breastpiece:* NIV. Paul spoke figuratively of the "breastplate of righteousness" for Christians (Eph. 6:14).

BREASTS. See *Paps.*

BREATH. The air which a person inhales to sustain life. Job recognized this process as God's gift to His creatures (Job 12:10).

BREATH OF GOD. A symbolic phrase used to portray God as the source of life (Job 33:4). His breath demonstrates His power and creative ability (2 Sam. 22:14–16). In the N.T., God "breathed" the Holy Spirit upon His disciples (John 20:22).

BREECHES (UNDERGARMENTS). Trousers, or perhaps an undergarment, worn by priests (Exod. 28:42). *Undergarments:* NIV, NRSV.

BRIBERY. The act of giving gifts or favors inappropriately to influence others—a practice condemned often in the Bible (Amos 5:12).

BRICK. A building block made of clay, which was mixed with straw, then baked in the sun or placed in a kiln for curing. The Israelites made bricks during their enslavement in Egypt (Exod. 1:14). See also *Tile.*

BRICK-KILN. An oven or furnace for curing bricks (2 Sam. 12:31). See also *Furnace.*

BRIDE. A newly married woman. In the N.T., the Church is spoken of figuratively as the bride of Christ (Eph. 5:25–33). See also *Church.*

BRIDEGROOM. A newly married man. The N.T. speaks figuratively of Christ as the Bridegroom (John 3:29) and of the Church as His bride (Eph. 5:25–33).

BRIER. A shrub or plant with thorns and thistles. The word is often used figuratively to describe man's sinful nature (Mic. 7:4).

BRIGANDINE (COAT OF MAIL). Flexible body armor, probably worn by kings and commanders (1 Sam. 17:38; Jer. 46:4). *Coat of mail:* NRSV.

BRIMSTONE (BURNING SULFUR). A bright yellow mineral which burns easily and emits a strong odor. The cities of Sodom and Gomorrah were destroyed with burning brimstone (Gen. 19:24–25). *Burning sulfur:* NIV.

BRONZE SEA. See *Brasen Sea*.

BRONZE SNAKE. See *Brass Serpent*.

BROOM. See *Juniper*.

BROTHER. A male sibling. The word is also used figuratively for all Christian believers (Matt. 23:8). Christians are counseled not to offend a weak brother (Rom. 14:10–13). See also *Believers*.

BROTHERS OF CHRIST. The four earthly brothers, or half brothers of Jesus—James, Joses (Joseph), Simon, and Juda (Jude)—who were born by natural conception to Joseph and Mary after the virgin birth of Christ (Mark 6:3). James was leader of the church in Jerusalem (Acts 15:13–21) and likely the author of the epistle of James (Jas. 1:1). Jude wrote the N.T. epistle which bears his name (Jude 1).

BUCKLER (SHIELD). A small piece of protective armor worn on the arm by warriors (Song of Sol. 4:4). *Shield:* NIV. See also *Shield*.

BUKKI. A leader of the tribe of Dan, appointed by Moses to help divide the land of Canaan after its occupation by the Israelites (Num. 34:22).

BUL. The eighth month of the Hebrew year, roughly equivalent to parts of our October and November (1 Kings 6:38).

BULL. A general term for the male of the ox or cattle species (Job 21:10).

BULLOCK. A young bull used in animal sacrifices (Num. 15:24).

BULRUSH (PAPYRUS). A reedlike plant which grew in marshy areas of the Nile River and was used for making papyrus, an ancient writing material. The infant Moses was placed in a basket made of this plant (Exod. 2:3). *Papyrus:* NIV, NRSV. See also *Paper; Reed*.

BULWARK (RAMPARTS). A tower in a city's defensive wall which provided a better position for firing on the enemy below (Ps. 48:13). *Ramparts:* NIV, NRSV.

BURIAL. The ceremonial disposal of a body by placement in the ground or a tomb. In Bible times, burial usually took place as soon as possible because of the warm climate and because a body was considered ceremonially unclean (Deut. 21:23). Jesus' body was prepared for burial with aromatic oils and spices and wrapped in a linen cloth (John 19:39–40). See also *Funeral; Sepulchre.*

BURNING AGUE (FEVER). A severe fever, possibly a symptom of a serious illness, such as typhoid or malaria (Lev. 26:16). *Fever:* NIV, NRSV.

BURNING BUSH. The flaming shrub through which God spoke to Moses. As the bush burned, God expressed compassion for His captive people and called Moses to return to Egypt to deliver them from bondage (Exod. 3:9–10).

BURNING SULFUR. See *Brimstone.*

BURNT OFFERING. A meat sacrifice consisting of an unblemished animal, which was totally consumed by fire, except for the hide (Lev. 7:8). Burnt sacrifices were made to atone for sin and to restore the broken relationship between man and God (Num. 6:10–11).

BUSHEL. A dry measure of about one peck (Matt. 5:15).

BUSYBODY (MEDDLER, MISCHIEF MAKER). A gossip and troublemaker. This type of behavior is inappropriate for believers (1 Pet. 4:15). *Meddler:* NIV; *Mischief maker:* NRSV. See also *Gossip.*

BUTLER. See *Cupbearer.*

BUZZARD. See *Vulture.*

BYWORD. A degrading saying or remark, usually delivered in taunting fashion (1 Kings 9:7).

-C-

CAB (KAB). The smallest unit of measure for dry material, equal to about three pints (2 Kings 6:25). *Kab:* NRSV.

CAESAR. A formal title for several emperors of the Roman Empire. Four separate Caesars are mentioned in the N.T.:

1. Caesar Augustus (reigned about 27 B.C. to A.D. 14), who issued the taxation or census

Remains of an aqueduct, or water channel, built by the Romans at Caesarea near the Mediterranean Sea.

Courtesy Israel Ministry of Tourism

decree which required Joseph to go to Bethlehem, where Jesus was born (Luke 2:1).

2. Caesar Tiberius (reigned about A.D. 14–37), whose administration paralleled the public ministry of Jesus. Tiberius was known for his strict discipline of subject nations and his intolerance of potential rivals (John 19:12).

3. Caesar Claudius (reigned about A.D. 41–54), who sought to reduce strife throughout his empire. One of his tactics was to expel all the Jewish people living in Rome (Acts 18:2).

4. Caesar Nero (reigned about A.D. 54–68), the first emperor under whom the Christians were persecuted. As a Roman citizen, Paul appealed to him (Acts 25:8–12).

CAESAREA. A Roman coastal city founded about 10 B.C. and named for the Roman emperor Caesar Augustus. As the political capital of Palestine during N.T. times, it was the city of residence for Roman rulers of the district, including Agrippa II, before whom Paul appeared (Acts 26:28–32).

CAESAREA PHILIPPI. A city at the foot of Mt. Hermon in northern Palestine where Peter confessed Jesus as the Messiah (Matt. 16:13–28). Named for the Roman tetrarch Philip who rebuilt the city, it was called Caesarea Philippi to distinguish it from the city of Caesarea on the Mediterranean coast in central Palestine.

CAESAR'S HOUSEHOLD. A group of converts probably associated with the palace of the emperor in Rome. Paul sent greetings from this group to the church at Philippi (Phil. 4:22).

CAIAPHAS. The Jewish high priest who presided at the trial of Jesus and advised that He be put to death (Matt. 26:65–66; John 18:12–14). After Jesus' resurrection, the apostles John and Peter also appeared before Caiaphas (Acts 4:6).

CAIN. The oldest son of Adam and Eve who murdered his brother Abel. Exiled by God, he built a city which he named for his son (Gen. 4:1–17).

CAINAN. See *Kenan*.

CALAH. An ancient city of Assyria built by Nimrod (Gen. 10:8–12).

CALAMUS (FRAGRANT CANE, AROMATIC CANE). A reedlike plant known for its sweet fragrance (Song of Sol. 4:14). It was used in anointing oil (Exod. 30:23). *Fragrant cane:* NIV; *Aromatic cane:* NRSV.

CALDRON. A large kettle used by priests for boiling meats for sacrificial purposes (2 Chron. 35:13). See also *Kettle*.

CALEB. One of the twelve spies who scouted Canaan. Along with Joshua, he recommended that Israel attack the Canaanites immediately (Num. 13:30). He lived to enter the land forty years later and was given the city of Hebron for his faithfulness (Josh. 14:6–14). See also *Spies*.

CALF. A young cow prized as a delicacy (Gen. 18:7) and often sacrificed as a burnt offering (Lev. 9:8). See also *Fatling*.

CALF, GOLDEN. An idol built and worshiped by the Israelites in the wilderness as they waited for Moses to come down from Mt. Sinai (Exod. 32:1–4). It was probably an image of Apis, a sacred bull worshiped by the Egyptians. In later years, King Jeroboam of Israel set up pagan golden

Modern Cana, the village where Jesus performed His first miracle. *Courtesy Israel Ministry of Tourism*

calves at Dan and Bethel (1 Kings 12:26–33). See also *Idol*.

CALLING. The special summons to service which all Christians receive as part of their salvation experience (1 Cor. 7:20). See also *Vocation*.

CALNEH/CALNO. An ancient city built in southern Mesopotamia by Nimrod (Gen. 10:9–10). This may be the same city as Canneh (Ezek. 27:23). *Calno:* Isa. 10:9.

CALVARY (THE SKULL). A hill just outside the city walls of Jerusalem where Jesus was crucified (Luke 23:33). The word comes from a Latin word which means "skull," thus "place of the skull." The Aramaic form of this word is *Golgotha* (Mark 15:22). *The Skull:* NIV, NRSV. See also *Cross*.

CAMEL. A hardy, humpbacked animal ideally suited to the desert climate of Palestine and used as a riding animal and beast of burden (Gen. 24:64).

CAMP. A place where tent dwellers and nomads pitch their tents. The Israelites camped in many different places during their years of wandering in the wilderness

(Num. 33:1–49). See also *Wilderness Wanderings*.

CAMPHIRE (HENNA). A plant which produced a valuable red dye, used by women to adorn their lips and fingernails (Song of Sol. 1:14). *Henna:* NIV, NRSV.

CANA OF GALILEE. A village near Capernaum in the district of Galilee where Jesus performed His first miracle—the transformation of water into wine at a wedding feast (John 2:1–11).

CANAAN.
1. A son of Ham whose descendants founded several tribal peoples in and around Palestine (Gen. 10:1, 6, 15–18).
2. The region between the Red Sea and the Jordan River where Canaan's descendants settled and the territory which God promised to Abraham and his descendants (Gen. 15:3–7). *Chanaan:* Greek form (Acts 7:11). See also *Land of Promise*.

CANAANITES.
1. The original inhabitants of Canaan who settled the land before Abraham arrived about 2000 B.C. (Gen. 12:5–6). They were eventually forced out of the land by Israel at God's command because of their pagan religious practices. Intermarriage with Canaanites by the Israelites was distinctly prohibited by God (Deut. 7:3).
2. Members of a Jewish sect in N.T. times known for their fanatical opposition to the rule of Rome. Jesus' apostle Simon the Canaanite may have been a member of, or a sympathizer with, this sect (Matt. 10:4). They were also known as the *zelotes* or *zealots*.

CANDACE. A title of the queens of Ethiopia in N.T. times (Acts 8:27).

CANDLE (LAMP). A shallow clay bowl filled with oil and a burning wick, used for illumination (Matt.· 5:15). *Lamp:* NIV, NRSV.

CANDLESTICK (LAMPSTAND). A stand which held several small oil-burning lamps (Mark 4:21). *Lampstand:* NIV, NRSV.

CANKER (GANGRENE). A disease which led to rapid deterioration of the flesh (2 Tim. 2:17). *Gangrene:* NIV, NRSV.

CANKERWORM (LOCUST). A locust or grasshopper in the caterpillar stage of its growth (Joel 1:4). *Locust:* NIV, NRSV. See also *Locust; Palmerworm*.

CAPERNAUM. A city on the northwestern shore of the Sea of Galilee which served as the headquarters for Jesus during His Galilean ministry (Matt. 9:1; Mark 2:1). Capernaum was the home of His disciples Matthew (Matt. 9:9), Simon Peter, Andrew, James, and John (Mark 1:21–29).

CAPH. The eleventh letter of the Hebrew alphabet, used as a heading over Ps. 119:81–88.

CAPHTOR. The original home of the Philistines, probably the island of Crete (Jer. 47:4). See also *Crete; Philistines.*

CAPITALS. See *Pommels.*

CAPPADOCIA. A Roman province of Asia Minor. Christians of Cappadocia were addressed by Peter (1 Pet. 1:1).

CAPTAIN. A title for a civil or military officer (Judg. 4:7). This is also a title for Christ (Heb. 2:10). *Author:* NIV; *Pioneer:* NRSV.

CAPTIVITY. The carrying away of the citizens of a country by a conquering nation. The nation of Israel (the Northern Kingdom) was carried into captivity by the Assyrians about 722 B.C. (2 Kings 15:29), while

Judah (the Southern Kingdom) suffered the same fate at the hand of the Babylonians in 587 B.C. (2 Chron. 36:6–7). See also *Dispersion.*

CARBUNCLE (BERYL, EMERALD). A precious stone of deep red color in the breastplate of the high priest (Exod. 28:17). *Beryl:* NIV; *Emerald:* NRSV. See also *Emerald.*

CARCHEMISH/CHARCHEMISH. An ancient city near the Euphrates River in Mesopotamia (Jer. 46:2), where the Assyrian army was victorious over the Egyptians. *Charchemish:* 2 Chron. 35:20–24.

CARMEL, MOUNT. A prominent mountain in northern Palestine where the prophet Elijah demonstrated the power of God in a dramatic encounter with the priests of the pagan god Baal (1 Kings 18:17–39).

CARNAL (WORLDLY). To give in to the desires of the flesh. Following their natural desires led the Christians of Corinth into division and strife (1 Cor. 3:1–5). *Worldly:* NIV.

CARNELIAN. See *Sardine; Sardius.*

CARPUS. A friend to whom Paul entrusted his cloak (2 Tim. 4:13).

CARRION VULTURE. See *Gier Eagle.*

CART. A two-wheeled wagon, usually pulled by oxen (1 Sam. 6:7–8). See also *Wagon.*

CASLUHIM (CASLUHITES). An ancient people descended from Mizraim (the Hebrew word for Egypt), son of Ham (Gen. 10:14). *Casluhites:* NIV. See also *Egypt; Mizraim.*

CASSIA. The dried bark of a tree similar to the cinnamon which was prized for its pleasing fragrance. Cassia was used as an ingredient of holy oil (Exod. 30:24).

CASTAWAY. A word for "worthlessness" or "rejection." Paul used this word to express the idea of "disqualified" or "rejected" (1 Cor. 9:27).

CASTLE (BARRACKS). A fortress or defense tower. The "castle" into which Paul was taken was the quarters of the Roman soldiers at Jerusalem in the fortress of Antonia near the temple (Acts 21:34). *Barracks:* NIV, NRSV.

CASTOR AND POLLUX (TWIN BROTHERS). The twin sons of Zeus in Greek and Roman mythology who were considered special protectors of sailors. Paul's ship to Rome featured a carving of these two pagan gods (Acts 28:11). *Twin Brothers:* NRSV.

CATHOLIC EPISTLES. See *General Epistles.*

CAVE. A natural passageway or cavern within the earth. Caves were used as residences (Gen. 19:30) and burial places (Gen. 49:29). See also *Sepulchre.*

CEDAR. A cone-bearing evergreen tree which produces a reddish, fragrant wood. Lumber from the cedars of Lebanon was used in the temple in Jerusalem (1 Kings 5:1–10).

CEDRON. See *Kidron.*

CENCHREA (CENCHRE-AE). A harbor of Corinth through which Paul passed during the second missionary journey (Acts 18:18). This was the site of a church mentioned by Paul (Rom. 16:1), perhaps a branch of the church at Corinth. *Cenchreae:* NRSV.

CENSER. A small, portable container in which incense was burned (Num. 16:6–39). See also *Firepan; Incense.*

CENSUS. A count of the population of a country or region (2 Sam. 24:1–9; Luke 2:1–3).

CENTURION. A Roman military officer who commanded a force of one hundred soldiers (Acts 10:1, 22).

CEPHAS. See *Simon,* No. 1.

CHAFF. The leftover husks of threshed grain, separated when the grain is tossed into the air. The ungodly are compared to chaff (Ps. 1:4). See also *Winnowing.*

CHALCEDONY (AGATE). A precious stone cut from multicolored quartz and used in the foundation of the heavenly city, or New Jerusalem (Rev. 21:19). *Agate:* NRSV. See also *Agate.*

CHALDEA, CHALDEANS. See *Babylonia.*

CHALKSTONE. A soft and easily crushed rock, similar to limestone (Isa. 27:9).

CHAMBER. A word for a room or an enclosed place in a house or public building (2 Kings 23:12).

CHAMBERLAIN (EUNUCH). An officer in charge of the royal chambers or the king's lodgings and wardrobe, and perhaps his harem (Esther 2:3). *Eunuch:* NIV, NRSV. See also *Eunuch.*

CHAMELEON. See *Mole.*

CHAMOIS (MOUNTAIN SHEEP). A word which probably refers to a wild goat or a wild mountain sheep (Deut. 14:5). *Mountain sheep:* NIV, NRSV.

CHANAAN. See *Canaan.*

CHANCELLOR (COMMANDING OFFICER, ROYAL DEPUTY). A high official of the Persian kings whose exact duties are unknown (Ezra 4:8). *Commanding officer:* NIV; *Royal deputy:* NRSV.

CHARCHEMISH. See *Carchemish.*

CHARGER (PLATTER). A dish or shallow basin used in sacrificial ceremonies (Num. 7:13, 79). The head of John the Baptist was placed on a charger (Matt. 14:11). *Platter:* NIV, NRSV. See also *Platter.*

CHARIOT. A two-wheeled carriage drawn by horses. High

government officials rode in chariots, and they were also used as instruments of war (Judg. 4:15).

CHARIOT CITIES. The cities where Solomon stored or head-quartered his chariots and chariot forces (1 Kings 9:19).

CHARIOT OF FIRE. The fiery chariot with blazing horses which came between Elijah and Elisha as Elijah was taken into heaven by a whirlwind (2 Kings 2:11). See also *Elijah*.

CHARIOTS OF THE SUN. Chariots dedicated to the sun—a popular custom among the Persians, who worshiped this heavenly body. All chariots devoted to this practice among the Israelites were burned by King Josiah of Judah (2 Kings 23:11). See also *Sun*.

CHARITY. An old English word for "love" (1 Cor. 13). See *Love*.

CHARMERS. Magicians who claimed to be able to commune with the dead (Isa. 19:3). See also *Magic; Medium; Necromancer*.

CHARRAN. See *Haran*.

CHASTISEMENT (DISCI-PLINE). Punishment or discipline inflicted by God for guiding and correcting His children (Heb. 12:8). *Discipline:* NIV, NRSV. See also *Discipline*.

CHASTITY. A term for inward cleanliness, generally referring to sexual purity (2 Cor. 11:2). See also *Clean*.

CHEBAR. A river or canal of Babylonia where Jewish captives settled during the Exile. Ezekiel's visions came to him at Chebar (Ezek. 1:3; 10:15, 20).

CHEDORLAOMER. A king of Elam who invaded Canaan in Abraham's time (Gen. 14:1–16).

CHEEK. To strike a person on the cheek was considered a grave insult (Job 16:10). Jesus taught believers to react to such acts with kindness (Luke 6:29).

CHEMOSH. The chief pagan god of the Moabites and Ammonites to which children were sacrificed (2 Kings 23:13; Judg. 11:24). See also *Human Sacrifice*.

CHERETHITES/CHERE-THIM. A tribe of the Philistines in southwest Palestine (1 Sam. 30:14). *Cherethim:* Ezek. 25:16.

CHERITH. A brook where the prophet Elijah hid and where he was fed by ravens during a famine (1 Kings 17:3–5).

CHERUBIM. An order of angelic, winged creatures (Gen. 3:24). Their function was to praise God and glorify His name (Ezek. 10:18–20).

CHETH. The eighth letter of the Hebrew alphabet, used as a heading over Ps. 119:57–64.

CHIEF. Head of a tribe or family (Num. 3:24, 32). See also *Duke*.

CHIEF SEATS. Places of honor sought by the scribes and Pharisees. Jesus taught His followers that the highest honor is to serve others (Mark 12:31, 38–39).

CHILD SACRIFICE. See *Human Sacrifice*.

CHILDREN. Children were looked upon as blessings from God (Ps. 127:3), and childlessness was considered a curse (Deut. 7:14). The word is also used symbolically of those who belong to Christ (Rom. 8:17). See also *Parents*.

CHILEAB/DANIEL. A son of David; also called *Daniel* (2 Sam. 3:3; 1 Chron. 3:1).

CHILION. The son of Elimelech and Naomi and brother-in-law of Ruth (Ruth 1:2–5).

CHINNEROTH. See *Galilee, Sea of.*

CHIOS. An island in the Aegean Sea passed by Paul on his way to Jerusalem after the third missionary journey (Acts 20:15).

CHISLEU (KISLEV, CHISLEV). The ninth month of the Hebrew year, roughly equivalent to parts of our November and December (Neh. 1:1). *Kislev:* NIV; *Chislev:* NRSV.

CHITTIM. See *Cyprus*.

CHLOE. A Christian disciple at the place from which Paul sent his first epistle to the Corinthians—probably Philippi (1 Cor. 1:11).

CHORAZIN. A city north of the Sea of Galilee where Jesus did many mighty works. He pronounced a woe on this city because of its unbelief (Matt. 11:21).

CHOSEN LADY. See *Elect Lady*.

CHRIST. The Anointed One, the O.T. Hebrew Messiah. See *Jesus Christ*.

CHRISTIAN. A disciple or follower of Christ. The name apparently was first used of the believers in the church at Antioch (Acts 11:26). Other words which express the same idea are saint (Acts 9:13) and brethren (Acts 6:3). See also *Way, The*.

CHRONICLES, BOOKS OF FIRST AND SECOND. Two historical books of the O.T. which cover several centuries of history, beginning with a genealogy of Adam and his descendants (1 Chron. 1–9) and ending with the return of Jewish captives to their homeland about 538 B.C. following a period of exile among the Babylonians and Persians (2 Chron. 36).

Major events covered in the books include: (1) the death of King Saul (1 Chron. 10); (2) the reign of King David (1 Chron. 10–29); (3) the reign of King Solomon (2 Chron. 1–9); and (4) the reigns of selected kings of Judah after the division of the kingdom into two nations following Solomon's death (2 Chron. 10–36).

CHRYSOLYTE (CHRYSOLITE). A precious stone, possibly yellow topaz, used in the foundation of the heavenly city, or New Jerusalem (Rev. 21:20). *Chrysolite:* NIV, NRSV. See also *Beryl*.

CHRYSOPRASUS (CHRYSOPRASE). A precious stone, green in color and similar to agate, used in the foundation of the heavenly city, or New Jerusalem (Rev. 21:20). *Chrysoprase:* NIV, NRSV. See also *Beryl*.

CHURCH. A local body of believers assembled for Christian worship (Acts 15:4; 1 Cor. 1:2) as well as all the redeemed of the ages who belong to Christ (Gal. 1:13; Eph. 5:27). The word *church* is a translation of a Greek term which means "an assembly." Christ is head of His body the Church and His will is to be preeminent (Col. 1:18) by virtue of His redeeming work and lordship (Col. 1:14; 3:15–17). The Church's mission is to win the lost (Luke 4:18) and minister to others in the world. See also *Assembly; Congregation; People of God; Saint*.

CHUSHAN-RISHATHAIM (CUSHAN-RISHATHAIM). A king of Mesopotamia who oppressed the Israelites. He was defeated by the first judge, Othniel (Judg. 3:8–10). *Cushan-rishathaim:* NIV, NRSV.

CILICIA. A province of Asia Minor whose major city was Tarsus, Paul's hometown. Paul visited Cilicia after his conversion (Acts 9:30; Gal. 1:21).

CIRCUMCISION. The removal of the foreskin of the male sex organ, a ritual performed generally on the eighth day after birth (Exod. 12:44). This practice, probably initiated with Abraham (Gen. 17:9–14), signified the covenant between God and His people, the Hebrews. In the N.T., the word is often used symbolically for the casting off of sin or worldly desires (Col. 2:11).

CIRCUMSPECT. Prudent and holy. Paul charged the Ephesian Christians to live circumspectly (Eph. 5:15).

CISTERN. A large pit or hole in the ground which served as a water reservoir (2 Kings 18:31). Empty cisterns were sometimes used as dungeons or prisons (Gen. 37:24). See also *Pit; Prison.*

CITIES OF REFUGE. Six cities assigned to the Levites and set aside as sanctuaries for those who killed other persons by accident. These cities, scattered throughout Palestine, were Bezer, Golan, Hebron, Kedesh, Ramoth-gilead, and Shechem (Josh. 20:7–9). See also *Avenger of Blood; Manslayer.*

CITIES OF THE PLAIN. Five cities on the plain of Jordan destroyed in Abraham's time because of the great sin of their inhabitants. These cities were Admah, Bela or Zoar, Gomorrah, Sodom, and Zeboiim (Gen. 19:22–30).

CITRON WOOD. See *Thyine Wood.*

CITY. A population center where trade and commerce flourished. Many biblical cities were protected by a massive defensive wall. The first city mentioned in the Bible was built by Cain (Gen. 4:17). See also *Fenced City.*

CITY CLERK. See *Town clerk.*

CITY GATE. A massive wooden door in a city wall, often reinforced with brass or iron for greater strength. Goods were often bought and sold and legal matters were discussed just inside the gate (Ruth 4:11). Gates in the wall of Jerusalem mentioned by specific name in the Bible include the Beautiful Gate (Acts 3:10), Fish Gate (Neh. 3:3), Horse Gate (2 Chron. 23:15), and Water Gate (Neh. 3:26). See also *Fenced City*.

CITY OF DAVID. A title applied to Bethlehem and Jerusalem because of David's close association with these cities (Neh. 3:15; Luke 2:11). See also *Bethlehem; Jerusalem*.

CITY OF GOD. A name applied to the city of Jerusalem, religious capital of the nation of Israel (Ps. 46:4–5).

CLAUDA. A small island about fifty miles from Crete, where Paul's ship sought protection during a storm (Acts 27:16).

CLAUDIA. A Christian believer mentioned by Paul (2 Tim. 4:21).

CLAUDIUS. See *Caesar,* No. 3.

CLAUDIUS LYSIAS. A Roman military officer who rescued Paul from an angry mob at Jerusalem (Acts 21:30–35; 23:22–30).

CLAY. Fine soil used for making bricks and pottery (Jer. 18:1–6). While still moist, squares of clay were also written on, then baked to produce a hard, permanent tablet. See also *Nuzi Tablets; Ras Shamra Tablets*.

CLAY TABLET. See *Tile*.

CLEAN. A word used by the Hebrews to describe things that were ceremonially pure (Lev. 11). The word is also used symbolically to signify holiness or righteousness (Ps. 24:4). See also *Purification; Wash*.

CLEAVE. To hold firmly to or to remain faithful. Husbands are instructed to cleave to their wives (Matt. 19:5).

CLEMENT. A Christian believer at Philippi commended by Paul (Phil. 4:3).

CLEOPAS. A Christian believer to whom Christ appeared on the road to Emmaus after His resurrection (Luke 24:18).

CLEOPHAS (CLOPAS). The husband of Mary, one of the women who viewed the crucifixion of Jesus (John 19:25). *Clopas:* NIV, NRSV.

CLOKE/CLOAK. A one-piece, sleeveless garment, similar to a short robe, worn by both men and women in Bible times (Matt. 5:40). *Cloak:* NIV, NRSV. See also *Mantle.*

CLOTH. See *Handkerchief; Napkin.*

CLOUD. A mass of water vapor in the sky. Clouds are often associated with God's presence and protection (Exod. 16:10). At His second coming, Christ will come in "the clouds of heaven" (Matt. 24:30). See also *Pillar of Fire and Cloud.*

CLUB. See *Maul.*

CNIDUS. A harbor city in southern Asia Minor passed by Paul during his voyage to Rome (Acts 27:7).

COAT OF MAIL. See *Brigandine.*

COCK. A rooster. The crowing of the cock in Mark 13:35 refers to the third watch of the night, just before daybreak.

COCKATRICE (VIPER, ADDER). A poisonous snake (Isa. 11:8). *Viper:* NIV; *Adder:* NRSV.

COCKLE (WEED). A weed which grows in fields of grain (Job 31:40). *Weed:* NIV, NRSV.

COLOSSE (COLOSSAE). A city about 100 miles east of Ephesus and the site of a church to which Paul wrote one of his epistles (Col. 1:2). *Colossae:* NRSV. Whether Paul visited this city is uncertain.

COLOSSIANS, EPISTLE TO THE. A short epistle of the apostle Paul on the theme of Christ's glory and majesty and His work of redemption (chaps. 1–2). Paul also challenged the Christians at Colosse to put on the character of Christ and to express His love in their relationships with others (chaps. 3–4).

COLT. A young donkey. Christ rode a colt into Jerusalem (Matt. 21:1–7). See also *Ass.*

COMFORTER (COUN-SELOR, ADVOCATE). A title for the Holy Spirit which means "to strengthen" or "to bolster" (John 14:16–26). *Counselor:* NIV; *Advocate:* NRSV. See also *Advocate; Helper; Holy Spirit; Paraclete.*

COMMANDMENT. An order imposed by a person of rank or authority (Neh. 11:23). Jesus described the statute to love God and man as the greatest commandment (John 13:34). See also *Statute*.

COMMANDING OFFICER. See *Chancellor*.

COMMANDMENTS, TEN. See *Ten Commandments*.

COMMISSION. A special assignment from a person of authority (Ezra 8:36). Jesus' Great Commission to all His followers is to make disciples of all people everywhere (Matt. 28:19–20).

COMPACT. See *League*.

COMPANION. See *Yokefellow*.

COMPASSION. An attitude of mercy and forgiveness. As the compassionate Savior (Matt. 15:32), Jesus expects His followers to show compassion toward others (Matt. 18:33). See also *Mercy*.

CONCEIT. Vanity or pride; to have an exaggerated opinion of oneself. Paul warned Christians against such behavior (Rom. 11:25). See also *Pride; Vanity*.

CONCUBINE. A female slave or mistress; a secondary or common-law wife. Concubines were common among the patriarchs of the O.T. (Gen. 35:22), but Jesus taught the concept of monogamy—marriage to one person only (Matt. 19:4–9). See also *Paramour*.

CONCUPISCENCE (EVIL DESIRES). Sinful desire or sexual lust. Paul warned Christians of the dangers of this sin (Col. 3:5). *Evil desires:* NIV, NRSV.

CONDEMNATION. To declare a sinner guilty and deserving of punishment (Rom. 5:18). Jesus' mission was not to condemn but to save (John 3:17–18).

CONDUIT. A pipe or aqueduct through which water was channeled. King Hezekiah of Judah cut a conduit through solid rock to pipe water into Jerusalem (2 Kings 20:20). See also *Hezekiah*.

CONEY (BADGER). A small, furry animal which lived among the rocky cliffs of Palestine, probably the rock badger (Prov. 30:26). *Badger:* NRSV.

CONFESS. To admit or acknowledge one's sin (Josh. 7:19) and to proclaim one's faith in a bold and forthright manner (Rom. 10:9–10).

CONGREGATION. A gathering of people for worship or religious instruction (Acts 13:43). See also *Assembly*.

CONIAH. See *Jehoiachin*.

CONSECRATION. To dedicate or set apart for God's exclusive use. Believers are encouraged to consecrate or sanctify themselves to God's service (2 Tim. 2:21). See also *Ordain; Sanctification*.

CONSOLATION. A word which expresses the idea of comfort combined with encouragement. Believers find consolation in Jesus Christ and His Holy Spirit (Rom. 15:5).

CONTENTION (DISAGREEMENT). Severe disagreement which leads to sharp divisions among people, including Christian believers (Acts 15:39). Christians are encouraged to pursue peace with others (Rom. 12:18–21). *Disagreement:* NIV, NRSV. See also *Discord; Strife*.

CONTENTMENT. Satisfaction; freedom from worry and anxiety. This state of mind was modeled for all believers by Paul (Phil. 4:11).

CONTRITE. A meek or humble attitude (Ps. 51:17). A contrite person also shows genuine grief or sorrow over his sin (2 Cor. 7:10). See also *Humility; Meekness; Repentance*.

CONVERSATION. A word for behavior or lifestyle. Paul urged Christians to live in accordance with the gospel of Christ (Phil. 1:27).

CONVERSION. See *New Birth*.

CONVERT. See *Proselyte*.

CONVICTION. An awareness of one's sin and guilt (John 8:9) which leads to confession and repentance. The Holy Spirit is the agent of conviction (Heb. 3:7). See also *Holy Spirit; Repentance*.

CONVOCATION. A sacred assembly of the people of Israel for worship in connection with observance of the Sabbath or one of their major religious festivals, such as Passover or Pentecost (Lev. 23:2–8). See also *Assembly*.

COOS. A small island in the Mediterranean Sea which Paul passed on his way to Jerusalem at the close of the third missionary journey (Acts 21:1).

COPPER. See *Brass*.

COR. The largest liquid measure used by the Hebrew people, possibly equivalent to fifty or more gallons (Ezek. 45:14).

CORAL. A precious substance formed in the sea from the bodies of tiny sea creatures (Ezek. 27:16). Coral was apparently used for making beads and other fine jewelry (Job 28:18). See also *Ruby*.

CORBAN. A Hebrew word meaning a sacred gift, or an offering devoted to God. Jesus condemned the Pharisees for encouraging people to make such gifts while neglecting to care for their own parents (Mark 7:11–13).

CORD. See *Line; Rope*.

CORE. See *Korah*.

CORIANDER. A plant whose seeds were used as a medicine and as a seasoning for food (Num. 11:7).

CORINTH. A major port city in Greece on the trade route between Rome and its eastern provinces where Paul lived for eighteen months, establishing a church (Acts 18:1–11). The city was known for its immorality, paganism, and corruption.

CORINTHIANS, FIRST AND SECOND EPISTLES TO THE. Two letters of the apostle Paul to the church at Corinth, written to believers who were struggling to move beyond their pagan background and lifestyle.

First Corinthians deals mainly with problems in the church, including divisions (chaps. 1–4), sexual immorality (chaps. 5–6), and abuses of the Lord's Supper and spiritual gifts (chaps. 11–12; 14).

The themes of Second Corinthians include Paul's view of ministry and reconciliation (chaps. 1–6), support of the impoverished Christians at Jerusalem (chaps. 8–9), and Paul's example of suffering and abuse and defense of his credentials as an apostle (chaps. 10–13).

CORMORANT (DESERT OWL, HAWK). A large bird cited by Isaiah as a symbol of desolation and destruction (Isa. 34:11). *Desert owl:* NIV; *Hawk:* NRSV. See also *Pelican*.

CORN (GRAIN). A generic term for several different grains, including wheat, barley, and millet (Matt. 12:1).

Grain: NIV, NRSV. See also *Wheat.*

CORNELIUS. A Roman soldier from Caesarea who sought out the apostle Peter at Joppa and became the first Gentile convert to Christianity (Acts 10:1–48). This event showed clearly that the church was meant for Gentiles as well as Jews (Acts 15:7–11).

CORNER STONE. A stone strategically placed to align two walls and tie the building together. This is also a title for Christ as the keystone of the church (Eph. 2:20). See also *Foundation.*

CORNET (HORN). A musical instrument similar to the horn or trumpet (Dan. 3:5–7). *Horn:* NIV, NRSV.

COULTER (PLOWSHARE). An agricultural instrument of metal, probably the tip of a plow (1 Sam. 13:21). *Plowshare:* NIV, NRSV. See also *Plowshare.*

COUNCIL/SANHEDRIN. The highest court of the Jewish nation in N.T. times, composed of seventy-one priests, scribes, and elders; and presided over by the high priest. The Council accused Jesus of blasphemy against God, but it didn't have the power to put Jesus to death. It brought Him before Pilate, the Roman procurator, for sentencing (Matt. 26:65–66; John 18:31; 19:12). The Council also brought charges against Peter and John and the other apostles (Acts 4:1–23; 5:17–41) and Paul (Acts 22–24). *Sanhedrin:* NIV.

COUNSELLOR (COUNSELOR). A person who gives wise counsel or imparts advice. Kings employed counselors (1 Chron. 27:33). This is also one of the messianic titles of Christ (Isa. 9:6). *Counselor:* NIV, NRSV. See also *Comforter; Holy Spirit; Paraclete.*

COUNTENANCE. A word for the face or the expression on a person's face (Dan. 5:6).

COURAGE. Fearlessness and bravery in the face of danger (Acts 28:15). Moses exhorted Joshua to have courage (Deut. 31:7–8).

COURIER. See *Post.*

COURT. An enclosed yard or patio attached to a house or public building. Both the tabernacle (Exod. 27:9) and the temple in Jerusalem had courts or courtyards (1 Kings 6:36).

79

COURT OF THE GENTILES. An outer court in the Jewish temple beyond which Gentile worshipers could not go. The splitting of the curtain between this court and the inner court at Jesus' death symbolized the Gentiles' equal access to God (Matt. 27:51; Eph. 2:11–14). See also *Gentile; Middle Wall of Partition.*

COUSIN. A general term denoting any degree of relationship among blood relatives—cousin, nephew, aunt, uncle, etc. (Luke 1:36).

COVENANT. An agreement between two people or groups, particularly that between God and His people which promised His blessings in return for their obedience and devotion (Gen. 15:1–21). Through His sacrificial death, Jesus became the mediator of a new covenant, bringing salvation and eternal life to all who trust in Him (Heb. 10:12–17). See also *Testament.*

COVERED COLONNADE. See *Portico.*

COVETOUSNESS. Greed, or a burning desire for what belongs to others. This sin is specifically prohibited by the Ten Commandments (Exod. 20:17), and Paul warned against its dangers (Col. 3:5). See also *Greed.*

COW. See *Kine.*

CREATION. The actions of God through which He brought man and the physical world into existence. God existed before the world, and He produced the universe from nothing (Gen. 1:1–2). As the sovereign, self-existing God, He also rules over His creation (Ps. 47:7–9). See also *Creature.*

CREATOR. A title for God which emphasizes that He is the maker of all things and the sovereign ruler of His creation (Isa. 40:28; John 1:1–3; Col. 1:15–16). See also *Almighty; Sovereignty of God.*

CREATURE (CREATION). Any being created by God, including man (Gen. 2:19). Through God's redemption, a believer becomes a new creature (2 Cor. 5:17). *Creation:* NIV, NRSV. See also *Creation.*

CREEPING THING. A phrase for winged insects and reptiles (Lev. 11:21).

CRESCENS. A disciple who left Paul and went to Galatia (2 Tim. 4:10).

A rocky hill in Jerusalem known as "Gordon's Calvary," the site where Jesus was crucified, according to one tradition.

Courtesy Israel Ministry of Tourism

CRETE. A large island in the Mediterranean Sea by which Paul sailed during his voyage to Rome (Acts 27:1–13). Titus apparently served as leader of a church on Crete (Titus 1:4–5). See also *Titus.*

CRIMINAL. See *Malefactor.*

CRIMSON. See *Scarlet.*

CRISPING PIN (PURSE, HANDBAG). A purse or bag for carrying money (Isa. 3:22). *Purse:* NIV; *Handbag:* NRSV. See also *Purse.*

CRISPUS. Chief ruler of the synagogue at Corinth who became a Christian believer (Acts 18:8) and was baptized by Paul (1 Cor. 1:14).

CROCUS. See *Rose.*

CROSS. A wooden stake with a cross beam on which Jesus was put to death by the Roman authorities—a common form of capital punishment in N.T. times. Attached to the cross with nails or leather thongs, the victim generally suffered for two or three days before dying from exposure, exhaustion, and the loss of body fluids. But Jesus died after only six hours on the cross (John 19:30–33). His sacrificial death freed believers from the power of sin (Rom. 6:6–11) and sealed their reconciliation to God (2 Cor. 5:19). See also *Atonement; Redeem; Savior.*

CROWD. See *Multitude.*

CROWN. An ornamental headdress worn by kings and queens as a symbol of power and authority (2 Kings 11:12). The word is also used symbolically for righteous behavior befitting a believer (2 Tim. 4:8) and God's gift of eternal life (Jas. 1:12). See also *Diadem.*

CRUCIBLE. See *Fining Pot.*

CRUCIFIXION. See *Cross.*

CRUSE (JUG). A small earthen jug or flask for holding liquids (1 Kings 17:14–15). *Jug:* NIV, NRSV. See also *Pitcher.*

CRYSTAL. A transparent, colorless rock, perhaps a form of quartz (Rev. 22:1).

CUBIT. The standard unit for measurement of length, equivalent to about eighteen inches (Gen. 6:15–16).

CUCKOW (SEA GULL). A bird considered unclean by the Hebrews, probably a type of sea bird (Lev. 11:16). *Sea gull:* NRSV.

CUCUMBER. A climbing vine which produced vegetables probably similar to our cucumbers (Num. 11:5).

CUMMIN. A plant which produced seeds used for medicines and for seasoning food (Isa. 28:25–27). Jesus criticized the Pharisees for their shallow legalism in tithing the seeds from this insignificant plant while ignoring more important matters, such as mercy and faith (Matt. 23:23).

CUP. A drinking utensil (Gen. 44:12). The cup is also symbolic of the blood of the new covenant established by Christ (Matt. 20:22; 1 Cor. 10:16).

CUPBEARER. A royal household servant who tasted wine before serving to make sure it had not been poisoned (Neh. 1:11). The butler imprisoned with Joseph was probably a cupbearer to the Egyptian pharaoh (Gen. 40:1–13).

CURSE. A call for evil or misfortune against another (Gen.

4:11). Jesus taught that Christians are to return kindness for such actions (Luke 6:28).

CURTAIN. See *Veil*, No. 1.

CUSH. Ham's oldest son and a grandson of Noah (1 Chron. 1:8–10).

CUSHAN-RISHATHAIM. See *Chushan-rishathaim.*

CUSHI. A messenger sent by Joab to announce Absalom's death to King David (2 Sam. 18:21–32).

CUTH/CUTHAH. A city or district of Babylonia which provided colonists who settled the Northern Kingdom after it fell to the Assyrians (2 Kings 17:30). *Cuthah:* 2 Kings 17:24.

CYMBALS. Curved metal plates used as musical instruments (1 Cor. 13:1).

CYPRESS. See *Box Tree; Fir; Gopher Wood.*

CYPRUS/CHITTIM/KITTIM. A large island in the Mediterranean Sea about 125 miles off the coast of Palestine which Paul and Barnabas visited during the first missionary journey (Acts 13:4–5). Barnabas was a native of Cyprus (Acts 4:36). *Chittim:* Jer. 2:10; *Kittim:* Gen. 10:4.

CYRENE. A Greek city in North Africa and home of the Simon of Cyrene who carried the cross of Jesus (Matt. 27:32).

CYRENIUS (QUIRINIUS). The Roman governor of Syria at the time of Jesus' birth (Luke 2:1–4). *Quirinius:* NIV, NRSV.

CYRUS. The founding king of the Persian empire (reigned about 559–530 B.C.). After defeating the Babylonians, he allowed the Jewish captives to return to their homeland about 536 B.C. (2 Chron. 36:22–23; Ezra 1:1–4). See also *Persia.*

-D-

DAGON. The chief pagan god of the Philistines, which apparently had the head of a man and the tail of a fish. This idol fell before the ark of the covenant in the pagan temple at Ashdod (1 Sam. 5:1–5). See also *Philistines.*

DALETH. The fourth letter of the Hebrew alphabet, used as a heading over Ps. 119:25–32.

Excavated ruins of the ancient city of Dan in northern Israel.
Courtesy Israel Ministry of Tourism

DALMANUTHA. A place on the western shore of the Sea of Galilee visited by Jesus (Mark 8:10).

DALMATIA. A province on the eastern coast of the Adriatic Sea visited by Titus (2 Tim. 4:10).

DAMARIS. A woman of Athens converted under Paul's ministry (Acts 17:33–34).

DAMASCUS (SYRIA-DAMASCUS). The capital city of Syria, located north of Mt. Hermon in northern Palestine. Paul was traveling to Damascus to persecute Christians when he met the risen Lord in a life-transforming vision (Acts 9:1–8). Damascus is considered the oldest continually inhabited city in the world. *Syria-damascus:* 1 Chron. 18:6. See also *Syria.*

DAMNATION. Judgment and consignment to everlasting punishment; the fate of the wicked or those who reject Christ (Mark 16:16). See also *Hell; Judgment, Last; Perdition.*

DAMSEL. A word for a young woman (Mark 5:39–42).

DAN.
1. Jacob's fifth son and ancestor of one of the tribes

of Israel (Gen. 30:6; Num. 1:38–39). See also *Tribes of Israel.*

2. A village in the territory allotted to the tribe of Dan. It was located farther north than any other city of Palestine during most of the O.T. era. The phrase "from Dan even to Beersheba" (Judg. 20:1) described the entire territory of the Hebrew nation from north to south. *Laish:* Isa. 10:30.

DANCE. Rhythmic body movements, usually to musical accompaniment, to express joy and gratitude to God (Exod. 15:20–21). King David danced when the ark of the covenant was recovered and brought to Jerusalem (2 Sam. 6:14–16).

DANIEL.

1. A prophet of the O.T. known for his faithfulness to the God of Israel among the pagan Babylonians and Persians. Refusing to worship King Darius, he was thrown into a den of lions but was miraculously delivered by the Lord (Dan. 6:1–24). *Belteshazzar:* Persian form (Dan. 1:7).

2. Another name for Chileab, a son of David (1 Chron. 3:1). See *Chileab.*

DANIEL, BOOK OF. An apocalyptic book of the O.T. known

for its images of horns and beasts that are similar to those described in the Revelation to John in the N.T. The two major sections of Daniel are (1) the trials and tribulations suffered by Daniel and his three friends as captives of the Babylonians and Persians (chaps. 1–7) and (2) Daniel's visions and dreams about the future (chaps. 8–12). The prophet's famous "seventy weeks" prophecy has been interpreted as a period of 490 years (seventy weeks, representing seventy years, multiplied by seven) from Daniel's time until the coming of the Messiah (9:20–27). See also *Apocalypse.*

DARIC. See *Dram.*

DARIUS. A title for the kings of Persia. Four different kings with this title are mentioned in the O.T.:

1. Darius I or Darius the Great (reigned about 522–485 B.C.). Successor to Cyrus, he continued Cyrus's policy of restoring the Jewish people to their homeland (Ezra 6:1–12).

2. Darius II or Darius the Persian (Neh. 12:22), who reigned about 424–405 B.C

3. Darius III or Darius Codomannus (reigned about 336–330 B.C.). He is probably the "fourth" king of Persia

mentioned by the prophet Daniel (Dan. 11:2).

4. Darius the Mede, who made Daniel ruler over several provincial leaders (Dan. 6:1–2). Some scholars believe this is the same king as Darius II.

DARKNESS. The absence of light. Darkness ruled the world before God's creation of light (Gen. 1:2). Thus, darkness is symbolic of man's sin, rebellion, and ignorance (Job 24:13–17). See also *Light*.

DART (JAVELIN, SPEAR). A javelin or short spear. Absalom was killed by darts (2 Sam. 18:14). *Javelin:* NIV; *Spear:* NRSV. See also *Javelin; Spear*.

DATHAN. A leader of the rebellion against Moses in the wilderness. All the rebels were destroyed by an earthquake (Num. 16:1–35).

DAUGHTER. A word used for female offspring of parents as well as a distant female relative, such as a granddaughter or niece (Gen. 20:12; 24:48).

DAUGHTER OF ZION. A symbolic expression for the city of Jerusalem and its inhabitants (Ps. 9:14). See also *Jerusalem*.

DAVID. The popular king of Judah described by God as "a man after mine own heart" and an earthly ancestor of the promised Messiah, Jesus Christ (Luke 2:4–7). A descendant of the tribe of Judah (1 Chron. 28:4), he was a native of Bethlehem (1 Sam. 17:12). As a shepherd boy, he defeated the Philistine giant Goliath (1 Sam. 17:44–52). He served as King Saul's musician and armor bearer (1 Sam. 16:14–21) and was later anointed king after Saul's sin and disobedience (1 Sam. 16:11–13).

Forced to flee from Saul's jealousy and wrath (1 Sam. 21:10), David was befriended by Saul's son Jonathan (1 Sam. 19:1–3). After he became king, he united the Hebrew tribes into one nation with Jerusalem as the capital city (2 Sam. 5:1–10) and defeated many enemy nations (2 Sam. 8:1–15).

In a moment of weakness, David committed adultery with Bath-sheba (2 Sam. 11:1–4), but he later repented (Ps. 32; Ps. 51). He was forgiven and restored, but the consequences of his sin remained (2 Sam. 12:13–14). He suffered family tragedies (2 Sam. 12:15–20; 18:31–33) and wrote many psalms (see Pss. 54, 59, 65). He was succeeded as king by his

Camels graze at the En-gedi Oasis near the Dead Sea, where David hid from King Saul. *Courtesy Israel Ministry of Tourism*

son Solomon (1 Kings 2:12). In the N.T., Jesus was often called the "son of David" (Matt. 1:1; Mark 10:48). See also *Absalom; Bethlehem; Jerusalem.*

DAVID, TOWER OF. Fortress built by David at an unknown location (Song of Sol. 4:4).

DAY. The twenty-four hour period during which the earth rotates on its own axis. The Hebrews measured their day from sunset to sunset (Exod. 12:18). The twelve hours of daylight began with the first hour at sunup (about 6:00 A.M.). Midday or noon was the sixth hour, and the twelfth hour ended at sundown, or about 6:00 P.M.

DAY OF THE LORD. A phrase usually interpreted as a period in the end-time when God will bring His purpose for man and the world to fulfillment. This will be a day of judgment for the rebellious and sinful (Jer. 46:10) and a time of deliverance for the godly (Joel 2:28–32). Any time—whether now or in the distant future—when the Lord acts, intervening in history for the purpose of deliverance and judgment, may also be described as the "day of the Lord" (Isa. 13:6). See also *Damnation; Judgment, Last; Punishment.*

87

The Dead Sea, also known as the Salt Sea, in southern Palestine. *Courtesy Israel Ministry of Tourism*

DAY STAR/LUCIFER (MORNING STAR). A star which appears just before daybreak, signaling the beginning of a new day (2 Pet. 1:19). *Morning star:* NIV. The word for day star is also translated as *Lucifer* (Isa. 14:12), and used as a name for the king of Babylon. See also *Morning Star.*

DAY'S JOURNEY. The distance that could be traveled in one day by camel or horse, probably about twenty-five miles (Jon. 3:3–4).

DAYSMAN (UMPIRE). A word for a mediator, umpire, or judge between contending parties (Job 9:33). *Umpire:* NRSV.

DAYSPRING. A word for dawn or daybreak (Job 38:12).

DEACON. An officer or servant of the church. The first "deacons" were probably the seven men of Greek background who were appointed by the church at Jerusalem to coordinate the distribution of food to the needy (Acts 6:1–7). The strict qualifications for deacons (1 Tim. 3:8–13) show this was an important office in the early church. Phoebe, a female believer, is called a "deacon" in the NRSV translation of Rom. 16:1 (*Servant:* KJV).

DEAD SEA/SALT SEA/ EAST SEA. A body of water (about fifty miles long by ten miles wide) into which the Jordan River empties at the lowest point on earth in southern Palestine. Because of the hot, dry climate, the water evaporates, leaving a high concentration of salt and other minerals. *Salt Sea:* Josh. 3:16; *East Sea:* Joel 2:20.

DEAD SEA SCROLLS. A group of scrolls or ancient manuscripts discovered since 1947 in caves around the Dead Sea. Written between 250 B.C. and A.D. 68 and placed in clay jars, the scrolls were preserved by the dry climate of the area. Among the scrolls was a complete manuscript of the book of Isaiah, written in Hebrew. See also *Qumran, Khirbet.*

DEAF. Unable to hear. The word is also used symbolically of spiritual coldness or apathy (Isa. 42:18–19).

DEATH. The end of physical existence. Death is the price man pays for his sin and rebellion against God, but God provides salvation and eternal life for believers through the atoning death of Jesus Christ (Rom. 6:23). "Second death" is eternal separation from God—the fate of unbelievers (Rev. 20:6).

DEBASED. See *Reprobate.*

DEBAUCHERY. See *Lasciviousness.*

DEBIR
1. A king of Eglon and one of the five Amorite kings killed by Joshua's army (Josh. 10:3–26).
2. A Canaanite city captured by Joshua (Josh. 10:38–39). *Kirjath-sanna:* Josh. 15:49; *Kirjath-sepher:* Judg. 1:11.

DEBORAH. A prophetess and judge of Israel who, along with Barak, defeated the Canaanite forces of Sisera (Judg. 4:4–14). She celebrated the victory in a triumphant song (Judg. 5:1–3). See also *Sisera.*

DEBT. Borrowed property or money which must be repaid. The Hebrews were encouraged not to charge interest to their own countrymen (Lev. 25:35–38), but foreigners could be charged (Deut. 23:20). See also *Usury.*

DECALOGUE. See *Ten Commandments.*

DECAPOLIS. A Roman province or district with a large Greek population which was situated mostly on the eastern side of the Jordan River in northern Palestine (Matt. 4:25).

DECEIT. See *Guile*.

DECEIVER. One who misleads another. Deception is one of the evil tricks used by Satan (2 John 7). See also *Satan*.

DECISION, VALLEY OF. See *Jehoshaphat, Valley of*.

DECREE. A command or official order issued by a king. Mary and Joseph were affected by the decree of the Roman emperor Caesar Augustus (Luke 2:1). See also *Statute*.

DEDICATION, FEAST OF. An eight-day festival commemorating the Jewish victories which restored the temple during the era of the Maccabees about 160 B.C. Jesus attended one of these festivals in Jerusalem (John 10:22–23). This feast was also known as the *Feast of Lights* or *Hanukkah*.

DEER. A fleet-footed animal which could be eaten by the Hebrews (Deut. 14:5). See also *Hart; Hind*.

DEFILEMENT. Contamination; to make something impure by acts of sin and rebellion. The O.T. law emphasized ceremonial cleanliness (Num. 9:13; Lev. 15:24), but Jesus emphasized the need for ethical living and moral purity (Mark 7:1–23).

DEGREES, SONGS OF. A title used in fifteen psalms of the book of Psalms (Pss. 120–134). The Hebrew word for degrees means "goings up." These songs of ascent may have been pilgrim psalms, sung by worshipers as they were "going up" to the temple at Jerusalem.

DEHAVITES. An Assyrian tribe which settled in Samaria after the defeat of the Northern Kingdom by the Assyrians. In later years the Dehavites opposed the rebuilding of the Jewish temple at Jerusalem (Ezra 4:9–16). See also *Samaritan*.

DELEGATION. See *Ambassage*.

DELILAH. A woman, probably a Philistine, who cut off Samson's long hair—the source of his strength—so he could be captured by his Philistine enemies (Judg. 16:13–21). See also *Samson*.

DEMAS. A fellow believer who deserted Paul (2 Tim. 4:10) after having worked with him on earlier occasions (Philem. 24; Col. 4:14).

DEMETRIUS.
1. A silversmith at Ephesus who made replicas of the temple where the pagan goddess Diana was worshiped. When his livelihood was threatened by Paul's preaching, Demetrius incited a riot against the apostle (Acts 19:24–31). See also *Diana*.
2. A Christian believer commended by John (3 John 12).

DEMON. An evil spirit with destructive power who opposes God. In His healing ministry, Jesus cast demons out of several people (Matt. 12:22–24; Luke 8:27–39).

DEMON POSSESSION. Invasion and control of a person by evil spirits. In N.T. times, these demons often caused disease (Mark 9:25), mental anguish (Matt. 8:28), and antisocial behavior (Luke 8:27–39). Jesus cast demons out of several people—an act which showed His power over the demonic forces of Satan (Mark 1:25; 9:29).

DEN OF LIONS. A deep cavern where lions were kept by the Persian kings, probably for the sport of lion hunting. Daniel was thrown into one of these pits, but he was miraculously delivered by God's hand (Dan. 6:16–24). See also *Daniel*, No. 1.

DENARIUS. See *Penny*.

DEPOSIT. See *Earnest*.

DEPRAVED. See *Reprobate*.

DEPUTY. A person empowered to act for another (1 Kings 22:47). See also *Proconsul*.

DERBE. A city or village of the province of Lycaonia visited by Paul and Barnabas during the first missionary journey (Acts 14:6–20).

DESERT. A dry, barren, wilderness place (Isa. 48:21; Luke 1:80). See also *Wilderness*.

DESERT OWL. See *Cormorant; Hawk; Pelican*.

DESIRE OF ALL NATIONS (DESIRED OF ALL NATIONS, TREASURE OF ALL NATIONS). A title for the coming Messiah which emphasizes His universal rule and power (Hag. 2:6–7). *Desired* *of all nations:* NIV; *Treasure of all nations:* NRSV.

DEUTERONOMY, BOOK OF. A book of the O.T. containing a series of speeches which Moses delivered to the Hebrew people as they prepared to enter and conquer the land of Canaan. This book repeats many of the laws of God revealed to Moses on Mt. Sinai about two generations earlier—thus its name *Deuteronomy,* which means "second law."

In these speeches (chaps. 1–33), Moses cautioned the people to remain faithful to God in the midst of the pagan Canaanite culture they were about to enter. The final chapter (34) recounts the death of Moses and the succession of Joshua as the leader of the Hebrew people. See also *Moses; Pentateuch.*

DEVIL. A title for Satan which emphasizes his work as a liar and deceiver (Luke 4:3). See also *Satan.*

DEW. Moisture which condenses on the earth during the night (Exod. 16:13–14; Judg. 6:37–40). The heavy dews of Palestine during the dry season from April to September provide moisture for the growing crops (Gen. 27:28).

DIADEM (CROWN). A headpiece decorated with precious stones and worn by a king (Isa. 28:5). *Crown:* NIV. See also *Crown.*

DIAL. An instrument which shows the hour of the day through its shadow cast by the sun (Isa. 38:8).

DIAMOND (EMERALD, MOONSTONE). A precious stone in the breastplate of the high priest (Exod. 28:18). *Emerald:* NIV; *Moonstone:* NRSV.

DIANA (ARTEMIS). The Roman name for the pagan goddess of hunting and virginity. Paul's preaching at Ephesus, a center of Diana worship, caused an uproar among craftsmen who earned their living by making images of Diana (Acts 19:24–35). *Artemis:* NIV, NRSV. See also *Demetrius,* No. 1; *Ephesus.*

DIBON. An Amorite town taken by Israel during the years of wilderness wandering (Num. 32:3).

DIDYMUS. See *Thomas.*

DILL. See *Anise.*

DINAH. The daughter of Jacob who was assaulted by Shechem (Gen. 34:1–24).

DINAITES. An Assyrian tribe which populated Samaria after the Northern Kingdom fell to the Assyrians (Ezra 4:9). See also *Samaritan*.

DIONYSIUS. A member of the Areopagus of Athens who believed Paul's testimony about Jesus the Messiah (Acts 17:34). See also *Areopagus*.

DIOTREPHES. A church leader condemned by the apostle John for his false teachings (3 John 9–10).

DISAGREEMENT. See *Contention*.

DISCERNING OF SPIRITS (DISTINGUISHING BETWEEN SPIRITS). A spiritual gift which enables certain believers to tell the difference between true and false teachers and teachings (1 Cor. 12:10). *Distinguishing between spirits:* NIV.

DISCIPLE. A person who follows and learns from another person or group, especially a believer who observes the teachings of Jesus (Acts 6:1–7). See also *Apostle*.

DISCIPLINARIAN. See *Schoolmaster*.

DISCIPLINE. To train or teach, as parents impart important truths to a child (Prov. 22:6). A disciplined person also controls his impulses, speech, and actions (1 Pet. 3:10). God disciplines His children through corrective actions (Heb. 12:6). See also *Chastisement*.

DISCORD. Disagreement produced by a contentious spirit (Prov. 6:14). Discord is a sign of worldliness among believers (1 Cor. 3:3). See also *Contention*.

DISGRACE. See *Shame*.

DISH. See *Platter*.

DISPERSION. A word which refers to the scattering of the Jewish people among other nations. Jeremiah predicted such a scattering (Jer. 25:34), and this happened when the Babylonians overran Judah in 587 B.C. and carried its leading citizens into exile. See also *Captivity*.

DISPUTATION. Argument or dissension. Paul cautioned believers against such behavior (Phil. 2:14).

DISTAFF. The staff around which flax or wool was wound for spinning (Prov. 31:19). See also *Spinning; Warp; Weaver.*

DISTINGUISHING BE-TWEEN SPIRITS. See *Discerning of Spirits.*

DIVIDING WALL. See *Middle Wall of Partition.*

DIVINATION. Foretelling the future or determining the unknown through performing acts of magic or reading signs (Jer. 14:14). This practice was condemned by God (Deut. 18:10). See also *Magic; Soothsayer.*

DIVINER. See *Soothsayer.*

DIVORCE. A breaking of the ties of marriage. The divine ideal is for permanence in marriage (Matt. 19:3–6), and divorce violates the oneness which God intended (Gen. 2:24; Matt. 19:5–6). Under the Mosaic Law, divorce was permitted in certain situations (Deut. 24:1–4), but this provision was greatly abused (Matt. 19:8). Christ regarded adultery as the only permissible reason for divorce (Matt. 5:31–32; 19:9; Mark 10:11; Luke 16:18), and He reprimanded the Jews for their insensitive divorce practices (Matt. 19:3–9). Unfaithfulness to God was regarded as spiritual adultery (Hos. 2:2). See also *Marriage.*

DIZAHAB. A place in the wilderness of Sinai where Moses gave one of his farewell addresses to the Hebrew people (Deut. 1:1).

DOCTORS (TEACHERS). Teachers of the Law of Moses who were held in high esteem by the Jewish people. At the age of twelve, Jesus discussed the law with some of these teachers in Jerusalem (Luke 2:46). *Teachers:* NIV, NRSV. See also *Lawyer.*

DOCTRINE. A system of religious beliefs which followers pass on to others. Paul impressed upon young Timothy the importance of sound doctrinal teachings (1 Tim. 4:6).

DOEG. An overseer of King Saul's herds who betrayed the high priest Ahimelech for assisting David and his soldiers (1 Sam. 22:9–10).

DOG. An unclean animal (Deut. 23:18) looked upon with contempt by the Jewish people. Gentiles were called "dogs" (Matt. 15:26). See also *Gentile.*

DOME. See *Firmament.*

DOMINION. Authority to govern or rule. After his creation by God, man was given dominion over God's creation (Gen. 1:26–28).

DOOR (GATE). An opening through which a house or public building is entered. Jesus spoke of Himself as the doorway to salvation and eternal life (John 10:7–10). *Gate:* NIV, NRSV. See also *Gate.*

DOORKEEPER. A person who stood guard at the entrance of a public building (Ps. 84:10). See also *Gate Keeper; Porter.*

DOR. A royal Canaanite city captured by Joshua (Josh. 12:23).

DORCAS. See *Tabitha.*

DOTHAN. A city west of the Jordan River near Mt. Gilboa. Dothan was the place where Joseph was sold into slavery by his brothers (Gen. 37:17–28).

DOVE. See *Pigeon; Turtledove.*

DOWRY. Compensation paid by the groom to the bride's family for loss of her services as a daughter (Gen. 24:47–58). See also *Betrothal; Marriage.*

DOXOLOGY. A brief hymn or declaration which proclaims God's power and glory (1 Chron. 29:11; Luke 2:14).

DRAGON. A mythical sea creature or winged lizard. The name is applied to Satan (Rev. 12:9) and the Antichrist (Rev. 12:3). See also *Antichrist.*

DRAM (DRACHMA, DARIC). A Persian coin of small value (Neh. 7:70). *Drachma:* NIV; *Daric:* NRSV.

DRAWER OF WATER (WATER CARRIER). A person who carried water from the spring or well back to the household—a menial chore assigned to women, children, or slaves (Josh. 9:27). *Water carrier:* NIV.

DREAMS AND VISIONS. Mediums of revelation often used by God to make His will known. Joseph distinguished himself in Egypt by interpreting dreams for the pharaoh and his officers (Gen. 40–41). Daniel interpreted King Nebuchadnnezzar's dream that he would fall from power (Dan. 4:18–27). Paul's missionary thrust into Europe began with his vision of a man from Macedonia appealing for help (Acts 16:9–10).

DREGS. Waste which settled to the bottom of the vat in the wine-making process (Ps. 75:8). The word is also used symbolically of God's wrath and judgment (Isa. 51:17). See also *Lees*.

DRINK OFFERING. An offering of fine wine, usually given in connection with another sacrifice, such as a burnt offering (Num. 29:11–18).

DROMEDARY (YOUNG CAMEL). A distinct species of camel with one hump and known for its swiftness (Jer. 2:23). *Young camel:* NRSV.

DROPSY. A disease which causes fluid buildup in the body. Jesus healed a man with this disease on the Sabbath (Luke 14:2).

DROSS. Impurities separated from ore or metal in the smelting process (Prov. 25:4). The word is used symbolically of God's judgment against the wicked (Ps. 119:119).

DROUGHT. Lack of rainfall for an extended time (Ps. 32:4). The prophet Jeremiah spoke symbolically of a spiritual drought throughout the land (Jer. 14:1–7). See also *Famine*.

DRUNKARD. See *Winebibber*.

DRUNKENNESS. A state of intoxication caused by consuming too much wine or strong drink. This vice is condemned in both the O.T. and the N.T. (Deut. 21:20; 1 Cor. 5:11).

DRUSILLA. The wife of Felix, Roman governor of Judea, who heard Paul's defense (Acts 24:24–25.)

DUKE (CHIEF). A leader or chief of a clan (Gen. 36:15–43). *Chief:* NIV. See also *Chief*.

DULCIMER (PIPES). A musical instrument used in Babylonia, probably similar to the bagpipe (Dan. 3:5–15). *Pipes:* NIV.

DUMB. Unable to speak, or the temporary loss of speech (Ezek. 33:22). The word is also used figuratively of submission (Isa. 53:7).

DUNG (RUBBISH). Excrement of humans or animals (2 Kings 9:37). Dried dung was used for fuel in Palestine (Ezek. 4:12–15). The word is also used figuratively to express worthlessness (Phil. 3:8). *Rubbish:* NIV, NRSV.

DUNGEON. An underground prison. Some of these were little more than cisterns with the water partially drained. Joseph and Jeremiah were imprisoned in dungeons (Gen. 39:20; 40:15; Jer. 37:7–16). See also *Cistern; Pit; Prison.*

DURA. A plain in Babylonia where the golden image of King Nebuchadnezzar of Babylonia was set up (Dan. 3:1). See also *Adoraim.*

DUST. Dried earth in powdered form. Sitting in the dust was a symbol of dejection and humiliation (Lam. 3:29). The word is also used symbolically of man's mortality (Gen. 3:19).

DWELLING. See *Pavilion.*

DYSENTERY. See *Flux.*

-E-

EAGLE. A large bird of prey, considered unclean by the Hebrews (Lev. 11:13). Many scholars believe the eagle of the Bible was actually the griffon vulture.

EAR. The ears of the unregenerate are called dull or unhearing (Matt. 13:15). The "ears of the Lord" (1 Sam. 8:21) signify that He hears prayers, in contrast to dumb idols (Ps. 115:6).

EARLY RAIN. See *Former Rain.*

EARRING. A piece of jewelry worn suspended from the earlobe (Gen. 35:4).

EARNEST (DEPOSIT, FIRST INSTALLMENT). A down payment given as a pledge toward full payment of the loan. The Holy Spirit is given as a pledge of the believer's inheritance of eternal life (2 Cor. 1:22). *Deposit:* NIV; *First installment:* NRSV.

EARTHQUAKE. A violent shaking of the earth (Ps. 77:18). These earth tremors are a token of God's wrath and judgment (Judg. 5:4).

EAST SEA. See *Dead Sea.*

EAST WIND. A violent, scorching desert wind, also known as the sirocco (Job 27:21). See also *Wind.*

EASTER. A word which refers to the Passover festival (Acts 12:4). Easter as a celebration of the resurrection of Jesus developed among Christians many years after the N.T. era.

EBAL. A rocky mountain in Samaria, or the territory of Ephraim, where Joshua built an altar after destroying the city of Ai (Josh. 8:30).

EBED-MELECH. An Ethiopian eunuch who rescued Jeremiah from a dungeon (Jer. 38:7–13).

EBENEZER. Site of Israel's defeat by the Philistines (1 Sam. 5:1). Years later, Samuel erected an altar on this site and called it Ebenezer, meaning "the stone of help," to commemorate Israel's victory over the Philistines (1 Sam. 7:10–12).

EBER. A great-grandson of Shem (Gen. 10:21–24) and ancestor of the Hebrew race (Gen. 11:16–26).

EBONY. A hard, durable wood used for decorative carvings and musical instruments (Ezek. 27:15).

ECBATANA. See *Achmetha*.

ECCLESIASTES, BOOK OF. A wisdom book of the O.T., probably written by King Solomon, which declares that life derives joy and meaning not from riches, fame, or work but from reverence for God and obedience to His commandments. One of the book's most memorable passages is the poem on the proper time for all of life's events: "A time to be born, and a time to die; . . . A time to weep, and a time to laugh; . . .a time to keep silence, and a time to speak" (see 3:1–9).

EDEN, GARDEN OF. The fruitful garden created specifically by the Lord as the home for Adam and Eve. The four rivers of Eden, including the Euphrates, suggest that it may have been located in Mesopotamia. Because of their sin and rebellion against God, Adam and Eve were expelled from the garden (Gen. 2:8–3:24). See also *Adam; Eve.*

EDIFICATION. The process by which believers grow in holiness, wisdom, and righteousness (1 Cor. 14:3). See also *Sanctification.*

EDOM.
1. The name given to Esau, Jacob's brother, after he traded away his birthright (Gen. 25:30). See also *Esau.*
2. The land where the descendants of Esau settled. It was in extreme southern Palestine in the barren territory below the Dead Sea. Mount Seir was located in this territory (Gen. 36:8). Edom was referred to by the Greeks and Romans as *Idumaea* (Mark 3:8).

EDOMITES. The descendants of Esau who were enemies of the Israelites. The king of Edom refused to allow the Hebrews to pass through his territory after the Exodus (Num. 20:14–21). In later years, David conquered the Edomites (2 Sam. 8:14). But they apparently existed with a distinct territory and culture for several centuries (see Ps. 137:7). See also *Edom; Esau.*

EDREI. A capital city of Bashan. King Og was defeated here by the Israelites (Num. 21:33–35).

EGLAH. One of David's wives (2 Sam. 3:2–5).

EGYPT. The ancient nation along the Nile River which held the Hebrew people in slavery for more than 400 years before their miraculous deliverance by the Lord at the hand of Moses. Egypt had flourished as a highly civilized culture for several centuries before the time of Abraham about 2000 B.C. Soon after entering Canaan in response to God's call, Abraham moved on to Egypt to escape a famine (Gen. 12:10). This same circumstance led Jacob and his family to settle in Egypt after his son Joseph became a high official of the Egyptian pharaoh (Gen. 45–46). Ham's son *Mizraim* apparently was the ancestor of the Egyptians (1 Chron. 1:8). See also *Mizraim; Nile River; Pharaoh.*

EHUD. The second judge of Israel, who killed Eglon, king of Moab (Judg. 3:15). See also *Judges of Israel.*

EKRON. One of the five chief Philistine cities. It was captured by Judah the judge and allotted to Dan (Judg. 1:18). See also *Philistines.*

ELAH.
1. A valley in Judah where David killed the Philistine giant Goliath (1 Sam. 17:2, 49).
2. A king of Israel (reigned about 886–885 B.C.) who was assassinated and succeeded by Zimri (1 Kings 16:6–10).

ELAM. A son of Shem and ancestor of the Elamites (Gen. 10:22).

ELAMITES. Descendants of Elam who lived in Mesopotamia in the area later populated by the Medes and Persians (Jer. 25:25). See also *Persia.*

EL-BETHEL. See *Bethel.*

ELDER.
1. In the O.T., an older member of a tribe or clan who was a leader and official representative of the clan (Num. 22:7).
2. In the N.T., a local church leader who served as a teacher and ministered to the sick (1 Tim. 5:17; Jas. 5:14–15). See also *Bishop; Pastor.*

ELEAZAR. A son of Aaron who succeeded his father as high priest (Num. 20:25–28), serving under Moses and Joshua. He helped divide the land of Canaan among the twelve tribes of Israel (Josh. 14:1).

ELECT LADY (CHOSEN LADY). The person, or perhaps a local church, to which the Second Epistle of John is addressed (2 John 1:1). *Chosen lady:* NIV.

ELECTION, DIVINE. The doctrine which deals with God's choice of persons who will be redeemed. Conflicts between God's electing grace and Christ's invitation that "whosoever will" may come to Him are not easily resolved. God's intentional will is for all to "come to repentance" and be saved (2 Pet. 3:9), but those who reject His Son will be lost (John 5:40). God's grace is unmerited (Rom. 9:11–16), but it will be lavished on those who are committed to His truth and His will for their lives (2 Thess. 2:13). The elect are characterized by Christlikeness (Rom. 8:29), holiness (Eph. 1:4), good works (Eph. 2:10), and eternal hope (1 Pet. 1:2–4). See also *Foreknowledge; Predestination.*

EL-ELOHE-ISRAEL. A name, meaning "God, the God of Israel," given by Jacob to the altar which he built at Shechem after he was reconciled to his brother Esau (Gen. 33:20).

ELEVATION OFFERING. See *Wave Offering.*

ELI. A high priest of Israel with whom the prophet Samuel lived during his boyhood years (1 Sam. 1–4). Eli's own two sons, Phinehas and Hophni, were unworthy of the priesthood (1 Sam. 2:12–25). They were killed in a battle with the Philistines. Eli died upon learning of their death (1 Sam. 4:1–18).

ELIADA. See *Beeliada.*

ELIAKIM.
1. A son of Hilkiah and overseer of the household of King Hezekiah of Judah. Eliakim was praised by the prophet Isaiah for his role in mediating peace with the invading

Assyrian army (2 Kings 18:18; Isa. 22:20–25).

2. Another name for *Jehoiakim*, a king of Judah. See *Jehoiakim*.

ELIAS. See *Elijah*.

ELIDAD. A leader of the tribe of Benjamin, appointed by Moses to help divide the land of Canaan after its occupation by the Israelites (Num. 34:21).

ELIHU. A friend who spoke to Job after Eliphaz, Bildad, and Zophar had failed to answer Job's questions satisfactorily (Job 32:2–6).

ELIJAH/ELIAS. A courageous prophet who opposed King Ahab and his successor, Ahaziah, because of their encouragement of Baal worship throughout the Northern Kingdom. Because of Ahab's wickedness, Elijah predicted a drought would afflict the land (1 Kings 17:1–24). He wiped out the prophets of Baal after a dramatic demonstration of God's power on Mt. Carmel (1 Kings 18:17–40). After selecting Elisha as his successor, Elijah was carried into heaven in a whirlwind (2 Kings 2:1–11). The coming of the Messiah was often associated in Jewish thought with Elijah's return. Some people

even thought Jesus was Elijah (Luke 9:8). *Elias:* Greek form (Matt. 17:4). See also *Elisha*.

ELIM. The second encampment of the Israelites after they crossed the Red Sea (Exod. 15:27).

ELIMELECH. The husband of Naomi and the father-in-law of Ruth. He died in Moab, leaving his family destitute (Ruth 1:2–17).

ELIPHALET/ELPALET/ ELIPHELET. A son of David, born in Jerusalem to Bathsheba (2 Sam. 5:16). *Elpalet:* 1 Chron. 14:5; *Eliphelet:* 1 Chron. 3:5–6.

ELIPHAZ.
1. A son of Esau (Gen. 36:2–4).
2. One of Job's friends or "comforters" (Job 2:11). In his speeches, Eliphaz defended the justice, purity, and holiness of God (Job 2:11; 4:1; 15:1; 22:1; 42:7–9).

ELISABETH (ELIZABETH). The mother of John the Baptist and a relative of Mary, earthly mother of Jesus. Elisabeth rejoiced with Mary over the coming birth of the Messiah (Luke 1:36–45). *Elizabeth:* NIV, NRSV. See also *Mary*, No. 1.

ELISHA/ELISEUS. The prophet selected and anointed by Elijah as his successor (1 Kings 19:16–21). He followed Elijah for several years and was present at his ascension into heaven when the mantle of leadership fell upon him (2 Kings 2:9–14). Elisha served as a counselor and advisor to four kings of the Northern Kingdom—Jehoram, Jehu, Jehoa-haz, and Joash—across a period of about fifty years (850–800 B.C.). *Eliseus:* Greek form (Luke 4:27). See also *Elijah.*

ELISHAMA/ELISHUA. A son of David, born in Jerusalem (1 Chron. 3:1–6). *Elishua:* 2 Sam. 5:15.

ELISHEBA. The wife of Aaron and mother of Abihu, Eleazar, Nadab, and Ithamar (Exod. 6:23).

ELIZAPHAN. A leader of the tribe of Zebulun, appointed by Moses to help divide the land of Canaan after its occupation by the Israelites (Num. 34:25).

ELON. A minor judge of Israel, from the tribe of Zebulun (Judg. 12:11–12). See also *Judges of Israel.*

ELOTH. An Edomite seaport city on the Red Sea captured by David, then later turned into a station for trading ships by King Solomon (1 Kings 9:26).

ELPALET. See *Eliphalet.*

EL-PARAN. See *Paran.*

ELUL. The sixth month of the Hebrew year, roughly equivalent to our September (Neh. 6:15).

ELYMAS. See *Bar-jesus.*

EMBALM. To prepare a body for burial to protect it from decay. This art was practiced by the Egyptians. Joseph was embalmed for burial (Gen. 50:2–26).

EMBROIDERY. The art of fancy needlework (Exod. 28:39).

EMERALD. A precious stone of pure green color used in the high priest's breastplate (Exod. 28:18) and the foundation of New Jerusalem (Rev. 21:19). See also *Diamond.*

EMERODS (TUMORS, UL-CERS). A strange disease, exact nature unknown, which struck the Philistines when they placed the stolen ark of the covenant next to their false god Dagon (Deut. 28:27). *Tumors:* NIV; *Ulcers:* NRSV.

EMIMS (EMITES, EMIM). A race of giants east of the Dead Sea (Gen. 14:5). They were closely related to another race of giants known as the *Anakims* (Deut. 2:10–11). *Emites:* NIV; *Emim:* NRSV. See also *Anakims*.

EMMANUEL/IMMANUEL. The name given to the Christ child, meaning "God with us" (Matt. 1:23). The birth of a Savior bearing this name was foretold by the prophet Isaiah (Isa. 7:14; *Immanuel*). As this symbolic name suggests, God Incarnate came in the person of Jesus Christ (1 John 4:2). See also *Jesus Christ; Messiah; Son of God; Son of Man*.

EMMAUS. A village near Jerusalem where Jesus revealed Himself to two of His followers shortly after His resurrection (Luke 24:13–33).

EMPTY. See *Void*.

ENCHANTER (MEDIUM, SOOTHSAYER). A person who used magical chants and rituals to drive away evil spirits (Jer. 27:9). *Medium:* NIV; *Soothsayer:* NRSV. See also *Medium; Soothsayer*.

EN-DOR. A city in the territory of Manasseh (Josh. 17:11). King Saul sought advice from a witch in this city (1 Sam. 28:1–10).

EN-GEDI. An oasis on the western shore of the Dead Sea where David hid from King Saul (1 Sam. 23:29–24:1).

ENGINES (MACHINES). A word which refers to the ingenuity of a machine or apparatus. The "engines" in 2 Chron. 26:15 (*Machines:* NIV, NRSV) were used to hurl objects from the walls of besieged cities upon the enemy below. See also *Fenced City; Siege; Wall*.

ENGRAVER. A craftsman who engraved metals or carved wood and stone (Exod. 35:35).

ENMITY. Deep animosity toward another (Gen. 3:15). This sin is characteristic of unredeemed persons (Rom. 1:29–30). See also *Hate*.

ENOCH.
1. The firstborn son of Cain and the name of a city built by Cain and named after Enoch (Gen. 4:17).
2. The father of Methuselah who was taken into God's presence without experiencing physical death (Gen. 5:18–24). *Henoch:* 1 Chron. 1:3.

ENOS (ENOSH). A son of Seth and a grandson of Adam (Gen. 5:6) who is listed in the N.T. ancestry of Jesus (Luke 3:38). *Enosh:* NIV.

ENSIGN (BANNER). A symbol on a long pole which identified an army or tribe (Num. 2:2). *Banner:* NIV. See also *Standard.*

ENVY. Resentment toward another person's good fortune (Prov. 27:4). Paul cautioned Christians against the dangers of this sin (Rom. 13:13). See also *Jealousy.*

EPAENETUS (EPENETUS). A fellow believer at Rome greeted and commended by Paul (Rom. 16:5). *Epenetus:* NIV.

EPAPHRAS. A leader of the Colossian church (Col. 1:7–8) whom Paul called his "fellow prisoner" in Rome (Philem. 23).

EPAPHRODITUS. A believer from Philippi who brought a gift to Paul while he was imprisoned in Rome (Phil. 4:18).

EPENETUS. See *Epaenetus.*

EPHAH. A dry measure equal to about one bushel (Exod. 16:36).

EPHESIANS, EPISTLE TO THE. A letter from the apostle Paul to the church at Ephesus on the theme of the risen Christ as Lord of creation and head of His body, the Church. The first three chapters of the epistle focus on the redemption made possible by the atoning death of Christ and His grace that is appropriated through faith— "not of works, lest any man should boast" (2:9). Chapters 4–6 call on the Ephesian Christians to model their lives after Christ's example and to remain faithful in turbulent times.

EPHESUS. The chief city of Asia Minor and a center of worship of the pagan goddess Diana where Paul spent two to three years, establishing a church (Acts 18:19–21; 19:1–10). Archaeologists have uncovered the remains of the temple of Diana and a Roman theater on this site. See also *Diana.*

EPHOD. A sleeveless linen garment, similar to a vest, worn by the high priest while officiating at the sacrificial altar (2 Sam. 6:14).

EPHPHATHA. An Aramaic word, meaning "be opened," spoken by Jesus to heal a deaf man (Mark 7:34).

Excavated ruins of an ancient market or shopping mall at Ephesus. *Courtesy Rayburn W. Ray*

EPHRAIM.

1. The second son of Joseph who became the founder of one of the twelve tribes of Israel (Gen. 48:8–20). Joshua was a member of this tribe. See also *Tribes of Israel*.

2. A name often used symbolically for the nation of Israel (Hos. 11:12; 12:1).

3. A city in the wilderness to which Jesus and His disciples retreated (John 11:54).

4. A forest where the forces of Absalom were defeated by David's army (2 Sam. 18:6).

EPHRATAH, EPHRATH. See *Bethlehem*.

EPHRON. A Hittite who sold the cave of Machpelah to Abraham as a burial site (Gen. 23:8–20). See also *Machpelah*.

EPICUREANS. Followers of the Greek philosopher Epicurus, who believed the highest goal of life was the pursuit of pleasure, tempered by morality and cultural refinement. Epicureans were among the crowd addressed by Paul in the city of Athens (Acts 17:18). See also *Athens; Stoicks*.

EPISTLE. A type of correspondence best described as a "formal letter." Twenty-two of the twenty-seven N.T. books were written as epistles.

ERASTUS. A Christian believer, apparently from Ephesus, whom Paul sent into Macedonia (Acts 19:22).

ERECH. One of the cities of Nimrod's kingdom in the land of Shinar on the Euphrates River (Gen. 10:10).

ESAIAS. See *Isaiah*.

ESAR-HADDON. A son of Sennacherib who succeeded his father as king of Assyria (reigned about 681–669 B.C.; 2 Kings 19:37). Esar-haddon apparently was the king who resettled Samaria with foreigners after the fall of the Northern Kingdom (Ezra 4:1–2). See also *Samaritan*.

ESAU/EDOM. The oldest son of Isaac who sold his birthright to his twin brother Jacob for a bowl of stew (Gen. 25:26–34). Esau was the ancestor of the Edomites. *Edom:* Gen. 36:8. See also *Edom; Edomites*.

ESDRAELON. See *Jezreel, No. 3*.

ESEK. A well in the valley of Gerar which the servants of

Isaac and Abimelech quarreled over (Gen. 26:20).

ESH-BAAL. See *Ish-bosheth*.

ESHCOL. A valley or brook near Hebron explored by the spies sent into Canaan (Deut. 1:24).

ESPOUSED. See *Betrothal*.

ESSENES. A religious group of N.T. times which practiced strict discipline, withdrawal from society, and communal living. Although they are not mentioned by name in the Bible, many scholars believe they are the group which preserved the Dead Sea Scrolls in caves at Qumran near the Dead Sea. See also *Dead Sea Scrolls; Qumran*.

ESTHER. A young Jewish woman who became queen under King Ahasuerus of Persia and used her influence to save her countrymen. Her Persian name was *Hadassah* (Esther 2:7). See also *Ahasuerus; Haman*.

ESTHER, BOOK OF. A historical book of the O.T. named for its major personality, Queen Esther of Persia, who saved her people, the Jews, from annihilation by the evil and scheming

Haman—a high official of the Persian king. The book shows clearly that God protects and sustains His people.

ETERNAL LIFE. Life without end, or everlasting existence. Eternal life was promised to believers at their conversion by Christ (John 11:25–26) and affirmed by the appearance of Moses and Elijah to Jesus and the three disciples (Matt. 17:2–9). Through His resurrection, Christ became the "firstfruits" of eternal life for all believers (1 Cor. 15:12–58). Life everlasting represents man's final victory over sin and death (Rev. 21:4).

ETHAN. See *Jeduthun*.

ETHANIM. The seventh month of the Hebrew year, corresponding roughly to our October (1 Kings 8:2).

ETHIOPIA. An ancient nation south of Egypt. Moses married an Ethiopian woman (Num. 12:1). Philip witnessed to a servant of the queen of Ethiopia (Acts 8:27).

EUBULUS. A Christian at Rome who sent greetings to Timothy (2 Tim. 4:21).

EUNICE. The mother of Timothy. She was commended for her great faith by the apostle Paul (2 Tim. 1:5). See also *Timothy*.

EUNUCH. Male household servant of a king. These servants were often emasculated to protect the king's harem (2 Kings 9:32). See also *Chamberlain*.

EUODIAS. A Christian woman at Philippi (Phil. 4:2).

EUPHRATES. A major river in the territory of the ancient Babylonians and Persians in Mesopotamia which is also mentioned as one of the rivers of the Garden of Eden (Gen. 2:14). See also *Tigris*.

EUROCLYDON (NORTH-EASTER). A violent wind which struck Paul's ship bound for Rome (Acts 27:14). *Northeaster:* NIV, NRSV.

EUTYCHUS. A young man who went to sleep and fell from a window during Paul's sermon at Troas. He was restored by Paul (Acts 20:9–12).

EVANGELIST. A person who traveled from place to place, preaching the gospel. Philip was one of the zealous evangelists of the early churches (Acts 21:8).

EVE. The name given by Adam to his wife as the mother of the human race (Gen. 3:20). Fashioned from one of Adam's ribs, she was created to serve as his helpmate and companion (Gen. 2:18–23). Because of her sin and rebellion, Eve was to experience pain and sorrow, especially in connection with the birth of children (Gen. 3:16). See also *Adam; Fall of Man*.

EVERLASTING LIFE. See *Eternal Life*.

EVIL. A force which stands in opposition to God and righteousness. This evil force originates with Satan, the archenemy of good, truth, and honesty (Matt. 13:19). In the end-time, God will triumph over evil, and Satan will be thrown into a lake of fire (Rev. 20:10). See also *Iniquity; Sin; Wickedness*.

EVIL-MERODACH. A successor of Nebuchadnezzar II as king of Babylonia (reigned about 562–560 B.C.). He released King Jehoiachin of Judah from prison (2 Kings 25:27–30). See also *Babylonia*.

EVIL DESIRES. See *Concupiscence*.

EWE LAMB. A female sheep (Gen. 21:30).

EXHORTATION. A strong message of encouragement or warning (Heb. 12:5).

EXILE. See *Captivity*.

EXODUS, BOOK OF. A book of the O.T. which recounts the release of the Hebrew people from Egyptian enslavement and the early years of their history as a nation in the wilderness.

Important events covered in the book include: (1) God's call of Moses to lead the people out of slavery (chaps. 3–4); (2) the plagues upon the Egyptians (chaps. 7–12); (3) the release of the Israelites and the crossing of the Red Sea at God's hand (chap. 14); (4) God's miraculous provision for His people in the wilderness (16:1–17:7); (5) Moses' reception of the Ten Commandments and other parts of the law (chaps. 20–23); and (6) the building of the tabernacle for worship at God's command (chaps. 36–40). See also *Moses*.

EXPANSE. See *Firmament*.

EYE. An organ of sight (Matt. 6:22). The word is also used symbolically to portray sinful desire (1 John 2:16).

EZEKIAS. See *Hezekiah.*

EZEKIEL. A prophet of Judah who was carried into exile by the Babylonians and who prophesied faithfully to his countrymen for more than twenty years. He is the author of the book of Ezekiel in the O.T.

EZEKIEL, BOOK OF. A prophetic book of the O.T. addressed to the Jewish captives in Babylon about 585 B.C. and offering God's promise that His people would be restored to their homeland after their period of suffering and exile was over. This promise from God is exemplified by Ezekiel's vision of a valley of dry bones, "I. . .shall put my spirit in you, and ye shall live, and I shall place you in your own land" (37:13–14).

EZION-GEBER/EZION-GABER. A place on the coast of the Red Sea where the Israelites camped during their years of wandering in the wilderness (Num. 33:35). This settlement later became a town, serving as a harbor for Solomon's trading ships (2 Chron. 8:17). *Eziongaber:* Deut. 2:8.

EZRA. A scribe and priest who led an important reform movement among the Jewish people after the Babylonian Exile. He is the author of the book of Ezra. See also *Nehemiah.*

EZRA, BOOK OF. A historical book of the O.T. which describes events in Jerusalem after the Jewish captives began returning to their homeland about 500 B.C. following their period of exile in Babylonia and Persia. After the rebuilding of the temple (6:14–15), the people under Ezra's leadership committed themselves to God's law, put away foreign wives (Ezra 10:1–17), and confessed their sins and renewed the covenant (Neh. 9–10).

-F-

FABLE. A story in which inanimate things are personalized, as in Jotham's narrative of the trees and the bramble (Judg. 9:1–15).

FACE. The front part of the head. This word is often used symbolically of God's presence (Deut. 31:18).

FAIR HAVENS. A harbor on the southern side of the island of Crete where Paul stopped during his voyage to Rome (Acts 27:8).

FAITH. Belief and confidence in the testimony of another, particularly God's promise of salvation and eternal life for all who place their trust in Jesus Christ (John 5:24). A gift of God, faith is essential to salvation (Eph. 2:8). The word also refers to the teachings of Scripture, or the "faith which was once delivered unto the saints" (Jude 3). See also *Trust*.

FALL OF MAN. A phrase which refers to Adam and Eve's state of sorrow and misery which followed their sin and rebellion against God (Gen. 2–3). Their original sin has afflicted the human race ever since (Rom. 3:23)—a condition cured only by the atoning death of Christ (Rom. 5:6). See also *Adam; Eve; Man; Sin*.

FALLOW DEER. A distinct species of deer, common in Mesopotamia in Bible times, and a clean animal to the Hebrews (Deut. 14:4–5). See also *Deer*.

FALLOW GROUND (UN-PLOWED GROUND). A field plowed and left idle for a short time before planting again (Jer. 4:3). *Unplowed ground:* NIV.

FALSE PROPHETS. Persons who deliver a false or misleading message under the pretense that it comes from God. Believers are warned to beware of false prophets (Matt. 24:11, 24; 2 Pet. 2:1).

FALSE WEIGHTS. Deceptive measurements used in weighing merchandise—a practice condemned by the Lord (Deut. 25:13–14).

FALSE WITNESS (FALSE TESTIMONY). A person who gives false testimony or tells lies about others in an attempt to undermine their credibility or slander their character. Such testimony is specifically prohibited by the Ten Commandments (Exod. 20:16). *False testimony:* NIV.

FAMILIAR SPIRIT. The spirit of a dead person which a sorcerer "calls up" in order to communicate with that person (Deut. 18:11). The spirit of Samuel was called up by a witch at En-dor (1 Sam. 28:3–20). Such sorcery was considered an abomination by God. See also *Sorcery; Witchcraft*.

FAMILY. A group of persons related to one another by blood kinship and the ties of marriage. The N.T. implies that all

Christians are related to one another in a spiritual sense, since we are all members of the "household of faith" (Gal. 6:10). See also *Kindred*.

FAMILY RECORDS. See *Register*.

FAMINE. A time, often an extended period, when food or water is in short supply because of lack of rain and the failure of crops (Gen. 12:10). See also *Drought*.

FAN (FORK). A wooden pitchfork for winnowing grain (Isa. 30:24). The grain was thrown into the wind to separate it from the straw (Matt. 3:12). The fan is also spoken of as a symbol of God's judgment (Jer. 15:7). *Fork:* NIV, NRSV. See also *Winnowing*.

FARMER. See *Husbandman*.

FARTHING (PENNY). A Roman coin of small value (Matt. 10:29). *Penny:* NIV, NRSV. See also *Penny*.

FASTING. The practice of giving up eating and drinking for a specified time, generally as part of a religious ritual in times of peril. Elijah and Jesus each fasted for forty days (1 Kings 19:8; Matt. 4:2).

FAT CALF. See *Fatling*.

FATHER. The male head of a household who was the undisputed authority in the family. This word was also used by Jesus as a title for God (Matt. 11:25).

FATHOM. A nautical measure, equal to about seven feet. The term is mentioned in the account of Paul's shipwreck (Acts 27:28).

FATLING (FAT CALF). A young animal fattened for slaughter (Matt. 22:4). *Fat calf:* NRSV. See also *Calf*.

FEAR. An emotion aroused by danger or risk to one's safety (1 Sam. 21:10). The word is also used for respect or reverence toward God (Deut. 10:20).

FEAST. A festival, or a major religious holiday which marked some great event in Jewish history. The Jews celebrated several major festivals.

FEAST OF BOOTHS. See *Tabernacles, Feast of*.

FEAST OF HARVEST. See *Pentecost*.

FEAST OF INGATHERING. See *Tabernacles, Feast of*.

111

FEAST OF LIGHTS. See *Dedication, Feast of.*

FEAST OF UNLEAVENED BREAD. See *Passover and Feast of Unleavened Bread.*

FEAST OF WEEKS. See *Pentecost.*

FEET. The removal of sandals and the washing of one's feet upon entering a house or a holy place was a token of respect, similar to our custom of taking off the hat (Exod. 3:5).

FELIX. The governor of Judea who heard Paul's defense at Caesarea (Acts 23:24; 24:10–27).

FELLOWSHIP. A mutual sharing or friendly association, particularly that between believers who have a common faith in Jesus Christ (1 Cor. 1:9).

FENCED CITY (FORTIFIED CITY). A city with a strong defensive wall (2 Sam. 20:6). *Fortified city:* NIV, NRSV. The wall was erected to provide protection against enemies in times of war. See also *City; Siege; Wall.*

FERRET (GECKO). A burrowing animal considered unclean by the Hebrews (Lev. 11:30). *Gecko:* NIV, NRSV.

FESTUS. Successor of Felix as Roman governor of Judea. Paul made his defense before Festus (Acts 24:27).

FETTERS (SHACKLES). Metal bands for binding the wrists or ankles of prisoners (2 Kings 25:7). *Shackles:* NIV. See also *Stocks.*

FEVER. See *Burning Ague.*

FIELD OF BLOOD. See *Aceldama.*

FIERY SERPENTS (VENOMOUS SNAKES, POISONOUS SERPENTS). Snakes which attacked the Israelites in the wilderness. Moses erected a brass serpent on a pole as an antidote for those who were bitten (Num. 21:6–9). *Venomous snakes:* NIV; *Poisonous serpents:* NRSV. See also *Brass Serpent.*

FIG. The pear-shaped fruit of the fig tree. The spies sent into Canaan brought back figs to show the bounty of the land (Deut. 8:8). Figs were pressed into cakes and also preserved by drying (1 Sam. 25:18). The fig tree was considered a symbol of prosperity (1 Kings 4:25).

FIGHTING MEN. See *Mighty Men.*

FILTH. See *Offscouring.*

FILTHY LUCRE. A phrase for money (1 Tim. 3:3), which is condemned as an unworthy motive for ministry (1 Pet. 5:2). See also *Money.*

FINER (SILVERSMITH, SMITH). A craftsman who refined or shaped precious metals (Prov. 25:4). *Silversmith:* NIV; *Smith:* NRSV. See also *Smith.*

FINGER.
1. A digit of the human hand. The word is also used symbolically of God's power (Exod. 8:19).
2. A measure of length, equal to about three-fourths of an inch (Jer. 52:21).

FINING POT (CRUCIBLE). A vessel for melting and purifying metal (Prov. 17:3). *Crucible:* NIV, NRSV.

FIR (PINE, CYPRESS). An evergreen tree which grew on Mount Lebanon. Its lumber was used in the construction of Solomon's temple in Jerusalem (1 Kings 6:15, 34). *Pine:* NIV; *Cypress:* NRSV.

FIRE. Burning material used for cooking and in religious ceremonies. Fire is often associated with the presence and power of God (Exod. 3:2) as well as the final punishment of the wicked (Matt. 13:49–50). See also *Pillar of Fire and Cloud.*

FIREPAN. A vessel in which incense was burned during worship ceremonies in the tabernacle (Exod. 27:3). See also *Censer.*

FIRKIN. A liquid measure equal to about five or six gallons (John 2:16).

FIRMAMENT (EXPANSE, DOME). A word for the heavens, or the limitless sky above the earth (Gen. 1:6–8). *Expanse:* NIV; *Dome:* NRSV.

FIRST DAY OF THE WEEK. Sunday, or the day of Christ's resurrection, which was adopted as the day of worship by the early church (Acts 20:7).

FIRST INSTALLMENT. See *Earnest.*

FIRSTBORN. First child born into a family (Gen. 49:3). The firstborn son received a double portion of his father's property as his birthright and assumed leadership of the family. See also *Birthright; Inheritance.*

FIRSTFRUITS. The first or best of crops and livestock.

113

According to Mosaic Law, these were to be presented as sacrifices and offerings to the Lord (Exod. 23:19).

FISH GATE. A gate in the wall of Jerusalem, probably so named because fish from the Mediterranean Sea were brought into the city through this gate (Neh. 3:3).

FISHER, FISHERMAN. One who makes his living by fishing. Several of Jesus' disciples were fishermen, and He promised to make them "fishers of men" (Matt. 4:19).

FITCH (SPELT). A plant which produces grain similar to oats or rye (Ezek. 4:9). *Spelt:* NIV, NRSV. See also *Rie*.

FLAG (RUSH). A coarse grass which grows in marshes or wetlands (Isa. 19:6). *Rush:* NIV, NRSV.

FLAGON.
1. A cake of dried grapes or raisins served as a delicacy or dessert (Song of Sol. 2:5).
2. A flask or leather bottle for holding liquids (Isa. 22:24). See also *Spoon; Vial*.

FLASK. See *Vial*.

FLAX. A plant grown in Egypt and Palestine for its fiber, which was woven into linen cloth (Exod. 9:31). See also *Linen*.

FLEA. A tiny insect which sucks the blood of animals or humans. David used this word as a symbol of insignificance (1 Sam. 24:14).

FLEECE. Wool which grows on a sheep. Gideon used a fleece to test God's call (Judg. 6:36–40). See also *Sheep; Wool*.

FLESH. A word for the human body in contrast to the spirit (Matt. 26:41). The word is also used for unredeemed human nature and carnal appetites or desires which can lead to sin (Gal. 5:16–17). See also *Carnal*.

FLESHHOOK (MEAT FORKS). Large pronged fork used to handle meat for sacrificial purposes (2 Chron. 4:16). *Meat forks:* NIV.

FLINT. A very hard stone, perhaps a variety of quartz (Deut. 8:15). The word is also used symbolically to denote firmness (Ezek. 3:9).

FLOCK. A group of sheep or birds (Gen. 4:4). The word is also used to designate a Christian congregation under a pastor's leadership (1 Pet. 5:2).

FLOGGING. See *Scourging*.

FLOOD, THE. The covering of the earth by water in Noah's time; the instrument of God's judgment against a wicked world. This great deluge came after forty days of continuous rainfall, but Noah and his family and the animals in the ark were saved by the hand of God (Gen. 6–8). See also *Noah; Ark, Noah's*.

FLOUR. Wheat or barley ground into a fine powder and used for baking bread. Flour was often offered as a sin offering (Lev. 5:11–13). See also *Bread; Wheat*.

FLUTE (PIPE). A musical instrument, played by blowing, similar to the modern flute (Dan. 3:5–15). *Pipe:* NRSV. Flute players were hired for funerals during N.T. times (Matt. 9:23–24). See also *Organ; Pipe*.

FLUX (DYSENTERY). KJV word for dysentery, a common disease in the Mediterranean world. Paul healed Publius of this ailment (Acts 28:8). *Dysentery:* NIV, NRSV.

FOAL. A colt, or young donkey. Jesus rode a colt on His triumphant entry into Jerusalem (Matt. 21:5), an event foretold in the O.T. (Zech. 9:9). See also *Ass*.

FODDER. See *Provender*.

FOOD. Plants and animals eaten for nourishment. Specific foods mentioned in the Bible include lentils (Gen. 25:34), honey, nuts, and spices (Gen. 43:11). The meats of certain animals were considered unclean and unfit for eating (Lev. 11; Deut. 14).

FOOL. An absurd person; one who reasons wrongly (Prov. 29:11).

FOOLISH. Actions which show a lack of wisdom or faulty and shallow reasoning (Prov. 26:11). Jesus described the five virgins who were unprepared for the wedding feast as foolish (Matt. 25:1–13).

FOOT. See *Feet*.

FOOTMAN. A member of the infantry or walking unit of an army (Jer. 12:5); a swift runner who served as a messenger for a king (1 Sam. 22:17). See also *Post*.

FOOTSTOOL. A low stool upon which the feet are rested. The word is also used symbolically to describe the fate of God's enemies (Ps. 110:1).

FOOT-WASHING. An expression of hospitality bestowed upon guests in Bible times. Foot-washing was generally performed by lowly domestic servants, but Jesus washed His disciples' feet to teach them a lesson in humble ministry (John 13:5–15).

FORBEARANCE (TOLERANCE). Restraint and tolerance. God, in His forbearance or patience, gives people opportunity for repentance (Rom. 2:4). *Tolerance:* NIV. See also *Longsuffering; Patience.*

FORD. A crossing through shallow water across a brook or river (Gen. 32:22).

FOREHEAD. The part of the human face above the eyes. God's people were instructed to learn the law so well that it would be as if it were written on their foreheads (Deut. 6:8). See also *Frontlet.*

FOREIGNER (TEMPORARY RESIDENT). A word for an outsider or stranger—a person who was not of the same ethnic stock as the Hebrews and who had no loyalty to Israel's God (Exod. 12:45). *Temporary resident:* NIV. See also *Alien; Sojourner.*

FOREKNOWLEDGE. God's knowledge of events before they happen and His ability to influence the future by actually causing such events (Isa. 41:4). See also *Election, Divine; Predestination.*

FORERUNNER. One who goes before and makes preparations for others to follow (Heb. 6:20). John the Baptist was a forerunner of Christ.

FORESAIL. See *Mainsail.*

FORESKIN. The fold of skin which covers the male sex organ. This foreskin is removed in the rite of circumcision (Gen. 17:11). See also *Circumcision.*

FORGIVENESS. To pardon or overlook the wrongful acts of another person; God's free pardon of the sin and rebellion of man. Our sin separates us from God, but He forgives us and reestablishes the broken relationship when we repent and turn to Him in faith (Acts 10:43). Just as God forgives believers, He expects us to practice forgiveness in our relationships with others (Matt. 5:43–48). See also *Pardon*.

FORK. See *Fan*.

FORMER RAIN (AUTUMN RAIN, EARLY RAIN). The first rain of the growing season, essential for the germination of seed and the growth of young plants (Joel 2:23). *Autumn rain:* NIV; *Early rain:* NRSV.

FORNICATION (SEXUAL IMMORALITY). Sexual relations between two persons who are not married to one another; any form of sexual immorality or unchastity. Paul cited fornication as a sin which believers should scrupulously avoid (1 Cor. 6:18). *Sexual immorality:* NIV. See also *Adultery; Chastity*.

FORT. A high wall or fortification built to provide protection against one's enemies in times of war (Isa. 25:12). See also *Fenced City; Wall*.

FORTIFIED CITY. See *Fenced City*.

FORTRESS. See *Misgab*.

FORTUNATUS. A Christian from the city of Corinth who visited Paul (1 Cor. 16:17).

FORUM OF APPIUS. See *Appii Forum*.

FOUNDATION. The strong base on which a building is erected. The apostle Paul described Christ as the sure foundation for believers (1 Cor. 3:11). See also *Corner Stone*.

FOUNTAIN. A source of fresh, flowing water; a spring (Deut. 8:7). The word is also used symbolically of God's blessings upon His people (Jer. 2:13).

FOUNTAIN GATE. A gate in the wall of Jerusalem, perhaps named for the fountain or pool of Siloam (Neh. 12:37).

FOWLER. A person who captures birds by nets, snares, or decoys (Hos. 9:8). The word is also used symbolically of temptations (Ps. 91:3). See also *Hunter*.

FOX. An animal of the dog family known for its cunning (Judg. 15:4). See also *Jackal*.

FRAGRANT CANE. See *Calamus*.

FRANKINCENSE (INCENSE). The yellowish gum of a tree, known for its pungent odor when burned as incense during sacrificial

117

ceremonies (Neh. 13:9). Frankincense was one of the gifts presented to the infant Jesus by the Wise Men (Matt. 2:11). *Incense:* NIV. See also *Incense.*

FREEDMEN. See *Libertines.*

FREEWILL OFFERING. An offering given freely and willingly (Amos 4:5), in contrast to one made to atone for some misdeed (Num. 15:3).

FRIEND. An intimate acquaintance who is loved and esteemed. Abraham was called "the Friend of God" (Jas. 2:23).

FRINGE (TASSEL). An ornament worn on the edges of one's robe as a profession of piety and commitment to God (Deut. 22:12). *Tassel:* NIV, NRSV. See also *Hem.*

FROG. An amphibious animal sent by the Lord as the second plague upon Egypt (Exod. 8:2–14).

FRONTLET. A small leather case with passages of Scripture, worn upon the forehead as a literal obedience of Deut. 6:6–9. See also *Forehead; Phylactery.*

FRUITFULNESS. Productive; reproducing abundantly. Paul declared that believers should be fruitful in righteousness and goodness toward others (Col. 1:10).

FULLER (LAUNDERER). A laborer who treated or dyed clothes and also did ordinary laundry work (Mal. 3:2). *Launderer:* NIV.

FULLER'S FIELD (WASHERMAN'S FIELD). A place near the wall of Jerusalem where fullers worked and perhaps where they spread their laundry to dry (2 Kings 18:17). *Washerman's Field:* NIV.

FUNERAL. A ceremony honoring the dead before burial. These ceremonies were sometimes accompanied by sad music and the loud wailing of friends and professional mourners (Eccles. 12:5; Matt. 9:23). See also *Burial; Minstrel.*

FURLONG. A Greek measure of length, equal to about 650 feet or one-eighth of a mile (Luke 24:13).

FURNACE (SMOKING FIREPOT). An enclosed oven for baking (Gen. 15:17), (*smoking firepot:* NIV, NRSV), smelting (Gen. 19:28), or drying and firing bricks (Dan. 3:15–17). See also *Brick-kiln.*

-G-

GAASH, MOUNT. A mountain in the hill country of Ephraim where Joshua was buried (Josh. 24:30).

GABBATHA. See *Pavement, The.*

GABRIEL. An archangel who appeared to Daniel (Dan. 8:16), Zacharias (Luke 1:18–19), and the Virgin Mary (Luke 1:26 –38). See also *Archangel*.

GAD. The seventh son of Jacob, born of Zilpah (Gen. 30:10–11), and ancestor of one of the twelve tribes of Israel. Known as a fierce, warlike people, the Gadites settled east of the Jordan River (Josh. 13:24–25). See also *Tribes of Israel*.

GADARA. A Greek city about six miles southeast of the Sea of Galilee. In N.T. times, Gadara was the capital city of the Roman province of Perea.

GADARENES/GERGE-SENES. People from the area of Gadara in Perea. Jesus healed a wild, demon-possessed man in this area (Mark 5:1–20). *Gergesenes:* Matt. 8:28.

GADDI. One of the twelve spies who scouted the land of Canaan, representing the tribe of Manasseh (Num. 13:11). See also *Spies*.

GADDIEL. One of the twelve spies who scouted the land of Canaan, representing the tribe of Zebulun (Num. 13:10). See also *Spies*.

GAIN. See *Lucre*.

GAIUS.
1. A Macedonian and companion of Paul (Acts 19:29).
2. A man of Derbe and companion of Paul (Acts 20:4).
3. A Corinthian baptized under Paul's ministry (1 Cor. 1:14).
4. The person to whom John addressed his third letter (3 John 1, 5).

GALATIA. A territory of central Asia Minor which contained several cities visited by Paul during the first missionary journey—Antioch of Pisidia, Derbe, Iconium, and Lystra (Acts 13–14)—all located in southern Galatia. Paul's letter to the Galatians (Gal. 1:1–2) was apparently addressed to churches in and around these cities.

GALATIANS, EPISTLE TO THE. A short epistle of the apostle Paul to the churches of Galatia on the themes of Christian liberty and justification by faith alone. The content of the epistle includes: (1) a defense of Paul's apostleship and the gospel (chaps. 1–2); (2) his argument that salvation comes by God's grace through faith, not through obeying the law (chaps. 3–4); and (3) the practical dimension of one's faith —living in obedience to God and in harmony with others (chaps. 5–6).

GALBANUM. A gum from a plant used to produce sacred incense, which was burned at the altar (Exod. 30:34).

GALE. See *Whirlwind*.

GALILEAN. A native of the province of Galilee. All of Jesus' disciples except Judas were Galileans. Peter was recognized as a Galilean because of his distinct accent (Mark 14:70).

GALILEE, (GALILEE OF THE GENTILES). A Roman province in northern Palestine during N.T. times and the area where Jesus spent most of His earthly ministry (Mark 3:7). Because of its far-north location, Galilee had a mixed population of Jews and Gentiles. The prophet Isaiah referred to it as "Galilee of the nations" (Isa. 9:1). *Galilee of the Gentiles:* NIV.

GALILEE, SEA OF/SEA OF CHINNEROTH/LAKE OF GENNESARET/SEA OF TIBERIAS. A freshwater lake about fourteen miles long and seven miles wide which took its name from the surrounding Roman province. Fed by the Jordan River, it provided the livelihood for many commercial fishermen, including several disciples of Jesus: James, John, Peter, and Andrew (Mark 1:16–20). Jesus calmed the waters of this lake after He and His disciples were caught in a boat in a sudden storm (Mark 4:35–41). *Sea of Chinneroth:* Josh. 12:3; *Lake of Gennesaret:* Luke 5:1; *Sea of Tiberias:* John 21:1.

GALL. A bitter, poisonous herb used to make a pain-killing substance. While on the cross, Jesus was offered a drink containing gall (Matt. 27:34).

GALLIO. The Roman provincial ruler of Achaia who refused to get involved in the dispute between Paul and the

The Church of the Beatitudes near the site where Jesus delivered His Sermon on the Mount in Galilee.

Courtesy Israel Ministry of Tourism

Jewish leaders in Corinth (Acts 18:12–17).

GALLOWS. A structure used for executing people by hanging. The wicked Haman was hanged on the gallows which he had prepared for Mordecai (Esther 5:14; 7:10). See also *Haman.*

GAMALIEL. A teacher of the law under whom Paul studied (Acts 22:3). As a member of the Jewish Sanhedrin, he advised against persecution of the apostles and the early church (Acts 5:33–39). See also *Council.*

GAME. See *Venison.*

GANGRENE. See *Canker.*

GARDEN. A fenced plot generally outside the walls of a city where fruit trees or vegetables were grown. The most famous garden in the Bible is the Garden of Eden (Gen. 2:8–10). See also *Orchard.*

GARLAND (WREATH). A ceremonial wreath woven from flowers or leaves and worn on the head (Acts 14:13). *Wreath:* NIV.

GARLICK (GARLIC). A vegetable or herb similar to the onion which was used to flavor food. The Hebrews longed for this vegetable after leaving Egypt (Num. 11:5). *Garlic:* NIV, NRSV.

GARRISON. A company of soldiers stationed in a fortified military post (1 Sam. 13:3–4)

GASHMU. An influential Samaritan leader who opposed the Jewish people while they were rebuilding Jerusalem's walls under Nehemiah after the Exile (Neh. 6:6).

GATE. An entrance, door, or opening, particularly the strong gate in the walls of a fortified city (Judg. 16:3). The word is also used symbolically of salvation (Matt. 7:13) and heaven (Rev. 21:25). See also *Door*.

GATE KEEPER. A person who guarded the gate in a walled city (1 Chron. 9:19). See also *Doorkeeper; Porter*.

GATH. Royal Philistine city captured by David (1 Chron. 18:1) and home of the giant Goliath. (1 Sam. 17:4). See also *Philistines*.

GATH-HEPHER/GITTAH-HEPHER. A city in the territory of Zebulun and home of the prophet Jonah (2 Kings 14:25). *Gittah-hepher:* Josh. 19:13.

GAZA/AZZAH. A Philistine city where Samson was killed when he destroyed the temple of their pagan god Dagon (Judg. 16:21–30). *Azzah:* Jer. 25:20. See also *Philistines*.

GAZELLE. See *Roe*.

GAZER. See *Gezer*.

GEBAL. An ancient seaport town of the Phoenicians near the city of Tyre (Ezek. 27:9).

GECKO. See *Ferret*.

GEDALIAH. A friend of the prophet Jeremiah (Jer. 39:14; 40:5–6). After the fall of Jerusalem to the Babylonians in 587 B.C., Gedaliah was made supervisor of the vinedressers left in the land (2 Kings 25:22–25).

GEDEON. See *Gideon*.

GEHAZI. A servant of the prophet Elisha who was struck with leprosy because of his dishonesty and greed (2 Kings 5).

GEHENNA. See *Hell; Hinnom, Valley of*.

Ancient olive trees in the Garden of Gethsemane, the site where Jesus was delivered to His enemies by Judas.

Courtesy Israel Ministry of Tourism

GENEALOGY. A record of the descendants of a person or family (1 Chron. 5:1–5). These records were important to the Jewish people because they documented inheritance rights and the right of succession as a clan leader, king, or high priest. See also *Register*.

GENERAL EPISTLES. The epistles of Hebrews; James; 1 and 2 Peter; 1, 2, and 3 John; and Jude—so named because they are addressed to broad, general problems rather than to local, specific issues. They are also referred to as *Catholic Epistles*.

GENERATION. A single step or stage in the line of descent from one's ancestors (Gen. 5:1; Matt. 24:34). The word is used in a more general sense to designate a period or age (Gen. 7:1).

GENESIS, BOOK OF. The first book of the O.T., often referred to as "the book of beginnings" because of its accounts of the world's creation and the early history of the Hebrew people.

Major events and subjects covered in the book include:

1. God's creation of the physical world and Adam and Eve's life in the Garden of Eden; Adam and Eve sinned and introduced sin to mankind (chaps. 1–3);

2. Adam's descendants and the great flood (chaps. 4–9);

3. the tower of Babel and the scattering of mankind (chap. 11); and

4. the life stories of the Hebrew patriarchs: Abraham and Isaac (chaps. 12–27), Jacob (chaps. 25–35), and Joseph (chaps. 37–50).

GENNESARET. See *Galilee, Sea of.*

GENTILE. A member of any ethnic group other than the Jewish race. The Jews looked down upon other races as barbarous and unclean (Jer. 9:26). Jesus, however, abolished this distinction through His atoning death and His acceptance of all people through repentance and faith (Gal. 3:28). See also *Heathen.*

GERAH. A coin of small value, equal to one-twentieth of a shekel (Lev. 27:25). See also *Shekel.*

GERAR. An ancient city of southern Canaan, or Philistia, where Abraham was reprimanded by Abimelech for lying about his wife Sarah's identity (Gen. 20:1–18).

GERGESENES. See *Gadarenes.*

GERIZIM, MOUNT. A mountain in central Canaan where Joshua pronounced God's blessings for keeping God's laws when the Hebrew people entered the land (Deut. 11:29; 27:4–26). In later years, this mountain was considered a sacred worship place by the Samaritans (John 4:20–23). See also *Samaritan.*

GESHEM. An Arabian who opposed the rebuilding of Jerusalem's walls under Nehemiah after the Exile (Neh. 2:19; 6:2).

GETHSEMANE. A garden near the Mount of Olives outside Jerusalem where Jesus prayed in great agony of soul on the night before He was betrayed and arrested (Mark 14:32–46). The garden was probably a grove of olive trees, since Gethsemane means "oil press."

GEUEL. One of the twelve spies who scouted the land of Canaan, representing the tribe of Gad (Num. 13:15). See also *Spies.*

GEZER/GAZER. A Canaanite city captured by Joshua (Josh. 10:33) and assigned to the Levites (Josh. 21:21). In later years, Solomon turned Gezer into an important military center (1 Kings 9:15–19). *Gazer:* 2 Sam. 5:25; 1 Chron. 14:16.

GHOST (SPIRIT). An old English word for spirit (Matt. 27:50; 28:19). *Spirit:* NIV, NRSV.

GIANTS. People of unusually large size, such as the Philistine Goliath (2 Sam. 21:22). Races of giants mentioned in the Bible are the *Anakims* (Deut. 2:11), *Emims* (Deut. 2:10), *Rephaims* (Gen. 14:5), and *Zamzummins* (Deut. 2:20).

GIBBETHON. A Canaanite town captured by Joshua and assigned to the Levites (Josh. 21:23).

GIBEAH/GIBEATH. The native city of King Saul and capital of his kingdom (1 Sam. 14:16; 15:34). This was apparently the same city destroyed by the Israelites during the period of the judges (Judg. 20:20–40). *Gibeath:* Josh. 18:28.

GIBEON. A royal Canaanite city whose inhabitants surrendered to Joshua to avoid the fate of Jericho and Ai (Josh. 9:6–15).

GIBEONITES. Inhabitants of Gibeon who were made slaves following their surrender to Joshua (Josh. 9:21).

GIDEON/GEDEON/JERUB-BAAL. The famous judge of Israel who delivered the Israelites from oppression by defeating the mighty Midianite army with a force of only 300 warriors. Gideon came from an obscure family of the tribe of Manasseh, but he trusted God at every step of his military campaign and thus was successful (see Judg. 6–8). He is listed in the N.T. as one of the heroes of the faith (Heb. 11:32; *Gedeon*). *Jerubbaal:* Judg. 6:25–32. See also *Midianites*.

GIER EAGLE (OSPREY, CARRION VULTURE). Bird of prey considered unclean by the Hebrews (Lev. 11:18). *Osprey:* NIV; *Carrion vulture:* NRSV. This is probably the same bird as the Egyptian vulture.

GIFTS, SPIRITUAL. See *Spiritual Gifts*.

GIHON.
1. One of the four rivers of the Garden of Eden, associated with Ethiopia (Gen. 2:13). Some scholars believe this was either the Nile or the Ganges.
2. A place near Jerusalem

where Solomon was anointed and proclaimed king (1 Kings 1:33).

GILBOA, MOUNT. A mountain range in the territory of Issachar where King Saul died after his defeat by the Philistines (1 Chron. 10:1–8).

GILEAD.
1. A fertile, flat tableland east of the Jordan River (Judg. 20:1), known in N.T. times as the region of Perea.
2. A mountain or hill overlooking the plain of Jezreel where Gideon divided his army for battle against the Midianites (Judg. 7:1–7).

GILEAD, BALM OF. See *Balm of Gilead.*

GILGAL. A site between the Jordan River and the city of Jericho where the Hebrew people erected memorial stones to commemorate God's faithfulness in leading them into the Promised Land (Josh. 4:19–20). Gilgal apparently served as Joshua's headquarters in his campaign against the Canaanites (Josh. 6:11–14; 10:1–43). In later years, Saul was crowned as Israel's first king at Gilgal (1 Sam. 11:15).

GIMEL. The third letter of the Hebrew alphabet, used as a heading over Ps. 119:17–24.

GIRDLE (BELT). A belt or sash made of cloth or leather and worn by men and women to hold their loose outer garments (2 Kings 1:8). *Belt:* NIV, NRSV.

GIRGASITES/ GIRGASHITES. Members of an ancient tribe, descendants of Canaan (Gen. 10:15–16), which inhabited part of the land of Canaan before the arrival of the Hebrew people. *Girgashites:* Deut. 7:1.

GITTAH-HEPHER. See *Gath-hepher.*

GITTITES. Inhabitants of the Philistine city of Gath (Josh. 13:3).

GITTITH. A musical instrument or tune associated with the city of Gath. The word is used in the titles of Pss. 8, 81, and 84.

GLASS. A clear liquid mineral used to make utensils, ornaments, and vases. The "sea of glass" in John's vision probably represented God's purity or holiness (Rev. 4:6).

GLEANING. The gathering of grain left behind by the reapers—a courtesy offered to the needy (Lev. 19:9–10). Ruth gleaned in the fields of Boaz (Ruth 2:2–23).

GLEDE (RED KITE). Bird of prey, probably the kite or hawk (Deut. 14:13). *Red kite:* NIV.

GLORY. Splendor, honor, or perfection. The "glory of the Lord" signifies the supreme perfection of His nature (Exod. 16:7). Jesus also partook of the glory of His Father (John 2:11). He shares His divine glory with all believers (John 17:5–6). See also *Transfiguration of Jesus*.

GLUTTONY. The act of eating or drinking to excess—a sin against which believers are warned (Prov. 23:1–8, 21).

GNASH. See *Tooth*.

GNAT. A small, stinging insect considered a great pest in the marshlands of Egypt and Palestine (Matt. 23:24). See also *Lice*.

GNOSTICISM. A heretical movement of N.T. times which taught that salvation came through superior knowledge. While gnosticism is not mentioned by name in the N.T., it was probably what Paul condemned when he declared that true knowledge comes from God and does not consist of idle speculation (Col. 2:8–23).

GOAD. A sharp, pointed stick or rod used in guiding oxen. Shamgar used a goad as a weapon against the Philistines (Judg. 3:31). See also *Ox*.

GOAT. A domesticated animal used for food (Gen. 27:9), clothing (Num. 31:20), and in religious sacrifices (Exod. 12:5). See also *Kid*.

GOAT DEMON. See *Satyr*.

GOB. A place on the plain of Gezer where the Hebrews fought the Philistines (2 Sam. 21:18–19).

GOD. The Creator and ruler of the universe (Isa. 40:28–31); the first person of the triune Godhead: God the Father, God the Son, God the Spirit (Matt. 28:19; 2 Cor. 13:14) who reveals Himself through the natural world, the Bible, and His Son Jesus Christ (Col. 1:19). God is infinite in being and character: omnipresent (Jer. 23:23– 24), all-powerful (Rev. 19:6), perfect in holiness (Lev. 11:44), and infinite in mercy (Ps. 136), wisdom (Col. 2:2–3), and truth (Titus 1:2).

God is active in salvation history. He covenanted with Abraham to "make of thee a great nation" and to make the Hebrew people a blessing to the rest of the world (Gen. 12:1–4). He called Moses to deliver the Israelites from Egyptian bondage (Exod. 3:9 –10). He promised a Savior to rule Israel (Isa. 9:6–7). This promise was fulfilled in Jesus Christ (Matt. 1:18–21), God's love gift of salvation to the world (John 3:16, 36).

God's Spirit convicts unbelievers of sin and coming judgment (John 16:8–11). Man can know God through faith in Christ (John 14:1, 6) and obedience to the Father's will (Matt. 7:21; Mark 3:35). God welcomes the worship and fellowship of His adopted children (John 4:23–24; Rom. 8:15–17). See also *I Am; Jehovah; Yahweh.*

GODDESS. A female deity or idol. Goddesses were prominent in the pagan cultures of Mesopotamia, Egypt, Canaan, Greece, and Rome. For example, Ashtaroth was the wife of Baal in Canaanite mythology (1 Kings 11:33; Ashtoreth: plural form). Diana (or Artemis) was worshiped in the great temple at Ephesus (Acts 19:24–28). See also *Ashtaroth; Diana.*

GODLINESS. Holy living and righteous behavior which issues from devotion to God. Godliness also leads to love for others (1 Thess. 4:7–9). See also *Righteousness.*

GOG, PRINCE OF MAGOG. The leader of a tribal people, enemies of the Israelites, who was condemned by the prophet Ezekiel (Ezek. 38:2; 39:1). In the book of Revelation, Gog and Magog represent the forces of evil which oppose God and His people (Rev. 20:8).

GOLAN. A city in the territory of Manasseh designated as one of the six cities of refuge (Deut. 4:43). See also *Cities of Refuge.*

GOLD. A precious mineral used to make coins, jewelry, and utensils. Used extensively in Solomon's temple (1 Kings 7:48–50), gold also symbolized the splendor of the heavenly city, or New Jerusalem (Rev. 21:18).

GOLD FILIGREE SETTINGS. See *Ouches.*

GOLGOTHA. See *Calvary.*

GOLIATH. A Philistine giant from the city of Gath who defied the entire army of King Saul. He was killed by David the shepherd boy with a single stone from his sling (1 Sam. 17:4–54).

GOMER. The unfaithful wife of the prophet Hosea. After her unfaithfulness, Gomer left Hosea and was sold into slavery, but the prophet restored her as his wife at God's command. His forgiveness of Gomer represented God's unconditional love for His wayward people (Hos. 1; 3). See also *Hosea*.

GOMORRAH/GOMORRHA. A city near the Dead Sea destroyed by God with earthquake and fire because of the sin and wickedness of its inhabitants (Gen. 19:23–29). The city was cited in later years as an example of God's punishment (Isa. 1:9) *Gomorrha:* Matt. 10:15. See also *Cities of the Plain; Sodom*.

GOODMAN (LANDOWNER). A word for the head of a household, head of the house, or "master of the house," as rendered by some translations (Matt. 20:11). *Landowner:* NIV, NRSV.

GOODNESS. Purity and righteousness; a fruit of the Spirit which should characterize followers of Christ (Gal. 5:22). True goodness comes from God, who is holy, righteous, merciful, and loving (Ps. 31:19; Rom. 15:14). See also *Grace; Love; Righteousness*.

GOPHER WOOD (CYPRESS). The wood used in building Noah's ark, probably cypress (Gen. 6:14). *Cypress:* NIV, NRSV.

GOSHEN.
1. An Egyptian district where the Israelites settled and lived during their years in Egypt (Gen. 45:10).
2. A region and city in southern Judah (Josh. 10:41).

GOSPEL. The "good news" that God has provided salvation for all people through the atoning death of His Son (Mark 1:1–15). The word is also used of the teachings of Jesus and the apostles (Col. 1:5).

GOSPELS, FOUR. The four books at the beginning of the N.T. which describe the life and ministry of Jesus: Matthew, Mark, Luke, and John. Each Gospel tells the story from a slightly different perspective, giving us a fuller picture of the

Savior than we would get from a single narrative. See also *Synoptic Gospels*.

GOSSIP. Idle talk, rumors, or fruitless tales. This type of speech is associated with the wicked and troublemakers (Prov. 16:28; 1 Tim. 5:13). See also *Busybody; Talebearer*.

GOURD. A poisonous plant which produces fruit similar to the common melon (2 Kings 4:39). Jonah sat under the shade of a gourd vine (Jon. 4:6–10).

GOVERNMENT. A system of power and authority through which stability and order are maintained in society. Governments have a vital function and should be supported by Christians, as long as they do not intrude into the role which belongs to God alone (Mark 12:13–17).

GOVERNOR (RULER). A general term for rulers or officials of differing rank or status (1 Kings 10:15). The chief in command of a Roman province was called a governor (Matt. 27:2; Acts 23:24). This title was applied to Christ (Matt. 2:6). *Ruler:* NIV, NRSV. See also *Lieutenant; Tirshatha*.

GOVERNOR'S HEADQUARTERS. See *Praetorium*.

GOZAN. A town, district, or river of Mesopotamia to which the people of the Northern Kingdom were deported after the fall of Samaria to the Assyrians (2 Kings 18:11).

GRACE. God's unmerited favor and love which leads Him to grant salvation to believers through the exercise of their faith in Jesus Christ (Titus 2:11; Acts 15:11). Salvation cannot be earned; it is a gift of God's grace (Eph. 2:8). See also *Mercy; Salvation*.

GRAIN. See *Corn; Wheat*.

GRAIN OFFERING. See *Oblation*.

GRAPE. A fruit used for food and wine-making. It was one of the most important agricultural crops of Palestine (Num. 13:23). See also *Wine*.

GRASS. A word for various types of common plants, such as that which livestock grazed. It is used symbolically of the brevity of life (Ps. 90:5–6). See also *Hay*.

GRASSHOPPER. An insect of the locust species which deby the Hebrews (Lev. 11:22), the grasshopper was a symbol of insignificance (Isa. 40:22). See also *Locust*.

GRATITUDE. See *Thanksgiving*.

GRAVE. A burial place for the dead. In Bible times, bodies were buried in pits (Gen. 35:8), caves (Gen. 25:9), and sepulchres hewn in rocks (Matt. 27:60). See also *Cave; Sepulchre*.

GRAVEN IMAGE (IDOL). An image of a false god made from wood or stone and set up in a prominent place as an object of worship (Exod. 20:4). The prophets warned God's people against such idolatry (Isa. 44:9–10; Hos. 11:2). *Idol:* NIV, NRSV. See also *Idol*.

GRAVING TOOL. An instrument or tool used for carving or engraving. Aaron used this tool to shape the golden calf (Exod. 32:4).

GREAT LIZARD. See *Tortoise*.

GREAT OWL. A species of owl considered unclean by the Hebrews (Deut. 14:16).

GREAT SEA. See *Mediterranean Sea*.

GREAVES. Armor for the legs, covering the area from the knees to the ankles (1 Sam. 17:6).

GRECIAN JEWS, GRECIANS. See *Greeks*.

GREECE/JAVAN. An ancient world power which reached its greatest strength in the time between the testaments, about 400 B.C. to A.D. 1. The O.T. word for Greece was *Javan* (Gen. 10:2). See also *Athens*.

GREED. Excessive desire for material things. The Bible warns that this sin leads to disappointment and destruction (Luke 22:3–6; 1 Tim. 6:9). See also *Covetousness*.

GREEKS (GRECIAN JEWS, HELLENISTS). Natives of Greece or people of Greek heritage or descent. The N.T. often uses the word for people influenced by Greek traditions who were not Jews (John 12:20). The word *Grecians* is used of Greek-speaking Jews (Acts 6:1). *Grecian Jews:* NIV; *Hellenists:* NRSV.

GREYHOUND (STRUTTING ROOSTER). An animal cited as an example of gracefulness (Prov. 30:31). *Strutting rooster:* NIV, NRSV.

GRIDDLE. See *Pan*.

GROVE. A wooden pole which represented the Canaanite fertility goddess Ashtoreth (2 Kings 21:7).

GUARANTEE. See *Surety*.

GUARD. A soldier who provided personal protection for a ruler; a bodyguard (2 Chron. 12:11).

GUILE (DECEIT). Craftiness, cunning, or deception (Ps. 55:11). Nathanael was commended by Jesus as an Israelite without guile—a model of honesty and truthfulness (John 1:47). *Deceit:* NRSV.

GUILT. Remorse for sin and wrongdoing (Lev. 6:4). The guilt of sin is covered for believers by the sacrificial death of Christ (Rom. 5:1–2). See also *Conviction; Repentance*.

GUM RESIN. See *Stacte*.

GUTTER (WATERING TROUGH). A drinking trough for animals (Gen. 30:38). *Watering trough:* NIV.

-H-

HABAKKUK. A prophet of Judah who was probably a contemporary of Jeremiah; and author of the book which bears his name (Hab. 1:1; 3:1).

HABAKKUK, BOOK OF. A short prophetic book of the O.T. which questions the coming suffering and humiliation of God's people at the hands of the pagan Babylonians (1:1–4; 1:12–2:1). God's response makes it clear that He is using the Babylonians as an instrument of judgment against His wayward people (1:5–11; 2:2 –20). The book closes with a psalm of praise to God for His mercy and salvation (chap. 3).

HABERGEON. An old English word for the priest's breastplate (Exod. 28:32; 39:23). See also *Breastplate*.

HABITATION. A place of residence (Num. 15:2; Acts 17:26).

HADAD. An Edomite prince or ruler who became an enemy of King Solomon (1 Kings 11:14–25).

HADADEZER/HADAR-EZER. A king of Zobah in Syria. He was defeated by David and

Joab (2 Sam. 8:3–13; 10:16–19). *Hadarezer:* 1 Chron. 18:10.

HADASSAH. See *Esther*.

HADES. See *Hell*.

HAGAR/AGAR. Sarah's Egyptian slave who became the mother of Ishmael by Abraham (Gen. 16). She was driven into the wilderness with her son because of conflict with Sarah, but God intervened to save them (Gen. 21:9–21). *Agar:* Gal. 4:24. See also *Ishmael*.

HAGGAI. A prophet after the Babylonian Exile; and author of the book which bears his name.

HAGGAI, BOOK OF. A short prophetic book of the O.T. written to encourage the Jewish captives who had returned to their homeland after three generations under the Babylonians and Persians. The people were encouraged to finish the task of rebuilding the temple in Jerusalem (1:1–2:9) and to remain faithful to God in difficult times (2:10–23).

HAGGITH. A wife of David and the mother of Adonijah (2 Sam. 3:4).

HAI. See *Ai*.

HAIL. Frozen rain (Job 38:22). The word is also used as a symbol of God's judgment (Rev. 8:7).

HAIR. Fibers on the human body, especially the head. They are used as a symbol of God's special care of believers (Matt. 10:30).

HAKELDAMA. See *Aceldama*.

HALAH. A region in Assyria where captives from the Northern Kingdom were carried (2 Kings 17:6).

HALF-SHEKEL TAX. A temple tax, also called the two-drachma tax (Exod. 30:13–14; Matt. 17:24–27). See also *Tribute*.

HALF-TRIBE OF MANASSEH. A phrase which refers to the two distinct settlements of the tribe of Manasseh—one in central Palestine and the other east of the Jordan River (Num. 32:33–34; Josh. 22:10). See also *Manasseh*.

HALLELUJAH. See *Alleluia*.

HALLOW. To set apart for holy use; to make holy (Exod. 20:11; Luke 11:2). See also *Consecration*.

HAM. The youngest son of Noah. Ham's four sons are thought to be the ancestors of the people of several nations: Canaan (Canaanites), Cush and Phut (Africa and Ethiopia), and Mizraim (Egypt). See Gen. 10:6.

HAMAN. An aide to King Ahasuerus of Persia who plotted to kill the Jewish leader Mordecai and all the Jews, only to be hanged himself on the gallows which he had built for Mordecai's execution (Esther 3:1–9:25). See also *Esther; Mordecai.*

HAMATH/HEMATH (LEBO-HAMATH). A Hittite city north of Damascus (Josh. 13:5). *Lebo-Hamath:* NIV, NRSV. *Hemath:* Amos 6:14.

HAMMER. A driving tool (Judg. 4:21). It is used as a symbol of the power of God's Word (Jer. 23:29).

HAMMOTH-DOR/ HAMMATH/HAMMON. A city of refuge in the territory of Naphtali (Josh. 21:32). This is probably the same city as *Hammon* (1 Chron. 6:76) and *Hammath* (Josh. 19:35).

HAMMURABI, CODE OF. An ancient and influential law code named for an early king of Babylonia. The code was discovered in 1901–02 by an archaeologist at Susa.

HANAMEEL (HANAMEL). A cousin of Jeremiah the prophet (Jer. 32:7). *Hanamel:* NIV, NRSV. Jeremiah bought a field from Hanameel during the siege of Jerusalem by the Babylonians to signify hope for the future for God's people (Jer. 32:8–12).

HANANI. Nehemiah's brother, who became governor of Jerusalem (Neh. 7:2). Hanani brought news of the suffering citizens of Jerusalem to Nehemiah in Persia (Neh. 1:2–3).

HANANIAH. See *Shadrach.*

HAND OF GOD. A symbolic expression for the power of God (Exod. 9:3) and the guidance which He provides for His people (Ps. 63:8).

HANDBAG. See *Crisping Pin.*

HANDBREADTH. A measure of length (about four inches) based on the width of the palm of one's hand (Exod. 25:25). It is also symbolic of the frailty and brevity of life (Ps. 39:5).

HANDKERCHIEF (CLOTH). A small cloth for wiping the face

or hands (Acts 19:12) and also a burial cloth placed over the face of corpses (John 20:7). *Cloth:* NIV, NRSV. See also *Napkin.*

HANDMAID (MAIDSER-VANT). A female servant (Gen. 29:24). *Maidservant:* NIV. This word also signified humility, as in Ruth's conversation with Boaz (Ruth 2:13–14).

HANDS, LAYING ON OF. See *Laying on of Hands.*

HANGING. A form of capital punishment (2 Sam. 18:10). Haman, the enemy of the Jews, was hanged on the gallows which he had prepared for Mordecai (Esther 7:9–10). See also *Haman.*

HANNAH. The mother of Samuel the prophet. She prayed earnestly for Samuel to be born (1 Sam. 1:5–11), devoted him to God's service (1 Sam. 1:24–28), and offered a beautiful prayer of thanksgiving for God's blessings (1 Sam. 2:1–10). See also *Samuel.*

HANNIEL. A representative of the tribe of Manasseh, appointed by Moses to help divide the land of Canaan after its occupation by the Israelites (Num. 34:23).

HANUKKAH. See *Dedication, Feast of.*

HANUN. An Ammonite king defeated by David (2 Sam. 10:2–14).

HARA. A site in Assyria where some of the captives from the Northern Kingdom were settled after the fall of their nation (1 Chron. 5:26).

HARAN/CHARRAN. A city of Mesopotamia known as a center of pagan worship (2 Kings 19:12). Abraham lived in Haran for a time before he left at God's command to settle in Canaan (Gen. 12:4–5). *Charran:* Acts 7:2, 4.

HARDNESS OF HEART. A symbolic expression for rebellion or a stubborn and unyielding spirit, such as that exemplified by the pharaoh of Egypt in refusing to free the Hebrew slaves (Exod. 9:35).

HARE (RABBIT). A rabbit-like animal with long ears and legs (Deut. 14:7). Hares were considered unclean by the Israelites (Lev. 11:6). *Rabbit:* NIV.

HAREM. A group of women married to one man, especially a king. Esther was a member of the harem of King Ahasuerus of Persia (Esther 2:8–14).

HARLOT (PROSTITUTE). Harlotry was forbidden among God's people (Lev. 19:29). Engaging in prostitution was often compared to the spiritual adultery of God's people (Isa. 57:7–9; Rev. 17:1–18). *Prostitute:* NIV.

HAROD. A spring or well near the mountains of Gilboa by which Gideon and his army camped (Judg. 7:1).

HARP (LYRE). A stringed musical instrument frequently used in worship (2 Chron. 29:25). David calmed King Saul by playing his harp (1 Sam. 16:16, 23). *Lyre:* NRSV. See also *Psaltery.*

HARPIST. See *Minstrel.*

HARROW. An agricultural tool or implement, probably used to level a plowed field for planting (Job 39:10).

HART (DEER). A male deer. The word is used to illustrate spiritual thirst (Ps. 42:1) and conversion (Isa. 35:6). *Deer:* NIV, NRSV. See also *Deer.*

HARVEST. The gathering of mature crops (Lev. 23:10). This word is used to illustrate the ripe spiritual harvest (Matt. 9:37–38). See also *Reaper.*

HARVEST, FEAST OF. See *Pentecost.*

HATE. Extreme dislike or animosity toward another. Jesus enjoined believers not to hate their enemies but to return love for malice (Luke 6:27). See also *Enmity; Malice.*

HAUGHTINESS. An arrogant spirit. God's Word indicates that haughty persons will be humbled (Prov. 16:18; Isa. 2:11, 17). See also *Conceit; Pride.*

HAURAN. A fertile district east of the Jordan River near Mt. Hermon (Ezek. 47:16).

HAWK. A bird of prey considered unclean by the Israelites (Deut. 14:15). See also *Cormorant.*

HAY (GRASS). A word for grass, which was cut and fed to livestock while fresh and green (Isa. 15:6). *Grass:* NIV, NRSV. See also *Grass.*

HAZAEL. A leader who was anointed king of Syria at God's command by the prophet Elijah (1 Kings 19:15). He murdered Ben-hadad in order to take the throne (2 Kings 8:7–15). Hazael conducted military campaigns against both Judah (2 Kings 12:17–18) and Israel (2 Kings 10:32). See also *Syria*.

HAZEL (ALMOND). A tree from which Jacob cut a rod or switch (Gen. 30:37). *Almond:* NIV, NRSV. See also *Almond*.

HAZEROTH. A camping place for the Israelites in the wilderness (Num. 11:35) where Aaron and Miriam rebelled against Moses (Num. 12:1–2).

HAZOR. A royal Canaanite city destroyed by Joshua (Josh. 11:1–13). The rebuilt fortress city was later ravaged by Deborah and Barak during the period of the judges (Judg. 4:2–24). Hazor was ultimately destroyed by King Tiglathpileser of Assyria (2 Kings 15:29).

HE. The fifth letter of the Hebrew alphabet, used as a heading over Ps. 119:33–40.

HEALING. The process of restoring a person to good health. Jesus' healing ministry showed His compassion and God's power over sickness and death (Mark 1:34). See also *Balm of Gilead; Medicine*.

HEART. To the Hebrews, the heart was the center of one's existence, including emotions (Gen. 42:28), wisdom or skill (Exod. 35:35), and even physical life (Deut. 6:5). A person acts and speaks from the heart, so he should guard it carefully (Matt. 15:18–19).

HEATH. A dense shrub or bush which grew in the desert regions of Palestine (Jer. 17:6).

HEATHEN (NATIONS, GENTILES). A word for ethnic groups besides the Jews (Ezek. 22:15). *Nations:* NIV, NRSV. It was also used for unbelievers, pagans, or Gentiles (Gal. 1:16). *Gentiles:* NIV, NRSV. See also *Gentile*.

HEAVE OFFERING. An offering which consisted of the firstfruits of the harvest (Num. 15:19–21) and a tenth of all tithes (Num. 18:21–28). It was presented to God before being given to the priests. This was also known as a *peace offering* (Josh. 22:23).

HEAVEN. A word for (1) the atmosphere or the sky (Ps. 146:6), (2) the place where God dwells (1 Kings 8:45), and (3) the future home of all believers (Col. 1:5), who will dwell with

God eternally (Isa. 65:17). See also *Heavenly City; Paradise.*

HEAVENLY CITY. The future city built by God as a dwellingplace for those who belong to Him (Heb. 11:10–16). It will be known as "New Jerusalem," the place where God dwells eternally among the redeemed (Rev. 21:2–10). See also *Heaven; Paradise.*

HEBREWS, EPISTLE TO THE. An epistle of the N.T., author unknown, written to a group of believers of Jewish background to show that Jesus had replaced the O.T. ceremonial law and sacrificial system. Hebrews declares that Jesus is superior to angels (1:1–2:18) and Moses (3:1–16) and that He is our great High Priest who offered Himself—rather than a sacrificial animal—as an atoning sacrifice for our sins (chaps. 4–10). The book closes with an appeal to believers to remember the great heroes of the faith (chap. 11) and to remain steadfast and true in their commitment to Christ (chaps. 12–13).

HEBRON/KIRJATH-ARBA. An ancient town in Canaan where Abraham lived and where Sarah died (Gen. 23:2–6). After the conquest of Canaan, it was designated one of the six cities of refuge. *Kirjath-arba:* Josh. 14:15. See also *Cities of Refuge.*

HEIFER. A young cow (Gen. 15:9). This word is sometimes used figuratively of contentment or complacency (Jer. 50:11).

HEIR. See *Inheritance.*

HELAM. The place where David won a decisive victory over the Syrians (2 Sam. 10: 16–19).

HELI. Father of Joseph (husband of Mary) in the ancestry of Jesus (Luke 3:23).

HELL. The place of eternal torment reserved for unbelievers. *Sheol,* a Hebrew word rendered as "hell" in the O.T., corresponds to the Greek word *Hades,* which means "unseen underworld" or "place of the dead." In the N.T. both *Hades* and *Gehenna* are rendered as "hell." *Gehenna* is derived from the Valley of Hinnom, a site for heathen worship that became a dumping ground near Jerusalem where filth and dead animals were burned; hence hell's association with the final state of lost souls in a place of eternal fire (Mark 9:47–48).

Hell is described as a "lake of fire" (Rev. 19:20), "everlasting destruction" (2 Thess. 1:9), and the "second death" (Rev. 20:14). See also *Damnation; Hinnom, Valley of; Lake of Fire.*

HELLENISTS. Greek-speaking Jews. See *Greeks.*

HELMET. An armored covering for the head to protect soldiers in combat. Paul spoke of the "helmet of salvation" which protected believers in spiritual warfare (Eph. 6:17).

HELPER. One who assists another. This word is used for the Holy Spirit's comfort and intercession on behalf of believers (Rom. 8:26). See also *Advocate; Comforter; Holy Spirit; Paraclete.*

HELP MEET (HELPER). A helper, companion, or mate. God created Eve as a helper for Adam (Gen. 2:18). *Helper:* NIV, NRSV.

HEM. A decorative border or fringe on a piece of clothing, worn to remind the Jews of God's commandments (Exod. 28:33–34). See also *Fringe.*

HEMAN. A talented musician under David and a grandson of Saul (1 Chron. 6:33; 15:16–17).

Heman was regarded as a person of spiritual insight (1 Chron. 25:5).

HEMATH. See *Hamath.*

HEMLOCK (WORMWOOD). A bitter and poisonous plant (Amos 6:12). *Wormwood:* NRSV.

HENA. A city on the Euphrates River captured by the Assyrians (2 Kings 18:34).

HENNA. See *Camphire.*

HENOCH. See *Enoch,* No. 2.

HEPHZI-BAH. A symbolic name, meaning "my delight is in her," which would be used for Jerusalem after her restoration to God's grace and favor (Isa. 62:4).

HERALD. A person sent by a high government official to deliver a formal and public message or to announce good news (Dan. 3:4)

HERB. A plant used to promote healing or to season food (Gen. 1:29). The Israelites used bitter herbs in their bread at the first Passover (Exod. 12:8). See also *Mallows.*

HERD. A group of cattle, sheep, or oxen (1 Sam. 11:5). In O.T.

times, a person's wealth was measured by the size of his herd (2 Sam. 12:1–3).

HERDMAN (SHEPHERD). A tender or keeper of livestock. The prophet Amos was a herdman and farmer (Amos 7:14). *Shepherd:* NIV. See also *Shepherd.*

HERESY. False teachings that deny essential doctrines of the Christian faith—a serious problem condemned by Paul (1 Cor. 11:19). See also *Doctrine; Gnosticism; Judaizers.*

HERMAS. A fellow believer at Rome greeted and commended by Paul (Rom. 16:14).

HERMES
1. A fellow believer at Rome greeted and commended by Paul (Rom. 16:14).
2. NIV, NRSV word for the pagan god Mercurius. See *Mercurius.*

HERMOGENES. A believer from the province of Asia who turned away from Paul (2 Tim. 1:15).

HERMON, MOUNT/SIRION/SHENIR/SENIR. The highest mountain in Syria, with an elevation of almost 10,000 feet (Josh. 12:1). It was also called *Sirion* and *Shenir* (Deut. 3:9) and *Senir* (Ezek. 27:5).

HEROD. The name of several Roman rulers in Palestine during N.T. times:
1. Herod the Great (ruled 37 to 4 B.C.), in power when Jesus was born, who ordered the slaughter of innocent children (Matt. 2:3–10). Herod reconstructed the temple at Jerusalem and completed other ambitious building projects.
2. Herod Archelaus (ruled 4 B.C. to A.D. 6), the son and successor of Herod the Great as Roman ruler in Judea soon after the birth of Jesus (Matt. 2:22).
3. Herod Antipas (ruled 4 B.C. to A.D. 39), who granted his wife's request that John the Baptist be executed. This was the Herod who returned Jesus for sentencing by Pilate (Luke 23:6–12).
4. Herod Philip (ruled 4 B.C. to A.D. 33), ruler in extreme northern Galilee at the time when Jesus began His public ministry (Luke 3:1, 19–20).
5. Herod Agrippa I (ruled A.D. 37–44), who persecuted the apostles and executed James, leader of the Jerusalem church (Acts 12:1–19).
6. Herod Agrippa II (ruled A.D. 50–100), before whom Paul made his defense at Caesarea (Acts 25:13–26:32).

HERODIANS. An influential Jewish group that favored Greek customs and Roman law in New Testament times. The Herodians joined forces with the Pharisees against Jesus (Mark 3:6).

HERODIAS. The wife or queen of Herod Antipas, the Roman provincial ruler of Palestine, who had John the Baptist executed. Herodias was angry at John because of his criticism of her immorality and illicit marriage (Matt. 14:1–11).

HERODION. A believer at Rome greeted and commended by Paul, who called him "my kinsman." (Rom. 16:11).

HERON. An unclean bird which lived in the lakes and marshes of Palestine (Deut. 14:18).

HESHBON. An ancient Moabite city east of the Jordan River captured by the Amorite king Sihon (Num. 21:25–34).

HETH. A son of Canaan and ancestor of the Hittites. Abraham dealt with the sons of Heth in securing a burial place for Sarah (Gen. 23:3–20).

HEWER (WOODCUTTER, STONECUTTER). A woodcutter (Josh. 9:21). *Woodcutter:* NIV, or stonecutter (2 Kings 12:12). *Stonecutter:* NIV, NRSV.

HEZEKIAH/EZEKIAS. The godly king of Judah (ruled about 716–686 B.C.) who implemented religious reforms by abolishing idol worship, restoring and reopening the temple in Jerusalem, and leading in celebration of major religious festivals, such as the Passover (2 Kings 18:4; 2 Chron. 29:3–36). Preparing for a siege against Jerusalem by the Assyrians, Hezekiah cut a tunnel through solid rock to bring water from a spring outside the city wall into the city (2 Kings 20:20). *Ezekias:* Matt. 1:9.

HIDDEKEL. See *Tigris River.*

HIEL. A native of Bethel who rebuilt the city of Jericho in King Ahab's time (1 Kings 16:34). This was a fulfillment of Joshua's curse against the city (Josh. 6:26).

HIERAPOLIS. A city of the district of Phrygia in Asia Minor. This city was mentioned by Paul, implying that Christianity had been planted here (Col. 4:13).

HIGGAION. A musical term translated "meditation" in Ps. 9:16, perhaps signifying a soft, quiet sound.

HIGH PLACE. An elevated place where worship of false gods was conducted (2 Kings 12:3). These shrines of idolatry provoked God's wrath (Ps. 78:58). See also *Altar*.

HIGH PRIEST. The chief priest or head of the priesthood—an office filled by succession of the oldest son of each generation through the lineage of Aaron, Israel's first high priest (Exod. 28). Jesus is called our "great high priest" (Heb. 4:14) because He laid down His life as a living "sacrifice" on our behalf (Heb. 9:26). See also *Priest*.

HIGHWAY. The "highways" of the Bible were little more than paths or crude trails, and they generally connected large cities or major trading centers (Isa. 19:23). See also *Road*.

HILKIAH. A high priest during the reign of King Josiah of Judah who found the lost Book of the Law and used it to bring about religious reforms (2 Kings 22:8–23:4).

HILL. An elevated site. Pagan altars were often built on hills (1 Kings 14:23). See also *High Place*.

HILL COUNTRY (MOUNTAIN REGION). A region of low, rugged mountains in southern Lebanon and northern Judea (Josh. 13:6). *Mountain region:* NIV.

HIN. A unit of measure, equal to about one and one-half gallons (Exod. 29:40).

HIND (DEER). A female deer. The word is used symbolically to show spiritual resilience (Hab. 3:19; Ps. 18:33; *Deer:* NIV, NRSV. See also *Deer*.

HINNOM, VALLEY OF. A deep, narrow ravine southwest of Jerusalem where pagan worship involving child sacrifice was conducted (2 Chron. 28:3; Jer. 19:2–4). Some scholars believe this site in N. T. times became a garbage dump for the city of Jerusalem known as *Gehenna*—a word translated as "hell" (Matt. 5:22; Mark 9:43). See also *Hell*.

HIRAM/HURAM. The king of Tyre—or perhaps a son and his successor—who assisted David and Solomon with their building projects in Jerusalem by providing materials and skilled workmen (2 Sam. 5:11; 1 Kings 5:7–11). *Huram: 2 Chron. 2:3–12.* See also *Tyre.*

HIRELING (LABORER, HIRED HAND). A common laborer hired for a short time to do farm chores (Job 7:1–2). *Laborer:* NRSV. Unlike a hireling, Jesus as the Good Shepherd takes a personal interest in His sheep (John 10:12–13). *Hired hand:* NIV, NRSV. See also *Laborer.*

HISS. A sound made by forcing air between the tongue and the teeth to show scorn and contempt (Job 27:23; Isa. 5:25–26).

HITTITES. An ancient people who lived in Canaan apparently before Abraham's time, since he bought a burial cave from Ephron, who was probably a Hittite (Gen. 23:10–20). Hittites also served in David's army (2 Sam. 11:6, 15).

HIVITES. Descendants of Canaan (see Gen. 10:6) who lived in the Promised Land before and after the Hebrew people occupied their territory (Deut. 7:1). Some scholars believe these are the same people as the Horites. See also *Horites.*

HOBAB. See *Jethro.*

HOE. See *Mattock.*

HOHAM. An Amorite king defeated by Joshua near the cave at Makkedah (Josh. 10:1–27).

HOLINESS. Moral purity; to be set apart and sanctified for service to God. God is holy (Exod. 15:11), and He expects holiness of His people (Rom. 12:1). Since Jesus was the perfect example of holiness, He was called the "Holy One of God" (Mark 1:24). See also *Righteousness.*

HOLY GHOST. An old English phrase for Holy Spirit (Acts 5:3). See *Holy Spirit.*

HOLY OF HOLIES (HOLY PLACE). The sacred innermost sanctuary of the temple and tabernacle, containing the ark of the covenant and the mercy seat, which only the high priest could enter. Even he could go in only one day a year on the Day of Atonement, when he made a special sacrifice for the sins of the people (Heb. 9:2–3, 7). *Holy Place:* NRSV. See also *Ark of the Covenant; Atonement, Day of; Mercy Seat.*

HOLY PLACE. KJV phrase for the section of the tabernacle just outside the holy of holies (Exod. 28:29).

HOLY SPIRIT. The third person of the trinity. The O.T. contains glimpses and promises of the Holy Spirit (Gen. 1:2, 6:3; Zech. 4:6) and the Spirit rested on Jesus from His birth (Luke 1:35), but the full manifestation of the Spirit's power occurred at Pentecost after Jesus' resurrection and ascension to the Father (Acts 2:1–21). Jesus promised He would send the Holy Spirit as a comforter and advocate in His absence (John 14:16; 1 John 2:1). The Spirit would glorify the Son (John 15:16), empower believers (John 14:12–27), and convict unbelievers of sin and coming judgment (John 16:8–11).

Another function of the Holy Spirit is to inspire the Scriptures, thus providing guidance and direction to believers. See also *Advocate; Comforter; Helper; Paraclete.*

HOMER. The standard unit of dry measure, equal to about six bushels (Ezek. 45:11).

HOMOSEXUALITY. The practice of sexual activity among persons of the same sex—a sin strictly forbidden by the O.T. law (Lev. 18:22). Paul also condemned this practice (Rom. 1:26–27; 1 Cor. 6:9).

HONESTY. Speaking the truth and acting fairly and without deceit in human relationships. This is a virtue which all believers should practice (2 Cor. 13:7).

HONEY. A sweet liquid substance produced naturally from bees and artificially from fruit. It was used to sweeten food (Exod. 16:31). The word is also used symbolically for abundance (Exod. 3:8, 17).

HONEYCOMB. The wax cells built by bees to hold their eggs and honey (1 Sam. 14:27).

HONOR. Respect and esteem toward God and other people. The Ten Commandments enjoin honor toward one's parents (Exod. 20:12). God and His Son Jesus Christ are worthy of our highest honor (John 5:23).

HOOK. A metal grasping tool. Different types of hooks mentioned in the Bible include fleshhooks (Exod. 27:3), fish hooks (Matt. 17:27), pruning hooks (Isa. 18:5), and the hooks which supported the tabernacle curtains.

HOOPOE. See *Lapwing.*

HOPE. A sure and steady faith in God's promises. The believer has hope in God's promise of salvation (1 Thess. 5:8), resurrection (Acts 26:6–7), and eternal life (1 Cor. 15:19–26). See also *Promise.*

HOPHNI. A sinful and immoral son of Eli the high priest who was not considered worthy of conducting priestly duties (1 Sam. 1:3; 2:22–25). Along with his evil brother Phinehas, he was killed by the Philistines (1 Sam. 4:1–11). See also *Phinehas,* No. 2.

HOPHRA. See *Pharaoh,* No. 5.

HOR, MOUNT. A mountain in the territory of the Edomites where Moses' brother Aaron died and was buried (Num. 20:22–29). A different mountain with the same name was located in northern Palestine (see Num. 34:7–8).

HORAM. A king of Gezer defeated by Joshua's forces (Josh. 10:33).

HOREB, MOUNT. See *Sinai.*

HORITES/HORIMS. Inhabitants of Mt. Hermon who were driven out by Esau's descendants (Gen. 36:20). These may have been the same people as the Hivites of Joshua's time. *Horims:* Deut. 2:22. See also *Hivites.*

HORMAH. See *Zephath.*

HORN. A bonelike protrusion from an animal's head. The word is also used as a symbol of strength (Hab. 3:4; Rev. 13:1). See also *Cornet.*

HORNET. A wasplike insect with a painful sting, portrayed as a symbol of God's judgment against the enemies of His people (Exod. 23:28).

HORNS OF THE ALTAR. Projections at the four corners of an altar (Exod. 27:1–2). The blood of a sacrificial animal was sprinkled on these four projections (Exod. 29:12). See also *Altar.*

HORSE. An animal used for transportation (Gen. 47:17) as well as in warfare. God warned his people not to "multiply" horses for use in war (Deut. 17:16).

HORSE GATE. A gate in the old wall of Jerusalem, mentioned by Nehemiah as having been destroyed and then rebuilt under his supervision (Neh. 3:28).

HORSELEACH (LEECH). A parasite which attaches to humans and animals and sucks blood; probably a leech (Prov. 30:15). *Leech:* NIV, NRSV.

HOSANNA. A triumphal shout by the crowds as Jesus entered Jerusalem a few days before His crucifixion (Matt. 21: 9, 15). The expression means "save us now."

HOSEA/OSEE. A prophet who delivered God's message of judgment to the Northern Kingdom in the years shortly before this nation fell to the Assyrians in 722 B.C. Author of the book of Hosea, he is best known for his marriage to a prostitute in obedience of God's command (Hos. 1:2–9). *Osee:* Rom. 9:25.

HOSEA, BOOK OF. A prophetic book of the O.T. which compares the spiritual adultery or idolatry of God's people with the physical adultery of the prophet's wife, Gomer (1:2–5; 2:2–5). Just as Hosea redeemed her from slavery and restored her as his mate, God promised that He would eventually restore His people as His own after a period of punishment at the hand of their enemies (4:1–14:9). This book is one of the greatest treatises in the Bible on the nature of God, emphasizing His demand for righteousness and impending punishment as well as His steadfast love. See also *Gomer*.

HOSEN (TROUSERS). An old English word for "trousers," possibly referring to the tunic or inner garment worn during Bible times (Dan. 3:21). *Trousers:* NIV, NRSV.

HOSHEA.
1. The original name of Joshua (Deut. 32:44). See *Joshua*.
2. The last king of Israel (reigned about 730–722 B.C.) who paid tribute to King Shalmaneser of Assyria. After Hoshea rebelled, Israel was defeated, and Hoshea was taken to Assyrian as a captive (2 Kings 17:1–6).

HOSPITALITY. The gracious provision of food and lodging to strangers. Kindness toward travelers and strangers was encouraged in both O.T. and N.T. times (Lev. 19:33–34; 1 Pet. 4:9).

HOST. A hospitable person who entertained guests (Heb.

146

13:2) or a multitude or crowd of people (Gen. 2:1).

HOSTS, LORD OF (LORD ALMIGHTY). A title of God which emphasizes His sovereignty (Isa. 1:9; 10:23). *Lord Almighty:* NIV.

HOST OF HEAVEN. Heavenly beings created by God and associated with His rule of the universe. These beings ("a multitude of the heavenly host") praised God at the angels' announcement of the birth of Jesus (Luke 2:13).

HOUR. A twelfth part of the working day between sunrise and sunset—a unit which varied with the season and the duration of daylight (Matt. 20:1–12).

HOUSE (TENT). A building or residence for a family (1 Sam. 9:18). The word is also used of a clan or all the descendants of a family (1 Sam. 20:16) as well as the believer's final dwellingplace in heaven (2 Cor. 5:1). *Tent:* NIV, NRSV. See also *Tent.*

HOUSEHOLD. Members of a family who lived together in the same dwelling or a compound of dwellings, perhaps including several generations (2 Sam.

6:11). Believers are members of God's household (Eph. 2:19).

HOUSEHOLD IDOLS. Images of pagan gods kept in the house in the belief that they protected the family (Gen. 31:19–35). See also *Teraphim.*

HOUSEHOLDER (OWNER). The head of a household or owner of a house (Matt. 13:27). *Owner:* NIV.

HULDAH. The wife of Shallum and a prophetess who foretold the collapse of Jerusalem (2 Kings 22:14–20).

HUMAN SACRIFICE. The practice of sacrificing children to a pagan god (2 Kings 3:26–27). This was common among the pagan religions of Bible times, but the custom was specifically prohibited by God (Lev. 20:2–5; Deut. 18:10). See also *Hinnom, Valley of; Jephthah.*

HUMILITY. The opposite of arrogance and pride; an attitude which grows out of the recognition that all we are and everything we own are gifts from God (Rom. 12:3; 1 Pet. 5:5). See also *Meekness.*

HUNTER. A person who stalks and kills wild animals. Nimrod, a descendant of Noah, was a "mighty hunter" (Gen. 10:9). See also *Fowler.*

HUR. A man who helped Aaron hold up the arms of Moses to give the Israelites victory over the Amalekites (Exod. 24:14).

HURAM. See *Hiram.*

HUSBAND. The male partner in a marriage relationship. Husbands had total authority over their wives in Bible times, but Paul called on male believers to love their wives (Eph. 5:25).

HUSBANDMAN (FARMER). A farmer or tiller of the soil (Gen. 9:20). In N.T. times a husbandman, like a tenant farmer, often took a share of the crops as payment for his labor (2 Tim. 2:6). *Farmer:* NIV, NRSV.

HUSHAI. A friend and advisor of King David (2 Sam. 15:32–37). Hushai remained loyal to David during Absalom's revolt (2 Sam. 17:1–16).

HUSKS (PODS). The fruit of the carob tree, a type of locust. The prodigal son in Jesus' parable was reduced to eating this coarse and unappetizing food in order to survive (Luke 15:16). *Pods:* NIV, NRSV.

HYMENAEUS. An early Christian who denied the faith and was excommunicated by Paul (1 Tim. 1:19–20; 2 Tim. 2:16–17).

HYMN. A song of praise and thanksgiving to God (Eph. 5:19). Jesus and His disciples sang a hymn after they finished the last supper (Matt. 26:30).

HYPOCRITE. A person who pretends to be something he or she is not. Jesus called the Pharisees hypocrites because they did good deeds to gain the praise of others and pretended to be godly and righteous but were actually insensitive to God's truth (Matt. 23:13–29).

HYSSOP. A plant used in purification ceremonies (Exod. 12:22). It was also symbolic of spiritual cleansing (Ps. 51:7). Hyssop was used to relieve Jesus' thirst on the cross (John 19:29).

-I-

I AM. The name by which God revealed Himself to Moses at the burning bush. It shows His eternity, self-existence, and unsearchableness (Exod. 3:14). See also *God; Jehovah; Yahweh.*

IBEX. See *Pygarg*.

IBHAR. A son of David, born at Jerusalem after he became king (1 Chron. 3:6).

IBZAN. A judge of Israel for seven years. A native of Bethlehem, he had thirty sons and thirty daughters (Judg. 12:8 –10). See also *Judges of Israel*.

I-CHABOD. The son of Phinehas and grandson of Eli. He was given this symbolic name, meaning "inglorious," by his dying mother when she learned the ark of the covenant had been captured and that Eli and Phinehas were dead (1 Sam. 4:19–22).

ICONIUM. An ancient city in Asia Minor near Lystra and Lycaonia. Paul and Barnabas introduced Christianity here on the first missionary journey (Acts 13:51; 14:1, 21–22). Paul apparently also visited Iconium on the second journey (Acts 16:1–7).

IDDO. A leader of the tribe of Manasseh who served as an aide or government official under David (1 Chron. 27:21).

IDLENESS. Inactivity or laziness. This behavior is condemned in Proverbs (Prov. 24:30–34) and by Paul (2 Thess. 3:10). See also *Sluggard*.

IDOL, IDOLATRY. The worship of false gods or something created rather than the Creator (Rom. 1:25). Idolatry was prohibited by the first two of the Ten Commandments (Exod. 20:3–4). Abraham migrated to Canaan to escape idol worship (Josh. 24:2–3). Prominent idols mentioned in the Bible are the golden calves of Aaron (Exod. 32:4) and King Jeroboam (2 Chron. 11:15) and the grain god of the Philistines known as Dagon (Judg. 16:23). Elijah helped overthrow Baal worship in Israel (1 Kings 18:17–40), and the prophet Isaiah described the folly of idolatry (Isa. 44:9–20). In the N.T., idolatry is anything that comes between the believer and God (Col. 3:5). See also *Graven Image*.

IDUMAEA. See *Edom*, No. 2.

IGAL. One of the twelve spies who scouted the land of Canaan, representing the tribe of Issachar (Num. 13:7). See also *Spies*.

IGNORANCE. Lack of knowledge or understanding. While sins of ignorance are less grievous than premeditated sins (Lev. 4:2–14; Num. 15:30–31), they are still destructive (Hos.

149

4:6) and require repentance (Acts 17:30–31). At Pentecost, Peter declared Christ was crucified out of ignorance—a sin which required repentance (Acts 3:17, 19).

ILLYRICUM. A district on the eastern coast of the Adriatic Sea. Paul mentioned Illyricum as the furthermost point to which he had traveled (Rom. 15:19).

IMAGE. An exact likeness or representation of some object of idolatrous worship. God warned Israel to destroy such pagan images (Exod. 34:13–17).

IMAGE OF GOD. Human beings were created to perfectly reflect God's image, marred that image by sinning, but have the potential to be molded back into that image (Rom. 8:28–30). Jesus is the image of the "invisible God" (Col. 1:15), and man expresses God's image when he is in right relation with his Creator and faithfully tends God's creation (Gen. 1:26–28). Man's unique attributes of human reason, will, and personality are further evidences of divine image.

IMMANUEL. See *Emmanuel.*

IMMORALITY. Behavior which violates established moral principles or laws. This word is used to condemn illicit sexual activity outside of marriage (Prov. 2:16; Rom. 1:26–27) and to describe Israel's worship of pagan gods (Ezek. 23:8, 17). See also *Adultery; Fornication.*

IMMORTALITY. See *Eternal Life.*

IMMUTABILITY. An attribute of God's nature which refers to His unchangeableness (Mal. 3:6). The unchangeable nature of Christ assures us that God's mercy is constant (Heb. 13:8). God, who cannot lie, offers an anchor of hope for all believers, who are the "heirs of promise" (Heb. 6:17–19). See also *God.*

IMPARTIALITY. Justness and fairness. God is impartial in His loving concern for all persons (2 Pet. 3:9) and in His command for repentance (Rom. 3:6). Peter learned that all persons who are cleansed by the Lord are brothers (Acts 10:15, 34–35).

IMPUTATION. To transfer something to another person. Adam's sin was imputed to all persons (Rom. 5:12). Our iniquity was laid on Jesus (Isa. 53:5–6), and He bore our sins (John 1:29). Jesus, the "second Adam," imputed grace and righteousness to all who put their trust in Him (Rom. 5:17–19).

INCARNATION OF CHRIST. The birth and existence of Christ in human form. This was foretold by the O.T. prophets (Isa. 7:14). When Jesus was born into the world, He was described as "the Word . . .made flesh" (John 1:14). Belief in the incarnation of Christ is a mark of the Christian (1 John 4:2–3). See also *Advent of Christ; Virgin Birth.*

INCENSE. Sweet perfume extracted from spices or gums and used in worship ceremonies. Incense was burned on the altar of incense in the tabernacle by the priest (Exod. 30:7–8). See also *Censer; Frankincense.*

INCEST. Sex relations with members of one's own family. Prohibited by the Levitical Law (Lev. 18:6–12), incest was considered such a serious offense that it was punishable by death (Lev. 20:11–17). Lot committed incest with his two daughters (Gen. 19:30–38) and Reuben with his father's concubine (Gen. 35:22).

INDIA. A region near the Indus River which served as the eastern limit of the Persian Empire (Esther 1:1; 8:9). Scholars believe this "India" covered essentially the same region as the modern nations of India and Pakistan.

INDIFFERENCE. Lack of interest and concern—behavior characteristic of unbelievers and backsliders (Rev. 3:15–16). Indifference breeds moral callousness (Matt. 27:3–4; Acts 18: 12–16).

INFIDEL (UNBELIEVER). An unbeliever (1 Tim. 5:8). *Unbeliever:* NIV, NRSV. Infidelity is caused by an unregenerate heart (Rom. 2:5) and hatred of the light (John 3:20). An infidel will be punished by eternal separation from God (2 Thess. 1:8–9). See also *Atheism; Unbelief.*

INHERITANCE. A gift of property or rights passed from one generation to another. In ancient Israel, a father's possessions were passed on to his living sons, with the oldest receiving a double portion (Deut. 21:17). Reuben lost his inheritance because he committed incest with Bilhah (Gen. 35:22;

151

49:4). Esau traded his birthright as the oldest son to his brother Jacob for a bowl of soup (Gen. 25:29–34).

Christians enjoy a spiritual birthright (Eph. 1:13–14). All the redeemed, including Gentiles, become God's adopted children with full inheritance rights (Gal. 4:5–7). See also *Adoption; Birthright; Firstborn.*

INIQUITY (WICKEDNESS). Sin, wickedness, or evil. Jesus taught that evil or iniquity originates in the heart, or from within (Matt. 23:28). Christ redeems believers from their iniquity, purifies them, and sets them apart for His service (Titus 2:14). *Wickedness:* NIV. See also *Wickedness.*

INK. Writing fluid. The earliest ink was probably a mixture of water, charcoal or soot, and gum. The scribe Baruch used ink to write Jeremiah's prophecies (Jer. 36:18). See also *Paper; Writing.*

INKHORN. A carrying case for pens and ink, probably made from the horn of an animal and carried on a belt (Ezek. 9:2–11).

INN. A shelter which provided lodging for travelers. Inns were often crude stopping places with no indoor accommodations. Jesus was born at a stable of an inn, which provided shelter for people and their animals (Luke 2:7).

INSANE. See *Mad.*

INSCRIPTION. See *Superscription.*

INSPECTION GATE. See *Miphkad.*

INSPIRATION. Divine influence. God's inspiration is the source of human understanding (Job 32:8). Scripture is inspired by God for our correction and instruction (2 Tim. 3:16). The Holy Spirit moved holy men to prophesy and record God's message (2 Pet. 1:20–21). God has communicated with man in various ways, including a voice (Rev. 1:10–11), dreams (Dan. 7:1), and visions (Ezek. 11:24–25).

INTELLIGENT. See *Prudent.*

INTERCESSION. Prayer offered on behalf of others. Christ made intercession for those who were crucifying Him (Luke 23:34) and for His disciples (John 17:9–26). Elders of the early church were instructed to pray for the sick (Jas. 5:14–16). Paul prayed for Israel to be saved (Rom. 10:1) and for the Colossians to grow spiritually (Col. 1:9–12). Christ, our high priest, lives to make intercession for us (Heb. 7:25–26). The Holy Spirit helps us intercede for others (Rom. 8:26). See also *Petition; Prayer*.

INTERCESSOR. An advocate for others (Isa. 59:16). Abraham interceded for Sodom to be spared (Gen. 18:23–32). Paul encouraged intercession for all people (1 Tim. 2:1–2). Christ is the Christian's advocate or intercessor (Heb. 7:25–26).

INTEREST. See *Usury*.

INTERMARRIAGE. Marriage between members of different races or religions. Intermarriage of the Israelites with the idolatrous Canaanites was forbidden by God (Josh. 23:12–13). Paul counseled the Corinthian Christians not to marry unbelievers (2 Cor. 6:14–17). See also *Marriage*.

INTERMEDIATE STATE. Some believe this to be a condition of believers between death and the resurrection. Paul characterized this state as being "absent from the body" (2 Cor. 5:8) while awaiting the resurrection (1 Thess. 4:13–18) and anticipating a glorified body like that of Jesus (Phil. 3:20–21). This condition is also characterized as a sleeplike state (John 11:11) that is enjoyable (Ps. 17:15) and unchangeable (2 Cor. 5:1).

INWARD PARTS. See *Bowels*.

IRON
1. A fortified city in the territory of Naphtali (Josh. 19:38), also known as *Beth-shemesh* and *Yiron*.
2. An ancient metal first mentioned in Gen. 4:22. Iron was used to make weapons (Job 20:24) and tools (1 Kings 6:7).

IR-SHEMESH. See *Beth-shemesh*.

ISAAC. The son born to Abraham and Sarah in their old age (Gen. 21:1–3) and thus the person through whom God's Chosen People, the Israelites, were descended (Gen. 21:9–13). He married Rebekah (Gen. 24:57 –67)—a union to which twin sons Jacob and Esau were born (Gen. 25:19–26). Isaac was considered a man of faith (Heb. 11:9, 20), a patriarch of Israel (Exod. 32:13), and an ancestor of Christ (Luke 3:34). See also *Rebekah*.

ISAIAH/ESAIAS. A major prophet of Judah whose career spanned forty years (about 740–701 B.C.). The son of Amoz, he was married to a "prophetess" (Isa. 8:3). Working in the capital city of Jerusalem, Isaiah was the confidant of King Uzziah (Azariah) and his successors (Isa. 1:1). He warned that the city and nation would be destroyed by Assyria, but a righteous remnant would be saved (Isa. 1:2–9; 11:11). He gave his two sons symbolic names to underscore his message (Isa. 8:1–4; 7:3–4).

Isaiah encouraged King Hezekiah but foretold the king's death (2 Kings 20:1). He was the author of the book of Isaiah, which prophesied the coming of the Messiah (Isa. 7:14), His rejection (Isa. 53), and the conversion of the Gentiles (Isa. 61:10–11). *Esaias:* Greek form (Matt. 4:14).

ISAIAH, BOOK OF. A major prophetic book of the O.T. noted for its prediction of the coming Messiah (7:14; 9:7) and particularly its emphasis on the Messiah as God's "suffering servant" (42:1–9; 49:1–6; 50:4–9; 52:13–53:12). These messianic passages occur in the midst of the prophet's prediction that God would punish the nation of Judah because of its rebellion and idolatry (1:1–12:6). Other prophecies in the book are directed at the pagan nations surrounding Judah (13:1–23:18).

Many Bible students call Isaiah the "fifth Gospel" because it echoes the N.T. themes of salvation and redemption. Jesus began His public ministry by identifying with this book's promise of comfort and healing for God's people: "The Spirit of the Lord God is upon me; because the Lord hath anointed me to preach good tidings unto the meek; he hath sent me to bind up the brokenhearted, to proclaim liberty to the captives" (Isa. 61:1; see also Luke 4:18–19). See also *Messiah.*

ISCARIOT, JUDAS. The disciple who betrayed Jesus (John 13:2, 26; 18:1–8). The word *Iscariot* identifies Judas as a citizen of Kerioth, a city in southern Judah (Josh. 15:25), to distinguish him from Judas (or Jude), brother of James, who was also one of the Twelve (Luke 6:16). Judas Iscariot apparently served as the treasurer for Jesus and His disciples (John 13:29). After realizing the gravity of his act of betrayal, Judas committed suicide (Matt. 27:3–5). See also *Twelve, The.*

ISH-BOSHETH/ESH-BAAL. The youngest son of Saul who became king of Israel for two years (2 Sam. 2:8–10). He was eventually defeated by David and assassinated in his bed (2 Sam. 4:8–12). *Eshbaal:* 1 Chron. 8:33.

ISHI. A symbolic name, meaning "my husband," to be given to God when the Israelites returned to Him (Hos. 2:16–17). Ishi was to be used instead of Baali because the name Baal was associated with a pagan god.

ISHMAEL. Abraham's son born to Sarah's Egyptian maid Hagar (Gen. 16:1–11). After conflicts with Sarah, Hagar fled with Ishmael into the desert, where she was assured by angels that Ishmael would have many descendants (Gen. 21:8–18). Tradition holds that the Arab peoples are descendants of Ishmael. See also *Hagar.*

ISHMAELITES. Descendants of Ishmael, Abraham's son by Hagar (Gen. 16:15). God promised to bless the Ishmaelites, although Ishmael was not Abraham's covenant son (Gen. 21:12–13). Ishmael had twelve sons, whose descendants lived as nomads in the deserts of northern Arabia. Most modern-day Arabs claim descent from Ishmael. See also *Arabia.*

ISH-TOB. See *Tob.*

ISRAEL.
1. Another name for Jacob. Jacob was renamed Israel by an angel at Penuel because of his influence with God and man (Gen. 32:28; 35:10). His name was extended to the nation of Israel (Exod. 3:16) and finally narrowed to designate the Northern Kingdom after the nation divided following Solomon's administration. See also *Jacob.*
2. The Northern Kingdom. This nation was formed in 931 B.C. when the ten northern tribes rebelled against the two southern tribes and established its own kingship under Rehoboam (1 Kings 12). Samaria was established as the capital city. After about two centuries, the Northern Kingdom was carried into captivity by Assyria in 722 B.C. and Samaria was populated by foreigners (2 Kings 17:23–24). See also *Samaritan.*

ISRAELITES. Descendants of Israel, or Jacob (Lev. 23:42 –43), a nation which was designated by God as His special people. The Israelites were regarded as children of the covenant and heirs of the promises which God made to Abraham (Gen. 12:1–3; Rom. 9:4; 11:1). See also *Jews*.

ISSACHAR. Jacob's fifth son by Leah; father of one of the twelve tribes of Israel (Gen. 30:17–18). The tribe occupied fertile land bounded on the north by Zebulon and Naphtali, on the east by the Jordan River, and on the south and west by Manasseh. The judges Deborah and Barak are assumed to be Issacharites, since they came from this territory (see Judg. 4–5). See also *Tribes of Israel*.

ITALIAN BAND (ITALIAN COHORT, ITALIAN REGIMENT). A unit of the Roman army stationed in Caesarea. Cornelius, one of the first Gentile converts to Christianity, was attached to this unit (Acts 10:1). *Italian Regiment:* NIV; *Italian Cohort:* NRSV.

ITALY. The boot-shaped country between Greece and Spain which juts into the Mediterranean Sea (Acts 18:2). Its capital city, Rome, was the seat of the Roman Empire in N.T. times. Paul sailed to Rome as a prisoner (Acts 27:1–6; 28:14–16).

ITCH. See *Scall*.

ITHAMAR. The youngest son of Aaron who was consecrated as a priest (Exod. 6:23). He oversaw the tabernacle during the wilderness wanderings (Exod. 38:21).

ITHREAM. A son of David, born at Hebron (2 Sam. 3:5).

ITUREA. A small province in Palestine at the base of Mt. Hermon. This area was ruled by Herod Philip when John the Baptist began his ministry (Luke 3:1).

IVAH, IVVAH. See *Ahava*.

IVORY. Decorative trim from the tusks of elephants which was a symbol of luxury. King Ahab's house was known as the "ivory house" (1 Kings 22:39). See also *Ahab*.

IYYAR. See *Zif*.

-J-

JAAZER. See *Jazer*.

JABBOK. A small stream which enters the Jordan River about twenty miles north of the Dead Sea (Num. 21:24).

Beside this stream, at a point later called Peniel, Jacob wrestled with an angel (Gen. 32:24–31).

JABESH-GILEAD. A city of Gilead about twenty miles south of the Sea of Galilee. King Saul defended this city against Nahash, king of the Ammonites (1 Sam. 11:1–11).

JABIN.
1. The Canaanite king of Hazor who was killed by Joshua at the Merom Brook (Josh. 11:1–14).
2. Another king of Hazor who was defeated by Deborah and Barak at the Kishon River (Judg. 4).

JACHIN (JAKIN) AND BOAZ. Two ornamental bronze pillars, constructed by Hiram of Tyre, which stood in front of Solomon's temple at Jerusalem (1 Kings 7:13–22). *Jakin:* NIV.

JACINTH. A precious stone, perhaps the same as sapphire, used in the foundation of the heavenly city, or New Jerusalem (Rev. 21:20). See also *Ligure.*

JACKAL. A wild dog, or a scavenger which ran in packs. The "foxes" which Samson used to destroy crops of the Philistines may have been jackals (Judg. 15:4). See also *Fox.*

JACOB. The son of Isaac and Rebekah and father of several sons who became the ancestors of the twelve tribes of Israel. Jacob was the twin brother of Esau, who was the firstborn son and thus entitled to the birthright of his father Isaac. But he bought Esau's birthright for a pot of stew (Gen. 25:23–34). With his mother Rebekah's help, he deceived his father and received his blessing as well (Gen. 27:6–29). While fleeing his brother's wrath, Jacob struggled with an angel and was given the name *Israel,* meaning "prince with God" (Gen. 32:22–30). His descendants were known as Israelites, or descendants of Israel.

In his later years, after the birth of many children to his wives Rachel and Leah and their handmaids, Jacob mourned his favorite son Joseph, whom he presumed dead. But his joy was restored when Joseph was discovered alive and well in Egypt. Jacob died in Egypt after moving there at Joseph's initiative to escape a famine in Canaan. He was returned to his homeland for burial (Gen. 37–50). See also *Israel; Israelites.*

JACOB'S WELL. The well dug by Jacob and the site where Jesus offered the Samaritan woman "living water" (John 4:1–26). Not mentioned in the O.T., the site today is associated with the ancient city of Shechem (Tell Balatah) near the highway from Jerusalem to Galilee.

JAEL. The wife of Heber the Kenite who killed Sisera, a commander of the forces of King Jabin of Hazor (Judg. 4:17–22). See also *Sisera*.

JAFFA. See *Joppa*.

JAH. See *Jehovah*.

JAIR. The eighth judge of Israel, a member of the tribe of Gilead, who led the nation for twenty-two years (Judg. 10:3 –5). See also *Judges of Israel*.

JAIRUS. A ruler of the synagogue near Capernaum whose daughter was raised from the dead by Jesus (Mark 5:22–23).

JAKIN. See *Jachin*.

JAMBRES. Magician of the Egyptian pharaoh who opposed Moses. While he is not mentioned in the O.T., Jambres was cited by Paul as one who resisted God's truth (2 Tim. 3:8).

JAMES.

1. A son of Zebedee and a disciple of Jesus. He and his brother John were called "sons of thunder" by Jesus because of their fiery temperament (Mark 3:17).

2. A son of Alphaeus and a disciple of Jesus (Matt. 10:3).

3. The half brother of Jesus who became a leader in the church at Jerusalem (Acts 21:17–18; Gal. 1:19). He was probably the author of the epistle of James. See also *Brothers of Christ*.

JAMES, EPISTLE OF. A short N.T. epistle—written probably by James, the half brother of Jesus—known for its plain language and practical application of the gospel to the believer's daily life. According to James, the true test of Christianity is in the living and doing of its truth rather than in speaking, hearing, and even believing its doctrines (1:22–27). Authentic faith results in acts of ministry to others, or as James puts it, "Faith, if it hath not works, is dead" (2:17). Other emphases in James are equality of all people before God (2:1–10) and the power of the tongue (3:3–10).

JANNES. A magician of the Egyptian pharaoh who opposed Moses. While he is not mentioned in the O.T., Jannes was cited by Paul as one who resisted God's truth (2 Tim. 3:8).

JAPHETH. A son of Noah who was saved in the ark (Gen. 5:32). Japheth is considered the father of the Indo-European races (Gen. 9:19–27; 10:2–5).

JAPHIA.
1. The king of Lachish and one of the five Amorite kings killed by Joshua's army (Josh. 10:3–27).
2. A son of David, born at Jerusalem after he became king (2 Sam. 5:15).

JAPHO. See *Joppa.*

JAR. See *Cruse; Pitcher.*

JARMUTH. A royal Canaanite city captured by Joshua (Josh. 10:3–27). Centuries later, Jarmuth was resettled by the Israelites after the Exile (Neh. 11:29).

JASHER. See *Book of Jasher.*

JASHOBEAM. The chief of David's mighty men, or brave warriors, who helped him become king and kept his kingdom strong (1 Chron. 11:10 –11). See also *Mighty Men.*

JASON. A citizen of Thessalonica who was persecuted because he provided lodging for Paul and Silas (Acts 17:5–9). This may be the same Jason whom Paul referred to as "my kinsman" (Rom. 16:21).

JASPER. A precious stone, probably a type of quartz, used in the breastplate of the high priest (Exod. 28:20) and in the foundation of the heavenly city, or New Jerusalem (Rev. 21:19).

JAVAN. A son of Japheth and grandson of Noah. Javan was the father of the Ionians, or Greeks (Gen. 10:2; Isa. 66:19). See also *Greece.*

JAVELIN (SPEAR). A short spear or dart. A javelin was used by King Saul (1 Sam. 19:9–10) and by the high priest Phinehas (Num. 25:7). *Spear:* NIV, NRSV. See also *Dart; Spear.*

JAZER/JAAZER. A fortified Amorite city east of the Jordan River (2 Sam. 24:5) noted for its fertile land (Num. 32:1) and occupied by the conquering Israelites (Josh. 13:24–25). *Jaazer:* Num. 21:32.

JEALOUSY. Ill feelings toward others because of their blessings or favored position. Jacob's sons were jealous of their brother Joseph because he was their father's favorite (Gen. 37:11). Christians are counseled not to participate in such behavior (Rom. 13:13). See also *Envy*.

JEBUS. See *Jerusalem*.

JEBUSITES. Tribal enemies of the Israelites who were descended from Canaan (Gen. 10:15–16). They controlled Jerusalem (known as Jebus at that time) before David conquered the city (2 Sam. 5:6–8) and turned it into his capital. Remnants of the Jebusites became bondservants during Solomon's reign (1 Kings 9:20–21). See also *Jerusalem*.

JECONIAH. See *Jehoiachin*.

JEDIDIAH. A name for Solomon, meaning "beloved of Jehovah," bestowed at birth by Nathan the prophet (2 Sam. 12:25). This name suggests that David's sin of adultery had been forgiven.

JEDUTHUN/ETHAN. A Levite musician and writer of psalms (1 Chron. 9:16) who led in praise services when the ark of the covenant was returned to Jerusalem (1 Chron. 16:41–42). *Ethan:* 1 Chron. 6:44.

JEHOAHAZ.
1. The son and successor of Jehu as king of Israel (reigned 814–798 B.C.; 2 Kings 10:35). A wicked king, he led Israel into sin and idolatry (2 Kings 13:2).
2. The son and successor of Josiah as king of Judah about 610 B.C. A sinful monarch, he reigned only three months before being deposed by Pharaoh Nechoh of Egypt (2 Kings 23:31–34). *Shallum:* 1 Chron. 3:15.
3. Another name for Ahaziah, king of Judah about 850 B.C. See *Ahaziah,* No. 2.

JEHOASH. See *Joash,* No. 1.

JEHOIACHIN/CONIAH/ JECONIAH/JECHONIAS. The son and successor of Jehoiakim as king of Judah (reigned only three months, about 597 B.C.). Evil like his father, Jehoiachin was king when the nation was captured by Nebuchadnezzar and the people were deported to Babylonia (2 Kings 24:8–16). He was released after thirty-seven years in prison (Jer. 52:31–34). Jehoiachin is listed as an ancestor of Christ (Matt. 1:11–12). *Coniah:* Jer. 22:24; *Jeconiah:* 1 Chron. 3:16–17; *Jechonias:* Matt 1:11–12.

JEHOIADA.
1. A military leader at Hebron who apparently recruited 3,700 of his countrymen to serve in David's army (1 Chron. 12:27).
2. A high priest who protected young King Joash from Queen Athaliah until Joash was crowned king of Judah. Jehoiada also led out in reducing Baal worship (2 Kings 11:3–21). See also *Joash*, No. 1.

JEHOIAKIM/ELIAKIM. The son and successor of Josiah as king of Judah (reigned about 609–597 B.C). An evil ruler who exploited the people and led them into idolatry, Jehoiakim died while Jerusalem was under siege by the Babylonians (2 Chron. 36:6). The prophet Jeremiah foretold his defeat (Jer. 22:17–19). *Eliakim:* 2 Kings 23:34.

JEHORAM/JORAM.
1. The wicked king of Judah (reigned about 848–841 B.C.) who murdered his own brothers (2 Chron. 21:2–13) in order to succeed his father Jehoshaphat (1 Kings 22:50). Struck down by God, he died in disgrace, as predicted by the prophet Elijah, from a mysterious disease (2 Chron. 21: 12–20). *Joram:* 2 Kings 8:21.
2. Ahab's son and successor as Israel's king (reigned about 852–841 B.C.; 2 Kings 1:17). He died in battle against the Syrians (2 Kings 8:28–29). *Joram:* 2 Kings 8:16.

JEHOSHABEATH/ JEHOSHEBA. The daughter of King Jehoram of Judah who hid her nephew Joash from Queen Athaliah's wrath until Joash was crowned king (2 Chron. 22:11–12). *Jehosheba:* 2 Kings 11:2.

JEHOSHAPHAT/ JOSAPHAT. The son and successor of Asa as king of Judah (reigned about 870–848 B.C.). A reformer like his father, Jehoshaphat attacked idolatry and sent teachers to help people learn about God (2 Chron. 17:6–9). He was rebuked by the prophet Jehu for forming an alliance with King Ahab of Israel (2 Chron. 19:1–3). *Josaphat:* Matt. 1:8.

JEHOSHAPHAT, VALLEY OF. A place where God will judge the nations in the endtime, according to the prophet Joel (Joel 3:2–14). This site is believed to be part of the Kidron Valley between Jerusalem and the Mount of Olives. The name may refer to a symbolic "valley of decision," where God will judge all nations.

JEHOSHEBA.
See *Jehoshabeath*.

JEHOSHUA. See *Joshua*.

JEHOVAH/JAH. A translation of *Yahweh*, a Hebrew word for God in the O.T. which indicated his eternity and self-existence. This word is based on a Hebrew verb meaning "to be"; thus the name "I Am" by which God revealed himself to Moses at the burning bush. Yahweh is rendered as "Lord" and printed in capital and small capital letters (LORD) in most English versions of the Bible, although some translations use *Yahweh* or *Jehovah*. *Jah* is an abbreviated form of the word (Ps. 68:4) See also *I Am; Lord; Yahweh*.

JEHOVAH-JIREH. A name for God meaning "the Lord will provide." It was used by Abraham to commemorate God's provision of a ram in place of Isaac as a sacrifice (Gen. 22:14).

JEHOVAH-NISSI. A name for God meaning "the Lord is my banner." Moses used this name to show God's victory over the Amalekites (Exod. 17:15–16).

JEHOVAH-SHALOM. The name of an altar built by Gideon, meaning "the Lord is peace" (Judg. 6:24).

JEHOVAH-SHAMMAH. The name of a city of the future envisioned by the prophet Ezekiel, indicating that "the Lord is there" (Ezek. 48:35).

JEHOVAH-TSIDKENNU. The name for the coming Messiah used by the prophet Jeremiah, meaning "the Lord our righteousness" (Jer. 23:6).

JEHU.
1. A violent and deceitful king of Israel (reigned about 841–814 B.C.) who gained the throne by killing King Ahab's descendants (2 Kings 9:2– 10:36).
2. A prophet who delivered a message of doom to King Baasha of Israel (1 Kings 16:1– 2) and rebuked King Jehoshaphat of Judah for forming alliances with King Ahab (2 Chron. 19: 1–3).

JEMIMA. The first of Job's three daughters to be born after his recovery from suffering and affliction (Job 42:14).

JEPHTHAH/JEPHTHAE. A judge of Israel who delivered the nation from the Ammonites. After making a rash and foolish vow, Jepthah sacrificed his only child as an offering to God

162

(Judg. 11:1–39). *Jephthae:* Heb. 11:32. See also *Judges of Israel.*

JEREMIAH/JEREMIAS/
JEREMY. A major prophet of the O.T. who preached God's message of doom to the nation of Judah for about forty years during the reigns of the last five kings of the nation: Josiah, Jehoahaz, Jehoiakim, Jehoiachin, and Zedekiah (Jer. 1:2–3). Called to his prophetic ministry even before he was born (Jer. 1:4–10), he wept openly over the sins of Judah (Jer. 9:1) and declared that the nation would fall to a foreign enemy as punishment for its sin and idolatry (Jer. 16:1–13). After Judah was overrun by the Babylonians, Jeremiah remained in Jerusalem while most of his countrymen were deported to Babylonia. Eventually he was taken to Egypt, where he continued to preach to a remnant of Jewish people (Jer. 43:5–13). *Jeremy:* Matt. 2:17; 27:9; *Jeremias:* Greek form (Matt. 16:14)

JEREMIAH, BOOK OF. A major prophetic book of the O.T. noted for its stern warnings to the nation of Judah that it was destined to fall to the Babylonians unless the people repented and turned back to God. After being called and assured of God's guidance and presence (1:1–19), Jeremiah pronounced prophecies of doom against Judah (2:1–45:5) and then the surrounding pagan nations (46:1–51:64). The book closes with a description of the destruction of Jerusalem (52:1–23) and the deportation of the influential people of Judah to Babylonia (52:24–30).

The concept of a new covenant (Jer. 31) is unique to the book of Jeremiah. This new agreement between God and His people, based on grace and forgiveness, was needed because the old covenant of law had failed to keep the people on the path of righteousness and holiness. See also *Babylonia.*

JERICHO. A fortified Canaanite city near the Jordan River and the Dead Sea (Deut. 32:49) which was captured by Joshua when the Israelites entered the Promised Land (Josh. 6:1–22). In N.T. times, Jesus encountered Zacchaeus at Jericho (Luke 19:1–10), a city which had been built near the site of O.T. Jericho. It is regarded as one of the world's oldest cities, probably inhabited as early as 7000 B.C.

JEROBOAM.
1. Jeroboam I. The first king of Israel (reigned about 931–910

B.C.) after the kingdom of Solomon split into two separate nations following the death of Solomon. An official in Solomon's administration, Jeroboam led the ten northern tribes to rebel against the two southern tribes when Rehoboam succeeded Solomon as king (1 Kings 12:17–20). He established idol worship in the cities of Bethel and Dan (1 Kings 12:26–30) and was ultimately defeated by King Abijah of Judah and struck down by the Lord (2 Chron. 13:19–20).

2. Jeroboam II. A wicked king of Israel (reigned about 782–753 B.C.) who succeeded his father Jehoash (2 Kings 14:23–29). He was denounced by the prophet Amos for his evil deeds and encouragement of idol worship (Amos 7:7–9).

JERUBBAAL/JERUBBE-SHETH. A name given to the judge Gideon by his father after he destroyed the altar of Baal at Ophrah (Judg. 6:32). It probably means "let Baal contend." Another name given to Gideon was *Jerubbesheth* (2 Sam. 11:21; *Jerubbaal:* NRSV), probably meaning "contender with the idol." See also *Gideon*.

JERUEL. A wilderness in southern Judah where the prophet Jahaziel predicted King Jehoshaphat of Judah would meet the Ammonite and Moa-bite armies (2 Chron. 20: 14–16).

JERUSALEM/JEBUS/SALEM. The religious and political capital of the Jewish people. Situated forty-eight miles from the Mediterranean Sea and eighteen miles west of the Jordan River, Jerusalem was known as *Salem* in Abraham's time (Gen. 14:18) and as *Jebus* when the people of Israel entered Canaan, or the Promised Land (Josh. 15:8).

David captured the city from the Jebusites, renamed it, and turned it into his capital (2 Sam. 5:6–9). It was often called the "city of David" (2 Chron. 32:5). Solomon built the magnificent temple in Jerusalem as the center of worship for the Jewish people about 950 B.C. (1 Kings 5:5–8). The city fell to the Babylonians in 587 B.C., and its leading citizens were taken away as captives (Jer. 39:1–8).

After the Persians defeated the Babylonians, King Cyrus of Persia allowed Jewish exiles to return to their homeland and rebuild Jerusalem, including the temple and the city wall (Ezra 1:1–4; Neh. 12:27–47; Zech. 4). In N.T. times, Christ wept over the city because of its sin and spiritual indifference

The Dome of the Rock, a Moslem mosque which sits on the site once occupied by Solomon's temple in Jerusalem.

Courtesy Israel Ministry of Tourism

(Luke 19:41–42). He predicted its destruction (Luke 19:43–44), entered Jerusalem as a conquering spiritual leader (Matt. 21:9–10), and was crucified on a hill just outside the city wall (Luke 9:31). As Jesus predicted, Jerusalem was destroyed in A.D. 70 during a fierce battle between the Roman army and Jewish zealots.

The church was launched in Jerusalem, where it experienced spectacular growth (Acts 2). The apostle John described the future heavenly city as "New Jerusalem" (Rev. 21: 1–3). See also *City of David; Jebusites; Zion.*

JERUSALEM COUNCIL. A conference held during the early days of the Christian movement to determine how Gentile believers would be received into the church. Participants representing the church at Antioch and the church in Jerusalem included Peter, Paul, Barnabas, and James. The issue was whether Gentile converts first had to identify with Judaism by being circumcised before they could be baptized and received as full members of the church (Acts 15:6).

The council concluded that since Gentile and Jewish

believers are saved by grace alone, circumcision was unnecessary (Acts 15:8–19). This solution averted a conflict that would have hampered missionary efforts and could have made Christianity a sect of Judaism. See also *Judaizers*.

JESHANAH GATE. See *Old Gate*.

JESHUA

1. A priest who returned to Jerusalem with Zerubbabel after the Babylonian Exile and helped rebuild the temple and reestablish worship (Ezra 2:2; 3:2–9).

2. Another name for Joshua (Neh. 8:17). See *Joshua*.

JESSE. The father of David and an ancestor of Christ. Jesse presented his eight sons to the prophet Samuel, who anointed David as the future king of Israel (1 Sam. 16: 10–13). Jesse is mentioned in Scripture as the root or shoot that would produce the royal line of David (Isa. 11:1, 10; Rom. 15:12) and ultimately the Savior (Matt. 1:5–6).

JESUS CHRIST. The Son of God and Savior of the world. Jesus is the Greek form of the name *Joshua,* meaning "Savior." Christ means "the anointed

one," identifying Him as the promised Messiah of O.T. prophecy (Gal. 4:4–5).

Jesus was born during the reign of Herod the Great as Roman ruler over Palestine, some time before 4 B.C., the date of Herod's death (Matt. 2:1). After a public ministry of perhaps three years, He was crucified about A.D. 30. He preexisted as the eternal Word of God (John 1:1, 18; 8:58) and participated in the creation of the world (John 1:3). His advent in human form, including His virgin birth in Bethlehem (Isa. 7:14; Mic. 5:2), was foretold in the O.T. (Ps. 2:7–8; Isa. 9:6–7). As the God-man, Jesus was incarnated to reveal God in an understandable way (Matt. 1:23; John 1:14–18) and "to make reconciliation for the sins of the people" (Heb. 2:17–18).

As a boy, Jesus grew physically and advanced in knowledge (Luke 2:51–52). Yet, He had a consciousness of His divine mission (Luke 2:49). He was baptized by John the Baptist to "fulfill all righteousness" and to identify with humanity (Matt. 3:15–17). In resisting Satan's temptations at the beginning of His public ministry, the sinless Savior refused to break dependence on the Father and to establish His kingdom in any fashion other than by

A view of Bethlehem, the village where Jesus was born, from inside the bell tower of the Church of the Nativity.

Courtesy Israel Ministry of Tourism

suffering (Matt. 4:7–10).

Jesus' public ministry was short and revolutionary (John 17:4). He came preaching and healing (Mark 1:38–42), teaching (Luke 6:6), and seeking the lost (Luke 19:10). After an early campaign in Judea in southern Palestine, He began a major campaign in the region of Galilee in northern Palestine with Capernaum as His home base. His hometown synagogue in Nazareth rejected Him, but the common people heard Him gladly (Luke 4:16–32). He proclaimed a spiritual kingdom which required repentance and faith rather than blind and ritualistic obedience to the law and the legalistic demands of the Pharisees (Matt. 6:10, 33; Luke 13:3). His later ministry was devoted to training His disciples and preparing them for His death and their witness to others in the Holy Spirit's power (Luke 24:46–49).

Jesus' actions such as denouncing the Pharisees (Matt. 23), healing on the Sabbath (Matt. 12:8–14), and cleansing the temple angered the religious leaders among the Jews and disturbed Roman officials (Matt. 21:23). His triumphal entry into Jerusalem on a donkey disappointed His followers who wanted an earthly king (Luke 24:19–21). After observing the Passover with His disciples and instituting the Lord's Supper, He was betrayed into enemy hands (Luke 22:15–21).

In His trial before Pilate, Jesus acknowledged His kingship but declared His kingdom "not of this world" (John 18:36–37). Nevertheless, He was charged with treason and crucified between two thieves (John 19:14–16; Luke 23:33). On the third day He arose from the grave, conquering sin and death for believers (Acts 13:30; 1 Cor. 15:57). Jesus ascended to the Father, where He "ever liveth to make intercession" (Heb. 7:25). He will return for righteous judgment (Acts 17:31), to raise the dead (1 Thess. 4:14–17), and to usher in the time when all must confess that "Jesus Christ is Lord" (Phil. 2:9–11; Rev. 11:15).

See also *Emmanuel; Messiah; Son of God; Son of Man.*

JETHRO/REUEL/HOBAB. The father-in-law of Moses who was a priest of Midian. Moses married his daughter Zipporah (Exod. 2:16–22; 4:18). Jethro visited Moses in the wilderness and advised him to select leaders to share the responsibility of dispensing justice and settling disputes among the Hebrews (Exod. 18:17–26). *Reuel:* Exod. 2:18; *Hobab:* Judg. 4:11.

JEWELS. Precious stones used as ornaments or jewelry. The breastplate of Aaron the high priest contained twelve jewels, symbolizing the twelve tribes of Israel (Exod. 25:7).

JEWS. A word for the Israelites which came into general use during the period after the Babylonian Exile. In the N.T., it designates Israelites as opposed to Gentiles. See also *Israelites.*

JEZEBEL. The scheming wife of King Ahab who promoted Baal worship in the nation of Israel. She led Ahab to erect pagan altars (1 Kings 16:32–33), killed several prophets of the Lord (1 Kings 18:4–13), and plotted the death of Elijah (1 Kings 19:1–2), who prophesied her death (1 Kings 21:23). King Jehu had her assassinated when he came into power, in fulfillment of Elijah's prophecy (2 Kings 9:7–37). See also *Ahab.*

JEZREEL.
1. A symbolic name given

by the prophet Hosea to his son to show that King Jehu and his family would be punished for murdering King Ahab's family. The name means "God scatters" or "God sows" (Hos. 1:3–5).

2. A fortified city where King Ahab's palace was located (1 Kings 21:1) and where his family was assassinated by Jehu's forces (2 Kings 10:1–10).

3. The name of a valley in O.T. times which separated Samaria from Galilee. Many major battles have occurred here. Some scholars believe the battle of Armageddon in which Satan will be overthrown will be fought in this valley (Rev. 16:16; 20:1–10). The Greek word for this valley is *Esdraelon*.

JOAB. The commander of King David's army during most of David's reign (1 Kings 11:14–17). He became commander because he was the first to launch an attack against the Jebusites in their fortified city known as Jebus (later called Jerusalem; see 1 Chron. 11:6). His military exploits included victories over the Edomites (2 Sam. 2:13–16) and the Ammonites (2 Sam. 10:6–14). Joab carried out David's plan to have Uriah the Hittite killed in battle (2 Sam. 11:14). Joab was murdered on orders from the king when Solomon succeeded David as ruler of Judah (1 Kings 2:5, 31–34).

JOANNA. A woman who was a faithful follower of Jesus (Luke 8:1–3). She prepared spices for His burial and proclaimed His resurrection (Luke 23:55–56; 24:1–10).

JOASH.

1. The eighth king of Judah (reigned about 798–782 B.C.) who succeeded his father Ahaziah (2 Kings 11:2) at age seven. He was hidden by his aunt from the wicked queen Athaliah to prevent his assassination (2 Kings 11:1–3). Jehoiada the priest served as his counselor (2 Kings 11:12, 17). Joash brought needed religious reforms to Judah (2 Kings 12:4–5), but he turned to idol worship after Jehoiada's death (2 Chron. 24:17–19). He was assassinated by his own officers (2 Chron. 24:24–25). *Jehoash:* 2 Kings 11:21.

2. The son and successor of Jehoahaz as king of Israel (reigned about 798–782 B.C.). He led the nation into sin through his idolatry (2 Kings 13:10–25).

JOATHAM. See *Jotham.*

JOB. A godly man of the O.T. whose faith sustained him

through fierce trials and sufferings. Afflicted by Satan with God's permission (Job 1:6–19), Job refused to blame or curse God for his misfortune (1:20–22; 2:10), although he did complain to God, lamenting the day he was born (3:1–3). He and his three friends had long discussions about his misfortunes and what they meant. Job eventually came to a greater understanding of God's ways of dealing with man (42:3–6), and God restored his family and possessions (42:10–15). He was praised by James in the N.T. for his patience and faith (Jas. 5:11).

JOB, BOOK OF. A wisdom book of the O.T. which addresses the issue of human suffering, particularly the question of why the righteous suffer. The book is written in the form of a poetic drama revolving around the discussion of this problem by Job and his three friends: Eliphaz, Bildad, and Zophar.

After Job lost his children and earthly possessions (1:1– 2:13), his three friends arrived to "comfort" him and discuss the reason for Job's suffering (3:1–37:24). God assured Job that He is the sovereign, almighty God who doesn't have to defend His actions (38:1– 41:34). Armed with a new understanding of God and His nature ("I have heard of thee by the hearing of the ear: but now mine eye seeth thee"; 42:5), Job was rewarded by the Lord with the restoration of his family and possessions (42:10–15). See also *Wisdom Literature.*

JOBAB. A member of a confederacy of Canaanite kings defeated by Joshua at the Merom Brook (Josh. 11:1–12).

JOCHEBED. The mother of Moses, Aaron, and Miriam (Exod. 6:20). She is listed as one of the heroes of the faith (Heb. 11:23).

JOD. The tenth letter of the Hebrew alphabet, used as a heading over Ps. 119:73–80. See *Jot.*

JOEL.
1. A prophet of Judah in the days of King Uzziah and author of the O.T. book which bears his name. He predicted the outpouring of God's Spirit at Pentecost (Joel 2:28–32; Acts 2:16–21), proclaimed salvation through Christ (Joel 2:32), sounded the note of God's universal judgment (Joel 3:1–16), and pictured the eternal age with blessings for God's people (3:17–21).
2. The son of Samuel and a

corrupt judge of Israel. Joel's dishonesty, along with that of his brother Abiah, led the people to ask Samuel to appoint a king to rule the nation (1 Sam. 8:2–5).

JOEL, BOOK OF. A brief prophetic book of the O.T. which uses a devastating swarm of locusts (chap. 1) as an early warning sign of God's judgment in order to call His people to repentance. The prophet predicted the outpouring of God's spirit (2:28–32), an event which happened on the day of Pentecost (Acts 2:16–21); proclaimed salvation through Christ (2:32); and pictured the eternal age with blessings for God's people (3:17–21). See also *Pentecost*.

JOHANAN. A supporter of Gedaliah, governor of Judah (2 Kings 25:22–23), who took a remnant of the Jews to Egypt, in spite of the prophet Jeremiah's warning (Jer. 41:16–18; 43:4–6).

JOHN THE APOSTLE. A fisherman from Galilee, the son of Zebedee and brother of James, who became one of the twelve apostles of Jesus (Matt. 4:21–22). He was described as the disciple "whom Jesus loved" and a member of Christ's inner circle of disciples, which included his brother James and Simon Peter (Mark 5:37; 9:2; 14:33). John was ambitious for position and prestige in Christ's kingdom (Mark 10:35–37), but he showed a willingness to die for Jesus (Mark 10:38–39). Associated with Peter in bold evangelism in Jerusalem after Jesus' ascension (Acts 4:13; 8:14–15), he left Jerusalem about A.D. 65 for Ephesus, where he wrote the fourth Gospel and the three epistles of John. He wrote the Revelation while ex-iled as a political prisoner on the island of Patmos (Rev. 1:9–11).

JOHN THE BAPTIST. The prophet of righteousness and preacher of repentance who prepared the way for Christ. John's birth, Nazarite lifestyle, and unique role as the Messiah's forerunner was revealed to his father Zechariah (Luke 1:13–17) and his mother Elizabeth, a cousin of Mary—the earthly mother of Jesus (Luke 1:5–9, 39–41). He preached repentance and baptized converts in the Jordan River (Matt. 3:1–6), reluctantly agreeing to baptize Jesus after proclaiming Him as the "Lamb of God" (Matt. 3:13–17; John 1:29).

John denounced the hypocrisy of the Pharisees and the

immorality and adultery of Herod Antipas, a Roman ruler in Palestine (Matt. 3:7–8; 14:4). He was executed by Herod at the request of his wife Herodias's dancing daughter (Matt. 14:3–12). John always magnified Jesus rather than himself (John 3:30), and Jesus commended him highly for his faithfulness (Luke 7:24–28).

JOHN, EPISTLES OF. Three short epistles of the N.T. written by John, one of the twelve disciples of Jesus. First John, the longest of the three, focuses on such themes as the incarnation of Christ (1:1–5), Christian discipleship (1:6–10), false teachings about Christ (2:1–8), and the meaning of love and fellowship (2:15–5:3). Second John calls on believers to abide in the commandments of God (vv. 1–10) and reject false teachers (vv. 7–13). Third John commends the believers Gaius (vv. 1–8) and Demetrius (v. 12), while condemning Diotrephes (vv. 9–11). The apostle John probably wrote these epistles from Ephesus about A.D. 95. See also *Elect Lady; Demetrius,* No. 2; *Gaius,* No. 4; *John the Apostle.*

JOHN, GOSPEL OF. One of the four Gospels of the N.T., written by the apostle John to show that "Jesus is the Christ, the Son of God" (20:31). John is unique among the Gospels in that it majors on the theological *meaning* of the events in Jesus' life rather than the events themselves. Many of the miracles of Jesus are interpreted as "signs" of His divine power and unique relationship to the Father (2:1–12; 5:2–16).

The "I am" sayings of Jesus, in which He reveals selected attributes or characteristics of His divine nature, are also unique to the Gospel of John: The bread of life (6:35), light of the world (8:12), the door of the sheep (10:7), the good shepherd (10:11), the way, the truth, and the life (14:6), and the vine (15:5). See also *John the Apostle; Synoptic Gospels.*

JOKSHAN. A son born to Abraham and his concubine Keturah (Gen. 25:1–2; 1 Chron. 1:32).

JOKTAN. A son of Eber and descendant of Shem. He was an ancestor of several tribes in the Arabian desert (1 Chron. 1:19–27).

JONAH/JONAS. An O.T. prophet who was swallowed by a "great fish" while fleeing from God's call to preach to the pagan citizens of Nineveh in

Assyria (Jon. 1:17). In predicting His death and resurrection, Jesus referred to Jonah's experience (Luke 11:30; *Jonas*). See also *Assyria; Nineveh.*

JONAH, BOOK OF. A short prophetic book of the O.T. which emphasizes God's universal love. Jonah, the "reluctant prophet" (1:1–2:10) finally preached to the citizens of Nineveh in Assyria, a pagan nation noted for its cruelty and opposition to Israel. To his surprise and disappointment, the pagans repented and turned to God (4:1–10). Through this experience, Jonah learned that God is concerned for all people, not just the citizens of his native land (4:1–11). See also *Assyria.*

JONATHAN.

1. King Saul's oldest son (1 Sam. 14:49), who was a loyal friend of David, even while his father was trying to kill David (1 Sam. 20:17–42). David mourned Jonathan (2 Sam. 1:17–26) after he was killed by the Philistines (1 Sam. 31:2–8). See also *Mephibosheth.*

2. A supporter of David during Absalom's rebellion. Jonathan hid in a well to warn David of Absalom's plans (2 Sam. 17:17–21).

JOPPA/JAPHO/JAFFA. A coastal city on the Mediterranean Sea where Peter had his vision on full acceptance of the Gentiles (Acts 10:9–23). This area is known today as *Jaffa*, a part of the city of Tel Aviv. *Japho:* Josh. 19:46.

JORAM. See *Jehoram.*

JORDAN RIVER. The largest and most important river in Palestine. It runs the length of the country, from the Sea of Galilee in the north to the Dead Sea in the south. Jesus was baptized by John in the Jordan (Matt. 3:5–13).

JOSAPHAT. See *Jehoshaphat.*

JOSEPH.

1. The son of Jacob by Rachel who was sold to a band of traders by his jealous brothers. Enslaved and imprisoned in Egypt, Joseph became an important official under the pharaoh. He was eventually reunited with his father and brothers when they came to Egypt to buy grain. A model of faith and forgiveness, Joseph saw God at work in human events (Gen. 37–50; Heb. 11:22). He was called *Zaphnathpaaneah* by the Egyptian pharaoh (Gen. 41:45).

2. The husband of Mary,

Jesus' mother. A descendant of King David (Matt. 1:20), he was a carpenter (Matt. 13:55) and a righteous man (Matt. 1:19). Joseph took Mary as his wife after an angel explained Mary's condition (Matt. 1:19–25). He was with Mary when Jesus was born in Bethlehem (Luke 2:16). He took his family to Egypt to escape Herod's wrath, then returned later to Nazareth, where the young Jesus was obedient to His earthly parents (Matt. 2:13–23; Luke 2:51). Since Joseph does not appear later in the Gospels, it is likely that he died before Jesus' public ministry.

3. A devout man of Arimathaea (Luke 23:50–51) and secret disciple of Jesus (John 19:38) who prepared Jesus' body for burial and placed Him in his own tomb (Mark 15:43–46; Luke 23:53).

4. A half brother of Jesus. See *Brothers of Christ.*

JOSES.

1. A half brother of Jesus (Mark 6:3). See *Brothers of Christ.*

2. Another name for Barnabas. See *Barnabas.*

JOSHUA/OSHEA/HOSHEA/ JEHOSHUAH/JESHUA.

Moses' successor who led the Israelites into the Promised Land and rallied the people to victory over the Canaanites. One of two spies who gave Moses a favorable report on Canaan (Num. 13:8), he was the Lord's choice as Moses' successor (Num. 27:18–20). After his conquest of Canaan (Josh. 10–12), Joshua divided the land among the twelve tribes (Josh. 13–19). Before his death, he led the people to renew their covenant with God (Josh. 24:15–27). *Oshea:* Num. 13:8; *Hoshea:* Deut. 32:44; *Jehoshuah:* 1 Chron. 7:27; *Jeshua:* Neh. 8:17.

JOSHUA, BOOK OF.

A book of the O.T. that details the conquest and settlement of the land of Canaan by the Israelites under the leadership of Joshua. Major events covered by the book include: (1) Joshua's succession of Moses as leader of the people and their spiritual preparation for conquest (1:1–5:15); (2) battles against the Canaanites and allied tribes (6:1–13:7); (3) division of the land among the tribes of Israel (13:8–19:51); (4) the cities of refuge and Levitical cities (20:1–21:45); and (5) the farewell address and death of Joshua (23:1–24:33). See also *Cities of Refuge; Joshua; Levitical Cities.*

JOSIAH/JOSIAS. The son and successor of Amon as king of Judah (reigned 640–609 B.C.; 2 Kings 21:26). Crowned at age eight, he made a covenant to obey God (2 Kings 23:3) and led an important reform movement to reestablish God's law, repair the temple (2 Kings 22:3–9), and abolish idolatry (2 Kings 23:4–24). *Josias:* Jesus' ancestry (Matt. 1:10–11).

JOT. The English word for the jod (yod), the smallest letter in the Hebrew alphabet (Matt. 5:18), used figuratively by Jesus for a matter of minor importance. See *Jod.*

JOTHAM/JOATHAM. The son and successor of Azariah (Uzziah) as king of Judah (reigned about 750–732 B.C.). A contemporary of the prophets Isaiah, Hosea, and Micah (Isa. 1:1; Mic. 1:1), he was a good king but failed to destroy places of pagan worship (2 Kings 15:34–35). Jotham improved the temple, strengthened the city wall, and fortified buildings throughout Judah (2 Chron. 27:3–4). *Joatham:* Matt. 1:9.

JOY. Great delight or positive feelings. Joy attended Christ's birth (Luke 2:10) and resurrection (Matt. 28:8). A believer's spiritual joy is produced by the Holy Spirit (Luke 10:21; Phil. 4:4).

JUBAL. A son of Lamech, descendant of Cain, and a skilled musician regarded as the ancestor of those who play the harp and the flute (Gen. 4:21).

JUBILE (JUBILEE). A year of celebration devoted to liberty and justice and observed every fifty years by the Israelites. During this year, Israelites serving as indentured servants were released from their debts and set free. All properties given up because of indebtedness since the last jubilee were returned to the original owners. Cropland was allowed to go unplanted as a conservation measure (Lev. 25:8–55). *Jubilee:* NIV, NRSV.

JUDAH.

1. A son of Jacob and Leah and ancestor of the tribe of Judah (Gen. 29:35). Judah interceded for his brother Joseph to be sold rather than killed (Gen. 37:26–27). He offered himself as a ransom for his brother Benjamin before Joseph in Egypt (Gen. 43:8–9; 44:32–34). His father Jacob bestowed Reuben's birthright on Judah, declaring "the sceptre shall not depart from

Judah" (Gen. 49:10). He is listed as an ancestor of Christ (Matt. 1:2–3) and called *Juda* in Luke's ancestry (Luke 3:33). The tribe Judah is spelled *Juda* in the N.T. (Heb. 7:14). See also *Tribes of Israel*.

2. The Southern Kingdom, or nation of Judah. Founded after Solomon's death, the Southern Kingdom was composed largely of the tribes of Judah and Benjamin, while the rebellious ten northern tribes retained the name of Israel. Solomon's son Rehoboam was the first king of Judah, with the capital at Jerusalem (1 Kings 14:21). The nation drifted into paganism and idolatry under a succession of kings, turning a deaf ear to great prophets such as Isaiah and Jeremiah, who tried to bring them back to worship of the one true God. Judah was overrun and taken into exile by the Babylonians about 587 B.C. A remnant returned to rebuild Jerusalem about 530 B.C. (2 Chron. 36:20–23).

JUDAIZERS. An early Christian sect which advocated that Gentiles must be circumcised before they could become Christians (Acts 15:1). They were denounced by Paul, who insisted that believers are justified by faith alone (Acts 15:12; Gal. 6:15). The Judaizers were also opposed by Peter and James at the Jerusalem Council (Acts 15:8–19). See also *Circumcision; Jerusalem Council*.

JUDAS. See *Iscariot, Judas; Jude*.

JUDAS, BROTHER OF JAMES/LEBBAEUS/ THADDAEUS. One of the twelve disciples of Jesus, also called *Lebbaeus* (Matt. 10:3) and *Thaddaeus* (Mark 3:18). He was called "brother of James" to set him apart from the Judas who betrayed Jesus (Luke 6:16). See also *Twelve, The*.

JUDE/JUDAS. The half brother of Christ and author of the N.T. epistle which bears his name. He did not believe in Jesus in the beginning (John 7:5), but he apparently became a disciple after His resurrection (Acts 1:14). *Judas:* Matt. 13:55. See also *Brothers of Christ*.

JUDE, EPISTLE OF. A short N.T. letter written like a brief essay or tract and addressed to the problem of false teachings in the early church. Jude called on believers to root their faith in the true doctrine taught by the apostles (v. 17) as well as the love of Christ (v. 21).

JUDEA. A district in southern Palestine in N.T. times. The name was derived from "Jewish," a word describing Jewish exiles who returned to southern Palestine from the Babylonian Exile about 530 B.C. Judea was a Roman province annexed to Syria when Jesus was born (Matt. 2:1).

JUDGES, BOOK OF. A historical book of the O.T. which records the exploits of several different judges, or military deliverers, in Israel's history. The key to understanding Judges is the phrase, "The children of Israel again did evil in the sight of the Lord" (see 4:1), which occurs several times throughout the book. After each period of sin against God, He would send enemy oppressors in judgment. The Israelites would repent and pray for a deliverer, and God would answer their prayer. After their deliverance at the hand of a judge, the cycle of sin / oppression / repentance / deliverance would start all over again. See also *Judges of Israel*.

JUDGES OF ISRAEL. Popular military leaders or deliverers who led Israel between the time of Joshua's death and the beginning of the kingship (about 1380–1050 B.C.). Israel's judges served in times of dis-

unity and spiritual decline among the twelve tribes (Judg. 17:6; 21:25) as well as times when all the tribes were oppressed by their enemies. While some judges were weak or wicked, noteworthy exploits include Deborah and Barak's defeat of the Canaanite king Jabin (4:4–24), Gideon's 300 warriors who subdued the Midianites (7:1–8:21), and Samson's massacre of the Philistines (15:14–16).

Judges of Israel

Othniel ....Judg. 3:9–10
Ehud .... Judg. 3:15–30
Shamgar..............Judg. 3:31
Deborah and
Barak ....Judg. 4:4–8
Gideon .... Judg. 6:11–40
Abimelech.......Judg. 9:1–54
Tola ....Judg. 10:1–2
Jair..................Judg. 10:3–5
Jephthah ....Judg. 12:1–7
Ibzan ....Judg. 12:8–10
Elon............ Judg. 12:11–12
Abdon .... Judg. 12:13–15
Samson..............Judg. 15:20
Eli............... 1 Sam. 4:15–18
Samuel............. 1 Sam. 7:15
Samuel's sons. 1 Sam. 8:1–3
Bedan.............. 1 Sam. 12:11

JUDGMENT. Divine retribution against human activities. God's judgment is designed to punish evil (Exod. 20:5), to correct the misguided (2 Sam. 7:14–15), and to deter His people from wrongdoing (Luke 13:3–5). His judgment is an expression of His chastening love for the believer (Heb. 12:5–6). Jesus, God's resurrected Son, has authority to judge all mankind (John 5:27; Acts 17:31). Believers in Jesus will avoid condemnation and enter eternal life (John 3:16–17). See also *Punishment; Retribution*.

JUDGMENT, LAST. Final judgment of unbelievers of all ages. The final judgment is called a day of wrath for unbelievers (Rom. 2:5–8) but a day when believers will enter into eternal life (Rom. 2:7). The Lord will appear suddenly to gather His elect (Matt. 24:32, 42) and to separate unbelievers for judgment (Matt. 25:31–33). We should be prepared for this time (1 Thess. 5:1–9) and avoid self-deception regarding God's final judgment (Matt. 7:21–27). See also *Day of the Lord; Hell; Tribulation, Great*.

JUG. See *Cruse*.

JULIA. A female believer at Rome to whom the apostle Paul sent greetings (Rom. 16:15).

JULIUS. A Roman soldier who guarded Paul and other passengers during their trip to Rome (Acts 27).

JUNIA (JUNIAS). A fellow believer at Rome greeted and commended by Paul (Rom. 16:7). *Junias:* NIV.

JUNIPER (BROOM). A bush with dense twigs which was used for charcoal (Ps. 120:4). *Broom:* NIV, NRSV.

JUPITER (ZEUS). The chief god of Roman mythology and a name applied to Barnabas by the superstitious citizens of Lystra (Acts 14:12). The Greek name for this god was *Zeus* (NIV, NRSV).

JUSTICE. Fair and impartial treatment; righteousness. Justice is characteristic of God's nature (Deut. 32:4) and descriptive of Christ (Acts 3:14) and believers (Heb. 12:14). Just dealings with others by God's people was demanded by the O.T. prophets (Mic. 6:8; Amos 5:24). God's justice is fair and merciful (Acts 17:31).

JUSTIFICATION. The act or event when God both declares and makes a person just or right with him (Rom. 5:9). Justification is not accomplished by personal merit or good works (Gal. 2:16) but by God's grace through personal faith in Christ (Eph. 2:8–9). To be justified is to have peace with God and hope for eternity (Titus 3:5–7). See also *Atonement; Propitiation; Reconciliation.*

JUSTUS. A friend and believer at Corinth with whom the apostle Paul lodged (Acts 18:7).

-K-

KAB. See *Cab.*

KADESH/KADESH-BARNEA. A wilderness region between Canaan and Egypt which served as the southern boundary of the Promised Land (Num. 34:4). The Israelites camped in this area during the wilderness wandering years before they entered the Promised Land (Num. 32:8; 27:14). *Kadesh-barnea:* Josh. 14:7. See also *Wilderness Wanderings.*

KANAH. A stream between the territories of Ephraim and Manasseh (Josh. 16:8–9; 17:9), likely the same as present-day Wadi Kanah, which runs into the Mediterranean Sea north of Joppa.

KEDAR. A son of Ishmael, grandson of Abraham, and founder of an Arabic tribe which lived in the desert between Arabia and Babylonia (Gen. 25:12–13).

KEDESH.
1. One of the six cities of refuge, situated in the territory of Naphtali in northern Palestine (Josh. 20:1–7). This city is now called *Keder.* See also *Cities of Refuge.*
2. A Canaanite town captured by Joshua (Josh. 12:7, 22) and allotted to the tribe of Issachar (1 Chron. 6:72). *Kishion:* Josh. 19:20; *Kishon:* Josh. 21:28.

KEILAH. A fortified city of southern Judah near Hebron taken from the Philistines by David's army (1 Sam. 23:1–5).

KEMUEL. A leader of the tribe of Ephraim who helped Moses divide the land of Canaan after its occupation by the Israelites (Num. 34:24).

KENAN/CAINAN. A son of Enoch and grandson of Adam who lived in the days before the great flood (1 Chron. 1:1–2). *Cainan:* Gen. 5:9.

KENITES. A nomadic Midianite tribe associated with the Amalekites (Gen. 15:19). Friendly toward the Israelites, this tribe was likely absorbed into Judah (1 Sam. 27:10).

KENIZZITES. A Canaanite tribe whose land was promised to Abraham's descendants (Gen. 15:18–19).

KENOSIS. Relating to the dual nature of Christ—His divinity and humanity. Citing Phil. 2:7, advocates of this theory claim that God's Son laid aside or "emptied himself" of certain divine attributes when He became human. Most scholars reject the notion that Jesus stopped being God or that He gave up any divine attributes. Rather, the phrase refers to Christ's voluntary servanthood (John 17:5).

KERIOTH. A town in southern Judah (Josh. 15:25). This may have been the hometown of Judas Iscariot, Jesus' disciple and betrayer, since Iscariot means "man of Kerioth."

KETTLE. A vessel used for cooking and in worship rituals (1 Sam. 2:14). The Hebrew word for kettle is also translated as "basket," "caldron," or "pot" (Jer. 24:2; Job 41:20). See also *Caldron*.

KETURAH. The wife of Abraham after Sarah's death (Gen. 25:1). The six sons born to their union were ancestors of six Arabian tribes in Palestine or Arabia (1 Chron. 1:33).

KEY. A tool used to unlock a door. In Bible times, keys were long rods with metal pins (Judg. 3:25). The word is also used figuratively as a symbol of authority (Isa. 22:22; Rev. 1:18).

KID. A young goat. Kids were used as sacrificial offerings or butchered for special occasions (Luke 15:29). See also *Goat*.

KIDNEY. See *Reins*.

KIDRON/CEDRON. A valley or ravine with a wet-weather stream near Jerusalem. David crossed the Kidron Brook while fleeing from his son Absalom (2 Sam. 15:23–30). Idols from pagan cults were burned in this valley (1 Kings 15:13). Jesus probably crossed this valley on the night of His arrest (John 18:1; *Cedron*).

KINDNESS. Cordiality toward others. Believers are to be kind and forgiving, following the example of Jesus (Eph. 4:32).

KINDRED. Relatives, or members of one's immediate or extended family. The clan or tribe was the basic family unit in early Hebrew history. Family members considered it their duty to protect one another (Gen. 34). See also *Family*.

KINE (COW). An archaic word for cow or ox (Gen. 32:15). The prophet Amos used this word for the oppressive, indulgent leaders of Israel (Amos 4:1–3). *Cow:* NIV, NRSV.

KING. The monarch or supreme ruler of a nation. Beginning with the first king, Saul, who was anointed with God's authority (1 Sam. 10:1), Judah and Israel had a succession of kings across several centuries until both nations were overrun by foreign powers. The books of 1 and 2 Samuel, 1 and 2 Kings, and 1 and 2 Chronicles report on the reigns of many of these kings. A few were godly and kind rulers who honored God and followed His law, but most were evil and corrupt. They led God's people into sin and idolatry.

The believer should remember that God is our eternal king, worthy of all honor (1 Tim. 1:17). Christ, our ultimate ruler, is Lord of Lords and King of Kings (John 18:37; Rev. 17:14).

KINGDOM OF GOD. The spiritual reign of God in the hearts of believers (Luke 17:20–21).

Partially attained in this life for those who seek God's will, God's kingdom will be fully established in the world to come (John 18:36). Jesus preached the "gospel of the kingdom" (Mark 1:14) and taught His disciples to seek His kingdom (Matt. 6:33) and to pray for its arrival on earth (Matt. 6:10). Unrepentant sinners cannot inherit this kingdom (Eph. 5:5). It is reserved for those who repent (Matt. 3:2) and experience spiritual rebirth (John 3:3–5). Other phrases for this kingdom are "kingdom of heaven" (Matt. 4:17) and "kingdom of Christ" (Col. 1:13).

KINGS, BOOKS OF. Two historical books of the O.T. which cover a period of roughly four centuries in Jewish history—from about 970 to 587 B.C. First Kings records the reign of Solomon as successor to David (1 Kings 1:1–11:43); the division of the kingdom into two separate nations, Judah and Israel (12:1–14:31); and the reigns of selected kings in both these nations until the time of Ahaziah of Israel (about 853–852 B.C.).

Second Kings continues the narrative of Ahaziah's reign (1:1–18) and reports on the reigns of selected kings in both nations up until the time of the fall of the Northern Kingdom under Hoshea (reigned about 730–722 B.C.; chap. 17). Chapters 18 through 25 cover the final years of the surviving nation of Judah, until it fell to the Babylonians in 587 B.C. See also *King*.

KING'S DALE/SHAVEH. The ancient name for a valley east of Jerusalem where Abraham met the king of Sodom and Melchizedek (Gen. 14:17–18). Also called *Shaveh,* this is perhaps the same place as the Valley of Jehoshaphat (Joel 3:2). See *Jehoshaphat, Valley of.*

KING'S GARDEN. A royal garden in the city of Jerusalem (2 Kings 25:4).

KING'S HIGHWAY. An important road linking Damascus and Egypt which ran through Israel. While in the wilderness, the Israelites were denied passage on this road as they traveled toward Canaan (Num. 20:17–21).

KINSMAN-REDEEMER. A close relative who had first option to buy back or redeem personal freedom or property that had been forfeited by impoverished members of the clan (Lev. 25:48–49). Boaz, a near kinsman of Naomi, acted

as a redeemer in his marriage to Ruth (Ruth 4). Jesus is our "elder brother" who redeems the believer (Heb. 2:11–17).

KIRIOTH/KERIOTH. A fortified city in Moab and possibly its capital in the eighth century B.C., since the prophet Amos predicted its destruction (Amos 2:2). *Kerioth:* Jer. 48:24, 41.

KIRJATH-ARBA. See *Hebron.*

KIRJATH-JEARIM/ BAALAH. A fortified city of the Gibeonites where the ark of the covenant was kept for twenty years before being taken to Jerusalem (1 Chron. 13–16). *Baalah:* Josh. 15:9.

KIRJATH-SANNA, KIRJATH-SEPHER. See *Debir,* No. 2.

KISHION/KISHON. See *Kedesh,* No. 2.

KISHON/KISON. A river in the valley of Jezreel in northern Palestine where Elijah killed the prophets of Baal (1 Kings 18:40). *Kison:* Ps. 83:9.

KISLEV. See *Chisleu.*

KISS. A sign of affection practiced by parents and children (Gen. 27:26). Jesus was betrayed by Judas with a kiss (Matt. 26:49).

KITE. A bird of prey belonging to the hawk family and regarded as unclean by the Israelites (Deut. 14:12–13).

KITTIM. See *Cyprus*.

KNEADINGTROUGH. A large bowl used to knead dough to prepare it for baking (Exod. 12:34).

KNEEL. A symbol of respect (Ps. 95:6) or subjection and surrender (2 Kings 1:13). Kneeling was also a customary stance in prayer, indicating reverence for God (Luke 22:41). See also *Bowing.*

KNIFE. A sharp-edged weapon or tool made of flint or bronze (Josh. 5:2).

KNOP. An old English word for the ornamental cap on a column. The word is also used for a decoration on the golden candlesticks in the tabernacle (Exod. 25:31–36).

KNOWLEDGE. A body of facts or information gained through study and experience. The prophets of the O.T. lamented the Israelites' lack of knowledge (Isa. 5:13). Paul indicated that knowledge of God is to be desired above all else (Phil. 3:8). The verb "to know" was often used in the O.T. for sexual intimacy (Gen. 4:1).

KOHATH. The second son of Levi (Gen. 46:8, 11) and founder of the Kohathites, priests who cared for the ark of the covenant and other accessories used in the tabernacle in the wilderness (Num. 3:30–31). Moses and Aaron were Kohathites (Exod. 6:18–20).

KOPH. The nineteenth letter of the Hebrew alphabet, used as a heading over Ps. 119:145–152.

KORAH/CORE. A grandson of Kohath who incited a rebellion against Moses and Aaron in the wilderness. Korah and his followers were swallowed by the earth as punishment for their sin (Num. 16:30–33). *Core:* Greek form (Jude 11).

-L-

LABAN. A brother of Jacob's mother Rebekah and father of Leah and Rachel, who were given in marriage to Jacob. Jacob visited Laban to escape the wrath of his brother Esau (Gen. 27:43). He worked seven years for Laban for the privilege of marrying Rachel, only to be tricked into marrying Leah instead. Then Jacob worked another seven years for Rachel (Gen. 29:18–36).

LABORER. An unskilled worker who performed such menial tasks as tilling the fields and gathering the crops in Bible times (Ruth 2:2; Ps. 90:10). See also *Hireling*.

LACHISH. An Amorite city in southern Judah captured by Joshua (Josh. 10:31–35) and later besieged by King Sennacherib of Assyria (2 Kings 18:13–14). Lachish was reoccupied by the Israelites after the Babylonian Exile (Neh. 11:30).

LAISH. See *Dan,* No. 2.

LAKE OF FIRE. The place of final punishment. Filled with burning brimstone (Rev. 19:20), this place is described as the "second death" (Rev. 20:14). Those consigned to the lake of fire include Satan (Rev. 20:10), persons not named in the Book of Life (Rev. 20:15), and unbelieving sinners (Rev. 21:8). See also *Hell*.

LAKE OF GENNESARET. See *Galilee, Sea of.*

LAMB. A young sheep, used for food (2 Sam. 12:4), clothing (Prov. 27:26), and religious sacrifices (Exod. 12:5, 7). A lamb also symbolized the sufferings of Christ (Isa. 53:7) and the reign of the Messiah (Isa. 11:6). See also *Sheep*.

LAMB OF GOD. A title of Christ which emphasizes the sacrificial nature of His life and His atoning death. This aspect of His ministry was foretold by the prophet Isaiah (Isa. 53:7). John the Baptist greeted Jesus with this title (John 1:29). As the Lamb of God, Jesus is worthy of eternal honor and praise (Rev. 5:12–13). See also *Atonement; Cross.*

LAME. Inability to walk, due to an injury (2 Sam. 4:4) or a birth defect (Acts 3:2). Persons with this disability were healed by Jesus (Matt. 11:5) and Peter (Acts 3:2–7).

LAMECH. A son of Methuselah and a man of faith who found "comfort" in the birth of his son Noah (Gen. 5:25–31). Lamech is listed in the ancestry of Jesus (Luke 3:36).

LAMED. The twelfth letter of the Hebrew alphabet, used as a heading over Ps. 119:89–96.

LAMENTATIONS OF JERE-MIAH. A short O.T. book which expresses in poetic form the prophet Jeremiah's deep grief and anguish at the destruction of Jerusalem and the Jewish temple by the pagan Babylonians. Chapter 4 paints a bleak picture of life in Jeru-salem during the extended siege against the city. See also *Babylonia; Jeremiah.*

LAMP. See *Candle.*

LAMPSTAND. See *Candlestick.*

LANCE. See *Spear.*

LAND OF PROMISE. Canaan, or the land inhabited by the Israelites. This land was promised by God to Abraham's descendants (Gen. 12:1–7). The promise was fulfilled centuries later when Joshua led the Israelites to take the land from the Canaanites (Josh. 10–12). See also *Canaan, No. 2; Palestine.*

LANDMARK (BOUNDARY STONE, MARKER). A marker, usually consisting of a pile of stones, which indicated property lines. Removal of a landmark was forbidden (Deut. 19:14). *Boundary stone:* NIV; *Marker:* NRSV.

LANDOWNER. See *Goodman.*

LANTERN. A torch covered with skin or transparent horn for outdoor use. On the night before His crucifixion, Jesus was arrested by armed men with lanterns (John 18:3). See also *Torch.*

LAODICEA. A major city in Asia Minor, located on the Lycus River. One of the seven churches addressed in the book of Revelation was located in Laodicea (1:11). This church was rebuked because of its complacency (Rev. 3:14–18).

LAPIDOTH (LAPPIDOTH). The husband of Deborah the prophetess (Judg. 4:4). *Lappidoth:* NIV, NRSV. See also *Deborah.*

LAPWING (HOOPOE). A small European bird, considered unclean by the Hebrews, which wintered in Palestine (Lev. 11:19; Deut. 14:12, 18). *Hoopoe:* NIV, NRSV.

LASCIVIOUSNESS (DE-BAUCHERY, LICENTIOUS-NESS). Unbridled lust, a sin characteristic of life apart from Christ (1 Pet. 4:3; *debauchery:* NIV; *licentiousness:* NRSV), which believers are warned to avoid.

According to Paul, victory over lasciviousness requires repentance (2 Cor. 12:21) and living in the spirit of Christ (Gal. 5:22–25).

LASHARON. A Canaanite town near Tabor captured by Joshua (Josh. 12:1–18). This may be the same city as Lasha (Gen. 10:19).

LAST SUPPER. See *Lord's Supper*.

LATCHET (THONGS). A strap which fastened a sandal to the foot (Gen. 14:23). John the Baptist declared he was unworthy to untie the latchet of Christ's sandals (Mark 1:7). *Thongs:* NIV, NRSV. See also *Sandal*.

LATTER RAIN (SPRING RAIN). The rain which fell late in the growing season, allowing crops to reach full maturity before the harvest (Jer. 3:3). *Spring rain:* NIV, NRSV. See also *Former Rain; Rain*.

LATTICE. A screened opening or porch on a house to provide privacy and let in night breezes (Judg. 5:28; 2 Kings 1:2).

LAUNDERER. See *Fuller*.

LAVER (BASIN). A container placed near the altar outside the tabernacle where priests could wash their hands and feet before offering animal sacrifices (Exod. 30:18–21). *Basin:* NIV, NRSV. See also *Bason*.

LAW, LAW OF MOSES. The authoritative rule of conduct spelled out in the Ten Commandments and the Pentateuch—the books of Genesis, Exodus, Leviticus, Numbers, and Deuteronomy. This code was revealed to Moses by the Lord on Mt. Sinai (Deut. 5:1–2). While many of the regulations are ceremonial or procedural in nature, the moral law embodied in the Law of Moses is eternal and unchangeable (Rom. 7: 7–12). It was fulfilled by the gospel and confirmed by Christ (Matt. 5:17–18). See also *Moses*.

LAWYER. An interpreter or teacher of the law in the synagogues and schools of N.T. times (Matt. 22:34–40), also called a *scribe* (Luke 11:53). See also *Scribe*.

LAYING ON OF HANDS. A ritual blessing or ordination for service. This ritual was used by the high priest on the Day of Atonement. By placing his hands on the scapegoat, he ritually transferred the sins of the people to the animal (Lev. 16:21). The patriarchs placed their hands on their descendants to confirm birthright or convey special blessings (Gen. 48:14, 18). The church at Antioch laid hands on Paul and Barnabas to confirm their calling as missionaries and to set them apart for this service (Acts 13:2–3).

LAZARUS. A brother of Mary and Martha whom Jesus raised from the dead. This event impressed the common people (John 11:41–45) but provoked the Jewish leaders to seek the death of both Jesus and Lazarus (John 11:47–57; 12:10–11).

LEAD. A heavy metal cast into weights (Zech. 5:8). It was also a useful agent for refining gold and silver (Num. 31:22–23). The word is used figuratively for the cleansing of Israel (Jer. 6:29).

LEAGUE (COMPACT, TREATY). An alliance of nations for fostering common interests and providing protection against enemies (2 Sam. 5:3). *Compact:* NIV (1 Kings 5:12). *Treaty:* NIV, NRSV. Leagues with the Canaanites and other pagan nations were prohibited (Exod. 23:31–33). See also *Alliance.*

LEAH. Laban's oldest daughter and Jacob's first wife (Gen. 29:19–27). She bore seven children (Gen. 29:32–35; 30:17–21) and remained loyal to Jacob when he had to flee from Laban (Gen. 31:17–20). See also *Jacob.*

LEANNOTH. A musical term of uncertain meaning in the title of Ps. 88.

LEARNED. See *Prudent.*

LEATHER. Treated animal skins used for clothing (Lev. 13:48), tent coverings (Exod. 26:14), sandals (Ezek. 16:10), and water and wine containers (Matt. 9:17). See also *Tanner.*

LEAVEN (YEAST). A fermentation agent used in making bread or wine (Hos. 7:4). Jesus used the term to warn against the teachings of the Pharisees and Sadducees (Matt. 16:11–12). *Yeast:* NIV, NRSV.

LEBANON. A rugged mountainous region in northern Palestine. Cedar and fir trees from Lebanon were used in the construction of the temple in Jerusalem under Solomon (1 Kings 5:6–10; 7:2).

LEBBAEUS. See *Judas, Brother of James.*

187

LEBO-HAMATH.
See *Hamath*.

LEECH. See *Horseleach*.

LEEK. An onionlike plant. In the wilderness, the Israelites longed for this vegetable which they had enjoyed in Egypt (Num. 11:5).

LEES (DREGS). The waste which settled to the bottom of the container in the process of wine-making (Isa. 25:6). The term is used figuratively for indifference or laziness (Jer. 48:11; Zeph. 1:12). *Dregs:* NIV, NRSV. See also *Dregs*.

LEGION
1. A Roman military division, consisting of several thousand foot soldiers plus cavalrymen (John 18:3–12).
2. Any large number, such as angels available to Jesus (Matt. 26:53) or demons inhabiting a demoniac (Luke 8:30).

LEHI. A site in the hill country of Judah where Samson killed 1,000 Philistines with the jawbone of a donkey (Judg. 15:9–15).

LEMUEL. An unknown king mentioned in the book of Proverbs (Prov. 31:1). Some scholars identify Lemuel as Solomon.

LENTIL. A plant of the pea family used in Jacob's pottage, or stew. Esau sold his birthright to Jacob for a bowl of this stew (Gen. 25:29–34).

LEOPARD. A wild animal of the cat family noted for its speed and fierceness (Jer. 5:6). The reign of the Messiah is pictured as a time when leopards will lie down with goats (Isa. 11:6).

LEPROSY. A variety of dreaded skin diseases. The Mosaic Law required a leper to live in isolation from others and to cry "unclean" so people could avoid him (Lev. 13:45–46). Jesus healed ten lepers and sent them to the priest for verification and purification (Luke 17:11–15).

LETTER. See *Jot*.

LEVI.
1. The third son of Jacob and Leah (Gen. 29:34) and ancestor of the Levites (Exod. 2:1; Num. 1:49). His three sons were ancestors of the three major branches of the Levitical priesthood: Kohathites, Gershonites, and Merarites (Gen. 46:11). See also *Levites; Tribes of Israel*.

2. Another name for Matthew. See *Matthew*.

LEVIATHAN. A sea monster, believed by some scholars to be the crocodile (Job 41:1). The word is also used figuratively to describe one of Israel's enemies, probably Egypt (Isa. 27:1).

LEVIRATE MARRIAGE. The marriage of a man to the widow of a deceased relative if she had no male heir. The purpose of this law was to provide an heir and an estate for the deceased relative and to provide for widows (Deut. 25:5–10). The union of Boaz and Ruth was a Levirate marriage (see Ruth 3–4). See also *Widow*.

LEVITES. Members of one of the twelve tribes of Israel who were descendants of Levi, third son of Jacob and Leah (Gen. 29:34). The Levites were responsible for taking care of the tabernacle and assisting the priests in their ceremonial duties (Num. 3:5–10). Moses and Aaron were Levites of the family of Kohath, Levi's son. When Canaan was divided, the Levites were assigned forty-eight towns in various tribal territories rather than a specific part of the land (Josh. 21:1–8). See also *Levitical Cities*.

LEVITICAL CITIES. Forty-eight cities assigned to the tribe of Levi instead of one specific territory (Num. 35:2–7). This arrangement gave the priestly class access to the spiritual needs of the other tribes. Six of these cities were designated as cities of refuge to protect those who accidentally killed persons from avenging relatives (Josh. 20:1–6). See also *Cities of Refuge*.

LEVITICUS, BOOK OF. An O.T. book filled with instructions about sanctification of the priests, regulations for worship and ceremonial offerings, and personal purification and dietary laws. The theme of the book is holiness. Because God is a holy God, He demands a holy and separated people who are totally committed to Him. This holiness is obtained through rituals of acceptable sacrifice, the emphasis of the first part of the book (1:1–17:16); and rituals of sanctification, the theme of the book's second major section (18:1–27:34).

These instructions in holiness and appropriate worship were revealed by the Lord to Moses during the Hebrews' wandering years in the wilderness of Sinai. See also *Clean; Sacrifice; Unclean Animals*.

LIAR. One who tells untruths. Satan is the father of lies (John 8:44), and liars are his agents (Acts 5:3). Lying is associated with idolatry and perversion of truth (Rom. 1:18, 25).

LIBERALITY. A generous spirit of helpfulness toward those in need. Ministering in such a spirit validates our faith (Gal. 6:10). Those who are generous will be treated with generosity (Luke 6:38).

LIBERTINES (FREEDMEN). Jews carried to Rome by Pompey as captives (63 B.C.) and later freed. Members of the Jerusalem synagogue who opposed Stephen were Libertines (Acts 6:9). *Freedmen:* NIV, NRSV.

LIBYA/PHUT/LUBIM. The Greek name for the continent of Africa west of Egypt (Acts 2:10). Persons from Libya were in Jerusalem on the day of Pentecost (Acts 2:10). The man who carried Jesus' cross was from Cyrene, Libya's chief city (Matt. 27:32). In the O.T., Libya was also called *Phut* (Ezek. 27:10) and *Lubim* (Nah. 3:9). See also *Phut.*

LICE (GNATS). Small biting insects, perhaps sand ticks, gnats, or mosquitoes. An invasion of lice was the third plague sent by God to persuade the pharaoh to allow the Israelites to leave Egypt (Exod. 8:16–18). *Gnats:* NIV, NRSV. See also *Gnat.*

LICENTIOUSNESS. See *Lasciviousness.*

LIE. See *Liar.*

LIEUTENANT (SATRAP). A military officer (Ezra 8:36). Also, a general title for the governor of a Persian province (Esther 3:12). *Satrap:* NIV, NRSV. See also *Satrap.*

LIFE, ETERNAL. See *Eternal Life.*

LIGHT. Illumination. God's first act of creation was to bring light into existence (Gen. 1:3–5). The word is used figuratively in the Bible to represent truth and goodness (Ps. 119:105), which dispel the darkness of ignorance and wickedness (Matt. 4:16; 5:15). See also *Darkness.*

LIGHTS, FEAST OF. See *Dedication, Feast of.*

LIGN ALOES. A tree from which perfume was made (Num. 24:6).

LIGURE (JACINTH). A precious stone in the breastplate of the high priest (Exod. 28:19). *Jacinth:* NIV, NRSV. See also *Jacinth.*

LILY. A general term for any flower resembling the lily (Song of Sol. 5:13; Matt. 6:28).

LIME. Powdered limestone, used for plaster and cement work (Isa. 33:12).

LINE (CORD). A method of measuring land with a cord (Josh. 2:18). *Cord:* NIV, NRSV. Amos told Amaziah the priest that the Lord's punishment would include division of his land by line (Amos 7:17). See also *Cord; Rope.*

LINEN. Cloth made from flax. The rich wore "fine linen" (1 Chron. 15:27), while the poor wore garments of unbleached flax. Linen was also used for curtains and veils in the tabernacle (Exod. 26:1). See also *Flax.*

LINTEL. A beam of wood over a door (Amos 9:1). In Egypt, the Hebrews were commanded to place blood from a sacrificial lamb over the lintels of their doors to avoid the angel of death (Exod. 12:22–23).

LINUS. A Christian at Rome whose greetings were sent by Paul to Timothy (2 Tim. 4:21).

LION. A large catlike animal which preyed upon sheep (1 Sam. 17:34–36). Those who offended the king of Persia were thrown into a den of lions (Dan. 6:7–28).

LIPS. A part of the human body associated with speaking. Moses described his poor speaking skills as "uncircumcised lips" (Exod. 6:12, 30). Covering of the lips was a gesture of shame or mourning (Mic. 3:7). See also *Mouth; Throat; Tongue.*

LIQUOR. A fermented beverage associated with both festive occasions (Luke 15:23, 32) and drunkenness (Rom. 13:13). Paul counseled that believers should be "filled with the spirit" rather than strong drink (Eph. 5:18).

LITTER. A portable chair on poles upon which people were carried. A covering provided protection from the sun and rain (Isa. 66:20).

LIZARD. A reptile regarded as unclean by the Mosaic Law (Lev. 11:30). Numerous species of lizards are found in Palestine.

LOAF. See *Bread*.

LO-AMMI. A symbolic name, meaning "not my people," given by Hosea to his second son to signify God's rejection of rebellious Israel (Hos. 1:8–9). See also *Hosea*.

LOAN. Borrowed money which had to be repaid with interest. To secure a loan, a debtor often pledged his children or himself (2 Kings 4:1; Amos 8:6). The Mosaic Law specified that loans to the poor were not to accrue interest (Exod. 22:25). See also *Debt; Usury*.

LOCUST. A migratory, plant-eating insect similar to the grasshopper. Swarms of locusts were sent as a plague upon the Egyptians to convince the pharaoh to free the Israelite people (Exod. 10:1–4). See also *Cankerworm; Grasshopper; Palmerworm*.

LOD/LYDDA. A town near Joppa built by Shemed, a descendant of Benjamin (1 Chron. 8:12). Peter healed a lame man here (Acts 9:32–35; *Lydda*).

LOFT (UPPER ROOM, UPPER CHAMBER). The small room or upper story built on the flat roof of a house (1 Kings 17–19). *Upper room:* NIV; *Upper chamber:* NRSV. See also *Upper Room*.

LOG. A unit of liquid measure, equal to about one-twelfth of a hin (Lev. 14:10). See also *Hin*.

LOGOS. A Greek term which means both "the Word" and "reason." Jesus came into the world as the Logos, or the Word of God incarnate—in human form (John 1:1–3; Col. 1:15 –17). See also *Word of God*.

LOINS. The midsection of the human body, just below the stomach. The Jewish people wrapped their loose garments around their loins when working or traveling to give greater freedom of movement (2 Kings 4:29). The word is used figuratively by Peter to counsel readiness for Christ's return (1 Pet. 1:13).

LOIS. The grandmother of Timothy who was commended by Paul for her faith (2 Tim. 1:5). See also *Timothy*.

LONGSUFFERING (PATIENT). Forbearance or patience; an attribute of God's nature (Exod. 34:6). His long-suffering is intended to bring people to repentance (2 Pet.

3:9). *Patient:* NIV, NRSV. See also *Forbearance; Patience.*

LOOPS. Fasteners which joined the curtains of the tabernacle together in a continuous unit (Exod. 26:3–11).

LORD. A rendering of various Hebrew words which refer to the God of Israel, Jesus, and persons in authority such as kings. The word is also used as a translation of the divine name *Yahweh,* which the Hebrews did not pronounce out of reverence (Gen. 12:8; Exod. 3:15–16). See also *Jehovah; Yahweh.*

LORD ALMIGHTY. See *Hosts, Lord of.*

LORD'S DAY. Sunday, the first day of the week, and the Christian day of worship (Rev. 1:10). The Jewish day of rest and worship fell on Saturday, the last day of the week. But after Christ's resurrection on the first day, Christians adopted this as their normal day of worship (Acts 20:7). The Christian custom of Sunday worship was already well established when the Roman emperor Constantine instituted the day as a Christian holiday in A.D. 321.

LORD'S PRAYER. Jesus' model prayer which He taught to His disciples in response to their request, "Lord, teach us to pray" (Luke 11:1). The prayer teaches us to approach God reverently (Matt. 6:9–10), to ask Him to meet our physical needs, and to seek His forgiveness and protection (Matt. 6:11–13). See also *Prayer; Sermon on the Mount.*

LORD'S SUPPER. Jesus' final meal with His disciples which He observed as a Passover ritual to symbolize His approaching death (Luke 22:15–16). In this act, He established a memorial supper, symbolizing His broken body and shed blood (Matt. 26:26–28), which Christians are enjoined to observe until the Lord's return (1 Cor. 11:26). See also *Love Feast.*

LO-RUHAMAH. A symbolic name for the prophet Hosea's daughter, meaning "unloved." It expressed God's displeasure with rebellious Israel (Hos. 1:6).

LOT. Abraham's nephew. He accompanied Abraham to Canaan and traveled with him to Egypt to escape a famine (Gen. 12:5; 13:1). His uncle gave him first choice of Canaan's land on which to settle. He selected the fertile Jordan Valley (Gen. 13:10–11) and settled with his family near the pagan city of Sodom. Lot escaped the destruction of this city, but his wife looked back on their possessions and was turned into a pillar of salt (Gen. 19:16–26). Lot was an ancestor of the Moabites and the Ammonites, tribes which became bitter enemies of the Israelites in later centuries (Gen. 19:37–38). See also *Ammonites; Lot's Wife; Moabites.*

LOTAN. See *Moab,* No. 2.

LOTS, CASTING OF. Decision making by casting small stones out of a container, similar to our modern practice of "drawing straws" (Josh. 18:6). It was believed that God made His will known through this method (Prov. 16:33). Matthias was chosen as an apostle to succeed Judas by casting lots (Acts 1:26).

LOT'S WIFE. The wife of Abraham's nephew who was turned into a pillar of salt as she looked back on Sodom (Gen. 19:26). Jesus used her experience to warn of the dangers of delay and disobedience (Luke 17:32).

LOVE. Unselfish, benevolent concern for other persons (1 Cor. 13:4–7; *charity:* KJV). To love God supremely and others unselfishly are the two most important commands of Jesus (Matt. 22:37–40). Christ's sacrificial death was the supreme expression of love (John 13:1; 15:13). See also *Agape.*

LOVE FEAST. Meal observed by the early churches in connection with the Lord's Supper. The purpose of the meal was to promote Christian fellowship and brotherly love (Acts 2:42, 46; 1 Cor. 10:16–17). Paul condemned some of the Corinthian Christians for their sinful behavior and selfish indulgence at such love feasts (1 Cor. 11:20–22). See also *Lord's Supper.*

LOVER. See *Paramour.*

LOVINGKINDNESS. God's gentle and steadfast love and mercy which He extends freely to His people (Pss. 63:3; 69:16; 103:4–12). See also *Mercy.*

LUBIM. See *Libya.*

LUCAS. See *Luke.*

LUCIFER (MORNING STAR, DAY STAR). A name for the pompous king of Babylonia used by the prophet Isaiah

(14:12). *Morning Star:* NIV; *Day Star:* NRSV. Some scholars believe this passage describes the fall of Satan (see Luke 10:18). See also *Devil; Satan.*

LUCIUS. A Jewish Christian and kinsman of Paul who greeted believers at Rome (Rom. 16:21). He may be the same person as Lucius of Antioch (Acts 13:1).

LUCRE (GAIN). Material wealth, represented by money or goods (1 Sam. 8:3; Titus 1:7, 11). *Gain:* NIV, NRSV. See also *Filthy Lucre; Money.*

LUDIM (LUDITES, LUD). A people descended from Mizraim, a son of Ham (Gen. 10:13, 22). *Ludites:* NIV; *Lud:* NRSV.

LUKE/LUCAS. A Christian of Gentile descent, apparently a physician by vocation (Col. 4:14), who accompanied Paul on some of his missionary journeys (Acts 16:10; 20:5; 28:30). Luke wrote the Gospel which bears his name as well as the Book of Acts. Paul commended Luke for his loyalty and friendship (2 Tim. 4:11). *Lucas:* Philem. 24. See also *Acts of the Apostles.*

LUKE, GOSPEL OF. One of the four Gospels of the N.T., written by Luke—a physician of Gentile background—to portray Jesus as the Savior of all people, Gentiles as well as Jews. Luke shows that Jesus associated with all types of people, including sinners (5:30; 15:2), the poor and outcasts (6:20–23; 16:19–31), and the Samaritans (17:11–19). This theme of Christ as the universal Savior was continued in the Book of Acts, which Luke wrote as a sequel to his Gospel. Acts tells how the gospel eventually spread from Jerusalem, the center of Judaism, to Rome, the capital city and nerve center of the Roman Empire. See also *Luke; Acts of the Apostles; Roman Empire.*

LUKEWARM. Neither hot nor cold; a term for indifference or complacency. Members of the church at Laodicea were criticized for their tepid spirituality (Rev. 3:16).

LUST. Evil desire, usually associated with the sex drive. Unbridled lust leads to sin and produces death (Eph. 2:3; Jas. 1:14–15). Believers are warned to flee worldly lust (Titus 2:12) and "follow righteousness" (Gal. 5:16; 2 Tim. 2:22).

LUZ. See *Bethel.*

LYCAONIA. A Roman province in southern Asia Minor visited by Paul. Cities in this region where he preached included Derbe, Lystra, and Iconium (Acts 14:1–6).

LYCIA. A province of Asia Minor which juts into the Mediterranean Sea. Paul made stops in Patara (Acts 21:1) and Myra, Lycia's major cities.

LYDDA. See *Lod*.

LYDIA. A businesswoman of Thyatira, a dealer in purple cloth, who was apparently converted under Paul's ministry at Philippi. After her conversion, she invited Paul and his friends to spend time in her home (Acts 16:14–15). See also *Philippi*.

LYE. See *Nitre*.

LYRE. See *Harp; Psaltery; Sackbut; Viol*.

LYSANIAS. The governor of Abilene, a region in Syria, when Herod was ruler over Galilee and when John the Baptist began his ministry (Luke 3:1). See also *Abilene*.

LYSIAS, CLAUDIUS. See *Claudius Lysias*.

LYSTRA. A city in the province of Lycaonia in central Asia Minor. Paul preached and healed a lame man here and was stoned by unbelieving Jews (Acts 14:6–20).

-M-

MAACAH/MAACHAH. One of David's wives and the mother of Absalom (2 Sam. 3:3). *Maachah:* 1 Chron. 3:2.

MACCABEES. A family of Jewish patriots who headed a religious revolt against the Syrians in Palestine from 167 to 63 B.C. See also *Antiochus IV Epiphanes*.

MACEDONIA. A mountainous country north of Greece and the first European territory visited by the apostle Paul. He planted churches in the cities of Philippi and Thessalonica (see Acts 16, 17, 20). Paul was beckoned to visit this region through his famous "Macedonian call"— a vision of a man pleading, "Come over into Macedonia, and help us" (Acts 16:9).

MACHINES. See *Engines*.

MACHIR (MAKIR). The oldest son of Manasseh (Josh. 17:1), a grandson of Joseph (Gen. 50:23), and a military hero who became the ancestor of the Macherites (1 Chron. 7:17–18). The Macherites won significant victories over the Amorites during the conquest of Canaan (Num. 32:39). *Makir:* NIV.

MACHPELAH. A field with a cave which Abraham bought as a burial ground (Gen. 23:9–18). Buried here were Abraham and Sarah, Isaac and Rebekah, and Jacob and Leah (Gen. 25:9–10; 49:29–33).

MAD (INSANE). A term for insanity, but it may also refer to anger or confusion (1 Cor. 14:23). David pretended to be insane in order to escape from Achish (1 Sam. 21:13–15). *Insane:* NIV.

MADAI. A son of Japheth and ancestor of the Medes (Gen. 10:2). See also *Medes.*

MADIAN. See *Midian,* No. 2.

MAGDALA. A city of Galilee near Capernaum, and probably the home of Mary Magdalene (Matt. 27:56).

MAGDALENE. See *Mary,* No. 2.

MAGI. See *Wise Men.*

MAGIC. The practice of illusion and sleight of hand to bring benefits or to deceive. The Israelites were forbidden to consult magicians or sorcerers (Lev. 19:31). See also *Sorcery; Witchcraft.*

MAGISTRATE. Civil authority or ruler. Magistrates in Philippi beat and imprisoned Paul and Silas for healing a demented slave girl (Acts 16:18–23).

MAGNIFICAT. The poem or song of the Virgin Mary upon learning she would give birth to the Messiah (Luke 1:46–55). Mary praised God for remembering "the lowliness of his ser-vant" (NRSV) and for keeping His promise to bless Abraham and his descendants. See also *Mary,* No. 1.

MAGOG. See *Gog, Prince of Magog.*

MAHALATH, MAHALATH LEANNOTH. A phrase in the titles of Pss. 53 and 88 which probably refers to a musical instrument or a tune to be used in worship.

MAHANAIM. The name which Jacob gave to a site near the Jabbok River where he was visited by angels while waiting for his brother Esau (Gen. 32:1–2). The name means "two armies" or "two camps," perhaps referring to the meeting of his and Esau's forces or to the camps of Jacob and God. A city by the same name was established later on this site (Josh. 21:38).

MAHER-SHALAL-HASH-BAZ. The symbolic name given by the prophet Isaiah to his second son, meaning "hasten the booty" (Isa. 8:1–4). It signified that Assyria would conquer Israel and Syria.

MAHLON. Ruth's first husband and the elder son of Naomi. He died about ten years after his marriage to Ruth (Ruth 1:5).

MAID. A young unmarried woman, often of the servant class (Ruth 2:8). The word may also refer to a virgin or a female slave.

MAIDSERVANT. A female servant or handmaid (Ruth 3:9). Sometimes the word refers to a female slave. See also *Handmaid; Servant.*

MAIL, COAT OF. See *Brigandine.*

MAINSAIL (FORESAIL). The dominant or principal sail of a ship (Acts 27:40). *Foresail:* NIV, NRSV.

MAJESTY. A term referring to the dignity, power, and authority of a king or other high official (1 Chron. 29:24–25).

MAJOR PROPHETS. A term for the prophetic books which appear first in the O.T.—Isaiah, Jeremiah, Ezekiel, and Daniel—because of the longer length of their books. See also *Minor Prophets.*

MAKIR. See *Machir.*

MAKKEDAH. A royal Canaanite town captured by Joshua (Josh. 10:10–26) and assigned to the tribe of Judah (Josh. 15:20, 41).

MAKTESH. A district near Jerusalem where merchants bought and sold. They were denounced by the prophet Zephaniah for their sinful practices (Zeph. 1:11).

MALACHI. An O.T. prophet and the author of the book which bears his name. His name means "my messenger" (Mal. 1:1). He lived after the Babylonian Exile and was probably a contemporary of the prophet Nehemiah.

MALACHI, BOOK OF. A short prophetic book of the O.T. written about 100 years after the Babylonian Exile and directed against shallow and meaningless worship practices. The prophet condemned the people of Israel for presenting defective animals as sacrifices (1:8) and withholding tithes and offerings (3:8–10). The book closes with a note of hope regarding the future Messiah (chap. 4).

MALCHI-SHUA/MELCHI-SHUA (MALKI-SHUA). A son of King Saul who was killed by the Philistines in the battle at Gilboa (1 Sam. 14:49). *Malki-shua:* NIV. *Melchi-shua:* 1 Sam. 31:2.

MALCHUS. A servant of the high priest whose ear was cut off by Peter. Jesus rebuked Peter and restored the severed ear (John 18:10–11).

MALE SLAVE. See *Manservant.*

MALEFACTOR (CRIMINAL). A rebel or criminal. Christ was crucified between two malefactors (Luke 23:32–33). *Criminals:* NIV, NRSV.

MALICE. A burning desire or intention to hurt others. Christians are urged to renounce malice (Eph. 4:31) and pray for those guilty of this sin (Matt. 5:44). See also *Hate.*

MALKI-SHUA. See *Malchi-shua.*

MALLOWS (HERB). A wild plant or shrub which thrived in the dry, salty regions near the Dead Sea. It was sometimes eaten by the poor (Job 30:3–4). *Herb:* NIV.

MALTA. See *Melita.*

MAMMON (MONEY, WEALTH). Material wealth or possessions. Christ warned that money or physical goods were false gods that should not be worshiped (Matt. 6:24). He urged believers to seek kingdom interests and promised that their material needs would be met (Matt. 6:33). *Money:* NIV; *Wealth:* NRSV. See also *Filthy Lucre; Money.*

MAMRE.
1. A town or district near Hebron where Abraham lived (Gen. 13:18; 18:1).
2. An Amorite chief and supporter of Abraham who gave his name to the plain where Abraham lived (Gen. 14:13).

MAN. The being created by God in His image and for His glory (Gen. 1:26–27; 9:6; Isa. 43:7). The crown of God's creation, man was given dominion over the natural world (Ps. 8:4–6). Man's sin has separated him from God (Rom. 3:23), but he may be redeemed by God's grace through faith in Christ (Rom. 3:22–24). See also *Fall of Man; Sin.*

MANAEN. A prophet and teacher in the church at Antioch. Along with others, he laid hands on Paul and Barnabas, endorsing their call to missionary service (Acts 13:1–3).

MANASSEH.

1. Joseph's firstborn son whose descendants became one of the tribes of Israel (Gen. 48:4–6) and occupied both sides of the Jordan River (Josh. 16:4–9). *Manasses:* Rev. 7:6. See also *Tribes of Israel.*

2. The son and successor of Hezekiah as king of Judah (reigned about 687–642 B.C.; 2 Kings 20:21). A wicked ruler who encouraged pagan worship throughout Judah, Manasseh was captured and taken to Babylonia (2 Chron. 33:10–11). He later repented and was allowed to return to Jerusalem (2 Chron. 33:12–13).

He was succeeded as king by his son Amon (2 Chron. 33:20).

MANDRAKE. A plant with an aromatic fragrance (Song of Sol. 7:13). Its fruit was thought to generate fertility (Gen. 30:14–16).

MANEH (MINA). A Hebrew weight equal to fifty shekels, or about two pounds (Ezek. 45:12). *Mina:* NIV, NRSV.

MANGER. A feeding trough for livestock. The infant Jesus was laid in a manger after His birth (Luke 2:7–16).

MANNA. Food miraculously provided by the Lord for the Israelites in the wilderness (Num. 11:7–9). Called "bread from heaven," (Exod. 16:4) manna was provided daily except on the Sabbath for forty years. A different substance by this name drops from various trees, particularly the tamarisk, in the valleys near the Sinai wilderness. See also *Wilderness Wanderings.*

MANOAH. A member of the tribe of Dan and father of Samson (Judg. 13:1–25).

MANSERVANT (MALE SLAVE). A male domestic

servant, often a slave (Exod. 21:32). *Male slave:* NIV, NRSV.

MANSLAYER (SLAYER). A person who accidentally killed another. This person could seek asylum from the avenging relatives of the victim in a city of refuge (Num. 35:6–12). *Slayer:* NRSV. See also *Avenger of Blood; Cities of Refuge.*

MANTLE (CLOAK). An outer garment, similar to a robe, made of coarse cloth or sheepskin. Elijah's mantle was placed on Elisha as a symbol of succession and blessing (1 Kings 19:19–21). *Cloak:* NIV. See also *Cloke.*

MARA. A name, meaning "bitter," which was assumed by Naomi because it expressed her sorrow at the death of her husband and sons (Ruth 1:3–21).

MARANATHA. An Aramaic phrase, meaning "come, O Lord," which expresses hope for the second coming of Jesus (1 Cor. 16:22). See also *Second Coming.*

MARBLE. Crystalline limestone noted for its beauty and durability as a building material. Marble was used in the building of the temple in Jerusalem (1 Chron. 29:2).

MARCUS. See *Mark.*

MARDUK. See *Merodach.*

MARESHAH. A town of Judah (Josh. 15:20, 44) built for defensive purposes by King Rehoboam (2 Chron. 11:5, 8). A battle between King Asa of Judah and King Zerah of Ethiopia was fought here (2 Chron. 14:9–10).

MARINER. A seaman or sailor. Paul reassured the mariners on his ship during a storm (Acts 27:31–36). See also *Ship.*

MARK, JOHN/MARCUS. A relative of Barnabas who accompanied Paul and Barnabas on the first missionary journey as far as Perga and then returned to Jerusalem (Acts 13:3–5). After Paul's refusal to allow Mark to go with them on the second journey, Barnabas and Paul went their separate ways (Acts 15:36–41). In later years, Paul spoke of Mark with warmth and affection (Col. 4:10–11). Most scholars believe Mark was the author of the Gospel of Mark, drawing perhaps upon the reflections of Peter, who worked closely with Mark (1 Pet. 5:13; *Marcus*).

MARK, GOSPEL OF. One of the four Gospels of the N.T. and probably the first to be written, according to most scholars. A short Gospel of only sixteen chapters, Mark portrays Jesus as a person of action. He uses the words *immediately* (1:12; 2:8) and *straightway* (8:10) to show that Jesus was on an important mission for God and had no time to waste. While Mark makes it clear that Jesus was the Son of God (15:39), he also emphasizes the humanity of Jesus more than the other Gospel writers, including incidents which reveal His disappointment (8:12), anger (11: 15–17), sorrow (14:34), and fatigue (4:38). See also *Mark; Synoptic Gospels*.

MARKER. See *Landmark*.

MARKET, MARKETPLACE. A large open area in a city where trade, public trials, and discussions were conducted (Acts 16:19–20). Children often played in this area (Luke 7:32). The Greek word for marketplace is *agora*.

MARRIAGE. The union of a man and a woman in commitment to one another as husband and wife. First instituted by God in the Garden of Eden (Gen. 2:18), marriage was also confirmed by Christ (Matt. 19:5). Love for and submission to one's mate were enjoined by Paul (Eph. 5:22–29). The love of a husband and wife for one another is symbolic of Christ's love for the Church (Eph. 5:23–25). See also *Betrothal; Dowry*.

MARROW. Tissue in the cavities of the bones. This word is used to illustrate the piercing power of God's Word (Heb. 4:12).

MARS' HILL. See *Areopagus*.

MARTHA. The sister of Mary and Lazarus (John 11:1–2). Jesus rebuked Martha because of her unnecessary worry after she welcomed Him into her home (Luke 10:38–42). She grieved at the death of her brother Lazarus and sought Jesus' help (John 11:20–22).

MARTYRDOM. Death in defense of one's faith. A Christian who gives a faithful testimony of the power of Christ in his or her life may face such an end (Rev. 6:9). But the wicked will eventually give account for the blood of the martyrs (Luke 11:49–51).

MARY.
1. The earthly mother of Jesus (Matt. 1:16). A descendant of David from Bethlehem, Mary was engaged to

Joseph (Luke 1:27). She was informed by an angel that she had been divinely chosen to give birth to the Messiah (Luke 1:28–33). She traveled with Joseph to Bethlehem (Luke 2:4–5) and gave birth to Jesus in fulfillment of prophecy (Isa. 7:14). She was forced to flee to Egypt with Joseph to escape Herod's slaughter of innocent children (Matt. 2:13–18). After she and Joseph returned to Nazareth, she gave birth to other children (Mark 6:3).

Mary visited Jerusalem during the Passover feast with Joseph and Jesus (Luke 2:41–46). She attended a marriage in Cana of Galilee, where Jesus worked His first miracle (John 2:3). She was present at the cross when Jesus commended her to John's care (John 19:25–27). Mary was also present with one of the praying groups in the upper room after the ascension of Jesus (Acts 1:14).

2. Mary Magdalene. The woman who served Jesus faithfully after being delivered from seven demons (Luke 8:1–2). She witnessed the crucifixion and visited the tomb of Jesus (Matt. 27:55–61). She told the apostles of Jesus about the empty tomb (John 20:1–2) and was one of the first to see the risen Lord (Mark 16:9).

3. The sister of Martha and Lazarus. She was an eager listener at Jesus' feet while Martha performed household duties (Luke 10:38–41). She anointed the feet of Jesus and wiped them with her hair (John 12:1–3). Jesus defended her contemplative temperament (Luke 10:42).

4. The mother of the disciple James. This Mary is probably one of the women who provided food for Jesus and His disciples (Luke 8:2–3). She was also among those who went to the tomb to anoint Jesus' body and discovered He had been raised from the dead (Mark 16:1–8).

5. The mother of John Mark (Acts 12:12). Her house may have been a meeting place for the early Christians of Jerusalem.

6. A fellow believer at Rome greeted and commended by Paul in his letter to the Roman Christians (Rom. 16:6).

MASCHIL. A Hebrew word which appears in the titles of thirteen psalms, apparently giving directions for the melody to be sung (Pss. 32, 42, 44–45, 52–55, 74, 78, 88–89, 142).

MASON. A bricklayer or stoneworker. Phoenician masons were used by Solomon to build the temple in Jerusalem (1 Kings 5:17–18).

MASSAH AND MERIBAH. A site in the wilderness where the Israelites rebelled against Moses and Aaron (Exod. 17:4–7). Their complaints provoked the wrath of the Lord (Deut. 6:16). See also *Wilderness Wanderings*.

MAST. The rigging or wooden frame which held the sails on a ship (Ezek. 27:5). The word was used figuratively to show the strength of Israel's enemies (Isa. 33:23). See also *Ship*.

MASTER (TEACHER). Word meaning "teacher" which was often applied to Christ (Matt. 22:16, 24). *Teacher:* NIV, NRSV. The word was also used in the O.T. as a term of respect for one's superiors (Gen. 24:48–49). See also *Teacher*.

MATHUSALA. See *Methuselah*.

MATTANIAH. See *Zedekiah*.

MATTHEW/LEVI. A tax collector who became a disciple of Jesus (Matt. 9:9) and writer of the Gospel which bears his name. He was also known as *Levi* (Mark 2:13–17; Luke 5:27–32). See also *Publican*.

MATTHEW, GOSPEL OF. One of the four Gospels of the N.T., written by a tax collector who became one of the twelve apostles of Jesus. This Gospel apparently was written to show the Jewish people that Jesus was the Messiah promised in the O.T., since many events in His life are interpreted as fulfillment of the Scriptures (1:22; 4:14; 12:17; 21:4; 27:35). In Matthew's genealogies, Jesus' ancestry through Joseph, His earthly father, is traced to two of the greatest personalities in Jewish history—Abraham (1:2) and David (1:6).

Matthew's Gospel also emphasizes the teaching ministry of Jesus, particularly His instructions to His disciples in the Sermon on the Mount (5:1–7:27). Another prominent theme of this Gospel is the kingdom of God or the kingdom of heaven (5:3; 6:33; 8:11; 12:28; 13:43–46; 19:23; 21:31; 25:34). See also *Beatitudes; Kingdom of God; Sermon on the Mount*.

MATTHIAS. The person who replaced Judas as an apostle. Matthias was chosen by the other apostles through the casting of lots (Acts 1:15–26).

Excavated ruins of a Roman theater at Caesarea beside the Mediterranean Sea. *Courtesy Israel Ministry of Tourism*

See also *Lots, Casting of; Twelve, The.*

MATTOCK (HOE). An agricultural tool, similar to a crude hoe, used to loosen the soil and remove roots (Isa. 7:25). *Hoe:* NIV, NRSV.

MATURITY. See *Perfection.*

MAUL (CLUB). A heavy club used as a weapon of war. The head was often studded with spikes (Prov. 25:18). *Club:* NIV, NRSV (Jer. 51:20).

MAW (STOMACH). The stomach of an animal that chews the cud. Considered a delicacy by the Hebrews, the maw, shoulders, and cheeks became the priests' portion of sacrificial animals (Deut. 18:3). *Stomach:* NRSV.

MAZZAROTH. A constellation of stars cited by Job as evidence of the power and sovereignty of God (Job 38: 31–33).

MEAT FORK. See *Fleshhook.*

MEAT OFFERING. An offering of a sacrificial animal, made to atone for sin (1 Chron. 21:23).

MEDDLER. See *Busybody.*

MEDEBA. An old Moabite town taken by Israel from King Sihon (Num. 21:23–30) and assigned to the tribe of Reuben (Josh. 13:8–16).

MEDES, MEDIA. Descendants of Japheth (Gen. 10:2) and an ancient kingdom between the Tigris River and the Caspian Sea to which Sargon of Assyria brought Hebrew captives (2 Kings 17:6; 18:11).

MEDIATOR, CHRIST THE. A title of Christ which describes His work in reconciling us to God. His sacrificial death has made it possible for us to have peace with God and with each other (Eph. 2:13–16). As our Mediator, He has made a full and final sacrifice for our salvation (Heb. 7:27). See also *Atonement; Propitiation; Reconciliation.*

MEDICINE. A healing substance. In Bible times, medicine was made from herbs, fruits, and minerals. The Balm of Gilead was probably made from the gum of an evergreen tree (Jer. 8:22). See also *Balm of Gilead; Healing.*

MEDITATION. Contemplation of spiritual truths (Ps. 119:148) which produces understanding (Ps. 49:3) and spiritual satisfaction (Ps. 63:5–6). Meditation on God's commands encourages obedience (Josh. 1:8).

MEDITERRANEAN SEA/ GREAT SEA. The sea on Israel's western border which was also called the *Great Sea* (Josh 9:1). Solomon used the Phoenicians to provide import/ export services for Israel across this body of water (1 Kings 9:27). Paul often sailed the Mediterranean during his missionary journeys (Acts 9:30; 18:18; Acts 27).

MEDIUM. A communicator between humans and the spirit world. The Mosaic Law specified that professing mediums or wizards were to be stoned to death (Lev. 20:27). The prophet Isaiah warned against consulting the dead rather than listening to the Lord (Isa. 8:19–20; 19:3). See also *Enchanter; Familiar Spirit; Wizard.*

MEEKNESS. A kind, gentle, and humble spirit. The meek will find spiritual satisfaction (Ps. 22:26) and receive God's instruction (Ps. 25:9). Paul cited meekness as one of the fruits of the spirit (Gal. 5:22–23). Jesus declared that the meek will inherit the earth (Matt. 5:5). See also *Humility; Kindness.*

MEGIDDO/MEGIDDON. A fortified city west of the Jordan River in the plain of Jezreel associated with the great battle in the end-time. This city was the site of Barak's victory over Sisera (Judg. 4:14–16) and King Josiah's death in a battle with Pharaoh Necho of Egypt (2 Chron. 35:22–24). In this area the final battle between God and the forces of evil will occur (Zech. 12:11; Rev. 16:16). *Megiddon:* Zech. 12:11. See also *Armageddon.*

MELCHI-SHUA. See *Malchi-shua.*

MELCHIZEDEK/MEL-CHISEDEC. The mysterious king of Salem who received tithes from Abraham (Gen. 14:18–20) and who is depicted as a type of Christ because of his endless priesthood (Heb. 5:6–10; 7: 15–17). The Messiah who is to come was also described as a priest "after the order of Mel-chizedek" (Ps. 110:4). *Melchisedec:* Heb. 7:11.

MELITA (MALTA). An island south of Sicily in the Mediterranean Sea where Paul was shipwrecked while sailing to Rome (Acts 28:1–8). *Malta:* NIV, NRSV.

MELON. A fruit, apparently grown in Egypt, for which the Israelites longed during their wilderness wanderings (Num. 11:5). Various melons are grown today in Palestine.

MEM. The thirteenth letter of the Hebrew alphabet, used as a heading over Ps. 119:97–104.

MEMPHIS. See *Noph.*

MENAHEM. A cruel and idolatrous king of Israel (ruled about 752–742 B.C.) who killed Shallum in order to assume the throne. He paid tribute to Tiglath-pileser III, king of Assyria, in order to maintain his power. He was succeeded by his son Pekahiah (2 Kings 15:16–22).

MEPHIBOSHETH/MERIB-BAAL. The crippled son of David's friend Jonathan and a grandson of King Saul. He was dropped by his nurse and crippled at age five when she received the news that Jonathan and Saul had been killed by the Philistines (2 Sam. 4:4). David sought out Mephibosheth, restored his family's land, and gave him a place at the king's table. *Merib-baal:* 1 Chron. 8:34. See also *Jonathan,* No. 1.

MERARI. The third son of Levi and ancestor of the Merarites (Gen. 46:11; Exod. 6:19).

MERCHANDISE. Items bought and sold in business transactions. Many traders in caravans passed through Israel on their way to and from Egypt (Gen. 37:25–28). Solomon established maritime trading agreements with the king of Tyre (1 Kings 9:26).

MERCURIUS (HERMES). The Roman name for the pagan god Mercury—the god of commerce—and the name applied to Paul by the people of Lystra (Acts 14:12). *Hermes:* NIV, NRSV.

MERCY (COMPASSION). Compassion for others. God's mercies are abundant (1 Pet. 1:3) and fresh every morning (Lam. 3:22–23). Paul described God as "the father of all mercies" (2 Cor. 1:3). *Compassion:* NIV. Jesus commended the Samaritan who showed mercy for a wounded traveler (Luke 10:36–37). See also *Compassion; Lovingkindness; Pity.*

MERCY SEAT (COVER). The gold lid which covered the ark of the covenant. It was called the "mercy seat" because God was believed to be present to hear and answer prayers (Exod. 25:21–22). *Cover:* NIV. On the Day of Atonement, the high priest sprinkled blood of the sin offerings on the mercy seat as a propitiation for the people's sins (Lev. 16:11–16). See also *Ark of the Covenant; Atonement.*

MERIBAH. See *Massah and Meribah.*

MERIB-BAAL. See *Mephibosheth.*

MERODACH (MARDUK). The pagan Babylonian god of war whose overthrow was predicted by the prophet Jeremiah (Jer. 50:2). *Marduk:* NIV.

MERODACH-BALADAN. See *Berodach-baladan.*

MESHA.
1. The oldest son of Caleb (1 Chron. 2:42).
2. A king of Moab who led an unsuccessful invasion of Judah (2 Chron. 20). He offered his oldest son as a sacrifice to the pagan god Chemosh (2 Kings 3:4, 26–27).

MESHACH/MISHAEL. The Babylonian name for Daniel's friend who was thrown into the fiery furnace for refusing to worship an idol (Dan. 1:7).

He was saved through God's miraculous intervention. His Hebrew name was *Mishael* (Dan. 1:6). See also *Daniel.*

MESOPOTAMIA/ PADAN-ARAM. The territory between the Tigris and Euphrates rivers also known as *Padan-aram* (Gen. 25:20). Abraham and his family migrated from the city of Ur in this region (Gen. 11:31–32; Acts 7:2). The Babylonian Empire flourished in this general vicinity during O.T. times. Citizens of Mesopotamia were present in Jerusalem on the day of Pentecost (Acts 2:9). See also *Ur of the Chaldees.*

MESS. A portion of food served at a meal (2 Sam. 11:8). To receive a larger-than-usual mess or portion was considered an honor (Gen. 43:34).

MESSENGER. A person sent to deliver a special message. Jewish kings sent couriers to distant cities to proclaim laws and edicts (2 Chron. 36:22–23). John the Baptist was a messenger who prepared the people for the coming of Jesus (Matt. 11:10).

MESSIAH/MESSIAS (ANOINTED ONE). The title given by the Jewish people to a future leader whom they expected to restore their honor and glory after delivering them from their oppressors (Dan. 9:25–26). *Anointed one:* NIV. Jesus fulfilled their longing but in an unexpected way by becoming a spiritual Savior who delivered believers from sin (Rom. 6:1–9). *Messias:* Greek form: (John 1:41; 4:25). See also *Emmanuel; Jesus Christ; Son of God.*

METHUSELAH/MATHU- SALA. A son of Enoch (Gen. 5:21) and the grandfather of Noah. Methuselah lived to the age of 969, the oldest recorded age in the Bible. *Mathusala:* Luke 3:37.

MICAH. A prophet of the O.T., a contemporary of Isaiah, whose ministry paralleled the reigns of kings Jotham, Ahaz, and Hezekiah from about 750 to 687 B.C. (Mic. 1:1). A stern prophet of judgment, he denounced the social injustices of his time (Mic. 2:1–3).

MICAH, BOOK OF. A short prophetic book of the O.T. known for its prediction that the Messiah would be born in Bethlehem (5:2). The prophet also condemned the rich for oppressing the poor (2:1–2; 6: 7–13) and announced that God's judgment against the nations of Judah and Israel would be wrought by the conquering Assyrians (1, 3, 7:10–13).

MICAIAH. An O.T. prophet who predicted that King Ahab of Israel would be killed in a battle at Ramoth-gilead, in contrast to false prophets who assured the king he would be victorious (1 Kings 22:8–28). Micaiah was imprisoned for his stinging message, but his prediction was correct (1 Kings 22:29–39).

MICHAEL.
1. A son of Jehoshaphat, king of Judah. Michael was killed by his brother Jehoram, who became king (2 Chron. 21:2–4).
2. An archangel who was thought to serve as a prince and guardian over the nation of Israel (Dan.10:21; 12:1). See also *Archangel*.

MICHAL. A daughter of King Saul presented to David as a wife after David killed 200 Philistine warriors (1 Sam. 14:49; 18:25–27). She died without children (2 Sam. 6:21–23).

MICHMAS/MICHMASH (MICMASH). A town near Jerusalem occupied by Saul's army (1 Sam. 13:2–4) and the site of Jonathan's victory over the Philistines (1 Sam. 14:6–18). Some Jewish citizens returned to this city after the Babylonian Exile (Ezra 2:27). *Michmash:* Isa. 10:28; *Micmash:* NIV.

MICHTAM. A word in the titles of Ps. 16 and Pss. 56–60, perhaps designating a particular type of psalm.

MIDDLE WALL OF PARTITION (BARRIER, DIVIDING WALL). The curtain or barrier in the Jewish temple at Jerusalem which separated Jews and Gentiles. Christ's atonement removed this partition and brought reconciliation and peace to people of all races and nationalities (Eph. 2:14–18). *Barrier:* NIV; *Dividing wall:* NRSV. See also *Court of the Gentiles*.

MIDIAN/MADIAN.
1. A son of Abraham by Keturah and founder of the Midianites (Gen. 25:1–4; 1 Chron. 1:32–33).
2. A region in the Arabian desert east of the Jordan River, including Edom and the Sinai Peninsula, which was occupied by the Midianites (Exod. 2:15). *Madian:* Acts 7:29.

MIDIANITES. Nomadic traders who occupied the land of Midian. A band of Midianites probably bought Joseph and sold him as a slave in Egypt (Gen. 37:28). This tribe joined the Moabites in attacking Israel but failed (Num. 22). The Midianites were probably absorbed into the Moabites and the Arabs. See also *Gideon.*

MIDWIFE. A Hebrew woman who assisted other women in the process of childbirth. Many midwives refused the Egyptian pharaoh's orders to kill male children (Exod. 1:15–17).

MIGDOL. A place in northeastern Egypt where some citizens of Judah fled after their nation fell to the Babylonians about 587 B.C. (Jer. 44:1; 46:14).

MIGHTY MEN (FIGHTING MEN, WARRIORS). The brave and loyal warriors who risked their lives for David before and after he became king (2 Sam. 23:8–39). Joshua also had the support of courageous warriors known as "mighty men of valor" (Josh. 1:14; 10:7). *Fighting men:* NIV; *Warriors:* NRSV. See also *Jashobeam.*

MILCOM/MOLECH/ MOLOCH. The supreme god of the Ammonites (1 Kings 11:5). *Molech:* NIV. Solomon built a sanctuary for worship of this pagan god, but it was destroyed during King Josiah's reforms (2 Kings 23:12–13). *Molech:* Lev. 20:2. *Moloch:* Acts 7:43. See also *Ammonites.*

MILE. A Roman unit for measuring distance which equaled 1,000 paces, or 1,616 yards. Jesus used this term to teach His followers forgiveness and forbearance (Matt. 5:41).

MILETUS/MILETUM. A coastal city of Asia Minor about forty miles south of Ephesus. Paul met the leaders of the Ephesian church here and gave a moving farewell address (Acts 20:15–38). *Miletum:* 2 Tim. 4:20.

MILK. A liquid for drinking and cheese-making taken from cows, goats, sheep, and camels (Gen. 32:14–15). The word is also used figuratively to indicate abundance (Exod. 3:8) and the diet of immature Christians (1 Cor. 3:1–2).

MILL. A device for grinding grain into flour, consisting of two stones which pulverized the grain between them (Exod. 11:5; Matt. 24:41).

MILLENNIUM. A term for the period of 1,000 years described in Rev. 20:1–8. Opinions vary on how to interpret this period. Premillennialists expect a literal reign of 1,000 years by Christ on earth after His return. Postmillennialists believe that 1,000 years of peace will precede Christ's second coming, during which time much of the world will be converted. While believing in the Lord's return, amillennialists view Christ's millennial reign in a spiritual sense.

MILLET. A plant which produced small heads of grain, used for making bread (Ezek. 4:9).

MILLO.
1. A stronghold or fortress at Shechem whose occupants proclaimed Abimelech as their king (Judg. 9:6, 20). *Beth-millo:* NIV, NRSV.
2. A defensive fortress tower built by David near Jerusalem (2 Sam. 5:9) and improved by Solomon in anticipation of an Assyrian siege (1 Kings 9:15).

MINA. See *Maneh; Pound.*

MIND. The reasoning faculty of human beings. In the Bible, the word *heart* often means "mind" (see Ps. 19:14). Those who reject God have corrupt minds (Rom. 1:28), and the carnally minded are enemies of God (Rom. 8:6–7). Jesus urged His followers to love God with all their mind and heart (Matt. 22:37). Paul encouraged the Christians at Rome to have their minds renewed so they would know and follow the will of God (Rom. 12:2).

MINE. A place where metals were extracted from the earth. Iron and copper were mined in the area around the Dead Sea, especially during Solomon's reign (1 Kings 9:26–28).

MINISTER. A term for a person who serves others, often used interchangeably with the word *servant*. In addition to the religious meaning of the word, it is also applied to court attendants (1 Kings 10:5) and civil rulers (Rom. 13:4–6). All Christians are instructed to "preach the word" and perform duty as God's servants (2 Tim. 4:2–5). See also *Deacon; Pastor; Priest; Shepherd.*

MINISTRY. Service in the name of God. Such service demands a spirit of sacrificial service after the example of Christ (Matt. 20:26–28). All Christians are called to be ambassadors for Christ in the work of reconciliation (2 Cor. 5:18–20), to be fishers of men (Mark 1:17), and to perfect believers (Eph. 4:11–12).

MINOR PROPHETS. The twelve prophets of the O.T. whose books were placed last in the prophetic writings because of their shorter length—Hosea, Joel, Amos, Obadiah, Jonah, Micah, Nahum, Habakkuk, Zephaniah, Haggai, Zechariah, and Malachi. See also *Major Prophets*.

MINSTREL (HARPIST, MUSICIAN). A singer or musician (2 Kings 3:15; *Harpist:* NIV; *Musician:* NRSV), often employed at funerals or wakes, as in the case of the daughter of Jairus (Matt. 9:23).

MINT. A common, inexpensive herb used in medicine and for seasoning foods. Jesus mentioned mint as an object scrupulously tithed by the scribes and Pharisees (Matt. 23:23).

MIPHKAD (INSPECTION GATE, MUSTER GATE). A gate in the walls of Jerusalem or the temple rebuilt by Nehemiah (Neh. 3:31). *Inspection Gate:* NIV; *Muster Gate:* NRSV.

MIRACLE. God's intervention or suspension of the natural laws of the universe. Miracles are described in the N.T. as signs, wonders, mighty works, and powers. Most miracles in the Bible occurred during (1) the period of the Exodus (Exod. 7, 9, 10, 14); (2) Elijah's and Elisha's ministry (2 Kings 4:2–7); (3) the period of the Exile (Dan. 3:9–27); (4) the ministry of Jesus, when miracles attested to His divine power (Matt. 15:33–39); and (5) the ministry of the apostles, signifying their apostleship (Acts 3:6). Jesus worked miracles to relieve suffering (Matt. 8:14–17), to raise the dead (Matt. 9:23–25), to calm nature (Luke 8:22–25), or to give an object lesson (Mark 11:12–14). See also *Sign*.

MIRIAM. The sister of Aaron and Moses (1 Chron. 6:3). Miriam protected her baby brother Moses by arranging for their mother Jochebed to care for him (Exod. 2:4–10). She led a triumphant song of praise and thanksgiving to God after the Hebrews were delivered from the pursuing Egyptian army at the Red Sea (Exod. 15:2–21). She died and was buried in the wilderness at Kadesh (Num. 20:1). See also *Aaron; Jochebed; Moses*.

MISCHIEF MAKER. See *Busybody*.

MISGAB (STRONGHOLD, FORTRESS). An unknown site in Moab, perhaps a mountainous region or fortified outpost (Jer. 48:1). *Stronghold:* NIV; *Fortress:* NRSV.

MISHAEL. See *Meshach.*

MISHEAL (MISHAL). A city in the territory of Asher assigned to the Levites and designated as a city of refuge (Josh. 19:26). *Mishal:* NIV, NRSV. See also *Cities of Refuge.*

MISSIONS. The process of carrying out Jesus' Great Commission to disciple and teach all peoples. Even in the O.T., Abraham was called to be a blessing to all nations (Gen. 12:1–3), and Jonah was sent by the Lord to preach to the pagan citizens of Nineveh (Jon. 1:2). Missions is prompted by God's love (John 3:16) and mankind's lost condition (Rom. 3:9–31). Believers are equipped for this task by the Holy Spirit's presence (Acts 1:8), the Word of God (Rom. 10:14–15), and the power of prayer (Acts 13:1–4). Christ's followers are to evangelize all nations, baptize believers, and teach His commands (Matt. 28: 19–20). See also *Commission.*

MIST. A vapor or fog. The earth was watered by a mist before the first rainfall (Gen. 2:6). Mist and darkness are used figuratively to describe spiritual blindness (Acts 13:11).

MISTRESS. A woman with power or authority (Gen. 16:4–9). The Queen of Sheba (1 Kings 10:1–3) and Queen Jezebel (1 Kings 21:7–11) were women of authority.

MITE. The coin of smallest value in N.T. times, worth less than a penny. Jesus commended a poor widow's sacrificial gift of two mites (Mark 12:42).

MITRE (TURBAN). A headdress worn by the high priest (Lev. 8:9). *Turban:* NIV, NRSV. A gold plate inscribed with "holiness to the Lord" was attached to the mitre (Exod. 39:28–31).

MITYLENE. The principal city of the island of Lesbos in the Aegean Sea. Paul spent a night at Mitylene (Acts 20:13–15).

MIZPAH. A place where Jacob and his father-in-law Laban made a covenant and agreed to a friendly separation. They marked the site with a pile of stones (Gen. 31:44–53).

MIZRAIM
1. The second son of Ham and father of Ludim (Gen. 10:6–13). His descendants settled in Egypt (Gen. 45:20; 50:11).
2. The Hebrew name for Egypt (Gen. 50:11). See *Egypt.*

MNASON. A Christian from the island of Cyprus who accompanied Paul on his last visit to Jerusalem (Acts 21:16).

MOAB.
1. A son of Lot and an ancestor of the Moabites (Gen. 19:33–37).
2. The country of the Moabites, lying east of the Jordan River and the Dead Sea and south of the Arnon River (Deut. 1:5–7). Its earliest name was *Lotan* or *Lot,* since the inhabitants were descended from Lot (Gen. 19:37).

MOABITE STONE. A black memorial stone which confirms a significant event of the O.T.— the rebellion of King Mesha of Moab against King Ahaziah of Israel (2 Kings 3:4–27).

MOABITES. Pagan inhabitants of Moab, worshipers of Chemosh (Num. 21:29), and enemies of the Israelites. The strength of the Moabites varied across several centuries of Israel's history. The tribes of Reuben and Gad settled in northern Moab before the conquest of Canaan (Num. 32: 1–37). Ehud won a significant victory over their forces during the period of the judges (Judg. 3:15–30). David also fought and conquered the Moabites (2 Sam. 8:2). Ruth was a native of Moab (Ruth 1:22).

MODERATION. Temperance and forbearance. Paul described moderation as a quality of gentleness to be practiced before others (Phil. 4:5). Christians are counseled to be moderate in all things (1 Cor. 9:25). See also *Temperance.*

MOLE (CHAMELEON). A KJV word which probably refers to a chameleon or lizard since no true moles are found in Palestine (Lev. 11:30). *Chameleon:* NIV, NRSV.

MOLECH, MOLOCH. See *Milcom.*

MOLTEN SEA. A large bronze vessel made by King Hiram of Tyre for ceremonial use by the priests in Solomon's temple at Jerusalem (1 Kings 7:23). See also *Brasen Sea.*

MONEY. A medium of exchange. In O.T. times before

215

the Babylonian Exile, money was a specific weight of precious metal, such as silver or gold. The coins of N.T. times were issued by the Romans or Greeks (Matt. 17:27; Mark 12:42). The earliest coins used in Palestine before the N.T. era were Persian in origin. See also *Filthy Lucre; Mammon*.

MONEYCHANGERS. Independent agents, much like cashiers, who converted money into "shekels of the sanctuary," which could be used in the temple at Jerusalem. These "bankers" provided worshipers with the required temple tax, the half-shekel (Exod. 30:13–15). Jesus denounced these money-changers who were charging excess fees for their services. He overturned their tables and drove them out of the temple (Matt. 21:12).

MONOGAMY. The marriage of a man to one woman only—the pattern established by God in the Garden of Eden (Gen. 2: 18–24). Many of the O.T. patriarchs, such as Jacob, had more than one wife (Gen. 29:16–35). See also *Marriage; Polygamy*.

MONOTHEISM. The belief in one—and only one—supreme God, in contrast to polytheism, or the worship of several gods. The one true God is to be loved supremely and His commands taught to others (Deut. 6:4–7). God demands absolute loyalty, and He will not tolerate the worship of any other god by His people (Exod. 20:3–5). See also *Polytheism*.

MONTH. One of the twelve divisions of the year. The length of the Hebrew month was calculated from one new moon to the next (Num. 10:10; 28: 11–14).

MOON. The heavenly body or satellite which revolves around the earth, referred to as the "lesser light" in the account of creation (Gen. 1:16). Each new moon marked the beginning of another Jewish month, and its arrival was celebrated with special sacrifices (Num. 28: 11–15). The moon was worshiped under various names by pagan peoples, but God forbade this practice by the Hebrews (Deut. 4:19).

MOONSTONE. See *Diamond*.

MORDECAI. A Jewish exile in Persia who befriended Esther, helping her to become the king's favorite and assume the queenship (Esther 2:5–11). With Esther's help, Mordecai thwarted the plot of Haman to destroy the Jews (Esther 2:19–23). He was honored by the king and promoted (Esther 6:10–11; 8:1–2). See also *Ahasuerus; Esther; Haman.*

MOREH. A place near Shechem where Abraham built an altar after entering Canaan (Gen. 12:6–7).

MORESHETH-GATH. The birthplace of Micah the prophet in the lowland plain of Judah (Mic. 1:14).

MORIAH. The mountainous area in Jerusalem where Abraham was commanded by God to sacrifice his son Isaac (Gen. 22:1–13). After God provided a sacrifice other than Isaac, Abraham renamed the site Jehovahjireh, meaning "the Lord will provide" (Gen. 22:14).

MORNING STAR. The planet Venus as it appears at dawn and a figurative title for Christ (Rev. 22:16). Christ is described as the morning star, which outshines the light of prophetic witness (2 Pet. 1:19). See also *Day Star.*

MORTALITY. The human condition which leads eventually to physical death. Mortality is the common lot of all human beings, but it serves as the entrance to eternal life for believers (2 Cor. 5:4–6). For the Christian, bodily resurrection and eternal life are as certain as physical death (1 Cor. 15:21–23). See also *Eternal Life.*

MORTAR. A mixture of lime and sand used to build the tower of Babel (Gen. 11:3). The Israelites in Egypt worked with bricks and mortar (Exod. 1:14). See also *Untempered Mortar.*

MOSERA/MOSEROTH. A place in the wilderness where the Israelites camped on their way to Canaan. Aaron died and was buried here (Deut. 10:6). *Moseroth:* Num. 33:30–31.

MOSES. The great lawgiver and prophet of Israel who led the Hebrew people out of Egypt. His life is best understood in three forty-year periods.

Forty years in Egypt. Moses was born into slavery and hidden by his mother to escape the pharaoh's order that all male Hebrew babies should be killed (Exod. 1:22; 2:1–10). Discovered and "adopted" by the pharaoh's daughter, he was raised and schooled as an Egyptian (Exod. 2:10). After killing an Egyptian who was abusing an Israelite slave, he became a fugitive in the desert (Exod. 2:14–15).

Forty years in Midian. Moses became a shepherd (Exod. 3:1), married Zipporah, the daughter of a priest, and she bore two sons, Gershom and Eliezer (Exod. 18:3–4). He reluctantly answered God's call to lead His people out of slavery (Exod. 3:11–4:9), and returned to Egypt, where he enlisted his brother Aaron as his helper and spokesman (Exod. 4:27–31). After ten plagues sent by the Lord upon the Egyptians, the pharaoh finally released the Hebrews, who entered the wilderness area in the Sinai Peninsula under Moses' leadership.

Forty years in the wilderness. In the wilderness, Moses received the Ten Commandments (Exod. 20:1–24) and other parts of the Mosaic Law, exhorted the people to remain faithful to God, built the tabernacle at God's command (Exod. 36–40), and sent spies to investigate Canaan (Num. 13). He impatiently struck a rock for water at Kadesh (Num. 20:1–13), a sin which led God to deny his entrance into the Promised Land. He died in Moab at Canaan's border at the age of 120 (Deut. 34:1–8). See also *Aaron; Law.*

MOST HIGH. A name for God signifying His majesty (Acts 7:48–49). The title was used by nonbelievers in both the O.T. (Num. 24:16) and the N.T. (Acts 16:17). See also *I Am; Jehovah; Yahweh.*

MOTE (SPECK). A small particle of anything. Jesus used this word to indicate the hypocrisy of those who found small flaws in others while ignoring major defects of their own (Matt. 7:3–5). *Speck:* NIV, NRSV.

MOTH. A destructive insect. Since wealthy Jews stored clothes which could be destroyed by moths, Jesus used the word to indicate the fleeting nature of earthly riches (Matt. 6:19–20).

MOTHER. A term for a female parent as well as a grandmother and other female relatives. Eve is regarded as the "mother of all living" (Gen. 3:20). Mothers are worthy of honor and obedience by those who desire long life (Exod. 20:12; Eph. 6:1–3). The prophets alluded to Israel as "mother" in denouncing the nation's shameful sins (Jer. 50:12–13; Ezek. 19).

MOUNT OF THE AMALEKITES. A mountain in Ephraim where Abdon, one of the judges of Israel, was buried (Judg. 12:15).

MOUNT OLIVET. See *Olives, Mount of.*

MOUNT PARAN. See *Paran, Mount.*

MOUNTAIN REGION. See *Hill Country.*

MOUNTAIN SHEEP. See *Chamois.*

MOURN. To express grief or sorrow. The usual mourning period was seven days, but this was extended to thirty days for Moses and Aaron (Num. 20:29). Jesus mourned at the death of his friend Lazarus (John 11:33–36). See also *Sackcloth; Sorrow.*

MOUSE. A rodent (1 Sam. 6:5). Many species of these destructive animals are found in Palestine. They were "unclean," according to Mosaic Law (Lev. 11:29; Isa. 66:17).

MOUTH. The mouth has potential for good or evil. It may be used for praise and prayer (Ps. 34:1; 1 Sam. 1:12) or as an instrument of idolatry (1 Kings 19:18) and lying (1 Kings 22:13, 22). See also *Lips; Throat; Tongue.*

MUFFLER (VEIL, SCARF). A veil, or a long scarf worn about the head or chest (Isa. 3:19). *Veil:* NIV; *Scarf:* NRSV.

MULBERRY (BALSAM). A common tree of Palestine, probably the aspen, baca, or balsam (2 Sam. 5:23). *Balsam:* NIV, NRSV See also *Sycamine.*

MULE. A beast of burden of the horse family used extensively by the Hebrews. A runaway mule carried Absalom to his death (2 Sam. 18:9–15).

MULTITUDE (CROWD). A crowd or a large group of people. Jesus was often followed by "great multitudes" eager for learning or healing (Matt. 4:24–25). He miraculously fed two multitudes of several thousand (Matt. 14:15–21). *Crowd:* NIV, NRSV. See also *Host.*

MURDER. The unlawful killing of a human being, an act which was prohibited by Mosaic Law (Exod. 20:13). The Israelites exacted the death penalty for willful murder (Exod. 21:12; Lev. 24:17) but provided cities of refuge for persons guilty of manslaughter, or accidental killing (Num. 35: 11). Jesus warned of intense anger that could lead to murder (Matt. 5:20–25). See also *Avenger of Blood; Man-slayer*.

MURRAIN. A mysterious disease and the fifth plague which God brought against the Egyptians, attacking their animals (Exod. 9:1–6). It may have been anthrax.

MUSIC. Vocal and instrumental music was prominent in temple choirs (2 Sam. 6:5). Musical instruments were invented by Jubal, son of Lamech (Gen. 4:21). The Hebrews used cymbals, harps, organs, pipes, psalteries, and trumpets in their worship (1 Chron. 15: 16–22).

MUSICIAN. See *Minstrel*.

MUSTARD SEED. The tiny, almost microscopic seed from a common herb of Palestine. Jesus used this small seed to illustrate the power of faith in the believer's life (Luke 17:6). See also *Faith*.

MUSTER GATE. See *Miphkad*.

MUTH-LABBEN. A musical term in the title of Ps. 9, perhaps referring to the tune for the psalm.

MYRA. A town in the province of Lycia in Asia Minor where Paul changed ships during his voyage to Rome (Acts 27:5–6).

MYRRH (RESIN). An aromatic gum resin found chiefly in Arabia (Gen. 37:25). *Resin:* NRSV. It was one of the gifts presented to the infant Jesus (Matt. 2:11). Myrrh was used in incense perfume, anointing oil, embalming fluid, and medicine (Exod. 30:23; John 19:39).

MYRTLE. A common evergreen shrub of Palestine. Its branches were used at the Feast of Tabernacles (Neh. 8:15). A myrtle tree in the desert was symbolic of God's provision for His people (Isa. 41:19; 55:13).

MYSIA. A province in northwestern Asia Minor through which Paul and Silas passed on the second missionary journey (Acts 16:7–10).

MYSTERY (SECRET). Something unknown except through divine revelation (Rom. 16:25–26). The gospel is called a mystery (Eph. 3:8–9). Jesus taught in parables to reveal the mysteries of God's kingdom to His disciples (Luke 8:10). *Secret:* NIV, NRSV. Paul reveals that Christ within us inspires our hope to share in His glory (1 Cor. 15:51; Col. 1:26–27).

-N-

NAAMAN. A captain in the Syrian army who was healed of leprosy by the prophet Elisha. At first Naaman was reluctant to bathe in the Jordan River for healing, as commanded by Elisha. But he finally obeyed, received healing, and praised the God of Israel (2 Kings 5:1–15). Naaman was mentioned by Jesus (Luke 4:27).

NABAL. A wealthy herdsman who refused to provide food for the desperate David and his army in the wilderness. His wife Abigail secretly offered hospitality, and Nabal died ten days later (1 Sam. 25). See also *Abigail.*

NABOTH. An Israelite who was framed and killed by Jezebel so Ahab could take possession of his vineyard. God pronounced judgment against them for this despicable act (1 Kings 21:1–23).

NACHOR. See *Nahor.*

NADAB

1. The oldest son of Aaron who was destroyed, along with his brother Abihu, for offering "strange fire" to God (Lev. 10:1–2). See also *Abihu.*

2. A king of Israel (reigned about 910–909 B.C.), the son of Jeroboam I. Nadab was assassinated by Baasha, who succeeded him (1 Kings 15:25–31).

NAHASH. A king of Ammon who befriended David. David tried to return the favor to his son Hanun but was rejected (2 Sam. 10:1–4).

NAHBI. One of the twelve spies who scouted the land of Canaan, representing the tribe of Naphtali (Num. 13:14). See also *Spies.*

NAHOR/NACHOR. The grandfather of Abraham and father of Terah (Gen. 11:22–25). *Nachor:* Luke 3:34.

NAHUM. A prophet of Judah from Elkosh who prophesied against Nineveh before 612 B.C., probably during the reign of King Hezekiah (Nah. 1:1, 8, 13); author of the book of Nahum.

NAHUM, BOOK OF. A short prophetic book of the O.T. that predicted the downfall of the pagan nation of Assyria

(3: 7–19) because of the atrocities which it committed against God's people. The prophet portrays God as the sovereign Lord of history who has the final word in the conflict between good and evil (1:1–15). See also *Assyria*.

NAIN. A village south of Nazareth near the Sea of Galilee where Jesus raised a widow's son from the dead (Luke 7: 11–17).

NAIOTH. A place in Ramah where David fled from King Saul and where Samuel lived and conducted his school for prophets (1 Sam. 19:18–20).

NAME. The word or title by which someone or something is known. Adam gave names to the animals (Gen. 2:20). Persons and places in the Bible often bore symbolic names, such as the children of the prophets Isaiah (Isa. 8:3) and Hosea (Hos. 1:4).

NAOMI. The mother-in-law of Ruth. After marrying Elimelech, Naomi moved to Moab to escape a famine. Her husband and two sons died, leaving Naomi and her two daughters-in-law alone. She returned to Bethlehem with Ruth and helped arrange Ruth's marriage to Boaz (see Ruth 1–4).

NAPHTALI.
1. A son of Jacob by Bilhah, Rachel's maid (Gen. 30:1, 8). He received Jacob's blessing (Gen. 49:21–28), and his descendants became one of the twelve tribes of Israel.

2. The tribe consisting of Naphtali's descendants (Num. 1:42), who were assigned the fertile, mountainous territory in northern Palestine, including the cities of Hazor, Kedesh, and Ramah (Josh. 19:36–38; 20:7). Isaiah prophesied that Naphtali in "Galilee of the nations" would see a great light (Isa. 9:1–7). This was fulfilled in Jesus' Galilean ministry (Matt. 4:12–16). See also *Tribes of Israel*.

NAPHTUHIM (NAPTU-HITES). The inhabitants of central Egypt who were descendants of Mizraim, son of Ham (Gen. 10:13). *Naptuhites:* NIV (1 Chron. 1:11).

NAPKIN (CLOTH). A handkerchief or small piece of cloth (Luke 19:20) used for wiping perspiration and other purposes (Acts 19:12). A similar cloth was used for binding the face and head of the dead for burial (John 11:44; 20:7). *Cloth:* NIV, NRSV. See also *Handkerchief*.

NARCISSUS. A Christian in Rome whose household was greeted by Paul (Rom. 16:11).

NARD. See *Spikenard.*

NATHAN.
1. A son of David by Bathsheba, born after David became king (1 Chron. 3:5). A brother of Solomon (2 Sam. 5:14), he is listed as an ancestor of Jesus (Luke 3:31).
2. The brave prophet who used an allegory to rebuke King David for his sin with Bathsheba and his plot to kill Bathsheba's husband Uriah (2 Sam. 12:1–15). Nathan also assisted David when Adonijah attempted to seize the throne (1 Kings 1:8–45) and wrote histories of David's and Solomon's administrations (1 Chron. 29: 29; 2 Chron. 9:29).

NATHANAEL. See *Bartholomew.*

NATION. A word used in various ways in the Bible: (1) to describe all the inhabitants of a country or the country itself (Deut. 4:34); (2) to refer to natives of the same stock (Acts 26:4); (3) to denote the father or head of a tribe or clan; and (4) to refer to heathens or Gentiles (Isa. 9:1).

NATIONS. See *Heathen.*

NATURE. A word which refers to the physical universe as well as the essence or disposition of man. God created the natural world and gave man dominion over it (Gen. 1:1, 26–31). Adam and Eve's disobedience in the garden introduced sin and corrupted nature (Gen. 3:12–19). The natural world is intended to draw mankind to the Creator (Ps. 8; Rom. 1:20), but man's carnal nature has worshiped the creature instead of the Creator (Rom. 1:25). Fallen man's faith in Christ appropriates God's divine nature (2 Pet. 1:3–4).

NAVE (RIM). The hub or rim of a wheel into which spokes were fitted (1 Kings 7:33). *Rim:* NIV, NRSV.

NAVEL. The umbilical connection of a newborn child with its mother. Ezekiel compared Jerusalem's unfaithfulness and neglect to an untended newborn child whose navel cord had not been cut (Ezek. 16:1–4).

NAZARENE (NAZOREAN). A native or inhabitant of the city of Nazareth. Since this was His hometown, Jesus was referred to as a "Nazarene" (Matt. 2:23). *Nazorean:* NRSV (Mark 1:23–24).

NAZARETH. An obscure town in Galilee which was the boyhood home of Jesus (Mark 1:24). Mary, Joseph, and Jesus returned to Nazareth after their flight into Egypt (Matt. 2:20–23). The town was located in the district of Galilee beside the plain of Esdraelon, fifteen miles southeast of Mt. Carmel. Jesus was rejected by the townspeople of Nazareth at the beginning of His public ministry (Luke 4:16–30).

NAZARITE (NAZIRITE). A man or woman especially consecrated to God according to the law of the Nazarites (Num. 6:2). *Nazirite:* NIV, NRSV. Voluntarily or because of a devout parent's promise, a Nazarite assumed strict religious vows, including abstaining from strong drink and not cutting his hair. The vow might be for life or a fixed period. Samson (Judg. 13:4–7), Samuel (1 Sam. 1:11, 28), and John the Baptist (Luke 1:15) were Nazarites. See also *Asceticism.*

NEAPOLIS. A seaport at Philippi where Paul landed on the second missionary journey (Acts 16:11).

NEBO.
1. The highest point of Mount Pisgah in Moab near Jericho where Moses died after viewing the Promised Land and where he was buried (Deut. 32:49; 34:5–6). See also *Pisgah, Mount.*
2. The Babylonian god of science and knowledge. Mount Nebo was possibly a center of Nebo worship. Isaiah declared the vanity of such idols (Isa. 46:1).

NEBUCHADNEZZAR/ NEBUCHADREZZAR. The king of Babylonia (reigned about 605–561 B.C.) who captured Jerusalem and carried Judah into exile about 587 B.C. (see Dan. 1–4). The only strong Babylonian king, he was the son of Nabopolassar, founder of the empire. After a revolt by King Zedekiah of Judah, Nebuchadnezzar destroyed Jerusalem, burned the temple, and carried the nation's leading citizens into exile (2 Kings 25: 1–26). *Nebuchadrezzar:* Jer. 51:34. See also *Babylonia.*

NEBUZAR-ADAN. An officer in Nebuchadnezzar's army during the Babylonian siege of Jerusalem (2 Kings 25:8–20). He looked after the prophet Jeremiah, who remained in

Jerusalem after the siege (Jer. 39:11–14; 40:1–5).

NECHO. See *Pharaoh, No. 4.*

NECK. A word used figuratively for stubbornness ("stiffnecked," Deut. 9:6). It was also used to express the coming siege of Judah by Assyria (Isa. 8:8) and to represent the burden which circumcision would place on Gentile Christians (Acts 15:10).

NECKLACE. An ornament or jewelry worn around the neck. The pharaoh placed a gold chain around Joseph's neck, symbolizing his appointment as governor of Egypt (Gen. 41:41–43)

NECROMANCER. One who communicated with the dead in an effort to foretell the future (1 Sam. 28:7–20). This practice was forbidden by Mosaic Law (Deut. 18:11). See also *Familiar Spirit; Medium; Wizard.*

NEEDLE. A tool for sewing. Jesus compared the difficulty of the wealthy reaching heaven with putting a camel through the eye of a needle (Matt. 19:24).

NEEDLEWORK. Embroidery or delicate sewing. Embroidered robes and curtains were used in the tabernacle (Exod. 28:39; 36:37).

NEEDY. See *Poor.*

NEGEV. See *South Country.*

NEGINAH/NEGINOTH. Phrases in the titles of several psalms which may refer to stringed instruments (Pss. 4, 6, 54, 55, 61, 67, 76).

NEHEMIAH. The governor of Jerusalem (445–433 B.C.) who helped rebuild the city wall after the Babylonian Exile; author of the book of Nehemiah. The son of Hachaliah, he was cupbearer to King Artaxerxes of Persia (Neh. 1:11; 2:1). He received permission from the king to return to Jerusalem to assist the returned exiles in their rebuilding efforts (Neh. 2:3–6). In addition to rallying the people to rebuild the city wall, he led a religious reform with the assistance of Ezra the priest (Neh. 8:1–13; 12:36). See also *Ezra.*

NEHEMIAH, BOOK OF. A historical book of the O.T. which records the rebuilding of Jerusalem's defensive wall after the Babylonian Exile under the leadership of Nehemiah (1:1–7:73). The book also recounts the religious reforms undertaken by Nehemiah and Ezra. They led the people to renew the covenant and recommit themselves to God's law (8:1–13:31). See also *Ezra*.

NEHILOTH. A musical term in the title of Ps. 5, probably denoting a wind instrument such as the flute.

NEHUSHTAN. A bronze serpent worshiped by the Israelites in the wilderness (2 Kings 18:4).

NEIGHBOR. A fellow human being. Paul declared that Christians should love and speak truth to their neighbors (Rom. 13:9–10; Eph. 4:25). The Pharisees confined the meaning of "neighbor" to people of their own nation, but Jesus' parable of the Good Samaritan indicates all people are neighbors and should help each other (Luke 10:25–37).

NEPHEG. A son of David, born in Jerusalem after David became king (2 Sam. 5:13–15).

NEPHEW. A term for a grandson (Judg. 12:14) or other male relative (Job 18:19). Lot, however, was a true nephew of Abraham (Gen. 11:27).

NEREUS. A Christian at Rome to whom the apostle Paul sent greetings (Rom. 16:15).

NERGAL. A Babylonian god of war which was worshiped by the men of Cuth (2 Kings 17:30). Images of Nergal were placed throughout Israel by King Shalmaneser of Assyria (2 Kings 17:24, 30).

NERGAL-SHAREZER. A Babylonian prince of King Nebuchadnezzar's court during the capture of Jerusalem (Jer. 39:1–3). He helped release Jeremiah from prison (Jer. 39:13–14).

NERO. The fifth emperor of Rome (reigned A.D. 54–68) who severely persecuted Christians. Although he is not named in the Bible, he is probably the emperor under whom Paul and Peter were martyred. Secular history confirms that Nero placed blame for Rome's great fire (A.D. 64) on the Christians and had many put to death during his administration. See also *Roman Empire*.

NEST. The dwellingplace of birds. The loftiness of the eagle's nest demonstrated the foolishness of man's pride (Jer. 49:16; Obad. 4).

NET. A meshed fabric used to capture birds or fish. The word is also used figuratively for entrapment of the innocent and for winning others to Christ (Matt. 4:18).

NETHANEEL (NETHANEL). A priest who helped transport the ark of the covenant to Jerusalem (1 Chron. 15:24). *Nethanel:* NIV, NRSV.

NETHER, NETHERMOST. The lower or lowest part. The children of Israel assembled on the nether part of Mt. Sinai to receive a message from God (Exod. 19:17).

NETHINIM (TEMPLE SERVANTS). Persons assigned to do menial work as assistants to the priests in temple service. Many of the Nethinim were slaves or captives of war assigned to the Levites (Ezra 8:17–20). *Temple servants:* NIV, NRSV.

NETTLE. A shrub with prickly briars (Prov. 24:31), possibly a variety of acanthus which grew near the Mediterranean Sea (Isa. 34:13).

NETWORK. The brass grate or grid on the altar of burnt offering in the tabernacle (Exod. 27:4).

NEW BIRTH. A state of regeneration or resurrection from spiritual death (Rom. 6:4–8). The Holy Spirit brings regeneration (John 3:5–8) and produces a changed person. This comes about by God's grace through faith in Christ rather than through one's own efforts or good works (Eph. 2:8–9). Regeneration helps the believer overcome the world and lead a victorious life (1 John 5:4–5). The new birth is required before a person can enter the kingdom of God (John 3:3–7). See also *Regeneration; Salvation.*

NEW COVENANT. God's final covenant with His people through which His grace is expressed to all believers. Prophesied by the prophet Jeremiah (Jer. 31:31–34), the new covenant was symbolized by Jesus at the Passover meal with His disciples. He called the cup the "new covenant in my blood" (Luke 22:20, NIV, NRSV). Christ, mediator of a new and better covenant, assures our eternal inheritance (Heb. 8:6; 9:11–15). See also *Covenant; Jeremiah, Book of; Testament.*

NEW JERUSALEM. See *Jerusalem.*

NEW MOON. See *Month; Moon.*

NEW TESTAMENT. The second major division of the Bible, composed of twenty-seven books, also known as the "new covenant" to magnify the coming of the Messiah and His redemptive ministry of grace (Jer. 31: 31–34; Heb. 9:15). The complete N.T. in its current form was formally adopted by the Synod of Carthage in A.D. 397.

NIBHAZ. An idol of the Avites, a displaced Assyrian tribe that settled in Samaria (2 Kings 17:31). The name means "barker"; this pagan god was in the form of a dog-headed man.

NICANOR. One of the seven men chosen as "deacons" in the church at Jerusalem (Acts 6:1–5).

NICODEMUS. An influential Pharisee who talked with Jesus about the new birth. Impressed by Jesus' miracles, he came to Jesus at night. Jesus impressed upon him the necessity of being born of the Spirit (John 3:1–7). Later, Nicodemus cautioned the Jewish officials not to prejudge Jesus (John 7:50–51). He helped prepare Jesus' body for burial (John 19:39).

NICOLAITANES (NICOLAITANS). An early Christian sect whose origin is unknown. Their idolatrous practices were abhorrent to God, being compared to those of Balaam (Rev. 2:14). The church at Ephesus was commended for not tolerating the Nicolaitanes (Rev. 2:6), while the church at Pergamos was rebuked for its openness to their teachings (Rev. 2:15). *Nicolaitans:* NIV, NRSV.

NICOLAS (NICOLAUS). A person of Greek background who was one of the seven men chosen as "deacons" in the church at Jerusalem (Acts 6: 1–5). *Nicolaus:* NRSV.

NICOPOLIS. A city, probably in northern Greece, where Paul spent the winter (Titus 3:12).

NIGER. See *Simeon,* No. 3.

NIGHT. The period of the day when darkness prevails. The Creator established night along with the daylight hours (Gen. 1:5). The word is used figuratively to denote death (John 9:4) or sin (1 Thess. 5:5).

NIGHT HAWK (SCREECH OWL). An unclean bird, probably an owl or other night creature (Lev. 11:13–16; Deut. 14:15). *Screech owl:* NIV.

NILE RIVER. The great river of Egypt which begins in Africa and runs for more than 4,000 miles across Africa and Egypt, emptying finally into the Mediterranean Sea. In Bible times, Egypt's fertility depended on the annual overflow of the Nile (Isa. 23:10). God's judgment on Egypt was often depicted as a drying up of the Nile (Zech. 10:11). The baby Moses was hidden in the tall grass at the edge of the river (Exod. 2:3). See also *Egypt*.

NIMROD. Ham's grandson and son of Cush. A skilled hunter and warrior, he became a powerful king and empire builder in Babylonia, or Shinar (Gen. 10:8–12; 1 Chron. 1:8–10).

NINEVEH/NINEVE. The capital of Assyria on the Tigris River where the prophet Jonah preached God's message of judgment. Founded by Asshur, a son of Shem, Nineveh reached the height of wealth and splendor during Jonah's time (Jon. 3:3). It was taken by the Medes about 750 B.C. and destroyed by the Medes and Babylonia about 606 B.C. *Nineve:* Luke 11:32. See also *Assyria*.

NISAN. See *Abib*.

NISROCH. An Assyrian god with a temple at Nineveh where King Sennacherib was killed about 698 B.C. It was believed to have a human body with an eagle's head (2 Kings 19:36–37).

NITRE (SODA, LYE). A mineral used as a cleaning agent; probably lye or sodium carbonate (Jer. 2:22). *Soda:* NIV; *Lye:* NRSV.

NO (THEBES). A thriving Egyptian city on both sides of the Nile River which served as the capital of upper Egypt (Nah. 3:8). No was destroyed in 81 B.C., as predicted by Jeremiah (Jer. 46:25). *Thebes:* NIV, NRSV.

NOADIAH. A prophetess who tried to frighten Nehemiah and hinder his efforts to rebuild the wall of Jerusalem (Neh. 6:14).

NOAH/NOE. The person chosen by the Lord to preserve life on earth by building an ark to escape the great flood. Noah was the son of Lamech and the father of Shem, Ham, and Japheth. He "found grace in the eyes of the Lord" (Gen. 6:8) and was described in the N.T. as a preacher of righteousness (2 Pet. 2:5). After building the ark, he entered with his family and selected animals (Gen. 7:1–24).

Upon leaving the ark after the flood ended, he built an altar for worship (Gen. 8:18–22). God covenanted with Noah not to destroy the earth with water again (Gen. 9:1–19). After pronouncing blessings and curses on his sons, he died at the age of 950 (Gen. 9:29). *Noe:* Greek form (Luke 17:26). See also *Ark, Noah's.*

NOB. A Levitical city near Jerusalem (Isa. 10:32) where David fled to escape King Saul's wrath (1 Sam. 21:1–6). Saul ordered the slaughter of eighty-five priests here in retaliation for their kindness to David (1 Sam. 22:13–19).

NOBLEMAN (ROYAL OFFICIAL). A person of high rank or privileged position. A nobleman sought Jesus to heal his son who was seriously ill (John 4:46–54). *Royal official:* NIV, NRSV.

NOD. An unknown region east of Eden where Cain lived after murdering his brother Abel (Gen. 4:16–17). It may have been China, according to some scholars.

NOE. See *Noah.*

NOGAH. A son of David, born in Jerusalem after David became king (1 Chron. 3:7; 14:6).

NOMADS. Tent dwellers or herdsman who moved from one grazing ground to another with their flocks (Gen. 13:5–7). The children of Israel led a nomadic life in the wilderness for forty years (Num. 14:2). See also *Wilderness Wanderings.*

NOOSE. See *Snare.*

NOPH (MEMPHIS). An ancient royal city of the Egyptians (Jer. 46:19), *Memphis:* NIV, NRSV. Noph flourished about 3000 to 2200 B.C. on the west bank of the Nile River about thirteen miles south of modern Cairo. Many of the royal pyramids and the famous Spinx are located near the site of this ancient city.

NORTHEASTER. See *Euroclydon.*

NOSE JEWELS. Jeweled rings worn in the nose as ornaments (2 Kings 19:28).

NOSE, NOSTRILS. God created man and breathed life into his nostrils (Gen. 2:7). The word is figurative of God's power in parting the Red Sea for the Israelites (Exod. 15:8).

NOVICE (RECENT CONVERT). An inexperienced or recent Christian convert. Paul instructed Timothy that a novice in the faith lacked the maturity to serve as a pastor or bishop (1 Tim. 3:1, 6). *Recent convert:* NIV, NRSV.

NUMBERS, BOOK OF. An O.T. book which focuses on the Israelites in the wilderness of Sinai—a period of more than forty years between their departure from Egypt and their occupation of Canaan. The book describes the "numbering" of the people in two separate censuses (1–54; 26:1–51), their failure to trust God and fear of the Canaanites (chap. 13), their numerous rebellions and complaints in the wilderness (15:1–25:18), and their final preparation for entering the Land of Promise (26:1–36:13). See also *Wilderness Wanderings.*

NUN.
1. The father of Joshua and an Ephraimite servant of Moses who helped lead the Israelites across the Jordan River into the Promised Land (Josh. 1:1–2).
2. The fourteenth letter of the Hebrew alphabet, used as a heading over Ps. 119:105–112.

NURSE. A woman servant who breast-fed an infant or helped rear the child. Deborah, Rebecca's nurse, accompanied the family to Canaan (Gen. 24:59; 35:8).

NUZI TABLETS. Clay tablets of archaeological significance discovered during the 1920s on the site of the ancient city of Nuzi in present-day Iraq. These tablets describe life in ancient Mesopotamia from about the time of Abraham (2200 B.C.), listing goods produced, items traded, and other details of everyday life. The city of Nuzi is not mentioned in the Bible. See also *Clay; Ras Shamra Tablets.*

NYMPHAS (NYMPHA). A Christian of Laodicea to whom Paul sent greetings (Col. 4:15). *Nympha:* NIV, NRSV.

-O-

OAK. Several species of oak grew in Palestine. This word was often used to describe any strong tree or grove of trees (Gen. 35:8). Oak was used for carving idols (Isa. 44:9–15).

OAR. A paddle for pulling a ship through the water. Even large sailing vessels used oars when there was not enough wind to fill the sails (Isa. 33:21–23).

OATH. A solemn promise, often used to appeal to God to attest that a statement was true or to affirm a covenant (2 Sam. 21:7). The taking of an oath was accompanied by raising the hand or placing the hand under the thigh (Gen. 24:2–3). Jesus warned against careless oaths (Matt. 5:34–36).

OBADIAH.
1. A prophet of Judah and author of the O.T. book which bears his name (Obad. 1). He probably lived after the destruction of Jerusalem in 587 B.C. Nothing more is known about him.
2. A godly servant of King Ahab who hid 100 prophets in a cave so they could escape Jezebel's wrath (1 Kings 18: 3–16).

OBADIAH, BOOK OF. A prophetic book of only twenty-one verses—the shortest book in the O.T.—that pronounces judgment against the Edomites, the descendants of Esau (vv. 1, 6), because of their mistreatment of God's people, the Israelites (vv. 10–14). See also *Edomites; Esau.*

OBED-EDOM. A Philistine from the city of Gath. The ark of the covenant was left at his house for three months before its removal to Jerusalem (1 Chron. 13:13–14).

OBEY. To submit to authority. Children are commanded to obey their parents (Exod. 20:12; Eph. 6:1–3). Jesus was obedient to Joseph and Mary (Luke 2:51). Jesus was perfectly obedient to the Father, and He requires obedience of His followers (Heb. 5:8–9).

OBLATION (GRAIN OFFERING). An offering sanctified to God, consisting usually of meat, meal, firstfruits of the harvest, or land (Lev. 2:4). *Grain offering:* NIV, NRSV.

OBSERVER OF TIMES. A person who was thought to be able to foretell the future through reading signs (Deut. 18:10–14). See also *Omen; Witchcraft.*

ODED. A prophet of Samaria who urged kindness toward captives from Judah. His intervention led to the release of captives who were taken to Jericho (2 Chron. 28:9–15).

The hill known as the Mount of Olives in Jerusalem, with the Church of All Nations in the foreground.

Courtesy Israel Ministry of Tourism

OFFENSE. A charge or accusation against another. Reconciliation with an offended brother should take priority over making an offering (Matt. 5:24).

OFFERING. Something given to God as a confession, consecration, expiation, or thanksgiving, generally as a part of worship. Because of his sinfulness and frailty, man recognizes he cannot covenant with God without obedience and faith. Jesus offered Himself as a full and final sacrifice for sin (Heb. 7:25, 27). See also *Sacrifice*.

OFFSCOURING (SCUM, FILTH). Refuse; something vile or despised (Lam. 3:45). *Scum:* NIV; *Filth:* NRSV. Paul indicated that faithful Christians may be regarded as "scum of the earth" by the world (1 Cor. 4:13).

OFFSPRING. Children or descendants (Job 5:25). The risen Lord declared He was the "offspring of David" (Rev. 22:16). All people are regarded as offspring of the Creator (Acts 17:28–29). See also *Posterity; Seed*.

OG. An Amorite king of Bashan who was defeated by the

Israelites at Edrei (Num. 21: 33). His territory was assigned to the tribe of Manasseh (Deut. 3:1–13).

OIL. A liquid extracted from olives which was burned in lamps (Matt. 25:3) and used for anointing (Ps. 23:5), food preparation (1 Kings 17:12), and medicine (Luke 10:34). Olive groves were numerous throughout Palestine. See also *Anointing; Olive.*

OIL TREE (OLIVE). The olive tree or the oleaster shrub (Isa. 41:19). *Olive:* NIV, NRSV. The oleaster shrub resembled the wild olive, with its yellow flowers and olivelike fruit.

OINTMENT (PERFUME). A salve or perfumed oil made of olive oil and spices and used in anointing ceremonies. Jesus was anointed by devoted followers (Mark 14:3). *Perfume:* NIV (John 12:3). See also *Perfume.*

OLD GATE (JESHANAH GATE). A gate in the walls of Jerusalem rebuilt by Nehemiah (Neh. 3:6; 12:39). *Jeshanah Gate:* NIV.

OLD TESTAMENT. The first major section of the Bible, containing thirty-nine books, also known as the "old covenant" because it points to the coming of the new covenant in Jesus Christ. The O.T. begins with God's creation of the world, contains the books of the law and wisdom, and ends with prophecies which point to the Messiah's coming (Isa. 53; Jer. 31:31–34).

OLIVE. The fruit of the olive tree which was used for food and olive oil. The branch of an olive tree was a symbol of peace (Gen. 8:11). See also *Oil.*

OLIVES, MOUNT OF/ MOUNT OLIVET. A hill in eastern Jerusalem where Jesus was betrayed by Judas on the night before His crucifixion (Matt. 26:30, 47). The branches of olive trees from the Mount of Olives were used to make booths for the Feast of Tabernacles (Neh. 8:15). *Mount Olivet:* Acts 1:12.

OLYMPAS. A Christian in Rome greeted by the apostle Paul (Rom. 16:15).

OMEGA. See *Alpha and Omega.*

OMEN. A sign used to predict future events. Witchcraft and divination were forbidden by the Mosaic Law (Deut. 18:10). The Lord frustrates the efforts of fortune-tellers and astrologers (Isa. 44:25). See also *Observer of Times; Witchcraft.*

OMER. A dry measure of two to three quarts (Exod. 16:16).

OMNIPOTENCE. The unlimited and infinite power which belongs to God. This characteristic of God's nature is expressed by His names *almighty* (Gen. 17:1) and *omnipotent* (Rev. 19:6). God controls nature (Amos 4:13) and the destiny of nations (Amos 1:1–2:16). God's omnipotence is also expressed by the Holy Spirit's power to convict and save (Rom. 15:19). See also *God; Sovereignty of God.*

OMNIPRESENCE. The universal presence of God. No person can hide from God (Jer. 23:23–24). Christ is present with the multitudes or with two or three believers (Matt. 18:20). God's Spirit is our companion in all circumstances (John 14:3, 18). See also *God.*

OMNISCIENCE. The infinite knowledge of God. The all-wise and all-knowing God requires no counselor (Isa. 40:14). Christ is the key who opens all the hidden treasures of God's wisdom and knowledge (Col. 2:2–3). God's Spirit reveals the "deep things of God" to those who are spiritually receptive (1 Cor. 2:10–14). See also *God.*

OMRI. The king of Israel who built Samaria as the capital city of the Northern Kingdom (reigned about 885–874 B.C.; 1 Kings 16:23–28). He was a wicked king who led the nation into idolatry (1 Kings 16:26). Omri was the father of the wicked king Ahab, who succeeded him (1 Kings 16:29), and grandfather of the ruthless queen Athaliah of Judah (2 Kings 11:1–3). See also *Samaria.*

ON.

1. A Reubenite leader who joined Korah and others in the rebellion against Moses and Aaron in the wilderness (Num. 16:1–14).

2. A city of lower Egypt noted for its learning and its prominence as a center of sun worship. Joseph's wife Asenath was from this city (Gen. 41:45). *Aven:* Amos 1:5.

ONAN. The second son of Judah who was killed because of his failure to consummate a marriage union with Tamar, wife of his slain brother (Gen. 38:8–10).

ONESIMUS. A slave of Philemon who was converted under Paul. Onesimus escaped and fled to Rome, where he came under Paul's influence. After his conversion, he returned to his master Philemon with an epistle from Paul, who appealed for Onesimus to be treated with mercy (Col. 4:9; Philem. 10). See also *Philemon*.

ONESIPHORUS. A Christian from Ephesus who befriended Paul when he was a prisoner in Rome. Paul commended him for his service (2 Tim. 1:16–18; 4:19).

ONION. A popular vegetable in Egypt and Palestine (Num. 11:5).

ONYCHA. An ingredient in sacred incense which Moses was instructed to prepare (Exod. 30:34). It may have come from the mollusk shell. See also *Incense*.

ONYX. A precious stone in the breastplate of the high priest (Exod. 28:20). David collected onyx to decorate the temple in Jerusalem (1 Chron. 29:2). See also *Sardonyx*.

OPHEL. The southern side of ancient Jerusalem's eastern hill, perhaps a tower or other fortification. The Nethinim lived here after the Babylonian Exile (Neh. 3:26–27).

OPHIR.
1. A son of Joktan and great-grandson of Eber (Gen. 10:26–29).
2. The territory, probably in Arabia, populated by Ophir's descendants (Gen. 10:29–30). A famous gold-producing region, Ophir was visited by the ships of Solomon and the Phoenicians (1 Kings 9:26–28).

OPHRAH. Gideon's hometown in Manasseh where an angel assured him of the Lord's guidance and protection (Judg. 6:11–14).

OPPRESSOR. One who defrauds and mistreats others. The Egyptians oppressed the Hebrews by making them slaves (Exod. 3:9). See also *Taskmasters*.

ORACLE. A revelation or wise saying given to a person for his guidance (Rom. 3:2). Ministers are charged to preach God's message (1 Pet. 4:11).

ORCHARD. A garden planted with trees (Eccles. 2:5), particularly fruit-bearing trees (Song of Sol. 4:13). See also *Garden*.

ORDAIN. To set a person apart for special service. Matthias was ordained to replace Judas as an apostle (Acts 14:23). Christ ordained His disciples to bear enduring fruit (John 15:16). Christ was ordained to be a merciful high priest and judge of the living and the dead (Heb. 5:1). See also *Consecration*.

ORDINANCES. Baptism and the Lord's Supper, rituals or procedures intended to commemorate the great events of redemption. The Lord's Supper memorializes the shed blood and broken body of Christ (1 Cor. 11:23–26). Baptism symbolizes the death, burial, and resurrection of Jesus and the believer's victory over sin and death (Rom. 6:3–6). See also *Baptism; Lord's Supper*.

OREB. A Midianite priest killed by Gideon and the Ephraimites (Judg. 7:25). His name was given to the rock east of Jordan where he died (Isa. 10:26).

ORGAN (FLUTE, PIPE). A wind instrument made of reeds of various lengths and played by blowing across their open ends (Gen. 4:21). *Flute:* NIV *Pipe:* NRSV. See also *Pipe*.

ORION. A constellation of stars cited as evidence of God's power (Job 9:9).

ORNAMENTS. Items of jewelry, such as rings on the fingers, ears, and nose (Isa. 3:18–23). Bracelets and earrings were presented to Rebekah by Abraham's servant (Gen. 24:22).

ORNAN. See *Araunah*.

ORONTES. The major river of Syria. The important cities of Kadesh, Riblah (2 Kings 23:33–35), and Hamath (1 Kings 8:65) were situated on the Orontes.

ORPAH. A Moabite woman who married Chilion, son of Naomi and Elimelech. She returned to her own people after the death of her husband (Ruth 1:4–15).

ORPHANS. Children whose parents have died. Kindness toward orphans was commanded by the Mosaic Law (Deut. 24:17). Visiting orphans and widows was considered a mark of true religion, or godliness (Jas. 1:27). Jesus promised believers would not be treated as orphans (John 14:18).

OSEE. See *Hosea*.

OSHEA. See *Joshua*.

OSNAPPAR. See *Asnapper*.

OSPRAY (BLACK VULTURE). An unclean bird, perhaps similar to the eagle or hawk (Lev. 11:13). *Black vulture:* NIV. See also *Gier Eagle*.

OSSIFRAGE (VULTURE). An unclean bird, probably similar to the eagle, or perhaps the vulture (Deut. 14:12). *Vulture:* NIV, NRSV. See also *Vulture*.

OSTRICH. A large, flightless bird noted for its speed (Job 39:13–18) and its mournful cry (Mic. 1:8, NRSV). It was listed as "unclean" in the Mosaic Law (Lev. 11:16, NRSV).

OTHNIEL. The first judge of Israel who defeated the king of Mesopotamia (Judg. 3:9–11). See also *Judges of Israel*.

OUCHES (GOLD FILIGREE SETTINGS). Sockets or mountings in which precious stones were set in the ephod of the high priest (Exod. 28:11–14). *Gold filigree settings:* NIV, NRSV.

OUTCASTS. Dispossessed people. This word was used by the prophets to describe the Jews scattered among foreign nations (Isa. 11:12; Jer. 30:17).

Jesus had compassion on lepers who were social outcasts (Luke 17:11–19). See also *Remnant*.

OVEN. A large earthenware container filled with hot coals and ashes. Utensils with food were placed over the opening for cooking (Hos. 7:7).

OVERSEER. An elder, bishop, presbyter, or supervisor in charge of a congregation (Acts 20:28).

OWL. A bird of prey with large eyes and strong claws which hunts at night (Ps. 102:6). It was considered unclean by the Israelites (Lev. 11:11–17).

OWNER. See *Householder*.

OX. An animal of the cow family used for plowing (Deut. 22:10), for threshing grain (Deut. 25:4), and as a beast of burden (1 Chron. 12:40). Oxen also supplied milk and meat and were used as sacrifices (Lev. 17:3–4). See also *Bull; Bullock*.

OX GOAD. A spike used to drive oxen. Shamgar, judge and deliverer of Israel, killed six hundred Philistines with an ox goad (Judg. 3:31; 5:6).

OZIAS. See *Uzziah*.

238

-P-

PACE (STEP). A measure of length, based on the step of a man (2 Sam. 6:13). *Step:* NIV.

PADAN-ARAM
See *Mesopotamia.*

PADDLE. A spadelike tool at the butt end of a spear for digging a hole in the ground to cover waste (Deut. 23:13).

PAINT. A cosmetic cover. Hebrew women painted around their eyes, but the practice was condemned (Jer. 4:30). Paint was also used to color walls and adorn pagan temples (Ezek. 23:14).

PALACE. A residence for a king or other high official. Solomon's palace on Mount Zion near the temple featured an ivory throne (1 Kings 7:1–12; 10: 18). Jesus was tried in the hall of Herod's palace by Pilate (Mark 15:16) and in the palace of Caiaphas the high priest (Matt. 26:56–57).

PALESTINE/PALESTINA. The territory of the Canaanites which became known as the land of the people of Israel. The name *Palestine* referred originally to the territory of the Philistines, especially the coastal plain south of Mt. Carmel. The name was extended during the Christian era to include all of the Holy Land, including both sides of the Jordan River and the Dead Sea region south to Egypt. After the Canaanites were displaced, the country was called the land of Israel (1 Sam. 13: 19) and the "land of promise" (Heb. 11:9). Three great world religions—Judaism, Christianity, and Islam—originated here. *Palestina:* Exod. 15:14. See also *Canaan,* No. 2; *Land of Promise.*

PALM. A tropical tree (Exod. 15:27), so named because its leaf resembles a human hand. Most biblical references are to the date palm, which grows sixty to eighty feet tall.

PALMERWORM (LOCUST). A caterpillar or a distinct species of locust which ate vegetation (Joel 1:4). This insect or worm was sent as a plague upon rebellious Israel (Amos 4:9–10). *Locust:* NIV, NRSV. See also *Locust.*

PALSY. A disease which caused paralysis and possible loss of feeling (Acts 8:7). Although it was regarded as incurable, Jesus healed many people with palsy (Matt. 4:24).

PALTI. One of the twelve spies who scouted the land of Canaan, representing the tribe of Benjamin (Num. 13:9). See also *Spies*.

PALTIEL. A leader of the tribe of Issachar, appointed by Moses to help divide the land of Canaan after its occupation by the Israelites (Num. 34:26).

PAMPHYLIA. A coastal region in southern Asia Minor visited by Paul (Acts 13:13; 14:24). Perga was its capital and Attalia its main seaport (Acts 14:25). Residents of Pamphylia were present in Jerusalem on the day of Pentecost (Acts 2:10).

PAN (GRIDDLE). A utensil or cooking container (Lev. 6:21). *Griddle:* NIV, NRSV.

PANTHEISM. A doctrine which teaches that God and His universe are identical, or that physical things are merely attributes of an all-encompassing God. Jews and Christians reject this doctrine because God created the universe separate and apart from Himself (Gen 1:1). He exists apart from, in addition to, and above the world (see Ps. 8). See also *Creation*.

PAPER. Papyrus, or an ancient writing material made from reeds which grew on the banks of the Nile River in Egypt (2 John 12). See also *Bulrush; Ink; Reed; Writing*.

PAPHOS. A city on the island of Cyprus where Paul blinded Elymas the magician. This led to the conversion of the Roman governor, Sergius Paulus (Acts 13:6–13).

PAPS (BREASTS). An archaic old English word for "breasts" (Luke 11:27). *Breasts:* NRSV.

PAPYRUS. See *Bulrush*.

PARABLE. A short story drawn from daily life which is used to convey an important truth; a favorite teaching device used by Jesus (Matt. 13:3). In the O.T., Nathan told a parable to convict King David of his sin of adultery (2 Sam. 12:1–7). Jesus used parables to present truth to His receptive hearers and to conceal the lesson from those who were critical or unreceptive (Matt. 13:10–16, 35). Drawn from daily life, His parables revealed lessons about salvation, the kingdom, and the future life (Luke 15).

PARACLETE (COUNSELOR, ADVOCATE). A Greek word for the Holy Spirit which expresses the idea of a helper called to one's side. It is translated as "comforter" in the Gospels (John 14:16). *Counselor:* NIV; *Advocate:* NRSV. Also, as "advocate" in the epistle of John (1 John 2:1). See also *Advocate; Comforter; Helper; Holy Spirit.*

PARADISE. A word which describes the heavenly home of the redeemed (2 Cor. 12:4). Jesus used the term to comfort the repentant dying thief (Luke 23:43). See also *Heaven; Heavenly City.*

PARADOX. A contradictory statement which expresses a great truth; a favorite teaching device of Jesus. He declared that a person could find his life by losing it (Matt. 10:39) and that a person became great by serving others (Mark 10:43).

PARALYSIS. See *Palsy.*

PARALYTIC. A paralyzed person. Jesus honored the faith of a paralytic by offering forgiveness and healing (Matt. 9:1–7).

PARAMOUR (LOVER). A slave or concubine who provided sexual favors (Ezek. 23:20). *Lover:* NIV. See also *Concubine.*

PARAN/MOUNT PARAN/ EL-PARAN. A mountainous wilderness region in the Sinai Peninsula, sometimes called *Mount Paran* (Hab. 3:3) and *El-Paran* (Gen. 14:6). The Israelites camped here during their years in the wilderness (Num. 10:12; 12:16).

PARAPET. See *Battlement.*

PARCHED CORN (ROASTED GRAIN, PARCHED GRAIN). Roasted grains of wheat, barley, or millet (1 Sam. 25:18). *Roasted grain:* NIV; *Parched grain:* NRSV.

PARCHMENT. Writing material made from the skin of sheep or goats. Paul asked Timothy to bring parchments to him in prison (2 Tim. 4:13).

PARDON. Forgiveness. God will pardon those who repent and turn to the Lord (Isa. 55:7). The loving father in Jesus' parable had compassion on his repentant son, extended pardon, and celebrated his return (Luke 15:18–24). God promised to pardon the iniquity of Judah and Israel that led to their captivity and exile (Jer. 33:8–9). See also *Forgiveness; Remission.*

PARENTS. People who bear and rear children. The duty of parents is to train (Deut. 4:9; 6:6–7) and correct (Deut. 21:18–21) their children. They should avoid favoritism (Gen. 25:28) and anger (Eph. 6:4). God promised to bless parents who bring up children in the nurture of the Lord (Prov. 22:6; Eph. 6:4). See also *Children*.

PARLOR. A room in a house for entertaining guests (1 Sam. 9:22), a secret chamber for retreat (1 Chron. 28:11), or a room on the roof for enjoying cool breezes (Judg. 3:20–25).

PARMENAS. One of the seven men of Greek background chosen as "deacons" in the church at Jerusalem (Acts 6:1–5).

PAROUSIA. A Greek word which refers to the second coming of Christ. See also *Second Coming*.

PARTHIANS. Inhabitants of Parthia, a country north of Media and Persia. Parthians were in Jerusalem on the day of Pentecost (Acts 2:1, 9).

PARTIALITY. To show favoritism or preference toward some people over others. God's wisdom is available to all and free of favoritism or hypocrisy (Jas. 3:17).

PARTITION. See *Middle Wall of Partition*.

PARTRIDGE. A wild bird in Palestine prized for its meat and eggs. Jeremiah compared ill-gotten wealth to a partridge sitting on eggs that will not hatch (Jer. 17:11).

PARVAIM. An unidentified place which provided gold for Solomon's temple (2 Chron. 3:6). Some scholars believe this was the same place as *Ophir* (1 Kings 9:28).

PASCHAL LAMB. See *Passover*.

PASHUR. A priest who struck Jeremiah and had him imprisoned. Jeremiah predicted that Pashur and his household would die as captives in Babylonia (Jer. 20:3–6).

PASSOVER AND FEAST OF UNLEAVENED BREAD. A Jewish festival which commemorated the Exodus from Egypt (Josh. 5:10–12). The Passover celebrated how God "passed over" the Hebrew houses in Egypt that were sprinkled with blood while killing the firstborn of the Egyptians on the eve of the Exodus (Exod. 12). The seven-day Feast of Unleavened Bread recalled the haste with which the slaves left Egypt (Exod. 12:33–34). Jesus observed the Passover with His disciples on the night He was betrayed (Luke 22:15). Paul declared that Christ is our Passover (1 Cor. 5:7). *Paschal lamb:* NRSV.

PASTOR. One who leads and instructs a congregation. Jeremiah predicted the coming of faithful pastors who would lead Israel back to God (Jer. 3:15). Pastors are called of God to perfect the saints and build up the body of Christ (Eph. 4: 11–13). See also *Bishop: Elder; Minister; Shepherd.*

PASTORAL EPISTLES. The three letters of Paul—1 and 2 Timothy and Titus—which deal with pastoral concerns, or practical matters involving the operation and government of a local church.

PASTURE. Grazing lands for livestock. The word is also used figuratively for the protection of God's people under the Good Shepherd (Ps. 23:1–2; Ezek. 45:15).

PASTURE LANDS. See *Suburbs.*

PATARA. A port of Lycia in Asia Minor. Paul changed ships here on the way to Phoenicia (Acts 21:1–2).

PATH. A crude road. The word is also used figuratively for the route of one's life. The righteous are warned not to walk the paths of darkness (Prov. 2:13–15).

PATHROS (UPPER EGYPT). A name for upper Egypt where Egyptian civilization likely began. Jewish people lived here during the Babylonian Exile (Jer. 44:1, 15). *Upper Egypt:* NIV.

PATIENCE. Forbearance or restraint. God is the author of patience (Rom. 15:5), and Christ is its perfect model (2 Thess. 3:5). Believers are urged to labor with patience in the service of Christ (1 Thess. 5:14). See also *Forbearance; Longsuffering; Steadfastness.*

PATMOS. A desolate island in the Aegean Sea, used as a prison by the Romans, where the apostle John was exiled and where he wrote the book of Revelation. Christ revealed Himself to John and told him to send messages to the seven churches of Asia Minor (Rev. 1:9–19). See also *John the Apostle.*

PATRIARCH. Head of a tribe or clan in O.T. times who ruled by authority passed down from father to oldest son. Abraham, Isaac, and Jacob, along with the sons of Jacob and David, are notable examples of patriarchal rule (Acts 2:29; 7:8–9).

PATROBAS. A fellow believer at Rome greeted and commended by Paul (Rom. 16:14).

PAUL THE APOSTLE. The great apostle to the Gentiles; defender and advocate of the Christian faith in its early years through his thirteen N.T. letters. A complex personality, Paul demonstrated both toughness and tenderness in his devotion to Christ. His teachings are both profound and practical (Phil. 3:7–10). His Hebrew name as a Jew of Benjamite ancestry was *Saul,* but his Roman name was Paul (Acts 13:9). A Roman citizen born at Tarsus in Cilicia (Acts 22:3), he was a tentmaker by trade—a vocation by which he often supported himself as a minister to the churches which he established (Acts 18:3).

A strict Pharisee and member of the Jewish Sanhedrin, Paul opposed Christianity in its early years in Jerusalem. He consented to the death of Stephen, the first martyr of the church (Acts 7:58; 8:1). He was on his way to persecute Christians at Damascus when he was converted to Christianity in his famous "Damascus road" experience (Acts 9:1–19). From that point on, Paul was zealous for the cause of Christ.

Under the sponsorship of the church at Antioch in Syria, Paul undertook three great missionary journeys to the Roman world, extending westward through Cyprus and Asia Minor into Europe (Acts 16:9–10). His traveling companions on these tours included Barnabas, John Mark, Timothy, Silas, Titus, and Luke. Along with his successes in making disciples, healing, and planting churches, he suffered a "thorn in the flesh" (2 Cor. 12:7), was frequently arrested, was stoned, and imprisoned (Acts 16:22–23).

Falsely accused by his enemies, he appealed to the Roman emperor for justice (Acts 25: 10–12). After an arduous voyage by ship, he spent two years in Rome under house arrest. While guarded by Roman soldiers, he received friends and preached the gospel (Acts 28:30–31; Phil. 1:12–14). Four of his epistles—Ephesians, Colossians, Philippians, and Philemon—were written from Rome. Most scholars believe he was beheaded in Rome about

A.D. 67 during Nero's reign (Phil. 2:17; 2 Tim. 4:6–8).

PAULUS, SERGIUS. The Roman proconsul of Cyprus who was converted under Paul's ministry (Acts 13:4–12). See also *Cyprus; Paphos.*

PAVEMENT, THE/ GABBATHA. An area in Pilate's courtroom paved with stone where Jesus was judged, sentenced to crucifixion, and turned over to the mob (John 19:13–16). Its Aramaic name was *Gabbatha.*

PAVILION (DWELLING, SHELTER). A tent or booth for kings or other members of the royal family. The word is also used figuratively for the dwellingplace of God (Ps. 27:5). *Dwelling:* NIV; *Shelter:* NRSV.

PE. The seventeenth letter of the Hebrew alphabet, used as a heading over Ps. 119:129–136.

PEACE. Harmony and accord brought about by cordial relationships. Peace has its source in God (Phil. 4:7) through Christ (John 14:27) and the Holy Spirit (Gal. 5:22). Christians are urged to pursue peace and to live peaceably with all people (2 Cor. 13:11; 2 Tim. 2:22).

PEACE OFFERING. See *Heave Offering; Wave Offering.*

PEACOCK (BABOON). An exotic animal imported by King Solomon, probably from Spain (2 Chron. 9:21). *Baboon:* NIV.

PEARL. Precious stone found in the shells of oysters. Jesus likened the kingdom of heaven to a merchant seeking valuable pearls (Matt. 13:45–46).

PEDAHEL. A leader of the tribe of Naphtali, appointed by Moses to help divide the land of Canaan after its occupation by the Israelites (Num. 34:28).

PEG. See *Pin.*

PEKAH. A king of Israel (reigned about 740–732 B.C.) who assassinated Pekahiah to gain the throne. He was killed by Hoshea in a conspiracy (2 Kings 15:23–31).

PEKAHIAH. An evil king of Israel (reigned about 742–740 B.C.) who was murdered and succeeded by Pekah, one of his military officers (2 Kings 15:23–26).

PELEG/PHALEC. A descendant of Shem (Gen. 10:25, 32). *Phalec:* Luke 3:35.

PELETHITES. A unit or division of David's soldiers who remained loyal to him during the rebellions of Absalom and Sheba (2 Sam. 15:14–18; 20:7).

PELICAN (DESERT OWL). A large bird, considered unclean by the Israelites (Lev. 11:13, 18), which was cited as a symbol of loneliness and desolation (Ps. 102:6–7). *Desert owl:* NIV. This may be the same bird as the *cormorant* (Isa. 34:11). See also *Cormorant*.

PEN. A word for various writing instruments, including those which wrote on scrolls (Jer. 8:8), skin or parchment, and stones (Job 19:24). See also *Ink; Writing*.

PENKNIFE (SCRIBE'S KNIFE). A small knife used for sharpening the writing pen, or reed pen (Jer. 36:23). *Scribe's knife:* NIV.

PENCE. See *Penny*.

PENIEL/PENUEL. A place east of the Jordan River near the Jabbok River where Jacob wrestled with an angel (Gen. 32:24–32). *Penuel:* Judg. 8:8. See also *Jacob*.

PENITENCE. See *Repentance*.

PENNY/PENCE (DENARIUS). A silver coin of small value (Matt. 20:2–13). *Denarius:* NIV. It varied in value, but it generally equaled the daily wage of an unskilled worker. *Pence:* plural form (Luke 10:35). See also *Farthing*.

PENTATEUCH. The Greek name for the first five books of the O.T.: Genesis, Exodus, Leviticus, Numbers, and Deuteronomy. It was called the Torah or the Law of Moses by the Hebrews (Ezra 7:6). Jesus recognized the value of the law and came to fulfill its spiritual requirements (Matt. 5: 17–18; 12:5). See also *Law*.

PENTECOST/FEAST OF WEEKS/FEAST OF HARVEST. An annual Jewish feast or holy period, commemorating the end of the harvest, which fell on the fiftieth day after the Passover. This was the holiday being observed in Jerusalem when the Holy Spirit came in power upon the early Christian believers (Acts 2). This feast was also known as the *Feast of Weeks* and the *Feast of Harvest* (Exod. 34:22).

PENUEL. See *Peniel*.

PEOPLE OF GOD. A phrase for the nation of Israel as well as the people of the new covenant, or the Church. The Israelites were called by God as His special people (Deut. 8:6–9), but all whose hearts have been "circumcised" are also His people (Rom. 2: 28–29). Peter declared that believing Gentiles were also part of God's "chosen generation" (1 Pet. 2:9–10). God's people include every kindred, tongue, and nation (Rev. 5:9; 7:9). See also *Church; Congregation; Saint.*

PEOR. A mountain of Moab across the Jordan River from Jericho. From Peor, Balak and Balaam observed the camp of the Israelites with the intention to curse them (Num. 23:28; 24:1–2).

PERAZIM. See *Baal-perazim.*

PERDITION. The state of the damned, or those who have rejected Christ. Jesus called Judas the "son of perdition" because of his betrayal of Christ (John 17:12). Perdition is the final destiny of the ungodly (2 Pet. 3:7) as well as the final abode of the Antichrist (Rev. 17:8–11). See also *Damnation; Hell; Judgment, Last.*

PEREA. A word used by some translations of the Bible for the territory east of the Jordan River across from Judea and Samaria. Jews often traveled from Galilee to Judea by Perea to avoid going through the territory of the despised Samaritans (Matt. 4:15; 19:1). This region is called the land "beyond Jordan" in the KJV.

PEREZ. See *Pharez.*

PEREZ-UZZAH. A name given by David to the site where Uzza was struck down for touching the ark (2 Sam. 6:6–8).

PERFECTION (MATURITY). A state of completion or fulfillment. Believers are urged to advance to mature teachings and "perfection" or fulfillment in good works (Heb. 6:1). *Maturity:* NIV. While disclaiming perfection, Paul urged believers to keep striving for perfection by being like Christ (Phil. 3:12–15).

PERFUME. A sweet-smelling fragrance, usually an extract of spices used in ointments, incense, and oils (Prov. 27:9). See also *Oil; Ointment.*

PERFUMER. See *Apothecary.*

PERGA. The capital of Pamphylia and a city visited by Paul.

John Mark left Paul and Barnabas at Perga (Acts 13:13–14), and Paul preached here on the return to Antioch after the first missionary journey (Acts 14:25).

PERGAMOS (PERGAMUM). A city where one of the seven churches of Asia Minor addressed by John in Revelation was located. The church was rebuked for its toleration of sexual immorality and false teachings. The phrase "where Satan's seat is" is probably a reference to a pagan temple in the city (Rev. 2:12–17). *Pergamum:* NIV, NRSV.

PERIZZITES. Descendants of Perez who were subdued by Joshua's forces. Natives of the hill country, they were associated with the Canaanites (Josh. 3:10).

PERSECUTION. Oppression in matters of conscience or religious practice, or punishment because of one's convictions. Believers who are not well grounded in the faith cannot endure persecution (Matt. 13:21). Jesus declared that those who are persecuted because of their commitment to Him will inherit the kingdom of God (Matt. 5:10–12). See also *Affliction; Suffering; Tribulation.*

PERSEVERANCE. Persistence, or the ability to endure through difficult circumstances. Paul counseled steadfastness in the Lord's work because labor for Him is never in vain (1 Cor. 15:58). Endurance of God's chastening or discipline is a mark of God's sonship (Heb. 12:7–8). See also *Patience; Steadfastness.*

PERSIA. A great empire whose territory covered what is now western Asia and parts of Europe and Africa, reaching the height of its greatness around 486 B.C. under Cyrus. The Persians conquered Babylonia in 539 B.C. and allowed the Israelites to return to their native land (2 Chron. 36:20–23). The Persian king Artaxerxes allowed Nehemiah to return to Jerusalem to rebuild the city wall (Neh. 2:1–8). The Persians were defeated by the Greek military conqueror Alexander the Great in 330 B.C. (Ezek. 38:5). See also *Elam; Elamites.*

PERSIS. A fellow believer at Rome greeted and commended by Paul (Rom. 16:12).

PESTILENCE. A plague or widespread fatal disease (Hab. 3:5), usually coming as a result of God's judgment against sin

(Exod. 5:3; Ezek. 33:27). See also *Plague*.

PESTLE. A short, blunt tool used for grinding grain or crushing other material in a container known as a mortar (Prov. 27:22).

PETER. See *Simon,* No. 1.

PETER, EPISTLES OF. Two short N.T. epistles, probably from the apostle Peter, written to encourage Christians experiencing persecution and discouragement (1 Peter) and to warn them against false teachers (2 Peter). In response to scoffers who doubted the second coming of Christ—since He had not yet returned—Peter declared, "The Lord is not slack concerning his promise, as some men count slackness; but is longsuffering to us-ward, not willing that any should perish, but that all should come to repentance" (2 Pet. 3:9).

PETHOR. A town in northern Mesopotamia near the Euphrates River; home of Balaam, who was sent to curse the Israelites (Num. 22:5–7).

PETITION. An earnest request. King Ahasuerus granted Esther's petition to save her people (Esther 7:2–5). Believers are confident their petitions will be answered (1 John 5:14–15). See also *Intercession; Prayer*.

PETRA. An ancient city located south of the Dead Sea. Named for its rocky terrain, Petra was once the capital of Edom and later of Nabatea. Some scholars believe it was the same city as *Selah* (2 Kings 14:7).

PHALEC. See *Peleg*.

PHARAOH. The title of the king of Egypt. The pharaoh of Egypt, who is unnamed (Exod. 1:8–11), refused to release the Israelites from slavery until God killed the Egyptian firstborn throughout the land. The named pharaohs of the Bible are:

1. Shishak, who attacked Jerusalem and plundered the temple (1 Kings 14:25–26).

2. So, who made an alliance with King Hoshea of Israel (2 Kings 17:4).

3. Tirhakah, who aided King Hezekiah of Judah against Sennacherib of Assyria (2 Kings 19:9).

4. Nechoh, whose archers mortally wounded King Josiah of Judah at Megiddo (2 Kings 23:29). *Necho:* Jer. 46:2.

5. Hophra, whom God declared would fall to his enemies (Jer. 44:30).

PHAREZ/PEREZ/PHARES. One of Judah's twin sons by Tamar (Gen. 38:24–30) and founder of the family or clan of Pharzites (Num. 26:20–21). *Perez:* Neh. 11:4; *Phares:* Matt. 1:3.

PHARISEES. Members of a Jewish sect pledged to uphold the oldest traditions of Israel. In Jesus' time the Pharisees were the most powerful party —political or religious—among the Jews. Jesus exposed the hypocrisy of the Pharisees, who emphasized minute details of the law while neglecting more important issues such as justice, mercy, and love (Matt. 23:1–7). Pharisees in the N.T. who were known for their generosity and noble spirit were the apostle Paul, Nicodemus, Gamaliel, and Joseph of Arimathea. See also *Sadducees.*

PHARPAR. One of two rivers of Damascus mentioned by the Assyrian commander Naaman. He was offended when told by Elisha to bathe in the Jordan River rather than the rivers of Damascus (2 Kings 5:9–12). See also *Abana River.*

PHEBE (PHOEBE). A believer at Cenchrea near Corinth who was commended by Paul for her support of him and others (Rom. 16:1–2). *Phoebe:* NIV, NRSV.

PHENICE/PHENICIA (PHOENICIA). A Mediterranean coastal region, including the cities of Ptolemais, Tyre, and Sidon. The inhabitants of Phoenicia, descended from the Canaanites, became a seafaring and colonizing people. King Hiram of Tyre furnished cedar timber and craftsmen for the construction of Solomon's temple in Jerusalem (2 Sam. 5:11; 1 Kings 5:1–10). Jesus ministered in this region (Matt. 15:21), and Christians fled here to escape persecution after Stephen's death (Acts 11:19). *Phenicia:* Acts 21:2. *Phoenicia:* NIV, NRSV. See also *Hiram; Tyre.*

PHILADELPHIA. A city of Lycia in Asia Minor and site of one of the seven churches of Asia Minor addressed in the book of Revelation (Rev. 1:11). This church was commended for its faithfulness (Rev. 3:7–9).

PHILEMON. A Christian at Colossae to whom Paul wrote on behalf of Philemon's slave Onesimus (Philem. 1). See also *Onesimus.*

PHILEMON, EPISTLE TO. A short N.T. book written by Paul to help a runaway slave

Onesimus—a convert under Paul's ministry. Philemon, the owner of Onesimus and a fellow believer, was encouraged to welcome his slave back as a Christian brother (v. 16). Paul also hinted that Onesimus be given his freedom in the spirit of Christian love (v. 21).

PHILETUS. A teacher condemned by Paul for his false teachings about the resurrection (2 Tim. 2:17–18).

PHILIP.

1. One of the twelve apostles of Jesus. He responded to Jesus' invitation to discipleship and brought another disciple, Nathanael, to Jesus (John 1:43–51). He also brought a group of Greeks, or Gentiles, to see Jesus in Jerusalem (John 12:21). See also *Twelve, The*.

2. One of the seven men of Greek background chosen as "deacons" in the church at Jerusalem (Acts 6:5–6) and an evangelist in the early church. Philip preached extensively in Samaria and responded to God's call to the Gaza desert (Acts 8:25–27), where he led a eunuch to Christ and baptized him (Acts 8:32–38). He entertained Paul's group of missionaries (Acts 21:8–9) and was the father of four daughters who prophesied (Acts 21:9).

3. A Roman ruler in northern Palestine. See *Herod*, No. 4.

PHILIPPI. A city of Macedonia where Paul and Silas were imprisoned but miraculously rescued by God. This was the first city in Greece to receive the gospel, and Lydia became the first convert (Acts 16:12–34). While imprisoned in Rome, Paul wrote a letter to the Christians in the church at Philippi (Phil. 1:1). See also *Lydia*.

PHILIPPIANS, EPISTLE TO THE. A short N.T. epistle written by Paul to the church at Philippi—a group for whom the apostle expressed great appreciation, thanksgiving, and admiration (1:1–11). Paul appealed to these fellow believers to follow Christ's example of humility (chap. 2), to continue to grow toward maturity in Christian service (chap. 3), and to experience the peace and joy which Christ promises to all believers (chap. 4). Philippians has been called Paul's "epistle of joy" because of his exhortation, "Rejoice in the Lord alway: and again I say, rejoice" (4:4). See also *Kenosis; Philippi*.

PHILISTIA. A coastal region about forty miles long beside the Mediterranean Sea which served as the land of the Philistines in O.T. times (Gen. 21:32–34). The name *Palestine* was derived from *Philistia*. The chief cities of Philistia were Ashdod, Askelon, Ekron, Gath, and Gaza (Josh. 13:3). See also *Palestine*.

PHILISTINES/PHILISTIM. The people of Philistia who were enemies of the Israelites, especially during the days of Saul and David. After settling in Canaan, the Philistines often battled the Israelites (2 Sam. 5:17–25). Their chief pagan gods were Dagon (Judg.16:23) and Baalzebub (2 Kings 1:2–3). Their kingdom disappeared after the Babylonian Exile. *Philistim:* Gen. 10:14. See also *Caphtor*.

PHILOLOGUS. A Christian at Rome to whom Paul sent greetings (Rom. 16:15).

PHILOSOPHY. The study of truths regarding ultimate reality. The early Christians encountered Greek dualism and the teachings of the Stoics and Epicureans (Acts 17:18; Col. 2:8–10).

PHINEHAS.
1. Aaron's grandson who became Israel's high priest and chief of the Korahite branch of the Levites (1 Chron. 9:19–20). He killed Zimri and Cozbi at God's command for allowing Israel to be corrupted with idolatry (Num. 25:6–15).

2. A priest who corrupted his office by immorality and corrupt leadership (1 Sam. 2:22–24). Phinehas and his brother Hophni died in battle with the Philistines, as foretold by a prophet (1 Sam. 2:27, 34; 4:10–11). Phinehas's wife also died in childbirth (1 Sam. 4:19–20). See also *Hophni*.

PHLEGON. A fellow believer at Rome greeted and commended by Paul (Rom. 16:14).

PHOEBE. See *Phebe*.

PHOENICIA. See *Phenice*.

PHRYGIA. A region of central Asia Minor visited by Paul (Acts 16:6). Jews from Phrygia were in Jerusalem on the day of Pentecost (Acts 2:10).

PHUT/PUT. A son of Ham (Gen. 10:6). This reference may be to people related to the Egyptians, or possibly to the Libyans. *Put:* 1 Chron. 1:8. See also *Libya*.

PHYGELLUS (PHYGELUS). A believer condemned by Paul

because he deserted the apostle Paul in the Roman province of Asia (2 Tim. 1:15). *Phygelus:* NIV, NRSV.

PHYLACTERY. A verse of Scripture worn on the forehead or near the heart (Exod. 13:11–16; Deut. 6:4–9). Jesus denounced the conspicuous wearing of phylacteries (Matt. 23:5). See also *Forehead; Frontlet.*

PHYSICIAN. A healer or person who practiced medicine. Medical studies were prominent in Egypt (Gen. 50:2), with midwives and physicians practicing among the Israelites (2 Chron. 16:12). Luke was described as a "beloved physician" (Col. 4:14).

PIG. See *Swine.*

PIGEON. A bird used for sacrifices, particularly by the poor. The word is used interchangeably with *dove* in most Bible passages. Mary and Joseph offered bird sacrifices when Jesus was dedicated to God in the temple (Luke 2:24). See also *Turtledove.*

PILATE. The procurator or Roman governor of Judea (ruled about A.D. 26–36) who presided at Jesus' trial. An opportunist,

Pilate was unwilling to condemn Jesus as a criminal (John 18:30, 38), so he sought to have him tried by Herod at the next judicial level (Luke 23:11). Then he proposed that Jesus be the prisoner customarily dismissed at Passover, but this move also failed (John 18:39–40). Finally he released Jesus to be crucified but tried to dodge responsibility for the decision (Matt. 27: 24–25).

PILGRIMAGE. A stay in a foreign country (Exod. 6:4). The term is applied figuratively to the earthly life span (Heb. 11:13). See also *Alien; Foreigner.*

PILLAR OF FIRE AND CLOUD. Supernatural signs which guided the Israelites in the wilderness (Exod. 13:21). Given to protect the Hebrews, the signs represented God's presence with His people (Num. 14:13–14). These signs were repeated in the transfiguration of Christ (Matt. 17:5). See also *Cloud; Fire.*

PILLOW. A head rest for sleeping. The Hebrews used quilts, stones (Gen. 28:18), netting of goat's hair (1 Sam. 19:13), or a leather cushion (Mark 4:38).

PIN (PEG). A peg or stake. Copper or brass tent pins were used to hold the cords of the tabernacle (Exod. 27:19). *Peg:* NIV, NRSV. The Hebrew word for pin is also rendered as nail (Judg. 4:21).

PINE. See *Fir; Box Tree.*

PINNACLE. A wing of the temple, perhaps an elevated area over Solomon's porch. Satan tempted Jesus to impress the crowds with a spectacular leap from this high place (Matt. 4:5–7). *Highest point:* NIV.

PINT. See *Pound.*

PIPE (FLUTE). A musical instrument probably blown like a flute (Isa. 30:29). This may have been similar to the instrument called an organ in some passages. *Flute:* NIV, NRSV. See also *Flute; Organ.*

PIPES. See *Dulcimer.*

PISGAH, MOUNT. A mountain peak in Moab from which Moses viewed Canaan before his death (Deut. 34:1–6). Balaam built altars and offered sacrifices on this mountain. The highest point of Pisgah was called *Nebo.* See also *Nebo,* No. 1.

PISHON. See *Pison.*

PISIDIA. A large mountainous district in Asia Minor visited by Paul, who preached in the city of Antioch (Acts 13:14–16, 44). See also *Antioch of Pisidia.*

PISON (PISHON). One of four rivers which flowed out of the Garden of Eden (Gen. 2:10–14). *Pishon:* NIV, NRSV.

PIT (CISTERN). A hole in the ground. This word may refer to a deep hole lightly covered to trap animals (Jer. 18:22) as well as to an empty cistern like that into which Joseph was cast (Gen. 37:24). *Cistern:* NIV. Sometimes Sheol is referred to as a pit (Num. 16:30). See also *Cistern; Prison.*

PITCH. A tarlike substance used on Noah's ark, probably asphalt or bitumen found in the Dead Sea area (Gen. 6:14). It was used like mortar and caulk. See also *Slime.*

PITCHER (JAR). An earthenware vessel used to carry water (Gen. 24:14). *Jar:* NIV, NRSV. The word is also used symbolically of the human life span (Eccles. 12:6). See also *Cruse.*

PITHOM. An Egyptian city built by Hebrew slaves (Exod. 1:11). It was located in Goshen east of the Nile River.

PITY. Compassion toward others. James described God as "very pitiful and of tender mercy" (Jas. 5:11). God showed pity on the pagan peoples of Nineveh (Jon. 4:10–11) as well as His people, the Israelites (Isa. 63:9). See also *Mercy*.

PLAGUE. A disastrous affliction or epidemic. Plagues were often interpreted as signs of God's judgment (Exod. 9:14). Ten plagues were sent upon the Egyptians for their failure to release the Hebrew slaves (Exod. 7–11). The children of Israel were plagued for their complaining in the wilderness (Num. 11:1, 31–33). See also *Pestilence*.

PLAIN. A meadow or rolling expanse of land (Judg. 11:33). Given a choice by Abraham, Lot chose the fertile plain near Sodom rather than Canaan's hill country (Gen. 13:10–12).

PLASTER. A thick paste used as a coating for walls and stones (Lev. 14:42).

PLATTER (DISH, PLATE). A dish or utensil for food. Jesus used the word figuratively to condemn the scribes and Pharisees for their hypocrisy (Matt. 23:25–26). *Dish:* NIV; *Plate:* NRSV. See also *Charger*.

PLEDGE. A vow or something given for security of a debt. Under the Mosaic Law, an outer garment pledged by a poor man had to be returned at sunset for his use as a bed covering (Exod. 22:26–27). A creditor was forbidden to enter his neighbor's house to take a pledged item (Deut. 24:10–11). See also *Surety*.

PLEIADES. A constellation of stars cited as evidence of God's sovereignty (Job 9:9). See also *Seven Stars*.

PLOWSHARE. A piece of iron at the end of a plow shaft, used to till the soil. The word is also used figuratively for a coming age of peace (Isa. 2:4). See also *Coulter*.

PLUMBLINE. A tool used by carpenters to determine precise uprightness of a wall. The word is also used figuratively of God's test for the uprightness of His people (Amos 7:7–9).

PLUNDER. See *Spoil*.

PODS. See *Husks*.

POETIC WRITINGS. The five books of the O.T. which are written almost entirely in poetic form—Job, Psalms, Proverbs, the Song of Solomon, and Lamentations—as well as those sections of other books which use this form. Sections of several of the prophetic books, for example, appear in poetry.

POETRY, HEBREW. Unique form of Hebrew writing which uses a repetition technique known as parallelism rather than rhyming or alliteration to express ideas. In parallelism, one line of poetry is advanced, contrasted, or repeated by the next line to convey thought. For example, "Have mercy upon me, O Lord; for I am weak: / O Lord, heal me; for my bones are vexed" (Ps. 6:2).

POISON. A deadly substance when swallowed or introduced into the bloodstream. Dipping the tips of arrows into poison is probably referred to in Job 6:4. The word is also used figuratively for destructive speech (Jas. 3:8). See also *Venom*.

POISONOUS SERPENTS. See *Fiery Serpents*.

POLE. A staff upon which a standard or banner was flown. God instructed Moses to place a "fiery serpent" upon a pole (Num. 21:8–9). See also *Brass Serpent*.

POLLUX. See *Castor and Pollux*.

POLYGAMY. A family system under which a man is allowed to have more than one wife at the same time. The O.T. patriarchs practiced polygamy (for example, Abraham; Gen. 16:1 –4), but it was contrary to God's original plan (Gen. 2:24) and divine ideal of marriage (Matt. 19:5). See also *Monogamy*.

POLYTHEISM. The practice of worshiping many gods, in contrast to monotheism, which emphasized devotion to the one and only true God. The nations surrounding Israel worshiped multiple gods, a practice which led to immorality (Num. 25: 1–9), prostitution (2 Kings 23: 13–14), and child sacrifice (Jer. 7:29–34). The first two of the Ten Commandments make it clear that devotion to the one and only supreme God was not to be mixed with worship of any other false or pagan god (Exod. 20:3–5). See also *Monotheism*.

POMEGRANATE. A small tree which bore apple-shaped fruit that was popular in Palestine. The spies who explored Canaan discovered this tree (Deut 8:7–8).

POMMELS (CAPITALS). Round ornaments at the top of pillars or columns; an architectural feature used in

Solomon's temple at Jerusalem (2 Chron. 4:11–12). *Capitals:* NIV, NRSV.

PONTIUS PILATE. See *Pilate*.

PONTUS. A coastal region along the Black Sea in northern Asia Minor where Priscilla and Aquila settled (Acts 18:2; 1 Pet. 1:1).

POOL. A water reservoir which supplied water for cities (John 5:2). King Hezekiah of Judah built a pool with an aqueduct to pipe water into Jerusalem (2 Kings 20:20). See also *Bethesda; Siloam; Solomon, Pools of.*

POOR. Needy or impoverished people. The Hebrews were instructed by the Lord to show compassion on the poor (Luke 14:13–14). Gleanings of the harvest were left for the poor (Lev. 19:9–10; Ruth 2). Jesus showed compassion for widows and other poor persons (Mark 12:42–44). The early church appointed "deacons" to serve the neglected poor (Acts 6:1). See also *Alms; Beggar.*

POPLAR. A tree of the willow family. Jacob used poplar branches to produce speckled flocks (Gen. 30:37–39). See also *Willow.*

PORCH (PORTICO, VESTIBULE,). A veranda or covered deck around a building. Solomon's porch was along the east side of the temple in Jerusalem (1 Kings 6:3). *Portico:* NIV; *Vestibule:* NRSV. See also *Portico.*

PORCIUS FESTUS. See *Festus.*

PORK. The flesh of pigs, an unclean meat to the Jews (Lev. 11:7–8).

PORTER (GATEKEEPER, DOORKEEPER). A doorkeeper or watchman stationed at city gates (2 Sam. 18:26; *Gatekeeper:* NIV), and at private houses (Mark 13:34). *Doorkeeper*: NRSV. Porters were also assigned to guard duty in the temple at Jerusalem (1 Chron. 23:5). See also *Doorkeeper; Gatekeeper.*

PORTICO (COVERED COLONNADE). A porch. Jesus healed a paralytic lying on one of the porches of the Pool of Bethesda (John 5:2–8). *Covered colonnade:* NIV. See also *Porch.*

PORTION. See *Mess.*

POST (COURIER). A person who relayed messages for a

king or other high official. King Hezekiah used posts to order the Israelites to keep the Passover (2 Chron. 30:6–10). *Courier:* NIV, NRSV. See also *Footman.*

POSTERITY. One's children and grandchildren. The prophet Jehu told King Baasha of Israel that his sinful leadership would destroy him and his family (1 Kings 16:2–4). See also *Seed.*

POT. A kitchen vessel, usually made of clay (Isa. 29:16), but brass pots were used in the sanctuary (1 Kings 7:45).

POTENTATE (SOVER-EIGN). A person of great power or authority. Jesus Christ will be recognized as the only true Potentate (1 Tim. 6:15). *Sovereign:* NRSV.

POTIPHAR. A high Egyptian officer who had Joseph imprisoned because his wife accused Joseph of trying to seduce her (Gen. 39:1–20).

POTI-PHERAH. An Egyptian priest of the city of On whose daughter Asenath married Joseph (Gen. 41:45).

POTSHERD. A fragment of pottery, often used by the poor for a drinking vessel or for carrying coals (Ps. 22:15). See also *Pottery.*

POTTAGE (STEW). A thick vegetable soup (Hag. 2:12); the price paid by Jacob for his brother Esau's birthright (Gen. 25:29–34). *Stew:* NIV, NRSV.

POTTER. A craftsman who made vessels from clay on a revolving wheel (Jer. 18:3). To Isaiah, the power of the potter over the clay was symbolic of the Creator's sovereignty (Isa. 45:9).

POTTER'S FIELD. A burial place for poor people outside Jerusalem. This field was bought with the betrayal silver returned by Judas to Jewish officials (Matt. 27:6–8).

POTTERY. Vessels made from clay. The broken piece of pottery cited by Jeremiah was a symbol of Judah's coming destruction (Jer. 19:1–11). See also *Potsherd.*

POUND (PINT, MINA). A dry measure of uncertain volume. Mary of Bethany anointed Jesus with a pound of costly ointment (John 12:3). *Pint:* NIV. This term was also used of money (Luke 19:13). *Mina:* NIV.

PRAETORIUM (GOVER-NOR'S HEADQUARTERS). The Roman governor's official residence at Jerusalem. After being scourged by Pilate, Jesus was taken to Pilate's residence, where he was mocked by the soldiers (Mark 15:16). *Governor's headquarters:* NRSV.

PRAISE. Worship of God with honor and thanksgiving (Ps. 42:14). God is pleased and glorified with our praise (Ps. 50:23). Our praise of the Father is commanded in Jesus' model prayer (Matt. 6:9–13). See also *Thanksgiving.*

PRAYER. Communion with God. Elements of sincere prayer are adoration (Matt. 6:9–10), confession (1 John 1:9), supplication (1 Tim. 2:1–3), intercession (Jas. 5:15), and thanksgiving (Phil. 4:6). Jesus was a model for His followers in the practice of prayer. He arose early in the morning to pray (Mark 1:35), prayed all night before choosing the Twelve (Luke 6:12), prayed in Gethsemane on the night of His betrayal (Luke 22:44), and prayed on the cross for His enemies (Luke 23:34). He also gave His disciples a model prayer to follow in their communion with the Father (Matt. 6:9–13). See also *Intercession; Petition.*

PREACH. To proclaim the truths of the gospel. Paul's preaching was motivated by the lost condition of His hearers (Rom. 10:1–3). The prophets were anointed by God to preach good tidings of His deliverance (Isa. 61:1–2). Jesus urged His disciples to preach the gospel to everyone (Mark 16:15).

PRECEPT. A command or directive. Vain worship results when human precepts rather than God's commands are given priority (Matt. 15:9).

PREDESTINATION. God's plan for the eternal salvation of those who choose Him. God has ordained good for those who love Him and are called within His purpose (Rom. 8:28). Those called to salvation will be justified and will share God's glory (Rom. 8:30). Those chosen before the foundation of the world will be adopted by God, redeemed, and given an eternal inheritance (Eph. 1:4–11). See also *Election, Divine; Foreknowledge.*

PREPARATION DAY. The day before the Jewish Sabbath or the celebration of a religious festival (Matt. 27:62). Preparation for the Passover celebration involved cooking the Passover meal, baking unleavened bread, and choosing appropriate clothing for the occasion.

PRIDE. Arrogance, vanity, or conceit. This sin results in self-righteousness (Luke 18:11–12) and self-deception (Jer. 49:16). Paul, however, expressed justifiable pride in his fellowship with the Philippians (Phil. 1:3–6). See also *Conceit; Haughtiness; Vanity.*

PRIEST. A religious leader who made sacrificial offerings. The priesthood originated with Aaron, and his descendants were sanctified to the office (Exod. 29:9, 44). Jesus, our faultless high priest, paid for our sins once and for all by sacrificing Himself (Heb. 7: 26–28). See also *High Priest.*

PRIESTHOOD OF BELIEVERS. The doctrine that each believer has direct access to God. This was symbolized by the torn veil in the temple at Jerusalem when Jesus died on the cross, providing access to the holy of holies for all believers (Matt. 27:50–51). Christ is the only authorized mediator between God and man (Eph. 3:11–12). Therefore, we can come boldly and directly to Him (Heb. 4:15–16). As priests of God, believers should minister to others in a spirit of love (Gal. 3:28).

PRIESTHOOD OF CHRIST. One of Christ's offices as the Son of God, emphasizing His offering of Himself on our behalf. Christ obtained eternal redemption for believers by making a perfect sacrifice "by his own blood" (Heb. 9:11–12).

PRINCE (RULER). A leader or ruler; a title for tribal officials (Exod. 2:14). *Ruler:* NIV, NRSV. Also a title for Jesus, who is called the "Prince of life" (Acts 3:15) and the "prince of the kings of earth" (Rev. 1:5). The word is also applied to Satan as the ruler of evil (John 12:31).

PRINCESS. The daughter of a king. King Solomon had princesses among his hundreds of wives (1 Kings 11:3). Athaliah, daughter of King Ahab, killed all the royal descendants and usurped Judah's throne (2 Kings 11:1–3).

PRINCIPALITY. A powerful class of angels and demons. Christ is "far above" all earthly or cosmic powers (Eph. 1:21; 3:10). Believers will share His victory over hostile principalities (Col. 2:10).

PRISCILLA, PRISCA. See *Aquila*.

PRISON. A place of confinement for prisoners, often consisting of little more than a crude dungeon, cistern, or hole in the ground, particularly in O.T. times (Jer. 52:11). Paul wrote several epistles from prison and regarded his confinement as an opportunity to advance the gospel (2 Cor. 6:3–5; Phil. 1:12–14). See also *Cistern; Pit*.

PRIVY. Something kept private or secret. Solomon said Shimei's heart was privy to the wickedness plotted against King David (1 Kings 2:44).

PROCHORUS. One of the seven men of Greek background chosen as "deacons" in the church at Jerusalem (Acts 6:5).

PROCLAMATION. A reading or announcement of an official decree. King Cyrus of Persia proclaimed that the Jewish prisoners could return to Jerusalem to rebuild the temple (Ezra 1:1–3).

PROCONSUL. An official of a Roman province, perhaps the second in command. Paul was brought before the proconsul Gallio at Corinth (Acts 18:12).

See also *Deputy*.

PRODIGAL SON. The main character in Jesus' parable who spent his inheritance foolishly, fell into poverty, and finally returned to his father to ask forgiveness and reinstatement as a servant. His father, representing the love and forgiveness of God, welcomed him back as a son (Luke 15:11–32).

PROGNOSTICATOR. A fortune-teller, or one who foretold the future by consulting the stars. The Lord promised to judge Babylonia, in spite of the power of these astrologers (Isa. 47:12–14). See also *Astrologer*.

PROMISE. A pledge or guarantee, particularly of some blessing from God. Israel's history included significant promises from God: (1) Promise of a son to Abraham (Gen. 18:10); (2) the land of Canaan promised to Israel (Exod. 6:4); and (3) a Savior promised from the house of David (Isa. 7: 13–14; Matt. 1:20–23). See also *Hope*.

PROPHET. An inspired messenger called by God to declare His will (Ezra 5:2). Prophets were described as God's servants (Zech. 1:6), watchmen (Ezek. 3:17), and holy men

(2 Pet. 1:21). In the N.T. the prophets were cited as a noble example of patient suffering (Jas. 5:10). Another word for prophet is *seer*.

PROPHETESS. A female prophet or the wife of a prophet. Noted prophetesses include Miriam (Exod. 15:20), Deborah (Judg. 4:4), Huldah (2 Kings 22:14), and Anna (Luke 2:36). Four daughters of Philip were said to prophesy (Acts 21:8–9).

PROPITIATION. Atonement or expiation. Christ was appointed to be a propitiation for our sins through "faith in his blood" (Rom. 3:24–25). His sacrificial death is the supreme demonstration of love (1 John 4:10). See also *Atonement; Mediator, Christ the; Reconciliation*.

PROSELYTE (CONVERT). A Gentile who converted to Judaism. Some of these converts renounced their pagan lifestyle but refused to accept such Jewish practices as circumcision. Well-known proselytes of the Bible include Cornelius, Lydia, and Nicolas of Antioch (Acts 6:5). *Convert:* NIV.

PROSTITUTE. See *Harlot*.

PROVENDER (FODDER). Food for livestock, consisting of chopped straw mixed with barley, beans, or dates (Gen. 24:32). *Fodder:* NIV, NRSV.

PROVERBS, BOOK OF. A book of wisdom in the O.T. filled with short, pithy sayings on how to live with maturity and integrity under the watchful eye of God—the source of all wisdom. These wise sayings, written by Solomon as well as other sages of Israel, deal with such practical matters as strong drink (23:20–21), pride (16:18), work (6:6–11), family (22:6), friendship (17:17), anger (19:11), speech (15:1–4), sexual temptation (5:1–23), and honesty in business (11 1–4). See also *Solomon; Wisdom Literature*.

PROVIDENCE. Divine guidance of human events (Neh. 9:6). This doctrine affirms God's absolute lordship over His creation and the activities by which He preserves and governs. God is constantly working in accord with His purpose (Eph. 1:11). He sustains the moral universe by operating within spiritual principles (Gal. 6:7–9).

PROVINCE. A district or section of a nation, often the outlying area of an extended world power such as the Persian and the Roman empires (Esther 3:12). In the N.T. this word refers to districts conquered and controlled by the Romans (Acts 25:1).

PROVISION. A supply or ration of some substance, such as food. Solomon's court required a large provision of food (1 Kings 4:22–23).

PRUDENT (LEARNED, INTELLIGENT). To have discernment or understanding (Matt. 11:25). *Learned:* NIV; *Intelligent:* NRSV. The prudent person foresees evil (Prov. 22:3) and is crowned with knowledge (Prov. 14:18).

PRUNINGHOOK. A tool for cutting shrubs and vines. To beat pruninghooks into spears was a sign of war (Joel 3:10). To do the opposite was a sign of peace (Isa. 2:4).

PSALMS, BOOK OF. A poetic book of the O.T. filled with hymns of praise and prayers of thanksgiving to God as well as laments against one's enemies and misfortune. Its title is derived from a Greek word which implies that these psalms were to be sung to the accompaniment of a musical instrument. King David of Judah wrote many of these psalms (see 54,

59, 65). But many other unknown writers contributed to this book, which was probably compiled across many centuries of Jewish history. Generations of believers have found the psalms to be a rich source of devotional inspiration, with its emphasis on the goodness, stability, power, and faithfulness of God. See also *David; Poetic Writings; Poetry, Hebrew*.

PSALTERY (LYRE, HARP). A stringed musical instrument that was probably similar to the harp (1 Sam. 10:5). *Lyre:* NIV; *Harp:* NRSV. See also *Harp*.

PTOLEMAIS. See *Accho*.

PTOLEMY. The title of Greek kings who ruled throughout Egypt and Palestine from about 323 to 30 B.C. These kings are possibly referred to in Daniel's visions (see Dan. 11:5–30). Their kingdom eventually fell to the Romans.

PUBLICAN (TAX COLLECTOR). A Jewish citizen who purchased the right to collect taxes in a specific area of his country for the Roman government. Publicans were hated and looked upon as traitors by their fellow citizens (Matt. 5:46). Matthew (Matt. 9:9–11) and Zacchaeus (Luke 19:1–10)

An ibex—called a *pygarg* in the KJV—in the hills of En-gedi, a modern Israeli nature reserve near the Dead Sea.

Courtesy Israel Ministry of Tourism

were prominent publicans who followed Jesus. *Tax collector:* NIV, NRSV. See also *Matthew*.

PUBLIUS. A Roman official who entertained Paul on the island of Miletus after a shipwreck. Paul healed his father of a fever (Acts 28:7–8).

PUDENS. A believer at Rome who joined Paul in sending greetings to Timothy (2 Tim. 4:21).

PUL. See *Tiglath-pileser*.

PULSE (VEGETABLES). Food made of vegetables, such as peas or beans; the food eaten by Daniel and his friends instead of the king's provisions (Dan. 1:12–16). *Vegetables:* NIV, NRSV.

PUNISHMENT. A penalty for wrongdoing. Cain reacted to God's penalties for murdering Abel with "my punishment is greater than I can bear" (Gen. 4:13). Jesus urged forgiveness of offenders rather than the Mosaic tradition of "an eye for an eye" (Matt. 5:38–39). See also *Judgment; Retribution; Wrath.*

PURIFICATION. Ceremonial or spiritual cleansing. The

Mosaic Law prescribed purification rites for those ceremonially defiled by touching a corpse, by contact with bodily discharges, by childbirth, and by leprosy (see Lev. 14–15). The mother of Jesus offered turtledoves and pigeons as a sacrifice in her ceremonial cleansing (Luke 2:21–24). See also *Clean; Wash.*

PURIM, FEAST OF. A Jewish festival which celebrated the rescue of the Jews from Haman's oppression in Esther's time (Esther 9:21–32).

PURPLE. The color preferred by kings and other royal officials; a bright dye made from shellfish. Lydia was a businesswoman who sold purple cloth (Acts 16:14).

PURSE. A bag for carrying items (Luke 10:4), generally placed in the folds of the sash around the waist. The purse in Jesus' instructions to His disciples was probably a money bag (Mark 6:8). See also *Crisping Pin.*

PUT. See *Phut.*

PUTEOLI. A seaport city of Italy visited by Paul (Acts 28:13–14).

The caves of Qumran, where the ancient manuscripts known as the Dead Sea Scrolls were discovered.

Courtesy Israel Ministry of Tourism

PYGARG (IBEX). An animal of the deer family, perhaps the antelope or the addax. It was considered unclean by the Jews (Deut. 14:5). *Ibex:* NIV, NRSV.

-Q-

QUAILS. Small game birds provided miraculously by the Lord as food for the Israelites in the wilderness (Exod. 16:12–13).

QUARTUS. A Christian at Corinth from whom Paul sent greetings to the church at Rome (Rom. 16:23).

QUATERNION. A company of four soldiers who guarded prisoners during a night "watch" assignment consisting of three hours (Acts 12:4).

QUEEN. A woman who exercised royal power, or the wife or mother of a king. Esther exercised great power as the wife of King Ahasuerus of Persia (Esther 5:2). Solomon provided a seat at his right hand for his mother, Bathsheba (1 Kings 2:19).

QUEEN OF HEAVEN. A fertility goddess worshiped by the citizens of Jerusalem during the idolatrous days before the fall of the nation of Judah (Jer. 7:18; 44:17). This may have been the goddess Ashtaroth. See also *Ashtaroth*.

QUEEN OF SHEBA. See *Sabeans*.

QUICKEN. To preserve or give life. The psalmist praised God who will "quicken me again" (Ps. 71:20). The Father and Son have authority to raise the dead and give eternal life (John 5:21).

QUICKSANDS (SYRTIS). Sandbars and shifting sands off the African coast in the Mediterranean Sea which posed a hazard for ships (Acts 27:17). *Syrtis:* NRSV.

QUIRINIUS. See *Cyrenius*.

QUIVER. A sheath for arrows carried by foot soldiers or hung on the sides of chariots (Lam. 3:13). The word is also used figuratively for God's protection (Isa 49:2) and the blessing of children (Ps. 127:5).

QUMRAN, KHIRBET. A site near the Dead Sea where the Dead Sea Scrolls were discovered. See also *Dead Sea Scrolls; Essenes*.

-R-

RAAMSES. See *Rameses.*

RABBAH/RABBATH. The capital city of the Ammonites (Deut. 3:11–12) captured by David's army under Joab. The city's destruction was prophesied by Amos (Amos 1:14). *Rabbath:* Ezek 21:20.

RABBI/RABBONI (RABBOUNI). A title of great respect, meaning "master" or "teacher," used by Nicodemus in addressing Jesus (John 3:2). Its Aramaic form is *rabboni* (John 20:16). *Rabbouni:* NRSV.

RABBIT. See *Hare.*

RAB-SHAKEH. The chief cupbearer or aide for King Sennacherib of Assyria who demanded the surrender of Jerusalem from King Hezekiah (2 Kings 18:17; Isa. 36:13–22).

RACA. A term of insult, meaning "worthless" or "good for nothing," which was forbidden by Christ. Expressing such contempt for a fellow human being will lead to God's judgment and condemnation (Matt. 5:21–22).

RACE. This word in the N.T. refers to popular Grecian contests, such as races by foot, horseback, or chariot. It is also used figuratively of the Christian's call to pursue the goal of Christlikeness (Heb. 12:1).

RACHAB. See *Rahab.*

RACHEL/RAHEL. Jacob's favorite wife (Gen. 29:28–30) and the mother of his sons Joseph and Benjamin (Gen. 30:23–24; 35:16–18). She died giving birth to Benjamin and was buried near Bethlehem (Gen. 35:16–20). Jeremiah referred to Rachel weeping for her children carried into the Babylonian Exile (Jer. 31:15–17; *Rahel*). See also *Jacob.*

RAHAB/RACHAB. A harlot in Jericho who hid the spies sent by Joshua to scout the city (Josh. 2:1–6). Later she and her family were spared when Jericho fell to the invading Israelites (Josh. 6:22–25). In the N.T. Rahab was commended for her faith (Heb. 11:31). *Rachab:* Jesus' ancestry (Matt. 1:5).

RAHEL. See *Rachel.*

RAID. See *Road.*

RAIN. God's life-giving moisture from the sky was sometimes withheld because of the sin of His people (Deut. 11:17).

Excessive rain produced the great flood in Noah's time as an instrument of God's judgment (Gen. 7:4). See also *Former Rain; Latter Rain.*

RAINBOW. A colored arch in the clouds after the great flood, given by God as a promise that He would never again destroy the world with water (Gen. 9:9–17).

RAISINS. Dried grapes which were preserved in clusters (1 Sam. 25:18) and used in cakes known as flagons (Song of Sol. 2:5). See also *Flagon,* No. 1.

RAM.
1. A long beam used to batter down the gates of walled cities (Ezek. 4:2).
2. A male sheep used for food (Gen. 31:38) and favored as a sacrificial animal (Num. 15:6).

RAMA (RAMAH). A Benjamite city near Jerusalem and the probable site of Rachel's tomb (Matt. 2:18). *Ramah:* NIV, NRSV.

RAMAH. Another name for the town of Ramoth-gilead. See *Ramoth-gilead.*

RAMESES/RAAMSES. A fertile district of Egypt where Jacob and his descendants settled (Gen. 47:11). This name may have been given later to a royal treasure city built by the Hebrew slaves (Exod. 1:11; *Raamses*).

RAMOTH-GILEAD/RAMAH/RAMOTH. An ancient Amorite stronghold east of the Jordan River which became one of the six cities of refuge after its conquest by the Israelites (Deut. 4:43). *Ramah:* 2 Kings 8:29; *Ramoth:* 1 Kings 22:3. See also *Cities of Refuge.*

RAMPART. A low wall around a military trench or embankment, which served as the first line of defense for a walled city (Lam. 2:8; Nah. 3:8). See also *Bulwark.*

RAM'S HORN. The curved horn of a ram which was blown like a trumpet as a signal to worshipers and warriors (Josh. 6:4–13). See also *Trumpet.*

RANSOM. To redeem or buy by making a payment. Because of His atoning death, Christ is described as a "ransom for all" (1 Tim. 2:6).

RAPTURE, THE. A doctrine held by some which deals with the transformation of the redeemed into a glorified state at

Christ's return (Phil. 3: 20–21). The dead in Christ will be raised at Christ's return and given an incorruptible body (1 Cor. 15:51–53). They will be caught up into the air, along with living saints, to meet the Lord (1 Thess. 4:16–17). See also *Second Coming.*

RAS SHAMRA TABLETS. Clay writing tablets discovered by archaeologists at the ancient city of Ugarit in Syria. Dating from the fifteenth century B.C., these tablets describe the pagan religions mentioned in the O.T., particularly Baalism. See also *Clay; Nuzi Tablets.*

RAVEN. A bird of prey considered unclean under Mosaic Law (Lev. 11:15). God used ravens to sustain the prophet Elijah (1 Kings 17:4–6).

RAZOR. A sharp instrument made of flint, bronze, or steel, and used for cutting hair (Ezek. 5:1).

REAPER. A person who harvested grain (Ruth 2:3, 14). The spiritual law of the harvest declares we reap what we sow (Gal. 6:7–8). See also *Harvest.*

REBA. A Midianite chief killed by Joshua's army in the plains of Moab (Josh. 13:21).

REBEKAH/REBECCA. The wife of Isaac and the mother of his twin sons Jacob and Esau. She encouraged her favorite son Jacob to obtain Esau's birthright by deceiving the aging Isaac. Then she encouraged Jacob to flee to her relatives in Mesopotamia to escape Esau's wrath (Gen. 27). *Rebecca:* Greek form (Rom. 9:10). See also *Isaac.*

REBUKE. See *Reproof.*

RECENT CONVERT. See *Novice.*

RECHAB. The father of Jehonadab and founder of the Rechabites, a tribe committed to abstain from wine and live in tents. Because of their faithfulness, the prophet Jeremiah promised they would not cease to exist (Jer. 35:8–19). The descendants of this tribe still live in Iraq and Yemen.

RECOMPENSE. To pay back in kind (Prov. 12:14). Believers are assured their courage and faith will be rewarded (Heb. 10:35–36). See also *Reward.*

RECONCILIATION. The process of bringing opposing parties or people together. Believers, who are justified by faith and reconciled to God by

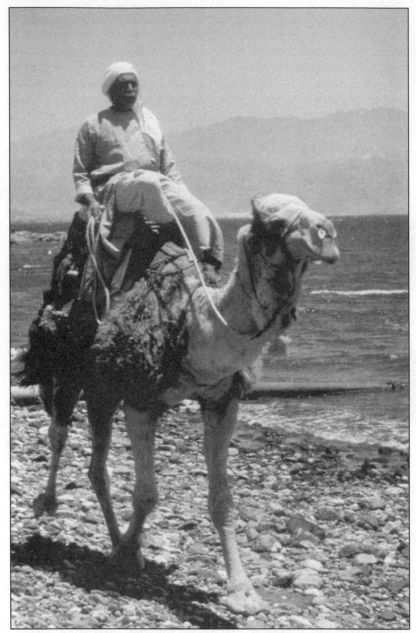

A Bedouin camel rider on the shore of the Red Sea.

Courtesy Israel Ministry of Tourism

Christ's victory over sin and death (Rom. 5:1, 10), are to be ambassadors of reconciliation for others (2 Cor. 5:18–20). See also *Atonement; Mediator, Christ the; Propitiation.*

RECORD (TESTIMONY). A witness or testimony to one's faithfulness. Jesus told His enemies, "my record is true" (John 8:14). *Testimony:* NIV, NRSV. Paul defended his record of faithfulness to God (Acts 20:26–27). See also *Testimony; Witness.*

RECORDER. An aide to a king who kept official records and served as a counselor or advisor (2 Kings 18:18, 37).

RED DRAGON. A name for Satan. After being cast out of heaven, Satan turned his fury on God's people (Rev. 12:3–17). See also *Satan.*

RED HEIFER. An unblemished cow or ox that had never been yoked. It was used as a sacrifice in a sin offering (Num. 19:1–9).

RED KITE. See *Glede; Vulture.*

RED SEA. The sea between Egypt and Arabia which the Israelites crossed miraculously through God's intervention when fleeing from the Egyptian army (Exod. 14:16; 15:4, 22). This body of water is also called the Sea of Reeds because of its reed-filled marshes at the head of the Gulf of Suez.

REDEEM. To buy back property which had been forfeited because of indebtedness or to buy back a person who had been sold into slavery (Exod. 6:6). This idea describes perfectly the work of Christ, who "bought us back" from sin and death through His atonement on the cross as our Redeemer (Matt. 20:28). See also *Atonement; Lamb of God.*

REED. A tall grass, common in marshes and swamps, used to make paper, musical instruments, and writing pens. The word is also used figuratively for weakness and fragility (Matt. 11:7). See also *Bulrush; Paper.*

REFINER. A craftsman who removed impurities from precious metals by melting the ore (Jer. 6:29)—an apt description for God, who purifies His people through affliction and chastisement (Isa. 48:10). See also *Finer.*

REFUGE, CITIES OF. See *Cities of Refuge.*

REFUSE (RUBBISH). Waste or worthless matter (Amos 8:6). Paul declared his accomplishments were as garbage, compared to the riches of knowing Christ (Phil. 3:8). *Rubbish:* NIV, NRSV. See also *Dung*.

REGENERATION. New birth; spiritual change brought about by the Holy Spirit in those who trust in Christ (2 Cor. 5:17–21). See also *New Birth; Salvation.*

REGISTER (FAMILY RECORDS, GENEALOGICAL RECORDS). A tablet on which census records or genealogical lists were inscribed, with the names of the living on one side and the dead on the other (Ezra 2:62). *Family records:* NIV; *Genealogical records:* NRSV. See also *Genealogy.*

REHOB. A city near the source of the Jordan River scouted by the spies who investigated the land of Canaan (Num. 13:21).

REHOBOAM/ROBOAM. Son and successor of Solomon as king of Judah (reigned about 931–913 B.C.). He refused to implement the reform measures requested by northern leaders after Solomon's death —a foolish act which resulted in the split of the ten northern tribes into the Northern Kingdom (1 Kings 12:1–24). *Roboam:* Jesus' ancestry (Matt. 1:7).

REHOBOTH. The name of a well dug by Isaac in the valley of Gerar south of Beer-sheba (Gen. 26:17, 22).

REINS. KJV word for the *kidneys*, a vital body organ in humans and animals. The reins of an animal were considered a special ceremonial sacrifice (Lev. 3:4–5). In humans, the kidneys were regarded as the seat of conscience and affection (Prov. 23:16).

REJOICE. To be glad or to express one's joy. Joy may result from God's blessings (Exod. 18:9) or assurance of salvation (Acts 8:39). See also *Joy.*

REKEM. A Midianite king killed by the Israelites under Moses (Num. 31:8; Josh. 13:21).

REMISSION. God's forgiveness or pardon of our sins. This forgiveness is based on Christ's atoning death (Matt. 26:28) and our repentance (Mark 1:4) and faith in Christ (Acts 10:43). See also *Forgiveness; Pardon.*

REMNANT (SURVIVORS). A small group of God's people

who remained loyal to Him in the midst of widespread sin and idolatry. The prophet Isaiah declared that Israel would be punished for its unfaithfulness (Isa. 1:9). *Survivors:* NIV, NRSV. However, a righteous remnant of His people would be preserved (Isa. 10:20–22). God continues to work through His righteous remnant, the church (Rom. 11:5). See also *Outcasts.*

REMPHAN (REPHAN). A star god of the Babylonians worshiped secretly by the Israelites —an act for which they were taken into exile by the Babylonians (Acts 7:41–43). *Rephan:* NIV, NRSV.

REND (TEAR). To tear apart by force. Rending one's clothes was a sign of great sorrow or repentance (Esther 4:1). *Tear:* NIV, NRSV.

REPENTANCE. The act of turning from sin and changing one's orientation from rebellion against God to acceptance of God's will and lordship. A patient God commands all persons to repent (Acts 17:30). Christ came to call sinners to repentance (Luke 5:32), and He also counsels believers to forgive a brother who repents (Luke 17:3). See also *Contrite;*

Conviction; Penitence.

REPHAIM (REPHAITES).
1. A race of giants in Palestine defeated by Chedorlaomer, a king of Elam, and allied kings (Gen. 14:5). *Rephaites:* NIV.
2. A fertile valley near Jerusalem where David defeated the Philistines (2 Sam. 5:18–22).

REPHAN. See *Remphan.*

REPHIDIM. A camping site of the Israelites between the wilderness of Sin and Mt. Sinai where Moses struck the rock and where Amalek was defeated (Exod. 17:1).

REPROACH. Shame, blame, or scorn. Jesus the Messiah suffered reproach for our sake (Isa. 53:3–6; Rom. 15:3).

REPROBATE (DEPRAVED, DEBASED). A person who is depraved, corrupt, or worthless—a term applied to those who reject God (Rom. 1:28). *Depraved:* NIV; *Debased:* NRSV.

REPROOF. A sharp rebuke for misconduct. John the Baptist reproved Herod for his incestuous marriage (Luke 3:19–20).

RESH. The twentieth letter of the Hebrew alphabet, used as a heading over Ps. 119:153–160.

RESIN. See *Myrrh*.

RESTITUTION. To make a fair settlement with a person for property lost or for wrong done. Restitution was strictly required by the Mosaic Law (Exod. 22:1). Zacchaeus promised to make fourfold restitution of what he had taken unlawfully as a tax collector (Luke 19:8).

RESURRECTION. A raising to life beyond physical death which leads to eternal life for believers. This truth was taught by Jesus (John 6:40, 44) and demonstrated by His miracles (Matt. 9:25) as well as His own resurrection (Acts 2:32). Paul taught that Christians will have a glorified body like that of Christ (Phil. 3:20–21) and that it will last through eternity (Rom. 2:7).

RESURRECTION OF CHRIST. The return of Jesus to physical life following His death. His resurrection was foretold in Psalms (Ps. 16:10–11) and prophecy (Isa. 53:10–12), announced by Christ Himself (Mark 9:9–10), and proclaimed by the apostles (Acts 2:32; 3:15). It validates our faith and witness (1 Cor. 15:14–15), assures believers of resurrection (1 Cor. 15:18–20), emphasizes our final victory over sin and death (1 Cor. 15:17, 26, 54, 57), and inspires faithfulness in Christian service (1 Cor. 15:58).

RETRIBUTION. A repayment for wrong done; God's wrath and punishment against man's rebellion and unbelief (Rom. 1:18). Only trust in Jesus and His atoning death can deliver us from God's retribution (1 Thess. 1:10). See also *Judgment, Last; Punishment; Tribulation, Great.*

REUBEN. The oldest son of Jacob and Leah and founder of one of the twelve tribes of Israel (Gen. 29:32). He lost his birthright by committing adultery with his father's concubines (Gen. 35:22; 49:3–4). Reuben likely saved Joseph's life when his brothers proposed to kill him (Gen. 37:21–22). The tribe of Reuben settled east of the Jordan River, along with Gad and Manasseh (Num. 32:1–25). See also *Tribes of Israel.*

REUEL. See *Jethro*.

REVELATION. The uncovering or presentation of truth at God's initiative (2 Cor. 12: 1–7). Christ, the only begotten Son, reveals the Father (John 1:18). God's searching Spirit (1 Cor.

2:10) interprets the divine purpose through the prophets (1 Pet. 1:12) and the apostles (Gal. 1:16).

REVELATION OF JOHN. The last book of the N.T., which consists of a series of seven visions revealed directly by the Lord to the apostle John. Through symbols such as angels, horsemen, and plagues, these visions are considered by some to portray the end of the present age and the coming of God's kingdom.

The seven visions serve as a convenient outline of the book: (1) Christ encouraging His church against attacks (1: 9–3:22); (2) Christ the Lamb with a sealed scroll (4:1–7:17); (3) seven angels blowing trumpets (8:1–11:19); (4) Satan and the beast persecuting the church (12:1–14:20); (5) seven bowls pouring out the wrath of Christ (15:1–16:21); (6) the judgment of Babylonia, or Rome (17:1–19:20); and (7) the final victory of God and His final judgment (19:11–21). The book ends on a triumphant note with God's promise of a new heaven and a new earth (21:1–22:21). See also *Apocalypse; John the Apostle; Seven Churches of Asia.*

REVENGE. Retaliation against another, or "getting even." Jesus rebuked His disciples for a vengeful spirit (Luke 9: 54–56) and commanded forbearance (Matt. 5:38–44). He commanded us to love our enemies and show mercy toward others (Luke 6:35–38). The Bible declares that vengeance should be exacted only by God (Prov. 20:22; Heb. 10:30).

REVERENCE. A feeling of deep respect and awe which believers are to show toward God and the sanctuary devoted to worship (Lev. 19:30; Ps. 89:8). Reverence should also be shown to kings (1 Kings 1:31), parents (Heb. 12:9), and family members (Eph. 5:33).

REVILER (SLANDERER). A mocker. Revilers will not inherit God's kingdom (1 Cor. 6:10). *Slanderer:* NIV. Those reviled for Christ's sake will be blessed and rewarded (Matt. 5:11–12).

REWARD. A. return or payment for service. God rewards those who diligently seek Him (Heb. 11:6). See also *Recompense.*

REZIN. The last king of Syria who was killed in the conquest by Tiglath-pileser of Assyria (2 Kings 15:37; 16:5–9).

RHEGIUM. A port in southern Italy where Paul landed on his way to Rome (Acts 28:13).

RHODA. A servant girl in the home of Mary, mother of John Mark, who answered the door for Peter after his miraculous release from prison (Acts 12:13–16).

RHODES. A Greek island in the Aegean Sea which Paul's ship passed when sailing from Assos to Palestine (Acts 21:1). This was the site of the ancient lighthouse known as the Colossus of Rhodes, one of the seven wonders of the ancient world.

RICHES. Material goods and earthly treasures, which are portrayed as deceitful (Matt. 13:22), fleeting (Prov. 23:5), and uncertain (1 Tim. 6:17). Jesus urged believers to lay up spiritual treasures in heaven rather than earthly possessions (Matt. 6:19–20).

RICH ROBE. See *Stomacher*.

RIDDLE. A story with a hidden meaning. Samson posed a riddle to the Philistines (Judg. 14:12–19).

RIE (SPELT). A common Egyptian grain plant which thrived in poor soil under hot, dry conditions (Exod. 9:32). *Spelt:* NIV, NRSV. See also *Fitch*.

RIGHT HAND. A symbol of power and strength (Ps. 77:10). Jesus is exalted in power at God's right hand (Eph. 1:20). See also *Hand of God*.

RIGHTEOUSNESS. An attribute of God which signifies His holiness, sinlessness, and justice (Ps. 35:24). Through faith in Christ, God's righteousness is imputed or granted to believers (Titus 3:5). Christians are encouraged to pursue the interests of God's righteous kingdom (Matt. 6:33). See also *Godliness; Goodness*.

RIM. See *Nave*.

RIMMON. A Syrian god worshiped by Naaman the leper (2 Kings 5:18), possibly a god of the sun or rain.

RING. A circular band worn as an ornament on fingers, wrists, ankles, and in ears and nostrils. The pharaoh of Egypt presented a ring to Joseph as a symbol of authority as his aide or advisor (Gen. 41:42).

RIVER. A freshwater stream. The largest rivers mentioned in the Bible are the Abana (2 Kings 5:12), Euphrates

(Gen. 2:14), Jordan (Matt. 3:6), Nile (Exod. 7:21), Pharpar (2 Kings 5:12), and Tigris, or Hiddekel (Gen. 2:14).

RIVER OF EGYPT (WADI OF EGYPT). A small stream flowing into the Mediterranean Sea which marked the old boundary between Egypt and Palestine (Num. 34:5). *Wadi of Egypt:* NIV, NRSV.

RIZPAH. The concubine of King Saul who was taken by Abner after Saul's death (2 Sam. 3:6–8). Her two sons were hanged by the Gibeonites during David's reign (2 Sam. 21:8–11).

ROAD (RAID). A path or trail for public travel, also called a highway or way (Mark 10:46). The word is also used as a figure of speech for a raid by robbers or invaders (1 Sam. 27:10). *Raid:* NRSV. See also *Highway*.

ROBBER. A person who steals from others. The traveler in Christ's parable of the Good Samaritan was beaten by robbers (Luke 10:30).

ROBE. A long outer garment similar to a tunic or mantle. The soldiers mocked Jesus at His crucifixion by dressing him in a purple robe (Matt. 27:28). See also *Mantle*.

ROBOAM. See *Rehoboam*.

ROCK. A stone. The word is used metaphorically for God to show His strength and stability (Ps. 18:31). Jesus changed Peter's name to "rock" or "rocklike" (Greek: *petras*) when He called him as His disciple (John 1:42).

ROCK BADGER. See *Coney*.

ROD (SHOOT). A staff or stick (Ps. 23:4). The word is used figuratively for a branch or offshoot of a tribe or family; for example, in reference to Christ (Isa. 11:1). *Shoot:* NIV, NRSV.

ROE/ROEBUCK (GAZELLE). A graceful deer noted for its swiftness (2 Sam. 2:18). *Gazelle:* NIV, NRSV. It was considered a clean animal by the Jews (Deut. 12:15, 22). *Roebuck:* 1 Kings 4:23. See also *Deer; Hart; Hind*.

ROLL (SCROLL). A strip of parchment that was written on, then rolled on a stick (Jer. 36:2). *Scroll:* NIV, NRSV. It was unrolled for reading, just as a modern reader turns the pages of a book. See also *Scroll*.

ROMAN EMPIRE. The powerful pagan empire that dominated the known world during N.T. times (Rom. 1:7). Founded on the Tiber River in 735 B.C. by Romulus, the nation was governed by kings until 509 B.C., when it became a republic. Rome extended her borders greatly during the republic period, eventually annexing Palestine and Syria in 63 B.C. Augustus Caesar became emperor of the far-reaching empire in 27 B.C. and was reigning at Jesus' birth (Luke 2:1–7). Jesus was crucified by Roman soldiers under sentence from Pilate, the Roman governor of Judea (Matt 27:24–26).

ROMANS, EPISTLE TO THE. An epistle of the N.T. on the themes of righteousness and salvation, written by the apostle Paul to the Christians at Rome. The most systematic and theological of all of Paul's epistles, Romans expresses his conviction that the gospel is the power of salvation to all who believe (1:16–17). Other themes discussed in the epistle include: (1) the truth that all people, both Jews and Gentiles, are unworthy of God's grace (1:18–3:20); (2) God's imputed righteousness, through which He justifies and sanctifies believers (3:21–8:39); (3) Israel in God's plan of redemption (9:1–11:36); and (4) the practical application of faith in the life of believers (12:1– 15:13). See also *Righteousness; Salvation.*

ROME. The capital city of the Roman Empire (Rom. 1:7) and the place where Paul was imprisoned during his final days and where he likely died as a martyr (Phil. 1:12–13; 4:22; 2 Tim. 4:6–8). His epistle to the Romans was addressed to the Christians in this city (Rom. 1:1–7). In the N.T., Rome is figuratively portrayed as Babylon (1 Pet. 5:13).

ROOT. The life-sustaining part of a plant. The word is also used figuratively to describe Christ's humiliation (Isa. 53:2) and exaltation (Isa. 11:10) and the believer's foundation in Christ (Col. 2:7).

ROPE/CORD. A heavy cord. Ropes on the head or neck signified distress (1 Kings 20:31–32) and perhaps submission, since cords were used to bind prisoners. *Cord:* Judg. 15:13. See also *Line.*

ROSE (CROCUS). A flowering plant, perhaps the narcissus—a fragrant flower which grew in the plain of Sharon (Isa. 35:1). *Crocus:* NIV, NRSV.

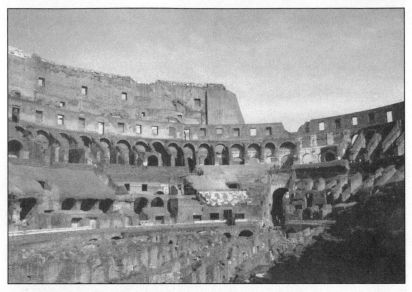

Interior view of the ruins of the ancient stadium or outdoor theater known as the Colosseum of Rome.

Courtesy Rayburn W. Ray

ROYAL DEPUTY. See *Chancellor.*

ROYAL OFFICIAL. See *Nobleman.*

RUBBISH. See *Dung; Refuse.*

RUBY (CORAL). A precious stone, perhaps coral or pearl (Prov. 3:15; Lam. 4:7). *Coral:* NRSV. See also *Coral.*

RUDDY. Having a reddish or fair complexion, in contrast to the dark skin of most people of the Middle East (1 Sam. 16:12).

RUE. An herb with a strong odor and bitter taste. Jesus denounced the Pharisees who were careful to tithe this insignificant plant while neglecting more important matters (Luke 11:42).

RUFUS. A fellow believer at Rome greeted and commended by Paul (Rom. 16:13). He was perhaps the son of Simon of Cyrene, who carried the cross of Jesus (Mark 15:21).

RUHAMAH. A symbolic name for Israel, meaning "having obtained favor," given by Hosea to his daughter to show that

Israel would be forgiven after their repentance (Hos. 2:1).

RULER. See *Governor; Prince.*

RUSH. A plant which grew in marshes, perhaps the same as the bulrush (Job 8:11). See also *Bulrush; Flag.*

RUST. A substance which corrodes metal. Jesus used this word to warn against the instability and uncertainty of earthly treasures (Matt. 6:19–20).

RUTH. A Moabite woman who remained loyal to her Jewish mother-in-law Naomi after the death of their husbands. Ruth moved with Naomi to Bethlehem (Ruth 1:16–19), where she gleaned grain in the fields of Boaz. She eventually married Boaz and became an ancestor of David and Christ (Ruth 4:9–22). See also *Boaz; Naomi.*

RUTH, BOOK OF. A short book of the O.T. which reads almost like a short story on the power of love in dismal circumstances. Love bound Ruth and her mother-in-law Naomi together in spite of the death of their husbands (1:1–2:23). And Ruth found happiness and security again through her marriage to Boaz, a kinsman of Naomi's family (3:1–4:22).

See also *Levirate Marriage.*

-S-

SABAOTH. A Hebrew word for "hosts." See *Hosts, Lord of.*

SABBATH. The Jewish day of worship and rest, established when God rested after the six days of creation (Gen. 2:1–3). The fourth of the Ten Commandments called for the Sabbath to be observed and "kept holy" (Exod. 20:8). The Pharisees placed restrictions on Sabbath observance that prohibited acts of mercy or necessity (Mark 2:23–24). But Jesus declared that "the sabbath was made for man and not man for the sabbath" (Mark 2:27–28). The O.T. Sabbath fell on the seventh day of the week, or our Saturday. Most Christian groups observe Sunday as the day of worship because of Christ's resurrection on the first day of the week (1 Cor. 16:2).

SABBATH DAY'S JOURNEY. The distance under law by which a person was permitted to travel on the Sabbath—2,000 paces outside the city wall, or about 3,000 feet (Exod. 16:29–30; Acts 1:12).

SABBATICAL YEAR. Every seventh year—or a Sabbath year—considered sacred to the Lord, when the land went uncultivated and debtors were released from their obligations (Lev. 25:20–21).

SABEANS. Natives or inhabitants of ancient Sheba in southwest Arabia, a country now known as Yemen. Job's livestock was stolen by Sabeans (Job 1:13–15). The wealthy queen of Sheba visited King Solomon (1 Kings 10).

SACKBUT (LYRE, TRIGON). A triangular-shaped stringed musical instrument similar to a harp (Dan. 3:5–10). *Lyre:* NIV; *Trigon:* NRSV.

SACKCLOTH. A coarse fabric made of goat's hair which was worn to express grief, sorrow, and repentance (Joel 1:8, 13). Jacob wore sackcloth in anguish when he thought his son Joseph was dead (Gen. 37:34). See also *Mourn.*

SACRAMENT. A ritual or religious act which serves as a channel of God's grace. While Roman Catholics and most orthodox churches observe seven sacraments, most Protestants admit only two—baptism and the Lord's Supper —and even these are called "ordinances" by most evangelical groups (see Matt. 3: 13–15).

SACRIFICE. An offering made to God or to false gods for the purpose of gaining favor or showing respect. In O.T. times, animals were sacrificed on the altar to atone for transgression against God and His law (Deut. 18:3). Christ offered Himself as the final and perfect sacrifice for our sins (Heb. 9:9–14). See also *Atonement; Burnt Offering; Redeem.*

SACRILEGE. See *Blasphemy.*

SADDUCEES. A priestly aristocratic party of N.T. times which—in contrast to the Pharisees—rejected the oral traditions of the Jewish faith and accepted only the original teachings of Moses as authoritative. They did not believe in a bodily resurrection (Matt. 22: 23) or angels and spirits (Acts 23:8). They often opposed Jesus and His teachings (Matt. 16:6, 12). See also *Pharisees.*

SAFFRON. A plant used in perfume, dyes, and medicines and for flavoring food and drinks (Song of Sol. 4:13–14).

SAINT. A N.T. word for a Christian believer set apart for God's service (Rom. 1:7; Heb. 6:10). In the O.T., the word refers to a pious Jew (Ps. 16:3). Spiritual blessings are reserved for the saints of God's kingdom (Col. 1:12). See also *Church; Congregation; People of God.*

SALAMIS. A town on the island of Cyprus where Paul and Barnabas preached during the first missionary journey (Acts 13:4–5).

SALEM. See *Jerusalem.*

SALIM. A place near Aenon west of the Jordan River where John the Baptist baptized (John 3:23).

SALMON. The father of Boaz, Ruth's husband, who is listed as an ancestor of Christ (Matt. 1:4–5).

SALOME. A woman who witnessed the Crucifixion and visited Jesus' tomb after His resurrection (Mark 15:40; 16:1). She may have been the mother of Jesus' disciples James and John.

SALT. A mineral used to season and preserve food. Jesus called His followers the "salt of the earth" but warned that compromise would diminish their witness (Matt. 5:13; Luke 14:34–35).

SALT, CITY OF. A city in the wilderness of Judah near the Dead Sea, or "Salt Sea" (Josh. 15:62).

SALT SEA. See *Dead Sea.*

SALT, VALLEY OF. A valley with heavy salt deposits near the Dead Sea where King David and King Amaziah were victorious in battle (2 Sam. 8:13; 2 Kings 14:7–8).

SALUTATION. An elaborate greeting, usually involving repeated bowing and embracing (Luke 15:20). Perhaps because of the urgency of their message, Jesus advised His disciples whom He sent out to "salute no man by the way" (Luke 10:4).

SALVATION. The total work of God in delivering us from sin and reconciling us to Himself. The apostle Peter declared that salvation is found in Christ alone (Acts 4:12). See also *New Birth; Regeneration.*

SAMARIA. The capital city of Israel, or the Northern Kingdom, and a name often applied to the surrounding region. The city was built by Omri, king of

Israel, about 900 B.C. It was destroyed about 722 B.C. when the Assyrians overran the Northern Kingdom (2 Kings 17:3–24). See also *Omri.*

SAMARITAN. An inhabitant of the district of Samaria between Judea and Galilee. These people were considered inferior by the Jews because of their mixed-blood ancestry going back to their intermarriage with foreign colonists placed here by the Assyrians (2 Kings 17:3–24). Jesus, however, associated with Samaritans (Luke 9:52; John 4:4–30) and even used a kindhearted Samaritan as an example of a good neighbor (Luke 10:29–37).

SAMECH. The fifteenth letter of the Hebrew alphabet, used as a heading over Ps. 119:113–120.

SAMGAR-NEBO. A prince of the family of Nebuchadnezzar of Babylonia who sat in the middle gate of Jerusalem while the city was being captured (Jer. 39:3).

SAMOS. An island of Greece off the coast of Lydia visited by the apostle Paul (Acts 20:15).

SAMOTHRACIA (SAMO-THRACE). An island in the Aegean Sea visited by Paul on his way to Macedonia (Acts 16:11). *Samothrace:* NIV, NRSV.

SAMSON. A judge of Israel set apart as a Nazarite before his birth. Samson had great physical strength, which he used effectively against the Philistines, as long as he was faithful to his vows. But his strength failed when he revealed his secret to Delilah, who cut his hair and turned him over to his enemies. Samson died, along with his captors, when he destroyed the pagan Philistine temple at Gaza (see Judg. 14–16). See also *Nazarite.*

SAMUEL/SHEMUEL. A prophet and the last judge of Israel who anointed the first two kings of Judah—Saul (1 Sam. 10:1) and David (1 Sam. 16:1–13). Samuel was dedicated to God's service by his mother Hannah even before his birth (1 Sam. 1:11–22), and he grew up under the tutelage of Eli the priest to prepare for priestly service (1 Sam. 3:1–20). A popular leader, he was mourned by the entire nation at his death (1 Sam. 25:1). *Shemuel:* 1 Chron. 6:33. See also *Hannah.*

SAMUEL, BOOKS OF. Two historical books of the O.T. named for the prophet Samuel, who anointed Saul and David as the first two kings of Israel. Their anointing marked the transition of the nation from a loose confederacy of tribes to a united kingdom under the leadership of a king.

Major events covered by these books include: (1) Samuel's rule as the last judge of Israel (1 Sam. 1:1–7:17); (2) King Saul's reign (1 Sam. 8:1–15:9); (3) the rivalry between Saul and David (1 Sam. 15:10–31:13); and (4) the accession of David to the throne; his military triumphs, shortcomings, and troubles (2 Sam.). Some of the information about David's administration in 2 Samuel is repeated in the book of 1 Chronicles. See also *Chronicles, Books of; David; Samuel; Saul.*

SANBALLAT. An influential Samaritan who plotted to kill Nehemiah to stop his rebuilding projects and reform projects in Jerusalem (Neh. 4:7–8; 6:1–4). See also *Tobiah.*

SANCTIFICATION. The process of consecrating or setting something apart for holy purposes. In the O.T., priests, Levites, and each family's firstborn child were consecrated to the Lord. In the N.T., sanctification was regarded as a work of grace following conversion (Phil. 1:6). God calls all believers to holiness and sanctification (1 Thess. 4:3, 7). Those sanctified are committed to God's truth and serve as witnesses to His power and grace in the world (Rom. 6:11–13). See also *Consecration.*

SANCTUARY. A holy place (Lev. 4:6), a place of public worship (Ps. 73:17), or a place of refuge where a person is safe under God's protection (Ezek. 11:16).

SAND. Fine, granular soil, which is seldom found in Palestine except along the seashore. The word is used figuratively for countless numbers or multitudes (Gen. 32:12).

SANDALS. Footwear, consisting of leather or wood bound to the feet with straps. They were removed before entering a house or holy place (Josh. 5:15; Luke 15:22). See also *Latchet.*

SANHEDRIN. See *Council.*

SAPPHIRA. An early believer at Jerusalem who was struck dead for lying and withholding money she had pledged to the church's common treasury (Acts 5:1–11). See also *Ananias.*

SAPPHIRE. A light blue gem or precious stone used in the breastplate of the high priest (Exod. 28:18) and in the foundation of New Jerusalem (Rev. 21:19).

SARAH/SARA/SARAI. A wife of Abraham and the mother of Isaac (Gen. 11:29; Rom. 9:9), also called *Sarai.* Although she was barren for many years, Sarah received God's promise that she would be "a mother of nations" (Gen. 17:15–16), and she bore Isaac past the age of ninety (Gen. 17:17–21; 21:2–3). She is commended in the N.T. for her faith and obedience (Heb. 11:11; *Sara:* Greek form). See also *Abraham.*

SARDINE (CARNELIAN). A precious stone (Rev. 4:3). *Carnelian:* NIV, NRSV. Probably the same as the sardius. See *Sardius.*

SARDIS. The chief city of Lydia in Asia Minor and site of one of the seven churches of Asia Minor. This church was characterized as "dead" (Rev. 3:1–5).

SARDIUS (CARNELIAN). A precious stone of blood-red color used in the high priest's breastplate (Exod. 28:17) and in the foundation of New Jerusalem (Rev. 21:20). *Carnelian:* NIV; NRSV.

SARDONYX (ONYX). A precious stone which combines the qualities of sardius and onyx, thus its name *sardonyx.* It was used in the foundation of New Jerusalem (Rev. 21:20). *Onyx:* NRSV. See also *Onyx; Sardius.*

SAREPTA. See *Zarephath.*

SARGON. The king of Assyria (reigned about 722–705 B.C.) who completed the siege of Samaria and carried the Northern King-dom into captivity (Isa. 20:1). See also *Assyria.*

SARON. See *Sharon.*

SATAN. An evil being who opposes God; the devil. In the Garden of Eden, Satan was represented as a serpent, who tempted Eve (Gen. 3:1–6). He falsely accused and harassed Job (Job 1:6–12). Jesus regarded Satan as a person (Matt. 4:1–10), whom He described as a murderer and the father of lies (John 8:44). While he is called "the prince of this world" (John 16:11), Satan is subject to God's greater power (1 John 4:4) and will be cast into the bottomless pit (Rev. 20:1–3). See also *Belial; Lucifer.*

SATRAP. NIV, NRSV word for the governor of a province in the ancient Persian Empire

(Dan. 6:1). *Prince:* KJV. See also *Governor; Lieutenant.*

SATYR (GOAT-DEMON). A Greek mythological figure which was an object of idolatrous worship (2 Chron. 11:15). The word also describes wild animals which would dance among the ruins of Babylon (Isa. 13:21). *Goat-demon:* NRSV.

SAUL.
1. The first king of Israel who displeased God by his disobedience and his insane jealousy against David. Anointed privately by Samuel (1 Sam. 10:1) and publicly proclaimed king at Gilgal (1 Sam. 11:15), he waged war against the Philistines during his administration (1 Sam. 17–18). He kept the spoils of war from at least one battle, assumed duties of the priestly office, and murdered Ahimelech and eighty-four other priests (1 Sam. 22:14–19)—acts which brought God's judgment. After his sons were killed, Saul committed suicide rather than be captured by the Philistines (1 Sam. 31:1–6).
2. The original name of Paul the Apostle. See *Paul.*

SAVIOR. A title for Christ which emphasizes His work of salvation (Matt. 1:20–21)—a ministry foretold by the prophet Isaiah (Isa. 61:1–3).

SAW. A tool with sharp teeth used in building the temple in Jerusalem and sometimes used to execute prisoners of war (2 Sam. 12:31).

SCAB. A sore on the skin; or a hardened, scaly spot left by a skin disease (Lev. 13:2, 6, 7–8).

SCABBARD. See *Sheath.*

SCALES. See *Balance, Balances.*

SCALL (ITCH). An inflammation of the scalp (Lev. 13:30–37). *Itch:* NIV, NRSV.

SCAPEGOAT (AZAZEL). A goat, symbolically bearing the sins of the people, sent into the wilderness by the high priest on the Day of Atonement (Lev. 16:8–22). *Azazel:* NRSV. This goat is a symbol of Christ, our sin bearer (see Isa. 53:6).

SCARF. See *Muffler.*

SCARLET (CRIMSON). A red color highly prized as a symbol of wealth and position (2 Sam. 1:24). *Crimson:* NRSV. Its brilliance symbolized Israel's glaring sin against God (Isa. 1:18).

SCENTED WOOD. See *Thyine Wood*.

SCEPTER. A staff or baton carried by a king or other high official as an emblem of authority (Esther 4:11).

SCEVA. Jewish priest at Ephesus whose sons tried in vain to cast out evil spirits in imitation of Paul (Acts 19:11–16).

SCHIN. The twenty-first letter of the Hebrew alphabet, used as a heading over Ps. 119:161–168.

SCHOOLMASTER (DISCIPLINARIAN). A household servant who accompanied children to school but did not function as a teacher. Paul used the word to show the shortcomings of the law. It could make a person aware of sin, but it fell short of providing salvation (Gal. 3:24–25). *Disciplinarian:* NRSV.

SCORN. Contempt and ridicule (Ps. 1:1). Scorners were regarded as foolish and wicked (Prov. 1:22).

SCORPION. An eight-legged insect with a poisonous tail (Deut. 8:15). The word is also used symbolically of a whip for scourging (2 Chron. 10:11–14). See also *Scourging*.

SCOURGING (FLOGGING). A severe beating with a leather strap containing bits of sharp metal. This punishment was limited to forty lashes (Deut. 25:3). Jesus was scourged before His crucifixion (Matt. 27:26). *Flogged:* NIV, NRSV.

SCREECH OWL. A bird noted for its strange cries at night (Isa. 34:14). See also *Bittern; Night Hawk*.

SCRIBE (TEACHER OF THE LAW). A public secretary who specialized in copying the law, in the days when documents had to be laboriously reproduced by hand. Many scribes became interpreters and teachers, and in N.T. times they were committed to preserving the law. Their burdensome technicalities brought Jesus' condemnation (Matt. 5:20). *Teacher of the law:* NIV. See also *Lawyer*.

SCRIBE'S KNIFE. See *Penknife*.

SCRIP (BAG). A small bag or satchel (Matt. 10:10) used for carrying food or other provisions on a journey (Luke 9:3). *Bag:* NIV, NRSV.

SCRIPTURE. See *Bible*.

SCROLL. A piece of papyrus or leather written on and then rolled on a stick. It was unrolled for reading (Rev. 6:14). See also *Roll*.

SCUM. See *Offscouring*.

SCURVY. A skin disease, caused by extended exposure and an unbalanced diet, characterized by dry, scaly skin with bright spots (Lev. 21:20; 22:22).

SCYTHIANS. Members of the nomadic tribes north of the Black Sea and the Caspian Sea. Paul used the word as a general term for barbaric persons (Col. 3:11).

SEA. A large body of salt water. In the O.T., the word is used for any large expanse of water, including rivers and lakes (Gen. 1:10; Isa. 19:5).

SEA GULL. See *Cuckow*.

SEA MONSTER. A giant sea creature of unspecified identity, perhaps a whale or large fish (Lam. 4:3).

SEA OF CHINNEROTH. See *Galilee, Sea of*.

SEA OF GLASS. A clear, crystal sea or lake which appeared to John in a vision, indicating God's purity and holiness and the victory of His redeemed people (Rev. 4:6).

SEA OF THE PLAIN. See *Dead Sea*.

SEA OF TIBERIAS. See *Galilee, Sea of*.

SEAL. See *Signet*.

SEBA. A son of Cush and grandson of Ham (Gen. 10:6–7); the nation made up of Seba's descendants (Ps. 72:10; Isa. 43:3).

SEBAT (SHEBAT). The eleventh month of the Hebrew year (Zech. 1:7). *Shebat:* NIV, NRSV.

SECOND COMING. Christ's return to earth to punish the wicked and unbelieving and to receive glory from believers (2 Thess. 1:9–10). This event will happen suddenly and will be "revealed from heaven with his mighty angels" (2 Thess. 1:7). He will raise the dead (1 Thess 4:13–18), destroy death (1 Cor. 15:25–26), gather the redeemed (Matt. 24:31), judge the world (Matt. 25:32), and reward God's people (Matt. 16:27). Christians should be prepared for His coming (Matt. 24:42) and remain faithful in Christian service (1 Cor. 15:58). See also *Maranatha; Rapture*.

SECRET. See *Mystery*.

SECT. A religious movement in Judaism (Pharisees, Sadducees, Essenes) as well as a political party (Herodians, zealots). Early Christians were regarded as "the sect of the Nazarenes" (Acts 24:5). The word is also applied to early perversions of Christian truth (Gal. 5:20).

SECUNDUS. A Christian who accompanied Paul on his third missionary journey (Acts 20:4).

SEED (OFFSPRING). A person's descendants and thus the means of transmitting life from one generation to another (Gen. 21:12). *Offspring:* NIV, NRSV. Believers in Christ were said to be born of "incorruptible seed" (1 Pet. 1:23) and true heirs of the promise made by God to Abraham (Gal. 3:29). See also *Offspring; Posterity*.

SEER. See *Prophet*.

SEIR, MOUNT. See *Edom, No. 2.*

SEIRATH (SEIRAH). A place in Mt. Ephraim where the judge Ehud hid after assassinating Eglon, king of Moab (Judg. 3:26). *Seirah:* NIV, NRSV.

SELAH. See *Petra*.

SELAH. A musical term in Psalms, possibly calling for a pause or a sudden outburst of voices or instruments (Ps. 44:8).

SELEUCIA. A seaport in Syria from which Paul and Barnabas set sail on the first missionary journey (Acts 13:4).

SELF-CONTROL. See *Sober; Temperance*.

SELF-DENIAL. Voluntary limitation of one's desires, a requirement of Jesus for His followers (Matt. 16:24). Paul also urged Christians to make an offering of themselves to God (Rom. 12:1). Sacrifices for Christ's sake will be rewarded (Luke 18:29–30).

SEM. See *Shem*.

SENIR. See *Hermon, Mount*.

SENNACHERIB. The king of Assyria (reigned about 705–681 B.C.) who captured all fortified cities of Judah except Jerusalem and then demanded tribute from King Hezekiah (2 Kings 18:13–16). Sennacherib was eventually assassinated by his own sons as he worshiped a pagan god (2 Kings 19:37). See also *Assyria*.

SENSIBLE. See *Sober*.

SENTINEL. See *Watchman*.

SEPHARVAIM. A city whose residents, the Sepharvaites, were sent to colonize the Northern Kingdom after Samaria was captured by the Assyrians (2 Kings 17:24–31). See also *Samaritan*.

SEPTUAGINT. The translation of the O.T. from Hebrew into the Greek language about 250 to 150 B.C.—a work accomplished by Jewish scholars who were brought to Alexandria, Egypt, especially for this purpose.

SEPULCHRE (TOMB). A natural cave or a place carved out of rock where bodies were buried (Gen. 23:6–9). *Tomb:* NIV. Some sepulchres were whitened for easy visibility (Matt. 23:27), since contact with a body made a person ceremonially unclean (Num. 19:16). Jesus was buried in a sepulchre or tomb prepared by Joseph of Arimathea (Matt. 27:57–60). See also *Cave; Grave*.

SERAIAH.
1. David's secretary or recorder who served also in Solomon's administration (2 Sam. 8:17). Also called *Sheva* (2 Sam. 20:25), *Shisha* (1 Kings 4:3), and *Shavsha* (1 Chron. 18:16).

2. A prince of Judah who carried Jeremiah's prophecy of doom to the city of Babylon (Jer. 51:59–61).

SERAPHIM (SERAPHS). Six-winged creatures which sang God's praises and also purified Isaiah's lips in his vision in the temple (Isa. 6:1–7). *Seraphs:* NIV, NRSV.

SERGIUS. See *Paulus, Sergius*.

SERMON ON THE MOUNT. Jesus' ethical teachings in Matt. 5–7, delivered to His followers on a hillside near Capernaum. Subjects covered include true happiness (5:2–12); Christian influence (5:14–16); relation of the law and Christian conduct (5:17–48); the practice of charity, prayer, and fasting (6:1–18); God and possessions (6:19–24); freedom from anxiety (6:25–34); judging others (7:1–6); the key to God's blessings (7:7–12); warn-ings about deception (7:13–23); and building life on a secure foundation (7:24–27). See also *Beatitudes*.

SERPENT. A snake. Satan in the form of a serpent tempted Adam and Eve to sin (Gen. 3: 1–5). Poisonous serpents were sent to punish the Israelites for complaining in the wilderness (Num. 21:6).

Moses' upraised serpent symbolized Jesus' future sacrificial death (John 3:14).

SERVANT. One who serves others; any person under the authority of another (Matt. 8:9). Isaiah depicted the coming Messiah as a Suffering Servant (Isa. 53:3–12). Jesus declared His mission was to serve and save (Matt. 20:28; Luke 22:27). See also *Maidservant; Manservant.*

SERVANT GIRL. See *Handmaid.*

SETH/SHETH. The third son of Adam and the father of Enoch (Gen. 4:25–26). *Sheth:* 1 Chron. 1:1.

SETHUR. One of the twelve spies who scouted the land of Canaan, representing the tribe of Asher (Num. 13:13). See also *Spies.*

SEVEN. A number often used symbolically because it was considered a round or perfect number. God's creation established an order of seven days (Gen. 2:2). Seven times or sevenfold suggested abundance (Matt. 18:21–22).

SEVEN CHURCHES OF ASIA. The seven churches in Asia Minor addressed by John in Revelation. The messages to these churches—located at Ephesus, Smyrna, Pergamos, Thyatira, Sardis, Philadelphia, and Laodicea (Rev. 1: 11)—ranged from warnings and rebukes to commendations for their faithfulness (see Rev. 2–3).

SEVEN SAYINGS FROM THE CROSS. The seven separate utterances which Jesus made as He suffered on the cross: (1) "Father, forgive them" (Luke 23:34); (2) "To day shalt thou be with me in paradise" (Luke 23:43); (3) "Woman, behold thy son" (John 19:26); (4) "My God, my God, why hast thou forsaken me?" (Matt. 27:46); (5) "I thirst" (John 19:28); (6) "It is finished" (John 19:30); and (7) "Father, into thy hand I commend my spirit" (Luke 23:46).

SEVEN STARS (PLEIADES). A brilliant cluster of stars named for the seven daughters of Atlas and Pleione in Greek mythology (Amos 5:8). *Pleiades:* NIV, NRSV. See also *Pleiades.*

SEVENTH MONTH FESTIVAL. See *Trumpets, Feast of.*

SEVENTY WEEKS. See *Daniel, Book of.*

SEXUAL IMMORALITY. See *Fornication*.

SHACKLES. See *Fetters; Stocks*.

SHADRACH. The Babylonian name of Hananiah, one of Daniel's friends, who was cast into the fiery furnace but miraculously delivered at God's hand (Dan. 3:1–28). See also *Daniel*.

SHALLUM. See *Jehoahaz*, No. 2.

SHALMANESER. An Assyrian king (reigned about 730–720 B.C.) who defeated Israel, or the Northern Kingdom, and carried its leading citizens into captivity (2 Kings 17:3–6.) See also *Assyria*.

SHAME. Disgrace or disrepute which produces a feeling of guilt. It may be caused by idleness (Prov. 10:5), excessive pride (Prov. 11:2), or evil companions (Prov. 28:7).

SHAMGAR. A judge who delivered Israel from oppression by killing 600 Philistines with an ox goad (Judg. 3:31). See also *Judges of Israel*.

SHAMHUTH. A captain in David's army who commanded 24,000 warriors (1 Chron. 27:8).

SHAMMUA

1. One of the twelve spies who scouted the land of Canaan, representing the tribe of Reuben (Num. 13:4). See also *Spies*.

2. Another name for Shimea, David's son. See *Shimea*.

SHAPHAN. A scribe who helped King Josiah carry out his religious reforms by recording temple contributions and proclaiming the law (2 Kings 22:3–13).

SHAPHAT. One of the twelve spies who scouted the land of Canaan, representing the tribe of Simeon (Num. 13:5). See also *Spies*.

SHARON/SARON. A fertile coastal plain between Joppa and Mt. Carmel along the Mediterranean Sea (1 Chron. 27:29). *Saron:* Acts 9:35.

SHAVEH. See *King's Dale*.

SHAVSHA. See *Seraiah*, No. 1.

SHEARING HOUSE. A place between Jezreel and Samaria where Jehu assassinated the family of King Ahaziah of Judah in order to become king (2 Kings 10:12–14).

SHEAR-JASHUB. A symbolic name, meaning "a remnant

shall return," given by Isaiah to his son to show God's promise to His people after their period of exile (Isa. 7:3–4).

SHEATH (SCABBARD). A carrying case for a dagger or sword (1 Sam. 17:51). *Scabbard:* NIV (John 18:11).

SHEBA. See *Sabeans*.

SHEBAT. See *Sebat*.

SHEBNA. A treasurer under King Hezekiah who made a sepulchre for himself. Isaiah predicted Shebna would die in exile (Isa. 22:15–19).

SHECHEM.
1. A tribal prince who was killed by Simeon and Levi for seducing their sister, Dinah (Gen. 34:1–29).
2. A city of refuge on a trade route in the territory of Ephraim (Josh. 20:7). *Sichem:* Gen. 12:6. *Sychem:* Acts 7:16. See also *Cities of Refuge*.

SHECHINAH. See *Shekinah*.

SHEEP. A domesticated animal prized for the food and fleece which it provided, and also used as a sacrificial offering (Lev. 9:2–4; 12:6). Large flocks of sheep were a sign of wealth (Job 1:3). Jesus spoke of straying sheep as a symbol of lost or sinful persons (Luke 15: 4–6). See also *Fleece; Lamb; Wool*.

SHEEP GATE. A gate in the wall of Jerusalem repaired under Nehemiah's leadership (Neh. 3:1, 32).

SHEEPFOLD. A strong enclosure which provided protection for sheep. Jesus is the Good Shepherd who protects His sheep (John 10:1–11).

SHEKEL. A Jewish coin or unit of measure. The silver shekel was worth about sixty cents; the gold shekel about eight dollars (Gen. 23:15; Neh. 10:32; Jer. 32:9).

SHEKELS OF SILVER. See *Silverlings*.

SHEKINAH. A visible manifestation of God's glory, usually as a bright light, fire, or cloud (Exod. 13:21; Matt. 17:5).

SHELTER. See *Pavilion*.

SHEM/SEM. The oldest son of Noah who was preserved in the ark (Gen. 5:32). Shem was the father of Elam, Asshur, Arphaxad, Lud, and Aram—ancestors of the Semitic nations known as the Jews, Arameans, Persians, Assyrians, and Arabians (Gen. 10:22). *Sem:* Greek form (Luke 3:36).

SHEMA, THE. The noted confession of faith quoted by faithful Jews each day: "Hear, O Israel: The Lord our God is one Lord" (Deut. 6:4–9). The complete Shema also includes Num. 15:37–41 and Deut. 11:13–21.

SHEMAIAH. Prophet of Judah who warned King Rehoboam not to attack Israel (1 Kings 12:22–24). He revealed that Pharaoh Shishak of Egypt was being used by the Lord to punish Judah for her sins (2 Chron. 12:5–9).

SHEMER. The landowner who sold King Omri of the Northern Kingdom a hill on which the capital city of Samaria was built (1 Kings 16:24). His name is reflected in the city's name.

SHEMINITH. A musical term appearing in the titles of Pss. 6 and 12 and 1 Chron. 15: 21. It may designate the manner of singing or the instrument to be used.

SHEMUEL.
1. Another name for Samuel the prophet. See *Samuel*.
2. A leader of the tribe of Simeon, appointed by Moses to help divide the land of Canaan

after its occupation by the Israelites (Num. 34:20).

SHENIR. See *Hermon, Mount*.

SHEOL. See *Hell*.

SHEPHATIAH. A son of David, born at Hebron to his wife Abital (2 Sam. 3:4).

SHEPHERD. A person who tends sheep, an honorable but dangerous vocation among the Jews (Gen. 31:38–40). The word is also used of ministers and of Christ, who referred to Himself as the "Good Shepherd" (John 10:11, 14). See also *Minister; Pastor*.

SHESHACH. See *Babylonia*.

SHESHAI. A descendant of Anak driven out of Hebron by Caleb and killed in battle (Judg. 1:10).

SHESH-BAZZAR. See *Zerubbabel*.

SHETH. See *Seth*.

SHEVA. See *Seraiah*, No. 1.

SHEWBREAD (BREAD OF THE PRESENCE). Unleavened bread kept in the temple or tabernacle for ceremonial purposes. Its name indicated it was exhibited in the presence of the Lord (Num. 4:7). *Bread of the Presence:* NRSV.

SHIBBOLETH. A password used to distinguish Ephraimites from Gileadites in battle. Unable to pronounce the first "h" in shibboleth, 42,000 Ephraimites were killed by the Gileadites (Judg. 12:5–6).

SHIELD. A piece of armor, made of wood and covered with hide or metal, and carried in battle for protection (1 Chron. 18:7). See also *Buckler*.

SHIGGAION. A musical term in the title of Ps. 7, possibly referring to an increased tempo for singing.

SHIHOR-LIBNATH. A brook that served as the southwestern boundary of the territory of Asher (Josh. 19:26).

SHILOAH. See *Siloam*.

SHILOH.
1. A town in the territory of Ephraim where the Philistines defeated the Israelites and captured the ark of the covenant (1 Sam. 4:3–11).
2. A title of the coming Messiah which identified Him as a descendant of Judah (Gen. 49:10).

SHIMEA/SHAMMUAH (SHAMMUA). A son of David and Bath-sheba, born at Jerusalem (1 Chron. 3:5). *Shammua:* NIV. *Shammuah:* 2 Sam. 5:14.

SHIMEI. A Benjamite who insulted David when he was fleeing from Absalom (2 Sam. 16:5–13). Pardoned by David, he was later executed by Solomon (1 Kings 2:36–46).

SHIMRON-MERON/SHIMRON. A town in upper Galilee conquered by Joshua (Josh. 12:20). *Shimron:* Josh. 11:1; 19:15.

SHINAR. See *Babylonia*.

SHIP. A seagoing vessel propelled by oars or sails (Jon. 1:4–5). The Jews were not mariners, since most of the Mediterranean coast was controlled by the Phoenicians and Phili-stines. Solomon's fleet was manned by Phoenicians (1 Kings 9:26–28). See also *Mariner*.

SHISHA. See *Seraiah,* No. 1.

SHISHAK. See *Pharaoh,* No. 1.

SHITTAH (ACACIA). A tree which produced lumber used in building the ark of the covenant and furnishing the tabernacle (Exod. 25:10–16; 30:1; Isa. 41:19). *Acacia:* NIV, NRSV.

SHITTIM.
1. The last campsite of the Israelites before they entered the land of Canaan. It was located across from Jericho in Moab on the eastern side of the Jordan River (Num. 25:1).
2. The wood or lumber produced from the shittah tree. See *Shittah*.

SHOA. A tribal enemy of the Jews. The prophet Ezekiel predicted these people would invade Judah (Ezek. 23:23–25).

SHOBAB. A son of David and Bath-sheba, born in Jerusalem after David became king (1 Chron. 3:5).

SHOBACH/SHOPHACH. A commander of the Syrian army who was killed in a battle with David's forces (2 Sam. 10:16 –18). *Shophach:* 1 Chron. 19:16.

SHOBI. An Ammonite who brought provisions to David at Mahanaim when he fled from Absalom (2 Sam. 17:27–29).

SHOE. See *Sandals*.

SHOOT. See *Rod*.

SHOPHACH. See *Shobach*.

SHOSHANNIM. A musical term, meaning "lilies," in the titles of Pss. 45, 69, and 80, possibly indicating the pitch or tune to which these psalms were to be sung.

SHOULDER. To drop the shoulder signified servitude (Gen. 49:15); to withdraw it denoted rebellion (Neh. 9:29); to put a responsibility upon a person's shoulder was to entrust it to his keeping (Isa. 9:6).

SHOVEL. A tool used by priests to remove ashes from the altar (Exod. 27:3). The word sometimes refers to a winnowing fork or fan (Isa. 30:24). See also *Fan*.

SHRINE. A miniature replica of the temple where the pagan goddess Diana was worshiped, placed in homes as objects of devotion. The silversmiths of Ephesus earned their livelihood by making and selling these trinkets (Acts 19:24). See also *Demetrius,* No. 1.

SHUAH. A son of Abraham by Keturah (Gen. 25:1–2).

SHUHITE. A member of an Arabic tribe which descended from Shuah, son of Abraham and Keturah. Job's friend Bildad was a Shuhite (Job 2:11).

SHULAMITE (SHULAM-MITE). A native of Shulam; the beloved or cherished one in Solomon's song (Song of Sol. 6:13). *Shulammite:* NIV, NRSV.

SHUNAMMITE. A woman from Shunem who provided food and lodging for Elisha. The prophet restored her son to life (2 Kings 4:8–37).

SHUR. A wilderness in southern Palestine (Gen. 16:7) where the Hebrew people wandered for three days after passing through the Red Sea (Exod. 15:22).

SHUSHAN/SUSA. A wealthy and powerful city where Persian kings lived and where Esther interceded for her people (Esther 1:2). *Susa:* NIV, NRSV.

SHUTTLE. A weaving device that shoots the thread rapidly from one side of the cloth to the other between threads of the warp. The word is used as a symbol of fleeting time (Job 7:6). See also *Warp; Weaver*.

SIBBOLETH. See *Shibboleth*.

SICHEM. See *Shechem,* No. 2.

SICKLE. A tool for cutting or harvesting grain (Deut. 16:9). The word is also used as a symbol of God's coming judgment (Rev. 14:14–19).

SIDON/ZIDON. A Canaanite city about twenty miles north of Tyre, founded by Sidon, the oldest son of Canaan (Gen. 10:15). Noted for its shipbuilding (Ezek. 27:8), silverware, and dyed fabrics, Sidon was often rebuked by the prophets for its idolatry (Isa. 23:4; Ezek. 28:21). Jesus ministered in this city (Matt. 15:21, 28). *Zidon:* Josh. 11:8.

SIEGE. An extended military assault and blockade against a walled city. King Sennacherib of Assyria besieged Jerusalem and other fortified cities of Judah (Isa. 36:1). See also *City; Fenced City*.

SIEVE. Cooking utensil for sifting flour or meal. Early sieves were made of bulrushes, horsehair, or papyrus (Amos 9:9).

SIGN. An event foretelling future happenings or a miracle confirming a person's faith (John 4:48). Jesus warned the wicked to heed the sign of Jonah's deliverance from the whale (Matt. 16:1–4). Jesus foretold signs of His return

(Matt. 24:3, 29–31). See also *Miracle; Token*.

SIGNET. An official or royal seal, used like a signature to legalize documents (Jer. 22:24).

SIHON. An Amorite king who refused to allow the Israelites to pass through his territory on their way to Canaan, only to be defeated by Moses (Num. 21:21–30).

SILAS/SILVANUS. A leader in the Jerusalem church who accompanied Paul on the second missionary journey and who was imprisoned with him at Philippi (Acts 15:40–41; 16:19, 23). He was also with Paul at Corinth and Thessalonica (2 Cor. 1:19). *Silvanus:* 2 Thess. 1:1.

SILK. A cloth derived from the silkworm (Rev. 18:12).

SILOAM/SHILOAH/SILOAH. A reservoir in Jerusalem supplied with water through King Hezekiah's underground tunnel from a spring outside the city (2 Kings 20:20). Jesus commanded a blind man to wash in the Pool of Siloam for healing (John 9:6–7). *Shiloah:* Isa. 8:6; *Siloah:* Neh. 3:15. See also *Hezekiah; Pool*.

SILVER. A precious metal used in utensils and jewelry (Gen. 44:2). First mentioned in the days of Abraham (Gen. 13:2), silver was used as a medium of exchange and was valued by weight (Ezek. 27:12).

SILVERLINGS (SILVER SHEKELS, SHEKELS OF SILVER). Bits of silver used like money as a medium of exchange (Isa. 7:23). *Silver shekels:* NIV; *Shekels of silver:* NRSV.

SILVERSMITH. A craftsman who formed silver into valuable objects. The Ephesian silversmiths made models of the temple of Diana (Acts 19:24–29). See also *Finer*.

SIMEON.
1. A son of Jacob by Leah (Gen. 29:33) and ancestor of one of the twelve tribes of Israel (Gen. 46:10). He was held hostage by Joseph to assure Benjamin's safe arrival in Egypt (Gen. 42:24, 36). See also *Tribes of Israel*.
2. A righteous man who blessed the child Jesus in the temple at Jerusalem (Luke 2:25–35).
3. A Christian prophet at Antioch associated with Paul and Barnabas (Acts 13:1). He was also called *Niger*.

SIMON.

1. Simon Peter, one of the twelve apostles or disciples of Christ and the leader of the church in Jerusalem after the resurrection and ascension of Jesus. A fisherman from Galilee, Peter followed Jesus after he was encouraged to do so by his brother Andrew (John 1:40–41). He was called *Cephas* by Jesus, a name meaning "stone" (John 1:42), perhaps indicating the promise which Jesus saw in him in spite of his reckless temperament and impetuous personality. Peter swore he would never forsake Christ, but he denied Him three times on the night before His crucifixion (Matt. 26:69–75). He went on to become a bold spokesman for Christ in the early years of the Christian movement (Acts 2:14–40). Peter's surname was *Bar-jona* (Matt. 16:17). *Son of Jonah:* NIV, NRSV. See also *Twelve, The.*

2. Another of the twelve apostles or disciples of Jesus, called Simon Zelotes (Luke 6:15) or Simon the Canaanite (Matt. 10:4) to distinguish him from Simon Peter. He may have been a zealot, a Jew fanatically opposed to Roman rule. See also *Canaanites,* No. 2; *Twelve, The; Zelotes.*

3. A magician or sorcerer condemned by the apostle Peter because he tried to buy the power of the Holy Spirit (Acts 8:18–21).

4. A tanner at Joppa and apparently a friend with whom the apostle Peter lodged (Acts 9:43; 10:6, 17, 32).

SIN.

Rebellion against God. Adam and Eve's disobedience in the Garden of Eden resulted in the introduction of sin into the human race (Rom. 5:12–14). Sin is committed against three parties: ourselves (Prov. 8:36), others (Rom. 5:12), and God (Ps. 51:4; 1 Cor. 8:12). Sin is described as transgression (Matt. 15:3), perversion of the right (1 John 5:17), disobedience (Rom. 5:19), rebellion (Isa. 1:2), and lawlessness (1 John 3:4). The consequence of unforgiven sin is spiritual death, but God's gift to the believer is eternal life through Jesus Christ (Rom. 6:23). See also *Evil; Iniquity.*

SIN OFFERING.

An offering of a sacrificial animal presented to God to gain forgiveness for sins, particularly those committed unintentionally or in ignorance (Lev. 4:2–3). A sin offering for all the people was made once a year by the high priest on the Day of Atonement (Lev. 16:6, 15). See also *Atonement, Day of; Sacrifice.*

SIN, WILDERNESS OF. A wilderness region between the Red Sea and Sinai where manna and quail were miraculously provided for the Israelites by the Lord (Exod. 16:1–8).

SINAI/SINA/HOREB. Mountain peak more than one mile high in the wilderness of Sinai where Moses tended sheep and saw the burning bush with God's call to deliver His people (Exod. 3:1–6). *Horeb:* KJV, NIV, NRSV. Later it was the site where Moses received the Ten Commandments and other parts of the law from God (Exod. 19–23). *Sina:* Greek form (Acts 7:30).

SINEW. A muscle along the thigh by which muscles are attached to bones (Job 10:11). Because of Jacob's thigh injury, Israelites avoided eating the sinew of the thigh (Gen. 32:25–32). See also *Thigh.*

SINIM (ASWAN, SYENE). An unidentified country or region—perhaps China, Egypt, or the wilderness of Sin—from which Jewish exiles would return (Isa. 49:12). *Aswan:* NIV; *Syene:* NRSV.

SINITES. Members of a tribe descended from Canaan who settled in northern Phoenicia (Gen. 10:17; 1 Chron. 1:15). They were perhaps inhabitants of Sin, a city near Mt. Lebanon.

SION. See *Zion.*

SIPHMOTH. A place in southern Judah where David hid from King Saul during his days as a fugitive (1 Sam. 30:26–28).

SIRION. See *Hermon, Mount.*

SISERA. A Canaanite commander killed by Jael, who drove a tent peg through his head while he slept (Judg. 4:2–22). See also *Deborah; Jael.*

SISTER. A general term for any near female relative, including a stepsister or half sister (2 Sam. 13:2; Matt. 13:56). The word is also used to denote members of the same spiritual family (Rom. 16:1).

SITNAH. The second well dug by Isaac near the Philistine city of Gerar after a dispute with herdsmen over water rights (Gen. 26:21).

SIVAN. The third month of the Hebrew year (Esther 8:9), corresponding closely to our June.

SKULL, THE. See *Calvary.*

SLANDER. A deceitful and destructive statement against another (Ps. 52:2). Such statements are uttered by the wicked against the righteous (Job 1: 9–11) and believers (1 Pet. 2:12).

SLANDERER. See *Reviler*.

SLAVE. A person who had been bought as a piece of property and pressed into service by his or her owners. Slavery was common in Bible times, but Christian teachings brought some moderation of the practice (Eph. 6:5–9). Paul appealed to Philemon to receive his runaway slave Onesimus as a brother in the faith (Philem. 15–18).

SLAVEMASTERS. See *Taskmasters*.

SLAYER. See *Manslayer*.

SLIME (TAR, BITUMEN). A tarlike substance, possibly bitumen or mortar, used in building the tower of Babel (Gen. 11:3). It was used as mortar for bricks and waterproofing (Exod. 2:3). *Tar:* NIV; *Bitumen:* NRSV. See also *Pitch*.

SLING. Weapon made of leather thongs and used to throw stones (Judg. 20:16).

David killed Goliath with a sling (1 Sam. 17:50).

SLUG. See *Snail*.

SLUGGARD. A lazy, inactive person. This habitual idleness will lead to poverty (Prov. 13:4; 20:4). Paul declared that those who won't work shouldn't eat (2 Thess. 3:10). See also *Idleness*.

SMITH. A metal worker who fabricated tools, weapons, and ornamental objects. Tubal-cain is the first smith mentioned in the Bible (Gen. 4:22). See also *Finer*.

SMYRNA. A city of Ionia about sixty miles north of Ephesus where one of the seven churches of Asia Minor was located (Rev. 1:11). The Lord encouraged this church, which was being persecuted by the "synagogue of Satan" (Rev. 2:8–11).

SNAIL (SLUG). A creature with a spiral shell which leaves a trail of slime. The psalmist expressed hope that his enemies would "melt away" even as a snail shrinks after depositing its slime (Ps. 58:7–8). *Slug:* NIV.

SNARE (NOOSE). A trap or net for catching animals. The word is used figuratively for

301

the pitfalls of the wicked (Job 18:10) *Noose:* NIV. It also represents calamity or death (2 Sam. 22:6).

SNOW. Frozen precipitation. One snowfall is recorded in the Bible (2 Sam. 23:20). The word is used figuratively of winter (Prov. 31:21) and moral purity (Matt. 28:3).

SNUFFER, SNUFFDISH. Two separate tools for ceremonial use, one for trimming the wicks of lamps in the tabernacle and the other for carrying away the trimmings (Exod. 25:38). See also *Tongs*.

SO. See *Pharaoh,* No. 2.

SOAP. See *Sope*.

SOBER (SENSIBLE, TEMPERATE, SELF-CONTROLLED). Moderation or seriousness, a quality desired in church leaders (1 Tim. 3:2). *Sensible:* NRSV (1 Tim. 3:11). *Temperate:* NIV, NRSV. This is an appropriate attitude for believers as we await the Lord's return (1 Thess. 5: 5–6). *Self-controlled:* NIV.

SODA. See *Nitre*.

SODOM/SODOMA. One of five cities destroyed by God because of its wickedness (Gen. 19:1–28). It is often mentioned in the Bible as a symbol of evil and as a warning to sinners (Isa. 1:9; Rev. 11:8). *Sodoma:* Greek form (Rom. 9:29). See also *Cities of the Plain; Gomorrah.*

SODOMITE (TEMPLE PROSTITUTE). A man who engaged in sexual activities with other men—a perversion condemned by God (Deut. 23:17–18). *Temple prostitute:* NRSV.

SOJOURNER. A person who lived temporarily in a foreign country (Heb. 11:9). Abraham sojourned in Egypt (Gen. 12:10) as did the Jews in captivity and exile (Ezra 1:4). The word is also used symbolically of Christians in the world (1 Pet. 1:17). See also *Alien; Foreigner.*

SOLDIER. A person engaged in military service (Num. 1:3). The concept is also used figuratively of Christian workers (Eph. 6:11–18).

SOLEMN ASSEMBLY. A religious gathering, usually occurring during a major Jewish festival, which was devoted to repentance, confession, and prayer (Lev. 23:36; Deut. 16:8).

SOLOMON. David's son and successor as king of Israel (reigned about 970–930 B.C.). Solomon got off to a good start by praying for divine wisdom and insight (1 Kings 3), and he developed fame as a wise and efficient king of great wealth (1 Kings 4:1–28). At God's command, he completed the building of the temple in Jerusalem (1 Kings 5–8). But he drifted away from commitment to the one true God through his marriages with pagan wives (1 Kings 11:1–8). He also oppressed his people with burdensome taxes to support his ambitious kingdom-building projects (1 Kings 12:4).

After Solomon's death, the ten northern tribes rebelled under Jeroboam and formed their own nation known as Israel, or the Northern Kingdom (1 Kings 12:1–19).

SOLOMON, POOLS OF. Water reservoirs built by King Solomon near Bethlehem to supply water for Jerusalem through a system of underground passages (Eccles. 2:6).

SOLOMON'S PORCH (SOLOMON'S COLONNADE, SOLOMON'S PORTICO). A porch on the eastern side of the temple in Jerusalem which featured a double row of elaborate columns about forty feet high (Acts 3:11). *Solomon's Colonnade:* NIV; *Solomon's Portico:* NRSV. Jesus entered the temple by Solomon's porch (John 10:23).

SOLOMON'S SERVANTS. Canaanites enslaved by Solomon and forced to work on the temple and other building projects (1 Kings 5:17–18).

SON. A male descendant. The birth of a son brought joy and celebration, since a family's heritage and traditions were passed on through its sons (Gen. 21:2).

SON OF GOD. A title of Christ which emphasizes His deity. An angel revealed to Mary that she would give birth to the "Son of God" (Luke 1:35). After Jesus was baptized, a voice from heaven declared, "This is my beloved Son" (Matt. 3:17). John's Gospel was written specifically to encourage belief in the Son of God (John 20:31). See also *Emmanuel; Jesus Christ; Messiah.*

SON OF MAN. A title of Christ, used often by Jesus Himself, which emphasized His humanity and Messiahship. This title was probably inspired by Daniel's prophecy of God's messenger who would come on a mission of redemption (Dan. 7:13–14). See also *Messiah*.

SONG OF SOLOMON. A short book of the O.T. filled with expressions of affection between two lovers (see 1:13; 4:1–11; 7:2–10). These words have been interpreted both sym-bolically and literally. Some insist the song symbolizes God's love for His people Israel, while others believe the book is a healthy affirmation of the joys of physical love between husband and wife. Most scholars believe Solomon wrote the book, since he is mentioned several times in the poems (1:1, 5; 3:7, 9, 11; 8:11–12). See also *Solomon*.

SOOTHSAYER (DIVINER). A fortune-teller who claimed to have the power to foretell future events (Josh. 13:22), reveal secrets (Dan. 2:27) and inter-pret dreams (Dan. 4:7). *Diviner:* NIV, NRSV. Paul and Silas healed a soothsayer in Philippi who was being exploited. See also *Enchanter; Medium*.

SOP. A small portion of food or bread, held in the hand in accordance with Palestinian dining customs, and used to soak up liquid foods, such as soup (John 13:26–30).

SOPATER. A Christian who accompanied Paul on the third missionary journey (Acts 20:4). This may be the same person as Sosipater (Rom. 16:21). See *Sosipater*.

SOPE (SOAP). An alkaline substance used for bathing and for purifying metals. Jeremiah indicated sope would clean externally but could not remove sin or iniquity (Jer. 2:22). *Soap:* NIV, NRSV.

SORCERY (MAGIC). The exercise of power received from evil or departed spirits to gain hidden knowledge (Exod. 7:11; Acts 8:9–24). *Magic:* NRSV. The practice of sorcery and witchcraft was specifically pro-hibited by God (Lev. 19:31). See also *Magic; Witchcraft*.

SOREK. A valley between Jerusalem and Ashdod; the home of Delilah, who betrayed Samson (Judg. 16:4).

SORROW. Grief or sadness, which may be caused by sin (Gen. 3:16–17), the death of a loved one (John 11:33–35), or persecution (Esther 9:22). The Christian's eternal hope is a source of comfort in times of sorrow (1 Thess. 4:13, 18). See also *Mourn*.

SOSIPATER. A kinsman of Paul whose greetings were sent to the church at Rome (Rom. 16:21). This may be the same person as Sopater (Acts 20:4). See *Sopater*.

SOSTHENES. A ruler of the synagogue at Corinth who was beaten by a mob when Paul was arrested for preaching there (Acts 18:17). This may be the same person as the believer greeted by Paul in 1 Cor. 1:1.

SOUL. The part of man's inner nature which is the seat of our appetites, passions, and sensations. Sometimes the word *soul* means "person" (Rom. 13:1). See also *Spirit*.

SOUR WINE. See *Vinegar*.

SOUTH COUNTRY (NEGEV, NEGEB). A hilly, wilderness region in southern Palestine around the Dead Sea. This region is also called "the South" and "the land of the South" (Judg. 1:16). *Negev:* NIV; *Negeb:* NRSV.

SOUTH RAMOTH. A place bordering the desert in southern Judah where David hid when fleeing from King Saul (1 Sam. 30:26–27).

SOVEREIGN. See *Potentate*.

SOVEREIGNTY OF GOD. A theological phrase which expresses the truth that God is in control of the universe. God's creation of man and the world implies His continuing rule and sovereignty (Gen. 1:1; Ps. 8:1–5). His supreme authority is also expressed by His title, "Almighty" (Rev. 1:8). In His holy character, the Sovereign must punish sin, but He has graciously provided salvation for all who trust Christ (Rom. 9:22–24). See also *Almighty; Omnipotence*.

SOWER. One who plants seeds, as in Jesus' parable of the sower (Matt. 13:3–23). Sowing was done mostly by hand.

SPAIN. A country in southwestern Europe which Paul expressed a desire to visit (Rom. 15:24, 28). It was known to ancient Greeks as Iberia and to Romans as Hispania. Jonah's ship was headed for Tarshish, Spain, when he was thrown overboard by the superstitious sailors (Jon. 1:3, 15).

SPAN. A measure of length equal to about nine inches (Exod. 28:16). The word was also used to indicate a small amount of space or time (1 Sam. 17:4; Isa. 40:12).

SPARROW. A small bird, common in Palestine, which was sold as food for the poor (Matt. 10:29, 31).

SPEAR. A weapon of war (2 Sam. 2:23), consisting of a metal point on the end of a long shaft (1 Sam. 13:22). It was similar to but bigger than a dart or javelin. See also *Dart; Javelin.*

SPEARMEN. Soldiers with light arms, such as spears (Acts 23:23).

SPECK. See *Mote.*

SPECKLED BIRD (BIRD OF PREY). A phrase of uncertain meaning. Jeremiah compared the nation of Israel to a speckled bird (Jer. 12:9). *Bird of prey:* NRSV.

SPELT. See *Fitch; Rie.*

SPICE. An aromatic vegetable compound used in perfumes and ointments (Exod. 30:23–36) and also used to prepare bodies for burial (Mark 16:1).

SPIDER. An insect whose frail web provided a lesson on the fleeting schemes of the wicked (Job 8:14; Isa. 59:5).

SPIES. The twelve scouts, one from each of the twelve tribes of Israel, sent to investigate Canaan and report on their findings (Num.13:1–3, 30–33).

SPIKENARD (NARD). An expensive and highly prized perfume or ointment (Song of Sol. 4:13–14) which was used to anoint Jesus' hands and feet (John 12:3). *Nard:* NIV, NRSV.

SPINNING. The process of making yarn into cloth by hand on a rotating loom or wheel (Prov. 31:19). See also *Warp; Weaver.*

SPIRIT. A word which denotes man's reason, conscience, and nobler affections (2 Cor. 7:1; Eph. 4:23)—in contrast to the soul—our appetites, passions, and sensations. The root meaning of the word is "wind" (John 3:8). See also *Ghost; Soul.*

SPIRITIST. See *Wizard.*

SPIRITS IN PRISON. A much-debated phrase from 1 Pet. 3:18–20 which seems to indicate that Christ, in His spiritual existence, preached to the "spirits in prison" who disobeyed God during the days of Noah. Some scholars claim that Christ did not descend into hell but that His eternal spirit (which later was made alive in

His resurrection) preached to the spirits at the time of their disobedience.

SPIRITUAL GIFTS. Gifts bestowed freely by the Holy Spirit upon believers (Jas. 1:17) for the edification of fellow believers and the church (Rom. 1:11; 1 Cor. 12:28). Gifts listed in Romans are preaching, serving, teaching, encouraging, giving, leading, and helping others (Rom. 12:6–8). Gifts listed in 1 Corinthians are wisdom, knowledge, faith, healing, miracles, prophecy, discernment of spirits, tongues, and interpretation of tongues (1 Cor. 12:8–11). Love is the supreme spiritual gift (1 Cor. 12:31; 13:13).

SPIT. To spit was a gesture of extreme contempt (Num. 12:14), but Jesus used saliva to cure a man's blindness (Mark 8:23).

SPOIL (PLUNDER, BOOTY). Plunder taken in war or seized by bandits (Num. 31:9). *Plunder:* NIV; *Booty:* NRSV. David established strict regulations for division of the spoils of war among his soldiers (1 Sam. 30:20–25). See also *Booty*.

SPOON (PITCHER, FLAGON). A shallow dish or pan used as a censer for burning incense in the tabernacle and temple (Exod. 25:29). *Pitcher:* NIV; *Flagon:* NRSV. See also *Pitcher; Flagon*, No. 2.

SPRING RAIN. See *Latter Rain*.

STABLE. A shelter for animals. Ezekiel denounced the Ammonites by prophesying the city of Rabbah would become a stable for livestock (Ezek. 25:2, 5).

STACHYS. A fellow believer at Rome greeted and commended by Paul (Rom. 16:9).

STACTE (GUM RESIN). An ingredient used in the sacred incense burned in temple ceremonies, possibly a gum or spice from the styrax tree (Exod. 30:34). *Gum resin:* NIV.

STAFF. A long stick or rod used to goad animals, to remove fruit from trees (Isa. 28:27), and as support or defense for the old and infirm (Exod. 21:19).

STALL. A stable and storage area. King Solomon had at least 4,000 stalls "for horses and chariots" (2 Chron. 9:25).

STANDARD (ENSIGN). Banner, flag, or streamer to

identify groups of troops or warriors. In the wilderness, each tribe of Israel marched under its own unique banner (Num. 2:2, 34). *Ensign:* NRSV. See also *Ensign*.

STANDARD BEARER. A person who carried the flag or standard of his army or his people, a highly regarded position (Isa. 10:18).

STAR. A luminous body visible in the sky at night. The Hebrews regarded all heavenly bodies as stars, except the sun and moon (Gen. 1:16). The stars were considered a noble mark of God's creative power (Ps. 19:1). Stars were used symbolically for rulers, princes, angels, and ministers (Job 38:7; Dan. 8:10; Rev. 1:16–20). Christ was called "the bright and morning star" (Rev. 22:16).

STARGAZERS. Astrologers; persons who predicted the future by the movement of the stars. The Babylonians were noted for their reliance on astrology (Isa. 47:1, 13). See also *Astrologer; Wise Men*.

STATUTE (DECREE). A law, commandment, or official pronouncement which regulates behavior and conduct (Exod. 18:16). *Decree:* NIV. See also *Commandment; Decree*.

STEADFASTNESS. Persistence and patience in one's faith and activities (Heb. 3:6, 14). Believers are encouraged to endure chastening (Heb. 12: 7) and persecution (Rom. 8:35–37). See also *Patience; Perseverance*.

STEEL. KJV word for copper or brass (Jer. 15:12). See also *Brass*.

STEP. See *Pace*.

STEPHANAS. A Christian from the city of Corinth who visited Paul (1 Cor. 1:16).

STEPHEN. A zealous believer who became the first martyr of the Christian cause. A Jewish believer of Greek background, Stephen was among the seven "deacons" selected by the early church to provide relief for other Greek-speaking Christians (Acts 6:5–8). His criticism of O.T. laws and traditions brought him into conflict with Jewish leaders, and he was stoned to death on a charge of blasphemy (Acts 7:55–58).

STEW. See *Pottage*.

STEWARD. A person employed as a custodian, manager, or administrator, usually of a large household (Gen. 43:19). Christians are urged to be faithful stewards of God's gifts (1 Cor. 4:1–2). See also *Treasurer*.

STEWARDSHIP. Wise and responsible use of one's God-given resources. Christian stewardship is based on God's ownership of all things (Gen. 1:1; Ps. 24:1–2) and man's assigned dominion of God's creation (Gen. 1:26; 2:15). Good stewardship involves faithfulness in use of one's time (Eph. 5:16), talents (2 Tim. 1:6; 2:15), and money (Mal. 3:10). See also *Tithe*.

STIFFNECKED. See *Neck*.

STOCKS (SHACKLES). A wooden frame for public punishment of offenders, containing holes for confining hands, feet, and sometimes the neck (Job 33:11). *Shackles:* NIV (Jer. 20:2–3). See also *Fetters*.

STOICKS (STOICS). A group of philosophers encountered by Paul in his visit to Athens (Acts 17:18). *Stoics:* NIV, NRSV. Highly independent moralists, the Stoics were fatalistic in their outlook on life. See also *Epicureans*.

STOMACH. See *Maw*.

STOMACHER (RICH ROBE). An expensive, festive robe worn by women (Isa. 3:24). *Rich robe:* NRSV.

STONE. See *Rock*.

STONECUTTER. See *Hewer*.

STONING. The Jewish mode of capital punishment, specified in the law for these offenses: Sacrificing children to idols (Lev. 20:2–5), breaking the Sabbath (Num. 15:32–36), idolatry (Deut. 17:2–7), rebellion of children against parents (Deut. 21:18–21), and adultery (Deut. 22:23–24). Godly men who were stoned for their faith included the prophets (Heb. 11:37), Stephen (Acts 7:59), and Paul, who was presumed dead (Acts 14:19–20).

STORE CITY (STORAGE TOWN). A city or a supply depot in a city for the storage of food, equipment, and weapons of war (2 Chron. 8:4). *Storage town:* NRSV. See also *Treasure City*.

STOREHOUSE. A building for storing food. Joseph built grain storehouses in Egypt to get ready for the years of famine (Gen. 41:48–49).

STORK. A long-necked migratory bird similar to the crane (Ps. 104:17); an unclean animal to the Jews (Lev. 11:19).

STORM. See *Tempest; Whirlwind.*

STRANGER. See *Foreigner.*

STRAW. A food for livestock. Also used as a strengthening and binding ingredient in bricks (Exod. 5:7, 16).

STREET. A traffic lane in a city. Streets were mostly crude, crooked, and narrow, much like a dirty alley (Jer. 37:21). The street in Damascus called Straight was exceptionally wide (Acts 9:11).

STRIFE. Bitter conflict caused by self-seeking (Luke 22:24) or a worldly spirit (1 Cor. 3:3). Strife may be avoided by unselfishness and a brotherly spirit (Gen. 13:7–8; Phil. 2:3). See also *Contention.*

STRONG DRINK. See *Wine.*

STRONGHOLD. See *Misgab; Tower.*

STRUTTING ROOSTER. See *Greyhound.*

STUBBLE. The short stumps of grain stalks left in the ground after harvesting (Exod. 5:12). Regarded as worthless, stubble symbolized instability and impermanence (Isa. 33:11).

STUMBLINGBLOCK. A hindrance to belief or understanding. Israel's iniquity and idolatry were a stumblingblock (Jer. 18:15). Paul urged Christians not to offend or serve as a hindrance to a weak brother (Rom. 14:13). The preaching of "Christ crucified" was a stumblingblock to the Jews (1 Cor. 1:23).

SUBURBS (PASTURE-LANDS). The open country around a city used for grazing livestock or other purposes (Josh. 21:11). *Pasture lands:* NIV, NRSV.

SUCCOTH. The Hebrews' first camping site in the wilderness after leaving Rameses in Egypt (Exod. 12:37).

SUCCOTH-BENOTH. An idol set up in Samaria by the pagan peoples who colonized the area after Israel fell to the Assyrians (2 Kings 17:29–30).

SUCKLING. An infant or young animal not yet weaned from its mother's milk. As judge, Samuel offered a suckling lamb as a burnt offering to the Lord (1 Sam. 7:9).

SUFFERING. Pain or distress. Suffering for Jesus' sake may be regarded as fellowship with Christ (Phil. 3:10) and as a stewardship (Phil. 1:29). See also *Affliction; Anguish*.

SUICIDE. To take one's own life. Suicide may be brought on by hopelessness (Judg. 16: 28–30), sin (1 Kings 16:18–19), disappointment (2 Sam. 17:23), and betrayal (Matt. 27:3–5). This act violates the principles of life's sacredness (Gen. 9:5–6; 1 Cor. 6:19) and God's sovereign rule (Rom. 9:20–21).

SUKKIIM (SUKKITES). An African or Ethiopian tribe allied with Pharaoh Shishak of Egypt when he invaded Judah (2 Chron. 12:3). *Sukkites:* NIV.

SULFUR. See *Brimstone*.

SUMER. The southern division of ancient Babylonia (now southern Iraq), consisting largely of the fertile plain between the Tigris and Euphrates rivers. In the O.T., it was called Shinar (Gen. 10:10) or Chaldea (Jer. 50:10). See also *Babylonia*.

SUN. The luminous solar body that provides light and heat to Earth. Some of the ancient civilizations surrounding Israel worshiped the sun, and even the Israelites burned incense to the sun on occasion (2 Kings 23:5). God is spoken of figuratively as a sun and shield (Ps. 84:11).

SUPERSCRIPTION (IN-SCRIPTION). Words engraved on coins or other surfaces. The superscription "King of the Jews" was placed above Jesus on the cross (Mark 15: 26). *Inscription:* NRSV.

SUPERSTITION. Ideas or impressions based on ignorance or fear. Many superstitions grow out of ignorance of the one true God (Rom. 1:25, 32).

SUPPER. The main daily meal of ancient times, usually the evening meal (Luke 14:16) as observed by Jews, Greeks, and Romans. In the N.T. the word is used of the Passover (John 13:1–2) and the Lord's Supper (1 Cor. 11:20).

SUPPLICATION (PETITION). An earnest prayer or request. Paul urged supplication with thanksgiving as an antidote to anxiety (Phil. 4:6). *Petition:* NIV. See also *Petition.*

SUPPLY CITY. See *Store City; Treasure City.*

SUPREME COMMANDER. See *Tartan.*

SUR. A gate of Solomon's temple in Jerusalem (2 Kings 11:6), also called "gate of the foundation" (2 Chron. 23:5).

SURETY (GUARANTEE). One who guarantees payment of another person's debt or obligation. Jesus' perfect priesthood was a surety or guarantee of a better covenant (Heb. 7:22). *Guarantee:* NIV, NRSV.

SURVIVORS. See *Remnant.*

SUSA. See *Shushan.*

SUSANNA. A female follower of Jesus who apparently provided food and lodging for Him and perhaps His disciples (Luke 8:2–3).

SWADDLING CLOTHES, SWADDLINGBANDS. Square cloth like a quilt or a blanket which was wrapped around a newborn baby (Luke 2:7–12). This cloth was held in place by swaddlingbands—narrow strips of cloth (Job 38:9).

SWALLOW. Swift bird which nests in buildings and makes a mournful sound (Ps. 84:3; Prov. 26:2).

SWAN (WHITE OWL, WATER HEN). An unclean water bird, perhaps the ibis or water hen (Lev. 11:18). *White owl:* NIV; *Water hen:* NRSV.

SWEARING. See *Oath.*

SWINE (PIGS). Pigs or hogs. The flesh of swine was forbidden as food (Lev. 11:7). *Pigs:* NIV, NRSV. Swine were regarded as offensive to the Lord (Isa. 65:2–4).

SWORD. A sharp blade carried by soldiers as a weapon of war. Simeon and Levi used swords in the massacre at Shechem (Gen. 34:25).

SYCAMINE (MULBERRY). A tree or shrub which bore a fruit similar to blackberries (Luke 17:6). *Mulberry:* NIV, NRSV. See also *Mulberry.*

SYCHAR. A city of Samaria where Jesus talked to the woman at Jacob's well (John 4:5–40).

SYCHEM. See *Shechem,* No. 2.

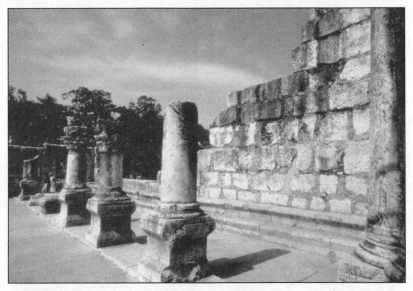

Excavated ruins of a synagogue at Capernaum, a city associated with Jesus' ministry in Galilee.

Courtesy Israel Ministry of Tourism

SYCOMORE (SYCAMORE). A fig-bearing tree valued for its fruit and soft, durable wood (Luke 19:4). *Sycamore:* NIV, NRSV.

SYENE. See *Sinim.*

SYMBOL. A word, action, or object which stands for truths or spiritual realities. Circumcision was a symbol of God's covenant with Israel (Rom. 4:11). The rainbow signified God's promise not to destroy the world by water again (Gen. 9:12–13). The tearing of the temple curtain at Christ's death represented the believer's direct access to God through Jesus (Matt. 27:50–51).

SYNAGOGUE. A house of worship for the Jews which developed during their period of exile in Babylonia and Persia. Synagogues shifted the emphasis of the Jews from animal sacrifices to worship and teaching of the law. Paul regularly proclaimed the message of Christ in Jewish synagogues on his missionary journeys outside Palestine (Acts 18:4).

SYNOPTIC GOSPELS. A phrase used for the Gospels of Matthew, Mark, and Luke, to set them apart from the Gospel of John. The synoptic Gospels are similar in their straightforward and factual treatment of the life of Jesus, while John gives the theological meaning of these facts and events.

SYNTYCHE. A female believer in the church at Philippi whom Paul exhorted, along with Euodias, to make peace with each other (Phil. 4:2).

SYRACUSE. A prosperous city on the eastern coast of Sicily visited by Paul (Acts 28:12).

SYRIA/ARAM. A nation northeast of Israel which was a persistent enemy of the Jews across several centuries (1 Kings 15: 18–20), particularly from David's administration until Syria fell to the Assyrians about 700 B.C. This nation was allied with Babylonia and Assyria at one point in its history; thus its name *Syria*. When Jesus was born, Syria was a province under Roman control (Luke 2: 2). This nation was also known as *Aram* (Num. 23:7). See also *Damascus*.

SYRIA-DAMASCUS. See *Damascus*.

SYRO-PHOENICIAN. An inhabitant of Phoenicia during the time when Phoenicia was part of the Roman province of Syria. Jesus ministered in this area (Mark 7:25–31).

SYRTIS. See *Quicksands*.

-T-

TAANACH/TANACH. A Canaanite city west of the Jordan River conquered by Joshua and assigned to the Levites (Josh. 12:21). *Tanach:* Josh. 21:25.

TABERAH. A camping site in the wilderness where many Israelites were killed by fire because of their complaining (Num. 11:1–3).

TABERNACLE/TENT OF MEETING. A tent or portable sanctuary built in the wilderness at God's command as a place of worship for the Israelites (Exod. 40:2–8). It was also called the *Tent of Meeting* be-cause it was considered a place of encounter between God and His people. The tabernacle foreshadowed Christ's incarnation when "the Word was made flesh and dwelt among us" (John 1:14). See also *Holy Place; Holy of Holies*.

Mount Tabor on the plains of Jezreel near Nazareth in Galilee.
Courtesy Israel Ministry of Tourism

TABERNACLES, FEAST OF/ FEAST OF BOOTHS. A festival, also known as the Feast of Booths and the Feast of Ingathering (Exod. 23:16; Num. 29:12), observed annually during the harvest season to commemorate Israel's wilderness wandering experience. The people lived in tents or booths in remembrance of their days as tent dwellers while waiting to enter Canaan (Lev. 23:39–43).

TABITHA/DORCAS. A Christian widow at Joppa whom Peter restored to life (Acts 9:36–40). Her Greek name was *Dorcas*.

TABLET. A flat piece of stone on which the Ten Commandments were engraved by the finger of God (Exod. 24:12).

TABOR, MOUNT. A mountain on the border of the territories of Zebulun and Issachar about six miles from Nazareth in Galilee. From this mountain the judge Deborah sent Barak to defeat Sisera and the Canaanites (Judg. 4:6–14).

TABRET (TAMBOURINE). A musical instrument which was probably similar to the tambourine (Gen. 31:27). *Tambourine:* NIV, NRSV.

315

TADMOR (TAMAR). A trading center between the city of Damascus in Syria and the Euphrates River which was rebuilt by King Solomon about 1000 B.C. (1 Kings 9:17–18). *Tamar:* NRSV.

TAHPANHES/TAHAPANES/ TEHAPHNEHES. An Egyptian city on the Nile River to which citizens of Judah fled after the fall of Jerusalem to the Babylonians (Jer. 43:7–10). *Tahapanes:* Jer. 2:16; *Tehaphnehes:* Ezek. 30:18.

TAHPENES. Queen of the Egyptian pharaoh in King Solomon's time (1 Kings 11:18–22).

TALEBEARER (GOSSIP). A person who gossips about or slanders another with destructive words (Prov. 18:8). *Gossip:* NIV. See also *Busybody; Gossip.*

TALENT. A common unit of weight or measure of monetary value used by the Hebrews, Greeks, and Romans (Matt. 25:14–30).

TAMAR.
1. The widow of Er and Onan, sons of Judah, who eventually bore Judah's twin sons, Perez and Zerah (Gen. 38:6–30). *Thamar:* Jesus' ancestry (Matt. 1:3).
2. Absalom's sister who was sexually assaulted by her half brother Amnon. Absalom avenged the crime by killing Amnon (2 Sam. 13:1–32).
3. NRSV word for Tadmor (1 Kings 9:17–18). See *Tadmor.*

TAMARISK. A small tree or shrub. King Saul and his sons were buried under a tamarisk (1 Sam. 22:6).

TAMBOURINE. See *Tabret; Timbrel.*

TANNER. A person who cured animal skins. This probably was not a reputable vocation among the Jews because of the problem of defilement by touching unclean animals. Peter lodged with a tanner at Joppa (Acts 10:5–6). See also *Leather.*

TAPESTRY. An expensive curtain or cloth embroidered with artwork and owned generally by the wealthy (Prov. 7:16; 31:22).

TAR. See *Slime.*

TARE. A weed, now known as the darnel plant, which resembles wheat. In Jesus' parable, tares represent wicked seed sown by Satan that will ultimately be separated and destroyed (Matt. 13:25–40).

TARPELITES. A tribe which colonized Samaria after the citizens of the Northern Kingdom were carried to Assyria as captives about 722 B.C. (Ezra 4:9). See also *Samaritan*.

TARSHISH/THARSHISH. A coastal city, probably in Spain, which was the destination of the ship boarded by the prophet Jonah (Jon. 1:3). *Tharshish:* 1 Kings 10:22.

TARSUS. Capital city of the Roman province of Silicia and the place where Paul was born (Acts 9:11). Once an important center of learning, Tarsus was on the Cydnus River about ten miles north of the Mediterranean Sea.

TARTAK. A false god worshiped by the Avites, a people who colonized Samaria after the Northern Kingdom fell to the Assyrians (2 Kings 17:31).

TARTAN (SUPREME COMMANDER). The title of the commander of the Assyrian army who demanded the surrender of Jerusalem from King Hezekiah (2 Kings 18:17). *Supreme commander:* NIV.

TASKMASTERS (SLAVEMASTERS). Egyptian overseers or supervisors who forced the Hebrew slaves to do hard labor at the command of the pharaoh (Exod. 1:11–14). *Slavemasters:* NIV.

TASSEL. See *Fringe*.

TATNAI (TATTENAI). A Persian official who appealed to King Darius of Persia to stop the Jews from rebuilding the temple in Jerusalem (Ezra 5:3–9). *Tattenai:* NIV, NRSV.

TAU. The twenty-second and last letter of the Hebrew alphabet, used as a heading over Ps. 119:169–176.

TAVERNS, THE THREE. A station on the Roman road known as the Appian Way about thirty miles south of Rome where believers met the apostle Paul (Acts 28:15).

TAX COLLECTOR. See *Publican*.

TAXES. Money, goods, or labor paid by citizens to a government. The Hebrews originally paid taxes known as tithes or firstfruits to support priests and Levites. The tax burden grew heavier under kings, particularly Solomon, and rebellion against his son and successor Rehoboam eventually split the kingdom (1 Kings 12:4, 8). The Romans sold the privilege of collecting taxes to independent contractors, resulting in great extortion (Luke 19:2, 8). See also *Toll*.

TEACHER. A person who communicates knowledge or religious truth to others. Teachers are mentioned along with pastors as persons whose skill and ministry are needed in the church (Eph. 4:11–12). See also *Master*.

TEACHER OF THE LAW. See *Scribe*.

TEAR. See *Rend*.

TEARS. Visible signs of sorrow. Jesus shed tears over the unbelief of Jerusalem (Luke 13:34) and wept at the grave of his friend Lazarus (John 11:35).

TEBETH. The tenth month of the Hebrew year (Esther 2:16).

TEETH. See *Tooth*.

TEHAPHNEHES. See *Tahpanhes*.

TEIL (TEREBINTH). A common tree in Palestine which resembled the elm or oak (Isa. 6:13). *Terebinth:* NIV, NRSV.

TEKOA/TEKOAH. A fortress city of Judah near Bethlehem; home of Amos the prophet (Amos 1:1). *Tekoah:* 2 Sam. 14:4.

TEL, TELL. An Arabic word for "mound," or a hill marking the site of an ancient city which has been built up over centuries of occupation. See also *Archaeology of the Bible*.

TEL-ABIB. A Babylonian city on the Chebar River where Ezekiel lived with the other Jewish captives (Ezek. 3:15).

TEMPERANCE (SELF-CONTROL). Moderation, restraint, or self-discipline— behavior that should characterize believers (2 Pet. 1:6). *Self-control:* NIV, NRSV. See also *Moderation; Sober*.

TEMPEST (STORM). A furious storm. Jesus calmed a tempest on the Sea of Galilee to save His disciples (Matt. 8:24–26). *Storm:* NIV.

TEMPLE. The central place of worship for the Jewish people. Three separate temples were built on the same site in Jerusalem.

The first was Solomon's temple, built about 961–954

B.C. A partition divided the holy place from the holy of holies (1 Kings 6:2; 20, 31). Ten golden candlesticks, the table of shewbread, and the ark of the covenant were housed in this temple.

Zerubbabel's temple was completed in 515 B.C. by Jews who returned to Jerusalem after a period of exile among the Babylonians and Persians. The partition was replaced by a veil or curtain. The ark, which had been destroyed by the Babylonians, was not replaced.

About 10 B.C. Herod the Great began reconstruction of Zerubbabel's temple. The third temple was more ornate and larger than its predecessors, with outer courts added. The infant Jesus was brought to this temple for dedication, and here Jesus taught and drove out the moneychangers (Mark 11: 15; John 2:14–15). This temple was destroyed by the Romans in A.D. 70. A Moslem mosque stands on the site today. See also *Herod, No. 1; Zerubbabel.*

TEMPLE PROSTITUTE. See *Sodomite.*

TEMPLE SERVANTS. See *Nethinim.*

TEMPORARY RESIDENT. See *Foreigner.*

TEMPTATION. Testing, or enticement to sin (Matt. 4:1–10). Jesus' temptation experiences provide a guide to help believers resist Satan the tempter (Matt. 4:10; Heb. 2: 18). God promises a means of escape for every temptation (1 Cor. 10:13).

TEN COMMANDMENTS. The ethical commands given by God to Moses on Mt. Sinai. Also called the *Decalogue,* the Ten Commandments summarize the basic moral laws of the O.T. Four of these commandments enjoin duties to God (Exod. 20: 1–11), while six deal with obligations to other people (Exod. 20:12–17). Jesus summed up these commandments in two great principles—supreme love for God and loving our neighbors as ourselves (Matt. 22: 37–40).

TENT. The house or dwelling-place of nomadic peoples (Gen. 12:8). Tents were made of goat hair and supported by poles and ropes tied to stakes. See also *House.*

TENT OF MEETING. See *Tabernacle.*

TENTH DEAL. A dry measure equaling one-tenth of an

ephah (Exod. 29:40). See also *Ephah*.

TENTMAKER. A skilled workman who made tents, a lucrative trade in Bible times. Paul supported himself as a tentmaker. (Acts 18:3).

TERAH/THARA. The father of Abraham and a native of Ur in Chaldea or ancient Babylonia. Through his sons Abraham, Nahor, and Haran, he was an ancestor of the Israelites, Ishmaelites, Midianites, Moabites, and Ammonites (Gen. 11:26–31). *Thara:* Jesus' ancestry (Luke 3:34).

TERAPHIM. Small images representing human figures which were venerated in households as guardians of good fortune (Judg. 17:5). Rachel stole her father's teraphim when Jacob left for Canaan (Gen. 31:19, 35). See also *Household Idols*.

TEREBINTH. See *Teil*.

TERTIUS. Paul's scribe who took dictation for the epistle to the Romans (Rom. 16:22).

TERTULLUS. A lawyer who accused Paul of desecrating the temple in a hearing before Felix at Caesarea (Acts 24:1–8).

TESTAMENT. A covenant or agreement with legal standing. The Old and New Testaments are covenants ratified first by the blood of sacrificial animals and then by the blood of Christ (Exod. 24:8; Matt. 26:28). See also *Covenant*.

TESTIMONY. A declaration of truth, based on personal experience (Acts 4:20). The testimony of Paul and Barnabas at Iconium was confirmed by their performance of miracles (Acts 14:3). See also *Record; Witness*.

TETH. The ninth letter of the Hebrew alphabet, used as a heading over Ps. 119:65–72.

TETRARCH. The governor or ruler of a Roman province (Luke 3:1). See also *Governor*.

THADDAEUS. See *Judas, Brother of James*.

THAMAR. *See Tamar, No. 1*

THANK OFFERING. A sacrificial animal presented to God as an expression of thanks for an unexpected special blessing (2 Chron. 29:31). See also *Sacrifice*.

THANKSGIVING. The act of expressing one's gratitude. The psalmist praised the Lord for

Excavated ruins of an ancient Roman theater at Beth-shan.
Courtesy Israel Ministry of Tourism

His goodness and blessings (Ps. 116:12–19). Our Christian inheritance of salvation and eternal life should inspire our thanksgiving to God (Col. 1:12). See also *Praise*.

THARA. See *Terah*.

THARSHISH. See *Tarshish*.

THEATER. An outdoor meeting place, similar to a stadium, where dramatic performances and sporting events were held. The theater at Ephesus was an impressive Roman structure made of stone and marble which seated thousands (Acts 19:29–31).

THEBES. See *No*.

THEBEZ. A fortified city near Shechem where Abimelech died when a stone was dropped on his head from a defense tower (Judg. 9:50–55).

THEOCRACY. A government in which God is the ruler. Israel was an imperfect example of this form of rule, beginning with their deliverance from Egypt (Exod. 15:13) and the giving of the law at Mt. Sinai (Exod. 19:5–8), until Samuel agreed to the people's demand for a king (1 Sam. 8:5).

THEOPHANY. Visible appearance of God. Examples are the burning bush (Exod. 3:1–6), the pillar of cloud and fire (Exod. 13:21–22), and the cloud and fire at Mt. Sinai (Exod. 24:16–18). Some scholars believe theophanies before the incarnation of Jesus were visible manifestations of the pre-incarnate Son of God (John 1:1, 18).

THEOPHILUS. A friend of Luke to whom he addressed his writings—the Gospel of Luke and the Book of Acts (Luke 1:3; Acts 1:1). See also *Luke*.

THESSALONIANS, EPISTLES TO THE. Two N.T. epistles written by the apostle Paul to the believers in the church at Thessalonica. The theme of both letters is the second coming of Christ, although Paul also included instructions on sexual morality (1 Thess. 4:1–8) and the need for diligent labor rather than idle speculation (1 Thess. 4:9–12; 2 Thess. 3:6–15). Paul declared that the believer's assurance in Christ's return should motivate them to righteous living (1 Thess. 3:13; 5:23) but that uncertainty about the exact time of His return should make them watchful and alert (1 Thess. 5:1–11).

THESSALONICA. A city on the Macedonian coast where Paul preached and founded a church. It was also the scene of a riot incited by Jews who opposed the preaching of Paul and Silas (Acts 17:1–9).

THEUDAS. The leader of an unsuccessful revolt mentioned by Gamaliel before the Sanhedrin. Gamaliel probably named this person to discourage premature action that might result in bloodshed (Acts 5:35–36).

THIEF. A robber. Double restitution for theft was required under Mosaic Law. Those who did not conform to this requirement could be sold as slaves (Exod. 22:3–7).

THIGH. The part of the leg between the hip and the knee. Placing the hand under the thigh signified obedience or subjection. Abraham's servant swore by this method that a Canaanite wife would not be chosen for Abraham's son Isaac (Gen. 24:2–9). See also *Sinew*.

THIRTY PIECES OF SILVER. The blood money given to Judas to betray Christ—the usual price for a slave. A remorseful Judas threw his silver on the temple floor and hanged himself (Matt. 27:3–8).

THISTLE. A briar or thorn, which was used for hedges and burned for fuel (Isa. 33:12; Hos. 2:6). The word was also used figuratively of neglect and desolation (Prov. 24:30–31).

THOMAS. One of the twelve apostles or disciples of Jesus, also called *Didymus* or "twin" (Luke 6:15), who refused to believe that Christ was alive until he could actually see and feel the wounds on Christ's resurrected body. Upon touching His hands and side, Thomas cried, "My Lord and my God" (John 20:25–28). See also *Twelve, The.*

THONG. A strip of leather. Paul was bound with thongs at Jerusalem (Acts 22:25–29). See also *Latchet.*

THORN. A plant with heavy briars or thistles. A crown of thorns was placed on Jesus' head in mockery as He hung on the cross (Matt. 27:29).

THORN IN THE FLESH. An unknown affliction from which the apostle Paul prayed to be delivered (2 Cor. 12:7–8). Some scholars believe it was an eye ailment, since he normally dictated his epistles and apologized for his own large handwriting (Gal. 6:11).

THORNBUSH. See *Bramble.*

THRESHINGFLOOR. A place where grain was threshed, or separated from the stalk and husk after harvesting (2 Sam. 6:6). See also *Fan; Winnowing.*

THROAT. The throat was compared to an "open sepulchre" because of the deadly falsehoods which it could utter through the mouth (Ps. 5:9; Rom. 3:13). See also *Lips; Mouth; Tongue.*

THRONE. An ornate chair occupied by kings (1 Kings 2:19), and sometimes priests and judges (1 Sam. 1:9; Jer. 1:15) as a symbol of their power and authority. The word is also used to designate the Lord's supreme authority (Isa. 6:1).

THUMB. The thumb was involved in the ceremony consecrating Aaron and his sons to the priesthood. The blood of rams was smeared on their thumbs as well as their ears and feet (Exod. 29:19–20).

THUMMIN. See *Urim and Thummin.*

THUNDER. Since thunder was rare in Palestine, it was considered a form of speaking by the Lord (Job 40:9) and often regarded as a sign of His displeasure (Exod. 9:23; 1 Sam. 12:7).

THYATIRA. A city in the Roman province of Asia and home of Lydia, a convert under Paul's ministry (Acts 16:14). Noted for its dye industry, Thyatira was also the site of one of the seven churches of Asia Minor addressed by the apostle John. This church was commended for its faith and good works but condemned for its tolerance toward the false prophetess Jezebel and her heretical teachings (Rev. 2:18–24).

THYINE WOOD (CITRON WOOD, SCENTED WOOD). A valuable wood resembling cedar used for fine cabinet work (Rev. 18:12). *Citron wood:* NIV. *Scented wood:* NRSV. It was also burned as incense because of its fragrance.

TIBERIAS. A city on the western shore of the Sea of Galilee (John 6:1, 23) built by Herod Antipas and named for the Roman emperor Tiberius. It was shunned by many Jews because it was built on a cemetery site. Tiberias became a center of learning after the fall of Jerusalem in A.D. 70.

TIBERIUS. See *Caesar,* No. 2.

TIBNI. A king of Israel (reigned about 885–880 B.C.) who ruled at the same time as Omri. Upon Tibni's death, Omri became the sole claimant to the throne (1 Kings 16:21–22).

TIGLATH-PILESER III/ TILGATH-PILNESER III/ PUL. A powerful Assyrian king (reigned about 745–727 B.C.) who defeated the Northern Kingdom and carried Jewish captives to Assyria (2 Kings 15:29; 16:1–10). *Tilgath-pilneser:* 2 Chron. 28: 20. *Pul:* 1 Chron. 5:26.

TIGRIS. A major river of southwest Asia which is possibly the same as the *Hiddekel* of the Garden of Eden (Gen. 2:14). Beginning in the Armenian mountains, the Tigris flows southeastward for more than 1,100 miles until it joins the Euphrates River. Mesopotamia, or "the land between the rivers," lies between these two streams. See also *Euphrates.*

TILE (CLAY TABLET, BRICK). A slab of baked clay used as roofing on houses (Ezek. 4:1). *Clay tablet:* NIV; *Brick:* NRSV. The tiles were removed from a roof to give a paralyzed man access to Jesus for healing (Luke 5:18–19). See also *Brick.*

TILGATH-PILNESER. See *Tiglath-pileser.*

TIMBREL (TAMBOURINE). A small hand drum or percussion instrument believed to resemble the tambourine (Exod. 15:20). *Tambourine:* NIV, NRSV. See also *Tabret.*

TIMNATH-SERAH/ TIMNATH-HERES. A town in the territory of Ephraim given to Joshua as an inheritance and the place where he was buried (Josh. 24:29–30). *Timnath-heres:* Judg. 2:9.

TIMON. One of the seven men chosen as "deacons" in the church at Jerusalem (Acts 6:1–5).

TIMOTHY/TIMOTHEUS. A young missionary friend of Paul, also called *Timotheus* (see Rom. 16:21), who accompanied the apostle on some of his travels and briefly shared his imprisonment at Rome (Heb. 13:23). Born to a Greek father and a Jewish mother (Acts 16:1), Timothy was reared by his mother Eunice and grandmother Lois in a godly home (2 Tim. 1:5). He was converted during Paul's first visit to Lystra (Acts 16:1) and served for a time as leader of the church at Ephesus (1 Tim.

1:3; 4:12). Paul addressed two of his pastoral epistles to Timothy. See also *Eunice.*

TIMOTHY, EPISTLES TO. Two short epistles of the apostle Paul to his young friend and fellow missionary, Timothy. The first epistle is practical in scope, instructing Timothy to teach sound doctrine (1:1–20), organize the church appropriately (2:1–3:16), beware of false teachers (4:1–16), administer church discipline (5:1–25), and exercise his pastoral gifts with love and restraint (6:1–21).

Second Timothy is perhaps Paul's most personal epistle, in which he expresses tender affection for the young minister (1: 1–2:20) and speaks of approaching days of persecution for the church (3:1–4:5) as well as the possibility of his own execution (4:6–22). See also *Pastoral Epistles; Timothy.*

TIN. A well-known and malleable metal (Num. 31:22) brought by ship from Tarshish and used in making bronze (Ezek. 27:12).

TINDER. See *Tow.*

TIPHSAH. A place which designated the eastern boundary of Solomon's kingdom (1 Kings

4:24), identified today as Thapsacus on the Euphrates River.

TIRE. A headdress, such as a turban, or an ornament worn in the hair by a high priest, a bridegroom, or women (2 Kings 9:30; Isa. 3:18).

TIRHAKAH. See *Pharaoh,* No. 3.

TIRSHATHA (GOVERNOR). The title of the governor of Judea under Persian rule. Both Zerubbabel and Nehemiah were appointed by Persian kings to this position (Ezra 2:63; Neh. 7:65). *Governor:* NIV, NRSV. See also *Governor; Lieutenant.*

TIRZAH. A Canaanite town captured by Joshua (Josh. 12:24). In later years it served as a capital of the Northern Kingdom until Samaria was built (1 Kings 14:17).

TISHBITE. An inhabitant of Tishbeh, a city of Gilead. The prophet Elijah was called a Tishbite (1 Kings 17:1).

TITHE. One-tenth of a person's income presented as an offering to God. Abraham paid tithes to Melchizedek (Gen. 14:18–20), and Jacob vowed to give tithes in accordance with God's blessings (Gen. 28:20–22). In N.T. times, the Pharisees were scrupulous tithers (Matt. 23:23). Jesus encouraged generosity and promised to bless sacrificial giving (Luke 6:38). Paul endorsed the principle of proportionate giving (1 Cor. 16:2). See also *Stewardship.*

TITTLE. A dot or other small mark which distinguished similar letters of the alphabet. Jesus used the word to emphasize the enduring quality of the law's most minute requirement (Matt. 5:18).

TITUS. A Greek Christian and traveling companion of Paul who was sent by the apostle to correct problems in the church at Corinth (2 Cor. 7:6; 8:6, 23). Titus also served as a church leader in Crete (Titus 1:5–3:11). See also *Crete.*

TITUS, EPISTLE TO. A short epistle written by the apostle Paul to his helper and companion Titus, who apparently was serving as a leader of the church on the island of Crete (1:5). Paul dealt with several practical church matters, including the qualifications of elders (1:5–9), dealing with false teachers (1:10–16), and the behavior of Christians in an immoral world (3:1–11). See also *Pastoral Epistles*.

TOB/ISH-TOB. A place in Syria east of the Jordan River where the judge Jephthah took refuge (Judg. 11:3, 5). The soldiers of Tob sided with the Ammonites against David (2 Sam. 10:6, 8). *Ish-tob:* 2 Sam. 10:8.

TOBIAH. An Ammonite servant of Sanballat who ridiculed the Jews and opposed Nehemiah's reconstruction of Jerusalem's wall (Neh. 2:10, 19; 4:3, 7). See also *Sanballat*.

TOI/TOU. King of Hamath who sent his son with presents to congratulate King David on his victory over King Hadadezer of Zobah in Syria (2 Sam. 8:9–12). *Tou:* 1 Chron. 18:9.

TOKEN (SIGN). A sign or signal. Circumcision was a token of God's covenant with Abraham (Gen. 17:11). The blood on the Israelites' doorposts was a sign for the death angel to "pass over" these houses (Exod. 12:13). *Sign:* NIV, NRSV. See also *Miracle; Sign*.

TOLA. A minor judge of Israel who succeeded Abimelech and ruled for twenty-three years (Judg. 10:1–2). See also *Judges of Israel*.

TOLERANCE. See *Forbearance*.

TOLL (TAX). A tax or fee levied against the citizens of a conquered nation (Ezra 4: 13). *Tax:* NIV. See also *Taxes; Tribute*.

TOMB. See *Sepulchre*.

TONGS. A tool for handling hot coals or trimming burning lamps (Exod. 25:38; Num. 4:9); probably the same as *snuffer*. See also *Snuffer*.

TONGUE. The organ of the body associated with speech. The tongue may be used as an instrument of punishment (Gen. 11:1–9) or blessing (Acts 2:1–13) and for good or evil (Jas. 3:5–10). See also *Lips; Mouth; Throat*.

TONGUES, SPEAKING IN. Glossolalia or ecstatic utterances; a spiritual gift exercised by some believers in the N.T. church. This gift apparently first occurred on the day of Pentecost with the outpouring of God's spirit on believers (Acts 2:1–13). Paul also mentioned this gift in 1 Cor. 14:2–28, although it is unclear whether this is the same as the phenomenon described in Acts.

TOOTH. The gnashing or grinding of one's teeth symbolized frustration or despair (Matt. 8:12).

TOPAZ (CHRYSOLITE). A precious stone, thought to resemble modern chrysolite, used in the high priest's breastplate (Exod. 28:17). *Chrysolite:* NRSV. It is also used in the foundation of New Jerusalem (Rev. 21:20). See also *Chrysolyte*.

TOPHET (TOPHETH). A place of human sacrifice in the Valley of Hinnom near Jerusalem (Jer. 7:31–32). *Topheth:* NIV, NRSV. See also *Hell; Hinnom, Valley of*.

TORAH. A Hebrew word, meaning "teaching" or "instruction," and used for the Pentateuch or the law, the first five books of the O.T. See also *Law, Law of Moses; Pentateuch*.

TORCH. A burning brand made of resinous wood or twisted flax and used to light one's path at night (John 18:3). See also *Lantern*.

TORTOISE (GREAT LIZARD). A reptile regarded as unclean by the Jews (Lev. 11:29). *Great lizard:* NIV, NRSV.

TOU. See *Toi*.

TOW (TINDER). The waste or refuse produced from flax when spinning thread. Isaiah used the word figuratively of the weakness of sinful people when facing God's punishment (Isa. 1:31). *Tinder:* NIV, NRSV.

TOWER (STRONGHOLD). A defensive turret in a city wall or a tall structure used as a watchtower. The word is also used figuratively of God's protection (2 Sam. 22:3). *Stronghold:* NIV, NRSV.

TOWNCLERK (CITY CLERK). An official of the city of Ephesus who restored order after a riot against Paul (Acts 19:29–41). *City clerk:* NIV.

TRADITION. An unwritten code or interpretation of the law which the Pharisees considered as binding as the written law itself (Matt. 15:2).

TRANCE. A state of semiconsciousness, often accompanied by visions. Peter's trance at Joppa prepared him for a ministry to Cornelius the Gentile. See also *Dreams and Visions*.

TRANSFIGURATION OF JESUS. A radical transformation in the Savior's appearance through which God was glorified. Accompanied by His disciples Peter, James, and John, Jesus went to a mountain at night to pray. Moses and Elijah appeared and discussed Jesus' death, emphasizing Jesus as the fulfillment of the law and the prophets. Shining with God's glory from within, Christ was overshadowed by a cloud and a voice declaring, "This is my beloved Son...hear ye him" (Matt. 17:1–8). These experiences attested Christ's divinity and mission and helped prepare Jesus and His disciples for the events leading to His death.

TRANSGRESSION. A violation of God's law, which may be personal (1 Tim. 2:14), public (Rom. 5:14), or premeditated (Josh. 7:19–25). Transgression produces death (1 Chron. 10:13) and destruction (Ps. 37:38), but it may be forgiven by confession (Ps. 32:1, 5) through the atoning death of Christ (Isa. 53:5–6).

TRANSJORDAN. A large mountainous plateau or tableland east of the Jordan River, generally referred to in the KJV as the land "beyond Jordan" (Gen. 50:10; Matt. 4:15). This is the area from which Moses viewed the Promised Land (Deut. 34:1–4). After the conquest of Canaan, it was occupied by the tribes of Reuben, Gad, and East Manasseh.

TRAVAIL. The labor pains associated with childbirth (Gen. 38:27). The word is also used figuratively of the birth of God's new creation (Rom. 8:22–23).

TREASURE CITY (STORE CITY, SUPPLY CITY). A fortified city in which a king stored his valuables. The Hebrew slaves built treasure cities at Pithom and Raamses for the Egyptian pharaoh (Exod. 1:11). *Store city:* NIV; *Supply city:* NRSV. See also *Store City.*

TREASURE OF ALL NATIONS. See *Desire of All Nations.*

TREASURER (STEWARD). An important financial officer in a king's court, charged with accounting for receipts and disbursements (Isa. 22:15–23). S*teward:* NIV, NRSV. See also *Steward.*

TREASURY. The place in the temple where offerings were received (Mark 12:41–44). Thirteen trumpet-shaped receptacles for offerings were placed in the outer court.

TREATY. See *League*.

TREE OF KNOWLEDGE OF GOOD AND EVIL. A specific tree placed in the Garden of Eden to test the obedience of Adam and Eve. Eating of the fruit of this tree was specifically prohibited by the Lord (Gen. 2:9–17). After they ate the forbidden fruit, Adam and Eve were banished from the garden and became subject to toil and death (Gen. 3:3–24).

TREE OF LIFE. A tree in the Garden of Eden with fruit which would bring eternal life if eaten (Gen. 3:22). In the heavenly Jerusalem there will also be a tree of life, with leaves for the healing of the nations (Rev. 22:2).

TRESPASS OFFERING. A sacrificial animal offering presented for lesser sins or offenses after full restitution to persons wronged had been made (Lev. 5:6–7, 15–19). See also *Sacrifice*.

TRIALS OF JESUS. A series of trials or appearances of Jesus before Jewish and Roman authorities which ended with His death. Jesus appeared before Annas, the former high priest (John 18:12–23); Caiphas, the current high priest, and the full Jewish Sanhedrin (Matt. 26:57–68); Pilate, the Roman governor (John 18:28–38); and Herod Antipas, ruler of Galilee (Luke 23:6–12); before finally being sentenced to death by Pilate (Mark 15:6–15).

TRIBES OF ISRAEL. The tribes which descended from the sons of Jacob—Asher, Benjamin, Dan, Gad, Issachar, Judah, Levi, Naphtali, Reuben, Simeon, and Zebulon (Gen. 49:1–28)—plus the two sons of Joseph, Ephraim and Manasseh (Gen. 48:5). After the conquest of Canaan, these tribes were assigned specific territories in the land, with the exception of Levi, the priestly tribe. The Levites were assigned to forty-eight different towns and scattered among all the other tribal territories to perform ceremonial duties. See also *Levites*.

TRIBULATION. Affliction and trouble caused by persecution (1 Thess. 3:4) and severe testing (Rev. 2:10, 22). The tribulation of believers may be overcome by patience (Rom. 8:35–37, 12:12) and a joyful spirit (2 Cor. 7:4). See also *Affliction; Persecution*.

TRIBULATION, GREAT. A time of great suffering and affliction in the end-time, sent upon the earth by the Lord to accomplish His purposes (Dan. 12:1; Rev. 7:14). Students of the Bible disagree on whether this event will precede or follow Christ's millennial reign or come before the ushering in of the new heavens and new earth. See also *Millennium; Persecution.*

TRIBUTE. A toll or tax imposed on citizens by a government. Every Hebrew male over age twenty paid an annual tribute of a half-shekel to support temple services (Exod. 30:13; Matt.17:24–27). See also *Half-Shekel Tax; Taxes; Toll.*

TRIGON. See *Sackbut.*

TRINITY, THE. God as expressed through the Father, the Son, and the Holy Spirit. The word *trinity* does not appear in the Bible, but the reality of the triune God was revealed in the O.T. at the creation of the world (Gen. 1:1–3, 26). In the N.T., the trinity was revealed at Christ's baptism (Matt. 3:16–17) and in His teachings (John 14:26; 15:26) as well as His Great Commission (Matt. 28:19). The Holy Spirit, whom Christ sent, convicts of sin, inspires believers, and empowers them for service (John 16:8, 13). The Father gives converts to Christ, and they hear His voice and follow Him (John 10:27, 29).

TRIUMPHAL ENTRY OF JESUS. Jesus' entry into Jerusalem on the Sunday before His crucifixion the following Friday. He was greeted by shouts of joy from the crowds, who were looking for an earthly king. With His entry, Jesus acknowledged He was the promised Messiah—but a spiritual deliverer rather than a conquering military hero (Matt. 21:2–11).

TROAS. An important city on the coast of Mysia where Paul received a vision. A man across from Troas in Macedonia pleaded, "Come. . .and help us" (Acts 16:8–10).

TROGYLLIUM. A city near Ephesus where Paul stopped after his third missionary journey (Acts 20:15).

TROPHIMUS. A Christian who accompanied Paul on the third missionary journey (Acts 20:4).

TROUSERS. See *Hosen.*

331

TRUMPET. A wind musical instrument made of animal horn or metal. Trumpets were used in temple ceremonies (1 Chron. 16:6–9). See also *Ram's Horn*.

TRUMPETS, FEAST OF. A Jewish religious festival, also called the *Seventh Month Festival* (Lev. 16:29). It was ushered in by the blowing of trumpets and observed by reading the law and presenting burnt offerings (Lev. 23:24–25; Neh. 8:2–3, 8–12). The exact reason for its observance is not clear.

TRUST. To put one's confidence in a person or thing. God's name and His Word are worthy of our trust (Ps. 33:21; 119:42). Christ warned that humans may deceive and be unworthy of trust (Matt. 10:17–21), but we may place ultimate trust and confidence in Him (John 6:35–37). See also *Faith*.

TRUTH. That which is reliable and consistent with God's revelation. Truth is established by God's law (Ps. 119:142– 144) and personified by Jesus Christ (John 14:6). Believers are purified by obedience to the truth (1 Pet. 1:22) and worshiping God in spirit and truth (John 4:23–24).

TRYPHENA. A fellow believer at Rome greeted and commended by Paul (Rom. 16:12).

TRYPHOSA. A fellow believer at Rome greeted and commended by Paul (Rom. 16:12).

TUBAL. The fifth son of Japheth (Gen. 10:2) and ancestor of a tribe descended from Tubal and Japheth. Isaiah mentioned Tubal as a people who would declare God's glory among the Gentiles (Isa. 66:19).

TUMORS. See *Emerods*.

TURBAN. See *Mitre*.

TURTLEDOVE (DOVE). A migratory bird noted for its plaintive cooing and affection for its mate (Song of Sol. 2:12). A turtledove was an acceptable sacrificial offering for the poor (Lev. 12:6–8). *Dove:* NIV. See also *Pigeon*.

TWELVE, THE. The twelve apostles or disciples chosen by Jesus. They were Andrew; Bartholomew (Nathanael); James, son of Alphaeus; James, son of Zebedee; John; Judas; Lebbaeus (Thaddaeus); Matt-hew; Philip; Simon the Can-aanite; Simon Peter; and Thomas (Matt. 10:1–4; Mark 3:13–19; Luke 6:12–16).

TWIN BROTHERS. See *Castor and Pollux.*

TYCHICUS. A Christian who accompanied Paul on his third missionary journey (Acts 20:4).

TYPE. A person or thing which foreshadows something else. For example, the brass serpent placed upon a pole by Moses in the wilderness (Num. 21:4–9) pointed to the atoning death of Jesus on the cross (John 3:14–15).

TYRANNUS. A man of Ephesus who allowed Paul to use his lecture hall. Paul taught here for two years after he was banned from the local synagogue (Acts 19:8–10).

TYRE/TYRUS. An ancient coastal city of Phoenicia north of Palestine. Hiram, Tyre's ruler, helped David and Solomon with their building projects (1 Kings 5:1–10). In the prophet Ezekiel's day, the city was a thriving trade center. He predicted Tyre's destruction because of its sin and idolatry (Ezek. 28:6–10). Jesus visited the city (Mark 7:24), and Paul landed here (Acts 21:3, 7). *Tyrus:* Amos 1:10.

TZADDI. The eighteenth letter of the Hebrew alphabet, used as a heading over Ps. 119:137–144.

-U-

UCAL. An unknown person to whom proverbs in the book of Proverbs are addressed (Prov. 30:1).

ULAI. A river of Persia beside which Daniel was standing when he saw the vision of the ram and goat (Dan. 8:2–16).

ULCERS. See *Emerods.*

UMPIRE. See *Daysman.*

UNBELIEF. Refusal to believe in God and to acknowledge His works (John 16:9). Unbelief is caused by Satan's power (John 8:43–47), an evil heart (Heb. 3:12), and self-glorification and pride (John 5:44). Those who refuse to believe and reject the gospel are in turn rejected by God (John 3:18–20; 8:24). See also *Atheism; Infidel.*

UNBELIEVER. See *Infidel.*

UNCIRCUMCISED. A Jewish term for impurity or wickedness of any kind (Jer. 6:10) as well as a general reference to

333

Gentiles (Rom. 2:25–29). See also *Circumcision*.

UNCLEAN. A term for physical, spiritual, or ritual impurity—a condition for which rituals of purification were prescribed (Lev. 11–15). See also *Clean*.

UNCLEAN ANIMALS. Under Mosaic Law, only animals that chewed the cud and were cloven-footed were considered "clean" and suitable for eating (Lev. 11:2–3). Even touching the flesh of an "unclean" animal made a person unclean (Lev. 11:8).

UNDERGARMENT. See *Breeches*.

UNDERSTANDING. See *Knowledge; Wisdom*.

UNICORN (WILD OX). A large animal of great strength, probably the wild ox (Num. 23:22). Yoking it and harnessing its power was considered impossible (Job 39:9–11). *Wild ox:* NIV, NRSV.

UNLEAVENED BREAD, FEAST OF. See *Passover and Feast of Unleavened Bread*.

UNPARDONABLE SIN. Blasphemy against the Holy Spirit, or attributing the work of Christ to Satan, as the critics of Jesus did: "By the prince of the devils casteth he out devils" (Mark 3:22–30). Many inter-preters believe this sin consists of decisively and finally rejecting the testimony of the Holy Spirit regarding Christ's person and work.

UNPLOWED GROUND. See *Fallow Ground*.

UNTEMPERED MORTAR (WHITEWASH). A thin layer of clay used as a protective coating on the exterior walls of buildings. The term is used figuratively of the futile promises of false prophets (Ezek. 13:10–15; 22:28). *Whitewash:* NIV, NRSV.

UPHAZ. A place in Arabia where gold was obtained, perhaps the same place as Ophir (Jer. 10:9).

UPPER EGYPT. See *Pathros*.

UPPER ROOM. A chamber or room usually built on the roof of a house and used in the summer because it was cooler than the regular living quarters (Mark 14:15). Such a room was the site of Jesus' last meal with His disciples (Luke 22:12). See also *Loft*.

UR OF THE CHALDEES (UR OF THE CHALDEANS).

A city in Mesopotamia where Abraham spent his early life with his father Terah and his wife Sarah before he was called by the Lord to go to Canaan (Gen. 11:28, 31). *Ur of the Chaldeans:* NIV, NRSV. Excavation has revealed that Ur was a thriving city and center of moon worship. See also *Mesopotamia.*

URBANE (URBANUS).

A fellow believer greeted and commended by Paul (Rom. 16:9). *Urbanus:* NIV, NRSV.

URIAH

1. A Hittite warrior in David's army whose wife Bathsheba was taken by David after the king plotted to have Uriah killed in battle (2 Sam. 11:15, 24–27). *Urias:* Greek form (Matt. 1:6).

2. NIV, NRSV name for the prophet Urijah. See *Urijah.*

URIJAH (URIAH).

A faithful prophet in Jeremiah's time who was killed by King Jehoiakim for predicting God's judgment on Judah (Jer. 26:20). *Uriah:* NIV, NRSV.

URIM AND THUMMIN.

Two objects in the breastplate of the high priest (Exod. 28:30), possibly colored stones cast as lots to help determine God's will (Num. 27:21). See also *Lots, Casting of.*

USURY (INTEREST).

Interest on money loaned. Under the Mosaic Law, Jews could exact interest only from non-Jews, not from their own countrymen (Lev. 25:36–37). *Interest:* NIV, NRSV. Nehemiah denounced those who were breaking this law (Neh. 5:7, 10). See also *Debt; Loan.*

UZ.

A place in southern Edom west of the Arabian desert where Job lived (Job 1:1; Jer. 25:20).

UZZA (UZZAH).

An Israelite who was struck dead for touch-ing the ark of the covenant while carting it to Jerusalem (1 Chron. 13:7–11). *Uzzah:* NIV, NRSV.

UZZIAH/AZARIAH/OZIAS.

The son and successor of Amaziah as king of Judah (reigned about 767–740 B.C.). A godly king, excellent general, and noted city builder (2 Chron. 26:1–15), he contracted leprosy as a divine punishment for assuming duties that belonged to the priesthood (2 Chron. 26:16–21). *Azariah:* 2 Kings 14:21; *Ozias:* Jesus' ancestry (Matt. 1:8).

-V-

VAGABOND (WANDERER).
A wanderer or fugitive. Life as a fugitive was part of the curse against Cain for murdering his brother Abel (Gen. 4:12). *Wanderer:* NIV, NRSV. The "vagabond Jews" of Acts 19:13 were professional exorcists.

VALE OF SIDDIM. A valley of tar pits near the Dead Sea where Sodom and Gomorrah were located (Gen. 14:2–10).

VALLEY OF DRY BONES. A vision of the prophet Ezekiel. When Ezekiel addressed the bones, representing Israel's exile in a foreign land, they came to life by God's Spirit. This served as God's assurance that His people would return one day to their native land (Ezek. 37:1–14). See also *Ezekiel, Book of.*

VANITY. Emptiness and futility. Life is vain and empty unless it is lived in obedience to God and His will (Ecc. 12:13).

VASHTI. The queen of Ahasuerus of Persia who refused the king's command to appear with the royal court and was replaced by Esther (Esther 1:10–12; 2:2, 15–17).

VAU. The sixth letter of the Hebrew alphabet, used as a heading over Ps. 119:41–48.

VEGETABLES. See *Pulse.*

VEIL (CURTAIN).
1. A screen or curtain which separated the holy place and the holy of holies in the tabernacle and temple. This veil was torn at Christ's death to symbolize direct access of all people to God's salvation through Jesus Christ (Matt. 27:51) *Curtain:* NIV, NRSV (Heb. 4:14–16). See also *Court of the Gentiles; Middle Wall of Partition.*
2. NIV word for *muffler.* See *Muffler.*

VENGEANCE. See *Revenge.*

VENISON (GAME). The flesh of any wild animal used for food. Isaac loved his son Esau because he was a "cunning hunter" who cooked venison (Gen. 25:27–28). *Game:* NIV, NRSV. See also *Hunter.*

VENOM (POISON). A poisonous fluid secreted by animals such as snakes and scorpions. The word is used figuratively of the destructive power of wine (Deut. 32:33). *Poison:* NRSV. See also *Poison.*

The Via Dolorosa, Jesus' crucifixion route through the old city of Jerusalem. *Courtesy Israel Ministry of Tourism*

VENOMOUS SNAKES. See *Fiery Serpents*.

VERMILION. A bright red substance used for ornamentation and painting of houses and images (Ezek. 23:14).

VESTIBULE. See *Porch*.

VIA DOLOROSA. The name, meaning "way of sorrow," for the traditional route which Jesus took from Pilate's judgment hall to Calvary for His crucifixion. It is impossible to determine the precise route, since Jerusalem was destroyed by the Romans in A.D. 70 and then rebuilt. This name does not appear in the Bible.

VIAL (FLASK). A bottle or flask which held oil or other liquids (1 Sam. 10:1). *Flask:* NIV.

VILLAGE. A collection of houses or a small town not protected by a defensive wall (Ezek. 38:11).

VINE. A plant which bore grapes. The word is also used figuratively of Israel (Hos. 10:1). Jesus referred to Himself as the "true vine" (John 15:1).

VINE OF SODOM. A plant which grew near the Dead Sea and produced a beautiful fruit which was unfit to eat—a fitting description of Israel's idolatry (Deut. 32:32).

VINEGAR (SOUR WINE). A beverage consisting of wine or strong drink that was excessively fermented until it turned sour. This drink was offered to Jesus on the cross (Matt. 27:34, 48) *Sour wine:* NRSV.

VINEYARD. A field or orchard of grapevines. The word is used symbolically for Israel (Ps. 80:8, 15–16).

VINTAGE. The time of year for making wine. Grapes were gathered with shouts of joy (Jer. 25:30), then put in baskets and carried to the winepress (Jer. 6:9). See also *Wine*.

VIOL (LYRE). A stringed musical instrument probably similar to the psaltery (Isa. 5:12). *Lyre:* NIV. See also *Harp; Psaltery*.

VIPER. See *Asp*.

VIRGIN. A general term for a young unmarried woman (Gen. 24:16).

VIRGIN BIRTH. The miraculous conception of Jesus by the Holy Spirit and His birth to the Virgin Mary. This event

A model of ancient Jerusalem, showing its massive outer wall with built-in defense towers. *Courtesy Israel Ministry of Tourism*

was foretold by the prophet Isaiah (Isa. 7:14) and revealed to Mary by an angel (Luke 1:26– 33). The Messiah's supernatural conception in a human mother corresponds to His unique role as God-man. See also *Advent of Christ, The First; Incarnation of Christ.*

VIRTUE. Moral excellence in association with power and ability—a characteristic of Jesus (Luke 6:19).

VISION. See *Dreams and Visions.*

VOCATION (CALLING). A calling based on God's purpose and grace (2 Tim. 1:9). Paul urged believers to "walk worthy" of their Christian vocation (Eph. 4:1). *Calling:* NIV, NRSV. See also *Calling.*

VOID (EMPTY). Containing nothing; empty. The earth was formless and void before God shaped it and filled it with life through His creative power (Gen. 1:2). *Empty:* NIV.

VOW. A pledge or agreement to perform a service for God in return for some expected benefit (Gen. 28:20–22).

VOW OFFERING. A gift or freewill offering which accompanied a vow to the Lord (Deut. 23:23).

VULTURE (RED KITE, BUZZARD). A large bird which fed mostly on dead animals or other wastes and was thus considered unclean (Lev. 11:14). *Red kite:* NIV; *Buzzard:* NRSV. See also *Ossifrage*.

-W-

WADI. A riverbed which is dry except during the rainy season (Gen. 26:19). This word does not occur in the Bible, but Palestine has hundreds of these wadis.

WADI OF EGYPT. See *River of Egypt*.

WAFER. A thin cake made of fine, unleavened flour and anointed with oil for meal offerings (Exod. 29:2). Wafers were sometimes sweetened with honey (Exod. 16:31).

WAGES. Payment for work rendered by field hands or common laborers. Wages were paid daily, at the end of the workday (Lev. 19:13).

WAGON. A crude wooden cart pulled by oxen (Gen. 45:19). See also *Cart*.

WALL. A massive fence of stone or brick around a city for protection against enemy attack (2 Sam. 18:24). Defense towers and even houses were often built on these walls (Isa. 2:15). See also *Fenced City; Siege*.

WALL OF PARTITION. See *Middle Wall of Partition*.

WANDERER. See *Vagabond*.

WAR. Armed conflict between nations or tribes. The Hebrews considered their conflicts with enemy nations as the Lord's battles (Num. 10:9). Early skirmishes were fought by spearmen, archers, and slingers; horses and chariots were a later development in Israel's history. The prophets envisioned an age without war (Mic. 4:3).

WARD. A prison cell or lockup room. This word is also used for a detachment of soldiers on guard duty (Acts 12:10). See also *Prison*.

WARDROBE. A place where royal robes or priestly vestments were kept (2 Kings 22:14).

WARP. The long threads in hand-spun cloth. These threads are extended lengthwise in the loom and crossed by the *woof,* or threads running in the opposite direction. See also *Weaver*.

WARRIORS. See *Mighty Men*.

WASH. To cleanse (Matt. 27:24). The Hebrews emphasized cleanliness and ceremonial purity. Washing the hands before meals or the feet after a journey were considered religious duties (Matt. 15:2). See also *Clean; Purification*.

WASHERMAN'S FIELD. See *Fuller's Field*.

WATCHMAN (SENTINEL). A guard or sentry stationed at city gates. These watchmen also patrolled the streets and called out the hours of the night (2 Sam. 18:24–27). *Sentinel:* NRSV.

WATCHTOWER. A tall guard station or lookout post which provided early warning of approaching dangers (Isa. 21:5–11).

WATER. In Palestine's arid climate, water was a precious commodity. People were dependent on wells or cisterns during the dry summer and fall. Public wells or reservoirs were provided for travelers (Gen. 26:19). Jesus promised the "water of life" to a sinful Samaritan woman (John 4:10–14). See also *Well*.

WATER CARRIER. See *Drawer of Water*.

WATER HEN. See *Swan*.

WATER OF JEALOUSY. A mixture of water with dust prescribed as a test for a woman accused of adultery by her husband (Num. 5:11–31).

WATER OF SEPARATION (WATER OF CLEANSING). Water mixed with ashes to purify a person after defilement through contact with the dead (Num. 19:13–22). *Water of cleansing:* NIV. See also *Bitter Water*.

WATERING TROUGH. See *Gutter*.

WATERPOT. A large clay vessel in which water for the household was stored (John 2:6–7).

WATERS OF MEROM. A lake ten miles north of the Sea of Galilee through which the Jordan River flows on its southward passage (Josh. 11:5–7).

WAVE OFFERING (ELEVATION OFFERING). A sacrificial animal presented to God to celebrate restoration of a right relationship with God. The sacrifice was "waved" before the Lord to gain acceptance (Exod.

29:24). *Elevation offering:* NRSV. See also *Sacrifice.*

WAX. A substance formed by bees while making honey. The word is also used figuratively for the punishment of the wicked in God's presence (Ps. 68:2).

WAY OF THE SEA. A road which ran from Sidon in Phoenicia to Egypt, passing through Palestine (Isa. 9:1). See also *Highway; Road.*

WAY, THE. A term of contempt for the Christian faith used by the enemies of the early church (Acts 9:2; 24:14, 22).

WEALTH. See *Mammon; Money.*

WEASEL. An unclean animal, possibly the mole or polecat (Lev. 11:29).

WEAVER. A craftsman who made cloth from several different raw materials, including wool and camel hair (Exod. 35:35; Lev. 13:47). The Hebrews may have learned the art of weaving in Egypt.

WEDDING. A marriage ceremony. A Jewish wedding was a festive occasion with the entire community participating. The bride wore jewels and an ornamented white robe with a veil. The bridegroom, accompanied by friends and musicians, proceeded to the bride's home to conduct her to the wedding hall. Festivities continued for seven days (Matt. 25:6–10; Luke 12:36; 14:8). See also *Betrothal; Dowry; Marriage.*

WEED. See *Cockle.*

WEEKS, FEAST OF. See *Pentecost.*

WELL. A large pit dug in the ground to reach groundwater. Wells were usually covered with stone slabs or surrounded by low stone walls (John 4:6). The word is also used figuratively of salvation (Isa. 12:3) and wisdom (Prov. 16:22). The phrase "wells without water" shows the futility of wickedness (2 Pet. 2:17). See also *Water.*

WHALE. A large sea-dwelling mammal (Gen. 1:21). The "great fish" that swallowed Jonah is thought to be an enormous white shark, common in the Mediterranean Sea (Jon. 1:17).

WHEAT. A grain which was ground and baked into bread (1 Kings 5:11). The wheat harvest was observed as a festival and time of celebration (Exod. 34:22). See also *Corn*.

WHIRLWIND (GALE, STORM). A great storm or tempest (Job 37:9). Elijah was transported to heaven by a whirlwind (2 Kings 2:1, 11). The word was also used figuratively for swift and sudden destruction (Isa. 17:13). *Gale:* NIV; *Storm:* NRSV. See also *Tempest*.

WHITE OWL. See *Swan*.

WHITED SEPULCHRE. See *Sepulchre*.

WHITEWASH. See *Untempered Mortar*.

WICKEDNESS. Evil, malice, and wrongdoing. See *Evil; Iniquity; Sin*.

WIDOW. A woman whose husband had died. Fair and just treatment of widows was enjoined under Mosaic Law (Exod. 22:22). In the N.T., visiting the fatherless and widows was cited as evidence of true religion (Jas. 1:27). See also *Levirate Marriage*.

WIFE. A married woman. Wives are urged to love and respect their husbands and to be faithful to them (Eph. 5:33; Prov. 31:11–12). Husbands and wives are to be mutually committed to each other and fulfill each other's needs (1 Cor. 7:2–5). See also *Family; Husband*.

WILD OX. See *Unicorn*.

WILDERNESS. A dry, desolate, uncultivated region where little vegetation grew. John the Baptist preached in the Judean wilderness (Matt. 3:1). See also *Desert*.

WILDERNESS WANDERINGS. The aimless course taken by the Hebrew people in the Sinai Peninsula for forty years after they left Egypt— God's punishment for their sin of disobedience (Deut. 1:1; Josh. 5:6). God provided food and guidance through Moses until they arrived in Canaan (Exod. 16:35; Neh. 9:24).

WILL OF GOD. God's desire and wish for His people. The Father's will is that those who believe on the Son will have eternal life and that none will be lost (John 6:39–40). The disciples of Jesus were taught to pray for God's will to be done on earth as it is in heaven (Matt. 6:10). Paul urged the Christians at Rome to allow God to transform their minds to know the perfect will of God (Rom. 12:2).

WILLOW (POPLAR). A tree which grew by streams; perhaps the weeping willow (Ps. 137:1–2). Its branches were used for booths at the Feast of Tabernacles (Lev. 23:40). *Poplar:* NIV. See also *Poplar*.

WIMPLE (CLOAK). A mantle, scarf, or shawl worn around the neck by women (Isa. 3:22). *Cloak:* NIV, NRSV.

WIND. The movement of the air. The Bible speaks of the "four winds" (Jer. 49:36): The north wind (Job 37:22), the warm south wind (Luke 12:55), the cool west wind bringing rain (Luke 12:54), and the scorching east wind from the desert (Job 27:21). Jesus illustrated the freedom of the Holy Spirit with the mysteries of the wind (John 3:8).

WINDOW. A small opening in a house or public building which let in light and cool breezes (1 Chron. 15:29). These openings were probably covered with shutters or latticework.

WINE/STRONG DRINK. The juice of grapes, fermented to produce a strong beverage which was very popular among the Jews (Gen. 40:11). Commonly referred to as *strong drink* (Prov. 31:6), wine was prohibited to Nazarites (Num. 6:3) as well as to priests before they officiated at the altar (Lev. 10:9). Excessive consumption of wine was denounced (Prov. 20: 1; Eph. 5:18). See also *Grape*.

WINEBIBBER (DRUNK-ARD). A person addicted to wine (Prov. 23:20–21). Jesus was accused of being a winebibber because He befriended sinners (Matt. 11:19). *Drunkard:* NIV, NRSV.

WINEPRESS. A vat or tank where juice was squeezed from grapes in the wine-making process. Usually hewn out of rock, the winepress had an upper vat where the grapes were crushed and a lower vat that received the juice (Judg. 6:11; Isa. 63: 2–3). See also *Grape*.

WINESKIN. See *Bottle*.

WING. A symbolic expression for God's protection. He delivers His people on the wings of eagles (Exod. 19:4).

WINNOWING. The process of separating chaff or straw from the grains of wheat by beating the stalks and throwing them into the air; symbolically, to rid oneself of sin or worldly desire (Matt. 3:12). See also *Fan; Threshingfloor*.

WINTERHOUSE (WINTER APARTMENT). A dwelling used by kings in the winter months (Jer. 36:22). *Winter apartment:* NIV, NRSV.

WISDOM. Knowledge guided by insight and understanding. Reverence for God is the source of wisdom (Prov. 9:10). Wisdom is more valuable than riches (Prov. 8:11) and produces good fruit (Jas. 3:17). Christ is the key that opens the hidden treasures of God's wisdom (Col. 2:3).

WISDOM LITERATURE. A distinct category of literature in the Bible, including Job, Proverbs, Ecclesiastes, and some of the psalms, so named because they deal with some of the most important ethical and philosophical issues of life—the meaning of suffering, the nature and purpose of God, human relationships, etc.

WISE MEN. Astrologers from Mesopotamia or Persia, often referred to as the *magi,* who brought gifts to the infant Jesus in Bethlehem (Matt. 2: 10–11). See also *Astrologer.*

WITCHCRAFT. The practice of sorcery or black magic by witches and wizards—an activity denounced by God (Deut. 18:10; Mic. 5:12). King Saul displeased God by asking the witch of En-dor to summon the spirit of Samuel from the dead (1 Sam. 28:3–25). See also *Magic; Sorcery.*

WITNESS. One who gives testimony regarding an event or another person's character. Under Mosaic Law, the testimony of at least two persons was required to convict a person of a capital offense (Deut. 17:6). False witnesses were punished severely (Deut. 19: 18–19). Believers are empowered to serve as witnesses for Christ (Acts 1:8). See also *Record; Testimony.*

WIZARD (SPIRITIST). A male witch, or practitioner of black magic, who claimed to have secret knowledge given by a spirit from the dead (2 Kings 21:6). *Spiritist:* NIV. Under Mosaic Law, wizards were to be put to death by stoning (Lev. 20:27). See also *Familiar Spirit.*

WOE. An expression of extreme grief or distress (Matt. 24:19). The word also expressed the threat of future punishment (Jer. 48:46).

WOLF. A fierce wild animal of the dog family which posed a threat to sheep (Isa. 11:6). Jesus also used the word figuratively of false prophets (Matt. 7:15).

WOMB. Barren women regarded themselves as cursed by the Lord (1 Sam. 1:5–10). Children were described as "fruit of the womb" and a blessing from God (Ps. 127:3–5). See also *Barren; Children.*

WOODCUTTER. See *Hewer.*

WOOF. See *Warp.*

WOOL. The furlike coat of sheep which was highly prized by the Jews for making clothes (Prov. 31:13). Its vulnerability to moths was a problem (Matt. 6:19). See also *Fleece; Sheep.*

WORD OF GOD. God's revelation of Himself to man, especially through Jesus and the Bible (Heb. 4:12). The written Scriptures, which Christians accept as the Word of God, testifies to Jesus as the eternal and living Word of God (John 1:1; 5:39). See also *Bible; Logos.*

WORK. Labor in a worthwhile cause; fruitful activity. A Christian's work should be performed as service to the Lord (Eph. 6:6–8).

WORKS. Good deeds performed as an expression of a believer's commitment to Christ. Works cannot save or justify (Eph. 2:9), but they do fulfill God's purpose for His people. We are created in Jesus Christ in order to perform good works for the building of God's kingdom (Eph. 2:10).

WORLDLY. See *Carnal.*

WORM. An insect which destroyed plants and consumed dead flesh (Job 7:5). The word is also used symbolically of human helplessness or insignificance (Isa. 41:14) and frailty (Ps. 22:6).

WORMWOOD. A plant noted for its bitter taste (Jer. 9:15). The phrase "gall and wormwood" describes something offensive or sorrowful (Deut. 29:18). See also *Hemlock.*

WORSHIP. The praise and adoration of God expressed both publicly and privately (Deut. 6; 1 Chron. 16:29). The Jews worshiped in the tabernacle until the temple became their worship center. After their period of exile among the Babylonians and Persians, they worshiped in neighborhood synagogues. The book known as Psalms contains many spiritual songs and hymns chanted or sung in public worship. See also *Hymn; Praise; Psalms, Book of.*

WORTHY. Of value or merit. The Lamb of God is worthy of praise because He redeemed us, made us kings and priests, and will share His reign with us (Rev. 5:9–14).

WRATH. Strong anger or indignation. Human wrath may be kindled by false accusation (Gen. 31:36) or disobedience (Num. 31:14–18), but God's wrath is exercised against ungodliness (Rom. 1:18), idolatry (Ps. 78:58–59), and unbelief (John 3:36). See also *Judgment; Punishment.*

WREATH. See *Garland.*

WRITING. The Hebrews probably learned writing from the Egyptians. Earliest writing was done on stone, clay tablets, papyrus, and animal skins. See also *Ink; Paper.*

-X-

XERXES. See *Ahasuerus.*

-Y-

YAHWEH. The Hebrew spelling of the major name for God in the O.T., translated in most English Bibles as "Lord" or "Jehovah." See *Jehovah.*

YARN. Thread used in weaving cloth. Yarn was produced from linen and wool fiber as well as the hair of camels and goats (Exod. 35:25–26). See also *Warp; Weaver.*

YEAR OF JUBILEE. See *Jubile.*

YEAST. See *Leaven.*

YIRON. See *Iron,* No. 1.

YOKE. A wooden collar or harness placed on the neck of draft animals and attached to plows and other agricultural tools (Jer. 31:18). The word was also used to denote servitude or oppression (1 Kings 12:4–14). Jesus declared His yoke is not burdensome (Matt. 11:29–30).

YOKEFELLOW (COMPANION). A fellow worker or comrade in a common cause. Paul appealed to an unnamed "yokefellow" in Philippi to help two women resolve their differences (Phil. 4:3). *Companion:* NRSV.

-Z-

ZABULON. See *Zebulun*.

ZACCHAEUS. A wealthy tax collector who, after a conversation with Jesus at Jericho, vowed to give half of his wealth to the poor and make fourfold restitution to those whom he had cheated. Jesus declared that salvation had come to Zacchaeus (Luke 19:1–10). See also *Publican*.

ZACHARIAH. The son and successor of Jeroboam II as king of Israel. Zachariah ruled only about three months (about 753–752 B.C.). before being assassinated by Shallum (2 Kings 14:29; 15:8–12).

ZACHARIAS (ZECHARIAH). A godly priest and the father of John the Baptist. Zacharias was stricken speechless for his reluctance to believe a son would be born to him in his old age (Luke 1:18–22). *Zechariah:* NIV, NRSV.

ZADOK. The priest who anointed Solomon king. He served as high priest for a time under both David and Solomon (2 Sam. 8:17; 1 Kings 1:39; 2:35).

ZAIN. The seventh letter of the Hebrew alphabet, used as a heading over Ps. 119:49–56.

ZALMONAH. A place in the wilderness where the Israelites camped (Num. 33:41–42).

ZALMUNNA. A Midianite king killed by Gideon's army (Judg. 8:4–21). See also *Zebah*.

ZAMZUMMIMS (ZANZUM-MITES, ZAMZUMMIM). A race of giants who lived in the region later occupied by the Ammonites (Deut. 2:20, 21). *Zanzummites:* NIV; *Zamzummim:* NRSV. See also *Zuzim*.

ZAPHNATH-PAANEAH. See *Joseph,* No. 1.

ZAREAH. See *Zorah*.

ZARED (ZERED). A brook and valley near the Dead Sea crossed by the Israelites during their wilderness wandering (Num. 21:12). *Zered:* NIV, NRSV.

ZAREPHATH/SAREPTA. A coastal town of Phoenicia where Elijah restored a widow's son to life. Elijah lodged with her during a drought (1 Kings 17:10–24). *Sarepta:* Luke 4:26.

The tomb of the prophet Zechariah, in the Kidron Valley outside the old city wall of Jerusalem.

Courtesy Israel Ministry of Tourism

ZEAL. Ardent desire and determination (Phil. 3:6). Isaiah predicted the "zeal of the Lord" would establish the Messiah's kingdom (Isa. 9:7).

ZEALOTS. See *Zelotes*.

ZEBADIAH. A commander in David's army who directed 24,000 warriors (1 Chron. 27:7).

ZEBAH. A Midianite king killed by Gideon's army (Judg. 8:21). See also *Zalmunna*.

ZEBEDEE. A Galilean fisherman and father of two of Jesus' disciples, James and John (Matt. 4:21–22).

ZEBOIM/ZEBOIIM. One of the five cities near the Dead Sea destroyed along with Sodom and Gomorrah because of its sin (Deut. 29:23). *Zeboiim:* Gen. 14:8. See also *Cities of the Plain*.

ZEBULUN/ZABULON. The sixth son of Jacob and Leah (Gen. 30:19–20) and the tribe descended from Zebulun's three sons (Num. 26:26). This tribe settled in the fertile hill country of Galilee (Josh. 19: 10–16). *Zabulon:* Greek form (Matt. 4:13). See also *Tribes of Israel*.

349

ZECHARIAH.

1. A prophet after the Babylonian conquest of Judah who probably helped rebuild the temple in Jerusalem (Ezra 5:1), and author of the O.T. book which bears his name.

2. NIV, NRSV name for *Zacharias*. See *Zacharias*.

ZECHARIAH, BOOK OF. A

prophetic book of the O.T. written to encourage the Jewish people during the difficult years back in their homeland following their period of exile among the Babylonians and Persians. Zechariah, through a series of eight visions (1:7–6:8) and four specific messages from God (7:4–8:23), encouraged the people to complete the task of rebuilding the temple in Jerusalem. The prophet also presented God's promises for the future, including the coming of the Messiah (9: 9–10:12), the restoration of the nation of Israel (10:1–12), and the universal reign of God (14:1–14). See also *Messiah*.

ZEDEKIAH/MATTANIAH.

The last king of Judah (reigned about 597–587 B.C.), who was renamed and placed on the throne as a puppet ruler by King Nebuchadnezzar of Babylonia (2 Kings 24:15, 17). Ignoring Jeremiah's advice, he rebelled against the Babylonians, only to be blinded and taken to Babylon in chains after seeing his sons put to death (2 Kings 25:6–7). His original name was *Mattaniah* (2 Kings 24:17).

ZEEB. A Midianite prince killed by Gideon's army (Judg. 7:25).

ZELAH (ZELA). The place where King Saul and his son Jonathan were buried in the territory of Benjamin (2 Sam. 21:14). *Zela:* NIV, NRSV.

ZELOPHEHAD. A member of the tribe of Manasseh whose five daughters petitioned for the right to inherit his property because he had no sons. Their request was granted on the condition that they not marry outside the tribe (Num. 26:33; 27:1–8).

ZELOTES (ZEALOT). A member of a political-religious party of zealous Jews in N.T. times whose aim was to overthrow Roman rule and establish a Jewish theocracy. Jesus' disciple known as Simon the Canaanite may have been a member of this party or sympathetic with its views (Luke 6:15). *Zealot:* NIV, NRSV. See also *Canaanites*, No. 2.

ZENAS. A Christian lawyer whom Paul asked Titus to bring while the apostle was spending the winter at Nicopolis (Titus 3:12–13).

ZEPHANIAH. A priest and friend of Jeremiah and author of the O.T. book which bears his name. Zephaniah often served as a messenger between Jeremiah and King Zedekiah of Judah (Jer. 21:1–2). After Jerusalem fell, he was killed by the Babylonians (Jer. 52:24–27).

ZEPHANIAH, BOOK OF. A short prophetic book of the O.T. known for its vivid portrayal of the certainty of God's judgment against the nation of Judah (1:1–2:15). The prophet also declared that God would spare a faithful remnant (3:13), through which His promise of a future Messiah would be accomplished.

ZEPHATH/HORMAH. A Canaanite town near Kadesh destroyed by the tribes of Simeon and Judah. It was occupied by the tribe of Simeon and renamed *Hormah* (Num. 21:3; Judg. 1:17).

ZERED. See *Zared*.

ZERUBBABEL/ZOROBABEL/SHESH-BAZZAR. A leader of the second group of Jews who returned to Jerusalem about 520 B.C. after their period of exile in Babylonia and Persia (Ezra 2:2). He supervised the rebuilding of the temple and helped restore religious practices among his people (Zech. 4:1–14; Ezra 6:14–22). He apparently was appointed governor of Judah by King Cyrus of Persia (Hag. 2:21). *Zorobabel:* Jesus' ancestry (Matt. 1:12). *Shesh-bazzar:* Ezra 5:14.

ZEUS. See *Jupiter*.

ZIBA. A former servant of King Saul who helped David locate Jonathan's son Mephibosheth. He became Mephibosheth's servant on the land restored by the king (2 Sam. 9:2–11).

ZIDON. See *Sidon*.

ZIF (ZIV). The second month of the Hebrew year, corresponding to *Iyyar* in the later Jewish calendar (1 Kings 6:1, 37). *Ziv:* NIV, NRSV.

ZIGGURAT. A tall Mesopotamian temple tower, built like a pyramid with staircases outside and a shrine for pagan worship on top. The tower of Babel was a ziggurat (Gen. 11:1–9). See also *Babel, Tower of.*

ZIKLAG. A city on the border of Judah assigned to David by King Achish of Gath as a place of refuge from King Saul (1 Sam. 27:5–6).

ZILPAH. Leah's maid who became a concubine of Jacob and bore two of his twelve sons, Gad and Asher (Gen. 30:9–13). See also *Jacob; Leah.*

ZIMRAN. A son of Abraham by his concubine Keturah (Gen. 25:1–2).

ZIMRI. A chariot commander under King Elah of Israel who killed the king and assumed the throne (about 885 B.C.), only to commit suicide seven days later to escape the wrath of Omri's army (1 Kings 16:8–18).

ZIN. A desert wilderness near the Dead Sea through which the Hebrews passed. Moses' sister Miriam died and was buried here (Num. 20:1).

ZION/SION. One of the hills on which Jerusalem was built and the site of an ancient Jebusite fortress before the city was captured by David. In Solomon's time this section of Jerusalem was extended to include the temple area. Sometimes all of Jerusalem is referred to as "Zion" (1 Kings 8:1). *Sion:* Rev. 14:1. See also *Jerusalem.*

ZIPH. A city in the hill country of Judah where David hid from King Saul (1 Sam. 23:14–18).

ZIPPORAH. A daughter of Jethro the Midianite priest, the wife of Moses, and mother of Moses' sons Gershom and Eliezer (Exod. 2:21–22).

ZIV. See *Zif.*

ZOAR/BELA. An ancient city of Canaan destroyed, along with Sodom and Gomorrah, because of its sin (Gen. 19:20–25). This city was also known as *Bela* (Gen. 14:2). See also *Cities of the Plain.*

ZOBAH/ZOBA/HAMATH-ZOBAH. A Syrian kingdom which warred bitterly against King Saul (1 Sam. 14:47). *Zoba:* 2 Sam. 10:6, 8. *Hamath-zobah:* 2 Chron. 8:3.

ZOPHAR. One of Job's friends or "comforters" (Job 2:11).

ZORAH/ZAREAH/ZOREAH. The place where the judge

Samson was born near Dan in the lowlands of Judah (Judg. 13:24–25). *Zareah:* Neh. 11:29. *Zoreah:* Josh. 15:33.

ZOROBABEL. See *Zerubbabel.*

ZUPH. The land where Saul first met the prophet Samuel while searching for his father's lost donkeys (1 Sam. 9:5–14).

ZUR. The Midianite king killed by Israelites during the wilderness wandering years (Num. 31:8).

ZUZIM (ZUZITES). A race of giants in the land east of the Jordan River (Gen. 14:5). *Zuzites:* NIV. Probably the same tribe as the *Zamzummims.* See also *Zamzummims.*

CONCORDANCE

George W. Knight

Abbreviations Used for Books of the Bible

Abbreviation	Bible Book	Abbreviation	Bible Book
Gen	Genesis	Eccl	Ecclesiastes
Ex	Exodus	Song	Song of Solomon
Lev	Leviticus	Isa	Isaiah
Num	Numbers	Jer	Jeremiah
Deut	Deuteronomy	Lam	Lamentations
Josh	Joshua	Ezek	Ezekiel
Judg	Judges	Dan	Daniel
Ruth	Ruth	Hos	Hosea
1 Sam	1 Samuel	Joel	Joel
2 Sam	2 Samuel	Amos	Amos
1 Kgs	1 Kings	Obad	Obadiah
2 Kgs	2 Kings	Jon	Jonah
1 Chr	1 Chronicles	Mic	Micah
2 Chr	2 Chronicles	Nah	Nahum
Ezra	Ezra	Hab	Habakkuk
Neh	Nehemiah	Zeph	Zephaniah
Esth	Esther	Hag	Haggai
Job	Job	Zech	Zechariah
Ps, Pss	Psalm(s)	Mal	Malachi
Prov	Proverbs		

Abbreviations Used for Books of the Bible

NEW TESTAMENT

Abbreviation	Bible Book	Abbreviation	Bible Book
Matt	Matthew	1 Tim	1 Timothy
Mark	Mark	2 Tim	2 Timothy
Luke	Luke	Titus	Titus
John	John	Phlm	Philemon
Acts	Acts	Heb	Hebrews
Rom	Romans	Jas	James
1 Cor	1 Corinthians	1 Pet	1 Peter
2 Cor	2 Corinthians	2 Pet	2 Peter
Gal	Galatians	1 John	1 John
Eph	Ephesians	2 John	2 John
Phil	Philippians	3 John	3 John
Col	Colossians	Jude	Jude
1 Thes	1 Thessalonians	Rev	Revelation
2 Thes	2 Thessalonians		

-A-

AARON (brother of Moses and first high priest of Israel). For a description of Aaron's life and work, see **Ex 4:14; 5:1; 7:10–20; 17:12; 28:1; 32:3–5,35 • Lev 8:2–27; 10:8 • Num 4:19; 16:3; 17:3–10; 20:12,28.** Aaron is also mentioned in 1 Chr 6:49 • Pss 105:26; 133:2 • Luke 1:5 • Acts 7:40 • Heb 5:4; 7:11; 9:4.

ABANA RIVER (a river of Syria). 2 Kgs 5:12.

ABASE [D]
Ezek 21:26 exalt him that is low, and *a* him that is high
Luke 18:14 every one that exalteth himself shall be *a'd*
Phil 4:12 I [Paul] know...how to be *a'd*...how to abound

ABATED
Gen 8:3 hundred and fifty days the waters were *a*
Deut 34:7 his [Moses'] eye was not dim, nor...natural force *a*

ABBA (an Aramaic word for "Father"). Mark 14:36 • Rom 8:15 • Gal 4:6.

ABDON (a judge of Israel). Judg 12:13,15.

ABED-NEGO (a companion of Daniel). Dan 2:49; 3:12–30. *Azariah:* Dan 1:7.

ABEL (a son of Adam). **Gen 4:2–25** • Matt 23:35 • Luke 11:51 • Heb 11:4; 12:24.

ABIA. See *Abijah.*

ABIATHAR (a high priest in David's time). 1 Sam 22:20–22; 23:6,9; 30:7 • 2 Sam 8:17; 15:24–35; 17:15; 19:11; 20:25 • 1 Kgs 1:7–42; 2:22–35; 4:4 • 1 Chr 15:11; 18:16; 24:6; 27:34 • Mark 2:26.

ABIDE [ING, TH]
1 Kgs 8:13 the earth a settled place for thee [God] to *a* in
Ps 15:1 LORD, who shall *a* in thy tabernacle?
Ps 91:1 *a* under the shadow of the Almighty
Ps 119:90 thou [God] hast established the earth...it *a'th*
Eccl 1:4 another generation cometh...earth *a'th* for ever
Nah 1:6 who can *a* in...fierceness of his [God's] anger?
Luke 2:8 shepherds *a'ing* in the field, keeping watch
Luke 9:4 whatsoever house ye enter into, there *a*
Luke 19:5 Zacchaeus...to day I [Jesus] must *a* at thy house
John 3:36 believeth not the Son...wrath...*a'th* on him

John 12:46 whosoever believeth on me [Jesus]...not *a* in darkness

John 14:16 another Comforter...may *a* with you for ever

John 15:4 A in me [Jesus], and I in you

John 15:5 He that *a'th* in me [Jesus]...bringeth...fruit

John 15:10 keep my [Jesus'] commandments...*a* in my love

1 Cor 3:14 any man's work *a* which he hath built

1 Cor 13:13 a'th faith, hope, charity...greatest...is charity

Phil 1:25 I [Paul] shall *a*... with you all for your...joy

1 Pet 1:23 Born...by the word of God...*a'th* for ever

1 John 2:10 He that loveth his brother *a'th* in the light

1 John 2:17 but he that doeth the will of God *a'th* for ever

1 John 2:28 a in him [Jesus]... confidence...at his coming

1 John 3:14 He that loveth not his brother *a'th* in death

1 John 3:15 no murderer hath eternal life *a'ing* in him

ABIGAIL (a wife of David). 1 Sam 25:3–42; 27:3; 30:5 • 2 Sam 2:2; 3:3 • 1 Chr 3:1.

ABIJAH (son and successor of Rehoboam as king of Judah).

2 Chr 11:20–22. *Abia:* Matt 1:7. *Abijam:* 1 Kgs 14:31; **15:1–8.**

ABIJAM. See *Abijah.*

ABILENE (a Roman section of Palestine). Luke 3:1.

ABIMELECH

1. A Philistine king in Abraham's time. Gen 20:2–18; 21:22–32; 26:1–31.

2. A son of Gideon. Judg 8: 31; **9:1–56;** 10:1 • 2 Sam 11:21.

ABIRAM (leader of a rebellion against Moses). **Num 16:1–27;** 26:9 • Deut 11:6 • Ps 106:17.

ABISHAG (David's nurse in his old age). 1 Kgs 1:3–4,15; 2:17,21–22.

ABISHAI (deputy commander in David's army). 1 Sam 26:6–9 • 2 Sam 2:18,24; 3:30; 10:10–14; 16:9–11; 18:2–12; 19:21; 20: 6,10; 21:17; 23:18 • 1 Chr 2:16; 11:20; 18:12; 19:11,15.

ABISHALOM. See *Absalom.*

ABLE TO DELIVER
Isa 36:14 Let not Hezekiah deceive...not be *a-t-d* you

Ezek 7:19 gold...not be *a-t-d* them in the day of the... LORD

Dan 3:17 God...is *a-t-d* us [Daniel's friends]

ABNER (commander of King Saul's army). 1 Sam 14:50–51; 17:55–57; 20:25; 26:5–15 • 2 Sam 2:8–30; 3:6–37; 4:1,12 • 1 Kgs 2:5,32 • 1 Chr 26:28; 27:21.

ABOLISH [ED]
Isa 2:18 the idols he [God] shall utterly *a*
Isa 51:6 my [God's] righteousness shall not be *a'ed*
Eph 2:15 *a'ed* in his [Jesus'] flesh...enmity...making peace
2 Tim 1:10 Jesus Christ, who hath *a'ed* death

ABOMINATION OF DESOLATION
Matt 24:15 see the *a-o-d*... stand in the holy place
Mark 13:14 see the *a-o-d*... standing where it ought not

ABOMINATION TO THE LORD, THINGS CONSIDERED AN
1. Graven images (Deut 7:25)
2. The froward, or wicked (Prov 3:32)
3. A false balance (Prov 11:1)
4. Lying lips (Prov 12:22)
5. Sacrifice of the wicked (Prov 15:8)
6. Thoughts of the wicked (Prov 15:26)
7. Every one that is proud in heart (Prov 16:5)

ABOUND [ED]
Rom 5:15 the grace of God... hath *a'ed* unto many
Rom 5:20 sin *a'ed,* grace did much more *a*
Rom 6:1 Shall we continue in sin, that grace may *a?*
Rom 15:13 *a* in hope, through the power of the Holy Ghost
2 Cor 8:7 in your love...see that ye *a* in this grace also
Eph 1:8 he [God] hath *a'ed* toward us in all wisdom
Phil 4:12 I [Paul] know...how to be abased...how to *a*
1 Thes 3:12 increase and *a* in love one toward another

ABOVE
Gen 1:7 God...divided the waters...*a* the firmament
Ex 19:5 a peculiar treasure unto me [God] *a* all people
Ex 20:4 not make...likeness of any thing...in heaven *a*
Deut 7:6 chosen thee to be a special people...*a* all people
1 Kgs 8:23 no God like thee, in heaven *a,* or on earth beneath
1 Chr 16:25 great is the LORD... to be feared *a* all gods
1 Chr 29:11 thou [God] art exalted as head *a* all

2 Chr 2:5 for great is our God *a* all gods

Esth 2:17 the king loved Esther *a* all the women

Ps 8:1 who [God] hast set thy glory *a* the heavens

Ps 57:5 Be thou exalted, O God, *a* the heavens

Ps 95:3 For the LORD is...a great King *a* all gods

Ps 99:2 The LORD...is high *a* all the people

Prov 31:10 a virtuous woman? For her price is far *a* rubies

Jer 17:9 The heart is deceitful *a* all things

Dan 6:3 Daniel was preferred *a* the...princes

Matt 10:24 The disciple is not *a* his master

John 8:23 Ye are from beneath; I [Jesus] am from *a*

1 Cor 10:13 God...not suffer you...tempted *a*...ye are able

Eph 1:21 Far *a* all principality, and power, and might

Eph 3:20 unto him [Jesus]... able to do...*a* all that we ask

Eph 4:6 One God...who is *a* all, and through all

Eph 6:16 A all, taking the shield of faith

Phil 2:9 given him [Jesus] a name...*a* every name

Col 3:1 seek those things which are *a*

Col 3:2 Set your affection on things *a,* not on...the earth

Jas 1:17 Every good...and... perfect gift is from *a*

Jas 3:17 Wisdom...from *a* is first pure, then...gentle

ABRAHAM (father of the nation of Israel). Also known as *Abram.* See **Gen 11:26–25: 10** for a sketch of Abraham.

1. Called by the Lord to a new land (Gen 12:1–6)

2. Promised many descendants (Gen 12:1–7; 13:14–18; 15:5–21; 17:1–9; 22:15–19)

3. Separated from Lot (Gen 13:1–12)

4. Blessed by Melchizekek (Gen 14:17–20)

5. Son Ishmael born to Hagar (Gen 16:15–16)

6. Name changed from Abram to Abraham (Gen 17:5)

7. Circumcised with his household (Gen 17:10–27)

8. Interceded for Sodom and Gomorrah (Gen 18:23–33)

9. Son Isaac born to Sarah (Gen 21:1–8)

10. Prevented from sacrificing Isaac (Gen 22:1–14)

11. Death of Sarah (Gen 23:1–20)

12. Death of Abraham (Gen 25:7–10)

Abraham is mentioned several times in the New Testament: Matt 1:1–2,17; 3:9; 8:11; 22:32 • Mark 12:26 • Luke 1:55,73; 3:8,34; 13:16,28; 16:23–25, 29–30; 19:9; 20:37 •

John 8:39–58 • Acts 3:13,25; 7:2–32; 13:26 • Rom 4:1–16; 9:7; 11:1 • 2 Cor 11:22 • Gal 3:6–18; 4:22 • Heb 2:16; 6:13; 7:1–9; 11:8,17 • Jas 2:21,23 • 1 Pet 3:6.

ABRAM. See *Abraham.*

ABSALOM (a son of King David who tried to seize his father's throne). 2 Sam 3:3; 13:1,4,20–39; 14:1–33; **15:1–18:33;** 19:1–10; 20:6 • 1 Kgs 1:6; 2:7 • 1 Chr 3:2 • 2 Chr 11:20–21. *Abishalom:* 1 Kgs 15:2–10.

ABUNDANCE
1 Kgs 18:41 Elijah said...there is a sound of *a* of rain
Ps 37:11 meek shall...delight... in the *a* of peace
Eccl 5:12 *a* of the rich will not suffer him to sleep
Matt 12:34 out of the *a* of the heart the mouth speaketh
Luke 12:15 life consisteth not in the *a*...he possesseth

ABUNDANT
1 Cor 12:24 more *a* honour to that part which lacked
2 Cor 4:15 *a* grace might... redound to the glory of God
2 Cor 11:23 in labours more *a,* in stripes above measure
1 Tim 1:14 grace of our Lord was exceeding *a* with faith

1 Pet 1:3 according to his [God's] *a* mercy...hath begotten us...a lively hope

ACCEPT [ED]
Job 42:9 the LORD also *a'ed* Job
Jer 14:12 I [God] will not *a* them...consume them by the sword
Jer 37:20 let my supplication... be *a'ed* before thee [God]
Amos 5:22 burnt offerings...I [God] will not *a* them
Mal 1:10 neither will I [God] *a* an offering at your hand
Luke 4:24 No prophet is *a'ed* in his own country
Acts 10:35 feareth him [God]... is *a'ed* with him

ACCEPTABLE
Ps 19:14 meditation of my heart...*a* in thy [God's] sight
Prov 21:3 To do justice...is more *a*...than sacrifice
Isa 61:2 To proclaim the *a* year of the LORD
Luke 4:19 To preach the *a* year of the Lord
Rom 12:1 bodies a living sacrifice...*a* unto God
Eph 5:10 Proving what is *a* unto the Lord
1 Tim 2:3 good and *a* in the sight of God
1 Pet 2:5 spiritual sacrifices, *a* to God by Jesus Christ

ACCESS

Rom 5:2 By whom [Jesus]...we have *a*...into this grace

Eph 2:18 through him [Jesus] we...have *a*...unto the Father

Eph 3:12 In whom [Jesus] we have...*a* with confidence

ACCOMPLISHED

Isa 40:2 Speak...to Jerusalem...her warfare is *a*

Jer 25:12 seventy years are *a*, that I [God] will punish the king of Babylon

Luke 2:6 days were *a* that she [Mary] should be delivered

Luke 12:50 how am I [Jesus] straitened till it be *a*

Luke 18:31 things...concerning the Son of man shall be *a*

John 19:28 Jesus knowing that all things were now *a*

ACCORD

Acts 1:14 These all continued with one *a* in prayer

Acts 2:1 Pentecost was...come, they were all with one *a*

Acts 2:46 one *a*...and breaking bread from house to house

Phil 2:2 having the same love, being of one *a*

ACCOUNT [ED]

Ps 144:3 the son of man, that thou makest *a* of him!

Matt 12:36 idle word that men...speak, they shall give *a*

Luke 16:2 *a* of thy stewardship...thou mayest be no longer steward

Luke 20:35 *a'ed* worthy...neither marry, nor are given in marriage

Luke 21:36 *a'ed* worthy to...stand before the Son of man

Luke 22:24 strife among them, which...be *a'ed* the greatest

Rom 14:12 every one...shall give *a* of himself to God

Gal 3:6 Abraham believed God...*a'ed*...for righteousness

Phil 4:17 I [Paul] desire fruit that may abound to your *a*

Phlm 1:18 oweth thee ought, put that on mine [Paul's] *a*

1 Pet 4:5 give *a* to him...ready to judge...the dead

ACCURSED

Josh 6:18 keep yourselves from the *a* thing

Josh 7:1 For Achan...took of the *a* thing

Rom 9:3 myself [Paul] were *a* from Christ for...kinsmen

1 Cor 12:3 no man speaking by the Spirit...calleth Jesus *a*

ACCUSATION

Matt 27:37 over his head his *a*...JESUS THE KING OF THE JEWS

Luke 6:7 Pharisees watched him [Jesus]...find an *a* against him

364

John 18:29 Pilate...said, What ***a*** bring ye against this man?

ACCUSE [D]
Matt 12:10 heal on the sabbath day...they might ***a*** him [Jesus]

Matt 27:12 ***a'd*** of the chief priests...he [Jesus] answered nothing

Luke 3:14 neither ***a*** any falsely...content with... wages

Luke 11:54 catch something out of his [Jesus'] mouth, that they might ***a*** him

Luke 23:2 ***a*** him [Jesus]...We found this fellow perverting the nation

ACELDAMA (a burial ground purchased with Judas's betrayal money). Acts 1:19.

ACHAIA (a Roman province of Greece visited by Paul). Acts 18:12,27; **19:21** • Rom 15:26; 16:5 • 1 Cor 16:15 • 2 Cor 1:1; 9:2; 11:10 • 1 Thes 1:7–8.

ACHAN (a warrior under Joshua executed for his disobedience). **Josh 7:1–26;** 22:20. *Achar:* 1 Chr 2:7.

ACHAZ. See *Ahaz.*

ACHISH (a Philistine king who aided David). 1 Sam 21:10–14; 27:2–12; 28:1–2; 29:6–9.

ACKNOWLEDGE
Ps 51:3 I ***a*** my transgressions...my sin is ever before me

Prov 3:6 ways ***a*** him [God], and he shall direct thy paths

Jer 3:13 ***a*** thine iniquity...that thou hast transgressed against the LORD

Jer 14:20 ***a,*** O LORD, our wickedness...sinned against thee

ACQUAINTED
Ps 139:3 Thou [God]...art ***a*** with all my ways

Isa 53:3 a man of sorrows, and ***a*** with grief

ACTS
Deut 11:7 eyes have seen all the great ***a*** of the LORD

1 Sam 12:7 reason with you... righteous ***a*** of the LORD

Ps 103:7 his [God's] ***a*** unto the children of Israel

Ps 106:2 ***a*** of the LORD? who can show forth all his praise?

Ps 145:4 One generation shall declare thy [God's] mighty ***a***

Ps 150:2 Praise him [God] for his mighty ***a***

ACTS OF THE APOSTLES, BOOK OF. The one book of history in the New Testament that traces the expansion of the early church from the ascension of Jesus to Paul's imprisonment in Rome—a period of about thirty-five years. Acts shows how the Christian witness spread in accordance with the Great Commission of Jesus (see Acts 1:8).

ADAM (the first person created by God). **Gen 2:19–5:5** • Deut 32:8 • 1 Chr 1:1 • Job 31:33 • Luke 3:38 • Rom 5:14 • 1 Cor 15:22,45 • 1 Tim 2:13–14 • Jude 14.

ADMAH (a city destroyed with Sodom and Gomorrah). Gen 10:19; 14:2,8 • Deut 29:23 • Hos 11:8.

ADMONISH [ING]
Rom 15:14 ye also are...able also to *a* one another
Col 3:16 a'ing one another in psalms and hymns
2 Thes 3:15 not as an enemy, but *a* him as a brother

ADONIJAH (a son of King David and rival of Solomon for the throne). 2 Sam 3:4 • **1 Kgs 1:5–53;** 2:13–28 • 1 Chr 3:2.

ADOPTION
Rom 8:15 Spirit of *a,* whereby we cry, Abba, Father
Rom 8:23 waiting for the *a*... the redemption of our body

Gal 4:5 them...under the law...receive the *a* of sons
Eph 1:5 predestinated us unto the *a* of children by Jesus

ADRIA (the Adriatic Sea). Acts 27:27.

ADULTERY
Ex 20:14 Thou shalt not commit *a*
Lev 20:10 a...neighbour's wife...adulterer...put to death
Deut 5:18 Neither shalt thou commit *a*
Prov 6:32 whoso committeth *a*...destroyeth his own soul
Jer 7:9 and commit *a*...and walk after other gods
Matt 5:28 looketh on a woman to lust...hath committed *a*
Mark 10:11 put away his wife, and marry another, committeth *a*
John 8:3 brought unto him [Jesus] a woman taken in *a*
Gal 5:19 works of the flesh are...*A,* fornication
2 Pet 2:14 eyes full of *a*...cannot cease from sin

ADVERSARY [IES]
Deut 32:43 he [God] will...render vengeance to his *a'ies*
1 Sam 2:10 a'ies of the LORD shall be broken
1 Kgs 5:4 hath given me rest... there is neither *a* nor evil

Esth 7:6 The *a* and enemy is this wicked Haman

Ps 69:19 mine *a'ies* are all before thee [God]

Ps 74:10 how long shall the *a* reproach?

Ps 109:29 Let mine *a'ies* be clothed with shame

Nah 1:2 LORD will take vengeance on his *a'ies*

Matt 5:25 Agree with thine *a*... in the way with him

Luke 18:3 widow...came...saying, Avenge me of mine *a*

Luke 21:15 wisdom, which all your *a'ies* shall not...resist

1 Cor 16:9 great door...is opened...many *a'ies*

1 Pet 5:8 *a* the devil...seeking whom he may devour

ADVERSITY

Ps 35:15 mine *a* they rejoiced, and gathered...together

Prov 17:17 a brother is born for *a*

Prov 24:10 faint in the day of *a,* thy strength is small

Isa 30:20 bread of *a,* and the water of affliction

ADVOCATE

1 John 2:1 we have an *a* with the Father, Jesus Christ

AFFECTION

Rom 1:31 Without understanding...without natural *a*

Col 3:2 Set your *a* on things above, not...on the earth

Col 3:5 uncleanness, inordinate *a,* evil concupiscence

2 Tim 3:3 Without natural *a,* trucebreakers, false accusers

AFFLICT [ED]

Ex 1:11 taskmasters to *a* them [Israelites] with their burdens

Ex 1:12 more they *a'ed* them [Israelites]...more they... grew

Ex 22:22 not *a* any widow, or fatherless child

Ruth 1:21 Almighty hath *a'ed* me [Naomi]

1 Kgs 11:39 I [God] will for this *a* the seed of David

2 Kgs 17:20 LORD rejected... Israel, and *a'ed* them

Job 34:28 he [God] heareth the cry of the *a'ed*

Ps 44:2 thou [God] didst *a* the people, and cast them out

Ps 88:15 I am *a'ed* and ready to die

Ps 90:15 the days wherein thou [God] hast *a'ed* us

Ps 119:71 I have been *a'ed*... learn thy [God's] statutes

Ps 140:12 maintain the cause of the *a'ed*

Isa 49:13 the LORD...will have mercy upon his *a'ed*

Isa 53:4 esteem him [God's servant] stricken...smitten... *a'ed*

Lam 1:12 LORD hath *a'ed* me in...his fierce anger

Lam 3:33 he [God] doth not *a* willingly nor grieve

Nah 1:12 Though I have *a'ed* thee [God], I will *a* thee no more

Matt 24:9 a'ed, and shall kill you...for my [Jesus']...sake

Heb 11:37 wandered about in sheepskins...*a'ed,* tormented

Jas 4:9 Be *a'ed*...your laughter be turned to mourning

Jas 5:13 a'ed? let him pray. Is any merry...sing psalms

AFFLICTION [S]

Gen 29:32 the LORD hath looked upon my [Leah's] *a*

Ex 3:7 I [God] have...seen the *a* of my people

Deut 16:3 unleavened bread... the bread of *a*

Deut 26:7 the LORD...looked on our *a*...and our oppression

Job 30:16 days of *a* have taken hold upon me

Ps 25:18 Look upon mine *a* and my pain

Ps 34:19 Many are the *a's* of the righteous

Ps 119:153 mine *a*...for I do not forget thy [God's] law

Ps 132:1 LORD, remember David, and all his *a's*

Isa 30:20 bread of adversity, and the water of *a*

Lam 1:3 Judah is gone into captivity because of *a*

2 Cor 4:17 light *a*...worketh for us...exceeding...glory

Col 1:24 fill up that...behind of the *a's* of Christ

2 Tim 4:5 endure *a's*...make full proof of thy ministry

Jas 1:27 visit the fatherless and widows in their *a*

AFRAID

Gen 3:10 I [Adam] was *a*...and I hid myself

Gen 28:17 he [Jacob] was *a*... How dreadful is this place

Ex 3:6 Moses...was *a* to look upon God

Ex 14:10 Egyptians marched after them [Israelites]... they were sore *a*

Num 22:3 Moab was sore *a* of the people [Israelites]

Deut 7:18 not be *a*...remember what the LORD...did

Deut 31:6 nor be *a*...thy God... will not fail thee

Josh 1:9 be not *a*...for the LORD...is with thee

1 Sam 18:12 Saul was *a* of David...the LORD was with him

Esth 7:6 Haman was *a* before the king and the queen

Job 3:25 that which I was *a* of is come unto me

Job 5:21 neither shalt thou be *a* of destruction

Ps 27:1 LORD...strength of my life; of whom shall I be *a?*

Ps 56:3 What time I am *a,* I will trust in thee [God]

Ps 56:11 In God have I put my trust...I will not be *a* what man can do unto me

Ps 91:5 Thou shalt not be *a* for the terror by night

Isa 12:2 not be *a*...Jehovah is my strength

Jer 1:8 be not *a*...I [God] am with thee to deliver thee

Jer 2:12 Be astonished...be horribly *a*...saith the LORD

Jer 42:11 not *a* of the king of Babylon...I [God]...with you

Jer 42:16 famine, whereof ye were *a*, shall follow

Dan 4:5 a dream...made me [Daniel] *a*...visions...troubled me

Jon 1:5 mariners were *a*, and cried every man unto his god

Matt 14:27 Jesus spake...it is I; be not *a*

Matt 17:7 Jesus...said, Arise, and be not *a*

Matt 25:25 I was *a*, and...hid thy talent in the earth

Matt 28:10 Be not *a*: go tell my [Jesus'] brethren that they go into Galilee

Mark 6:50 Be of good cheer: it is I [Jesus]; be not *a*

Mark 9:32 they [the disciples] understood not...and were *a* to ask him [Jesus]

Luke 2:9 and they [shepherds] were sore *a*

Luke 12:4 Be not *a* of them that kill the body

John 14:27 not your heart be troubled, neither let it be *a*

Acts 9:26 they [apostles] were all *a* of him [Paul]

Gal 4:11 I [Paul] am *a* of you, lest I...labour in vain

AGABUS (a prophet who warned of a famine and foretold Paul's arrest in Jerusalem). Acts 11:28; 21:10.

AGAG (a king of Amalek who was killed by Samuel). Num 24:7 • **1 Sam 15:8–33.**

AGAR. See *Hagar.*

AGREE [D]

Amos 3:3 Can two walk together, except they be *a'd*

Matt 5:25 **A** with...adversary quickly...in the way with him

Matt 20:13 didst not thou *a* with me for a penny?

Mark 14:56 false witness against him [Jesus], but their witness *a'd* not

AGRIPPA (a ruler before whom Paul made his defense at Caesarea). Acts 25:13–26; **26:1–32.**

AHAB (a king of Israel whose wicked reign led to idol worship). **1 Kgs 16:28–22:40** • 2 Kgs 1:1; 3:1,5; 9:7–29;

10:1–30; 21:3,13 • **2 Chr 18:1–34;** 21:6,13; 22:3–8 • Mic 6:16.

AHASUERUS (a king of Persia who married Esther). Esth 1:1–3:12; 6:2–10:3.

AHAVA (a town or river in Babylonia). Ezra 8:15,21,31.

AHAZ (a king of Judah who practiced idol worship). **2 Kgs 15:38–16:20** • **2 Chr 28:1–27** • Isa 1:1; 7:1–3,10–12; 14:28; 38:8 • Hos 1:1 • Mic 1:1. *Achaz:* Matt 1:9.

AHAZIAH
1. A king of Israel who worshiped the pagan god Baal. 1 Kgs 22:40,49–51 • 2 Kgs 1:2,18 • 1 Chr 3:11 • 2 Chr 20:35–37.
2. A king of Judah who fell into idol worship. 2 Kgs 8:24–9:28 • 2 Chr 22:1–9. *Azariah:* 2 Chr 22:6.

AHIJAH (a prophet in Solomon's time who foretold the division of the kingdom). **1 Kgs 11:29–39;** 14:2,18; 15:29 • 2 Chr 9:29; 10:15.

AHIMAAZ (a person who kept David informed about Absalom's rebellion). **2 Sam 15:27,36;** 17:17,20; 18:19–29 • 1 Chr 6:8–9,53.

AHIMELECH (high priest during King Saul's reign). 1 Sam 21:1–2,8; 22:9–20; 23:6 • 2 Sam 8:17 • 1 Chr 24:3,6,31.

AHITHOPHEL (one of David's aides who joined Absalom's rebellion against the king). 2 Sam 15:12–34; **16:15–23; 17:1–23** • 2 Sam 23:34 • 1 Chr 27:33–34.

AI (a Canaanite city captured by Joshua). **Josh 7:2–8:29;** 9:3; 10:1–2; 12:9 • Ezra 2:28 • Neh 7:32 • Jer 49:3. *Aiath:* Isa 10:28. *Aija:* Neh 11:31. *Hai:* Gen 12:8.

AIATH. See *Ai.*

AIJA. See *Ai.*

ALARM
Jer 4:19 the sound of the trumpet, the *a* of war
Joel 2:1 an *a*...for the day of the LORD cometh

ALIEN
Ex 18:3 I have been an *a* in a strange land
Job 19:15 a stranger: I [Job] am an *a* in their sight
Ps 69:8 stranger...*a* unto my mother's children

ALIVE
Gen 7:23 Noah only remained *a,* and they...with him

Ps 41:2 The LORD will preserve him, and keep him *a*

Mark 16:11 heard that he [Jesus] was *a*...had been seen

Luke 15:24 my son was dead, and is *a* again

Acts 1:3 he [Jesus] showed himself *a* after his passion

Rom 6:11 dead...unto sin, but *a* unto God through Jesus

1 Cor 15:22 even so in Christ shall all be made *a*

1 Thes 4:17 are *a*...caught up together...to meet the Lord

Rev 1:18 I [Jesus] am *a*...and have the keys...of death

Rev 2:8 first and the last, which was dead, and is *a*

ALMIGHTY GOD

Gen 17:1 I am the *A-G*...be thou perfect

Rev 19:15 treadeth the winepress of the...wrath of *A-G*

ALMS

Matt 6:1 do not your *a* before men, to be seen of them

Luke 12:33 give *a;* provide...a treasure...that faileth not

Acts 10:4 thine [Cornelius's] *a* are come up...before God

ALONE

Gen 2:18 not good that the man should be *a*

Gen 32:24 Jacob was left *a*... wrestled a man with him

Ex 24:2 Moses *a* shall come near the LORD

Num 11:14 I [Moses] am not able to bear all this people *a*

Job 7:16 let me *a;* for my [Job's] days are vanity

Ps 86:10 thou art great...thou art God *a*

Ps 148:13 praise the...LORD... his name *a* is excellent

Eccl 4:10 woe to him that is *a* when he falleth

Isa 2:11 the LORD *a* shall be exalted

Dan 10:7 And I Daniel *a* saw the vision

Matt 4:4 It is written, Man shall not live by bread *a*

Matt 14:23 a mountain...to pray...he [Jesus] was there *a*

Mark 1:24 Let us *a;* what have we to do with thee...Jesus

Mark 14:6 Let her *a*...she hath wrought a good work

Luke 5:21 Who can forgive sins, but God *a?*

John 12:24 a corn of wheat fall...and die, it abideth *a*

John 17:20 Neither pray I [Jesus] for these *a*

Jas 2:17 faith, if it hath not works, is dead, being *a*

ALPHA AND OMEGA (the first and last letters of the Greek alphabet). Rev 1:8,11; 21:6; 22:13.

ALPHAEUS. See *Cleophas.*

ALTAR [S]
1 Kgs 1:50 Adonijah...caught hold on the horns of the *a*
1 Kgs 8:22 Solomon stood before the *a*...in the presence of all... Israel
Ezek 6:4 *a's* shall be desolate, and...images...broken
Luke 1:11 angel...standing on the right side of the *a*
Acts 17:23 an *a* with this inscription, TO THE UN-KNOWN GOD

ALTARS BUILT BY OLD TESTAMENT PERSONALITIES
1. Noah (Gen 8:20)
2. Abraham (Gen 12:7)
3. Isaac (Gen 26:25)
4. Jacob at Shalem (Gen 33:20)
5. Jacob at Bethel (Gen 35:7)
6. Moses (Ex 17:15)
7. Joshua (Josh 8:30)
8. Gideon (Judg 6:24)
9. Saul (1 Sam 14:35)
10. David (2 Sam 24:25)

ALWAYS
Gen 6:3 My [God's] spirit shall not *a* strive with man
1 Chr 16:15 mindful *a* of his [God's] covenant
Ps 16:8 LORD *a* before me...he is at my right hand

Ps 103:9 He [God] will not *a* chide: neither...keep his anger for ever
Prov 5:19 be thou ravished *a* with her love
Mark 14:7 the poor with you *a*...me [Jesus] ye have not *a*
Luke 18:1 men ought *a* to pray, and not to faint
Acts 7:51 ye do *a* resist the Holy Ghost
Rom 1:9 I [Paul] make mention of you *a* in my prayers
1 Cor 1:4 I [Paul] thank my God *a* on your behalf
1 Cor 15:58 *a* abounding in the work of the Lord
2 Cor 4:10 *A* bearing about... the dying of the Lord
Eph 5:20 Giving thanks *a* for all things unto God

AMALEKITES (tribal enemies of the Israelites). Gen 14:7 • Num 13:29; 14:25,43–45 • Judg 6:3,33; 7:12; 10:12; 12:15 • 1 Sam 14:48; 15:6–8,15–32; 27:8; 30:1,18 • 2 Sam 1:1 • 1 Chr 4:43.

AMASA (commander of Absalom's rebel army). 2 Sam 17:25; 19:13; 20:4–12 • 1 Kgs 2:5,32 • 2 Chr 2:17.

AMAZED
Ex 15:15 dukes of Edom shall be *a*...inhabitants of Canaan shall melt away

372

Matt 12:23 people were *a*...Is not this the son of David?

Matt 19:25 disciples heard it, they were exceedingly *a*

Mark 1:27 all *a,* insomuch that they questioned

Mark 2:12 all *a*...We never saw it on this fashion

Mark 6:51 they were sore *a*... beyond measure

Mark 9:15 people...were...*a,* and...saluted him [Jesus]

Mark 10:32 Jesus went before them: and they were *a*

Luke 9:43 they were all *a* at the...power of God

Acts 2:7 they were all *a*...are not all these...Galilaeans?

Acts 2:12 were all *a*...saying... What meaneth this?

AMAZIAH (a king of Judah who worshiped the false gods of Edom). 2 Kgs 12:21; 13:12; 14:1–20 • **2 Chr 25:1–28.**

AMMONITES (tribal enemies of the Israelites). Deut 2:20 • 1 Sam 11:11 • 1 Kgs 11:1,5 • 2 Chr 20:1; 26:8; 27:5 • Ezra 9:1 • Neh 4:7 • Jer 27:3; 40:11,14; 41:10,15; 49:1–2 • Ezek 21:20,28; 25:2–10.

AMNON (a son of David who was murdered by his half brother Absalom). 2 Sam 3:2; **13:1–39.**

AMON (an evil king of Judah who was assassinated by his own servants). **2 Kgs 21:18–25** • **2 Chr 33:20–25** • Jer 1:2; 25:3 • Zeph 1:1 • Matt 1:10.

AMORITES (tribal enemies of the Israelites). Gen 10:16; 14:13; 15:16,21; 48:22 • Ex 3:8,17; 13:5; 23:23; 33:2; 34:11 • Num 13:29; 21:13–34; 22:2; 32:33,39; • Deut 1:4–44; 2:24; 3:2–9; 4:46–47; 7:1; 20:17; 31:4 • Josh 2:10; 3:10; 5:1; 7:7; 9:1,10; 10:5–12; 12:2,8; 13:4,10,21; 24:8–18 • Judg 1:34–36; 3:5; 6:10; 10:8,11; 11:19–23 • 1 Sam 7:14 • 2 Sam 21:2 • 1 Kgs 4:19; 9:20; 21:26 • 2 Kgs 21:11 • 1 Chr 1:14 • 2 Chr 8:7 • Ezra 9:1 • Neh 9:8 • Pss 135:11; 136:19 • Ezek 16:3,45 • Amos 2:9,10.

AMOS (a prophet against the Northern Kingdom and author of the book that bears his name). Amos is not mentioned outside the Book of Amos.

AMOS, BOOK OF. A prophetic book of the Old Testament written to call the people of the Northern Kingdom (Israel) back to worship of the one true God. According to Amos, true religion consists of following God's commands and treating others with justice (see Amos 5:24).

AMRAPHEL (a king of Shinar in Abraham's time). Gen 14:1,9.

ANAK (ancestor of a tribe of giants). **Num 13:22–33** • Deut 9:2 • Josh 15:13–14; 21:11 • Judg 1:20.

ANAKIMS (a tribe of giants). Deut 1:28; 2:10–11,21; 9:2 • Josh 11:21–22; 14:12,15.

ANAMMELECH (a pagan god of the Babylonians). 2 Kgs 17:31.

ANANIAS
1. A believer in the early church struck dead for lying. Acts 5:1–5.
2. A believer who befriended Paul after his conversion. Acts 9:10–17; 22:12.

ANATHOTH (a village north of Jerusalem). Josh 21:18 • 1 Kgs 2:26 • 1 Chr 6:60 • Ezra 2:23 • Neh 7:27; 11:32 • Isa 10:30 • Jer 1:1; 11:21,23; 29:27; 32:7–9.

ANCIENT OF DAYS (a title of God). Dan 7:9,13,22.

ANDREW (one of the twelve disciples of Jesus). Matt 4:18; 10:2 • Mark 1:16,29; 3:18; 13:3 • Luke 6:14 • John 1:40,44; 6:8; 12:22 • Acts 1:13.

ANGEL APPEARANCES
1. To Hagar during her pregnancy with Ishmael (Gen 16:7–11)
2. To Lot (Gen 19:1)
3. To Hagar and Ishmael in the wilderness (Gen 21:17)
4. To Abraham (Gen 22:11,15)
5. To Jacob at Haran (Gen 28:12; 31:11)
6. To Jacob at Mahanaim (Gen 32:1)
7. To Moses (Ex 3:2)
8. To Balaam (Num 22:22–35)
9. To Gideon (Judg 6:11–22)
10. To Samson's mother and father (Judg 13:3–21)
11. To Elijah (1 Kgs 19:5,7 • 2 Kgs 1:3,15)
12. To David (1 Chr 21:16)
13. To Gad (1 Chr 21:18)
14. To Ornan (1 Chr 21:20,27)
15. To Shadrach, Meshach, and Abed-nego (Dan 3:24–28)
16. To Zechariah (Zech 1:9)
17. To Joseph in Nazareth (Matt 1:20)
18. To Joseph in Bethlehem (Matt 2:13)
19. To Joseph in Egypt (Matt 2:19)
20. To Zacharias (Luke 1:11–29)
21. To Mary (Luke 1:26–38)
22. To shepherds at Jesus' birth (Luke 2:9–14)
23. To Jesus in the Garden of Gethsemane (Luke 22:43)

24. To Jesus at the resurrection (Matt 28:2)
25. To women at the tomb (Matt 28:5)
26. To Mary Magdalene at the empty tomb (John 20:11–12)
27. To the apostles (Acts 5:19)
28. To Philip (Acts 8:26)
29. To Cornelius (Acts 10:3)
30. To Peter in prison (Acts 12:7–11)
31. To Paul (Acts 27:23–24)
32. To John on the isle of Patmos (Rev 1:1)

ANGELS

Ps 8:5 thou [God] hast made him [man] a little lower than the *a*
Ps 148:2 Praise ye him, all his [God's] *a*
Matt 22:30 nor are given in marriage, but are as the *a*
Matt 25:31 Son of man shall come...holy *a* with him
Luke 15:10 joy in the presence of the *a*...over one sinner that repenteth
Rom 8:38 death, nor life, nor *a,* nor principalities
1 Cor 13:1 tongues of men and of *a,* and have not charity
Heb 13:2 some have entertained *a* unawares

ANGER

Gen 30:2 Jacob's *a* was kindled against Rachel
1 Sam 11:6 spirit of God came upon Saul...*a* was kindled
1 Sam 20:30 Saul's *a* was kindled against Jonathan
2 Sam 12:5 David's *a* was... kindled against the man
Ps 6:1 O LORD, rebuke me not in thine *a,* neither chasten
Ps 30:5 For his [God's] *a* endureth but a moment
Ps 78:58 provoked him [God] to *a* with their high places
Ps 103:8 LORD is merciful and gracious, slow to *a*
Prov 15:1 but grievous words stir up *a*
Prov 16:32 He that is slow to *a* is better than the mighty
Prov 21:14 A gift...pacifieth *a:* and a reward...wrath
Isa 63:6 I [God] will tread down the people in mine *a*
Jer 4:8 the fierce *a* of the LORD is not turned back
Lam 4:16 the *a* of the LORD hath divided them
Mic 5:15 I [God] will execute vengeance in *a* and fury upon the heathen
Nah 1:3 LORD is slow to *a*...will not...acquit the wicked
Mark 3:5 he [Jesus] looked... with *a*...for the hardness of their hearts
Eph 4:31 wrath, and *a*...and evil speaking, be put away
Col 3:8 put off all these; *a,* wrath, malice
Col 3:21 Fathers, provoke not your children to *a*

ANGER OF THE LORD

Ex 4:14 the ***a-o-t-L*** was kindled against Moses

Num 11:10 ***a-o-t-L*** was kindled...Moses also was displeased

Num 25:3 the ***a-o-t-L*** was kindled against Israel

2 Sam 6:7 the ***a-o-t-L*** was kindled against Uzzah

2 Sam 24:1 the ***a-o-t-L*** was... against Israel and he moved David against them

2 Kgs 24:20 through the ***a-o-t-L***...Zedekiah rebelled against...Babylon

2 Chr 25:15 the ***a-o-t-L*** was kindled against Amaziah

Jer 4:8 the fierce ***a-o-t-L*** is not turned back

Jer 12:13 be ashamed...because of the fierce ***a-o-t-L***

Jer 51:45 deliver ye every man his soul from the...***a-o-t-L***

ANGUISH

Job 15:24 ***a*** shall make him afraid; they shall prevail

Ps 119:143 ***a*** have taken...me: yet thy [God's] commandments are my delights

John 16:21 delivered of the child, she remembereth no more the ***a***

Rom 2:9 and ***a,*** upon every soul of man that doeth evil

2 Cor 2:4 and ***a***...I [Paul] wrote...with many tears

ANNA (a prophetess who praised the infant Jesus). Luke 2:36–38.

ANNAS (a high priest during Jesus' ministry). Luke 3:2 • John 18:13,24 • Acts 4:6.

ANNUNCIATION OF JESUS' BIRTH TO JOSEPH. Matt 1:18–25.

ANNUNCIATION OF JESUS' BIRTH TO MARY. Luke 1:26–38.

ANOINT [ED, EST, ING]

Ex 30:30 ***a*** Aaron and his sons, and consecrate them

Ex 40:15 ***a*** them [Aaron's sons]...that they may minister...in the priest's office

Lev 8:10 Moses...***a'ed*** the tabernacle...and sanctified them

Lev 8:12 the ***a'ing*** oil upon Aaron's head...sanctify him

Judg 9:8 trees went forth...to ***a*** a king over them

1 Sam 15:1 LORD sent me [Samuel] to ***a*** thee [Saul]

1 Sam 16:13 Samuel...***a'ed*** him [David] in the midst of his brethren

2 Sam 2:4 they ***a'ed*** David king over the house of Judah

1 Kgs 19:15 ***a*** Hazael to be king over Syria

2 Chr 6:42 turn not away... thine *a'ed:* remember... David

Ps 20:6 LORD saveth his *a'ed;* he will hear...from... heaven

Ps 23:5 thou [God] *a'est* my head with oil

Isa 45:1 Thus saith the LORD to his *a'ed,* to Cyrus

Isa 61:1 LORD hath *a'ed* me [God's servant]...to proclaim liberty

Mark 14:8 come...to *a* my [Jesus'] body to...burying

Mark 16:1 bought...spices, that they [women] might... *a* him [Jesus]

Luke 7:46 this woman hath *a'ed* my [Jesus'] feet

John 9:6 he [Jesus] *a'ed* the eyes of the blind man

John 12:3 Mary...*a'ed* the feet of Jesus

Heb 1:9 hath *a'ed* thee with the oil of gladness

Jas 5:14 *a'ing* him with oil in the name of the Lord

ANSWER

Job 31:35 that the Almighty would *a* me [Job]

Ps 27:7 have mercy...upon me, and *a* me

Ps 86:7 I will call upon thee [God]...thou wilt *a* me

Prov 15:1 A soft *a* turneth away wrath

Prov 26:4 *A* not a fool according to his folly

Jer 33:3 I [God] will *a* thee, and show thee great... things

Luke 21:14 not to meditate before what ye shall *a*

1 Pet 3:15 give an *a* to every man that asketh you a reason

1 Pet 3:21 baptism...the *a* of a good conscience toward God

ANTICHRIST (the archenemy of Christ). 1 John 2:18,22; 4:3 • 2 John 7.

ANTIOCH
1. A city in Syria. Acts 6:5; 11:19–27; 13:1; 14:26; 15:22–35; 18:22 • Gal 2:11.
2. A city in Pisidia. Acts 13:14; 14:19,21 • 2 Tim 3:11.

APOLLOS (a Jewish believer from Alexandria, Egypt). Acts 18:24; 19:1 • 1 Cor 3:4–6,22; 4:6; 16:12 • Titus 3:13.

APOSTLE [S]
Matt 10:2 names of the twelve *a's* are these

Mark 6:30 *a's* gathered...and told him [Jesus] all things

Luke 6:13 he [Jesus] chose twelve...he named *a's*

Acts 1:26 Matthias...numbered with the eleven *a's*

Acts 2:42 they continued stedfastly in the *a's'* doctrine

Acts 2:43 many wonders and signs were done by the *a's*

Acts 5:18 laid their hands on the *a's*...put them in... prison

Acts 8:1 they [believers] were... scattered...except the *a's*

Rom 1:1 Paul, a servant... called to be an *a*

Rom 11:13 I [Paul] am the *a* of the Gentiles

1 Cor 1:1 Paul, called to be an *a* of Jesus Christ

1 Cor 9:1 Am I [Paul] not an *a?* am I not free?

1 Cor 12:28 in the church, first *a's,* secondarily prophets

1 Cor 12:29 Are all *a's?* are all prophets? are all teachers?

1 Cor 15:9 I [Paul] am the least of the *a's*

2 Cor 11:13 transforming themselves into...*a's* of Christ

2 Cor 12:12 signs of an *a* were wrought among you

Eph 2:20 built upon the foundation of the *a's*

Eph 4:11 gave some, *a's;* and some, prophets

Heb 3:1 *A* and High Priest of our profession, Christ Jesus

APPEAR [ED, ETH, ING]

Gen 1:9 let the dry land *a:* and it was so

Gen 12:7 the LORD *a'ed* unto Abram...Unto thy seed will I give this land

Gen 35:9 God *a'ed* unto Jacob...and blessed him

Ex 3:2 Angel...*a'ed* unto him [Moses] in a flame

Ex 16:10 the glory of the LORD *a'ed* in the cloud

1 Sam 3:21 LORD *a'ed* again... revealed himself to Samuel

1 Kgs 9:2 LORD *a'ed* to Solomon...as he had...at Gibeon

2 Kgs 2:11 *a'ed* a chariot...Elijah went...by a whirlwind

Ps 42:2 when shall I come and *a* before God?

Ps 102:16 the LORD...shall *a* in his glory

Song 2:12 The flowers *a* on the earth

Mal 3:2 who shall stand when he [God] *a'eth?*

Matt 2:13 *a'eth*...take the... child...and flee into Egypt

Matt 2:19 Herod was dead... the Lord *a'eth*...to Joseph

Matt 17:3 *a'ed*...Moses and Elias talking with him [Jesus]

Matt 23:27 whited sepulchres, which...*a* beautiful outward

Matt 24:30 then shall *a* the sign of the Son of man

Mark 16:9 Jesus...*a'ed* first to Mary Magdalene

Mark 16:12 he [Jesus] *a'ed* in another form...two of them

Mark 16:14 he [Jesus] *a'ed* unto...eleven as they sat at meat

Luke 1:11 there *a'ed* unto him [Zacharias] an angel

Luke 24:34 The Lord...hath *a'ed* to Simon

Acts 2:3 there **a'ed** unto them cloven tongues like as of fire

2 Cor 5:10 all **a** before the judgment seat of Christ

Col 3:4 then shall ye also **a** with him [Jesus]

1 Tim 6:14 keep this commandment...until the **a'ing** of our Lord Jesus Christ

2 Tim 1:10 made manifest by the **a'ing** of our Saviour

2 Tim 4:1 judge the quick and the dead at his **a'ing**

2 Tim 4:8 unto all them...that love his [Jesus'] **a'ing**

Titus 2:13 the glorious **a'ing** of...our Saviour

Jas 4:14 It [life] is...a vapour, that **a'eth** for a little time

1 Pet 5:4 chief Shepherd shall **a,** ye shall receive a crown

APPII FORUM (a place south of Rome where believers greeted Paul). Acts 28:15.

APPOINT [ED]
Num 1:50 **a** the Levites over the tabernacle of testimony

Josh 20:2 **A** out for you cities of refuge

Job 14:5 thou hast **a'ed** his bounds that he cannot pass

Ps 104:19 He [God] **a'ed** the moon for seasons

Isa 1:14 your **a'ed** feasts my [God's] soul hateth

Luke 10:1 Lord **a'ed** other... and sent them two and two

Acts 6:3 seven men...whom we may **a** over this business

1 Thes 5:9 God hath not **a'ed** us to wrath, but to... salvation

2 Tim 1:11 I [Paul] am **a'ed** a preacher, and an apostle

Heb 1:2 whom he [God] hath **a'ed** heir [Jesus] of all things

Heb 9:27 **a'ed**...once to die, but after this the judgment

APPROVED
Acts 2:22 Jesus of Nazareth, a man **a**...by miracles

2 Tim 2:15 Study to show thyself **a** unto God

AQUILA (a believer who worked with Paul at Corinth). Acts 18:2,18,26 • Rom 16:3 • 1 Cor 16:19 • 2 Tim 4:19.

ARABAH (the Jordan River valley). Josh 18:18.

ARAM. See *Syria*.

ARARAT (a mountainous region in Armenia where Noah's ark came to rest). **Gen 8:4** • Jer 51:27.

ARAUNAH (a Jebusite from whom David bought a threshing floor). 2 Sam 24:16–24. *Ornan:* 1 Chr 21:15–28 • 2 Chr 3:1.

ARCHANGEL (a chief angel). 1 Thes 4:16 • Jude 9.

AREOPAGUS (a meeting place in Athens). Acts 17:19.

ARIEL (a name for Jerusalem). Isa 29:1–7.

ARIMATHAEA (a city northwest of Jerusalem). Matt 27:57 • Mark 15:43 • Luke 23:51 • John 19:38.

ARISE
Josh 1:2 now therefore *a,* go over this Jordan
Ps 7:6 **A,** O LORD...because of the rage of mine enemies
Ps 82:8 **A,** O God, judge the earth...inherit all nations
Prov 31:28 Her children *a* up, and call her blessed
Isa 60:1 **A,** shine; for thy light is come
Jer 18:2 **A**...go down to the potter's house...hear my [God's] words
Dan 7:17 Beasts...are four kings...*a* out of the earth
Jon 1:2 **A,** go to Nineveh, that great city...cry against it
Mal 4:2 shall the Sun of righteousness *a* with healing in his wings
Matt 2:13 angel...appeareth to Joseph...saying, **A**...take the young child
Matt 24:24 there shall *a* false Christs, and false prophets

Mark 5:41 Damsel, I [Jesus] say unto thee, *a*
Luke 5:24 I [Jesus] say...*A*... take up thy couch
Luke 15:18 *a* and go to my father...I have sinned
Luke 17:19 he [Jesus] said... **A,** go thy way: thy faith hath made thee whole
Acts 11:7 **A,** Peter; slay and eat
Acts 20:30 men *a,* speaking perverse things

ARISTARCHUS (a companion of Paul). Acts 19:29; 20:4; 27:2 • Col 4:10 • Phlm 24.

ARK OF MOSES (a basket in which the infant Moses was placed). Ex 2:3,5.

ARK OF NOAH (a wooden ship in which Noah's family escaped from the flood). **Gen 6:12–9:18** • Matt 24:38 • Luke 17:27 • 1 Pet 3:20.

ARK OF THE COVENANT (a wooden chest containing a pot of manna, Aaron's rod that budded, and stone tablets on which the Ten Commandments were inscribed). **Ex 25:10–22** • Num 10:33 • Deut 10:8; 31:9,25 • Josh 3:3–17; 4:7–18; 6:6–8; 8:33 • Judg 20:27 • 1 Sam 4:3–5 • 2 Sam 15:24 • 1 Kgs 3:15; 6:19; 8:1,6 • 1 Chr 15:25–29; 16:6,37; 17:1; 22:19; 28:2,18 • 2 Chr 5:2–7 • Jer

3:16. *Ark of the testimony:* Ex 25:22 • Num 7:89 • Josh 4:16.

ARK OF THE TESTIMONY. See *Ark of the Covenant.*

ARM OF THE LORD *Isa 51:9* O *a-o-t-L;* awake, as in the ancient days *Isa 53:1* to whom is the *a-o-t-L* revealed?

ARMAGEDDON (scene of the final conflict between God and the forces of evil). Rev 16:16.

ARNON (a river in southern Palestine). Num 21:13–28; 22:36 • Deut 2:24,36; 3:12,16; 4:48 • Josh 12:1–2; 13:9,16 • Judg 11:13–26 • 2 Kgs 10:33 • Isa 16:2 • Jer 48:20.

ARTAXERXES I (the Persian king in whose court Ezra and Nehemiah served). Ezra 4:7–23; 8:1 • Neh 2:1; 5:14; 13:6.

ASA (a king of Judah who led a religious revival). 1 Kgs 15:8–33; 16:8–29 • **2 Chr 14:1–13;** 15:2–19; 16:1–13 • Jer 41:9 • Matt 1:7–8.

ASAHEL (a captain in David's army). 2 Sam 2:18–32; 3:27,30; 23:24 • 1 Chr 2:16; 11:26; 27:7.

ASCEND [ED, ING] *Gen 28:12* ladder...the angels... *a'ing* and descending *Josh 10:7* Joshua *a'ed* from Gilgal, he...all the people of war *Ps 24:3* who shall *a* into the hill of the LORD *Ps 68:18* Thou hast *a'ed* on high...led captivity captive *Luke 19:28* he [Jesus] went before, *a'ing* up to Jerusalem *John 1:51* angels of God *a'ing*...upon the Son of man *John 6:62* see the Son of man *a* up where he was before *John 20:17* I [Jesus] am not yet *a'ed* to my Father *Eph 4:8* he [Jesus] *a'ed* up on high, he led captivity captive

ASCENSION OF JESUS. See *Jesus, Life and Ministry of.*

ASENATH (Joseph's Egyptian wife). Gen 41:45,50; 46:20.

ASER. See *Asher.*

ASHAMED *Gen 2:25* both naked, the man and his wife, and were not *a* *Ps 31:17* Let me not be *a*...for I have called upon thee [God] *Joel 2:27* your God...and my people shall never be *a* *Mark 8:38* of him also shall the Son of man be *a*

Rom 1:16 I [Paul] am not *a* of the gospel of Christ

Rom 10:11 Whosoever believeth on him [Jesus] shall not be *a*

2 Tim 2:15 a workman that needeth not to be *a*

1 John 2:28 not be *a* before him [Jesus] at his coming

ASHDOD (a major Philistine city). Josh 11:22; 15:46–47 • 1 Sam 5:1–7; 6:17 • 2 Chr 26:6 • Neh 13:23–24 • Isa 20:1 • Jer 25:20 • Amos 1:8; 3:9 • Zeph 2:4 • Zech 9:6.

ASHER (a son of Jacob and ancestor of one of the twelve tribes of Israel). Gen 30:13; 35:26; 46:17; 49:20 • Ex 1:4 • Num 26:46 • 1 Chr 2:2; 7:30,40. The tribe of Asher settled in northern Canaan. Josh 19:24–31. *Aser:* Luke 2:36.

ASHES

Job 2:8 he [Job] took...a potsherd to scrape himself... among the *a*

Isa 61:3 to give unto them beauty for *a*

Jer 25:34 Howl, ye shepherds... and wallow...in the *a*

ASHIMA (a pagan god of Hamath). 2 Kgs 17:30.

ASHKELON (a major Philistine city). Judg 14:19 • Jer 25:20; 47:5,7 • Amos 1:8 •

Zeph 2:4,7 • Zech 9:5. *Askelon:* Judg 1:18.

ASHTAROTH (a pagan goddess of the Philistines). Judg 2:13; 10:6 • 1 Sam 7:3–4; 12:10; 31:10. *Ashtoreth:* 1 Kgs 11:33.

ASIA (a Roman province in Asia Minor). Acts 2:9; 6:9; 16:6; 19:10,22,26–27,31; 20:4,16,18 • 1 Cor 16:19 • 2 Cor 1:8 • 2 Tim 1:15 • 1 Pet 1:1 • Rev 1:4,11.

ASK [ED]

Josh 4:6 your children *a*... What mean...these stones?

Judg 1:1 Israel *a'ed*...Who shall go up...against the Canaanites

1 Kgs 3:5 LORD appeared to Solomon in a dream...*A* what I shall give thee

Ps 105:40 people *a'ed,* and he [God] brought quails

Jer 37:17 king *a'ed* him [Jeremiah]...Is there any word from the LORD

Matt 6:8 Father knoweth what...ye...need...before ye *a*

Matt 7:7 **A,** and it shall be given you

Matt 7:9 if his son *a* bread, will he give him a stone

Matt 18:19 any thing...they shall *a,* it shall be done

Matt 21:22 ye shall *a*...believing, ye shall receive

Mark 14:61 high priest *a'ed* him [Jesus]...Art thou the Christ

Mark 15:2 Pilate *a'ed* him [Jesus], Art thou the King of the Jews

Luke 11:13 Your...Father give the Holy Spirit to them that *a* him

John 14:14 a any thing in my [Jesus'] name, I will do it

John 16:24 a, and ye shall receive...your joy may be full

Eph 3:20 exceeding abundantly above all that we *a*

Jas 1:5 If any of you lack wisdom, let him *a* of God

Jas 4:2 yet ye have not, because ye *a* not

1 John 5:14 a...according to his [God's] will, he heareth

ASKELON. See *Ashkelon.*

ASNAPPER (an Assyrian king). Ezra 4:10.

ASSHUR. See *Assyria.*

ASSUR. See *Assyria.*

ASSYRIA (a dominant power in the ancient world which overthrew the Northern Kingdom, enslaved many of its inhabitants, and resettled the region with foreigners). **2 Kgs 18:9–37;** 19:35–37 • Isa 7–8; 10:12; 14:24–25 • Hos 10:6 •

Nah 3:1–19. *Asshur:* Gen 10:11; Num 24:22–24. *Assur:* Ezra 4:2.

ATHALIAH (a daughter of Ahab and Jezebel who seized the throne as queen of Judah). 2 Kgs 8:26; **11:1–20** • 2 Chr 22:2–12; 23:12–21.

ATHENS (capital city of ancient Greece and the idolatrous city where Paul preached to the philosophers). **Acts 17:15–22;** 18:1 • 1 Thes 3:1.

ATONEMENT
Ex 29:36 offer...a bullock for a sin offering for *a*

Num 15:25 priest shall make an *a* for all...Israel

ATTAIN [ED]
Ps 139:6 knowledge is too wonderful...I cannot *a*...it

Phil 3:11 I [Paul] might *a* unto the resurrection of the dead

Phil 3:12 as though I [Paul] had already *a'ed*

Phil 3:16 already *a'ed,* let us walk by the same rule

1 Tim 4:6 nourished up in... faith and of good doctrine whereunto thou hast *a'ed*

ATTEND
Ps 17:1 O LORD, *a* unto my cry, give ear unto my prayer

Ps 86:6 O LORD...*a* to...my supplications

Prov 4:1 Hear...the instruction of a father, and *a* to know understanding

AUGUSTUS (emperor of the Roman Empire at the time when Jesus was born). **Luke 2:1** • Acts 25:21,25; 27:1.

AUTHORITY
Prov 29:2 When the righteous are in *a,* the people rejoice
Matt 8:9 I am a man under *a,* having soldiers under me
Matt 20:25 they that are great exercise *a* upon them
Matt 21:23 who gave thee [Jesus] this *a*
Matt 21:27 Neither tell I you by what *a* I [Jesus] do these things

Mark 1:22 he [Jesus] taught them as one that had *a*
Luke 9:1 he [Jesus] called his... disciples...gave them...*a* over all devils
1 Cor 15:24 when he [Jesus] shall have put down... all *a*
1 Tim 2:12 suffer not a woman...to usurp *a* over the man

AVEN. See *On,* No. 2.

AZARIAH. See *Abed-nego; Ahaziah,* No. 2; *Uzziah.*

AZZAH. See *Gaza.*

-B-

BAAL (a pagan Canaanite god of rain thought to provide fertility for crops and livestock and worshiped on occasion during Old Testament times by the Israelites). Num 22:41 • Judg 2:13; 6:25–32 • 1 Kgs 16:31–32; 18:19–40; 19:18; 22:53 • 2 Kgs 10:18–28; 11:18; 17:16; 21:3–4 • 2 Chr 23:17 • Jer 2:8; 7:9; 11:13,17; 12:16; 19:5; 23:13; 32:29,35 • Hos 2:8; 13:1 • Zeph 1:4. *Baalim:* 1 Sam 12:10.

BAALAH. See *Kirjath-jearim.*

BAAL-BERITH (a name under which the Canaanite god Baal was worshiped at Shechem). Judg 8:33; 9:4. *Berith:* Judg 9:46.

BAAL-PEOR (a name under which the Canaanite god Baal was worshiped by the Moabites). Num 25:1–9 • Deut 4:3–4 • Ps 106:28–29 • Hos 9:10. *Peor:* Num 31:1–18 • Josh 22:17.

BAAL-ZEBUB (a name under which the Canaanite god Baal was worshiped by the Philistines). 2 Kgs 1:2–16. *Beelzebub:* Matt 10:25; 12:24.

BAASHA (a king of the Northern Kingdom who gained the throne by murdering the heirs of King Jeroboam). **1 Kgs 15:16–33;** 16:1–13 • 2 Kgs 9:9 • 2 Chr 16:1–6 • Jer 41:9.

BABEL, TOWER OF. See *Tower of Babel.*

BABE [S]
Ps 8:2 Out of the mouth of *b's* and sucklings hast thou [God] ordained strength
Matt 21:16 Out of the mouth of *b's* and sucklings thou [God] hast perfected praise
Luke 1:41 when Elisabeth heard...Mary, the *b* leaped in her womb
Luke 2:16 Mary, and Joseph, and the *b* lying in a manger
1 Pet 2:2 As newborn *b's,* desire the...milk of the word

BABYLON (capital city of the Babylonian Empire). Citizens of the Southern Kingdom (Judah) were taken to Babylon as captives after the fall of Jerusalem in 587 B.C. (2 Chr 36:5–21). Most references to Babylon appear in the books of 2 Kings, Jeremiah, Ezekiel, and Daniel. In the Book of Revelation, Babylon is a symbol of evil and wickedness (Rev 14:8; 16:19; 17:5; 18:2,10,21).

BABYLONIA (a powerful nation that carried the Southern Kingdom [Judah] into exile about 587 B.C.). The Babylonians were defeated by the Persians about 539 B.C., fulfilling the prophecies of Isaiah and Jeremiah. **2 Chr 36:5–21** • Isa 14:22 • Jer 50:9. *Land of the Chaldeans:* Ezek 12:13. *Sheshach:* Jer 25:26. *Shinar:* Isa 11:11.

BACK [S]

Gen 19:26 But his [Lot's] wife looked *b*...and she became a pillar of salt

Ex 14:21 LORD caused the sea to go *b* by a strong...wind

Josh 7:8 Israel turneth their *b's* before their enemies

2 Sam 12:23 can I [David] bring him [David's child] *b*

Neh 9:26 they [the Israelites] were disobedient...cast thy [God's] law behind their *b's*

Job 39:22 neither turneth he [God] *b* from the sword

Ps 35:4 let them be turned *b* and brought to confusion

Ps 44:18 Our heart is not turned *b*

Prov 10:13 a rod is for the *b* of him...void of understanding

Prov 26:3 a bridle for the ass, and a rod for the fool's *b*

Isa 14:27 who shall turn it [God's hand] *b*

Isa 38:17 thou [God] hast cast all my sins behind thy *b*

Jer 4:8 anger of the LORD is not turned *b* from us

Ezek 23:35 thou hast...cast me [God] behind thy *b*

Dan 7:6 a leopard, which had upon the *b* of it four wings

Matt 24:18 Neither let him... return *b* to take his clothes

Luke 9:62 No man...looking *b,* is fit for the kingdom

John 6:66 many of his [Jesus'] disciples went *b*

Acts 20:20 I [Paul] kept *b* nothing...profitable unto you

BACKSLIDER

Prov 14:14 The *b* in heart shall be filled with his own ways

BACKSLIDING [S]

Jer 3:14 Turn, O *b* children, saith the LORD

Jer 14:7 our *b's* are many; we have sinned

Hos 4:16 For Israel slideth back as a *b* heifer

Hos 14:4 I [God] will heal their *b*...love them freely

BALAAM (a soothsayer or wizard hired by King Balak of Moab to curse the Israelites). **Num 22:1–24:25** • Deut 23:4–5 • Josh 13:22; 24:9–10 • Mic 6:5 • 2 Pet 2:15 • Jude 11 • Rev 2:14.

BALAC. See *Balak.*

BALAK (a king of Moab who hired Balaam the soothsayer to curse the Israelites). **Num 22:1–24:25** • Josh 24:9 • Judg 11:25 • Mic 6:5. *Balac:* Rev 2:14.

BALANCE [S]
Lev 19:36 Just *b's,* just weights, a just ephah
Job 31:6 Let me be weighed in an even *b*
Prov 11:1 A false *b* is abomination to the LORD
Isa 40:12 Who [God] hath measured...the hills in a *b*
Dan 5:27 Thou [Belshazzar] art weighed in the *b's,* and art found wanting
Amos 8:5 making the ephah small...falsifying the *b's*
Rev 6:5 he that sat on him [a black horse] had a pair of *b's* in his hand

BALM OF GILEAD (an aromatic gum, used for medicinal purposes, exported from Gilead in Arabia). Jer 8:22.

BAND [S]
Lev 26:13 I [God] have broken the *b's* of your yoke
Ps 119:61 The *b's* of the wicked have robbed me
Jer 2:20 I [God] have broken thy yoke, and burst thy *b's*

Hos 11:4 I [God] drew them... with *b's* of love
Matt 27:27 the soldiers...gathered unto him [Jesus] the whole *b* of soldiers
Luke 8:29 he [wild man among the tombs] brake the *b's*
John 18:12 the *b*...took Jesus, and bound him
Acts 10:1 Cornelius, a centurion of the *b* called...Italian *b*
Acts 16:26 prison...doors were opened, and every one's *b's* were loosed

BAPTISM
Matt 20:22 Are ye [James and John] able...to be baptized with the *b* that I [Jesus] am baptized with
Matt 21:25 The *b* of John, whence was it
Mark 1:4 John did...preach the *b* of repentance
Luke 12:50 I [Jesus] have a *b* to be baptized with
Rom 6:4 we are buried with him [Jesus] by *b* into death
Eph 4:5 One Lord, one faith, one *b*
Col 2:12 Buried with him [Jesus] in *b*
1 Pet 3:21 The like figure whereunto even *b* doth also now save us

BAPTISM OF JESUS. See *Jesus, Life and Ministry of.*

387

BAPTISM OF REPENTANCE

Luke 3:3 he [John the Baptist] came...preaching the **b-o-r** for the remission of sins

Acts 13:24 John...preached... the **b-o-r** to all the people

Acts 19:4 Then said Paul, John verily baptized with the **b-o-r**

BAPTIZE [D, ING]

Matt 3:11 he [Jesus] shall **b** you with the Holy Ghost

Matt 3:13 Then cometh Jesus... unto John, to be **b'd** of him

Matt 28:19 Go...and teach all nations, **b'ing** them in the name of the Father

Mark 1:8 but he [Jesus] shall **b** you with the Holy Ghost

Mark 16:16 He that believeth and is **b'd** shall be saved

Luke 3:7 Then said he [John the Baptist] to the multitude that came forth to be **b'd**

John 1:28 Bethabara beyond Jordan....John was **b'ing**

John 3:22 he [Jesus] tarried... and **b'd**

John 3:23 John also was **b'ing** in Aenon near to Salim

John 4:1 Jesus made and **b'd** more disciples than John

Acts 1:5 ye shall be **b'd** with the Holy Ghost

Acts 2:38 Repent, and be **b'd**... in the name of Jesus

Acts 2:41 they that gladly received his [Peter's] word were **b'd**

Acts 8:12 they [the Samaritans] were **b'd,** both men and women

Acts 8:36 what doth hinder me [the eunuch] to be **b'd**

Acts 9:18 he [Paul] received sight...arose, and was **b'd**

Acts 16:15 she [Lydia] was **b'd,** and her household

Acts 16:33 he [Philippian jailer]...was **b'd,** he and all his

Acts 22:16 arise, and be **b'd,** and wash away thy sins

Rom 6:3 so many of us as were **b'd** into Jesus Christ were **b'd** into his death

1 Cor 1:13 or were ye **b'd** in the name of Paul

1 Cor 1:17 Christ sent me [Paul] not to **b,** but to preach the gospel

1 Cor 12:13 by one Spirit are we all **b'd** into one body

1 Cor 15:29 what shall they do which are **b'd** for the dead

Gal 3:27 as many of you as have been **b'd** into Christ have put on Christ

BARABBAS (a notorious murderer and insurrectionist released by Pilate during the trial of Jesus). Matt 27:16–26 • Mark 15:7–15 • Luke 23:18 • John 18:40.

BARAK (a general who led the judge Deborah to victory over the Canaanites). **Judg 4:1–24** • Heb 11:32.

BARBARIAN (a word used by the Greeks to designate uncouth foreigners or citizens of other nations besides Greece). Acts 28:4 • Rom 1:14 • 1 Cor 14:11 • Col 3:11.

BAR-JESUS (a false prophet who opposed Paul and Silas). Acts 13:6–12. *Elymas:* Acts 13:8.

BARNABAS (a believer who befriended Paul and accompanied him on the first missionary journey). Acts 4:36–37; 9:27; 11:22–30; 12:25; **13:1–14:28;** 15:2–39 • 1 Cor 9:6 • Gal 2: 1,9,13. *Joses:* Acts 4:36.

BARREN
Gen 11:30 But Sarai was *b;* she had no child
Gen 29:31 he [God] opened her [Leah's] womb...Rachel was *b*
Ps 113:9 He [God] maketh the *b* woman to keep house
Luke 1:7 Elisabeth was *b,* and...well stricken in years
Luke 23:29 Blessed are the *b*... wombs that never bare
2 Pet 1:8 ye shall neither be *b* nor unfruitful in the knowledge of our Lord

BARTHOLOMEW (one of the twelve apostles of Jesus). Matt 10:3 • Mark 3:18 • Luke 6:14 • Acts 1:13. Probably the same person as *Nathanael:* John 1:45–46.

BARTIMAEUS (a blind beggar healed by Jesus). Mark 10:46–52.

BARUCH (friend and scribe of the prophet Jeremiah). Jer 32:12–16; 36:4–32; 43:1–7; 45:1–2.

BARZILLAI (a friend who helped King David during his flight from Absalom). **2 Sam 17:27–29;** 19:31–39 • 1 Kgs 2:7.

BASHAN (a fertile plain east of the Jordan River allotted to the half-tribe of Manasseh after the conquest of Canaan). Num 21:33–35 • Deut 3:13; 29:7 • Josh 13:11–12 • 2 Kgs 10:32–33 • Neh 9:22 • Ps 22:12 • Ezek 39:18 • Amos 4:1.

BASKET [S]
Gen 40:18 Joseph answered... The three *b's* are three days
Jer 24:2 One *b* had very good figs...like...figs...first ripe
Amos 8:1 and behold a *b* of summer fruit
Matt 14:20 they [the disciples] took up of the fragments

that remained twelve *b's* full

Mark 8:20 how many *b's* full of fragments took ye [the disciples] up

Acts 9:25 the disciples...let him [Paul] down...in a *b*

BATH-SHEBA (wife of Uriah who committed adultery with David and became his wife). **2 Sam 11:1–27; 12:24 • 1 Kgs 1:11,15–31; 2:13–25.** *Bathshua:* 1 Chr 3:5.

BATH-SHUA. See *Bath-sheba.*

BE STRONG

Deut 31:6 **B-s** and of a good courage, fear not

Josh 10:25 Joshua said...*b-s* and of good courage

1 Chr 28:10 chosen thee [Solomon] to build an house for the sanctuary: *b-s*...do it

Isa 35:4 **B-s**...your God will come with vengeance

Hag 2:4 **b-s,** all ye people of the land, saith the LORD

1 Cor 16:13 stand fast in the faith...*b-s*

Eph 6:10 **b-s** in the Lord, and in the power of his might

2 Tim 2:1 **b-s** in the grace that is in Christ Jesus

BEAM

1 Sam 17:7 the staff of his [Goliath's] spear was like a weaver's *b*

Matt 7:3 why...considerest not the *b*...in thine own eye

Luke 6:42 cast out first the *b* out of thine own eye

BEAR [ETH, ING]

Gen 4:13 Cain said unto the LORD, My punishment is greater than I can *b*

Gen 16:11 thou [Hagar]...shalt *b* a son...Ishmael

Gen 17:19 Sarah thy [Abraham's] wife shall *b*...a son

Ex 20:16 shalt not *b* false witness against thy neighbour

Ex 37:5 he [Bezaleel] put... staves into...rings by... sides of...ark, to *b* the ark

Lev 16:22 the goat shall *b* upon him all their iniquities

Lev 19:18 Thou shalt not avenge, nor *b* any grudge

Num 11:14 I [Moses] am not able to *b* all this people alone

Num 14:27 How long shall I [God] *b* with this evil congregation

Deut 5:20 Neither shalt thou *b* false witness against thy neighbour

Deut 32:11 As an eagle...*b'eth* them [her young] on her wings

Ps 91:12 They shall *b* thee up... lest thou dash thy foot against a stone

Ps 126:6 goeth forth and weepeth, *b'ing* precious seed

Prov 25:18 A man that **b'eth** false witness against his neighbour is a maul

Isa 7:14 a virgin shall...**b** a son...call his name Immanuel

Isa 46:4 I [God] will **b**...and will deliver you

Ezek 4:6 thou [Ezekiel] shalt **b** the iniquity of...Judah

Ezek 18:20 neither shall the father **b**...iniquity of the son

Ezek 36:7 the heathen...shall **b** their shame

Mic 7:9 I will **b** the indignation of the LORD

Matt 3:11 whose [Jesus'] shoes I [John the Baptist] am not worthy to **b**

Mark 15:21 compel one Simon...to **b** his [Jesus'] cross

Luke 4:11 they [angels] shall **b** thee [Jesus] up, lest...thou dash thy foot against a stone

Luke 13:9 if it **b** fruit, well: and if not...cut it down

Luke 14:27 whosoever doth not **b** his cross...cannot be my disciple

Luke 22:10 there shall a man meet you [the disciples], **b'ing** a pitcher

John 1:7 came for a witness, to **b** witness of the Light

John 5:31 If I [Jesus] **b** witness of myself, my witness is not true

John 8:18 Father that sent me [Jesus] **b'eth** witness of me

John 10:25 the works that I [Jesus] do...**b** witness of me

John 15:8 Herein is my [Jesus'] Father glorified, that ye **b** much fruit

John 16:12 many things to say unto you, but ye cannot **b** them

John 19:17 he [Jesus] **b'ing** his cross went forth into...the place of a skull

Acts 9:15 he [Paul] is a chosen vessel...to **b** my [Jesus'] name before the Gentiles

Rom 8:16 The Spirit itself **b'eth** witness with our spirit

Rom 15:1 We then that are strong ought to **b** the infirmities of the weak

1 Cor 13:7 [charity] **b'eth** all things, believeth all things

2 Cor 4:10 **b'ing** about...the dying of the Lord Jesus

2 Cor 11:1 Would to God ye could **b** with me [Paul] a little in my folly

Gal 6:2 **B** ye one another's burdens, and so fulfil the law of Christ

Gal 6:17 I [Paul] **b** in my body the marks of the Lord Jesus

Heb 9:28 Christ was once offered to **b** the sins of many

Heb 13:13 Let us go forth... **b'ing** his [Jesus'] reproach

1 John 5:6 it is the Spirit that *b'eth* witness, because the Spirit is truth

1 John 5:7 three that *b* record in heaven, the Father, the Word, and the Holy Ghost

BEAR FALSE WITNESS

Ex 20:16 Thou shalt not *b-f-w* against thy neighbour

Deut 5:20 Neither shalt thou *b-f-w* against thy neighbour

Matt 19:18 Thou shalt not steal, Thou shalt not *b-f-w*

Rom 13:9 Thou shalt not *b-f-w,* Thou shalt not covet

BEAR FRUIT

Isa 37:31 remnant...of the house of Judah shall...*b-f*

Luke 13:9 if it *b-f,* well: and if not...cut it down

John 15:4 branch cannot *b-f* of itself, except it abide in... vine

BEAT [ETH, ING]

Prov 23:14 *b* him with the rod...deliver his soul from hell

Isa 2:4 they shall *b* their swords into plowshares

Isa 3:15 What mean ye that ye *b* my [God's] people to pieces...grind the...poor

Joel 3:10 *B* your plowshares into swords

Jon 4:8 the sun *b* upon the head of Jonah

Matt 7:25 the winds blew, and *b* upon that house

Mark 4:37 the waves *b* into the ship, so that it was now full

Mark 12:5 him they killed, and many others; *b'ing* some

Acts 16:22 the magistrates... commanded to *b* them [Paul and Silas]

Acts 22:19 I [Paul] imprisoned and *b*...them that believed on thee [Jesus]

1 Cor 9:26 so fight I [Paul], not as one that *b'eth* the air

BEATITUDES. Matt 5:3–11.

BEAUTIFUL

1 Sam 16:12 he [David] was... of a *b* countenance

2 Sam 11:2 David...saw a woman...and the woman was very *b*

Eccl 3:11 He [God] hath made every thing *b* in his time

Isa 52:7 How *b* upon the mountains are the feet of him that bringeth good tidings

Matt 23:27 ye [scribes and Pharisees]...indeed appear *b* outward

Rom 10:15 as it is written, How *b* are the feet of them

BECKONED

Luke 5:7 they *b* unto their partners...in the other ship

Acts 21:40 Paul...*b* with the hand unto the people

Acts 24:10 Paul, after that the governor had *b* unto him to speak, answered

BEELZEBUB. See *Baal-zebub*.

BEER-SHEBA (a well that Abraham and Abimelech dug to seal their covenant and a city that grew up around the well). **Gen 21:31–33;** 26:32–33 • Judg 20:1 • 2 Sam 3:10 • Amos 5:5.

BEFOREHAND
Mark 13:11 take no thought *b* what ye shall speak
1 Tim 5:25 the good works of some are manifest *b*

BEGAN
Gen 6:1 men *b* to multiply on the face of the earth
2 Sam 5:4 David was thirty years old when he *b* to reign
2 Chr 3:1 Solomon *b* to build the house of the LORD
Jon 3:4 Jonah *b* to enter into the city a day's journey
Matt 4:17 Jesus *b* to preach, and to say, Repent
Matt 26:22 they [the disciples]... *b* every one of them to say unto him, Lord, is it I
Mark 6:7 he [Jesus] called... the twelve...*b* to send them forth
Mark 8:31 he [Jesus] *b* to teach them, that the Son of man must suffer

Luke 14:18 they all with one consent *b* to make excuse
Luke 15:14 famine...and he [the prodigal son] *b* to be in want
Luke 19:45 he [Jesus]...*b* to cast out them that sold therein
John 13:5 he [Jesus]...*b* to wash the disciples' feet

BEGINNING [S]
Gen 1:1 In the *b* God created the heaven and the earth
Job 42:12 the LORD blessed the latter end of Job more than his *b*
Ps 111:10 The fear of the LORD is the *b* of wisdom
Prov 1:7 The fear of the LORD is the *b* of knowledge
Eccl 7:8 Better is the end of a thing than the *b* thereof
Isa 40:21 hath it not been told you from the *b*
Isa 48:3 I have declared the former things from the *b*
Matt 19:4 Have ye not read... he which made them at the *b* made them male and female
Matt 20:8 give them their hire, *b* from the last unto the first
Mark 13:8 famines and troubles: these are the *b's* of sorrows
Luke 24:27 *b* at Moses...he [Jesus] expounded...the things concerning himself

John 1:1 In the *b* was the Word...Word was with God

John 6:64 Jesus knew from the *b* who...believed not

Col 1:18 he [Jesus] is the *b,* the firstborn from the dead

2 Thes 2:13 God hath from the *b* chosen you to salvation

Heb 7:3 [Melchisedec] having neither *b* of days

2 Pet 3:4 all things continue as they were from the *b*

1 John 1:1 That which was from the *b*...we have heard

1 John 2:13 ye have known him [Jesus] that is from the *b*

1 John 3:11 heard from the *b*... we should love one another

Rev 1:8 Alpha and Omega, the *b* and the ending

Rev 22:13 Alpha and Omega, the *b* and the end

BEGOTTEN

Ps 2:7 Thou art my Son; this day have I *b* thee

John 1:14 we beheld his [Jesus'] glory, the glory as of the only *b* of the Father

John 1:18 the only *b* Son...he hath declared him [God]

John 3:16 God so loved the world...gave his only *b* Son

1 Cor 4:15 for in Christ Jesus I [Paul] have *b* you through the gospel

1 Pet 1:3 God...hath *b* us again unto a lively hope

BEHAVE [D]

1 Sam 18:14 David *b'd* himself wisely...LORD was with him

Ps 101:2 I will *b* myself wisely in a perfect way

Ps 131:2 I have *b'd* and quieted myself, as a child

1 Cor 13:5 [charity] doth not *b* itself unseemly

2 Thes 3:7 we *b'd* not ourselves disorderly among you

BEHIND

Matt 9:20 behold, a woman... with an issue of blood... came *b* him [Jesus]

Matt 16:23 he [Jesus]...said unto Peter, Get thee *b* me

Phil 3:13 forgetting those things which are *b*

Col 1:24 fill up that which is *b* of the afflictions of Christ

Rev 1:10 I was in the Spirit... and heard *b* me a great voice

BEHOLD [EST, ETH, ING]

Gen 1:31 God saw every thing that he had made, and, *b,* it was very good

Ps 33:13 The LORD...*b'eth* all the sons of men

Ps 119:18 that I may *b* wondrous things out of thy [God's] law

Ps 133:1 *B,* how...pleasant it is for brethren to dwell together in unity

Prov 15:3 The eyes of the LORD are in every place, *b'ing* the evil and the good

Isa 7:14 B, a virgin shall conceive, and bear a son

Isa 40:26 b who hath created these things

Isa 42:1 B my [God's] servant, whom I uphold

Isa 59:1 B, the LORD's hand is not shortened, that it cannot save

Jer 32:27 B, I am the LORD, the God of all flesh

Jer 44:11 B, I [God] will set my face against you for evil

Mal 4:5 B, I [God] will send you Elijah the prophet

Matt 10:16 B, I [Jesus] send you forth as sheep in the midst of wolves

Matt 12:18 B my [God's] servant, whom I have chosen

Matt 12:49 B my [Jesus'] mother and my brethren

Mark 10:21 Then Jesus *b'ing* him [young ruler] loved him

Luke 1:38 Mary said, *B* the handmaid of the Lord

Luke 6:41 why *b'est* thou the mote...in thy brother's eye

John 1:36 he [John the Baptist] saith, *B* the Lamb of God

John 19:14 and he [Pilate] saith unto the Jews, *B* your King

1 Cor 15:51 B...We shall not all sleep...shall all be changed

2 Cor 5:17 b, all things are become new

Jas 1:23 a hearer...and not a doer...is like...a man *b'ing* his...face in a glass

1 John 3:1 B, what manner of love the Father hath bestowed upon us

Rev 3:11 B, I [Jesus] come quickly: hold...fast

Rev 3:20 B, I [Jesus] stand at the door, and knock

Rev 21:5 B, I [Jesus] make all things new

BELA. See *Zoar.*

BELIAL. See *Satan.*

BELIEVE [D, ING, TH]

Gen 15:6 he [Abraham] *b'd* in the LORD; and he counted it to him for righteousness

Ex 4:1 they will not *b* me [Moses], nor hearken unto my voice

Ps 119:66 I have *b'd* thy [God's] commandments

Jon 3:5 the people of Nineveh *b'd* God...put on sackcloth

Matt 18:6 whoso shall offend one of these little ones which *b* in me

Matt 21:22 whatsoever ye shall ask in prayer, *b'ing,* ye shall receive

Mark 5:36 he [Jesus] saith... Be not afraid, only *b*

Mark 9:23 If thou canst *b,* all things are possible

Mark 9:24 Lord, I *b;* help thou mine unbelief

Mark 11:24 b that ye receive them, and ye shall have them

Luke 24:25 O fools, and slow of heart to *b*

John 3:12 how shall ye *b,* if I tell you of heavenly things

John 3:16 whosoever *b'th* in him [Jesus] should not perish

John 3:18 he hath not *b'd* in the name of the only begotten Son of God

John 3:36 He that *b'th* on the Son hath everlasting life

John 4:48 Except ye see signs and wonders, ye will not *b*

John 6:29 This is the work of God, that ye *b* on him whom he hath sent

John 6:35 he that *b'th* on me [Jesus] shall never thirst

John 6:64 Jesus knew...who they were that *b'd* not

John 9:36 Who is he, Lord, that I might *b* on him

John 11:25 he that *b'th* in me [Jesus], though he were dead, yet shall he live

John 11:26 whosoever...*b'th* in me [Jesus] shall never die

John 11:27 Yea, Lord: I *b* that thou art the Christ

John 12:46 whosoever *b'th* on me [Jesus] should not abide in darkness

John 14:1 ye *b* in God, *b* also in me [Jesus]

John 20:25 Except I [Thomas]... thrust my hand into his [Jesus'] side, I will not *b*

John 20:29 blessed are they that have not seen, and yet have *b'd*

John 20:31 that ye might *b* that Jesus is the Christ

Acts 4:32 multitude of them that *b'd* were of one heart

Acts 8:37 And he [the eunuch] said, I *b* that Jesus Christ is the Son of God

Acts 16:31 B on the Lord Jesus Christ...thou shalt be saved

Rom 1:16 it [the gospel] is the power of God unto salvation to every one that *b'th*

Rom 4:3 Abraham *b'd* God, and it was counted unto him for righteousness

Rom 6:8 we *b* that we shall also live with him [Jesus]

Rom 10:4 Christ is the end of the law for righteousness to every one that *b'th*

Rom 10:9 b...that God hath raised him [Jesus] from the dead, thou shalt be saved

Rom 10:14 How then shall they call on him in whom they have not *b'd*

Rom 13:11 now is our salvation nearer than when we *b'd*

Rom 15:13 the God of hope fill you with all joy...in *b'ing*

1 Cor 1:21 it pleased God by the foolishness of preaching to save them that *b*

1 Cor 13:7 [charity] beareth all things, *b'th* all things

2 Tim 1:12 I [Paul] know whom I have *b'd*

Heb 11:6 he that cometh to God must *b* that he is

Jas 2:19 thou doest well: the devils also *b,* and tremble

1 John 3:23 we should *b* on the name of his Son Jesus

1 John 5:1 Whosoever *b'th* that Jesus is the Christ is born of God

1 John 5:10 He that *b'th* on the Son of God hath the witness in himself

BELIEVERS

Acts 5:14 *b* were the more added to the Lord

1 Tim 4:12 be thou an example of the *b,* in word...faith

BELONG [ED, ETH]

Ps 3:8 Salvation *b'eth* unto the LORD

Ps 94:1 O LORD God, to whom vengeance *b'eth,* show thyself

Dan 9:9 To the Lord our God *b* mercies and forgivenesses

Luke 23:7 he [Pilate] knew that he [Jesus] *b'ed* unto Herod's jurisdiction

1 Cor 7:32 He that is unmarried careth for the things that *b* to the Lord

BELOVED SON

Matt 3:17 This is my *b-S,* in whom I am well pleased

Matt 17:5 This is my *b-S,* in whom I am well pleased; hear ye him

Mark 1:11 Thou art my *b-S,* in whom I am well pleased

Mark 9:7 This is my *b-S:* hear him

Luke 3:22 Thou art my *b-S;* in thee I am well pleased

Luke 9:35 This is my *b-S:* hear him

Luke 20:13 send my *b-s:* it may be they will reverence him

1 Cor 4:17 I [Paul] sent unto you Timotheus, who is my *b-s*

2 Tim 1:2 To Timothy, my [Paul's] dearly *b-s:* Grace, mercy

BELSHAZZAR (last king of the Babylonian Empire whose fall was foretold by a mysterious hand writing on the wall).
Dan 5:1–31; 7:1; 8:1.

BELTESHAZZAR. See *Daniel.*

BENAIAH (a loyal supporter of David who later became commander-in-chief of Solomon's army). 2 Sam 8:18; 20:23; 23:20,22 • 1 Kgs 1:8–44; 2:25–46; 4:4 • 1 Chr 11:22,24; 18:17; 27:5–6.

BEN-AMMI (a son of Lot and ancestor of the Ammonites). Gen 19:30–38.

BENEFITS
Ps 68:19 Blessed be the Lord, who daily loadeth us with *b*
Ps 103:2 Bless the LORD, O my soul...forget not all his *b*
Ps 116:12 What shall I render unto the LORD for all his *b*

BEN-HADAD (a title for three different kings of Damascus, Syria).
1. Ben-hadad I, who invaded the Northern Kingdom in league with King Asa of Judah. 1 Kgs 15:18–21 • 2 Chr 16:2–4.
2. Ben-hadad II, who waged war against King Ahab of Israel. 1 Kgs 20:1–34 • 2 Kgs 6:24; 8:7–9.
3. Ben-hadad III, who was defeated by the Assyrians, as the prophet Amos predicted. 2 Kgs 13:3,24–25 • Amos 1:4.

BENJAMIN (a son of Jacob and ancestor of one of the twelve tribes of Israel). Gen 35:18,24; 42:4,36; 43:14–29; 45:12–14,22; 46:19,21 • Ex 1:3 • 1 Chr 2:2; 7:6; 8:1. The tribe of Benjamin settled in central Canaan. Josh 18:11–28.

BEREA (a city of Macedonia visited by Paul). Acts 17:10–14.

BEREAVE [D]
Gen 42:36 Me [Jacob] have ye *b'd* of my children
Jer 15:7 I [the LORD] will *b* them of children
Jer 18:21 let their wives be *b'd* of their children

BERITH. See *Baal-berith.*

BERNICE (a sister of Herod Agrippa II, Roman governor of Palestine before whom Paul appeared). Acts 25:13,23; 26:1–32.

BERODACH-BALADAN (a king of Babylon whose ambassadors viewed the treasures of King Hezekiah of Judah). 2 Kgs 20:12–19. *Merodach-baladan:* Isa 39:1.

BESEECH [ING]
1 Chr 21:8 *b* thee [God], do away...iniquity of thy servant
Ps 116:4 O LORD, I *b* thee, deliver my soul
Isa 64:9 see, we *b* thee [God], we are all thy people
Jer 38:20 Obey, I [Jeremiah] *b* thee, the voice of the LORD
Dan 9:16 I [Daniel] *b* thee [God], let thine anger...be turned away
Jon 4:3 O LORD, take, I [Jonah] *b* thee, my life from me

Matt 8:5 came unto him [Jesus] a centurion, *b'ing* him

Luke 7:3 he sent unto him [Jesus]...*b'ing* him that he would...heal his servant

Luke 9:38 Master, I *b* thee, look upon my son

Rom 12:1 I [Paul] *b* you therefore, brethren

1 Cor 4:16 I [Paul] *b* you, be ye followers of me

2 Cor 2:8 I [Paul] *b* you...confirm your love toward him

2 Cor 5:20 we are ambassadors for Christ, as though God did *b* you by us

Eph 4:1 I [Paul]...*b* you that ye walk worthy of the vocation wherewith ye are called

Phlm 10 I [Paul] *b* thee for my son Onesimus

1 Pet 2:11 I [Peter] *b* you... abstain from fleshly lusts

BEST

1 Sam 8:14 he [the king] will take your fields...the *b* of them

Luke 15:22 Bring forth the *b* robe, and put it on him

1 Cor 12:31 But covet earnestly the *b* gifts

BESTOW [ED]

Luke 12:17 What shall I do...no room where to *b* my fruits

John 4:38 I [Jesus] sent you to reap that whereon ye *b'ed* no labour

1 Cor 13:3 though I [Paul] *b* all my goods to feed the poor

Gal 4:11 I [Paul] am afraid of you, lest I have *b'ed* upon you labour in vain

1 John 3:1 what manner of love the Father hath *b'ed* upon us

BETHABARA (a place along the Jordan River where John the Baptist baptized). John 1:28.

BETHANY (a village outside Jerusalem where Lazarus, Mary, and Martha lived and the site from which Jesus ascended to heaven). Matt 21:17; 26:6 • Mark 11:1,11–12; 14:3 • Luke 19:29; 24:50–51 • John 11:1,18; 12:1.

BETHEL (a city where Jacob had a vision of angels on a staircase). Gen 12:8; 13:3–4; **28:10–19;** 35:1–15 • Josh 16:2 • 1 Sam 7:15–16; 10:3 • 1 Kgs 12:28–33 • 2 Kgs 23:4,15–20 • Jer 48:13 • Hos 10:15 • Amos 7:10–13. *El-bethel:* Gen 35:7. *Luz:* Gen 28:19.

BETHESDA (a pool in Jerusalem where Jesus healed a lame man). John 5:2–8.

399

BETH-HORON (twin towns—Upper and Lower—in the territory of Ephraim which served as important military outposts). Josh 10:10–14; 16:3–5 • 1 Sam 13:18 • 1 Chr 7:24 • 2 Chr 8:5.

BETHLEHEM (a town in southern Palestine near Jerusalem where Jesus was born in fulfillment of prophecy). Gen 35:19; 48:7 • Ruth 1:19,22; 2:4; 4:11 • 1 Sam 16:4; 17:15; 20:6,28 • 2 Sam 2:32; 23:14–16,24 • 1 Chr 11:16–26 • 2 Chr 11:6 • Ezra 2:21 • Neh 7:26 • **Mic 5:2** • Matt 2:1–16 • **Luke 2:4–7.** *Beth-lehem-judah:* Judg 19:18. *Ephratah:* Ruth 4:11. *Ephrath:* Gen 35:16–19.

BETH-LEHEM-JUDAH. See *Bethlehem.*

BETHPHAGE (a village outside Jerusalem mentioned in connection with Jesus' triumphal entry into the city). Matt 21:1 • Mark 11:1 • Luke 19:29.

BETHSAIDA (a fishing village on the Sea of Galilee; the home of Andrew, Peter, and Philip—apostles of Jesus). Matt 11:21 • Mark 6:45 • Luke 10:13 • **John 1:44; 12:21.**

BETRAY [ED, EST, ETH]
Matt 17:22 Son of man shall be *b'ed* into the hands of men
Matt 26:2 the Son of man is *b'ed* to be crucified
Matt 26:16 he [Judas] sought opportunity to *b* him [Jesus]
Matt 26:45 the Son of man is *b'ed* into the hands of sinners
Mark 14:10 Judas...went unto the chief priests, to *b* him [Jesus] unto them
Mark 14:21 but woe to that man by whom the Son of man is *b'ed*
Luke 22:21 the hand of him that *b'eth* me [Jesus] is with me on the table
Luke 22:48 Judas, *b'est* thou the Son of man with a kiss
John 6:64 Jesus knew...who should *b* him
1 Cor 11:23 the Lord Jesus the same night in which he was *b'ed* took bread

BETTER
1 Sam 15:22 Behold, to obey is *b* than sacrifice
2 Kgs 5:12 Are not Abana and Pharpar...*b* than all the waters of Israel
Ps 37:16 A little that a righteous man hath is *b* than the riches of many wicked
Ps 84:10 a day in thy [God's] courts is *b* than a thousand
Ps 118:8 b to trust in the LORD than to put confidence in man

Prov 8:11 For wisdom is *b* than rubies

Prov 15:16 *B* is little with the fear of the LORD than great treasure and trouble

Prov 16:16 How much *b* is it to get wisdom than gold

Prov 19:22 a poor man is *b* than a liar

Prov 27:5 Open rebuke is *b* than secret love

Prov 27:10 *b* is a neighbour... near than a brother far off

Eccl 4:9 Two are *b* than one; because they have a good reward for their labour

Eccl 4:13 *B* is a poor and a wise child than an old and foolish king

Eccl 6:9 *B* is the sight of the eyes than the wandering of the desire

Eccl 7:1 A good name is *b* than precious ointment

Eccl 7:8 *B* is the end of a thing than the beginning thereof

Eccl 9:18 Wisdom is *b* than weapons of war

Song 4:10 how much *b* is thy love than wine

Dan 1:20 found them [Daniel and his friends] ten times *b* than all the magicians

Jon 4:8 Jonah...said, It is *b* for me to die than to live

Matt 12:12 How much then is a man *b* than a sheep

Matt 18:8 it is *b* for thee to enter into life halt or maimed

1 Cor 7:9 for it is *b* to marry than to burn

Phil 1:23 having a desire...to be with Christ; which is far *b*

Heb 1:4 Being made so much *b* than the angels

Heb 7:22 was Jesus made a surety of a *b* testament

BEULAH (a symbolic name for Israel after the Exile in Babylon when the nation would be in a fruitful relationship with God). Isa 62:4.

BEZER (a city of refuge in the territory of Reuben). Deut 4:43 • Josh 20:8; 21:36 • 1 Chr 6:78.

BILDAD (one of the three friends who comforted Job). His speeches appear in Job 8:1–22; 18:1–21; 25:1–6.

BILHAH (a wife of Jacob and mother of two of his sons, Dan and Naphtali). Gen 29:29; 30:3–7; 35:22,25; 37:2; 46:25 • 1 Chr 7:13.

BIND [ETH, ING]
Gen 37:7 we [Joseph and his brothers] were *b'ing* sheaves in the field

Deut 6:8 thou shalt *b* them for a sign upon thine hand

Ps 147:3 He [God] healeth the broken in heart, and *b'eth* up their wounds

Prov 3:3 **b** them [mercy and truth] about thy neck

Isa 61:1 the LORD...hath sent me to **b** up the broken-hearted

Dan 3:20 he [the king] commanded...to **b** Shadrach, Meshach, and Abednego

Matt 12:29 how can one enter into a strong man's house... except he first **b**...man

Matt 16:19 whatsoever thou shalt **b** on earth shall be bound in heaven

Matt 23:4 they [Pharisees] **b** heavy burdens

Mark 5:3 no man could **b** him [demon-possessed man]

Acts 22:4 I [Paul] persecuted... **b'ing** and delivering...both men and women

BIRTH

Eccl 7:1 good name is better than...ointment...day of death than...day of...**b**

Matt 1:18 the **b** of Jesus Christ was on this wise

John 9:1 Jesus...saw a man which was blind from his **b**

Rev 12:2 she being with child cried, travailing in **b**

BIRTH OF JESUS. See *Jesus, Life and Ministry of.*

BIRTHRIGHT

Gen 25:31 Jacob said, Sell me this day thy [Esau's] **b**

Heb 12:16 Esau, who for one morsel of meat sold his **b**

BISHOP [S]

Phil 1:1 to all the saints...at Philippi, with the **b's**

1 Tim 3:1 If a man desire the office of a **b**, he desireth a good work

1 Tim 3:2 A **b** then must be blameless...husband of one wife

Titus 1:7 a **b** must be blameless, as the steward of God

1 Pet 2:25 ye are now returned unto the Shepherd and **B** of your souls

BITHYNIA (a Roman province of Asia Minor that Paul was prevented from entering). Acts 16:7.

BITTER

Ex 1:14 they [the Egyptians] made...lives **b** with... bondage

Ex 12:8 with **b** herbs they shall eat it [the Passover meal]

Ex 15:23 could not drink of the waters of Marah...they were **b**

Isa 24:9 strong drink shall be **b** to them that drink it

Jer 31:15 A voice was heard in Ramah...**b** weeping

Hab 1:6 I raise up the Chaldeans, that **b** and hasty nation

Jas 3:11 Doth a fountain send forth...sweet water and *b*

BITTER HERBS (herbs eaten by the Israelites during their Passover celebrations to help them remember their enslavement years in Egypt). Ex 12:8 • Num 9:11.

BITTERNESS
Job 9:18 He [God]...filleth me [Job] with *b*
Job 21:25 another dieth in the *b* of his soul
Acts 8:23 thou art in the gall of *b,* and in the bond of iniquity
Rom 3:14 Whose mouth is full of cursing and *b*
Eph 4:31 Let all *b,* and wrath... be put away from you

BLAMELESS
1 Cor 1:8 ye may be *b* in the day of our Lord Jesus
1 Tim 3:2 A bishop then must be *b,* the husband of one wife
1 Tim 3:10 use the office of a deacon, being found *b*
Titus 1:7 a bishop must be *b,* as the steward of God

BLASPHEME [D]
Ps 74:10 shall the enemy *b* thy [God's] name for ever
Ps 74:18 the foolish people have *b'd* thy [God's] name
Mark 3:29 he that shall *b* against the Holy Ghost hath never forgiveness

Rev 13:6 he opened his mouth... against God, to *b* his name

BLASPHEMY [IES]
Matt 12:31 *b* against the Holy Ghost shall not be forgiven
Matt 26:65 He [Jesus] hath spoken *b;* what further need have we of witnesses
Mark 2:7 Why doth this man [Jesus] thus speak *b'ies*
Col 3:8 put off all these; anger, wrath, malice, *b*
Rev 13:1 I [John]...saw a beast...and upon his heads the name of *b*

BLESS [ED, ING, INGS]
Gen 1:22 God *b'ed* them...Be fruitful, and multiply
Gen 2:3 God *b'ed* the seventh day, and sanctified it
Gen 9:1 And God *b'ed* Noah and his sons
Gen 12:2 I [God] will *b* thee [Abraham], and make thy name great
Gen 22:18 in thy [Abraham's] seed shall all the nations of the earth be *b'ed*
Gen 27:34 Esau...said unto his father, *B* me, even me also
Gen 39:5 the LORD *b'ed* the Egyptian's house for Joseph's sake
Ex 20:11 the LORD *b'ed* the sabbath day, and hallowed it
Num 6:24 The LORD *b* thee, and keep thee

Num 24:1 Balaam saw that it pleased the LORD to *b* Israel

Deut 8:10 thou shalt *b* the LORD...for the good land... he hath given thee

Deut 11:26 I set before you this day a *b'ing* and a curse

Deut 33:1 Moses...*b'ed* the children of Israel

Job 1:21 the LORD hath taken away; *b'ed* be the name of the LORD

Job 42:12 the LORD *b'ed* the latter end of Job more than his beginning

Ps 1:1 *B'ed* is the man that walketh not in the counsel of the ungodly

Ps 28:6 *B'ed* be the LORD, because he hath heard...my supplications

Ps 29:11 the LORD will *b* his people with peace

Ps 32:1 *B'ed* is he whose transgression is forgiven

Ps 33:12 *B'ed* is the nation whose God is the LORD

Ps 41:13 *B'ed* be the LORD God...from everlasting

Ps 66:20 *B'ed* be God, which hath not turned away my prayer, nor his mercy

Ps 67:1 God...*b* us; and cause his face to shine upon us

Ps 84:4 *B'ed* are they that dwell in thy [God's] house

Ps 94:12 *B'ed* is the man whom thou [God] chastenest

Ps 96:2 Sing unto the LORD, *b* his name

Ps 106:48 *B'ed* be the LORD God of Israel from everlasting to everlasting

Ps 115:18 we will *b* the LORD from this time forth

Ps 119:2 *B'ed* are they that keep his [God's] testimonies

Ps 128:1 *B'ed* is every one that feareth the LORD

Ps 145:1 I will *b* thy [God's] name for ever and ever

Prov 10:6 *B'ings* are upon the head of the just

Prov 31:28 Her children arise up, and call her *b'ed*

Ezek 34:26 there shall be showers of *b'ing*

Matt 5:3 *B'ed* are the poor in spirit

Matt 5:4 *B'ed* are they that mourn

Matt 5:5 *B'ed* are the meek

Matt 5:6 *B'ed* are they which do hunger...after righteousness

Matt 5:7 *B'ed* are the merciful

Matt 5:8 *B'ed* are the pure in heart

Matt 5:9 *B'ed* are the peacemakers

Matt 5:10 *B'ed* are they which are persecuted for righteousness' sake

Matt 5:11 *B'ed* are ye, when men shall revile you, and persecute you

Matt 5:44 Love your enemies, *b* them that curse you

Matt 16:17 *B'ed* art thou, Simon Barjona

Matt 26:26 Jesus took bread, and *b'ed* it, and brake it

Mark 10:16 he [Jesus]...put his hands upon them [the children], and *b'ed* them

Luke 1:28 b'ed art thou [Mary] among women

Luke 11:28 Yea rather, *b'ed* are they that hear the word of God, and keep it

John 20:29 b'ed are they that have not seen, and yet have believed

Rom 12:14 B them which persecute you: *b,* and curse not

1 Cor 4:12 being reviled, we *b*

1 Cor 10:16 The cup of *b'ing*... is it not the communion of the blood of Christ

Gal 3:9 they which be of faith are *b'ed* with...Abraham

Eph 1:3 who [God] hath *b'ed* us with all spiritual *b'ings*

1 Tim 6:15 who [Jesus] is the *b'ed* and only Potentate

Titus 2:13 that *b'ed* hope, and the glorious appearing of... our Saviour

Jas 1:12 B'ed is the man that endureth temptation

Jas 3:10 Out of the same mouth proceedeth *b'ing* and cursing

Rev 1:3 B'ed is he that readeth, and they that hear the words of this prophecy

Rev 5:12 Worthy is the Lamb... to receive...honour, and glory, and *b'ing*

Rev 22:7 b'ed is he that keepeth the sayings of the prophecy of this book

BLESS THE LORD

Ps 16:7 I will *b-t-L,* who hath given me counsel

Ps 34:1 I will *b-t-L* at all times: his praise shall continually be in my mouth

Ps 103:1 B-t-L, O my soul: and all that is within me, bless his holy name

Ps 103:2 B-t-L, O my soul, and forget not all his benefits

Ps 134:2 Lift up your hands in the sanctuary, and *b-t-L*

BLIND [ED]

Job 29:15 I was eyes to the *b,* and feet was I to the lame

Ps 146:8 The LORD openeth the eyes of the *b*

Isa 35:5 the eyes of the *b* shall be opened

Isa 42:7 To open the *b* eyes, to bring out the prisoners

Isa 43:8 Bring forth the *b* people that have eyes

Lam 4:14 They have wandered as *b* men in the streets

Mal 1:8 if ye offer the *b* for sacrifice, is it not evil

Matt 11:5 The *b* receive their sight, and the lame walk

Matt 20:30 two *b* men sitting by the way side...cried out

Matt 23:24 Ye *b* guides [Pharisees], which strain at a gnat

Mark 8:22 they bring a *b* man unto him [Jesus], and besought him

Mark 10:46 *b* Bartimaeus, the son of Timaeus, sat by the highway

Luke 4:18 Spirit...anointed me [Jesus] to preach... recovering of sight to the *b*

Luke 6:39 Can the *b* lead the *b*

Luke 7:22 tell John...that the *b* see, the lame walk

John 9:2 who did sin, this man, or his parents, that he was born *b*

John 12:40 He [God] hath *b'ed* their eyes...hardened their heart

Acts 13:11 thou [Elymas the sorcerer]...shalt be *b*

1 John 2:11 he that hateth his brother is in darkness, and...darkness hath *b'ed* his eyes

BLINDNESS

Gen 19:11 they [angels] smote the men...with *b,* both small and great

2 Kgs 6:18 And he [God] smote them with *b* according to the word of Elisha

Eph 4:18 being alienated from the life of God...because of the *b* of their heart

BLOOD

Gen 4:10 the voice of thy [Cain's] brother's *b* crieth unto me [God]

Gen 9:6 Whoso sheddeth man's *b,* by man shall his *b* be shed

Ex 7:21 there was *b* throughout all the land of Egypt

Ex 12:23 when he seeth the *b* upon the lintel...the LORD will pass over the door

Ex 24:8 Moses took the *b,* and sprinkled it on the people

Lev 7:27 Whatsoever soul eateth...*b*...shall be cut off

Lev 15:19 if...her issue in her flesh be *b,* she shall be put apart seven days

Lev 17:11 For the life of the flesh is in the *b*

Lev 20:9 he hath cursed his father or his mother; his *b* shall be upon him

Num 35:19 The revenger of *b*... shall slay the murderer

1 Kgs 18:28 they [the priests of Baal]...cut themselves... till the *b* gushed out

1 Kgs 22:38 the dogs licked up his [Ahab's] *b*

2 Kgs 9:33 her [Jezebel's] *b* was sprinkled on the wall

1 Chr 22:8 thou [David] hast shed much *b* upon the earth

Ps 30:9 What profit is there in my *b,* when I go...to the pit

Prov 1:16 their feet...make haste to shed *b*

Prov 6:17 a lying tongue, and hands that shed innocent *b*

Isa 1:11 I [God] delight not in the *b* of bullocks

Isa 1:15 I [God] will not hear: your hands are full of *b*

Isa 59:3 hands are defiled with
b...fingers with iniquity

Ezek 9:9 land is full of **b,** and
the city full of perverseness

Joel 2:31 The sun shall be
turned into darkness, and
the moon into **b**

Matt 9:20 a woman...with an
issue of **b** twelve years, came
behind him [Jesus]

Matt 16:17 for flesh and **b** hath
not revealed it unto thee
[Peter]

Matt 26:28 this is my [Jesus'] **b**
of the new testament, which
is shed for many

Matt 27:8 that field was called,
The field of **b,** unto this day

Matt 27:24 Pilate...washed his
hands...saying, I am innocent of the **b** of this...
person [Jesus]

Matt 27:25 Then answered all
the people...His [Jesus'] **b**
be on us

Luke 11:50 the **b** of all the
prophets...may be required
of this generation

Luke 22:44 his [Jesus'] sweat
was as...great drops of **b**

John 6:53 Except ye...drink his
[Jesus'] **b,** ye have no life

John 19:34 one of the soldiers...pierced his [Jesus']
side...came there out **b** and
water

Acts 2:20 sun shall be turned
into darkness...moon into **b**

Acts 17:26 And [God] hath
made of one **b** all nations of
men

Acts 18:6 Your **b** be upon your
own heads

Acts 20:28 feed the church of
God, which he [Jesus] hath
purchased with his own **b**

Rom 5:9 now justified by his
[Jesus'] **b,** we shall be saved
from wrath

1 Cor 10:16 The cup of blessing...is it not the communion of the **b** of Christ

1 Cor 15:50 flesh and **b** cannot
inherit the kingdom of God

Eph 2:13 ye who sometimes
were far off are made nigh
by the **b** of Christ

Eph 6:12 we wrestle not against
flesh and **b**

Col 1:14 In whom we have
redemption through his
[Jesus'] **b**

Heb 9:12 by his [Jesus'] own **b**
he entered in once into the
holy place

Heb 10:4 not possible that the
b of bulls...should take
away sins

Heb 13:12 he [Jesus] might
sanctify...with his own **b**

1 John 1:7 the **b** of Jesus Christ
his Son cleanseth us from
all sin

Rev 6:12 the sun became
black...and the moon be-
came as **b**

Rev 7:14 they...have washed their robes, and made them white in the *b* of the Lamb

Rev 16:3 the sea...became as the *b* of a dead man

BLOT [TED, TETH]

Ex 32:33 Whosoever hath sinned against me [God], him will I *b* out of my book

Ps 51:1 according unto...thy [God's] tender mercies *b* out my transgressions

Ps 51:9 Hide thy [God's] face from my sins, and *b* out all mine iniquities

Ps 69:28 Let them be *b'ted* out of the book of the living

Isa 43:25 I [God], even I, am he that *b'teth* out thy transgressions for mine own sake

Isa 44:22 I [God] have *b'ted* out...thy transgressions

Acts 3:19 Repent...that your sins may be *b'ted* out

Rev 3:5 I [God] will not *b* out his name out of the book of life...will confess his name

BOANERGES (a name, meaning "sons of thunder," given by Jesus to His disciples James and John). Mark 3:17.

BOAST [ETH, ING, INGS]

Ps 44:8 In God we *b* all the day long

Prov 25:14 Whoso *b'eth* himself of a false gift is like clouds... without rain

Prov 27:1 **B** not thyself of tomorrow

2 Cor 9:3 lest our *b'ing* of you should be in vain

Eph 2:9 Not of works, lest any man should *b*

Jas 3:5 the tongue is a little member...*b'eth* great things

Jas 4:16 ye rejoice in your *b'ings:* all such rejoicing is evil

BOAZ (the husband of Ruth and an ancestor of Christ). Ruth 2:1–23; 3:2,7; 4:1–21 • 1 Chr 2:11–12. *Booz:* Matt 1:5 • Luke 3:32.

BODY

Num 19:11 He that toucheth the dead *b*...shall be unclean

Deut 21:23 His *b* shall not remain all night upon the tree

Mic 6:7 give...the fruit of my *b* for the sin of my soul

Matt 6:23 eye be evil, thy whole *b* shall be full of darkness

Matt 26:26 Jesus took bread... Take, eat; this is my *b*

Mark 15:43 Joseph of Arimathaea...craved the *b* of Jesus

Luke 12:22 Take no thought... for the *b,* what ye...put on

Luke 23:55 the women... beheld...how his [Jesus'] *b* was laid

Rom 6:12 Let not sin therefore reign in your mortal *b*

Rom 7:24 who shall deliver me from the *b* of this death

Rom 12:5 we, being many, are one *b* in Christ

1 Cor 6:18 he that committeth fornication sinneth against his own *b*

1 Cor 10:17 we being many are one bread, and one *b*

1 Cor 12:12 the *b* is one, and hath many members

1 Cor 13:3 though I [Paul] give my *b* to be burned

1 Cor 15:44 It is sown a natural *b;* it is raised a spiritual *b*

2 Cor 5:8 absent from the *b*... present with the Lord

Gal 6:17 I [Paul] bear in my *b* the marks of the Lord Jesus

Phil 1:20 Christ shall be magnified in my [Paul's] *b*

Col 1:18 he [Christ] is the head of the *b,* the church

Jas 3:6 it [the tongue] defileth the whole *b*

1 Pet 2:24 Who [Jesus]...bare our sins in his own *b* on the tree

BODY OF CHRIST

Rom 7:4 ye also are become dead to the law by the *b-o-C*

1 Cor 10:16 The bread which we break, is it not the communion of the *b-o-C*

1 Cor 12:27 ye are the *b-o-C,* and members in particular

Eph 4:12 for the work of the ministry...edifying of the *b-o-C*

BOLD [LY]

Prov 28:1 The wicked flee... righteous are *b* as a lion

Acts 9:29 he [Paul] spake *b'ly* in the name of the Lord Jesus

Acts 19:8 he [Paul] went into the synagogue, and spake *b'ly*

Phil 1:14 many of the brethren...are much more *b* to speak the word without fear

Heb 4:16 Let us...come *b'ly* unto the throne of grace

BOLDNESS

Acts 4:13 they saw the *b* of Peter and John

Acts 4:31 they [the apostles]... prayed...spake the word of God with *b*

Eph 3:12 In whom [Jesus] we have *b*...with confidence

Phil 1:20 with all *b*...Christ... magnified in my [Paul's] body

1 John 4:17 that we may have *b* in the day of judgment

BOND [S]

Ps 116:16 thou [God] hast loosed my *b's*

Jer 27:2 Make thee *b's* and yokes, and put them upon thy [Jeremiah's] neck

Acts 26:29 that...all that hear me this day, were...such as I [Paul] am, except these *b's*

Gal 3:28 There is neither Jew nor Greek...*b* nor free

Eph 4:3 keep the unity of the Spirit in the *b* of peace

Eph 6:20 I [Paul] am an ambassador in *b's*

Phil 1:13 my [Paul's] *b's* in Christ are manifest in... palace

Col 3:11 there is neither...*b* nor free: but Christ is all

Col 3:14 put on charity, which is the *b* of perfectness

Phlm 10 son Onesimus, whom I [Paul] have begotten in my *b's*

BONDAGE

Ex 1:14 they [the Egyptians] made...lives bitter with hard *b*

Ex 6:6 I [God] will rid you [the Israelites] out of their *b*

John 8:33 We be Abraham's seed...never in *b* to any man

Rom 8:15 ye have not received the spirit of *b* again to fear

Gal 4:9 how turn ye...to... desire again to be in *b*

Gal 5:1 be not entangled again with the yoke of *b*

BOOK OF LIFE

Phil 4:3 help those...fellow-labourers, whose names are in the *b-o-l*

Rev 3:5 I will not blot out his name out of the *b-o-l*

Rev 20:12 another book was opened, which is the *b-o-l*

Rev 20:15 whosoever was not found written in the *b-o-l* was cast into the lake of fire

BOOZ. See *Boaz*.

BORN

Gen 17:17 Shall a child be *b* unto him [Abraham] that is an hundred years old

Gen 21:5 Abraham was an hundred years old, when his son Isaac was *b*

Job 3:3 Let the day perish wherein I [Job] was *b*

Job 5:7 man is *b* unto trouble, as the sparks fly upward

Job 14:1 Man that is *b* of a woman is of few days

Ps 58:3 The wicked...go astray as soon as they be *b*

Prov 17:17 A friend loveth at all times, and a brother is *b* for adversity

Eccl 3:2 A time to be *b,* and a time to die

Isa 9:6 unto us a child is *b,* unto us a son is given

Jer 20:14 Cursed be the day wherein I [Jeremiah] was *b*

Matt 2:1 when Jesus was *b* in Bethlehem of Judaea

Luke 1:35 that holy thing...*b* of thee [Mary] shall be called the Son of God

Luke 2:11 unto you is *b* this day...a Saviour

Luke 7:28 Among those...*b* of women...not a greater

prophet than John the Baptist

John 9:2 sin, this man, or his parents, that he was *b* blind

John 18:37 Thou sayest that I [Jesus] am a king. To this end was I *b*

Acts 22:28 And Paul said, But I was free *b*

1 Cor 15:8 he [Jesus] was seen of me [Paul] also, as of one *b* out of due time

1 John 3:9 Whosoever is *b* of God doth not commit sin

1 John 4:7 every one that loveth is *b* of God

BORN AGAIN

John 3:3 Jesus...said...Except a man be *b-a,* he cannot see the kingdom of God

John 3:7 Marvel not that I [Jesus] said unto thee [Nicodemus], Ye must be *b-a*

1 Pet 1:23 *b-a,* not of corruptible seed, but of incorruptible

BOSOM

Ex 4:6 he [Moses] put his hand into his *b:* and...his hand was leprous as snow

Prov 5:20 why wilt thou... embrace the *b* of a stranger

Isa 40:11 He [God] shall... carry them [lambs] in his *b*

Luke 16:22 the beggar died... carried...into Abraham's *b*

John 1:18 the only begotten Son...in the *b* of the Father

John 13:23 leaning on Jesus' *b* one of his disciples

BOTTLE [S]

Job 32:19 my belly...is ready to burst like new *b's*

Ps 56:8 put thou my tears into thy [God's] *b*

Luke 5:37 no man putteth new wine into old *b's*

BOTTOMLESS PIT

Rev 9:1 to him was given the key of the *b-p*

Rev 11:7 the beast that ascendeth out of the *b-p* shall make war

Rev 20:1 I saw an angel... having the key of the *b-p*

BOUGHT

Lev 27:24 the field shall return unto him of whom it was *b*

Jer 32:9 I [Jeremiah] *b* the field of Hanameel

Matt 13:46 he [merchant]... sold all...he had, and *b* it [pearl]

Mark 11:15 Jesus...began to cast out them that sold and *b* in the temple

Luke 14:18 I have *b* a piece of ground, and I must needs go and see it

1 Cor 6:20 ye are *b* with a price...glorify God

1 Cor 7:23 Ye are *b* with a price; be not ye the servants of men

BOUND

Gen 22:9 Abraham...laid the wood...and *b* Isaac his son

Judg 16:21 the Philistines took him [Samson]...and *b* him with fetters of brass

Dan 3:23 Shadrach, Meshach, and Abednego, fell down *b* into the...fiery furnace

Matt 14:3 Herod had laid hold on John, and *b* him

Matt 18:18 Whatsoever ye shall bind on earth shall be *b* in heaven

Mark 5:4 he [a demon-possessed man] had been often *b*

Luke 10:34 *b*...wounds... took care of him [wounded traveler]

John 11:44 he [Lazarus] came forth, *b*...with graveclothes

Acts 20:22 I [Paul] go *b* in the spirit unto Jerusalem

2 Tim 2:9 but the word of God is not *b*

Rev 20:2 he [an angel] laid hold on the dragon...and *b* him a thousand years

BOUNTIFUL [LY]

Ps 13:6 the LORD...hath dealt *b'ly* with me

Prov 22:9 He that hath a *b* eye shall be blessed

2 Cor 9:6 he which soweth *b'ly* shall reap also *b'ly*

BOWED

Ps 38:6 I am troubled; I am *b* down greatly

Ps 57:6 They...prepared a net for my steps...soul is *b* down

Isa 2:11 the haughtiness of men shall be *b* down

Matt 27:29 they *b* the knee before him [Jesus]...mocked him

Luke 13:11 a woman which had a spirit of infirmity... was *b* together

John 19:30 Jesus...*b* his head, and gave up the ghost

BOZRAH (ancient capital of Edom). Gen 36:33 • 1 Chr 1:44 • Isa 34:6; 63:1 • Jer 49:13,22 • Amos 1:12 • Mic 2:12.

BREAD OF LIFE, JESUS AS. See *"I Am" Statements of Jesus.*

BREAK [EST, ETH, ING]

Gen 32:24 there wrestled a man with him [Jacob] until the *b'ing* of the day

Job 9:17 For he [God] *b'eth* me with a tempest

Job 19:2 How long will ye [God]...*b* me...with words

Job 34:24 He [God] shall *b* in pieces mighty men

Ps 2:9 Thou shalt *b* them with a rod of iron

Ps 29:5 the LORD *b'eth* the cedars of Lebanon

Ps 46:9 he [God] *b'eth* the bow, and cutteth the spear

Ps 48:7 Thou [God] *b'est* the ships of Tarshish

Ps 58:6 *b* out the great teeth of the young lions, O LORD

Ps 89:34 My covenant will I [God] not *b*

Ps 94:5 They *b* in pieces thy people, O LORD

Eccl 3:3 a time to *b* down, and a time to build up

Isa 14:7 The whole earth is at rest...*b* forth into singing

Isa 42:3 A bruised reed shall he [God's servant] not *b*

Jer 1:14 Out of the north an evil shall *b* forth

Jer 19:11 Even so will I [God] *b* this people and this city

Jer 23:29 Is not my [God's] word like...a hammer that *b'eth* the rock

Hos 1:5 I [God] will *b* the bow of Israel

Matt 6:20 lay up...treasures in heaven...where thieves do not *b* through nor steal

Matt 12:20 A bruised reed shall he [Jesus] not *b*

Luke 24:35 he [Jesus] was known of them in *b'ing* of bread

Acts 2:42 they [believers] continued stedfastly in the apostles' doctrine...*b'ing* of bread

1 Cor 10:16 The bread which we *b,* is it not the communion of the body of Christ

BRIBE [S]

1 Sam 12:3 of whose hand have I received any *b*

Ps 26:10 and their right hand is full of *b's*

Amos 5:12 they afflict the just, they take a *b*

BUILDER [S]

Ps 118:22 stone which the *b's* refused is become the head stone of the corner

Mark 12:10 The stone which the *b's* rejected is become the head of the corner

Acts 4:11 This is the stone... set at nought of you *b's*

Heb 11:10 he [Abraham] looked for a city...whose *b* and maker is God

1 Pet 2:7 the stone which the *b's* disallowed...is made the head of the corner

BUILDING [S]

1 Kgs 7:1 Solomon was *b* his own house thirteen years

2 Chr 3:3 Solomon was instructed for the *b* of the house of God

Mark 13:2 Seest thou these great *b's?* there shall not be left one stone upon another

1 Cor 3:9 ye are God's husbandry, ye are God's *b*

2 Cor 5:1 we have a *b* of God, an house not made with hands, eternal

Eph 2:21 the *b* fitly framed together groweth unto an holy temple

BURDEN [S]

Ex 1:11 they [the Egyptians] did set over them taskmasters to afflict them with their *b's*

Ps 38:4 as an heavy *b* they [sins] are too heavy for me

Ps 55:22 Cast thy *b* upon the LORD...he shall sustain thee

Jer 17:22 Neither carry forth a *b*...on the sabbath day

Matt 11:30 my [Jesus'] yoke is easy, and my *b* is light

Matt 20:12 we have borne the *b* and heat of the day

Matt 23:4 they [the Pharisees] bind heavy *b's*

Gal 6:2 Bear ye one another's *b's*...fulfil the law of Christ

Gal 6:5 For every man shall bear his own *b*

BURIAL OF JESUS. See
Jesus, Life and Ministry of.

BURN [ED, ETH, ING]

Ex 3:2 the bush *b'ed* with fire, and...was not consumed

Ex 30:8 when Aaron lighteth the lamps...shall *b* incense

Neh 2:17 the gates [of Jerusalem] thereof are *b'ed*

Job 30:30 my [Job's] bones are *b'ed* with heat

Job 41:19 Out of his [God's] mouth go *b'ing* lamps

Ps 79:5 shall thy [God's] jealousy *b* like fire

Ps 97:3 A fire goeth before him [God], and *b'eth* up his enemies round about

Prov 6:27 Can a man take fire in his bosom, and his clothes not be *b'ed*

Jer 7:9 Will ye steal, murder... and *b* incense unto Baal

Jer 20:9 his [God's] word was in mine [Jeremiah's] heart as a *b'ing* fire

Jer 39:8 the Chaldeans *b'ed* the king's house

Dan 3:17 our God...is able to deliver us from the *b'ing* fiery furnace

Luke 3:17 the chaff he [God] will *b* with fire

Luke 24:32 Did not our heart *b* within us

Rom 1:27 the men...*b'ed* in their lust one toward another

1 Cor 3:15 If any man's work shall be *b'ed*...suffer loss

1 Cor 7:9 for it is better to marry than to *b*

1 Cor 13:3 though I [Paul] give my body to be *b'ed,* and have not charity

2 Pet 3:10 the earth also and the works...shall be *b'ed* up

Rev 19:20 beast...false prophet ...were cast...into a lake... *b'ing* with brimstone

BURNING BUSH RE-VEALED TO MOSES. Ex 3:1–5.

BURNT OFFERING, IN-STRUCTIONS FOR. Lev 1:1–17.

BUY [ETH]
Gen 42:3 Joseph's ten brethren went...to *b* corn in Egypt
Prov 23:23 *B* the truth, and sell it not; also wisdom
Prov 31:16 She considereth a field, and *b'eth* it
Amos 8:6 *b* the poor for silver... needy for a pair of shoes
Matt 13:44 a man...selleth all...he hath, and *b'eth* that field

John 6:5 he [Jesus] saith... Whence shall we *b* bread, that these may eat

BUYER
Isa 24:2 as with the *b,* so with the seller
Ezek 7:12 let not the *b* rejoice, nor the seller mourn

BYWORD
Deut 28:37 thou shalt become... a *b,* among all nations
1 Kgs 9:7 Israel shall be...a *b* among all people
Job 17:6 He [God] hath made me [Job] also a *b*
Ps 44:14 Thou [God] makest us a *b* among the heathen

-C-

CAESAREA (a city of Judah on the coast of the Mediterranean Sea where Paul was held as a prisoner). Acts 8:40; 9:30; 10:1,24; 11:11; 12:19; 18:22; 21:8–16; **23:23,33; 25:1–16.**

CAESAREA PHILIPPI (a city in northern Palestine where Peter confessed Jesus as the Messiah). Matt 16:13–20.

CAIAPHAS (high priest of the Jews before whom Jesus and the apostles Peter and John appeared). Matt 26:3,57 • Luke 3:2 • John 11:49; 18:13–14,24, 28 • Acts 4:6.

CAIN (oldest son of Adam and Eve who murdered his brother Abel). **Gen 4:1–25** • Heb 11:4 • 1 John 3:12 • Jude 11.

CAINAN. See *Kenan.*

CALEB (one of the twelve spies who scouted Canaan and recommended that Israel attack the Canaanites). **Num 13:6,30;** 14:6,24,30,38; 26:65; 32:12; 34:19 • Deut 1:36 • Josh 14:6,13–14; 15:13–18; 21:12 • Judg 1:12–20 • 1 Sam 25:3; 30:14 • 1 Chr 4:15; 6:56.

CALF

Ex 32:24 I [Aaron] cast it into the fire...there came out this *c*

Deut 9:16 ye had sinned...and had made you a molten *c*

Ps 106:19 They made a *c* in Horeb, and worshipped the molten image

Isa 11:6 shall lie down with... *c* and the young lion

Jer 34:18 they cut the *c* in twain, and passed between the parts thereof

Luke 15:23 bring hither the fatted *c,* and kill it

Acts 7:41 they made a *c*...and offered sacrifice unto the idol

CALL [ED, EST, ING]

Gen 1:5 God *c'ed* the light Day...the darkness...Night

Gen 2:19 whatsoever Adam *c'ed* every living creature, that was the name

Gen 12:8 he [Abraham] builded an altar...and *c'ed* upon the name of the LORD

Gen 17:5 Neither shall thy name any more be *c'ed* Abram, but...Abraham

Gen 17:19 thou [Abraham] shalt *c* his name Isaac

Gen 32:30 Jacob *c'ed* the name of the place Peniel

Gen 35:10 thy name shall not be *c'ed* any more Jacob

Gen 49:1 Jacob *c'ed* unto his sons, and said, Gather yourselves together

Ex 2:7 *c* to thee a nurse of the Hebrew women

Ex 2:10 she *c'ed* his name Moses...Because I drew him out of the water

Ex 3:4 God *c'ed* unto him [Moses] out of the midst of the bush

Ex 19:20 the LORD *c'ed* Moses up to the top of the mount

Deut 4:26 I [Moses] *c* heaven... to witness against you

Deut 28:10 all people...shall see that thou art *c'ed* by the name of the LORD

Judg 16:25 *C* for Samson, that he may make us sport

1 Sam 3:8 the LORD *c'ed* Samuel again the third time

1 Sam 12:18 So Samuel *c'ed* unto the LORD

1 Kgs 18:25 Elijah said...*c* on the name of your gods, but put no fire under

2 Kgs 5:11 I [Naaman] thought, He [Elisha] will surely...*c* on...the LORD

1 Chr 11:7 they *c'ed* it [Jerusalem] the city of David

1 Chr 16:8 *c* upon his [God's] name, make known his deeds

2 Chr 7:14 If my [God's] people, which are *c'ed* by my name, shall...pray

Job 27:10 will he always *c* upon God

Ps 4:1 Hear me when I *c,* O God of my righteousness

Ps 18:3 *c* upon the LORD, who is worthy to be praised

Ps 18:6 In my distress I *c'ed* upon the LORD

Ps 50:15 *c* upon me [God] in the day of trouble

Ps 72:17 all nations shall *c* him [God] blessed

Ps 86:5 thou, Lord, art...plenteous in mercy unto all them that *c* upon thee

Ps 105:1 give thanks unto the LORD; *c* upon his name

Ps 145:18 The LORD is nigh unto all them that *c* upon him

Prov 31:28 Her children arise up, and *c* her blessed

Isa 7:14 and bear a son, and shall *c* his name Immanuel

Isa 9:6 his [Messiah's] name shall be *c'ed* Wonderful

Isa 45:3 I, the LORD, which *c* thee by thy name, am the God of Israel

Isa 49:1 The LORD hath *c'ed* me from the womb

Isa 55:6 *c* ye upon him [God] while he is near

Isa 62:2 thou shalt be *c'ed* by a new name

Isa 62:4 but thou shalt be *c'ed* Hephzibah, and thy land Beulah

Isa 65:24 before they *c,* I [God] will answer

Jer 3:17 they shall *c* Jerusalem the throne of the LORD

Jer 33:3 C unto me [God], and I will answer thee

Dan 2:2 the king commanded to *c* the magicians

Hos 1:6 God said unto him [Hosea], *C* her name Loruhamah

Hos 11:1 then I [God]...*c'ed* my son out of Egypt

Joel 1:14 Sanctify ye a fast, *c* a solemn assembly

Joel 2:32 whosoever shall *c* on the name of the LORD shall be delivered

Jon 1:6 O sleeper [Jonah]? arise, *c* upon thy God

Matt 1:21 thou [Joseph] shalt *c* his name JESUS

Matt 1:25 and he [Joseph] *c'ed* his name JESUS

Matt 2:23 He [Jesus] shall be *c'ed* a Nazarene

Matt 5:9 the peacemakers... shall be *c'ed*...children of God

Matt 9:13 I [Jesus] am not come to *c* the righteous, but sinners to repentance

Matt 11:16 children sitting in the markets, and *c'ing* unto their fellows

Matt 18:2 Jesus *c'ed* a little child unto him

Matt 19:17 Why *c'est* thou me [Jesus] good

Matt 20:16 many be *c'ed,* but few chosen

Matt 21:13 My [God's] house shall be *c'ed*...house of prayer

Matt 23:9 c no man your father upon the earth

Matt 27:22 What shall I [Pilate] do then with Jesus which is *c'ed* Christ

Luke 1:13 thou [Zacharias] shalt *c* his name John

Luke 1:32 He [Jesus]...shall be *c'ed*...Son of the Highest

Luke 6:46 And why *c* ye me, Lord, Lord

Luke 9:1 he [Jesus] *c'ed* his twelve disciples together, and gave them...authority

Luke 14:13 c the poor, the maimed, the lame

Luke 15:21 I [prodigal son] have sinned...no more worthy to be *c'ed* thy son

John 1:42 thou [Peter] shalt be *c'ed* Cephas...a stone

Acts 2:21 whosoever shall *c* on...the Lord shall be saved

Acts 10:15 What God hath cleansed, that *c* not thou [Peter] common

Acts 11:26 disciples were *c'ed* Christians first in Antioch

Acts 13:2 Separate me Barnabas and Saul for the work whereunto I have *c'ed* them

Rom 1:1 Paul, a servant...*c'ed* to be an apostle

Rom 8:28 all things work together for good...to them who are the *c'ed*

Rom 10:12 the same Lord...is rich unto all that *c* upon him

Rom 10:13 whosoever shall *c* upon...the Lord shall be saved

Rom 10:14 How then shall they *c* on him in whom they have not believed

1 Cor 1:26 not many mighty, not many noble, are *c'ed*

1 Cor 7:20 Let every man abide in the same *c'ing*

Gal 5:13 brethren, ye have been *c'ed* unto liberty

Eph 4:1 walk worthy of the vocation...ye are *c'ed*

Phil 3:14 I [Paul] press toward the mark for the prize of the high *c'ing* of God

1 Thes 4:7 For God hath not *c'ed* us unto uncleanness, but unto holiness

2 Tim 2:22 follow righteousness...with them that *c* on the Lord out of a pure heart

Heb 11:8 Abraham, when he was *c'ed*...obeyed

Jas 5:14 Is any sick among you? let him *c* for the elders

1 Pet 2:9 the praises of him [Jesus] who hath *c'ed* you out of darkness

1 John 3:1 that we should be *c'ed* the sons of God

CALL ON THE LORD

2 Sam 22:4 I will *c-o-t-L,* who is worthy to be praised

2 Tim 2:22 follow righteousness...with them that *c-o-t-L* out of a pure heart

CALVARY (a hill near Jerusalem where Jesus was crucified). Luke 23:33. The word is from a Latin word which means "skull," thus "place of the skull." *Golgotha:* Mark 15:22 • John 19:17.

CANA OF GALILEE (a village where Jesus performed His first miracle—the turning of water into wine). **John 2:1–11;** 4:46–54; 21:2.

CANAAN

1. A son of Ham whose descendants founded several tribal peoples in and around Palestine. Gen 9:18–27; 10: 6,15–18 • 1 Chr 1:8,13.

2. The region where Canaan's descendants settled and the territory that God promised to Abraham. Gen 15:3–7. *Chanaan:* Acts 7:11.

CANDACE (a title of the queens of Ethiopia in New Testament times). Acts 8:27.

CANDLE

Ps 18:28 For thou [God] wilt light my *c*

Matt 5:15 Neither do men light a *c,* and put it under a bushel

Rev 22:5 they need no *c,* neither light of the sun

CAPERNAUM (a city on the shore of the Sea of Galilee which served as the headquarters for Jesus during His Galilean ministry). **Matt 4:13–17;** 8:5; 11:23; 17:24 • Mark 1:21; 2:1; 9:33 • Luke 4:23,31; 7:1; 10:15 • John 2:12; 4:46; 6:17,24,59.

CAPHTOR (the original home of the Philistines, probably the island of Crete). Deut 2:23 • Jer 47:4 • Amos 9:7.

CAPPADOCIA (a Roman province of Asia Minor). Acts 2:9 • 1 Pet 1:1.

CAPTIVE [S]
Ps 68:18 Thou hast ascended on high, thou hast led captivity *c*
Isa 61:1 LORD hath anointed me [God's servant]...to proclaim liberty to the *c's*
Jer 13:19 Judah shall be carried away *c*
Jer 39:9 Nebuzaradan...carried away *c* into Babylon the remnant of the people
Ezek 1:1 as I [Ezekiel] was among the *c's* by the river
Luke 4:18 he [God] hath anointed me [Jesus]...to preach deliverance to the *c's*

Eph 4:8 When he [Jesus] ascended...he led captivity *c*

CARCHEMISH (an ancient city in Mesopotamia where the Assyrian army defeated the Egyptians). Isa 10:9 • Jer 46:2. *Charchemish:* 2 Chr 35:20–24.

CARE [S, ST, TH]
Mark 4:19 the *c's* of this world...choke the word
Mark 4:38 *c'st* thou [Jesus] not...we [the disciples] perish
John 10:13 he is an hireling, and *c'th* not for the sheep
1 Cor 7:33 he that is married *c'th* for the things that are of the world
2 Cor 11:28 that which cometh upon me [Paul] daily, the *c* of all the churches
1 Tim 3:5 how shall he take *c* of the church of God
1 Pet 5:7 all your *c* upon him [Jesus]; for he *c'th* for you

CARMEL, MOUNT (a mountain where the prophet Elijah demonstrated the authority of God over the priests of the pagan god Baal). Josh 12:22; 19:26 • 1 Sam 15:12 • **1 Kgs 18:19–45** • 2 Kgs 2:25; 4:25; 19:23 • 2 Chr 26:10 • Song 7:5 • Isa 33:9; 35:2; 37:24 • Jer 46:18; 50:19 • Amos 1:2; 9:3 • Mic 7:14 • Nah 1:4.

CASLUHIM (an ancient people descended from Mizraim, son of Ham; Casluhim was the Hebrew word for Egypt). Gen 10:14 • 1 Chr 1:12.

CAST [ING]
Gen 37:20 slay him [Joseph], and *c* him into some pit
Ex 4:3 he [Moses] *c* it [his rod] on the ground, and it became a serpent
Ex 32:24 I [Aaron] *c* it into the fire...there came out this calf
Lev 16:8 Aaron shall *c* lots upon the two goats
Josh 18:10 Joshua *c* lots for them in Shiloh
Job 8:20 God will not *c* away a perfect man
Job 30:19 He [God] hath *c* me into the mire
Ps 37:24 Though he fall, he shall not be utterly *c* down
Ps 42:11 Why art thou *c* down, O my soul
Ps 51:11 *C* me not away from thy [God's] presence
Ps 55:22 *C* thy burden upon the LORD...he shall sustain thee
Ps 71:9 *C* me not off in the time of old age
Ps 77:7 Will the Lord *c* off for ever...be favourable no more
Ps 94:14 the LORD will not *c* off his people

Eccl 3:5 A time to *c* away stones, and a time to gather
Eccl 11:1 *C* thy bread upon the waters
Isa 31:7 every man shall *c* away his idols of silver
Jer 7:15 I [God] will *c* you out of my sight
Dan 3:21 these men...were *c* into the...fiery furnace
Dan 6:16 brought Daniel... *c* him into the den of lions
Jon 1:15 they [mariners]...*c* him [Jonah] forth into the sea
Zech 11:13 thirty pieces of silver, and *c* them to the potter
Matt 3:10 tree...bringeth not forth good fruit is...*c* into the fire
Matt 15:26 take the children's bread, and *c* it to dogs
Matt 21:12 Jesus...*c* out all them that sold and bought in the temple
Matt 27:5 And he [Judas] *c* down the pieces of silver
Matt 27:35 crucified him [Jesus], and parted his garments, *c'ing* lots
Mark 1:39 he [Jesus] preached...throughout all Galilee, and *c* out devils
Mark 12:43 this poor widow hath *c* more in
Luke 9:49 Master, we saw one *c'ing* out devils in thy name
John 8:7 He that is without sin...let him first *c* a stone

Rom 13:12 let us therefore *c* off the works of darkness

1 Pet 5:7 *C'ing* all your care upon him [Jesus]; for he careth for you

Rev 12:9 the great dragon was *c* out, that old serpent

Rev 20:15 not found...in the book of life was *c* into the lake of fire

CASTOR AND POLLUX (pagan gods who were considered protectors of sailors). Paul's ship to Rome featured a carving of these two gods. Acts 28:11.

CAUGHT
2 Sam 18:9 his [Absalom's] head *c* hold of the oak

Eccl 9:12 as the birds...*c* in the snare; so are the sons of men

Matt 14:31 Jesus stretched... his hand, and *c* him [Peter]

Acts 8:39 the Spirit of the Lord *c* away Philip

1 Thes 4:17 we...shall be *c* up together...in the clouds

CEASE [D, ING]
Gen 8:22 While the earth remaineth...day and night shall not *c*

Josh 5:12 And the manna *c'd* on the morrow

Neh 6:3 why should the work *c*...I [Nehemiah] leave it

Job 32:1 these three men *c'd* to answer Job

Ps 37:8 *C* from anger, and forsake wrath

Ps 85:4 O God...cause thine anger toward us to *c*

Prov 23:4 Labour not to be rich: *c* from thine...wisdom

Eccl 12:3 the grinders *c* because they are few

Ezek 26:13 I will cause the noise of thy songs to *c*

Jon 1:15 they...cast him [Jonah] forth...and the sea *c'd* from her raging

Mark 4:39 the wind *c'd,* and there was a great calm

Acts 5:42 they [the apostles] *c'd* not to teach and preach Jesus Christ

Acts 12:5 prayer was made without *c'ing* of the church unto God for him [Peter]

Rom 1:9 without *c'ing* I [Paul] make mention of you always in my prayers

1 Cor 13:8 whether there be tongues, they shall *c*

Col 1:9 since the day we heard it, do not *c* to pray for you

1 Thes 5:17 Pray without *c'ing*

CEDARS OF LEBANON
Judg 9:15 let fire come out... and devour the *c-o-L*

Ps 29:5 yea, the LORD breaketh the *c-o-L*

Ps 104:16 trees...are full of sap; the *c-o-L,* which he [God] hath planted

Isa 2:13 upon all the *c-o-L,* that are high and lifted up

Isa 14:8 the fir trees rejoice at thee, and the *c-o-L*

CEDRON. See *Kidron.*

CENCHREA (a harbor of Corinth through which Paul passed during his second missionary journey). **Acts 18:18 •** Rom 16:1.

CHALDEANS, LAND OF THE. See *Babylonia.*

CHANAAN. See *Canaan,* No. 2.

CHANGE [D, TH]
Jer 2:11 Hath a nation *c'd* their gods, which are...no gods
Jer 13:23 Can the Ethiopian *c* his skin...the leopard his spots
Dan 2:21 he [God] *c'th* the times and the seasons
Dan 5:6 the king's countenance was *c'd*
Hos 4:7 therefore will I [God] *c* their glory into shame
Rom 1:23 *c'd* the glory of the uncorruptible God
Rom 1:26 their women did *c* the natural use into that which is against nature
1 Cor 15:51 We shall not all sleep, but we shall all be *c'd*
Phil 3:21 Who shall *c* our vile body...like...his glorious body

CHARCHEMISH. See *Carchemish.*

CHARGE [D]
Deut 3:28 *c* Joshua, and encourage him
1 Kgs 2:1 David...*c'd* Solomon his son
Ps 91:11 For he [God] shall give his angels *c* over thee
Matt 16:20 Then *c'd* he...that they should tell no man that he was Jesus the Christ
Mark 8:15 And he [Jesus] *c'd* them, saying...beware of the leaven of the Pharisees
Luke 8:56 he [Jesus] *c'd* them... tell no man what was done
Acts 7:60 Lord, lay not this sin to their *c*
1 Tim 6:17 *C* them that are rich...they be not highminded

CHARITY
1 Cor 13:3 and have not *c,* it profiteth me nothing
Col 3:14 And above all these things put on *c*
1 Tim 4:12 be thou an example...in conversation, in *c*
1 Pet 4:8 *c* shall cover the multitude of sins
Rev 2:19 I [Jesus] know thy works, and *c,* and service

CHARRAN. See *Haran.*

CHASTEN [ED, EST, ETH, ING]
Ps 38:1 O LORD, rebuke me not...neither *c* me in thy hot displeasure
Ps 73:14 all the day long have I been...*c'ed* every morning
Ps 94:12 Blessed is the man whom thou *c'est,* O LORD
Prov 3:11 My son, despise not the *c'ing* of the LORD
1 Cor 11:32 we are judged, we are *c'ed* of the Lord
Heb 12:6 whom the Lord loveth he *c'eth*
Rev 3:19 As many as I love, I rebuke and *c*

CHEBAR (a river or canal of Babylonia where the prophet Ezekiel received his visions during the Exile). Ezek 1:1,3; 3:15,23; 10:15,20,22; 43:3.

CHEDORLAOMER (a king of Elam who invaded Canaan in Abraham's time). Gen 14:1–17.

CHEER
Matt 9:2 Son [man with palsy], be of good *c*
John 16:33 be of good *c;* I [Jesus] have overcome the world
Acts 23:11 Be of good *c,* Paul... so must thou bear witness also at Rome

CHEERFUL
Prov 15:13 A merry heart maketh a *c* countenance
Zech 9:17 corn shall make the young men *c*
2 Cor 9:7 let him give...for God loveth a *c* giver

CHEMOSH (chief pagan god of the Moabites and Ammonites to which children were sacrificed). Num 21:29 • Judg 11:24 • 1 Kgs 11:7,33 • 2 Kgs 23:13 • Jer 48:7,13,46.

CHERETHIMS. See *Cherethites.*

CHERETHITES (a tribe of the Philistines in southwest Palestine). 1 Sam 30:14 • Zeph 2:5. *Cherethims:* Ezek 25:16.

CHERITH (a brook where the prophet Elijah was fed by ravens during a famine). 1 Kgs 17:3–6.

CHILD
Gen 17:17 a *c* be born unto him...an hundred years old
Ex 22:22 Ye shall not afflict any widow, or fatherless *c*
1 Kgs 3:25 king [Solomon] said, Divide the living *c* in two
1 Kgs 17:22 the soul of the *c* came into him...he revived
2 Kgs 5:14 his [Naaman's] flesh came again like unto the flesh of a little *c*

Prov 22:6 Train up a *c* in the way he should go

Isa 9:6 unto us a *c* is born, unto us a son is given

Jer 1:6 behold, I [Jeremiah] cannot speak: for I am a *c*

Hos 11:1 When Israel was a *c,* then I [God] loved him

Matt 1:23 a virgin shall be with *c*...bring forth a son

Matt 2:21 he [Joseph]...took the young *c*...and came into the land of Israel

Matt 18:4 Whosoever...shall humble himself as this little *c,* the same is greatest

Mark 10:15 not receive the kingdom...as a little *c,* he shall not enter

Luke 2:17 they made known abroad the saying...concerning this *c*

Luke 2:40 the *c* [Jesus] grew, and waxed strong in spirit

1 Cor 13:11 When I [Paul] was a *c,* I spake as a *c*

2 Tim 3:15 from a *c* thou [Timothy] hast known the holy scriptures

CHILDREN

Gen 3:16 in sorrow thou [Eve] shalt bring forth *c*

Gen 37:3 Israel loved Joseph more than all his *c*

Ex 1:7 the *c* of Israel were fruitful, and increased

Ex 12:26 when your *c* shall say...What mean ye by this service

Ex 20:5 visiting the iniquity of the fathers upon the *c*

Num 8:17 the firstborn of the *c* of Israel are mine [God's]

Deut 24:16 The fathers shall not be put to death for the *c*

Josh 4:6 when your *c* ask their fathers...What mean ye by these stones

Josh 18:10 Joshua divided the land unto the *c* of Israel

Job 19:18 Yea, young *c* despised me [Job]

Ps 14:2 The LORD looked down...upon the *c* of men

Ps 34:11 Come, ye *c*...I will teach...the fear of the LORD

Ps 103:7 He [God] made known...acts unto the *c* of Israel

Ps 103:13 as a father pitieth his *c,* so the LORD pitieth them that fear him

Ps 115:14 The LORD shall increase...you and your *c*

Ps 127:3 Lo, *c* are an heritage of the LORD

Ps 127:4 As arrows are in the hand of a mighty man; so are *c* of the youth

Prov 4:1 Hear, ye *c,* the instruction of a father

Prov 13:22 A good man leaveth an inheritance to his children's *c*

Prov 20:7 his *c* are blessed after him [the just man]

Prov 31:28 Her *c* arise up, and call her blessed

Isa 54:13 all thy *c* shall be taught of the LORD

Jer 3:22 Return, ye backsliding *c*...I [God] will heal

Jer 31:15 Rahel weeping for her *c* refused to be comforted

Lam 1:16 my *c* are desolate, because the enemy prevailed

Hos 2:4 they be the *c* of whoredoms

Matt 2:16 Herod...slew all the *c*...in Bethlehem

Matt 7:11 know how to give good gifts unto your *c*

Matt 18:3 Except ye...become as little *c,* ye shall not enter into the kingdom

Matt 23:37 how often would I [Jesus] have gathered thy *c*

Matt 27:25 His [Jesus'] blood be on us, and on our *c*

Mark 10:13 they brought young *c* to him [Jesus]

Luke 16:8 the *c* of this world... wiser than the *c* of light

John 8:39 If ye were Abraham's *c,* ye would do the works of Abraham

John 12:36 that ye may be the *c* of light

1 Cor 14:20 Brethren, be not *c* in understanding

Gal 4:28 we, brethren...are the *c* of promise

Eph 4:14 That we henceforth be no more *c*

Eph 6:1 C, obey your parents in the Lord

Eph 6:4 fathers, provoke not your *c* to wrath

1 Thes 5:5 Ye are all the *c* of light...children of the day

1 John 2:1 My little *c*...write I unto you, that ye sin not

1 John 3:18 little *c,* let us not love in word...but in deed

1 John 5:21 Little *c,* keep yourselves from idols

3 John 4 no greater joy than to hear that my [John's] *c* walk in truth

CHILDREN OF GOD

Matt 5:9 Blessed are the peacemakers: for they shall be called the *c-o-G*

Rom 8:16 The Spirit...beareth witness...we are the *c-o-G*

Gal 3:26 ye are all the *c-o-G* by faith in Christ Jesus

1 John 5:2 know that we love the *c-o-G,* when we love God

CHILDREN WELCOMED BY JESUS. Matt 19:13–15 • Mark 10:13–16 • Luke 18: 15–17.

CHINNEROTH, SEA OF. See *Galilee, Sea of.*

CHITTIM. See *Cyprus.*

CHLOE (a believer in Corinth). 1 Cor 1:11.

CHOOSE [ING]

Deut 7:7 The LORD did not...*c* you, because ye were more in number

Deut 30:19 c life, that both thou and thy seed may live

Josh 24:15 c you this day whom ye will serve

Neh 9:7 Thou art the LORD the God, who didst *c* Abram

Phil 1:22 yet what I [Paul] shall *c* I wot not

Heb 11:25 C'ing rather to suffer affliction

CHORAZIN (a city near the Sea of Galilee upon which Jesus pronounced a woe because of its unbelief). Matt 11:21 • Luke 10:13.

CHOSEN

Deut 7:6 God hath *c* thee to be a special people

Judg 10:14 Go and cry unto the gods which ye have *c*

1 Chr 16:13 ye children of Jacob, his [God's] *c* ones

1 Chr 28:5 he [God] hath *c* Solomon my [David's] son to sit upon the throne

Ps 33:12 Blessed is...the people whom he [God] hath *c* for his own inheritance

Prov 22:1 A good name is rather to be *c* than great riches

Isa 43:10 Ye are...my [God's] servant whom I have *c*

Matt 12:18 Behold my [God's] servant, whom I have *c*

Matt 20:16 for many be called, but few *c*

Luke 10:42 Mary hath *c* that good part

John 15:16 Ye have not *c* me [Jesus], but I have *c* you

Acts 9:15 he [Paul] is a *c* vessel unto me [Jesus]

1 Cor 1:27 God hath *c* the foolish things of the world to confound the wise

2 Thes 2:13 God hath...*c* you to salvation

1 Pet 2:9 ye are a *c* generation, a royal priesthood

CHRONICLES, BOOKS OF FIRST AND SECOND. Two historical books of the Old Testament that cover several centuries of history, beginning with a genealogy of Adam and his descendants (1 Chr 1–9) and ending with the return of Jewish captives to their homeland about 538 B.C. following a period of exile (2 Chr 36).

CHURCH [ES]

Matt 16:18 thou art Peter, and upon this rock I [Jesus] will build my *c*

Matt 18:17 if he shall neglect to hear them, tell it unto the *c*

Acts 2:47 Lord added to the *c* daily such as should be saved

Acts 5:11 great fear came upon all the *c*

Acts 8:3 As for Saul, he made havock of the *c*

Acts 14:23 when they [Paul and Barnabas] had ordained them elders in every *c*

Acts 20:28 the Holy Ghost hath made you overseers, to feed the *c* of God

Rom 16:16 The *c'es* of Christ salute you

1 Cor 14:4 he that prophesieth edifieth the *c*

1 Cor 14:35 it is a shame for women to speak in the *c*

2 Cor 11:28 cometh upon me [Paul] daily, the care of all the *c'es*

Gal 1:13 I [Paul] persecuted the *c* of God

Eph 3:21 Unto him be glory in the *c* by Christ Jesus

Eph 5:25 Christ also loved the *c,* and gave himself for it

Col 1:18 he [Christ] is the head of the body, the *c*

1 Tim 3:5 how shall he take care of the *c* of God

1 Tim 3:15 *c* of the living God... pillar and ground of...truth

Jas 5:14 elders of the *c;* and let them pray over him

Rev 1:4 John to the seven *c'es* which are in Asia

Rev 2:1 Unto the angel of the *c* of Ephesus

Rev 2:8 unto the angel of the *c* in Smyrna

Rev 2:12 to the angel of the *c* in Pergamos

Rev 2:18 unto the angel of the *c* in Thyatira

Rev 3:1 unto the angel of the *c* in Sardis

Rev 3:7 to the angel of the *c* in Philadelphia

Rev 3:14 unto the angel of the *c* of the Laodiceans

CHUSHAN-RISHATHAIM (a king of Mesopotamia who was defeated by the judge Othniel). Judg 3:8–10.

CILICIA (a province of Asia Minor whose major city was Tarsus, the apostle Paul's hometown). Acts 6:9; 15:23,41; 21:39; 22:3; 23:34; 27:5 • Gal 1:21.

CIRCUMCISE [D]

Gen 17:11 ye shall *c* the flesh of your foreskin

Gen 17:24 Abraham was ninety years old and nine, when he was *c'd*

Lev 12:3 eighth day the flesh of his foreskin shall be *c'd*

Josh 5:2 *c* again the children of Israel the second time

Jer 4:4 *C* yourselves to the LORD, and take away the foreskins of your heart

Acts 15:1 certain men...from Judaea...said, Except ye be *c'd*...ye cannot be saved

Gal 5:2 if ye be *c'd,* Christ shall profit you nothing

429

Phil 3:5 **C'd** the eighth day, of the stock of Israel

CIRCUMCISION
Acts 10:45 they of the **c** which believed were astonished
Rom 3:1 or what profit is there of **c**
Rom 15:8 Christ was a minister of the **c** for the truth of God
1 Cor 7:19 **C** is nothing, and uncircumcision is nothing
Col 3:11 neither Greek nor Jew, **c** nor uncircumcision

CITIES OF REFUGE (six cities—Bezer, Golan, Hebron, Kedesh, Ramoth-gilead, and Shechem—set aside as sanctuaries for those who killed other persons by accident). Num 35:11,14 • Josh 20:2,8; 21:13, 21,27,32,38 • 1 Chr 6:57,67.

CLAUDA (a small island near Crete where Paul's ship anchored during a storm). Acts 27:16.

CLAUDIUS LYSIAS (a Roman military officer who protected Paul from his enemies). Acts 21:30–35; 23:22–30.

CLEAN AND UNCLEAN ANIMALS. Lev 11:1–47.

CLEANSE [D, TH]
Lev 16:30 shall the priest make an atonement...to **c** you
Neh 13:22 I [Nehemiah] commanded the Levites that they should **c** themselves
Ps 51:2 Wash me thoroughly... and **c** me from my sin
Ps 73:13 Verily I have **c'd** my heart in vain
Matt 11:5 the lepers are **c'd,** and the deaf hear
Matt 23:26 **c** first that which is within the cup
Mark 1:42 the leprosy departed...and he was **c'd**
Luke 17:17 Were there not ten **c'd?** but where are the nine
Acts 10:15 What God hath **c'd,** that call not thou [Peter] common
2 Cor 7:1 let us **c** ourselves from all filthiness
1 John 1:7 the blood of Jesus Christ...**c'th** us from all sin
1 John 1:9 he [Jesus] is faithful and just...to **c** us from all unrighteousness

CLEAVE [D, TH]
Gen 2:24 shall a man leave his father and his mother, and shall **c** unto his wife
Deut 10:20 to him [God] shalt thou **c**...swear by his name
Josh 23:8 But **c** unto the LORD your God
Job 19:20 My bone **c'th** to my skin and to my flesh

Job 29:10 their tongue *c'd* to the roof of their mouth

Ps 102:5 By reason...of my groaning my bones *c* to my skin

Ps 137:6 let my tongue *c* to the roof of my mouth; if I prefer not Jerusalem

Mark 10:7 shall a man leave his father and mother, and *c* to his wife

Rom 12:9 Abhor that which is evil; *c* to that which is good

CLEOPAS (a Christian believer to whom the resurrected Christ appeared on the road to Emmaus). Luke 24:18.

CLEOPHAS (the husband of Mary, one of the women who was present at the crucifixion of Jesus). John 19:25. *Alphaeus:* Matt 10:3.

CLOTHE [D, ING]

Gen 3:21 Unto Adam...wife did...God make coats of skins, and *c'd* them

2 Chr 6:41 O LORD God, be *c'd* with salvation

Job 7:5 My [Job's] flesh is *c'd* with worms

Ps 93:1 The LORD...is *c'd* with majesty

Ps 132:9 Let thy priests be *c'd* with righteousness

Prov 31:25 Strength and honour are her *c'ing*

Isa 50:3 I [God] *c* the heavens with blackness

Isa 61:10 For he [God] hath *c'd* me with the garments of salvation

Matt 7:15 Beware of false prophets...in sheep's *c'ing*

Matt 25:36 Naked, and ye *c'd* me; sick...ye visited me

Mark 1:6 John was *c'd* with camel's hair

Mark 12:38 the scribes...love to go in long *c'ing*

Mark 15:17 they *c'd* him [Jesus] with purple

Luke 12:28 how much more will he [God] *c* you, O ye of little faith

Luke 16:19 a certain rich man...*c'd* in purple

1 Pet 5:5 be subject one to another...*c'd* with humility

Rev 19:13 he was *c'd* with a vesture dipped in blood

CLOTHES

Gen 37:34 Jacob rent his *c*... put sackcloth upon his loins

Num 8:21 the Levites were purified...washed their *c*

Josh 7:6 Joshua rent his *c,* and fell to the earth

1 Kgs 1:1 covered him [David] with *c,* but he gat no heat

Prov 6:27 Can a man take fire in his bosom, and his *c* not be burned

Mark 5:28 she [woman with issue of blood] said, If I...

touch but his [Jesus'] *c*, I shall be whole

Luke 2:7 wrapped him [Jesus] in swaddling *c*

John 19:40 wound it [Jesus' body] in linen *c*

Acts 7:58 laid down...*c* at a young man's [Paul's] feet

CLOUD [S]

Gen 9:13 I [God] do set my bow in the *c*

Ex 13:21 LORD went before them [Israel]...pillar of a *c*

Ex 40:34 a *c* covered the tent of the congregation

1 Kgs 8:10 the *c* filled the house of the LORD

1 Kgs 18:44 there ariseth a little *c* out of the sea

Job 26:8 He [God] bindeth up the waters in his thick *c's*

Ps 78:14 he [God] led them [Israel] with a *c*

Ps 108:4 and thy [God's] truth reacheth unto the *c's*

Prov 3:20 By his [God's] knowledge...the *c's* drop down the dew

Isa 14:14 I will ascend above the heights of the *c's*

Isa 19:1 the LORD rideth upon a swift *c*

Isa 44:22 I [God] have blotted out, as a thick *c*, thy transgressions

Lam 3:44 Thou [God] hast covered thyself with a *c*

Joel 2:2 A day of darkness and...gloominess, a day of *c's*

Matt 24:30 the Son of man coming in the *c's*

Mark 9:7 voice came out of the *c*, saying, This is my beloved Son [Jesus]

Luke 21:27 Son of man coming in a *c* with power and great glory

Acts 1:9 he [Jesus] was taken up; and a *c* received him out of their sight

1 Thes 4:17 we...shall be caught up together with them in the *c's*

Heb 12:1 we also are compassed about with so great a *c* of witnesses

Rev 1:7 Behold, he [Jesus] cometh with *c's;* and every eye shall see him

COCK

Matt 26:34 before the *c* crow, thou [Peter] shalt deny me [Jesus] thrice

Mark 14:68 he [Peter] went out...and the *c* crew

Luke 22:61 Peter remembered...Before the *c* crow, thou shalt deny me [Jesus]

COLD

Ps 147:17 who can stand before his [God's] *c*

Prov 25:25 As *c* waters to a thirsty soul, so is good news

Matt 24:12 the love of many shall wax *c*
Rev 3:15 thou [church at Laodicea] art neither *c* nor hot

COLOSSE (a city near Ephesus and the site of a church to which Paul wrote one of his epistles). Col 1:2.

COLOSSIANS, EPISTLE TO THE. A short epistle of the apostle Paul on the theme of Christ's glory and majesty and His work of redemption (chaps. 1–2). Paul also challenged the Colossian Christians to express the love of Christ in their relationships with others (chaps. 3–4).

COMFORT [ED, ETH]
Job 2:11 Job's three friends...came...to *c* him
Ps 23:4 thy [God's] rod and thy staff they *c* me
Isa 40:1 *C* ye, *c* ye my people, saith your God
Isa 49:13 the LORD hath *c'ed* his people
Isa 61:2 To proclaim the acceptable year of the LORD...to *c* all that mourn
Jer 31:15 Rahel weeping for her children refused to be *c'ed* for her children
Lam 1:21 there is none to *c* me
Matt 5:4 Blessed are they that mourn: for they shall be *c'ed*

Luke 8:48 be of good *c*...faith hath made thee [woman with issue of blood] whole
2 Cor 1:3 Blessed be God...the Father of mercies, and the God of all *c*
2 Cor 1:4 Who *c'eth* us in all our tribulation
Phil 2:1 If there be therefore any consolation in Christ, if any *c* of love
1 Thes 4:18 *c* one another with these words

COMFORTER
John 14:26 the *C*...shall teach you all things
John 15:26 the *C*...shall testify of me [Jesus]
John 16:7 if I [Jesus] go not away, the *C* will not come unto you

COMMAND [ED, ETH, ING]
Gen 7:5 Noah did...all that the LORD *c'ed* him
Gen 21:4 Abraham circumcised his son Isaac...as God had *c'ed* him
Gen 49:33 Jacob had made an end of *c'ing* his sons
Ex 19:7 Moses...laid before their faces all these words which the LORD *c'ed*
Deut 4:2 Ye shall not add unto the word...I [God] *c* you
Deut 5:12 Keep the sabbath day to sanctify it, as the LORD...hath *c'ed*

Josh 1:9 Have not I [God] *c'ed* thee? Be strong and of a good courage

1 Sam 13:13 thou [Saul] hast not kept the commandment...which he [God] *c'ed* thee

1 Chr 16:15 the word which he [God] *c'ed* to a thousand generations

Ps 33:9 he [God] *c'ed,* and it stood fast

Ps 105:8 He [God] hath remembered...the word...he *c'ed*

Jer 1:17 speak unto them all that I [God] *c* thee [Jeremiah]

Dan 6:16 the king *c'ed,* and they...cast him [Daniel] into the den of lions

Matt 28:20 observe all things whatsoever I [Jesus] have *c'ed* you

Mark 1:27 with authority *c'eth* he [Jesus]...the unclean spirits

Mark 6:8 [Jesus] *c'ed* them that they should take nothing for their journey

Luke 4:3 *c* this stone that it be made bread

Luke 8:25 for he [Jesus] *c'eth* even the winds and water

John 8:5 Moses in the law *c'ed* us...such should be stoned

John 15:17 These things I [Jesus] *c* you...love one another

COMMANDMENT [S]

Ex 16:28 How long refuse ye to keep my [God's] *c's*

Ex 34:28 he [Moses] wrote upon the tables...the ten *c's*

Lev 27:34 These are the *c's*... for the children of Israel in mount Sinai

Deut 28:9 thou shalt keep the *c's* of the LORD thy God

1 Kgs 2:3 keep his [God's]...*c's,* and his judgments

2 Kgs 17:16 they left all the *c's* of the LORD

Ezra 9:10 for we have forsaken thy [God's] *c's*

Ps 111:7 all his [God's] *c's* are sure

Ps 119:10 let me not wander from thy [God's] *c's*

Ps 119:115 I will keep the *c's* of my God

Ps 147:15 He [God] sendeth forth his *c* upon earth

Prov 6:20 My son, keep thy father's *c*

Prov 10:8 The wise in heart will receive *c's:* but a prating fool shall fall

Eccl 12:13 keep his [God's] *c's*...this is the...duty of man

Amos 2:4 they have...not kept his [God's] *c's*

Matt 15:3 ye [Pharisees] also transgress the *c* of God by your tradition

Matt 22:40 On these two *c's* hang...the law and the prophets

Mark 12:28 Which is the first *c* of all

Mark 12:29 The first of all the *c's* is...The Lord our God is one Lord

John 13:34 A new *c* I [Jesus] give unto you, That ye love one another

John 14:15 If ye love me [Jesus], keep my *c's*

John 15:10 If ye keep my [Jesus'] *c's,* ye shall abide in my love

John 15:12 This is my [Jesus'] *c*...love one another, as I have loved you

1 Cor 7:19 Circumcision is nothing...but the keeping of the *c's* of God

Eph 6:2 Honour thy father and mother; which is the first *c* with promise

1 John 2:3 we know him [Jesus], if we keep his *c's*

2 John 6 this is love, that we walk after his [God's] *c's*

Rev 22:14 Blessed are they that do his [God's] *c's*

COMMANDMENT [S] OF THE LORD

Num 9:18 At the *c-o-t-L* the children of Israel journeyed

Num 14:41 Wherefore now do ye transgress the *c-o-t-L*

Deut 4:2 keep the *c's-o-t-L* your God

Deut 8:6 thou shalt keep the *c's-o-t-L* thy God

1 Sam 15:24 I [Saul] have transgressed the *c-o-t-L*

2 Kgs 17:16 they left all the *c's-o-t-L*...and made them molten images

Ps 19:8 the *c-o-t-L* is pure, enlightening the eyes

COMMEND [ED, ETH]

Prov 12:8 A man shall be *c'ed* according to his wisdom

Luke 16:8 the lord *c'ed* the unjust steward, because he had done wisely

Luke 23:46 Father, into thy hands I [Jesus] *c* my spirit

Rom 5:8 God *c'eth* his love toward us...Christ died for us

Rom 16:1 I [Paul] *c* unto you Phebe our sister

COMMIT [TED, TETH]

Gen 39:22 the keeper of the prison *c'ted* to Joseph's hand all the prisoners

Ex 20:14 Thou shalt not *c* adultery

Lev 18:29 the souls that *c* them shall be cut off

Lev 20:10 the man that *c'teth* adultery...shall surely be put to death

Josh 22:20 Did not Achan the son of Zerah *c* a trespass

Ps 31:5 Into thine [God's] hand I *c* my spirit

Prov 6:32 whoso *c'teth* adultery with a woman lacketh understanding

Prov 16:3 **C** thy works unto the Lord

Jer 2:13 my [God's] people have **c'ted** two evils

Matt 5:28 whosoever looketh on a woman to lust after her hath **c'ted** adultery

Matt 5:32 whosoever shall marry her that is divorced **c'teth** adultery

Mark 10:11 Whosoever shall put away his wife, and marry another, **c'teth** adultery

Mark 10:19 Thou knowest the commandments, Do not **c** adultery, Do not kill

John 5:22 Father...hath **c'ted** all judgment unto the Son

John 8:34 Whosoever **c'teth** sin is the servant of sin

1 Cor 6:18 he that **c'teth** fornication sinneth against his own body

1 Cor 10:8 Neither let us **c** fornication, as some of them

2 Cor 5:19 God...in Christ... hath **c'ted** unto us the word of reconciliation

1 Tim 6:20 Timothy, keep that which is **c'ted** to thy trust

2 Tim 1:12 he [Jesus] is able to keep that which I [Paul] have **c'ted**...against that day

2 Tim 2:2 the same **c** thou to faithful men

1 John 3:9 Whosoever is born of God doth not **c** sin

COMMON

Mark 12:37 the **c** people heard him [Jesus] gladly

Acts 2:44 all that believed... had all things **c**

Acts 10:14 I [Peter] have never eaten any thing that is **c** or unclean

1 Cor 10:13 There hath no temptation taken you but such as is **c** to man

COMMUNICATION [S]

Matt 5:37 let your **c** be, Yea, yea; Nay, nay

Luke 24:17 What manner of **c's** are these

Eph 4:29 Let no corrupt **c** proceed out of your mouth

COMMUNION

1 Cor 10:16 cup of blessing which we bless, is it not the **c** of the blood of Christ

2 Cor 6:14 what **c** hath light with darkness

2 Cor 13:14 and the **c** of the Holy Ghost, be with you all

COMPASSION [S]

Ex 2:6 she had **c** on him [Moses], and said, This is one of the Hebrews' children

Ps 86:15 thou, O Lord, art a God full of **c**

Ps 145:8 The LORD is gracious, and full of **c**

Jer 12:15 I [God] will return, and have *c* on them

Zech 7:9 show mercy and *c's* every man to his brother

Matt 14:14 Jesus...was moved with *c* toward them

Matt 18:27 the lord of that servant was moved with *c*, and loosed him

Mark 9:22 if thou canst do any thing, have *c* on us

Luke 10:33 a certain Samaritan...when he saw him, he had *c* on him

Luke 15:20 his father...had *c*, and ran, and fell on his neck

1 Pet 3:8 be ye all of one mind, having *c* one of another

1 John 3:17 seeth his brother have need, and shutteth up his bowels of *c* from him

COMPEL

Matt 5:41 *c* thee to go a mile, go with him twain

Mark 15:21 they *c* one Simon a Cyrenian...to bear his [Jesus'] cross

Luke 14:23 Go out into the highways and hedges, and *c* them to come in

CONCEIT [S]

Prov 26:5 Answer a fool...lest he be wise in his own *c*

Prov 28:11 The rich man is wise in his own *c*

Rom 12:16 Be not wise in your own *c's*

CONCEIVE [D]

Gen 21:2 Sarah *c'd,* and bare Abraham a son

Job 3:3 the day perish...in which it was said, There is a man child *c'd*

Ps 51:5 shapen in iniquity, and in sin did my mother *c* me

Isa 7:14 a virgin shall *c,* and bear a son

Matt 1:20 that...*c'd* in her [Mary] is of the Holy Ghost

Luke 1:31 thou [Mary] shalt *c*...and bring forth a son

Luke 1:36 thy [Mary's] cousin Elisabeth, she hath also *c'd* a son in her old age

Heb 11:11 Sara herself received strength to *c* seed

CONCERNING

Luke 2:17 they [shepherds] made known abroad the saying...*c* this child

Luke 18:31 all things that are written...*c* the Son of man shall be accomplished

Luke 24:27 he [Jesus] expounded...the things *c* himself

Acts 28:22 for as *c* this sect...it is spoken against

1 Cor 12:1 Now *c* spiritual gifts, brethren

Eph 5:32 I [Paul] speak *c* Christ and the church

1 Thes 5:18 this is the will of God in Christ Jesus *c* you

1 Pet 4:12 *c* the fiery trial which is to try you

2 Pet 3:9 The Lord is not slack *c* his promise

CONDEMN [ED, ETH]

Job 15:6 Thine own mouth *c'eth* thee

Prov 12:2 a man of wicked devices will he [God] *c*

Matt 12:37 by thy words thou shalt be *c'ed*

Luke 6:37 *c* not, and ye shall not be *c'ed*

John 3:17 God sent not his Son...to *c* the world

John 8:11 Neither do I [Jesus] *c* thee: go...sin no more

CONDEMNATION

John 3:19 the *c*...men loved darkness rather than light

Rom 8:1 no *c* to them which are in Christ Jesus

Jas 3:1 knowing that we shall receive the greater *c*

Jas 5:12 let your yea be yea... lest ye fall into *c*

CONFESS [ETH, ING]

Ps 32:5 I will *c* my transgressions unto the LORD

Mark 1:5 were all baptized of him [John the Baptist]... *c'ing* their sins

Luke 12:8 him shall the Son of man also *c*

Rom 10:9 if thou shalt *c* with thy mouth the Lord Jesus

Phil 2:11 every tongue should *c* that Jesus Christ is Lord

Jas 5:16 *C* your faults one to another

1 John 1:9 If we *c* our sins, he is faithful and just to forgive

1 John 4:2 Every spirit that *c'eth* that Jesus Christ is come in the flesh is of God

1 John 4:15 Whosoever shall *c* that Jesus is the Son of God, God dwelleth in him

Rev 3:5 I [Jesus] will *c* his name before my Father

CONFIDENCE

Ps 118:9 better to trust in the LORD than to put *c* in princes

Prov 14:26 In the fear of the LORD is strong *c*

Isa 30:15 in quietness and in *c* shall be your strength

Mic 7:5 put ye not *c* in a guide

Eph 3:12 In whom [Jesus] we have...access with *c*

1 John 2:28 when he [Jesus] shall appear, we may have *c*

CONFIDENT

Prov 14:16 but the fool rageth, and is *c*

2 Cor 5:8 We are *c*...willing... to be absent from the body

Phil 1:6 Being *c*...that he which hath begun a good work...will perform it

CONFIRM [ED, ETH, ING]

Deut 27:26 Cursed be he that *c'eth* not all the words of this law to do them

1 Chr 14:2 David perceived...
LORD had *c'ed* him king
Mark 16:20 the Lord working
with them, and *c'ing* the
word with signs
Acts 15:41 And he [Paul] went
through Syria and Cilicia,
c'ing the churches
Rom 15:8 Jesus Christ was a
minister...to *c* the promises
made unto the fathers
1 Cor 1:6 as the testimony of
Christ was *c'ed* in you
1 Cor 1:8 Who [Jesus] shall
also *c* you unto the end
2 Cor 2:8 *c* your love toward
him [Jesus]

CONFORMED
Rom 8:29 he [God] also did
predestinate to be *c* to the
image of his Son
Rom 12:2 be not *c* to this world:
but be ye transformed

CONIAH. See *Jehoiachin.*

**CONQUEST OF CANAAN
BY ISRAEL.** Josh 6–12.

CONSCIENCE
John 8:9 they [scribes and
Pharisees]...being convicted
by their own *c,* went out
Acts 23:1 I [Paul] have lived in
all good *c* before God
1 Cor 8:12 when ye...wound
their weak *c,* ye sin

1 Cor 10:27 eat, asking no
question for *c* sake
1 Tim 1:5 charity out of a pure
heart, and of a good *c*
1 Tim 3:9 mystery of the faith
in a pure *c*
Heb 9:14 the blood of Christ...
purge...*c* from dead works

CONSENT [ING]
Prov 1:10 if sinners entice thee,
c thou not
Luke 14:18 all with one *c* began
to make excuse
Acts 8:1 Saul was *c'ing* unto
his [Stephen's] death
Acts 22:20 I [Paul]...was...
c'ing unto his [Stephen's]
death
1 Cor 7:5 Defraud ye not...
except it be with *c* for a time

**CONSIDER [ED, EST, ETH,
ING]**
1 Sam 12:24 *c* how great things
he [God] hath done
Job 1:8 Hast thou [Satan] *c'ed*
my [God's] servant Job
Job 37:14 stand still, and *c* the
wondrous works of God
Ps 8:3 When I *c* thy [God's]
heavens, the work of thy
fingers...moon and...stars
Ps 25:19 *C* mine enemies; for
they are many
Ps 41:1 Blessed is he that *c'eth*
the poor
Ps 119:153 *C* mine affliction,
and deliver me

Prov 6:6 Go to the ant, thou sluggard; *c* her ways

Prov 31:16 She *c'eth* a field, and buyeth it

Isa 43:18 neither *c* the things of old

Hag 1:5 thus saith the LORD of hosts; *C* your ways

Matt 6:28 *C* the lilies of the field, how they grow

Matt 7:3 but *c'est* not the beam that is in thine own eye

Gal 6:1 *c'ing* thyself, lest thou also be tempted

Heb 3:1 *c* the...High Priest of our profession, Christ Jesus

CONSOLATION

Luke 2:25 man [Simeon] was just and devout, waiting for the *c* of Israel

Luke 6:24 But woe unto you that are rich! for ye have received your *c*

Acts 4:36 Barnabas...being interpreted, The son of *c*

Rom 15:5 the God of...*c* grant you to be likeminded

Phil 2:1 If there be therefore any *c* in Christ

CONTENT

Phil 4:11 whatsoever state I [Paul] am, therewith to be *c*

1 Tim 6:8 having food and raiment let us be therewith *c*

Heb 13:5 be *c* with such things as ye have

CONTINUE [D, ING, TH]

Luke 6:12 he [Jesus]...*c'd* all night in prayer

John 8:31 If ye *c* in my [Jesus'] word, then are ye my disciples indeed

John 15:9 so have I [Jesus] loved you: *c* ye in my love

Acts 1:14 These all *c'd* with one accord in prayer

Acts 2:46 they [the believers], *c'ing* daily with one accord

Acts 18:11 he [Paul] *c'd* there... teaching the word of God

Rom 6:1 Shall we *c* in sin, that grace may abound

Rom 12:12 patient in tribulation; *c'ing* instant in prayer

Gal 3:10 Cursed is every one that *c'th* not in all things... in the book of the law

Phil 1:25 I [Paul]...shall abide and *c* with you all for your... joy of faith

1 Tim 4:16 Take heed...unto the doctrine; *c* in them

Heb 13:1 Let brotherly love *c*

2 Pet 3:4 all things *c* as they were from the beginning

1 John 2:19 they would no doubt have *c'd* with us

CONVERSATION

Gal 1:13 ye have heard of my [Paul's] *c* in time past

Phil 3:20 our *c* is in heaven; from whence also we look for the Saviour

1 Tim 4:12 be thou an example ...in *c,* in charity

Heb 13:5 Let your *c* be without covetousness

2 Pet 3:11 what manner of persons ought ye to be in all holy *c* and godliness

CONVERSION

Acts 15:3 they [Paul and Barnabas] passed through ...declaring the *c* of the Gentiles

CONVERSION OF PAUL.
Acts 9:1–16.

CONVERT [ED, ETH, ING]

Ps 19:7 The law of the LORD is perfect, *c'ing* the soul

Ps 51:13 sinners shall be *c'ed* unto thee [God]

Matt 18:3 Except ye be *c'ed,* and become as little children

Acts 3:19 Repent ye therefore, and be *c'ed*

Jas 5:19 if any of you do err... and one *c* him

Jas 5:20 he which *c'eth* the sinner...shall save a soul

CORE. See *Korah.*

CORINTH (a major city in Greece where Paul lived for eighteen months and established a church). **Acts 18:1–18;** 19:1 • 1 Cor 1:2 • 2 Cor 1:1,23 • 2 Tim 4:20.

CORINTHIANS, FIRST AND SECOND EPISTLES TO THE. Two letters of the apostle Paul to the church at Corinth, dealing mainly with problems in the church, including divisions (1 Cor. 1–4), sexual immorality (1 Cor. 5–6), and abuses of the Lord's Supper and spiritual gifts (1 Cor. 11–12; 14).

CORNELIUS (a Roman soldier who became one of the first Gentile converts to Christianity). Acts 10:1–48.

CORRUPT [ED]

Gen 6:11 The earth also was *c* before God

Ex 8:24 land [Egypt] was *c'ed* by...swarm of flies

Job 17:1 My [Job's] breath is *c,* my days are extinct

Matt 6:20 treasures in heaven ...neither moth nor rust doth *c*

Luke 6:43 a good tree bringeth not forth *c* fruit

2 Cor 7:2 we have wronged no man, we have *c'ed* no man

Eph 4:29 no *c* communication proceed out of your mouth

Jas 5:2 Your riches are *c'ed*... garments are motheaten

CORRUPTION

Isa 38:17 thou [God] hast in love...delivered it [my soul] from the pit of *c*

Rom 8:21 delivered from...*c* into the glorious liberty of the children of God

1 Cor 15:42 It [the body] is sown in *c*...raised in incorruption

Gal 6:8 he that soweth to his flesh shall of the flesh reap *c*

COUNSEL OF THE LORD

Ps 33:11 The *c-o-t-L* standeth for ever

Prov 19:21 nevertheless the *c-o-t-L,* that shall stand

COUNT [ED, ETH]

Gen 15:6 and he [God] *c'ed* it... for righteousness

Job 31:4 Doth not he [God] see my ways...*c* all my steps

Ps 44:22 we are *c'ed* as sheep for the slaughter

Prov 17:28 a fool, when he holdeth his peace, is *c'ed* wise

Luke 14:28 sitteth not down first, and *c'eth* the cost

Acts 5:41 *c'ed* worthy to suffer shame for his [Jesus'] name

Rom 4:3 it was *c'ed* unto him [Abraham] for righteousness

Phil 3:7 gain to me [Paul], those I *c'ed* loss for Christ

Phil 3:8 I [Paul] *c* all things but loss

Phil 3:13 I [Paul] *c* not myself to have apprehended

2 Thes 1:5 that ye may be *c'ed* worthy of the kingdom of God

1 Tim 5:17 Let the elders that rule well be *c'ed* worthy

Jas 1:2 *c* it all joy when ye fall into divers temptations

2 Pet 3:9 The Lord is not slack concerning his promise, as some men *c* slackness

COURAGE

Deut 31:6 Be strong and of a good *c,* fear not

Ps 31:24 Be of good *c,* and he [God] shall strengthen your heart

Isa 41:6 every one said to his brother, Be of good *c*

COVENANT [S]

Gen 9:9 I [God] establish my *c* with you [Noah]

Gen 9:13 bow in the cloud... shall be for a token of a *c*

Gen 15:18 the LORD made a *c* with Abram

Ex 2:24 God remembered his *c* with Abraham

Ex 19:5 keep my [God's] *c,* then ye shall be a peculiar treasure

Ex 34:28 he [Moses] wrote... the words of the *c,* the ten commandments

Deut 4:23 Take heed...lest ye forget the *c* of the LORD

Deut 29:9 Keep therefore the words of this *c*

1 Sam 18:3 Jonathan and David made a *c*

Jer 11:3 Cursed be the man that obeyeth not...this *c*

Jer 31:31 I [God] will make a new *c* with...Israel

Ezek 16:62 I [God] will establish my *c* with thee

Rom 11:27 For this is my [God's] *c*...when I shall take away their sins

Eph 2:12 aliens...and strangers from the *c's* of promise

Heb 8:6 he [Jesus] is the mediator of a better *c*

Heb 13:20 through the blood of the everlasting *c*

COVET [ED, ETH]

Ex 20:17 Thou shalt not *c* thy neighbour's house

Prov 21:26 He *c'eth* greedily all the day long

Acts 20:33 I [Paul] have *c'ed* no man's silver

1 Cor 12:31 But *c* earnestly the best gifts

1 Tim 6:10 some *c'ed* after... erred from the faith

COVETOUSNESS

Ps 119:36 Incline my heart unto thy [God's] testimonies, and not to *c*

Luke 12:15 Take heed, and beware of *c*

Heb 13:5 Let your conversation be without *c*

CREATE [D]

Gen 1:1 In the beginning God *c'd* the heaven and the earth

Gen 1:27 God *c'd* man in his own image

Gen 6:7 I [God] will destroy man whom I have *c'd*

Ps 51:10 *C* in me a clean heart, O God...renew a right spirit

Ps 148:5 for he [God] commanded, and they were *c'd*

Isa 45:12 I [God] have made the earth...*c'd* man upon it

Isa 65:17 I [God] *c* new heavens and a new earth

Jer 31:22 the LORD hath *c'd* a new thing in the earth

Mal 2:10 Have we not all one father? hath not one God *c'd* us

1 Cor 11:9 Neither was the man *c'd* for the woman

Eph 2:10 we are his workmanship, *c'd* in Christ Jesus

Col 1:16 all things were *c'd* by him [Jesus], and for him

Rev 4:11 for thou [God] hast *c'd* all things

CREATION

Mark 10:6 beginning of the *c* God made...male and female

Rom 1:20 invisible things of him [God] from the *c* of the world are clearly seen

Rom 8:22 the whole *c* groaneth and travaileth in pain

CREATION OF MAN. Gen 1:26–2:7.

CREATION OF WOMAN.
Gen 2:18–25.

CREATION OF WORLD.
Gen 1:1–25.

CROOKED
Deut 32:5 they are a perverse and *c* generation

Eccl 7:13 make that straight, which he [God] hath made *c*

Isa 40:4 the *c* shall be made straight...rough places plain

Luke 3:5 the *c* shall be made straight...rough ways... smooth

Phil 2:15 sons of God...in the midst of a *c*...nation

CROSS
Matt 27:32 they compelled [Simon] to bear his [Jesus'] *c*

Matt 27:42 let him [Jesus] now come down from the *c*

Luke 9:23 take up his *c* daily, and follow me [Jesus]

John 19:17 And he [Jesus] bearing his *c* went forth into...the place of a skull

1 Cor 1:18 the preaching of the *c* is to them that perish foolishness

Gal 6:14 forbid that I [Paul] should glory, save in the *c*

Phil 2:8 he [Jesus]...became obedient unto...death of the *c*

Heb 12:2 who [Jesus] for the joy that was set before him endured the *c*

CROSSING OF JORDAN RIVER INTO CANAAN.
Josh 3:1–17.

CROSSING OF RED SEA.
Ex 14:21–31.

CROWN [ED, EDST]
Ps 8:5 thou [God]...hast *c'ed* him [man] with...honour

Prov 17:6 Children's children are the *c* of old men

Mark 15:17 platted a *c* of thorns, and put it about his [Jesus'] head

Phil 4:1 my joy and *c,* so stand fast in the Lord

2 Tim 4:8 laid up for me [Paul] a *c* of righteousness

Heb 2:7 thou *c'edst* him [Jesus] with glory and honour

Heb 2:9 But we see Jesus... *c'ed* with glory and honour

CROWN OF GLORY
Prov 16:31 The hoary head is a *c-o-g*

Isa 28:5 shall the LORD of hosts be for a *c-o-g*

Isa 62:3 Thou shalt...be a *c-o-g* in the hand of the LORD

1 Pet 5:4 chief Shepherd... appear, ye shall receive a *c-o-g*

CROWN OF LIFE
Jas 1:12 when he is tried, he shall receive the **c-o-l**
Rev 2:10 faithful unto death, and I will give thee a **c-o-l**

CRUCIFIXION OF JESUS.
See *Jesus, Life and Ministry of.*

CURSE [D, DST, ING, TH]
Gen 3:14 thou [the serpent] art **c'd** above all cattle
Gen 12:3 I [God] will...**c** him that **c'th** thee [Abraham]
Lev 20:9 one that **c'th** his father...shall be...put to death
Num 23:11 I [Balak] took thee [Balaam] to **c** mine enemies
Deut 11:26 I [Moses] set before you [Israel] this day a blessing and a **c**
Deut 27:15 **C'd** be the man that maketh any graven or molten image
Deut 30:19 I [Moses] have set before you life and death, blessing and **c'ing**
Josh 6:26 **C'd** be the man... that...buildeth...Jericho
Job 2:9 Dost thou [Job] still retain thine integrity? **c** God, and die
Jer 20:14 **C'd** be the day...I [Jeremiah] was born
Matt 5:44 Love your enemies, bless them that **c** you
Matt 15:4 He that **c'th** father... let him die
Matt 25:41 Depart from me [Jesus], ye **c'd,** into everlasting fire
Mark 11:21 fig tree which thou [Jesus] **c'dst** is withered
Mark 14:71 But he [Peter] began to **c**...saying, I know not this man [Jesus]
Acts 23:14 bound ourselves under a great **c**...eat nothing until we have slain Paul
Rom 12:14 Bless them which persecute you: bless...**c** not
Gal 3:13 Christ hath redeemed us from the **c** of the law
Jas 3:10 Out of the same mouth proceedeth blessing and **c'ing**

CUSTOM
Matt 9:9 he [Jesus] saw... Matthew...at the receipt of **c**
John 18:39 a **c,** that I [Pilate] should release unto you one at the passover
Rom 13:7 Render...to all their dues...**c** to whom **c**

CUTH (a Babylonian district whose citizens settled the Northern Kingdom [Israel] after it fell to the Assyrians). 2 Kgs 17:30. *Cuthah:* 2 Kgs 17:24.

CUTHAH. See *Cuth.*

CYPRUS (a large island in the Mediterranean Sea that Paul and Barnabas visited during the first missionary journey). Acts 4:36; 11:19–20; **13:4–13;** 15:39; 21:3,16; 27:4. *Chittim:* Jer 2:10. *Kittim:* Gen 10:4.

CYRENE (a city in Africa and home of the Simon who carried the cross of Jesus). Matt 27:32 • Mark 15:21 • Luke 23:26 • Acts 2:10; 6:9; 11:20; 13:1.

CYRENIUS (Roman governor of Syria at the time of Jesus' birth). Luke 2:1–4.

CYRUS (a king of the Persian empire who allowed the Jewish captives to return to their homeland about 536 B.C.). 2 Chr 36:22–23 • **Ezra 1:1–8;** 3:7; 4:3,5; 5:13–14,17; 6:3,14 • Isa 44:28; 45:1 • Dan 1:21; 6:28; 10:1.

-D-

DAGON (chief pagan god of the Philistines). Judg 16:23 • 1 Sam 5:1–7.

DALMANUTHA (a place near the Sea of Galilee visited by Jesus). Mark 8:10.

DALMATIA (a Roman province along the Adriatic Sea visited by Titus). 2 Tim 4:10.

DAMASCUS (capital city of Syria and the city to which Paul was traveling when he was converted). Gen 14:15 • 2 Sam 8:5–6 • 1 Kgs 15:18 • 2 Kgs 8:7–15 • Isa 8:4 • **Acts 9:1–8** • 2 Cor 11:32–33 • Gal 1:17. *Syria-damascus:* 1 Chr 18:6.

DAMNATION

Mark 3:29 blaspheme against the Holy Ghost...is in danger of eternal *d*

John 5:29 that have done evil, unto the resurrection of *d*

1 Cor 11:29 he...eateth and drinketh *d* to himself

DAN

1. A son of Jacob and ancestor of one of the twelve tribes of Israel. Gen 30:6; 35:25; 46:23; 49:16–17 • Ex 1:4 • Josh 19:47–48 • 1 Chr 2:2 • Ezek 27:19. The tribe of Dan settled in central Palestine and along the Mediterranean Sea. Judg 1:34; 5:17; 13:25; 18:2–30.

2. A village in the territory of Dan. Gen 14:14 • Judg 20:1 • 1 Chr 21:2 • 2 Chr 30:5. *Laish:* Isa 10:30.

DANIEL (a prophet who remained faithful to God among the pagan Babylonians and Persians). References to Daniel outside the Book of Daniel are found in Ezek 14:14, 20; 28:3 • Matt 24:15 • Mark 13:14. His Babylonian name was *Belteshazzar:* Dan 1:7.

DANIEL, BOOK OF. An apocalyptic book of the Old Testament known for its imagery that is similar to that in the Book of Revelation in the New Testament. The book describes the trials and tribulations suffered by Daniel and his three friends as captives of the Babylonians and Persians (Dan 1–7) and Daniel's visions and dreams about the future (Dan 8–12).

DARIUS (a title for four different kings of Persia).

1. Darius I or Darius the Great, who continued Cyrus's policy of restoring the Jewish people to their homeland. Ezra 6:1–12.

2. Darius II or Darius the Persian. Neh 12:22.

3. Darius III or Darius Codomannus, who is probably the "fourth" king of Persia mentioned by the prophet Daniel. Dan 11:2.

4. Darius the Mede, who made Daniel a ruler over several provincial leaders. Dan 6:1–2.

DARKENED

Isa 24:11 all joy is *d,* the mirth of the land is gone

Joel 3:15 The sun and the moon shall be *d*

Mark 13:24 after that tribulation, the sun shall be *d*

Rom 1:21 they [ungodly]... became vain...heart was *d*

DARKNESS

Gen 1:2 and *d* was upon the face of the deep

Ex 10:22 a thick *d* in all the land of Egypt three days

2 Sam 22:29 the LORD will lighten my *d*

Job 34:22 There is no *d,* nor shadow of death

Ps 18:9 He [God]...came down...*d* was under his feet

Isa 5:20 Woe unto them that... put *d* for light, and light for *d*

Isa 9:2 people that walked in *d* have seen a great light

Joel 2:31 sun shall be turned into *d*...moon into blood

Matt 4:16 people which sat in *d* saw great light

Luke 23:44 a *d* over all the earth until the ninth hour

John 1:5 the *d* comprehended it [the light] not

John 3:19 men loved *d* rather than light

John 12:46 whosoever believeth...not abide in *d*

Acts 2:20 The sun shall be turned into *d*

Acts 26:18 To open their eyes, and to turn them from *d* to light

2 Cor 4:6 God, who commanded the light to shine out of *d*... shined in our hearts

Eph 6:12 we wrestle...against the rulers...*d* of this world

1 Pet 2:9 who [Jesus] hath called you out of *d* into his marvellous light

1 John 1:5 God is light, and in him is no *d* at all

1 John 2:11 he that hateth his brother is in *d*

DAVID (a popular king of Judah and an earthly ancestor of the promised Messiah, Jesus Christ). See **1 Sam 16–31** • **2 Sam 1–24** • **1 Kgs 1:1–2:11** • **1 Chr 11–29** for a sketch of David.

1. Anointed as a boy by Samuel (1 Sam 16:1–13)

2. Musician and armorbearer for King Saul (1 Sam 16:14–23)

3. Killed the Philistine Goliath (1 Sam 17:1–54)

4. Hid from King Saul as a fugitive (1 Sam 19:1–30:31)

5. King over Judah (2 Sam 2:1–4:12)

6. Captured Jerusalem (Jebus) and turned it into his capital city (1 Chr 11:4–9)

7. King over all Israel (2 Sam 5:1–6:16)

8. His throne established by the Lord forever (2 Sam 7:1–29)

9. Committed adultery with Bathsheba (2 Sam 11:1–27)

10. Survived rebellion by his son Absalom (2 Sam 15:7–23)

11. Not allowed to build the temple (1 Chr 17:1–15)

12. Death of David (1 Kgs 2:10–11 • 1 Chr 29:26–28)

13. Succeeded by his son Solomon (1 Kgs 1:10–35)

The phrase "a psalm of David" appears in the titles of many psalms in the Book of Psalms, indicating either that David wrote these psalms or that they were written in his honor. Pss 2–9; 11–41; 51–65; 68–70; 86; 101–103; 108–110; 122; 124; 131–133; 138–145.

The prophets of the Old Testament often spoke of the promised Messiah who would fulfill God's promise to David. Isa 9:7; 55:3 • Jer 17:25; 33:17 • Ezek 37:24 • Zech 12:8.

In the New Testament, Jesus was called "the son of David" or "seed of David." Matt 9:27; 20:31 • Luke 18:38–39 • John 7:42 • Rom 1:3 • 2 Tim 2:8.

DAY

Gen 1:5 evening and the morning were the first *d*

Ex 13:3 Remember this *d*...ye came out from Egypt

Ex 20:11 LORD blessed the sabbath *d,* and hallowed it

Deut 4:4 ye that did cleave unto the LORD your God are alive...this *d*

Deut 11:26 Behold, I [Moses] set before you this *d* a blessing and a curse

Josh 4:14 On that *d* the LORD magnified Joshua

Josh 10:13 the sun stood still... and hasted not to go down about a whole *d*

Josh 24:15 choose you this *d* whom ye will serve

1 Kgs 18:36 known this *d* that thou art God in Israel

1 Chr 16:23 show forth from *d* to *d* his [God's] salvation

Job 3:3 the *d* perish wherein I [Job] was born

Job 19:25 he shall stand at the latter *d* upon the earth

Ps 1:2 in his [God's] law doth he meditate *d* and night

Ps 19:2 *D* unto *d* uttereth speech

Ps 50:15 call upon me [God] in the *d* of trouble

Ps 84:10 For a *d* in thy [God's] courts is better than a thousand

Ps 86:7 In the *d* of my trouble I will call upon thee [God]

Ps 91:5 shalt not be afraid... for the arrow that flieth by *d*

Ps 118:24 This is the *d* which the LORD hath made

Ps 121:6 sun shall not smite thee by *d*

Prov 27:1 knowest not what a *d* may bring forth

Isa 13:6 Howl ye, for the *d* of the LORD is at hand

Isa 60:19 sun shall be no more thy light by *d*

Jer 1:10 I [God] have this *d* set thee over the nations

Jer 9:1 I [Jeremiah] might weep *d* and night for the slain of my people

Jer 20:14 Cursed be the *d*...I [Jeremiah] was born

Joel 2:31 before...the terrible *d* of the LORD come

Amos 5:18 Woe unto you that desire the *d* of the LORD

Zech 2:11 many nations...be joined to the LORD in that *d*

Zech 14:6 in that *d,* that the light shall not be clear

Mal 3:2 who may abide the *d* of his [God's] coming

Matt 6:11 Give us this *d* our daily bread

Matt 7:22 Many will say to me in that *d,* Lord, Lord

Matt 25:13 know neither the *d* nor the hour wherein the Son of man cometh

Mark 14:25 I [Jesus] will drink no more of the fruit of the vine, until that *d*...I drink it new

Luke 2:11 born this *d* in the city of David a Saviour

Luke 9:22 Son of man must... be slain...raised the third *d*

Luke 19:9 This *d* is salvation come to this house

Luke 24:46 it behoved Christ to suffer...to rise from the dead the third *d*

John 9:4 I [Jesus] must work... while it is *d*

John 11:24 he [Lazarus] shall rise again...at the last *d*

1 Cor 16:2 Upon the first *d* of the week let every one of you lay by him in store

2 Cor 6:2 behold, now is the *d* of salvation

Phil 3:5 Circumcised the eighth *d*...stock of Israel

2 Tim 1:12 keep that...committed unto him [Jesus] against that *d*

Heb 13:8 Jesus Christ the same yesterday, and to *d*

2 Pet 3:8 one *d* is with the Lord as a thousand years

Rev 1:10 I [John] was in the Spirit on the Lord's *d*

Rev 6:17 the great *d* of his [God's] wrath is come

DAY OF ATONEMENT

Lev 23:27 a *d-o-a:* it shall be an holy convocation

Lev 23:28 a *d-o-a,* to make an atonement...before the LORD

Lev 25:9 in the *d-o-a* shall ye make the trumpet sound

DAY OF JUDGMENT

Matt 11:22 It shall be more tolerable for Tyre...at the *d-o-j,* than for you

Matt 12:36 every idle word... men...shall give account thereof in the *d-o-j*

1 John 4:17 that we may have boldness in the *d-o-j*

DAY OF THE LORD

Isa 2:12 the *d-o-t-L* of hosts... upon every one that is proud

Joel 1:15 Alas...for the *d-o-t-L* is at hand

Amos 5:20 Shall not the *d-o-t-L* be darkness, and not light? even very dark

Obad 15 the *d-o-t-L* is near upon all the heathen

Zech 14:1 Behold, the *d-o-t-L* cometh

Mal 4:5 send you Elijah the prophet before the...dreadful *d-o-t-L*

Acts 2:20 sun shall be turned into darkness...before that great...*d-o-t-L* come

1 Thes 5:2 the *d-o-t-L* so cometh as a thief in the night

2 Pet 3:10 the *d-o-t-L* will come as a thief in the night

DEACON [S]

1 Tim 3:10 use the office of a *d,* being found blameless

1 Tim 3:12 Let the *d's* be the husbands of one wife

1 Tim 3:13 used the office of a *d* well purchase to themselves a good degree

DEAD

Ex 12:30 great cry in Egypt... not a house where there was not one *d*

Josh 1:2 Moses my [God's] servant is *d*...therefore arise

2 Kgs 4:32 when Elisha was come into the house, behold, the child was *d*

Eccl 9:5 but the *d* know not any thing

Jer 22:10 Weep ye not for the *d,* neither bemoan him

Matt 2:19 when Herod was *d*... an angel...appeareth in a dream to Joseph

Matt 8:22 Follow me [Jesus]; and let the *d* bury their *d*

Matt 10:8 Heal the sick, cleanse the lepers, raise the *d*

Mark 6:16 I [Herod] beheaded: he [John the Baptist] is risen from the *d*

Mark 15:44 Pilate marvelled if he [Jesus] were already *d*

Luke 15:24 this my son was *d,* and is alive again

Luke 20:38 he is not a God of the *d,* but of the living

Luke 24:46 it behoved Christ to suffer...rise from the *d*

John 11:25 though he were *d,* yet shall he live

John 20:9 they knew not... that he [Jesus] must rise again from the *d*

Acts 17:32 when they heard of the resurrection of the *d,* some mocked

Acts 26:8 thought a thing incredible with you, that God should raise the *d*

Rom 1:4 declared to be the Son of God with power...by the resurrection from the *d*

Rom 6:4 Christ was raised up from the *d* by...the Father

Rom 10:9 if thou...shalt believe...that God hath raised him [Jesus] from the *d*

1 Cor 15:13 no resurrection of the *d,* then is Christ not risen

Gal 2:19 I [Paul] through the law am *d* to the law

Eph 2:1 you hath he [Jesus] quickened, who were *d* in trespasses and sins

Col 1:18 who [Jesus] is...the firstborn from the *d*

1 Thes 4:16 the *d* in Christ shall rise first

2 Tim 2:8 Jesus Christ...was raised from the *d* according to my gospel

Jas 2:17 Even so faith, if it hath not works, is *d*

1 Pet 4:5 to him that is ready to judge the quick and the *d*

Rev 1:17 I [John] saw him [Jesus], I fell at his feet as *d*

Rev 14:13 Blessed are the *d* which die in the Lord

DEAD SEA. See *Salt Sea.*

DEAF

Isa 35:5 the ears of the *d* shall be unstopped

Mark 7:32 they bring unto him [Jesus] one that was *d*

Luke 7:22 tell John...lepers are cleansed, the *d* hear

DEATH

Deut 30:15 I [Moses] have set before thee...*d* and evil

Deut 33:1 Moses...blessed the children of Israel before his *d*

2 Kgs 4:40 man of God, there is *d* in the pot

Job 16:16 on my [Job's] eyelids is the shadow of *d*

Ps 13:3 lighten mine eyes, lest I sleep the sleep of *d*

Ps 23:4 walk through the valley of the shadow of *d*

Ps 48:14 For this God...will be our guide even unto *d*

Ps 107:14 He [God] brought them out of...shadow of *d*

Ps 116:15 Precious in the sight of the LORD...*d* of his saints

Prov 14:12 but the end thereof are the ways of *d*

Isa 9:2 they that dwell in...the shadow of *d,* upon them hath the light shined

Isa 53:9 he [God's servant] made his grave with the wicked, and...rich in his *d*

Jer 21:8 I [God] set before you the way of life, and...*d*

Matt 4:16 to them which sat in the...shadow of *d* light is sprung up

Mark 14:34 My [Jesus'] soul is exceeding sorrowful unto *d*

Luke 2:26 he [Simon] should not see *d,* before he had seen the Lord's Christ

John 5:24 He that...believeth... is passed from *d* unto life

John 11:4 sickness is not unto *d,* but for the glory of God

Acts 8:1 Saul was consenting unto his [Stephen's] *d*

Rom 5:12 so *d* passed upon all men, for that all have sinned

Rom 6:4 we are buried with him [Jesus] by baptism into *d*

Rom 6:23 the wages of sin is *d*

Rom 7:24 who shall deliver me [Paul] from the body of...*d*

Rom 8:38 neither *d,* nor life, nor angels

1 Cor 11:26 ye do show the Lord's *d* till he come

1 Cor 15:26 The last enemy that shall be destroyed is *d*

1 Cor 15:55 O *d,* where is thy sting

Phil 2:8 he [Jesus] humbled himself...obedient unto *d*

Phil 3:10 being made conformable unto his [Jesus'] *d*

Heb 11:5 Enoch was translated that he should not see *d*

1 John 3:14 we have passed from *d* unto life, because we love the brethren

Rev 1:18 I [Jesus] am alive for evermore...and have the keys of hell and of *d*

Rev 20:14 *d* and hell were cast into the lake of fire

Rev 21:4 there shall be no more *d,* neither sorrow

DEATH OF JESUS. See *Jesus, Life and Ministry of.*

DEBORAH (a prophetess and judge of Israel who defeated the Canaanites). **Judg 4:4–16;** 5:1–31.

DEBT [S]

Matt 6:12 forgive us our *d's,* as we forgive our debtors

Matt 18:27 the lord of that servant...forgave him the *d*

Rom 4:4 to him that worketh is the reward...of *d*

DEBTOR [S]

Rom 1:14 I [Paul] am *d* both to the Greeks, and to the Barbarians

Rom 8:12 we are *d's,* not to the flesh, to live after the flesh

DECAPOLIS (a district with a large Greek population east of the Jordan River). Jesus visited this area several times. Matt 4:25 • Mark 5:20; 7:31.

DECEIVE [D, ING, TH]
Deut 11:16 Take heed...that your heart be not *d'd*
Prov 20:1 Wine is a mocker... and whosoever is *d'd* thereby is not wise
Luke 21:8 Take heed that ye be not *d'd:* for many shall come in my [Jesus'] name
Gal 6:3 think himself to be something, when he is nothing, he *d'th* himself
Gal 6:7 Be not *d'd;* God is not mocked
Eph 5:6 Let no man *d* you with vain words
Jas 1:22 be ye doers of the word, and not hearers only, *d'ing* your own selves
1 John 1:8 If we say that we have no sin, we *d* ourselves

DECEIVER [S]
Matt 27:63 *d* said...After three days I [Jesus] will rise again
2 John 7 many *d's* are entered into the world

DECLARE [D, ING]
1 Chr 16:24 *D* his [God's] glory among the heathen
Ps 9:11 *d* among the people his [God's] doings
Ps 19:1 The heavens *d* the glory of God
Ps 66:16 *d* what he [God] hath done for my soul
Ps 71:17 hitherto have I *d'd* thy [God's] wondrous works
Ps 96:3 *D* his [God's] glory among the heathen
Isa 12:4 Praise the LORD...*d* his doings among the people
Isa 48:3 I have *d'd* the former things from the beginning
John 1:18 the only begotten Son...he hath *d'd* him [God]
Acts 15:12 *d'ing* what miracles...God had wrought among the Gentiles
Acts 17:23 Whom therefore ye ignorantly worship, him [God] *d* I [Paul] unto you
Rom 1:4 *d'd* to be the Son of God with power
1 Cor 15:1 I [Paul] *d* unto you the gospel...I preached
1 John 1:3 That which we have seen...*d* we unto you
1 John 1:5 the message which we...*d* unto you

DEED [S]
1 Chr 16:8 Call upon his [God's] name, make known his *d's* among the people
Luke 23:41 we receive the due reward of our *d's*
John 3:19 men loved darkness... because their *d's* were evil
Rom 2:6 render to every man according to his *d's*

Rom 3:28 justified by faith without the *d's* of the law

Col 3:17 And whatsoever ye do in word or *d*

1 John 3:18 not love in word... but in *d* and in truth

DEFILE [D, TH]

Ezek 20:7 *d* not yourselves with the idols of Egypt

Dan 1:8 Daniel...would not *d* himself with...king's meat

Matt 15:20 to eat with unwashen hands *d'th* not a man

Mark 7:2 saw some of his [Jesus'] disciples eat bread with *d'd*...hands

Mark 7:18 thing from without entereth into the man, it cannot *d* him

John 18:28 went not into the judgment hall, lest they [Pharisees] should be *d'd*

1 Cor 3:17 If any man *d* the temple of God

Jas 3:6 the tongue...*d'th* the whole body

DEHAVITES (a tribe which settled in Samaria after the Northern Kingdom fell to the Assyrians). Ezra 4:9–16.

DELILAH (a woman who betrayed Samson to the Philistines). Judg 16:4–21.

DELIVER [ED, EDST, ETH, ING]

Ex 18:10 Jethro said...the LORD...hath *d'ed* you out of the hand of the Egyptians

Deut 1:27 the LORD...hath brought us forth...to *d* us into the hand of the Amorites

Deut 9:10 LORD *d'ed* unto me [Moses] two tables of stone

Josh 10:8 I [God] have *d'ed* them into thine hand

Judg 6:1 the LORD *d'ed* them into the hand of Midian

Judg 10:13 ye have forsaken me [God] and served other gods...I will *d* you no more

1 Sam 17:37 he [God] will *d* me [David] out of the hand of this Philistine

Job 16:11 God hath *d'ed* me [Job] to the ungodly

Job 33:28 He [God] will *d* his [man's] soul from...the pit

Ps 17:13 O LORD, *d* my soul from the wicked

Ps 25:20 keep my soul and *d* me: let me not be ashamed

Ps 34:4 the LORD...*d'ed* me from all my fears

Ps 34:17 the LORD...*d'eth* them out of all their troubles

Ps 41:1 the LORD will *d* him in time of trouble

Ps 72:12 he [God] shall *d* the needy when he crieth

Ps 107:6 and he [God] *d'ed* them out of their distresses

Ps 116:8 thou [God] hast **d'ed** my soul from death

Ps 120:2 **D** my soul, O LORD, from lying lips

Prov 11:4 righteousness **d'eth** from death

Isa 19:20 he [God] shall send them a saviour...and he shall **d** them

Isa 46:4 even I [God] will carry, and will **d** you

Jer 1:8 I am with thee to **d** thee, saith the LORD

Jer 20:13 he [God] hath **d'ed**... the poor from...evildoers

Dan 3:17 our God...is able to **d** us from the...furnace

Dan 6:20 is thy [Daniel's] God...able to **d** thee

Hos 11:8 how shall I [God] **d** thee, Israel

Joel 2:32 whosoever shall call on...the LORD shall be **d'ed**

Zeph 1:18 nor their gold shall... **d** them in the day of the LORD'S wrath

Matt 6:13 lead us not into temptation...**d** us from evil

Matt 24:9 Then shall they **d** you up to be afflicted

Matt 25:20 Lord, thou **d'edst** unto me five talents

Mark 10:33 Son of man shall be **d'ed** unto the chief priests

Mark 15:1 the chief priests... **d'ed** him [Jesus] to Pilate

Luke 2:6 days were accomplished that she [Mary] should be **d'ed**

Luke 9:44 Son of man shall be **d'ed** into the hands of men

Acts 22:4 I [Paul] persecuted... **d'ing** into prisons both men and women

Rom 7:24 who shall **d** me [Paul] from...this death

Gal 1:4 he [Jesus] might **d** us from this present evil world

Col 1:13 Who [Jesus]...**d'ed** us from the power of darkness

2 Tim 4:18 Lord shall **d** me from every evil work

2 Pet 2:9 Lord...knoweth how to **d**...out of temptations

DEMAS (a believer who deserted Paul). Col 4:14 • 2 Tim 4:10 • Phlm 24.

DEMETRIUS

1. A silversmith at Ephesus who incited a riot against the apostle Paul. Acts 19:24–38.

2. A believer commended by the apostle John. 3 John 12.

DENY [IED, IETH, ING]

Matt 10:33 him will I also **d** before my Father

Matt 26:72 And again he [Peter] **d'ied** with an oath, I do not know the man [Jesus]

Mark 14:30 thou [Peter] shalt **d** me [Jesus] thrice

Luke 9:23 let him **d** himself, and take up his cross daily

Luke 12:9 he that **d'ieth** me [Jesus] before men shall be **d'ied** before...God

1 Tim 5:8 hath **d'ied** the faith, and is worse than an infidel

2 Tim 2:12 if we **d** him [Jesus], he also will **d** us

Titus 2:12 **d'ing**...worldly lusts, we should live soberly

1 John 2:23 Whosoever **d'ieth** the Son...hath not the Father

DEPTH [S]

Ps 106:9 so he [God] led them through the **d's**

Ps 130:1 Out of the **d's** have I cried unto thee, O LORD

Jon 2:5 the **d** closed me [Jonah] round about

Mic 7:19 thou [God] wilt cast... their sins into...**d's** of the sea

Rom 8:39 Nor height, nor **d**... shall be able to separate us from the love of God

Rom 11:33 **d** of the riches both of the wisdom and knowledge of God

DERBE (a village in the province of Lycaonia visited by Paul and Barnabas). **Acts 14:6–20; 16:1; 20:4.**

DESCEND [ED, ING]

Gen 28:12 and behold...angels of God ascending and **d'ing** on it [a ladder]

Prov 30:4 Who hath ascended up into heaven, or **d'ed**

Matt 7:27 the rain **d'ed,** and the floods came

Matt 28:2 angel...**d'ed** from heaven...rolled back the stone

Mark 15:32 Let Christ...**d** now from the cross

Luke 3:22 Holy Ghost **d'ed**... like a dove

John 1:32 I [John] saw the Spirit **d'ing** from heaven like a dove

Rom 10:7 Who shall **d** into the deep...to bring up Christ

Eph 4:10 He [Jesus] that **d'ed**...also...ascended up far above all heavens

1 Thes 4:16 Lord himself shall **d** from heaven with a shout

Rev 21:10 that great city...holy Jerusalem, **d'ing** out of heaven from God

DESIRE [D, ING, S, TH]

Gen 3:16 **d** shall be to thy [Eve's] husband

Deut 5:21 Neither shalt thou **d** thy neighbour's wife

Ps 27:4 One thing have I **d'd** of the LORD

Ps 37:4 and he [God] shall give thee the **d's** of thine heart

Ps 38:9 all my **d** is before thee [God]...my groaning...not hid

Ps 73:25 none upon earth that I **d** beside thee [God]

Ps 145:16 Thou [God]...satisfiest the **d** of every living thing

Prov 21:25 The *d* of the slothful killeth him

Song 7:10 I am my beloved's, and his *d* is toward me

Isa 26:9 With my soul have I *d'd* thee [God] in the night

Ezek 24:16 I take away from thee the *d* of thine eyes

Hos 6:6 I [God] *d'd* mercy, and not sacrifice

Amos 5:18 Woe unto you that *d* the day of the LORD

Matt 12:46 his [Jesus'] mother ...stood without, *d'ing* to speak with him

Mark 9:35 any man *d* to be first, the same shall be last

Mark 11:24 What things soever ye *d,* when ye pray

Luke 22:31 Simon, behold, Satan hath *d'd* to have you

Rom 10:1 my [Paul's] heart's *d* ...for Israel is, that they might be saved

2 Cor 5:2 *d'ing* to be clothed upon with our house which is from heaven

Phil 1:23 having a *d* to depart, and to be with Christ

1 Tim 3:1 *d* the office of a bishop, he *d'th* a good work

Heb 11:16 now they *d* a better country, that is, an heavenly

1 Pet 2:2 As newborn babes, *d* the sincere milk of the word

DESTRUCTION [S]

Job 5:22 At *d* and famine thou shalt laugh

Ps 90:3 Thou [God] turnest man to *d*

Ps 107:20 He [God]...delivered them from their *d's*

Prov 16:18 Pride goeth before *d,* and a haughty spirit before a fall

Isa 13:6 day of the LORD... shall come as a *d* from the Almighty

Matt 7:13 broad is the way, that leadeth to *d*

DEUTERONOMY, BOOK OF.

An Old Testament book that contains a series of speeches delivered by Moses to the Israelites as they prepared to enter the land of Canaan. This book repeats many of the laws of God revealed to Moses on Mt. Sinai about two generations earlier—thus its name Deuteronomy, which means "second law."

DEVOUT

Luke 2:25 Simeon...was just and *d,* waiting for the consolation of Israel

Acts 2:5 there was dwelling at Jerusalem Jews, *d* men

DIANA

(a pagan goddess to whom a shrine was erected at Ephesus, a center of Diana worship). Acts 19:24–35.

DIE [D, ST, TH] *See also* **DYING**

Gen 2:17 day that thou eatest thereof [the forbidden tree] thou shalt surely *d*

Gen 45:28 I [Jacob] will...see him [Joseph] before I *d*

Ex 16:3 Would to God we had *d'd*...in the land of Egypt

Deut 4:22 I [Moses] must *d* in this land, I must not go over Jordan...ye shall go over

Deut 14:21 not eat of any thing that *d'th* of itself

Judg 16:30 Samson said, Let me *d* with the Philistines

Ruth 1:17 Where thou [Naomi] *d'st,* will I [Ruth] die

2 Sam 12:5 he [David] said... the man that hath done this thing shall surely *d*

2 Chr 25:4 every man shall *d* for his own sin

Job 2:9 Dost thou [Job] still retain thine integrity? curse God, and *d*

Job 3:11 Why *d'd* I [Job] not from the womb

Job 14:14 If a man *d,* shall he live again

Prov 10:21 but fools *d* for want of wisdom

Eccl 3:2 A time to be born, and a time to *d*

Isa 6:1 In the year that king Uzziah *d'd* I [Isaiah] saw also the Lord

Jer 16:6 the great and the small shall *d* in this land

Jer 31:30 every one shall *d* for his own iniquity

Ezek 18:32 I [God] have no pleasure in the death of him that *d'th*

Jon 4:3 it is better for me [Jonah] to *d* than to live

Matt 26:35 Though I [Peter] should *d* with thee [Jesus], yet will I not deny thee

John 6:50 bread...from heaven, that a man may eat...and not *d*

John 11:16 said Thomas...Let us also go, that we may *d* with him [Jesus]

John 11:21 Lord, if thou hadst been here, my [Martha's] brother had not *d'd*

John 11:50 it is expedient for us, that one man should *d* for the people

John 12:24 if it [grain of wheat] *d,* it bringeth forth much fruit

Acts 21:13 I [Paul] am ready... to *d* at Jerusalem for the name of...Jesus

Rom 5:6 in due time Christ *d'd* for the ungodly

Rom 5:7 scarcely for a righteous man will one *d*

Rom 5:8 while we were yet sinners, Christ *d'd* for us

Rom 6:9 Christ being raised from the dead *d'th* no more

Rom 14:7 none...liveth to himself...no man *d'th* to himself

Rom 14:8 whether we live...or *d,* we are the Lord's

1 Cor 15:3 how that Christ *d'd* for our sins according to the scriptures

1 Cor 15:22 in Adam all *d*...in Christ...all be made alive

2 Cor 5:14 if one *d'd* for all, then were all dead

2 Cor 5:15 he [Jesus] *d'd* for all, that they...should not... live unto themselves

Phil 1:21 to me [Paul] to live is Christ, and to *d* is gain

Heb 9:27 it is appointed unto men once to *d*

Rev 14:13 Blessed are the dead which *d* in the Lord

DINAH (Jacob's daughter who was assaulted by Shechem). Gen 30:20–21; **34:1–31.**

DINAITES (a tribe which settled in Samaria after the Northern Kingdom fell to the Assyrians). Ezra 4:9–16.

DIOTREPHES (a believer condemned for his false teachings by the apostle John). 3 John 9–10.

DISCERN [ING]

1 Kgs 3:9 that I [Solomon] may *d* between good and bad

Ezek 44:23 cause them to *d* between...unclean and... clean

Matt 16:3 ye hypocrites, ye can *d* the face of the sky

1 Cor 11:29 drinketh damnation to himself, not *d'ing* the Lord's body

1 Cor 12:10 another prophecy; to another *d'ing* of spirits

DISCIPLE

Matt 10:24 The *d* is not above his master

Luke 14:26 If any man...hate not his father...he cannot be my [Jesus'] *d*

John 19:38 Joseph of Arimathaea, being a *d* of Jesus

DISOBEDIENCE

Rom 5:19 For as by one man's [Adam's] *d* many were made sinners

Eph 5:6 cometh the wrath of God upon the children of *d*

DISOBEDIENT

Acts 26:19 I [Paul] was not *d* unto the heavenly vision

2 Tim 3:2 boasters, proud, blasphemers, *d* to parents

Titus 1:16 they deny him [God], being abominable, and *d* and...reprobate

1 Pet 2:7 unto them which be *d,* the stone...is made the head of the corner

DISTRESS [ED, ES]

Ps 18:6 In my *d* I called upon the LORD

Ps 107:13 he [God] saved them out of their ***d'es***

Zeph 1:15 That day is...a day of trouble and ***d***

Luke 21:23 for there shall be great ***d*** in the land

Rom 8:35 shall separate us from the love of Christ? shall tribulation, or ***d***

2 Cor 4:8 troubled on every side, yet not ***d'ed***

2 Cor 12:10 I [Paul] take pleasure...in ***d'es*** for Christ's sake

1 Thes 3:7 comforted over you [Thessalonians] in all our... ***d*** by your faith

DIVIDE [D, ING, TH]

Gen 1:6 let it [the firmament] ***d*** the waters from the waters

Ex 14:16 stretch out thine [Moses'] hand over the sea, and ***d*** it

Ex 14:21 the LORD...made the sea dry land...waters were ***d'd***

Num 33:54 ye shall ***d*** the land by lot for an inheritance

Judg 7:16 he [Gideon] ***d'd***... men into three companies

Job 26:12 He [God] ***d'th*** the sea with his power

Ps 78:13 He [God] ***d'd*** the sea... caused them to pass through

Prov 16:19 Better it is to be... with the lowly, than to ***d*** the spoil with the proud

Dan 5:28 Thy [Belshazzar's] kingdom is ***d'd,*** and given to the Medes and Persians

Zech 14:1 thy spoil shall be ***d'd*** in the midst of thee

Matt 25:32 he [Jesus] shall separate them...as a shepherd ***d'd*** his sheep from the goats

Luke 11:17 kingdom ***d'd*** against itself is brought to desolation

Luke 12:13 speak to my brother, that he ***d*** the inheritance with me

Luke 12:53 The father shall be ***d'd*** against the son

Luke 15:12 And he [prodigal son's father] ***d'd*** unto them his living

1 Cor 1:13 Is Christ ***d'd?*** was Paul crucified for you

2 Tim 2:15 a workman...not... ashamed, rightly ***d'ing*** the word of truth

DIVISION [S]

Luke 12:51 I [Jesus] tell you, Nay; but rather ***d***

John 9:16 How can a man...do such miracles? And there was a ***d*** among them

Rom 16:17 mark them which cause ***d's*** and offences

1 Cor 3:3 there is among you envying, and strife, and ***d's***

DIVISION OF CANAAN AMONG THE ISRAELITE TRIBES. Josh 14:1–19:51.

DIVORCE [D]

Lev 21:14 a widow, or a *d'd* woman...these shall he [a priest] not take

Jer 3:8 I [God] had put her [Israel] away, and given her a bill of *d*

Matt 5:32 whosoever shall marry her that is *d'd* committeth adultery

DOCTRINE [S]

Mark 11:18 the people was astonished at his [Jesus'] *d*

John 7:16 My [Jesus'] *d* is not mine, but his that sent me

Acts 2:42 they continued stedfastly in the apostles' *d*

Eph 4:14 be no more children... carried about with every wind of *d*

1 Tim 4:13 give attendance to reading, to exhortation, to *d*

2 Tim 3:16 All scripture is... profitable for *d*

2 Tim 4:3 For the time will come when they will not endure sound *d*

Heb 13:9 Be not carried about with divers and strange *d's*

2 John 9 He that abideth in the *d* of Christ

DOEG (a shepherd for King Saul who betrayed David). 1 Sam 21:7; **22:9–22.**

DOER [S]

Prov 17:4 A wicked *d* giveth heed to false lips

Rom 2:13 the *d's* of the law shall be justified

Jas 1:22 be ye *d's* of the word, and not hearers only

Jas 1:23 if any be a hearer of the word, and not a *d*

DOMINION [S]

Gen 1:28 God said...have *d* over the fish of the sea

Job 25:2 *D* and fear are with him [God]

Ps 8:6 Thou [God] madest him [man] to have *d* over the works of thy hands

Ps 72:8 He [God] shall have *d* also from sea to sea

Dan 4:3 his [God's] *d* is from generation to generation

Zech 9:10 and his [God's] *d* shall be from sea even to sea

Matt 20:25 princes of the Gentiles exercise *d*

Rom 6:9 death hath no more *d* over him [Jesus]

Col 1:16 by him [Jesus] were all things created...whether they be thrones, or *d's*

1 Pet 4:11 to whom [Jesus] be... *d* for ever and ever

Jude 25 To...God our Saviour, be...*d* and power

DOOR OF THE SHEEP, JESUS AS. See *"I Am" Statements of Jesus.*

DORCAS. See *Tabitha.*

DOTHAN (a city where Joseph was sold into slavery by his brothers). **Gen 37:17–28** • 2 Kgs 6:8–23.

DOUBT [ED, ING]
Matt 14:31 thou of little faith, wherefore didst thou *d*
Matt 28:17 they worshipped him [Jesus]: but some *d'ed*
1 Tim 2:8 men pray every where lifting up holy hands, without wrath and *d'ing*

DREAM
Gen 37:5 Joseph dreamed a *d,* and he told it his brethren
Gen 40:9 the chief butler told his *d* to Joseph
Gen 41:25 Joseph said...The *d* of Pharaoh is one
Dan 2:3 I [Nebuchadnezzar] have dreamed a *d,* and my spirit was troubled
Joel 2:28 pour out my [God's] spirit...old men shall *d* dreams
Acts 2:17 and your old men shall *d* dreams

DREAMS THROUGH WHICH GOD SPOKE TO PEOPLE
1. To Abimelech, king of Gerar (Gen 20:3)
2. To Jacob, son of Isaac (Gen 28:10–12)
3. To Laban, father-in-law of Jacob (Gen 31:24)

4. To Solomon, king of Judah (1 Kgs 3:5)
5. To Joseph, husband of Mary (Matt 1:20; 2:12–13,22)

DRINK [ETH, ING]
Ex 15:24 the people murmured against Moses, saying, What shall we *d*
Job 1:13 when his [Job's] sons and his daughters were eating and *d'ing* wine
Ps 69:21 in my thirst they gave me vinegar to *d*
Ps 78:15 He [God]...gave them *d* as out of the great depths
Prov 5:15 *D* waters out of thine own cistern
Prov 20:1 Wine is a mocker, strong *d* is raging
Prov 25:21 and if he [your enemy] be thirsty, give him water to *d*
Eccl 2:24 There is nothing better for a man, than that he should eat and *d*
Eccl 9:7 *d* thy wine with a merry heart
Isa 5:11 Woe unto them that rise up early...that they may follow strong *d*
Ezek 12:18 *d* thy water with trembling
Dan 1:12 give us [Daniel and his friends] pulse to eat, and water to *d*
Matt 6:31 What shall we eat? or, What shall we *d*
Matt 25:42 I was thirsty, and ye gave me no *d*

Mark 2:16 he [Jesus] eateth and *d'eth* with...sinners

Mark 10:38 can ye *d* of the cup that I [Jesus] *d* of

Mark 15:23 they gave him [Jesus] to *d* wine...with myrrh

Luke 5:30 Why do ye [Jesus] eat and *d* with publicans

Luke 7:33 John the Baptist came neither eating bread nor *d'ing* wine

Luke 10:7 eating and *d'ing* such things as they give

Luke 22:18 I [Jesus] will not *d* of the fruit...until the kingdom of God shall come

John 4:7 Jesus saith unto her [the Samaritan woman], Give me to *d*

John 4:14 *d'eth* of the water that I [Jesus] shall give him shall never thirst

John 6:53 Except ye...*d* his [Jesus'] blood, ye have no life in you

Acts 23:12 saying that they would neither eat nor *d* till they had killed Paul

Rom 12:20 if he [your enemy] thirst, give him *d*

Rom 14:17 the kingdom of God is not meat and *d*

1 Cor 10:31 Whether therefore ye eat, or *d*...do all to the glory of God

1 Cor 11:25 as oft as ye *d* it, in remembrance of me [Jesus]

1 Cor 11:29 eateth and *d'eth* damnation to himself

1 Tim 5:23 *D* no longer water, but use a little wine

Rev 16:6 thou hast given them blood to *d*

DRY BONES, EZEKIEL'S VISION OF. Ezek 37:1–14.

DUMB

Isa 53:7 as a sheep before her shearers is *d*

Mark 7:37 he [Jesus] maketh... the *d* to speak

Luke 1:20 thou [Zacharias] shalt be *d,* and not able to speak

1 Cor 12:2 Ye know that ye were Gentiles, carried away unto these *d* idols

DURA (a plain where an image of the Babylonian king was set up). Dan 3:1.

DYING (*See also* DIE)

2 Cor 4:10 in the body the *d* of the Lord Jesus

Heb 11:21 Jacob, when he was a *d,* blessed both the sons of Joseph

-E-

EARTH [LY]

Gen 1:1 God created the heaven and the *e*

Gen 6:6 it repented the LORD... he had made man on the *e*

Gen 9:1 Be fruitful, and multiply, and replenish the *e*

Gen 12:3 and in thee [Abraham] shall all families of the *e* be blessed

Deut 30:19 call heaven and *e* to record this day against you

1 Kgs 10:23 Solomon exceeded all the kings of the *e*...for wisdom

Job 1:8 there is none like him [Job] in the *e*

Job 19:25 he shall stand at the latter day upon the *e*

Job 38:4 Where wast thou [Job] when I [God] laid the foundations of the *e*

Ps 8:1 how excellent is thy [God's] name in all the *e*

Ps 24:1 The *e* is the LORD'S, and the fulness thereof

Ps 37:11 But the meek shall inherit the *e*

Ps 67:2 thy [God's] way may be known upon *e*

Ps 82:8 Arise, O God, judge the *e*...inherit all nations

Ps 96:1 O sing...a new song: sing unto the LORD, all the *e*

Ps 108:5 Be thou exalted, O God...and thy glory above all the *e*

Isa 6:3 the whole *e* is full of his [God's] glory

Isa 45:22 be ye saved, all the ends of the *e*

Isa 55:9 higher than the *e,* so are my [God's] ways higher than your ways

Isa 66:1 heaven is my [God's] throne...*e* is my footstool

Joel 3:16 and the heavens and the *e* shall shake

Hab 2:20 let all the *e* keep silence before him [God]

Matt 5:13 Ye are...salt of the *e*

Matt 6:10 Thy [God's] will be done in *e,* as it is in heaven

Matt 12:40 shall the Son of man be...three nights in the heart of the *e*

Matt 16:19 whatsoever thou shalt loose on *e* shall be loosed in heaven

Matt 24:35 Heaven and *e* shall pass away, but my [Jesus'] words shall not pass away

Matt 28:18 All power is given unto me [Jesus] in heaven and in *e*

Luke 2:14 on *e* peace, good will toward men

Luke 23:44 darkness over all the *e* until the ninth hour

John 3:12 I [Jesus] have told you *e'ly* things, and ye believe not

John 12:32 if I [Jesus] be lifted up from the *e*

Acts 1:8 ye shall be witnesses... the uttermost part of the *e*

2 Cor 5:1 our *e'ly* house of this tabernacle were dissolved

Col 3:2 Set your affection on things above, not on things on the *e*

Rev 7:1 four angels standing on the four corners of the *e*

Rev 21:1 I [John] saw a new heaven and a new *e*

EAST SEA. See *Salt Sea.*

EAT [EN, ER, ETH, ING]

Gen 2:17 the tree of...good and evil, thou shalt not *e*

Gen 3:11 Hast thou *e'en* of the tree...thou shouldest not *e*

Ex 16:35 the children of Israel did *e* manna

Lev 11:41 every creeping thing...shall not be *e'en*

Judg 14:14 Out of the *e'er* came forth meat

Ps 102:9 For I have *e'en* ashes like bread

Eccl 2:24 nothing better for a man, than that he should *e* and drink

Jer 31:29 fathers have *e'en* a sour grape

Ezek 3:1 *e* that thou [Ezekiel] findest; *e* this roll

Ezek 12:18 *e* thy [Ezekiel's] bread with quaking

Matt 6:25 Take no thought for your life, what ye shall *e*

Matt 9:11 Why *e'eth* your [disciples'] Master with publicans

Matt 15:20 to *e* with unwashen hands defileth not a man

Matt 26:26 they were *e'ing,* Jesus took bread...blessed it

Mark 7:28 dogs under the table *e* of the children's crumbs

Mark 14:18 One of you which *e'eth* with me [Jesus] shall betray me

Luke 5:30 Why do ye *e* and drink with...sinners

Luke 7:33 John the Baptist came neither *e'ing* bread nor drinking wine

Luke 15:23 bring...the fatted calf...let us *e,* and be merry

John 4:32 I [Jesus] have meat to *e* that ye know not of

John 6:50 This is...bread... from heaven, that a man may *e*...and not die

Acts 10:13 there came a voice... Rise, Peter; kill, and *e*

1 Cor 10:31 ye *e,* or drink...do all to the glory of God

1 Cor 11:26 as often as ye *e* this bread, and drink this cup

1 Cor 11:29 he that *e'eth*... unworthily, *e'eth*...damnation to himself

2 Thes 3:10 if any would not work, neither should he *e*

Rev 2:7 him that overcometh will I give to *e*...tree of life

EBAL (a mountain where Joshua built an altar after destroying the city of Ai). Deut 11:29; 27:4,13 • **Josh 8:30–35.**

EBED-MELECH (an Ethiopian eunuch who rescued Jeremiah from a dungeon). **Jer 38:7–13;** 39:15–18.

EBENEZER (a memorial site in Philistine territory that commemorated Israel's victory over the Philistines). 1 Sam 4:1–10; 5:1; **7:10–12.**

EBER (a great-grandson of Shem and ancestor of the Hebrew race). Gen 10:21–25; 11:14–17 • 1 Chr 1:18–23.

ECCLESIASTES, BOOK OF. A wisdom book in the Old Testament, probably written by King Solomon, which declares that life derives joy and meaning not from riches, fame, or work but from reverence for God and obedience to His commandments.

EDEN, GARDEN OF (the fruitful garden created specifically by the Lord as the home for Adam and Eve). **Gen 2:8–3:24;** 4:16 • Isa 51:3 • Ezek 28:13; 31:9,16–18; 36:35 • Joel 2:3.

EDIFY [IETH, ING]
1 Cor 14:4 speaketh in an unknown tongue *e'ieth* himself
Eph 4:12 for the *e'ing* of the body of Christ

1 Thes 5:11 comfort...and *e* one another

EDOM
1. The name given to Esau, Jacob's brother, after he traded away his birthright. Gen 25:30.
2. The land where the descendants of Esau settled. Gen 36:21,31–32,43 • Num 20:14–23; 34:3 • Josh 15:1,21 • Judg 11:17–18 • 2 Sam 8:14 • 2 Kgs 3:8–26 • Jer 25:21; 27:3; 40:11; 49:7–22 • Ezek 25:12–14 • Amos 1:6–11 • Obad 1,8. *Idumea:* Mark 3:8. See also *Esau.*

EGYPT (an ancient nation along the Nile River which held the Hebrew people in slavery before their miraculous deliverance). Gen 12:10; 37:28–36 • **Ex 1:7–14; 12:29–36** • Isa 19:3–25; 30:1–7; 36:6 • Jer 46:8 • Ezek 30:25 • Matt 2:13–15.

EHUD (a judge of Israel who killed King Eglon of Moab). Judg 3:15–26.

EKRON (a major Philistine city captured by Israel). Josh 13:3; 15:11,45–46; 19:43 • **Judg 1:18** • 1 Sam 5:10; 6:16–17; 7:14; 17:52 • 2 Kgs 1:2–6,16 • Jer 25:20 • Amos 1:8 • Zeph 2:4 • Zech 9:5,7.

ELAH

1. A valley where David killed the Philistine giant Goliath. **1 Sam 17:2,49;** 21:9.

2. A king of Israel who was assassinated and succeeded by Zimri. 1 Kgs 16:6–10.

ELAM (a son of Shem and ancestor of the Elamites). **Gen 10:22** • 1 Chr 1:17.

ELAMITES (descendants of Elam who lived in Mesopotamia in the area later populated by the Medes and Persians). Gen 14:1,9 • Ezra 4:9 • Isa 11:11; 21:2; 22:6 • Jer 25:25; 49:34–39 • Ezek 32:24 • Dan 8:2 • Acts 2:9.

EL-BETHEL. See *Bethel.*

ELDER [S]

Matt 15:2 Why do thy [Jesus'] disciples transgress the tradition of the *e's*

Luke 15:25 his [father of prodigal son] *e* son was in the field

Acts 14:23 they [Paul and Barnabas] had ordained them *e's*

Acts 20:17 he [Paul] sent to Ephesus, and called the *e's*

1 Tim 5:1 Rebuke not an *e,* but entreat him as a father

1 Tim 5:17 Let the *e's* that rule well be counted worthy

Jas 5:14 call for the *e's*...and let them pray over him

2 John 1 The *e* unto the elect lady and her children

Rev 4:10 four and twenty *e's* fall down before him [God]

ELEAZAR (a son of Aaron who succeeded his father as high priest). Ex 6:23–25; 28:1 • Lev 10:6–7 • Num 3:32; **20: 25–28** • Josh 14:1; 24:33.

ELECT

Isa 42:1 mine [God's] *e,* in whom my soul delighteth

Mark 13:27 he [Jesus] shall gather together his *e* from the four winds

Col 3:12 Put on...as the *e* of God...bowels of mercies

1 Pet 1:2 E according to the foreknowledge of God

ELECTION

Rom 11:5 a remnant according to the *e* of grace

2 Pet 1:10 give diligence to make your calling and *e* sure

ELI (a high priest of Israel with whom the prophet Samuel lived during his boyhood years). **1 Sam 1:9–3:17;** 4:15–18; 14:3 • 1 Kgs 2:27.

ELIAKIM

1. An aide to King Hezekiah of Judah who mediated

peace with the invading Assyrian army. **2 Kgs 18:18–19:2** • **Isa 22:20–25;** 36:3, 11,22; 37:2.

2. Another name for King Jehoiakim of Judah. See *Jehoiakim.*

ELIAS. See *Elijah.*

ELIHU (a man who criticized Job and his three friends). Job 32:2–6; 34:1; 35:1; 36:1.

ELIJAH (a courageous prophet who opposed King Ahab and his successor, Ahaziah, because of their encouragement of Baal worship throughout the Northern Kingdom). **1 Kgs 17–21** • **2 Kgs 1:1–18; 2:1–11;** 3:11; 9:36; 10:10,17 • 2 Chr 21:12 • Mal 4:5. *Elias:* Matt 17:3–4 • Mark 9:4–13 • Luke 9:30–54 • John 1:21,25 • Rom 11:2 • Jas 5:17.

ELIPHAZ
1. A son of Esau. Gen 36:10 • 1 Chr 1:35–36.
2. One of the three friends who comforted Job. His speeches appear in Job 4:1–5:27; 15:1–35; 22:1–30.

ELISABETH (mother of John the Baptist and a relative of Mary, earthly mother of Jesus). Luke 1:5–60.

ELISEUS. See *Elisha.*

ELISHA (a prophet selected and anointed by Elijah as his successor). 1 Kgs 19:16–19 • **2 Kgs 2:1–15;** 3:11–14; 4:1–38; 5:9–10,20,25; 6:1–32; 7:1; 8:1–14; 9:1; 13:14–21. *Eliseus:* Luke 4:27.

ELON (a minor judge of Israel). Judg 12:11–12.

ELOTH (a former Edomite city used as a port city by King Solomon). **1 Kgs 9:26** • 2 Chr 8:17; 26:2.

ELYMAS. See *Bar-jesus.*

EMMAUS (a village near Jerusalem where Jesus appeared to two of His followers after His resurrection). Luke 24:13–33.

END [ED, S]
Gen 2:2 on the seventh day God *e'ed* his work
Job 28:24 For he [God] looketh to the *e's* of the earth
Job 42:12 the LORD blessed the latter *e* of Job
Ps 22:27 the *e's* of the world shall...turn unto the LORD
Ps 39:4 make me to know mine *e*...measure of my days
Ps 102:27 thy [God's] years shall have no *e*

Prov 14:12 the *e* thereof are the ways of death

Eccl 7:8 Better is the *e* of a thing than the beginning

Eccl 12:12 of making many books there is no *e*

Isa 9:7 Of...his [the Messiah's] ...peace...there shall be no *e*

Jer 8:20 summer is *e'ed,* and we are not saved

Dan 12:9 words are...sealed till the time of the *e*

Matt 10:22 he that endureth to the *e* shall be saved

Matt 24:6 all these things must come to pass...*e* is not yet

Matt 28:20 I [Jesus] am with you alway, even unto the *e* of the world

John 18:37 Jesus answered... To this *e* was I born

Rom 10:4 Christ is the *e* of the law for righteousness

1 Cor 15:24 Then cometh the *e*

Eph 3:21 be glory in the church by Christ Jesus...world without *e*

1 Pet 4:7 But the *e* of all things is at hand

Rev 2:26 he that overcometh... keepeth my works unto the *e*

Rev 22:13 Alpha and Omega, the beginning and the *e*

END [S] OF THE EARTH

1 Sam 2:10 the LORD shall judge the *e's-o-t-e*

Ps 48:10 so is thy [God's] praise unto the *e's-o-t-e*

Ps 61:2 From the *e-o-t-e* will I cry unto thee [God]

Ps 67:7 all the *e's-o-t-e* shall fear him [God]

Isa 40:28 the Creator of the *e's-o-t-e,* fainteth not

Isa 42:10 Sing...his [God's] praise from the *e-o-t-e*

Isa 45:22 be ye saved, all the *e's-o-t-e*

Acts 13:47 thou [Paul] shouldest be for salvation unto the *e's-o-t-e*

EN-DOR (a city where King Saul sought advice from a fortune teller). Josh 17:11 • **1 Sam 28:1–10** • Ps 83:9–10.

ENDUED

Luke 24:49 tarry ye in...Jerusalem, until...*e* with power

Jas 3:13 Who is...*e* with knowledge among you

ENDURE [D, ING, TH]

Ex 18:23 then thou [Moses] shalt be able to *e*

1 Chr 16:34 his [God's] mercy *e'th* for ever

Esth 8:6 how can I [Esther] *e* to see the evil that shall come

Job 8:15 he shall hold it fast, but it shall not *e*

Ps 9:7 LORD shall *e* for ever

Ps 19:9 The fear of the LORD is clean, *e'ing* for ever

Ps 30:5 For his [God's] anger *e'th* but a moment

Ps 89:36 His [David's] seed shall *e* for ever

Ps 102:12 But thou, O Lord, shalt *e* for ever

Ps 107:1 give thanks unto... Lord...his mercy *e'th* for ever

Ps 145:13 thy [God's] dominion *e'th* throughout all generations

Prov 27:24 doth the crown *e* to every generation

Matt 10:22 he that *e'th* to the end shall be saved

Mark 13:13 he that shall *e* unto the end...shall be saved

1 Cor 13:7 [charity] hopeth all things, *e'th* all things

2 Tim 2:3 *e* hardness, as a good soldier of Jesus Christ

2 Tim 4:3 they will not *e* sound doctrine...having itching ears

2 Tim 4:5 watch thou in all things, *e* afflictions

Heb 6:15 after he [Abraham] had patiently *e'd*

Heb 12:2 who [Jesus] for the joy...set before him *e'd* the cross

Jas 1:12 Blessed is the man that *e'th* temptation

Jas 5:11 Behold, we count them happy which *e*

ENEMY [IES]

Deut 20:4 Lord...goeth...to fight...against your *e'ies*

1 Sam 18:29 Saul became David's *e* continually

Job 19:11 he [God] counteth me...as one of his *e'ies*

Ps 6:7 Mine eye...waxeth old because of all mine *e'ies*

Ps 9:3 *e'ies* are turned back, they shall fall

Ps 18:17 He [God] delivered me from my strong *e*

Ps 23:5 Thou [God] preparest a table...presence of mine *e'ies*

Ps 27:11 lead me in a plain path, because of mine *e'ies*

Ps 61:3 thou [God] hast been... a strong tower from the *e*

Ps 97:3 A fire...burneth up his [God's] *e'ies* round about

Ps 110:1 until I [God] make thine *e'ies* thy footstool

Prov 25:21 If thine *e* be hungry, give him bread

Matt 5:44 I [Jesus] say unto you, Love your *e'ies*

Rom 12:20 Therefore if thine *e* hunger, feed him

1 Cor 15:25 For he [Jesus] must reign, till he hath put all *e'ies* under his feet

1 Cor 15:26 The last *e* that shall be destroyed is death

Gal 4:16 Am I [Paul]...your *e,* because I tell you the truth

2 Thes 3:15 count him not as an *e,* but admonish him

Jas 4:4 a friend of the world is the *e* of God

EN-GEDI (an oasis near the Dead Sea where David hid from King Saul). Josh 15:62 • **1 Sam 23:29–24:1** • 2 Chr 20:2 • Song 1:14 • Ezek 47:10.

ENMITY
Gen 3:15 I [God] will put *e* between thee [the serpent] and the woman

Rom 8:7 Because the carnal mind is *e* against God

Jas 4:4 the friendship of the world is *e* with God

ENOCH
1. The firstborn son of Cain and a city named for him. Gen 4:17–18.

2. The father of Methuselah, who was taken into God's presence without experiencing physical death. Gen 5:18–24 • Luke 3:37 • Heb 11:5 • Jude 14. *Henoch:* 1 Chr 1:3.

ENTER [ED, ETH, ING]
Ps 100:4 **E** into his [God's] gates with thanksgiving

Prov 17:10 A reproof *e'eth* more into a wise man than an hundred stripes into a fool

Ezek 3:24 the spirit *e'ed* into me [Ezekiel]

Matt 6:6 when thou prayest, *e* into thy closet

Matt 7:21 Not every one that saith...Lord, Lord, shall *e* into the kingdom of heaven

Mark 7:18 thing from without *e'eth* into the man, it cannot defile him

Mark 14:38 pray, lest ye *e* into temptation

Luke 11:52 them that were *e'ing* in ye hindered

Luke 13:24 Strive to *e* in at the strait gate

Luke 18:25 easier for a camel... than for a rich man to *e* into the kingdom

Luke 22:3 Then *e'ed* Satan into Judas surnamed Iscariot

John 3:4 can he *e* the second time into his mother's womb, and be born

John 10:2 he that *e'eth* in by the door is the shepherd

Acts 11:8 nothing...unclean hath at any time *e'ed* into my [Peter's] mouth

Rom 5:12 by one man sin *e'ed* into the world

1 Cor 2:9 *e'ed* into the heart of man, the things which God hath prepared

Heb 9:12 he [Jesus] *e'ed* in once into the holy place

ENVY [IETH, ING]
Prov 3:31 **E** thou not the oppressor

Prov 27:4 but who is able to stand before *e*

Mark 15:10 chief priests had delivered him [Jesus] for *e*

Rom 13:13 Let us walk honestly ...not in strife and *e'ing*

1 Cor 13:4 charity *e'ieth* not... vaunteth not itself
Gal 5:26 not be desirous of... glory,...*e'ing* one another
Phil 1:15 Some...preach Christ even of *e* and strife
Titus 3:3 living in malice and *e*...hating one another
Jas 3:16 where *e'ing* and strife is, there is confusion

EPAPHRAS (a church leader who was called a "fellowprisoner" by the apostle Paul). Col 1:7–8; 4:12 • **Phlm 23.**

EPAPHRODITUS (a believer who visited Paul while he was imprisoned in Rome). Phil 2:25; **4:18.**

EPHESIANS, EPISTLE TO THE. A letter of the apostle Paul to the church at Ephesus on the theme of the risen Christ as Lord of creation and head of His body, the church.

EPHESUS (a major city of Asia Minor where Paul spent two to three years and established a church). **Acts 18:19–21; 19:1–10;** 20:16–17 • 1 Cor 15:32; 16:8 • Eph 1:1 • 1 Tim 1:3 • 2 Tim 1:18; 4:12 • Rev 1:11; 2:1.

EPHRAIM
1. A son of Joseph and ancestor of one of the twelve tribes of Israel. Gen 41:52;
48:1–20 • Num 26:28 • 1 Chr 7:20–22. The tribe of Ephraim settled in central Canaan. Josh 16:1–10.
2. A symbolic name for the nation of Israel, meaning "fruitful," used especially in the books of Isaiah, Jeremiah, and Hosea. Isa 7:2–17 • Jer 31:9–20 • Hos 5:3–14.
3. A city in the wilderness to which Jesus and His disciples retreated. John 11:54.
4. A forest where Absalom's forces were defeated by David's army. 2 Sam 18:6–18.

EPHRATAH. See *Bethlehem.*

EPHRATH. See *Bethlehem.*

EPHRON (a Hittite who sold a cave to Abraham). **Gen 23: 8–20;** 25:9; 49:29–30; 50:13.

EPICUREANS (followers of the Greek philosopher Epicurus whom Paul addressed in Athens). Acts 17:18.

EQUAL
Prov 26:7 The legs of the lame are not *e*
Ezek 18:25 Is not my [God's] way *e*...your ways unequal
John 5:18 he [Jesus]...said also that God was his Father, making himself *e* with God

Phil 2:6 Who [Jesus]...thought it not robbery to be *e* with God
Col 4:1 give unto your servants that which is just and *e*

ERASTUS (a believer whom Paul sent into Macedonia). Acts 19:22 • 2 Tim 4:20.

ERR [ED]
Job 6:24 understand wherein I [Job] have *e'ed*
Isa 9:16 leaders of this people cause them to *e*
Isa 63:17 why hast thou [God] made us to *e* from thy ways
Matt 22:29 Ye do *e,* not knowing the scriptures
1 Tim 6:10 they have *e'ed* from the faith
Jas 5:19 if any of you do *e* from the truth

ERROR
2 Sam 6:7 God smote him [Uzzah] there for his *e*
Matt 27:64 the last *e* shall be worse than the first
2 Pet 3:17 being led away with the *e* of the wicked

ESAIAS. See *Isaiah.*

ESAR-HADDON (a king of Assyria who succeeded his father, Sennacherib). **2 Kgs 19:37** • Ezra 4:2 • Isa 37:38.

ESAU (the oldest son of Isaac who traded his birthright for a bowl of stew). Esau was the ancestor of the Edomites. **Gen 25:26–34;** 26:34; 27:1–42; 28:6–9; 32:3–19; 33:1–16; 35:1,29; 36:1–43 • Josh 24:4 • 1 Chr 1:34–35 • Mal 1:2–3 • Rom 9:13 • Heb 12:16. *Edom:* Gen 36:8. See also *Edom.*

ESCAPE [D]
1 Sam 22:1 David...*e'd* to the cave Adullam
Job 19:20 I [Job] am *e'd* with the skin of my teeth
Ps 71:2 cause me to *e:* incline thine [God's] ear unto me
Isa 37:31 remnant that is *e'd* of the house of Judah
Jer 25:35 no way to flee, nor the principal of the flock to *e*
John 10:39 but he [Jesus] *e'd* out of their hand
1 Cor 10:13 God...will with the temptation also make a way to *e*
Heb 2:3 How shall we *e,* if we neglect so great salvation

ESEK (a well that the servants of Isaac and Abimelech quarreled over). Gen 26:20.

ESH-BAAL. See *Ish-bosheth.*

ESH-COL (a brook explored by the spies sent into Canaan). **Num 13:22–27;** 32:9 • Deut 1:24.

ESTABLISH [ED]

Gen 9:9 I [God] *e* my covenant with you [Noah]

Ps 7:9 e the just: for the righteous God trieth the hearts

Ps 78:5 he [God] *e'ed* a testimony in Jacob

Ps 90:17 e thou [God] the work of our hands

Prov 3:19 The LORD...by understanding hath...*e'ed* the heavens

Prov 12:19 The lip of truth shall be *e'ed* for ever

Prov 16:3 Commit...unto the LORD...thy thoughts shall be *e'ed*

Ezek 16:62 I [God] will *e* my covenant with thee

Matt 18:16 mouth of...witnesses every word...be *e'ed*

Acts 16:5 so were the churches *e'ed* in the faith

Rom 10:3 going about to *e* their own righteousness

Heb 8:6 he [Jesus] is the mediator of a better covenant... *e'ed* upon better promises

ESTHER (a young Jewish woman who became queen under King Ahasuerus of Persia and used her influence to save her countrymen). Esth 2–9.

ESTHER, BOOK OF. A historical book of the Old Testament named for its major personality, Queen Esther of Persia. This book shows that God protects and sustains His people.

ETERNAL

Deut 33:27 The *e* God is thy refuge

Mark 3:29 he that shall blaspheme against the Holy Ghost...is in danger of *e* damnation

John 17:3 life *e,* that they might know...God

2 Cor 4:18 things which are not seen are *e*

2 Cor 5:1 an house not made with hands, *e* in the heavens

1 Tim 1:17 unto the King *e,* immortal, invisible

Heb 5:9 he [Jesus] became the author of *e* salvation

Heb 9:12 by his [Jesus'] own blood he...obtained *e* redemption for us

ETERNAL LIFE

Mark 10:17 what shall I do that I may inherit *e-l*

John 3:15 whosoever believeth in him [Jesus] should not perish, but have *e-l*

John 6:54 Whoso eateth my [Jesus'] flesh...hath *e-l*

John 6:68 thou [Jesus] hast the words of *e-l*

John 10:28 I [Jesus] give unto them *e-l*

Rom 6:23 the gift of God is *e-l* through Jesus Christ

1 Tim 6:12 Fight the good fight of faith, lay hold on *e-l*

1 John 2:25 promise that he [Jesus] hath promised...*e-l*

1 John 3:15 no murderer hath *e-l* abiding in him

1 John 5:11 God hath given to us *e-l*...in his Son

Jude 21 mercy of our Lord Jesus Christ unto *e-l*

ETHIOPIA (an ancient nation south of Egypt). Gen 2:13 • 2 Chr 12:3 • Job 28:19 • Ps 68:31 • Isa 45:14 • Dan 11:43 • Amos 9:7 • Acts 8:27.

EUNICE (mother of Timothy who was commended for her faith by the apostle Paul). 2 Tim 1:5.

EUPHRATES (a major river in Mesopotamia). Gen 2:14; 15:18 • Josh 1:4 • 2 Sam 8:3 • 2 Kgs 23:29 • 2 Chr 35:20 • Jer 13:4–7 • Rev 9:14; 16:12.

EUTYCHUS (a young man who fell from a window during Paul's sermon at Troas). Acts 20:9–12.

EVANGELIST [S]

Acts 21:8 entered into the house of Philip the *e*

Eph 4:11 he [God] gave some... prophets; and some, *e's*

2 Tim 4:5 do the work of an *e*

EVE (first woman and mother of the human race). Gen 3:20; 4:1 • 2 Cor 11:3 • 1 Tim 2:13.

EVERLASTING

Deut 33:27 and underneath are the *e* arms

Ps 24:7 and be ye lift up, ye *e* doors

Ps 90:2 even from *e* to *e,* thou art God

Ps 100:5 For the LORD is good; his mercy is *e*

Ps 119:144 righteousness of thy [God's] testimonies is *e*

Isa 9:6 his [Jesus'] name shall be called...The *e* Father

Isa 26:4 in the LORD JEHOVAH is *e* strength

Isa 40:28 the *e* God...fainteth not, neither is weary

Isa 60:19 the LORD shall be unto thee an *e* light

Jer 31:3 I [God] have loved thee with an *e* love

Dan 7:14 his [God's] dominion is an *e* dominion

Matt 25:41 Depart from me [Jesus], ye cursed, into *e* fire

EVERLASTING COVENANT

Gen 9:16 the *e-c* between God and every living creature

Heb 13:20 Jesus, that great shepherd of the sheep, through the blood of the *e-c*

EVERLASTING LIFE

John 3:16 whosoever believeth in him [Jesus] should not perish, but have *e-l*

John 4:14 a well of water springing up into *e-l*

John 5:24 He that...believeth on him [God] that sent me [Jesus], hath *e-l*

John 6:47 He that believeth on me [Jesus] hath *e-l*

EVIL [S]

Gen 50:20 ye thought *e* against me [Joseph]; but God meant it unto good

Deut 30:15 I [Moses] have set before thee...death and *e*

Josh 24:15 if it seem *e* unto you to serve the LORD

1 Sam 16:14 an *e* spirit from the LORD troubled him [Saul]

Job 2:10 shall we receive good at the hand of God, and... not receive *e*

Job 28:28 to depart from *e* is understanding

Ps 23:4 valley of the shadow of death, I will fear no *e*

Ps 34:13 Keep thy tongue from *e,* and thy lips from...guile

Ps 38:20 They...that render *e* for good are...adversaries

Ps 51:4 Against thee [God]... have I...done this *e*

Ps 119:101 I have refrained my feet from every *e* way

Prov 3:7 fear the LORD, and depart from *e*

Prov 15:3 eyes of the LORD are in every place, beholding the *e* and the good

Prov 31:12 She will do him good and not *e*

Isa 5:20 Woe unto them that call *e* good, and good *e*

Jer 1:14 Out of the north an *e* shall break forth

Jer 2:13 my [God's] people have committed two *e's*

Matt 5:11 men...shall say all manner of *e* against you

Matt 6:13 lead us not into temptation...deliver us from *e*

Mark 3:4 lawful to do good on the sabbath...or to do *e*

Luke 11:13 ye then, being *e,* know how to give good gifts

John 3:19 men loved darkness... because their deeds were *e*

Rom 7:19 the *e* which I [Paul] would not, that I do

Rom 12:9 Abhor that which is *e;* cleave to...good

Rom 12:21 Be not overcome of *e*...overcome *e* with good

Eph 5:16 Redeeming the time, because the days are *e*

Eph 6:13 ye may be able to withstand in the *e* day

1 Thes 5:22 Abstain from all appearance of *e*

1 Tim 6:10 love of money is the root of all *e*

Heb 3:12 lest there be in any of you an *e* heart of unbelief

Jas 3:8 the tongue...is an unruly *e,* full of deadly poison

Jas 3:16 where envying...is, there is...every *e* work
3 John 11 Beloved, follow not that which is *e*

EVILDOER [S]

Ps 26:5 I have hated the congregation of *e's*
Ps 119:115 Depart from me, ye *e's*
1 Pet 4:15 let none of you suffer ...as an *e,* or...busybody

EVIL-MERODACH (a king of Babylonia who released King Jehoiachin of Judah from prison). **2 Kgs 25:27–30** • Jer 52:31.

EXALT [ED, ETH]

1 Chr 29:11 thou [God] art *e'ed* as head above all
Ps 34:3 let us *e* his [God's] name together
Ps 46:10 I [God] will be *e'ed* among the heathen
Ps 57:11 Be thou *e'ed,* O God, above the heavens
Ps 97:9 thou [God] art *e'ed* far above all gods
Ps 99:5 *E* ye the LORD...and worship at his footstool
Prov 14:34 Righteousness *e'eth* a nation
Isa 25:1 O LORD, thou art my God; I will *e* thee
Isa 40:4 Every valley shall be *e'ed*...hill...made low
Luke 14:11 he that humbleth himself shall be *e'ed*

Phil 2:9 God also hath highly *e'ed* him [Jesus]
1 Pet 5:6 that he [God] may *e* you in due time

EXAMPLE

Matt 1:19 Then Joseph her [Mary's] husband...not willing to make her a publick *e*
John 13:15 I [Jesus] have given you an *e*
1 Tim 4:12 be thou an *e* of the believers, in word

EXCEEDING [LY]

Gen 17:2 I [God]...will multiply thee [Abraham] *e'ly*
Ps 68:3 rejoice before God: yea, let them *e'ly* rejoice
Jon 3:3 Now Nineveh was an *e* great city
Jon 4:1 it displeased Jonah *e'ly,* and he was very angry
Matt 2:10 they [the wise men] rejoiced with *e* great joy
Matt 5:12 be *e* glad: for great is your reward in heaven
Matt 26:38 My [Jesus'] soul is *e* sorrowful, even unto death
Mark 15:14 cried out the more *e'ly,* Crucify him [Jesus]
2 Cor 4:17 our light affliction... worketh for us a far more *e*...weight of glory
Eph 2:7 he [God] might show the *e* riches of his grace
Eph 3:20 unto him [Jesus] that is able to do *e* abundantly above all...we ask

Jude 24 him [Jesus] that is able to...present you faultless before...his glory with *e* joy

EXCELLENT
Ps 8:9 how *e* is thy [God's] name in all the earth
Ps 150:2 praise him [God] according to his *e* greatness
Isa 12:5 for he [God] hath done *e* things
Dan 6:3 because an *e* spirit was in him [Daniel]
1 Cor 12:31 yet show I [Paul] unto you a more *e* way
Heb 8:6 hath he [Jesus] obtained a more *e* ministry
Heb 11:4 Abel offered...a more *e* sacrifice than Cain

EXCUSE
Luke 14:18 they all with one consent began to make *e*
Rom 1:20 they are without *e*

EXHORT [ED, ING]
1 Thes 2:11 we *e'ed* and comforted...every one of you
2 Tim 4:2 *e* with all longsuffering and doctrine
Titus 2:9 *E* servants to be obedient unto their own masters
Heb 10:25 Not forsaking the assembling of ourselves... but *e'ing* one another

EXODUS, BOOK OF.
An Old Testament book which recounts the release of the Hebrew people from Egyptian enslavement and the early years of their history as a nation. It describes God's miraculous provision for His people in the wilderness (16:1–17:7); Moses' reception of the Ten Commandments (chap. 20); and the building of the tabernacle in the wilderness (chaps. 36–40).

EXPEDIENT
John 11:50 *e*...that one man should die for the people
John 16:7 *e* for you that I [Jesus] go away
1 Cor 6:12 All things are lawful ...but all things are not *e*

EYE
Ex 21:24 *E* for *e,* tooth for tooth, hand for hand
Deut 34:7 when he [Moses] died...*e* was not dim, nor... natural force abated
Job 42:5 now mine [Job's] *e* seeth thee [God]
Ps 6:7 Mine *e* is consumed because of grief
Ps 17:8 Keep me as the apple of the *e*
Prov 28:22 He that hasteth to be rich hath an evil *e*
Matt 5:38 it hath been said...*e* for an *e*...tooth for a tooth
Matt 6:23 if thine *e* be evil, thy whole body...full of darkness
Mark 9:47 if thine *e* offend thee, pluck it out

Luke 6:41 the mote that is in thy brother's *e*

1 Cor 2:9 E hath not seen, nor ear heard

1 Cor 12:17 If the whole body were an *e*, where...hearing

1 Cor 12:21 the *e* cannot say unto the hand

1 Cor 15:52 in the twinkling of an *e*, at the last trump

Rev 1:7 he [Jesus] cometh with clouds...every *e* shall see him

EYE [S] OF THE LORD

Gen 6:8 Noah found grace in the *e's-o-t-L*

1 Kgs 15:5 David did...right in the *e's-o-t-L*

2 Chr 16:9 e's-o-t-L run to and fro throughout the...earth

Ps 33:18 the *e-o-t-L* is upon them that fear him

Prov 15:3 The *e's-o-t-L* are in every place, beholding the evil and the good

1 Pet 3:12 the *e's-o-t-L* are over the righteous

EYEWITNESSES

Luke 1:2 which...were *e*, and ministers of the word

2 Pet 1:16 we...were *e* of his [Jesus'] majesty

EZEKIAS. See *Hezekiah.*

EZEKIEL (a prophet of Judah carried into exile by the Babylonians and author of the book that bears his name). Ezek 1:3. He is not mentioned outside the Book of Ezekiel.

EZEKIEL, BOOK OF. A prophetic book of the Old Testament addressed to the Jewish captives in Babylon about 585 B.C., offering God's promise that His people would be restored to their homeland after their period of suffering and exile was over.

EZION-GABER. See *Ezion-geber.*

EZION-GEBER (a town with a harbor for King Solomon's trading ships). **1 Kgs 9:26–28; 22:48 • 2 Chr 8:17–18.** *Ezion-gaber:* Num 33:35–36 • Deut 2:8 • 2 Chr 20:36.

EZRA (a scribe and priest who led a reform movement among the Jews after the Exile and author of the book that bears his name). Ezra 7:1–25; 10:1–16 • Neh 8:1–13; 12:13–36.

EZRA, BOOK OF. A historical book of the Old Testament that describes events in Jerusalem after the Jewish captives began returning to their homeland about 500 B.C.

-F-

FABLES
1 Tim 1:4 Neither give heed to *f* and endless genealogies
1 Tim 4:7 refuse profane and old wives' *f*

FACE OF THE LORD
Ps 34:16 The *f-o-t-L* is against them that do evil
Luke 1:76 go before the *f-o-t-L* to prepare his ways
1 Pet 3:12 the *f-o-t-L* is against them that do evil

FAIR HAVENS (a harbor on the island of Crete where Paul stopped during his voyage to Rome). Acts 27:8.

FAITH
Hab 2:4 but the just shall live by his *f*
Matt 17:20 *f* as a grain of mustard seed
Acts 6:8 Stephen, full of *f* and power, did great wonders
Rom 1:17 righteousness of God revealed from *f* to *f*
Rom 3:28 justified by *f* without the deeds of the law
Rom 5:1 justified by *f*, we have peace with God
Rom 10:17 So then *f* cometh by hearing
1 Cor 13:13 abideth *f*, hope, charity, these three

Gal 2:20 I [Paul] live by the *f* of the Son of God
Gal 3:24 unto Christ, that we might be justified by *f*
Gal 5:22 fruit of the Spirit is love...goodness, *f*
Eph 2:8 by grace are ye saved through *f*
Eph 6:16 Above all, taking the shield of *f*
1 Tim 5:8 denied the *f*, and is worse than an infidel
1 Tim 6:12 Fight the good fight of *f*
2 Tim 4:7 finished my course, I [Paul] have kept the *f*
Heb 10:23 hold fast the profession of our *f*
Heb 11:1 Now *f* is the substance of things hoped for
Heb 12:2 Jesus the author and finisher of our *f*
Jas 2:17 *f*, if it hath not works, is dead, being alone
1 John 5:4 victory that overcometh the world, even our *f*
Jude 3 contend for the *f*... delivered unto the saints

FAITH CHAPTER OF THE BIBLE. Heb 11.

FAITHFUL [NESS]
Ps 31:23 for the LORD preserveth the *f*
Ps 119:90 Thy [God's] *f'ness* is unto all generations
Prov 27:6 *F* are the wounds of a friend

Lam 3:23 new every morning: great is thy [God's] *f'ness*

Matt 25:21 Well done, thou good and *f* servant

Luke 16:10 *f* in that which is least is *f* also in much

1 Cor 4:2 required in stewards, that a man be found *f*

1 Cor 10:13 God is *f,* who will not suffer you to be tempted

2 Thes 3:3 the Lord is *f,* who shall stablish you

1 John 1:9 he [Jesus] is *f* and just to forgive us our sins

Rev 2:10 be thou *f* unto death

FAITHLESS

Luke 9:41 O *f* and perverse generation

John 20:27 Thomas...be not *f*

FALL [EN, ETH, ING]

Ps 116:8 thou [God] hast delivered...my feet from *f'ing*

Ps 145:14 The LORD upholdeth all that *f*

Prov 16:18 Pride goeth before destruction...haughty spirit before a *f*

Eccl 4:10 woe to him that is alone when he *f'eth*

Dan 3:6 whoso *f'eth* not down and worshippeth shall...be cast into the...furnace

Hos 14:1 thou [Israel] hast *f'en* by thine iniquity

Luke 2:34 this child [Jesus] is set for the *f*...of many

Luke 6:39 shall they not both *f* into the ditch

John 12:24 corn of wheat *f* into the ground and die

1 Cor 10:12 thinketh he standeth take heed lest he *f*

Heb 10:31 It is a fearful thing to *f* into the hands of the living God

Jas 1:2 joy when ye *f* into divers temptations

Jude 24 Now unto him [Jesus] that is able to keep you from *f'ing*

Rev 14:8 Babylon is *f'en,* is *f'en,* that great city

FALL OF MAN. Gen 3:1–24.

FALSE [LY]

Ex 20:16 shalt not bear *f* witness against thy neighbour

Lev 19:11 Ye shall not steal, neither deal *f'ly*

Prov 11:1 A *f* balance is abomination to the LORD

Jer 29:9 prophesy *f'ly* unto you in my [God's] name

Matt 5:11 say all manner of evil against you *f'ly,* for my [Jesus'] sake

FALSE PROPHET [S]

Matt 7:15 Beware of *f-p's*...in sheep's clothing

Matt 24:11 many *f-p's* shall rise, and shall deceive many

Mark 13:22 *f-p's* shall rise... show signs and wonders

Acts 13:6 a *f-p,* a Jew, whose name was Bar-jesus

2 Pet 2:1 there were **f-p's** also among the people

1 John 4:1 many **f-p's** are gone out into the world

Rev 19:20 the beast was taken, and with him the **f-p**

FALSE WITNESS [ES]

Deut 5:20 Neither shalt...bear **f-w** against thy neighbour

Ps 35:11 **F-w'es**...laid to my charge things that I knew not

Prov 6:19 A **f-w** that speaketh lies

Prov 14:5 a **f-w** will utter lies

Mark 14:56 many bare **f-w** against him [Jesus]

FAST [ING]

Ps 109:24 knees are weak through **f'ing**

Matt 17:21 this kind goeth not out but by prayer and **f'ing**

Mark 2:20 bridegroom [Jesus] shall be taken away...then shall they **f**

1 Cor 16:13 Watch ye, stand **f** in the faith

Gal 5:1 Stand **f**...wherewith Christ hath made us free

1 Thes 5:21 Prove all things; hold **f** that which is good

Heb 10:23 hold **f** the profession of our faith

FATHER

Gen 2:24 shall a man leave his **f** and his mother

Gen 17:5 a **f** of many nations have I [God] made thee [Abraham]

Ex 20:12 Honour thy **f** and thy mother

Lev 20:9 one that curseth his **f**...shall be surely put to death

Ps 27:10 When my **f**...forsake me...LORD will take me up

Ps 103:13 Like as a **f** pitieth his children

Prov 4:1 Hear...the instruction of a **f**

Prov 15:20 A wise son maketh a glad **f**

Isa 9:6 his [Jesus'] name shall be...The everlasting **F**

Isa 64:8 LORD, thou art our **f**; we are the clay

Ezek 18:20 neither shall the **f** bear the iniquity of the son

Mal 2:10 Have we not all one **f**

Matt 5:48 even as your **F**...in heaven is perfect

Matt 6:9 Our **F**...in heaven

Matt 10:37 loveth **f** or mother more than me [Jesus] is not worthy of me

Matt 23:9 one is your **F,** which is in heaven

Matt 28:19 baptizing them in the name of the **F**

Mark 14:36 Abba, **F,** all things are possible unto thee

Luke 9:59 suffer me first to go and bury my **f**

Luke 15:22 the **f** said to his servants, Bring...the best robe

*Luke 23:34 **F,*** forgive them...
they know not what they do

Luke 24:49 I [Jesus] send the
promise of my ***F***

John 6:44 No man can come to
me [Jesus], except the ***F***
which...sent me draw him

John 10:30 I [Jesus] and my ***F***
are one

John 14:6 no man cometh unto
the ***F,*** but by me [Jesus]

John 14:16 I [Jesus] will pray
the ***F,*** and he shall give you
another Comforter

John 15:8 Herein is my [Jesus']
F glorified...bear much fruit

John 16:23 ask the ***F*** in my
[Jesus'] name, he will give it

John 20:21 my ***F*** hath sent me
[Jesus], even so send I you

Acts 1:7 not for you to know
the...seasons, which the ***F***
hath put in his own power

Eph 4:6 One God and ***F*** of all

Phil 2:11 confess that Jesus
Christ is Lord, to the glory
of God the ***F***

Col 1:19 For it pleased the ***F***
that in him [Jesus] should
all fulness dwell

Jas 1:17 good gift...cometh
down from the ***F*** of lights

Jas 2:21 Abraham our ***f*** justified by works

1 John 1:3 our fellowship is
with the ***F,*** and with his Son

1 John 2:1 we have an advocate
with the ***F,*** Jesus Christ

1 John 3:1 manner of love the
F hath bestowed upon us

FAULT [LESS, S]

Luke 23:4 I [Pilate] find no ***f*** in
this man [Jesus]

Gal 6:1 Brethren, if a man be
overtaken in a ***f***

Jas 5:16 Confess your ***f's*** one
to another

Jude 24 present you ***f'less***
before...presence of his
[Jesus'] glory

Rev 14:5 without ***f*** before the
throne of God

FEAR [ED, EST, ETH]

Gen 22:12 I [God] know that
thou [Abraham] ***f'est*** God

Deut 6:13 ***f*** the LORD thy God,
and serve him

Josh 4:14 ***f'ed*** him [Joshua], as
they ***f'ed*** Moses

1 Chr 16:25 he [God] also is to
be ***f'ed*** above all gods

Job 1:1 Job...was perfect...
and one that ***f'ed*** God

Job 1:9 Satan answered...Doth
Job ***f*** God for nought

Job 28:28 Behold, the ***f*** of the
Lord, that is wisdom

Ps 19:9 ***f*** of the LORD is clean,
enduring for ever

Ps 23:4 ***f*** no evil: for thou [God]
art with me

Ps 27:1 The LORD is my...salva-
tion; whom shall I ***f***

Ps 34:11 I will teach you the ***f***
of the LORD

Ps 46:2 will not we ***f,*** though
the earth be removed

Ps 103:13 the LORD pitieth
them that ***f*** him

Ps 111:10 *f* of the LORD is the beginning of wisdom

Ps 112:1 Blessed is the man that *f'eth* the LORD

Ps 118:6 I will not *f:* what can man do unto me

Prov 15:16 Better is little with the *f* of the LORD than great treasure and trouble

Eccl 12:13 *F* God, and keep his commandments

Mal 4:2 that *f* my name shall... Sun of righteousness arise

Matt 28:8 they [the women] departed quickly from the sepulchre with *f*

Mark 4:41 *f'ed* exceedingly... What manner of man is this

Luke 22:2 they [chief priests and scribes] *f'ed* the people

Acts 2:43 And *f* came upon every soul

Phil 2:12 work out your own salvation with *f*

2 Tim 1:7 God hath not given us the spirit of *f*

Heb 13:6 I will not *f* what man shall do unto me

1 John 4:18 perfect love casteth out *f*

Rev 15:4 Who shall not *f* thee, O Lord...glorify thy name

FEAR NOT

Gen 15:1 *F-n,* Abram: I [God] am thy shield

Gen 21:17 What aileth thee, Hagar? *f-n*

Dan 10:12 *F-n,* Daniel...thy words were heard

Joel 2:21 *F-n,* O land; be glad and rejoice

Matt 1:20 Joseph...*f-n* to take unto thee Mary

Matt 28:5 *F-n* ye [women at the tomb]: for I know that ye seek Jesus

Luke 1:13 *F-n,* Zacharias: for thy prayer is heard

Luke 1:30 *F-n,* Mary: for thou hast found favour with God

Luke 2:10 *F-n*...I [angel] bring you [shepherds] good tidings of great joy

Luke 12:32 *F-n*...it is your Father's good pleasure to give you the kingdom

Acts 27:24 Saying, *F-n,* Paul; thou must be brought before Caesar

Rev 1:17 *F-n;* I [Jesus] am the first and the last

FEARFUL [LY, NESS]

Ps 55:5 *F'ness* and trembling are come upon me

Ps 139:14 I am *f'ly* and wonderfully made

Matt 8:26 Why are ye *f,* O ye of little faith

Heb 10:31 a *f* thing to fall into the hands of the living God

FEAST OF HARVEST OR INGATHERING. See *Pentecost.*

FEAST OF WEEKS. See *Pentecost.*

485

FELIX (governor of Judea who heard Paul's defense at Caesarea). Acts 23:24–26; **24:3, 10–27;** 25:14.

FELLOWSHIP
Acts 2:42 continued stedfastly in the apostles' doctrine and *f*
2 Cor 6:14 what *f* hath righteousness...unrighteousness
Eph 5:11 have no *f* with the unfruitful works of darkness
Phil 3:10 That I [Paul] may know him [Jesus]...and the *f* of his sufferings
1 John 1:7 we have *f* one with another

FESTUS (successor of Felix as Roman governor of Judea before whom Paul made his defense). Acts 24:27; **25:1–24; 26:24–32.**

FIERY SERPENTS IN THE WILDERNESS. Num 21:4–9.

FILTHY
Ps 14:3 they are all together become *f*
Isa 64:6 all our righteousnesses are as *f* rags
1 Tim 3:8 must the deacons be grave...not greedy of *f* lucre

FINGER OF GOD
Ex 8:19 the magicians said... This is the *f-o-G*

Ex 31:18 gave unto Moses... two...tables of stone, written with the *f-o-G*
Luke 11:20 if I [Jesus] with the *f-o-G* cast out devils

FINISH [ED]
Gen 2:1 heavens and the earth were *f'ed*
Neh 6:15 wall was *f'ed* in the twenty and fifth day
Luke 14:28 counteth the cost, whether...sufficient to *f* it
John 4:34 My [Jesus'] meat is to...*f* his [God's] work
John 17:4 *f'ed* the work which thou [God] gavest me [Jesus]
John 19:30 It is *f'ed:* and he [Jesus]...gave up the ghost
2 Tim 4:7 I [Paul] have *f'ed* my course...kept the faith

FIRE AND BRIMSTONE
Ps 11:6 Upon the wicked he [God] shall rain snares, *f-a-b*
Luke 17:29 the same day that Lot went out of Sodom it rained *f-a-b*
Rev 14:10 he [worshiper of beast] shall be tormented with *f-a-b*

FIRSTFRUITS
Ex 23:19 first of the *f*...bring into...house of...God
Prov 3:9 Honour the LORD... with the *f* of...thine increase
1 Cor 15:20 now is Christ risen...*f* of them that slept

FLESH AND BLOOD

Matt 16:17 f-a-b hath not revealed it unto thee [Peter]

1 Cor 15:50 f-a-b cannot inherit the kingdom of God

Eph 6:12 wrestle not against *f-a-b,* but...principalities

FOOLISH [LY, NESS]

Ps 5:5 The *f* shall not stand in thy [God's] sight

Ps 69:5 O God, thou knowest my *f'ness*

Prov 10:1 a *f* son is the heaviness of his mother

Prov 12:23 the heart of fools proclaimeth *f'ness*

Prov 14:17 He that is soon angry dealeth *f'ly*

Prov 15:20 a *f* man despiseth his mother

Eccl 4:13 Better is...a wise child than an old and *f* king

Matt 7:26 likened unto a *f* man, which built his house upon the sand

Matt 25:3 They that were *f*... took no oil with them

1 Cor 1:23 Christ crucified... unto the Greeks *f'ness*

1 Cor 1:27 chosen the *f* things... to confound the wise

1 Cor 3:19 wisdom of this world is *f'ness* with God

Gal 3:1 f Galatians, who hath bewitched you

Titus 3:9 avoid *f* questions, and genealogies

FORGIVE [ING, TH]

Num 14:18 The LORD is long-suffering...*f'ing* iniquity

2 Chr 7:14 then will I [God] hear...and will *f* their sin

Ps 86:5 thou, Lord, art good, and ready to *f*

Ps 103:3 Who [God] *f'th* all thine iniquities

Matt 6:14 your heavenly Father will also *f* you

Matt 18:21 how oft shall my brother sin...and I [Peter] *f*

Mark 11:26 neither will your Father...*f* your trespasses

Luke 5:21 Who can *f* sins, but God alone

Luke 6:37 f, and ye shall be forgiven

Luke 23:34 f them; for they know not what they do

Eph 4:32 be ye kind...*f'ing* one another

1 John 1:9 he [Jesus] is faithful and just to *f* us our sins

FORGIVEN

Ps 32:1 Blessed is he whose transgression is *f*

Matt 12:31 blasphemy against the Holy Ghost shall not be *f*

Luke 6:37 forgive, and ye shall be *f*

Rom 4:7 Blessed are they whose iniquities are *f*

1 John 2:12 your sins are *f* you for his [Jesus'] name's sake

FORGIVENESS

Acts 26:18 that they may receive *f* of sins

Col 1:14 In [Jesus] we have redemption...the *f* of sins

FORNICATION

Matt 19:9 put away his wife, except it be for *f*

1 Cor 5:1 reported...that there is *f* among you

1 Cor 6:18 committeth *f* sinneth against his own body

Gal 5:19 Now the works of the flesh are...Adultery, *f*

1 Thes 4:3 this is the will of God...abstain from *f*

Rev 17:4 a golden cup in her [woman on scarlet beast] hand full...of her *f*

FOUNDATION [S]

Job 38:4 Where wast thou [Job] when I [God] laid the *f's* of the earth

Isa 28:16 I [God] lay in Zion for a *f* a stone

Matt 25:34 inherit the kingdom prepared for you from the *f* of the world

1 Cor 3:11 other *f* can no man lay than...Jesus Christ

Eph 2:20 built upon the *f* of the apostles

Heb 1:10 Thou, Lord...hast laid the *f* of the earth

Heb 11:10 city which hath *f's*...builder and maker is God

Rev 21:14 And the wall of the city had twelve *f's*

FREE [LY]

Gen 2:16 every tree of the garden thou mayest *f'ly* eat

Ps 51:12 uphold me with thy [God's] *f* spirit

Matt 10:8 *f'ly* ye have received, *f'ly* give

John 8:32 and the truth shall make you *f*

Rom 3:24 justified *f'ly* by his [God's] grace through... Christ Jesus

Rom 6:18 *f* from sin, ye became the servants of righteousness

Rom 8:2 Jesus hath made me *f* from the law of sin

1 Cor 9:19 though I [Paul] be *f* from all men

Gal 3:28 there is neither bond nor *f*

Gal 5:1 in the liberty wherewith Christ hath made us *f*

Col 3:11 neither Greek nor Jew...bond nor *f*

Rev 22:17 let him take the water of life *f'ly*

FRUIT OF THE SPIRIT. Gal 5:22–26.

-G-

GAASH, MOUNT (a mountain where Joshua was buried). **Josh 24:29–30** • Judg 2:9 • 2 Sam 23:30 • 1 Chr 11:32.

GABRIEL (an archangel who appeared to Daniel, Zacharias, and the Virgin Mary). Dan 8:16; 9:21 • Luke 1:19,26.

GAD (a son of Jacob and ancestor of one of the twelve tribes of Israel). Gen 30:11; 35:26; 46:16; 49:19 • Ex 1:4 • 1 Chr 5:11. The tribe of Gad settled east of the Jordan River. **Num 32:1–33** • Josh 13:24,28; 22:9–34.

GADARENES (people from the area of Gadara in Perea where Jesus healed a demon-possessed man). Mark 5:1–20 • Luke 8:26,37. *Gergesenes:* Matt 8:28.

GAIN [ED]
Matt 18:15 if he shall hear thee...hast **g'ed** thy brother
Mark 8:36 profit a man, if he shall **g** the whole world
Luke 19:16 thy pound hath **g'ed** ten pounds
1 Cor 9:20 I [Paul] became as a Jew, that I might **g** the Jews
Phil 1:21 to me [Paul] to live is Christ, and to die is **g**

1 Tim 6:6 godliness with contentment is great **g**

GALATIA (a territory of central Asia Minor visited by Paul during the first missionary journey). **Acts 16:6; 18:23** • 1 Cor 16:1 • Gal 1:2 • 2 Tim 4:10 • 1 Pet 1:1.

GALATIANS, EPISTLE TO THE. A short epistle of the apostle Paul to the churches at Galatia on the themes of Christian liberty and justification by faith alone.

GALILEE (a Roman province in northern Palestine where Jesus spent most of His earthly ministry). Mark 1:9–28; 3:7 • Luke 23:6–55 • John 4:3–54.

GALILEE, SEA OF. A freshwater lake in northern Palestine associated with the ministry of Jesus. Mark 1:16–20; 4:35–41; 7:31. *Lake of Gennesaret:* Luke 5:1. *Sea of Chinneroth:* Josh 12:3. *Sea of Tiberias:* John 21:1.

GALLIO (a Roman ruler of Achaia who refused to get involved in the dispute between Paul and the Jewish leaders in Corinth). Acts 18:12–17.

GAMALIEL (a teacher of the law under whom Paul studied). Acts 5:33–39; **22:3.**

GARDEN OF EDEN. Gen 2:8–3:24.

GASHMU (a Samaritan leader who opposed the rebuilding of Jerusalem's walls under Nehemiah). Neh 6:6.

GATH (a major Philistine city captured by David). Josh 11:22 • 1 Sam 5:8; 6:17; 17:4; 21:10–15; 27:3–12 • 2 Kgs 12:17 • **1 Chr 18:1** • 2 Chr 11:5–8 • Amos 6:1–3 • Mic 1:10.

GAZA (a major Philistine city where Samson was killed). Josh 10:41; 11:22; 15:47 • **Judg 16:21–30** • Amos 1:6–7 • Acts 8:26. *Azzah:* Jer 25:20.

GAZER. See *Gezer.*

GEDALIAH (a friend and supporter of the prophet Jeremiah). 2 Kgs 25:22–25 • Jer 39:14; **40:5–16;** 41:1–18; 43:6.

GEDEON. See *Gideon.*

GEHAZI (Elisha's servant who was struck with leprosy because of his greed). 2 Kgs 4:12–36; **5:20–27;** 8:4–6.

GENEALOGIES OF JESUS. See *Jesus, Life and Ministry of.*

GENERATION [S]

Gen 2:4 the **g's** of the heavens and of the earth

Num 32:13 all the **g,** that had done evil...was consumed

Ps 24:6 This is the **g** of them that seek him [God]

Ps 33:11 thoughts of his [God's] heart to all **g's**

Ps 71:18 I have showed thy [God's] strength unto this **g**

Ps 85:5 draw out thine [God's] anger to all **g's**

Ps 90:1 thou [God] hast been our dwelling place in all **g's**

Ps 100:5 his [God's] truth endureth to all **g's**

Prov 27:24 doth the crown endure to every **g**

Eccl 1:4 One **g** passeth away, and another **g** cometh

Dan 4:3 and his [God's] dominion is from **g** to **g**

Matt 24:34 **g** shall not pass, till...these things be fulfilled

Luke 3:7 **g** of vipers, who hath warned you

Luke 16:8 in their **g** wiser than the children of light

Col 1:26 mystery...hath been hid from ages and from **g's**

1 Pet 2:9 But ye are a chosen **g,** a royal priesthood

GENESIS, BOOK OF. The first book of the Old Testament

that describes the creation of the universe and recounts the early history of the people of Israel, including the patriarchs Abraham, Isaac, Jacob, and Joseph.

GENNESARET, LAKE OF. See *Galilee, Sea of.*

GENTILE [S]
Isa 42:6 a covenant of the people, for a light of the *G's*
Isa 60:3 *G's* shall come to thy [God's] light
Jer 16:19 *G's* shall come unto thee [God] from the ends of the earth
Mal 1:11 my [God's] name shall be great among the *G's*
Matt 12:18 Behold my [God's] servant...he shall show judgment to the *G's*
Mark 10:42 to rule over the *G's* exercise lordship
Luke 2:32 A light to lighten the *G's*...glory of...Israel
Acts 9:15 for he [Paul] is a chosen vessel...to bear my [God's] name before the *G's*
Acts 13:46 we [Paul and Barnabas] turn to the *G's*
Acts 14:27 he [God]...opened the door of faith unto the *G's*
Acts 18:6 from henceforth I [Paul] will go unto the *G's*
Rom 2:9 of the Jew first, and also of the *G*
Rom 3:29 God of the Jews only...not also of the *G's*

1 Cor 12:13 baptized into one body, whether...Jews or *G's*
Eph 3:6 *G's* should be...partakers of his [God's] promise

GERGESENES. See *Gadarenes.*

GERIZIM, MOUNT (a mountain considered a sacred worship place by the Samaritans). Deut 11:29; 27:12 • Josh 8:33 • Judg 9:7 • **John 4:5,20–21.**

GESHEM (an Arabian who opposed the rebuilding of Jerusalem's walls under Nehemiah). Neh 2:19; 6:1–2.

GETHSEMANE (a garden outside Jerusalem where Jesus agonized in prayer on the night before He was arrested). Matt 26:30–56 • Mark 14:32.

GEZER (a major Canaanite city captured by Joshua and settled by the Levites). **Josh 10:33;** 12:12; 16:3,10; **21:21** • Judg 1:29 • 1 Kgs 9:15–17 • 1 Chr 6:67; 7:28; 20:4. *Gazer:* 2 Sam 5:25 • 1 Chr 14:16.

GIBEAH (hometown and capital city of King Saul). **1 Sam 10:26; 15:34** • Judg 19:12–16; 20:4–43 • Hos 9:9; 10:9. *Gibeath:* Josh 18:28.

491

GIBEON (a Canaanite city whose inhabitants surrendered to avoid destruction by Joshua). **Josh 9:3–21;** 10:1–41 • 2 Sam 21:1–9.

GIDEON (a judge of Israel who defeated the Midianite army with a force of only three hundred warriors). Judg 6–8. *Gedeon:* Heb 11:32. *Jerubbaal:* Judg 6:25–32.

GIFT [S]
2 Chr 19:7 there is no iniquity... nor respect of persons, nor taking of *g's*
Prov 19:6 every man is a friend to him that giveth *g's*
Matt 2:11 they [wise men] presented...him [Jesus] *g's*
Matt 5:24 reconciled to thy brother, and then come and offer thy *g*
Luke 11:13 If ye then, being evil, know how to give good *g's* unto your children
John 4:10 If thou knewest the *g* of God
Rom 1:11 I [Paul] may impart unto you some spiritual *g*
Rom 12:6 *g's* differing according to the grace that is given to us
1 Cor 12:4 diversities of *g's,* but the same Spirit
1 Cor 12:31 But covet earnestly the best *g's*
1 Cor 13:2 though I [Paul] have the *g* of prophecy

2 Cor 9:15 Thanks be unto God for his unspeakable *g*
1 Tim 4:14 Neglect not the *g* that is in thee
Jas 1:17 Every good *g* and every perfect *g* is from above

GIFT OF GOD
Eccl 3:13 enjoy the good of all his labour, it is the *g-o-G*
Acts 8:20 thou [Simon the magician]...thought...the *g-o-G* may be purchased
Rom 6:23 *g-o-G* is eternal life through Jesus Christ
Eph 2:8 saved through faith... not of yourselves: it is the *g-o-G*
2 Tim 1:6 stir up the *g-o-G*

GIHON
1. One of the four rivers of the Garden of Eden, associated with Ethiopia. Gen 2:13.
2. A place near Jerusalem where Solomon was proclaimed king. 1 Kgs 1:33–45.

GILBOA, MOUNT (a mountain range where King Saul died). 1 Sam 31:1–8 • 2 Sam 1:6,21 • **1 Chr 10:1–8.**

GILEAD
1. A fertile, flat tableland east of the Jordan River settled by the tribes of Gad, Reuben, and Manasseh. **Deut 3:12–17** • 2 Sam 17:26 • 1 Kgs 17:1.

2. A hill where Gideon divided his army for battle against the Midianites. Judg 7:1–7.

GILGAL (a memorial site near the city of Jericho). **Josh 4:19–24;** 10:1–43 • 1 Sam 13:4–15 • Amos 4:4–5.

GIRGASHITES. See *Girgasites.*

GIRGASITES (an ancient tribe which inhabited Canaan). Gen 10:15–16. *Girgashites:* Deut 7:1.

GIVE [TH]
Gen 12:7 Unto thy [Abraham's] seed will I [God] *g* this land
Ex 20:12 that thy days may be long upon the land which the LORD...*g'th* thee
Num 6:26 The LORD lift up his countenance...*g* thee peace
Deut 16:17 Every man shall *g* as he is able
Josh 21:43 the LORD gave...all the land which he sware to *g* unto their fathers
1 Kgs 3:9 *G* therefore thy servant [Solomon] an understanding heart
1 Chr 16:34 *g* thanks unto the LORD; for he is good
Ps 5:1 *G* ear to my words, O LORD...my meditation
Ps 29:2 *G* unto the LORD the glory due unto his name

Ps 29:11 LORD will *g* strength unto his people
Ps 37:4 he [God] shall *g* thee the desires of thine heart
Ps 85:12 LORD shall *g* that which is good
Ps 91:11 he [God] shall *g* his angels charge over thee
Ps 107:1 *g* thanks unto the LORD, for he is good
Ps 119:125 I am thy [God's] servant; *g* me understanding
Ps 119:130 The entrance of thy [God's] words *g'th* light
Prov 2:6 For the LORD *g'th* wisdom
Prov 22:9 he *g'th* of his bread to the poor
Prov 25:21 If thine enemy be hungry, *g* him bread
Isa 7:14 the Lord...shall *g* you a sign...a virgin shall conceive...bear a son
Isa 49:6 I [God] will also *g* thee for a light to the Gentiles
Mic 6:7 shall I *g* my firstborn for my transgression
Matt 5:15 a candle...*g'th* light unto all...in the house
Matt 6:11 *G* us this day our daily bread
Matt 10:8 freely ye have received, freely *g*
Matt 11:28 Come unto me [Jesus]...I will *g* you rest
Matt 16:19 *g* unto thee the keys of the kingdom
Matt 20:28 Even as the Son of man came...to *g* his life a ransom for many

Mark 8:37 what shall a man *g* in exchange for his soul

Mark 10:40 sit on my [Jesus'] right hand...is not mine to *g*

Luke 12:32 for it is your Father's good pleasure to *g* you the kingdom

Luke 15:12 g me the portion of goods that falleth to me

Luke 20:22 Is it lawful for us to *g* tribute unto Caesar

John 4:14 water that I [Jesus] shall *g* him shall never thirst

John 10:11 good shepherd *g'th* his life for the sheep

John 13:34 new commandment I [Jesus] *g* unto you

John 14:16 and he [God] shall *g* you another Comforter

John 16:23 Whatsoever ye shall ask...in my [Jesus'] name, he [God] will *g* it you

Acts 6:4 g ourselves continually to prayer

Rom 14:12 every one...shall *g* account...to God

1 Cor 3:7 neither he that watereth; but God that *g'th* the increase

1 Cor 13:3 though I [Paul] *g* my body to be burned

1 Cor 15:57 thanks be to God, which *g'th* us the victory

2 Cor 3:6 the spirit *g'th* life

2 Cor 9:7 let him *g;* not grudgingly, or of necessity

1 Thes 5:18 In every thing *g* thanks...this is...will of God

Jas 4:6 God...*g'th* grace unto the humble

1 Pet 3:15 be ready always to *g* an answer

Rev 2:10 and I [Jesus] will *g* thee a crown of life

GIVING, PRINCIPLES OF.
2 Cor 8:1–24; 9:6–8.

GLAD [LY, NESS]

1 Chr 16:31 heavens be *g,* and let the earth rejoice

Ps 9:2 I will be *g* and rejoice in thee [God]

Ps 30:11 Thou [God] hast... girded me with *g'ness*

Ps 46:4 the streams...make *g* the city of God

Ps 68:3 let the righteous be *g*

Ps 100:2 Serve the LORD with *g'ness*

Ps 118:24 the day...the LORD hath made...rejoice and be *g* in it

Ps 122:1 g when they said unto me, Let us go into the house of the LORD

Prov 15:20 A wise son maketh a *g* father

Joel 2:21 be *g* and rejoice: for the LORD will do great things

Matt 5:12 be exceeding *g:* for great is your reward

Mark 12:37 common people heard him [Jesus] *g'ly*

Luke 15:32 meet that we should make merry, and be *g*

John 20:20 were the disciples *g,* when they saw the Lord

Acts 13:48 when the Gentiles heard this, they were *g*

Rom 10:15 beautiful are the feet...that...bring *g* tidings

2 Cor 12:15 I [Paul] will very *g'ly* spend and be spent

GLORIFY [IED, ING]

Ps 86:12 g thy [God's] name for evermore

Isa 49:3 art my [God's] servant...in whom I will be *g'ied*

Matt 5:16 see your good works, and *g* your Father

Matt 9:8 multitudes...marvelled, and *g'ied* God

Luke 2:20 shepherds returned, *g'ing* and praising God

Luke 7:16 came a fear on all: and they [crowd] *g'ied* God

Luke 23:47 centurion saw what was done, he *g'ied* God

John 12:23 hour is come...Son of man should be *g'ied*

John 14:13 that the Father may be *g'ied* in the Son

John 17:1 that thy Son also may *g* thee [God]

John 17:4 I [Jesus] have *g'ied* thee [God] on the earth

Rom 8:30 whom he [Jesus] justified, them he also *g'ied*

Rom 15:6 may with one mind and one mouth *g* God

1 Cor 6:20 g God in your body

2 Thes 1:12 name of our Lord... may be *g'ied* in you

1 Pet 4:16 but let him *g* God on this behalf

GLORY

1 Sam 4:21 named the child Ichabod...The *g* is departed

1 Chr 16:24 Declare his [God's] *g* among the heathen

1 Chr 29:11 Thine, O LORD, is the greatness...and the *g*

Ps 24:7 and the King of *g* shall come in

Ps 29:2 Give unto the LORD the *g* due unto his name

Ps 57:5 let thy [God's] *g* be above all the earth

Ps 72:19 let the whole earth be filled with his [God's] *g*

Ps 84:11 the LORD will give grace and *g*

Ps 96:3 Declare his [God's] *g* among the heathen

Ps 113:4 LORD is high above all nations, and his *g* above the heavens

Prov 17:6 the *g* of children are their fathers

Isa 6:3 the whole earth is full of his [God's] *g*

Isa 66:18 all nations and tongues...shall come, and see my [God's] *g*

Jer 13:16 Give *g* to the LORD your God

Hag 2:9 g of this latter house shall be greater

Matt 6:13 kingdom, and the power, and the *g*

Matt 6:29 Solomon in all his *g* was not arrayed

Mark 10:37 sit, one on thy [Jesus'] right hand...in thy *g*

Luke 21:27 the Son of man coming in a cloud with power and great *g*

John 1:14 we beheld his [Jesus'] *g*...full of grace

Rom 5:3 we *g* in tribulations

Rom 8:18 sufferings...are not worthy to be compared with the *g*...revealed

2 Cor 10:17 he that glorieth, let him *g* in the Lord

Gal 5:26 Let us not be desirous of vain *g*

Gal 6:14 forbid that I [Paul] should *g,* save in the cross

1 Tim 1:17 unto the King eternal...be...*g* for ever

Heb 2:7 thou [God] crownedst him [Jesus]with *g*...honour

1 Pet 4:13 when his [Jesus'] *g* shall be revealed

1 Pet 5:4 ye shall receive a crown of *g* that fadeth not

Rev 4:11 Thou art worthy, O Lord, to receive *g*

GLORY OF GOD

Ps 19:1 The heavens declare the *g-o-G*

John 11:4 sickness is not unto death, but for the *g-o-G*

Rom 3:23 all have sinned... come short of the *g-o-G*

1 Cor 10:31 whatsoever ye do, do all to the *g-o-G*

Phil 2:11 Jesus Christ is Lord, to the *g-o-G* the Father

GLORY OF THE LORD

Ex 24:16 the *g-o-t-L* abode upon mount Sinai

Ps 104:31 The *g-o-t-L* shall endure for ever

Isa 40:5 the *g-o-t-L* shall be revealed...all flesh...see it

Isa 60:1 the *g-o-t-L* is risen upon thee

Ezek 11:23 the *g-o-t-L* went up from the midst of the city

Hab 2:14 knowledge of the *g-o-t-L*, as the waters cover the sea

Luke 2:9 *g-o-t-L* shone round about them [shepherds]

GNASHING OF TEETH

Matt 8:12 there shall be weeping and *g-o-t*

Matt 22:13 cast him into outer darkness; there shall be weeping and *g-o-t*

Luke 13:28 weeping and *g-o-t,* when ye shall see...yourselves thrust out

GODLY [INESS]

2 Cor 7:10 *g* sorrow worketh repentance

1 Tim 4:8 *g'iness* is profitable unto all things

1 Tim 6:6 *g'iness* with contentment is great gain

2 Tim 3:5 a form of *g'iness,* but denying the power

2 Tim 3:12 all that will live *g* in Christ Jesus shall suffer persecution

Titus 2:12 live soberly, righteously, and *g*

GOG, PRINCE OF MAGOG (a tribal leader condemned by the prophet Ezekiel and a representative of the forces of evil which oppose God and His people). Ezek 38:2–18; 39:1–11 • Rev 20:8–15.

GOLAN (one of the six cities of refuge). Deut 4:43 • **Josh 20:8–9; 21:27.**

GOLGOTHA. See *Calvary.*

GOLIATH (a Philistine giant killed by David). **1 Sam 17:4–54;** 21:9; 22:10 • 2 Sam 21:19 • 1 Chr 20:5.

GOMER (unfaithful wife of the prophet Hosea). Hos 1:1–11; 3:1–5.

GOMORRAH (a city destroyed by God because of its wickedness). **Gen 19:23–29.** Referred to as an example of God's punishment in Deut 29:23; 32:32 • Isa 1:9–10; 13:19 • Jer 23:14; 49:18; 50:40 • Amos 4:11 • Zeph 2:9. *Gomorrha:* Matt 10:15 • 2 Pet 2:6.

GOOD SHEPHERD, JESUS AS. See *"I Am" Statements of Jesus.*

GOOD WORKS
Matt 5:16 see your *g-w,* and glorify your Father
Acts 9:36 Dorcas...was full of *g-w* and almsdeeds
Eph 2:10 we are his [God's] workmanship...unto *g-w*
2 Tim 3:17 man of God may be...furnished unto all *g-w*

GOODNESS
Ps 23:6 Surely *g* and mercy shall follow me
Ps 33:5 the earth is full of the *g* of the LORD
Ps 107:8 that men would praise the LORD for his *g*
Prov 20:6 Most men will proclaim every one his own *g*
Gal 5:22 fruit of the Spirit is... gentleness, *g,* faith

GOSHEN (an Egyptian district where the Israelites lived). Gen 45:10; 46:28–29,34; 47:1–27; 50:8 • Ex 8:22; 9:26.

GOSPEL
Matt 24:14 *g* of the kingdom... preached in all the world
Mark 16:15 preach the *g* to every creature
Luke 4:18 he [God] hath anointed me [Jesus] to preach the *g* to the poor
Rom 1:16 I [Paul] am not ashamed of the *g* of Christ
Rom 10:15 beautiful are the feet...preach the *g* of peace

1 Cor 9:14 they which preach the *g* should live of the *g*

Gal 1:7 some that...would pervert the *g* of Christ

Gal 4:13 I [Paul] preached the *g* unto you at the first

Eph 6:15 feet shod with the preparation of the *g* of peace

Phil 1:12 things...have fallen out rather unto the furtherance of the *g*

Phil 1:27 conversation be as it becometh the *g* of Christ

2 Tim 1:8 partaker of the afflictions of the *g*

2 Tim 2:8 Jesus...raised from the dead according to my [Paul's] *g*

1 Pet 4:17 end be of them that obey not the *g* of God

GOZAN (a place to which the people of the Northern Kingdom were deported after their defeat by the Assyrians). 2 Kgs 18:11.

GRACE

Gen 6:8 Noah found *g* in the eyes of the LORD

Ps 84:11 the LORD will give *g* and glory

John 1:14 beheld his [Jesus'] glory...full of *g* and truth

John 1:17 *g* and truth came by Jesus Christ

Rom 3:24 justified freely by his [God's] *g*

Rom 5:20 sin abounded, *g* did much more abound

Rom 6:1 Shall we continue in sin, that *g* may abound

2 Cor 8:9 ye know the *g* of our Lord Jesus Christ

2 Cor 9:8 God is able to make all *g* abound

2 Cor 12:9 My [God's] *g* is sufficient for thee

Eph 1:7 forgiveness of sins, according to the riches of his [Jesus'] *g*

Eph 2:8 by *g* are ye saved through faith

Eph 4:7 *g* according to the measure of the gift of Christ

Col 4:6 speech be alway with *g,* seasoned with salt

1 Tim 1:14 *g* of our Lord was exceeding abundant

Titus 3:7 being justified by his [Jesus'] *g,* we should be made heirs...of eternal life

Heb 4:16 Let us...come boldly unto the throne of *g*

Jas 4:6 God...giveth *g* unto the humble

2 Pet 3:18 grow in *g,* and in the knowledge of...Jesus

Rev 22:21 *g* of our Lord Jesus Christ be with you all

GRACE OF GOD

Luke 2:40 child [Jesus] grew... *g-o-G* was upon him

1 Cor 15:10 by the *g-o-G* I [Paul] am what I am

Eph 3:7 I [Paul] was made a minister, according to the gift of the *g-o-G*

Titus 2:11 the **g-o-G** that bringeth salvation

Heb 2:9 that he [Jesus] by the **g-o-G** should taste death for every man

1 Pet 4:10 as good stewards of the manifold **g-o-G**

GRACIOUS [LY]

Num 6:25 The LORD...be **g** unto thee

Ps 77:9 Hath God forgotten to be **g**

Ps 103:8 LORD is merciful and **g,** slow to anger

Ps 119:29 grant me thy [God's] law **g'ly**

Isa 33:2 O LORD, be **g** unto us

Amos 5:15 God...will be **g** unto the remnant of Joseph

Luke 4:22 bare him [Jesus] witness, and wondered at the **g** words

GRAVE [S]

Job 17:1 the **g's** are ready for me [Job]

Job 21:13 in a moment [the wicked] go down to the **g**

Ps 30:3 thou [God] hast brought up my soul from the **g**

Ps 88:3 my life draweth nigh unto the **g**

Eccl 9:10 no work...nor wisdom, in the **g**

Isa 53:9 he [God's servant] made his **g** with the wicked

Matt 27:52 **g's** were opened... bodies of the saints...arose

John 5:28 all that are in the **g's** shall hear his [Jesus'] voice

John 11:17 he [Lazarus] had lain in the **g** four days

1 Cor 15:55 O **g,** where is thy victory

1 Tim 3:8 must the deacons be **g,** not doubletongued

GREAT [ER]

Gen 1:16 two **g** lights; the **g'er** light to rule the day

Gen 12:2 I [God] will make of thee [Abraham] a **g** nation

1 Sam 12:24 how **g** things he [God] hath done for you

1 Chr 11:9 So David waxed **g'er** and **g'er**

1 Chr 16:25 **g** is the LORD, and greatly to be praised

Job 32:9 **G** men are not always wise

Ps 31:19 Oh how **g** is thy [God's] goodness

Ps 47:2 the LORD...is a **g** King over all the earth

Ps 48:1 **G** is the LORD, and greatly to be praised

Ps 77:13 who is so **g** a God as our God

Ps 95:3 LORD is...a **g** King above all gods

Ps 119:156 **G** are thy tender mercies, O LORD

Ps 126:3 The LORD hath done **g** things for us

Prov 22:1 good name is rather to be chosen than **g** riches

Isa 9:2 people that walked in darkness have seen a **g** light

Jer 10:6 thy [God's] name is *g* in might

Jer 32:17 thou [God]...made the...earth by thy *g* power

Dan 7:17 These *g* beasts, which are four, are four kings

Joel 2:31 sun shall be turned into darkness...before the *g*...day of the LORD

Jon 1:2 go to Nineveh, that *g* city, and cry against it

Hag 2:9 The glory of this latter house shall be *g'er*

Matt 4:16 people...in darkness saw *g* light

Matt 5:12 Rejoice...for *g* is your reward in heaven

Matt 11:11 least...is *g'er* than he [John the Baptist]

Matt 19:22 he [rich young ruler] went away sorrowful: for he had *g* possessions

Matt 20:26 *g* among you, let him be your minister

Mark 12:31 none other commandment *g'er* than these

Mark 13:26 Son of man coming...with *g* power

Luke 1:32 He [Jesus] shall be *g*...the Son of the Highest

Luke 2:5 Mary his [Joseph's] espoused wife, being *g* with child

Luke 10:2 harvest truly is *g,* but the labourers are few

Luke 22:44 his [Jesus'] sweat was as...*g* drops of blood

John 13:16 servant is not *g'er* than his lord

John 15:13 *G'er* love hath no man than this

Acts 16:26 a *g* earthquake... the foundations of the prison were shaken

Eph 5:32 a *g* mystery...concerning Christ and the church

Heb 2:3 escape, if we neglect so *g* salvation

Heb 4:14 Seeing then...we have a *g* high priest [Jesus]

Heb 12:1 compassed about...*g* a cloud of witnesses

Jas 3:5 Even so the tongue... boasteth *g* things

1 John 4:4 *g'er* is he...in you

3 John 4 no *g'er* joy than to hear...my [John's] children walk in truth

Rev 6:17 the *g* day of his [God's] wrath is come

GREAT COMMISSION. See *Jesus, Life and Ministry of.*

GREAT FLOOD. Gen 7:1–8:22.

GREAT SEA (the sea on Israel's western border, known today as the *Mediterranean Sea*). Josh 1:4; 9:1. *Sea of the Philistines:* Ex 23:31.

GREECE. See *Javan.*

GRIEF

Job 2:13 they saw that his [Job's] *g* was very great

Ps 6:7 Mine eye is consumed because of *g*

Prov 17:25 A foolish son is a *g* to his father

Isa 53:3 a man of sorrows [God's servant], and acquainted with *g*

Jer 45:3 LORD hath added *g* to my [Jeremiah's] sorrow

GRIEVE [D]

Gen 6:6 repented...he [God] had made man...it *g'd* him

Ps 78:40 oft did they...*g* him [God] in the desert

Ps 95:10 Forty years...was I [God] *g'd* with...generation

Mark 3:5 he [Jesus]...*g'd* for the hardness of their hearts

Mark 10:22 he [rich young ruler]...went away *g'd:* for he had great possessions

John 21:17 Peter was *g'd* because he [Jesus] said...the third time, Lovest thou me

Eph 4:30 *g* not the holy Spirit

GROW [ETH]

Ps 104:14 He [God] causeth the grass to *g* for the cattle

Matt 6:28 Consider the lilies of the field, how they *g*

Eph 2:21 the building...*g'eth* unto an holy temple

1 Pet 2:2 sincere milk of the word, that ye may *g* thereby

2 Pet 3:18 *g* in grace, and in... our Lord and Saviour

GUIDE [S]

Ps 48:14 this God...will be our *g* even unto death

Isa 58:11 the LORD shall *g* thee continually

Matt 23:24 Ye blind *g's,* which strain at a gnat

John 16:13 he [Holy Spirit] will *g* you into all truth

Acts 8:31 How can I [Ethiopian eunuch], except some man should *g* me

GUILT [Y]

Deut 19:13 put away the *g* of innocent blood from Israel

Matt 26:66 They...said, He [Jesus] is *g'y* of death

1 Cor 11:27 eat...drink... unworthily, shall be *g'y* of the...blood of the Lord

Jas 2:10 yet offend in one point, he is *g'y* of all

-H-

HABAKKUK (a prophet of Judah and author of the book that bears his name). Hab 1:1; 3:1.

HABAKKUK, BOOK OF. A short prophetic book of the Old Testament that struggles with the problem of the suffering of God's people at the hands of the pagan Babylonians.

HAGAR (Sarah's Egyptian slave who became the mother of Ishmael by Abraham). **Gen 16:1–16;** 21:9–17. *Agar:* Gal 4:24.

HAGGAI (a prophet after the Exile and author of the book that bears his name). Ezra 5:1; 6:14 • Hag 1–2.

HAGGAI, BOOK OF. A short prophetic book of the Old Testament written to encourage the Jewish captives who had returned to their homeland after three generations under the Babylonians and Persians.

HAI. See *Ai.*

HALAH (a region in Assyria where captives from the Northern Kingdom were settled). 2 Kgs 17:6; 18:11 • 1 Chr 5:26.

HALF TRIBE OF MANASSEH (a phrase referring to two distinct settlements of the tribe of Manasseh—one in central Palestine and the other east of the Jordan River). Num 32:33 • Deut 29:8 • Josh 22:10 • 1 Chr 6:61,71.

HAM (youngest son of Noah and ancestor of the people of several nations). Gen 5:32; 6:10; 7:13; 9:18,22; 10:1–20; 14:5 • 1 Chr 1:4,8.

HAMAN (an aide to King Ahasuerus of Persia who plotted to kill the Jews). Esth 3:1–9:25.

HAMATH-ZOBAH. See *Zobah.*

HANAMEEL (a cousin of Jeremiah from whom the prophet bought a field). Jer 32:7–12.

HANANI (Nehemiah's brother who brought news about the suffering citizens of Jerusalem). **Neh 1:2–3;** 7:2.

HAND OF GOD
Job 2:10 receive good at the *h-o-G,* and...not receive evil
Eccl 9:1 the wise, and their works, are in the *h-o-G*
Acts 7:56 I [Stephen] see...the Son of man standing on the right *h-o-G*

Col 3:1 things which are above, where Christ sitteth on the right *h-o-G*

1 Pet 3:22 Who [Jesus] is...on the right *h-o-G*

HANDWRITING ON A WALL. Dan 5:5–9.

HANNAH (mother of Samuel the prophet who prayed earnestly for Samuel to be born and devoted him to God's service). **1 Sam 1:5–28; 2:1–10.**

HARAN (a pagan city of Mesopotamia where Abraham lived for a time). **Gen 11:31–32; 12:4–5;** 27:43; 28:10; 29:4 • 2 Kgs 19:12 • Isa 37:12 • Ezek 27:23. *Charran:* Acts 7:2,4.

HATE [D, ST, TH]
Lev 19:17 Thou shalt not *h* thy brother in thine heart
Ps 5:5 thou [God] *h'st* all workers of iniquity
Ps 41:7 All that *h* me whisper... against me
Ps 69:4 They that *h* me without a cause are more than the hairs of mine head
Ps 119:163 I *h*...lying: but thy [God's] law do I love
Prov 8:13 The fear of the LORD is to *h* evil
Prov 13:24 He that spareth his rod *h'th* his son
Prov 14:20 poor is *h'd* even of his own neighbour

Eccl 3:8 A time to love, and a time to *h*
Isa 1:14 your appointed feasts my [God's] soul *h'th*
Amos 5:21 I [God] *h,* I despise your feast days
Matt 5:44 I [Jesus] say unto you...do good to them that *h* you
Matt 6:24 he will *h* the one, and love the other
Mark 13:13 *h'd* of all men for my [Jesus'] name's sake
Luke 14:26 and *h* not his father, and mother
John 12:25 he that *h'th* his life...shall keep it
John 15:18 it [the world] *h'd* me [Jesus] before it *h'd* you
John 15:23 He that *h'th* me [Jesus] *h'th* my Father also
1 John 2:9 He that saith he is in the light, and *h'th* his brother, is in darkness
1 John 4:20 If a man say, I love God, and *h'th* his brother, he is a liar

HAZAEL (a leader anointed king of Syria at God's command by the prophet Elijah). **1 Kgs 19:15–17** • 2 Kgs 8:8–29; 9:14–15; 10:32; 12:17–18; 13:3, 22–25 • 2 Chr 22:5–6 • Amos 1:4.

HAZOR (a royal Canaanite city destroyed by Joshua). **Josh 11:1–13;** 12:19; 19:36 • Judg

4:2,17 • 1 Sam 12:9 • 1 Kgs 9:15 • 2 Kgs 15:29.

HEAD [S]

Gen 3:15 it shall bruise thy [the serpent's] *h*

1 Sam 17:51 David...slew him [Goliath]...cut off his *h*

2 Sam 14:25 to the crown of his *h* there was no blemish in him [Absalom]

1 Chr 29:11 thou [God] art exalted as *h* above all

Job 1:20 Job arose...and shaved his *h*

Ps 3:3 thou, O Lord, art...the lifter up of mine *h*

Ps 23:5 thou [God] anointest my *h* with oil

Ps 24:7 Lift up your *h's,* O ye gates

Ps 118:22 The stone...is become the *h* stone

Ps 140:7 God...hast covered my *h* in the day of battle

Jer 9:1 Oh that my [Jeremiah's] *h* were waters

Dan 7:6 beast had also four *h's*

Matt 10:30 hairs of your *h* are all numbered

Matt 21:42 The stone which the builders rejected...is become the *h* of the corner

Matt 27:39 they...reviled him [Jesus], wagging their *h's*

Mark 6:28 brought his [John the Baptist's] *h* in a charger

Mark 14:3 a woman... brake the box, and poured it [ointment] on his [Jesus'] *h*

Mark 15:17 a crown of thorns, and put it about his [Jesus'] *h*

Luke 9:58 Son of man hath not where to lay his *h*

John 19:30 he [Jesus] bowed his *h,* and gave up the ghost

Acts 18:6 Your blood be upon your own *h's*

Rom 12:20 heap coals of fire on his [your enemy's] *h*

1 Cor 11:3 and the *h* of the woman is the man

1 Cor 12:21 eye cannot say... nor...the *h* to the feet, I have no need of you

Col 1:18 he [Jesus] is the *h* of the body, the church

Rev 1:14 His *h* and his hairs were white like wool

Rev 17:3 I [John] saw a woman...having seven *h's* and ten horns

HEAL [ING]

2 Chr 7:14 I [God will] hear from heaven...forgive their sin...*h* their land

Ps 41:4 Lord, be merciful unto me: *h* my soul

Eccl 3:3 A time to kill, and a time to *h*

Jer 3:22 I [God] will *h* your backslidings

Mal 4:2 Sun of righteousness arise with *h'ing* in his wings

Matt 4:23 Jesus went about... *h'ing* all manner of sickness

Matt 10:8 *H* the sick, cleanse the lepers, raise the dead

Luke 4:18 he [God] hath sent me [Jesus] to *h* the broken-hearted

Luke 9:2 he [Jesus] sent them [disciples]...to *h* the sick

1 Cor 12:30 Have all the gifts of *h'ing*...do all interpret

HEAR [EST, ETH, ING]

Deut 6:4 **H,** O Israel: The LORD our God is one

1 Sam 3:9 Speak, LORD, for thy servant [Samuel] *h'eth*

Job 35:13 Surely God will not *h* vanity

Job 42:5 I [Job] have heard of thee by the *h'ing* of the ear

Ps 4:3 the LORD will *h* when I call unto him

Ps 17:6 incline thine [God's] ear...and *h* my speech

Ps 55:17 and he [God] shall *h* my voice

Ps 65:2 O thou [God] that *h'est* prayer

Ps 69:33 For the LORD *h'eth* the poor

Ps 86:1 Bow down thine ear, O LORD, *h* me

Ps 115:6 They have ears, but they *h* not

Prov 4:1 **H,** ye children, the instruction of a father

Prov 13:1 wise son *h'eth* his father's instruction

Prov 18:13 answereth a matter before he *h'eth* it, it is folly

Prov 19:20 **H** counsel, and receive instruction

Eccl 7:5 better to *h* the rebuke of the wise, than...to *h* the song of fools

Isa 1:2 **H,** O heavens, and give ear, O earth

Isa 59:1 LORD's hand is not shortened...neither his ear heavy, that it cannot *h*

Isa 65:24 while they are yet speaking, I [God] will *h*

Jer 22:29 O earth...*h* the word of the LORD

Ezek 37:4 dry bones, *h* the word of the LORD

Matt 7:24 *h'eth* these sayings of mine [Jesus]...doeth them

Matt 13:9 Who hath ears to *h,* let him *h*

Matt 13:13 *h'ing* they *h* not, neither do they understand

Matt 13:16 blessed are your... ears, for they *h*

Matt 17:5 This is my [God's] beloved Son...*h* ye him

Mark 7:37 he [Jesus] maketh... the deaf to *h*

Luke 2:46 found him [Jesus]... sitting in the midst of the doctors...*h'ing* them

Luke 8:21 my [Jesus'] brethren are these which *h* the word of God, and do it

Luke 11:28 Yea...blessed are they that *h* the word of God, and keep it

John 3:8 wind bloweth...thou *h'est* the sound thereof

John 10:27 My [Jesus'] sheep *h* my voice...I know them

Acts 2:8 how *h* we every man in our own tongue

Acts 9:7 the men...stood speechless, *h'ing* a voice, but seeing no man

Acts 17:21 Athenians...spent their time...but...to *h* some new thing

Acts 28:28 salvation...is sent unto the Gentiles...that they will *h* it

Rom 10:14 how shall they *h* without a preacher

1 Cor 12:17 whole body were an eye, where were the *h'ing*

Jas 1:19 let every man be swift to *h,* slow to speak

1 John 5:14 if we ask any thing according to his [God's] will, he *h'eth* us

Rev 2:7 *h* what the Spirit saith unto the churches

Rev 3:20 any man *h* my [Jesus'] voice...open the door

Rev 22:17 let him that *h'eth* say, Come

HEARD [EST]

Gen 3:8 they [Adam and Eve] *h* the voice of the LORD God

Ex 3:7 I [God] have surely...*h* their [Israel's] cry

Job 42:5 I [Job] have *h*...by the hearing of the ear

Ps 28:6 the LORD...hath *h* the voice of my supplications

Ps 34:4 I sought the LORD, and he *h* me...delivered me

Ps 40:1 he [God] inclined unto me, and *h* my cry

Ps 116:1 I love the LORD, because he hath *h* my voice

Ps 119:26 I have declared my ways...thou [God] *h'est* me

Isa 6:8 *h* the voice of the Lord, saying, Whom shall I send

Isa 40:28 hast thou not *h*... God...fainteth not

Isa 42:2 He [God's servant] shall not...cause his voice to be *h* in the street

Jer 31:15 A voice was *h* in Ramah...bitter weeping

Matt 6:7 the heathen...think that they shall be *h* for their much speaking

Mark 12:37 common people *h* him [Jesus] gladly

Luke 2:20 shepherds returned... praising God for all...they had *h* and seen

Luke 12:3 spoken in darkness shall be *h* in the light

Acts 4:20 speak the things which we have seen and *h*

Acts 9:4 *h* a voice saying... Saul, Saul

Acts 11:1 apostles...*h* that the Gentiles had also received the word of God

Acts 17:32 *h* of the resurrection...some mocked

Rom 10:14 how shall they believe in him [Jesus] of whom they have not *h*

1 Cor 2:9 Eye hath not seen, nor ear *h*

Phil 4:9 things, which ye have... *h,* and seen...do

1 John 1:3 which we have seen and *h* declare we unto you

1 John 3:11 the message that ye *h* from the beginning

Rev 1:10 I [John] was in the Spirit on the Lord's day, and *h* behind me a great voice

HEART [S]

Ex 7:14 the LORD said...Pharaoh's *h* is hardened

Deut 6:5 love the LORD thy God with all thine *h*

Deut 10:16 Circumcise therefore the foreskin of your *h*

1 Sam 12:24 serve him [God] in truth with all your *h*

Ps 7:10 God...saveth the upright in *h*

Ps 13:5 my *h* shall rejoice in thy [God's] salvation

Ps 19:8 statutes of the LORD are right, rejoicing the *h*

Ps 19:14 Let the...meditation of my *h,* be acceptable

Ps 24:4 He that hath clean hands, and a pure *h*

Ps 37:4 he [God] shall give thee the desires of thine *h*

Ps 40:8 thy [God's] law is within my *h*

Ps 51:10 Create in me a clean *h,* O God

Ps 53:1 fool hath said in his *h,* There is no God

Ps 66:18 regard iniquity in my *h,* the Lord will not hear me

Ps 90:12 teach us to number our days, that we may apply our *h's* unto wisdom

Ps 119:11 Thy [God's] word have I hid in mine *h*

Ps 139:23 Search me, O God, and know my *h*

Ps 147:3 He [God] healeth the broken in *h*

Prov 2:2 apply thine *h* to understanding

Prov 3:5 Trust in the LORD with all thine *h*

Prov 15:13 merry *h* maketh a cheerful countenance

Prov 16:5 Every one that is proud in *h* is an abomination

Prov 17:22 A merry *h* doeth good like a medicine

Prov 21:2 but the LORD pondereth the *h's*

Eccl 9:7 and drink thy wine with a merry *h*

Jer 17:9 The *h* is deceitful above all things

Jer 29:13 ye shall...find me [God], when ye shall search...with all your *h*

Jer 31:33 I [God] will...write it [God's law] in their *h's*

Ezek 11:19 one *h,* and I will put a new spirit within you

Ezek 36:26 new *h* also will I [God] give you

Matt 5:8 Blessed are the pure in *h*...they shall see God

Matt 6:21 where your treasure is, there will your *h* be also

Matt 11:29 I [Jesus] am meek and lowly in *h*

Matt 15:8 honoureth me [Jesus] with their lips; but their *h* is far from me

Mark 12:30 love the Lord thy God with all thy *h*

Luke 2:19 Mary kept all these things...pondered...in her *h*

John 14:1 Let not your *h* be troubled

Acts 4:32 them that believed were of one *h*

Rom 1:24 God also gave them up...through the lusts of their own *h's*

Rom 5:5 love of God is shed abroad in our *h's*

Rom 10:9 believe in thine *h* that God hath raised him [Jesus] from the dead

2 Cor 3:2 Ye are our epistle written in our *h's*

2 Cor 4:6 God...hath shined in our *h's*

2 Cor 9:7 as he purposeth in his *h,* so let him give

Phil 4:7 peace of God...shall keep your *h's* and minds through Christ

2 Thes 3:5 Lord direct your *h's* into the love of God

Heb 3:12 lest there be in any of you an evil *h* of unbelief

Heb 3:15 harden not your *h's,* as in the provocation

Heb 4:12 word of God is quick... a discerner...of the *h*

Jas 4:8 purify your *h's,* ye double minded

HEAVEN [S]

Gen 1:1 God created the *h* and the earth

Deut 1:10 ye are this day as the stars of *h*

Deut 4:39 that the Lord he is God in *h* above

2 Sam 22:14 The Lord thundered from *h*

1 Kgs 8:23 no God like thee, in *h* above, or on earth beneath

2 Kgs 2:11 Elijah went up by a whirlwind into *h*

1 Chr 16:26 gods of the people are idols...Lord made the *h's*

2 Chr 7:14 will I [God] hear from *h*...forgive their sin

Job 28:24 For he [God]...seeth under the whole *h*

Ps 8:3 consider thy [God's] *h's,* the work of thy fingers

Ps 11:4 Lord's throne is in *h*

Ps 19:1 The *h's* declare the glory of God

Ps 57:5 Be thou exalted, O God, above the *h's*

Ps 89:6 who in the *h* can be compared unto the Lord

Ps 103:11 For as the *h* is high above the earth, so great is his [God's] mercy

Ps 108:5 Be thou exalted, O God, above the *h's*

Ps 121:2 help cometh from the Lord...made *h* and earth

Ps 136:26 thanks unto the God of *h*...mercy endureth for ever

Ps 139:8 If I ascend up into *h,* thou [God] art there

Eccl 3:1 a time to every purpose under the *h*

Isa 55:9 *h's* are higher than the earth, so are my [God's] ways higher than your ways

Jer 23:24 Do not I fill *h* and earth? saith the LORD

Jer 32:17 thou [God] hast made the *h* and the earth by thy great power

Jer 51:15 He [God]...hath stretched out the *h* by his understanding

Mal 3:10 prove me...if I [God] will not open you the windows of *h*

Matt 4:17 Jesus began to preach...Repent: for the kingdom of *h* is at hand

Matt 5:3 poor in spirit: for theirs is the kingdom of *h*

Matt 5:12 great is your reward in *h:* for so persecuted they the prophets...before you

Matt 5:34 Swear not at all; neither by *h*

Matt 5:48 even as your Father which is in *h* is perfect

Matt 6:9 Father which art in *h,* Hallowed be thy name

Matt 6:20 lay up for yourselves treasures in *h*

Matt 7:21 Not every one...shall enter...kingdom of *h*

Matt 16:19 give unto thee [Peter] the keys of the kingdom of *h*

Matt 18:3 become as little children, ye shall not enter into the kingdom of *h*

Matt 19:14 of such [little children] is the kingdom of *h*

Matt 26:64 shall ye see the Son of man...coming in the clouds of *h*

Matt 28:18 All power is given unto me [Jesus] in *h* and in earth

Mark 1:10 he [Jesus] saw the *h's* opened, and the Spirit... descending upon him

Mark 13:32 But of that hour knoweth no man, no, not the angels which are in *h*

Luke 3:22 voice came from *h,* which said...in thee [Jesus] I [God] am well pleased

Luke 16:17 easier for *h* and earth to pass, than one tittle of the law to fail

Luke 24:51 he [Jesus] was parted...carried up into *h*

John 3:27 receive nothing, except it be given him from *h*

John 6:38 I [Jesus] came down from *h,* not to do mine own will, but...him that sent me

Acts 1:11 men of Galilee, why stand ye gazing up into *h*

Acts 4:12 none other name under *h* given among men, whereby we must be saved

2 Cor 5:1 house not made with hands, eternal in the *h's*

Phil 2:10 every knee should bow, of things in *h*

1 Thes 4:16 Lord himself shall descend from *h* with a shout
Jas 5:12 swear not, neither by *h*...let your yea be yea
2 Pet 3:13 we...look for new *h's* and a new earth
Rev 5:3 no man in *h*...was able to open the book
Rev 20:1 angel come down from *h*, having the key of the bottomless pit
Rev 21:1 And I [John] saw a new *h* and a new earth

HEAVEN AND EARTH
Gen 14:19 Blessed be Abram... possessor of *h-a-e*
Ex 20:11 in six days the LORD made *h-a-e*
Ps 69:34 Let the *h-a-e* praise him [God], the seas
Ps 124:8 Our help is in...the LORD, who made *h-a-e*
Matt 5:18 Till *h-a-e* pass, one jot...shall in no wise pass
Matt 24:35 *H-a-e* shall pass away, but my [Jesus'] words shall not pass away
Acts 17:24 Lord of *h-a-e*, dwelleth not in temples made with hands

HEAVENLY
Matt 6:14 your *h* Father will also forgive you
Luke 2:13 with the angel a multitude of the *h* host
John 3:12 how shall ye believe, if I [Jesus] tell you of *h* things

Acts 26:19 I [Paul] was not disobedient unto the *h* vision

HEBREWS, EPISTLE TO THE. An epistle, author unknown, written to believers of Jewish background to show that Jesus had replaced the Old Testament ceremonial law and sacrificial system.

HEBRON (an ancient town in Canaan where Sarah died and that later became one of the six cities of refuge). Gen 13:18; **23:2–20;** 35:27; 37:14 • Josh 10:3–39 • Judg 1:10,20 • 2 Sam 3:2–32; 5:1–13 • 1 Chr 11:1–3 • 2 Chr 11:10. *Kirjatharba:* Gen 23:2 • Josh 14:15.

HEED
Josh 23:11 Take good *h*...that ye love the LORD
Prov 17:4 A wicked doer giveth *h* to false lips
Matt 6:1 Take *h* that ye do not your alms before men
Mark 8:15 Take *h*, beware of the...Pharisees
Luke 12:15 Take *h*, and beware of covetousness
Luke 21:8 Take *h*...be not deceived: for many shall come in my [Jesus'] name
1 Cor 3:10 every man take *h* how he buildeth thereupon
1 Cor 10:12 thinketh he standeth take *h* lest he fall

Heb 3:12 Take *h*...lest there be in...you an evil heart

HEIR [S]
Mark 12:7 This is the *h;* come, let us kill him
Gal 3:29 Abraham's seed, and *h's* according to the promise
Gal 4:7 if a son, then an *h* of God through Christ
Titus 3:7 justified by his [Jesus'] grace...be made *h's*
Heb 1:2 whom he [God] hath appointed *h* [Jesus] of all things
Heb 11:9 Isaac and Jacob, the *h's* with him [Abraham] of the same promise

HELL
Job 26:6 *H* is naked before him, and destruction hath no covering
Ps 18:5 sorrows of *h* compassed me about
Ps 139:8 make my bed in *h,* behold, thou [God] art there
Prov 27:20 *H* and destruction are never full
Jon 2:2 out of the belly of *h* cried I [Jonah]
Matt 5:22 say, Thou fool, shall be in danger of *h* fire
Matt 10:28 fear him...able to destroy...soul and body in *h*
Matt 16:18 gates of *h* shall not prevail against it [the church]
Luke 10:15 Capernaum...shalt be thrust down to *h*
Rev 1:18 I [Jesus]...have the keys of *h* and of death

Rev 20:14 death and *h* were cast into the lake of fire

HENOCH. See *Enoch,* No. 2.

HERMOGENES (a believer who deserted Paul). 2 Tim 1:15.

HERMON, MOUNT (a mountain in Syria that marked the northern limit of Joshua's conquest). **Josh 11:3,17;** 12:1,5 • Pss 89:12; 133:3. *Senir:* Ezek 27:5. *Shenir, Sirion:* Deut 3:9.

HEROD (the name of several Roman rulers in Palestine during New Testament times).
   1. Herod the Great, who ordered the slaughter of innocent children after Jesus was born. **Matt 2:1–22** • Luke 1:5.
   2. Herod Archelaus, son and successor of Herod the Great. Matt 2:22.
   3. Herod Philip, ruler in northern Galilee when Jesus began His public ministry. Luke 3:1,19–20.
   4. Herod Antipas, who executed John the Baptist. **Matt 14:1–12** • Mark 6:14–22; 8:15 • Luke 3:1,19; 9:7,9; 13:31; 23:7–12 • Acts 4:27; 13:1.
   5. Herod Agrippa I, who executed James, leader of the Jerusalem church. Acts 12:1–19.
   6. Herod Agrippa II, before whom Paul made his defense at Caesarea. Acts 25:13–26:32.

HERODIANS (an influential Jewish group that joined forces with the Pharisees against Jesus). Matt 22:16 • **Mark 3:6; 12:13.**

HERODIAS (wife of Herod Antipas who had John the Baptist executed). **Matt 14:1–11** • Mark 6:17.

HEZEKIAH (a godly king of Judah who implemented religious reforms). 2 Kgs 18:1–8; 19:1–37; 20:1–21 • **2 Chr 29:1–36; 31:1–21** • Isa 38:9–22. *Ezekias:* Matt 1:9.

HID [DEN]
Gen 3:8 Adam and his wife *h* themselves from...the LORD
Ex 3:6 Moses *h* his face; for he was afraid to look upon God
Ps 38:9 my groaning is not *h* from thee [God]
Ps 51:6 in the *h'den* part thou [God] shalt make me to know wisdom
Ps 119:11 Thy [God's] word have I *h* in mine heart
Isa 53:3 we *h*...our faces from him [God's servant]
Matt 5:14 A city that is set on an hill cannot be *h*
Matt 11:25 thou [God] hast *h* these things from the wise
Luke 13:21 It [kingdom of God] is like leaven, which a woman took and *h*

1 Cor 2:7 the *h'den* wisdom, which God ordained before the world unto our glory
Heb 11:23 Moses...was *h* three months of his parents

HIDE [ING, ST, TH]
Job 14:13 thou [God] wouldest *h* me in the grave
Ps 10:1 why *h'st* thou [God] thyself in times of trouble
Ps 13:1 how long wilt thou [God] *h* thy face from me
Ps 17:8 *h* me under the shadow of thy [God's] wings
Ps 51:9 *H* thy [God's] face from my sins
Ps 69:17 *h* not thy [God's] face from thy servant
Ps 119:114 Thou [God] art my *h'ing* place and my shield
Prov 19:24 A slothful man *h'th* his hand in his bosom
Isa 45:15 thou art a God that *h'st* thyself
Jer 23:24 Can any *h* himself in secret places that I [God] shall not see him
Rev 6:16 *h* us from the face of him that sitteth on the throne

HIERAPOLIS (a city in Asia Minor mentioned by Paul). Col 4:13.

HIGH [ER, EST, LY]
Gen 14:18 Melchizedek...was the priest of the most *h* God

Deut 28:1 God will set thee on *h* above all nations

Job 41:34 He [God] beholdeth all *h* things

Ps 7:17 I will...sing praise to the name of the LORD most *h*

Ps 47:2 the LORD most *h* is terrible...a great King

Ps 61:2 lead me to the rock that is *h'er* than I

Ps 69:29 let thy salvation, O God, set me up on *h*

Ps 91:1 He that dwelleth in the secret place of the most *H*

Ps 93:4 LORD on *h* is mightier than...many waters

Ps 97:9 thou, LORD, art *h* above all the earth

Ps 99:2 The LORD...is *h* above all the people

Ps 103:11 as the heaven is *h* above the earth, so great is his [God's] mercy

Ps 113:4 The LORD is *h* above all nations

Isa 6:1 I [Isaiah] saw also the Lord...*h* and lifted up

Isa 33:5 The LORD is exalted; for he dwelleth on *h*

Isa 52:13 my [God's] servant shall be exalted...be very *h*

Isa 55:9 heavens are *h'er* than the earth, so are my [God's] ways *h'er* than your ways

Matt 4:8 the devil taketh him [Jesus] up into an exceeding *h* mountain

Luke 1:28 Hail, thou [Mary] that art *h'ly* favoured

Luke 1:32 He [Jesus]...shall be called the Son of the *H'est*

Luke 2:14 Glory to God in the *h'est*...on earth peace

Luke 20:46 Beware of the scribes, which...love...the *h'est* seats in the synagogues

Luke 24:49 tarry...until... endued with power from on *h*

Rom 13:1 be subject unto the *h'er* powers

Eph 4:8 ascended up on *h,* he [Jesus] led captivity captive

Eph 6:12 wrestle...against spiritual wickedness in *h* places

Phil 2:9 God also hath *h'ly* exalted him [Jesus]

Phil 3:14 the prize of the *h* calling of God in Christ Jesus

HIGH PRIEST [S]

Matt 26:65 *h-p* rent his clothes, saying, He [Jesus] hath spoken blasphemy

John 18:19 *h-p* then asked Jesus of his...doctrine

Heb 3:1 Apostle and *H-P* of our profession, Christ Jesus

Heb 4:15 we have not an *h-p* which cannot be touched with...our infirmities

Heb 6:20 even Jesus, made an *h-p* for ever

Heb 7:27 Who [Jesus] needeth not daily, as those *h-p's,* to offer up sacrifice

HIGH PRIESTLY PRAYER OF JESUS. John 17:1–26.

HILKIAH (a high priest during King Josiah's reign who found the lost book of the Law). **2 Kgs 22:4–23:4** • 2 Chr 34:9–22.

HINNOM, VALLEY OF (a narrow ravine outside Jerusalem where pagan worship involving child sacrifice was conducted). Josh 15:8; 18:16 • 2 Kgs 23:10 • **2 Chr 28:3;** 33:6 • Neh 11:30 • Jer 7:31–32; **19:2–6.**

HIRAM (a king of Tyre who assisted David and Solomon with their building projects in Jerusalem). **2 Sam 5:11** • **1 Kgs 5:1–12;** 9:11–27; 10: 11,22 • 1 Chr 14:1. *Huram:* 2 Chr 2:3–12.

HITTITES (an ancient people who lived in Canaan). Gen 23:10–20 • 2 Sam 11:15–17 • 1 Kgs 15:5.

HOBAB. See *Jethro.*

HOLD [ING]
Ex 20:7 the LORD will not *h* him guiltless that taketh his name in vain
Job 6:24 Teach me, and I will *h* my tongue
Ps 83:1 Keep not thou silence, O God: *h* not thy peace
Ps 139:10 thy [God's] right hand shall *h* me

Jer 2:13 they have...hewed them out...cisterns, that can *h* no water
Luke 16:13 he will *h* to the one, and despise the other
Phil 2:16 **H'ing** forth the word of life...I [Paul] may rejoice
1 Thes 5:21 Prove all things; *h* fast that which is good
1 Tim 3:9 **H'ing** the mystery of the faith
Heb 4:14 we have a great high priest...Jesus...let us *h* fast our profession
Heb 10:23 h fast the profession of our faith
Rev 3:11 h that fast...that no man take thy crown

HOLY [INESS]
Ex 3:5 place whereon thou [Moses] standest is *h* ground
Ex 15:11 who is like thee [God], glorious in *h'iness*
Ex 20:8 Remember the sabbath day, to keep it *h*
Lev 11:44 ye shall be *h;* for I [God] am *h*
Lev 20:7 be ye *h:* for I am the LORD your God
Ps 11:4 The LORD is in his *h* temple
Ps 24:3 who shall stand in his [God's] *h* place
Ps 29:2 worship the LORD in the beauty of *h'iness*
Ps 51:11 take not thy [God's] *h* spirit from me

Ps 89:18 and the **H** One of
Israel is our king

Ps 96:9 worship the LORD in
the beauty of **h'iness**

Ps 99:5 worship at his [God's]
footstool; for he is **h**

Ps 103:1 all that is within me,
bless his [God's] **h** name

Ps 145:21 let all flesh bless his
[God's] **h** name for ever

Isa 6:3 one [seraphim] cried...
H, h, h, is the LORD of
hosts

Hab 2:20 the LORD is in his **h**
temple...earth keep silence

Rom 12:1 bodies a living sacrifice, **h,** acceptable unto God

Rom 16:16 Salute one another
with an **h** kiss

1 Cor 3:17 temple of God is **h,**
which temple ye are

Eph 5:27 it [the church] should
be **h** and without blemish

1 Thes 4:7 God hath...called us
unto...**h'iness**

1 Tim 2:8 men pray every
where, lifting up **h** hands

2 Tim 3:15 And that from a
child thou [Timothy] hast
known the **h** scriptures

1 Pet 1:16 it is written, Be ye **h;**
for I [God] am **h**

1 Pet 2:5 Ye also...are built
up...an **h** priesthood

1 Pet 2:9 ye are a chosen generation...an **h** nation

Rev 21:2 I John saw the **h** city,
new Jerusalem

HOLY GHOST

Matt 1:18 she [Mary] was
found with child of the **H-G**

Matt 3:11 he [Jesus] shall
baptize you with the **H-G**

Matt 12:31 blasphemy against
the **H-G** shall not be forgiven

Matt 28:19 baptizing them in
the name of the...**H-G**

Luke 1:35 The **H-G** shall come
upon thee [Mary]

Luke 1:67 Zacharias was filled
with the **H-G**

Luke 2:25 the **H-G** was upon
him [Simeon]

Luke 3:22 **H-G** descended...
like a dove upon him [Jesus]

John 14:26 the **H-G**...shall
teach you all things

Acts 1:8 receive power, after
that...**H-G** is come upon
you

Acts 6:3 look ye out...seven
men...full of the **H-G**

Acts 13:2 **H-G** said, Separate
me Barnabas and Saul

Rom 14:17 kingdom of God is...
joy in the **H-G**

1 Cor 12:3 and that no man
can say that Jesus is the
Lord, but by the **H-G**

2 Pet 1:21 holy men of God
spake...by the **H-G**

HONEST [LY, Y]

Acts 6:3 seven men of **h** report

Rom 13:13 Let us walk **h'ly**...
not in rioting

Phil 4:8 things are **h,** whatsoever things are just

1 Tim 2:2 lead a quiet...life in all godliness and *h'y*

HONOUR [ED, ETH]
Ex 20:12 H thy father and thy mother
1 Chr 16:27 Glory and *h* are in his [God's] presence
Ps 8:5 thou [God]...hast crowned him [man] with glory and *h*
Prov 3:9 H the LORD with thy substance...and...firstfruits
Prov 22:4 By...the fear of the LORD are riches, and *h*
Matt 13:57 Jesus said...A prophet is not without *h,* save in his own country
Mark 7:6 people *h'eth* me [Jesus] with their lips, but their heart is far from me
John 5:23 h'eth not the Son *h'eth* not the Father
John 12:26 if any man serve me [Jesus], him will my Father *h*
Rom 12:10 Be kindly affectioned one to another...in *h* preferring one another
1 Cor 12:26 one member be *h'ed,* all the members rejoice
Rev 4:11 Thou art worthy, O Lord, to receive glory and *h*

HOPE [D]
Job 7:6 My [Job's] days...are spent without *h*
Ps 38:15 in thee, O LORD, do I *h*...thou wilt hear
Ps 71:5 thou art my *h,* O Lord
Ps 119:114 Thou [God] art my... shield: I *h* in thy word
Ps 146:5 Happy is he...whose *h* is in the LORD
Jer 17:7 Blessed is the man... whose *h* the LORD is
Lam 3:24 LORD is my portion... therefore...I *h* in him
Rom 12:12 Rejoicing in *h;* patient in tribulation
Rom 15:13 the God of *h* fill you with all joy
1 Cor 13:13 now abideth faith, *h,* charity, these three
Col 1:27 which is Christ in you, the *h* of glory
1 Thes 4:13 that ye sorrow not... as others which have no *h*
Heb 11:1 faith is the substance of things *h'd* for
1 Pet 3:15 every man that asketh you a reason of the *h* that is in you

HOPHNI (an immoral son of Eli the high priest who was killed by the Philistines). 1 Sam 1:3; 2:12–17; **4:1–11.**

HOR, MOUNT (a mountain in Moab where Aaron died). **Num 20:22–29;** 21:4; 33:37–41 • Deut 32:50.

HOSEA (a prophet to the Northern Kingdom and author of the book that bears his name). Hos 1:1–2. *Osee:* Rom 9:25.

HOSEA, BOOK OF. A prophetic book of the Old Testament that compares the idolatry of God's people with the physical adultery of the prophet's wife, Gomer (1:2–5; 2:2–5). Just as Hosea redeemed her from slavery and restored her as his mate, God promised that He would eventually restore His people after a period of punishment by their enemies (4:1–14:9).

HOSHEA

1. The last king of Israel who was taken to Assyria as a captive. 2 Kgs 15:30; **17:1–6;** 18:1–10.

2. Another name for Joshua. See *Joshua.*

HOSPITALITY

1 Tim 3:2 A bishop then must be...given to *h,* apt to teach

1 Pet 4:9 Use *h* one to another without grudging

HOUR [S]

Matt 10:19 given you in that same *h* what ye shall speak

Matt 24:42 know not what *h* your Lord doth come

Matt 26:40 ye [Peter] not watch with me [Jesus] one *h*

Mark 13:32 of that day and that *h* knoweth no man

Luke 12:40 Son of man cometh at an *h* when ye think not

John 11:9 Are there not twelve *h's* in the day

John 12:23 h is come...Son of man should be glorified

HOUSE [S]

Gen 12:1 Get thee [Abraham]... from thy father's *h*

Gen 28:17 he [Jacob]...said... this is none other but the *h* of God

Gen 39:4 he [Potiphar] made him [Joseph] overseer over his *h*

Ex 12:7 blood...strike it...on the upper door post of the *h's*

Ex 20:2 I am...God, which have brought thee...out of the *h* of bondage

Ex 20:17 Thou shalt not covet thy neighbour's *h*

Deut 6:7 talk of them when thou sittest in thine *h*

Deut 25:14 not have in thine *h* divers measures

Josh 24:15 but as for me [Joshua] and my *h,* we will serve the LORD

2 Sam 12:10 sword shall never depart from thine [David's] *h*

1 Kgs 12:19 Israel rebelled against the *h* of David

1 Chr 17:1 I [David] dwell in an *h* of cedars

1 Chr 22:6 Then he [David]... charged him [Solomon] to build an *h* for the LORD

2 Chr 2:1 Solomon determined to build an *h* for the...LORD

2 Chr 7:16 sanctified this *h,* that my [God's] name may be there for ever

2 Chr 21:7 LORD would not destroy the *h* of David

Job 17:13 If I [Job] wait, the grave is mine *h*

Job 22:18 Yet he [God] filled their *h's* with good things

Ps 66:13 I will go into thy [God's] *h* with...offerings

Ps 69:9 the zeal of thine *h* hath eaten me up

Ps 84:4 Blessed are they that dwell in thy [God's] *h*

Ps 84:10 rather be a doorkeeper in the *h* of my God

Ps 127:1 Except the LORD build the *h*

Prov 12:7 the *h* of the righteous shall stand

Prov 15:25 The LORD will destroy the *h* of the proud

Isa 2:5 *h* of Jacob...let us walk in the light of the LORD

Jer 18:3 Then I [Jeremiah] went down to the potter's *h*

Jer 29:28 build ye *h's,* and dwell in them

Ezek 43:5 the glory of the LORD filled the *h*

Amos 3:15 great *h's* shall have an end, saith the LORD

Hag 2:9 glory of this latter *h*... greater than of the former

Mal 3:10 that there may be meat in mine [God's] *h*

Matt 2:11 they [wise men] were come into the *h,* they saw the young child [Jesus]

Matt 7:24 a wise man, which built his *h* upon a rock

Matt 10:6 go rather to the lost sheep of the *h* of Israel

Matt 13:57 Jesus said...A prophet is not without honour, save...in his own *h*

Matt 15:24 I [Jesus] am not sent but unto the lost sheep of the *h* of Israel

Matt 23:14 ye [scribes and Pharisees] devour widows' *h's*

Mark 3:25 if a *h* be divided against itself

Mark 11:17 My [God's] *h* shall be called...the *h* of prayer

Luke 14:23 compel them to come in...my *h* may be filled

Luke 19:9 This day is salvation come to this *h*

John 14:2 In my Father's *h* are many mansions

Acts 16:31 and thou shalt be saved, and thy *h*

Acts 28:30 Paul dwelt two... years in his own hired *h*

1 Cor 16:19 Aquila and Priscilla salute you...with the church...in their *h*

2 Cor 5:1 a building of God, an *h* not made with hands

1 Tim 3:5 if a man know not how to rule his own *h*

1 Tim 3:12 deacons...ruling... their own *h's* well

1 Tim 5:8 for those of his own *h,* he hath denied the faith

1 Pet 2:5 Ye also...are built up a spiritual *h*

1 Pet 4:17 judgment must begin at the *h* of God

HOUSE OF THE LORD
Deut 23:18 Thou shalt not bring...the price of a dog, into the *h-o-t-L*
1 Sam 3:15 Samuel...opened the doors of the *h-o-t-L*
1 Kgs 6:1 he [Solomon] began to build the *h-o-t-L*
1 Kgs 8:11 glory of the LORD had filled the *h-o-t-L*
1 Kgs 8:63 the king [Solomon] and all the children of Israel dedicated the *h-o-t-L*
1 Kgs 14:26 And he [Shishak] took away the treasures of the *h-o-t-L*
2 Kgs 22:8 I [Hilkiah] have found the book of the law in the *h-o-t-L*
2 Kgs 25:9 he [Nebuzar-adan] burnt the *h-o-t-L*
2 Chr 36:7 Nebuchadnezzar also carried of the vessels of the *h-o-t-L* to Babylon
Ps 23:6 I will dwell in the *h-o-t-L* for ever
Ps 27:4 I may dwell in the *h-o-t-L* all the days
Ps 122:1 glad when they said... Let us go into the *h-o-t-L*

HOUSEHOLD
Matt 10:36 a man's foes shall be they of his own *h*
Gal 6:10 do good unto...them who are of the *h* of faith

Eph 2:19 fellowcitizens with the saints, and of the *h* of God

HULDAH (a prophetess who foretold the collapse of Jerusalem). 2 Kgs 22:14–20 • 2 Chr 34:22–28.

HUMBLE [D, TH]
Ps 10:12 O God, lift up thine hand: forget not the *h*
Ps 35:13 clothing was sackcloth: I *h'd* my soul
Isa 5:15 and the mighty man shall be *h'd*
Matt 18:4 shall *h* himself as this little child...is greatest
Luke 18:14 he that *h'th* himself shall be exalted
Phil 2:8 he [Jesus] *h'd* himself... became obedient unto death
Jas 4:10 *H* yourselves...and he [God] shall lift you up

HUMILITY
Acts 20:19 Serving the Lord with all *h* of mind
1 Pet 5:5 be clothed with *h:* for God resisteth the proud

HUR (a man who held up the arms of Moses to give the Israelites victory over the Amalekites). Ex 17:8–13; 24:14.

HURAM. See *Hiram.*

HUSBAND [S]
Gen 3:16 thy [Eve's] desire shall be to thy *h*

Prov 12:4 A virtuous woman is a crown to her *h*

Isa 54:5 For thy Maker is thine *h;* the LORD of hosts is his name

Matt 1:19 Joseph her [Mary's] *h,* being a just man

Mark 10:12 if a woman shall put away her *h*...she committeth adultery

1 Cor 7:3 the *h* render unto the wife due benevolence

1 Cor 7:14 unbelieving *h* is sanctified by the wife

Eph 5:25 *H's,* love your wives... as Christ...loved the church

Col 3:19 *H's,* love your wives, and be not bitter against them

1 Tim 3:2 A bishop...must be blameless, the *h* of one wife

1 Tim 3:12 let the deacons be the *h's* of one wife

1 Pet 3:1 wives, be in subjection to your own *h's*

Rev 21:2 I John saw...new Jerusalem...prepared as a bride adorned for her *h*

HUSHAI (a friend of King David who remained loyal to the king during Absalom's rebellion). 2 Sam 15:32–37; 16:16–18; 17:5–15 • 1 Kgs 4:16 • 1 Chr 27:33.

HYMENAEUS (an early believer who denied the faith and was excommunicated by Paul). 1 Tim 1:19–20 • 2 Tim 2:16–18.

HYPOCRISY

Matt 23:28 within ye [Pharisees] are full of *h*

Mark 12:15 But he [Jesus], knowing their [Pharisees'] *h,* said...bring me a penny

HYPOCRITE [S]

Job 20:5 and the joy of the *h* but for a moment

Matt 6:2 do not sound a trumpet...as the *h's* do

Matt 6:16 be not, as the *h's,* of a sad countenance

Matt 7:5 *h,* first cast out the beam out of thine own eye

Matt 23:13 woe unto you, scribes and Pharisees, *h's*

Luke 13:15 *h,* doth not...you on the sabbath...lead him [ox] away to watering

-I-

I AM GOD
Ps 46:10 Be still, and know that *I-a-G*
Isa 45:22 be ye saved, all the ends of the earth: for *I-a-G*
Hos 11:9 I-a-G, and not man

"I AM" STATEMENTS OF JESUS IN JOHN'S GOSPEL
1. Bread of life (John 6:35)
2. Light of the world (John 8:12)
3. Door of the sheep (John 10:7)
4. Good shepherd (John 10:11,14)
5. Resurrection and the life (John 11:25)
6. Way, the truth, and the life (John 14:6)
7. True vine (John 15:1)

IBZAN (a minor judge of Israel). Judg 12:8–10.

ICHABOD (a grandson of Eli who was given this symbolic name, meaning "inglorious," when his mother learned that Eli and Phinehas were dead). 1 Sam 4:19–22.

ICONIUM (a city in Asia Minor visited by Paul and Barnabas). **Acts 13:51; 14:1, 19–22;** 16:1–7 • 2 Tim 3:11.

IDLE [NESS]
Prov 19:15 and an *i* soul shall suffer hunger
Prov 31:27 She...eateth not the bread of *i'ness*
Eccl 10:18 and through *i'ness* of the hands the house droppeth through
Matt 12:36 every *i* word that men shall speak, they shall give account
Luke 24:11 words seemed to them [the disciples] as *i* tales

IDOL [S]
Lev 19:4 Turn ye not unto *i's*
1 Chr 16:26 all the gods of the people are *i's*
Ps 135:15 The *i's* of the heathen are silver and gold
Ezek 14:6 Repent, and turn... from your *i's*
Acts 7:41 they made a calf... offered sacrifice unto the *i*
1 Cor 8:4 we know that an *i* is nothing in the world
2 Cor 6:16 what agreement hath...temple of God with *i's*
1 John 5:21 Little children, keep yourselves from *i's*

IDUMEA. See *Edom,* No. 2.

IGNORANCE
Num 15:27 And if any soul sin through *i*
Acts 17:30 And the times of this *i* God winked at
1 Pet 2:15 ye may put to silence the *i* of foolish men

IGNORANT [LY]

Acts 4:13 they [the Sanhedrin]... perceived that they [Peter and John] were...*i* men

Acts 17:23 Whom...ye *i'ly* worship, him [Jesus] declare I [Paul] unto you

1 Cor 12:1 concerning spiritual gifts...I [Paul] would not have you *i*

1 Thes 4:13 not have you to be *i*, brethren, concerning them which are asleep

2 Pet 3:8 be not *i* of this...one day is with the Lord as a thousand years

IMAGE [S]

Gen 31:19 Rachel had stolen the *i's* that were her father's

Ex 20:4 Thou shalt not make unto thee any graven *i*

Deut 7:25 graven *i's* of their gods shall ye burn with fire

2 Kgs 17:10 they set them up *i's* and groves

Ps 97:7 Confounded be all they that serve graven *i's*

Ps 106:19 They made a calf... and worshipped the molten *i*

Isa 21:9 all the graven *i's* of her [Babylon's] gods he [God] hath broken

Isa 42:8 my glory will I [God] not give...neither my praise to graven *i's*

Dan 3:18 we [Daniel's three friends] will not...worship the golden *i*

Mic 1:7 all the graven *i's*... shall be beaten to pieces

Mark 12:16 And he [Jesus] saith...Whose is this *i* and superscription

Rom 1:23 changed the glory of...God into an *i* made like to corruptible man

Rom 8:29 to be conformed to the *i* of his [God's] Son

1 Cor 15:49 we shall also bear the *i* of the heavenly

2 Cor 3:18 But we all...are changed into the same *i* from glory to glory

Col 1:15 Who [Jesus] is the *i* of the invisible God

IMAGE OF GOD

Gen 1:27 God created man...in the *i-o-G*

Gen 9:6 for in the *i-o-G* made he [God] man

2 Cor 4:4 the glorious gospel of Christ, who is the *i-o-G*

IMAGINATION [S]

Gen 6:5 God saw that...every *i* of the thoughts of his [man's] heart was only evil

Jer 16:12 ye walk every one after the *i* of his evil heart

Lam 3:61 Thou [God] hast heard...their *i's* against me

Luke 1:51 he [God]...scattered the proud in the *i* of their hearts

Rom 1:21 they glorified him not as God...but became vain in their *i's*

IMMORTALITY
1 Cor 15:53 For...this mortal must put on *i*

2 Tim 1:10 Jesus...hath brought life and *i* to light through the gospel

IMPOSSIBLE
Matt 17:20 and nothing shall be *i* unto you

Mark 10:27 With men it is *i,* but not with God

Luke 18:27 things...*i* with men are possible with God

Heb 11:6 without faith it is *i* to please him [God]

IMPUTE [D, ING, TH]
Ps 32:2 Blessed is the man unto whom the LORD *i'th* not iniquity

Rom 4:8 Blessed is the man to whom the Lord will not *i* sin

Rom 4:22 it was *i'd* to him [Abraham] for righteousness

2 Cor 5:19 To wit...God was in Christ...not *i'ing* their trespasses unto them

Jas 2:23 it was *i'd* unto him [Abraham] for righteousness

IN CHRIST
Rom 8:1 no condemnation to them which are *i-C*

Rom 12:5 we, being many, are one body *i-C*

1 Cor 4:10 fools for Christ's sake, but ye are wise *i-C*

1 Cor 15:19 in this life only we have hope *i-C*

1 Cor 15:22 as in Adam all die, even so *i-C* shall all be made alive

2 Cor 2:14 unto God, which... causeth us to triumph *i-C*

2 Cor 5:17 if any man be *i-C,* he is a new creature

2 Cor 5:19 To wit, that God was *i-C,* reconciling the world unto himself

Eph 1:10 he [God] might gather...in one all things *i-C*

Phil 2:1 If there be therefore any consolation *i-C*

Phil 2:5 Let this mind be in you, which was also *i-C*

Phil 3:14 the prize of the high calling of God *i-C*

1 Thes 4:16 the dead *i-C* shall rise first

IN THE BEGINNING
Gen 1:1 *I-t-b* God created the heaven and the earth

John 1:1 *I-t-b* was the Word, and the Word was with God

Heb 1:10 Thou, Lord, *i-t-b* hast laid the foundation of the earth

IN THE SIGHT OF GOD
Prov 3:4 find favour and good understanding *i-t-s-o-G*

Luke 16:15 that which is highly esteemed among men is abomination *i-t-s-o-G*

Gal 3:11 no man is justified by the law *i-t-s-o-G*

IN THE SPIRIT

Ezek 37:1 The hand of the LORD...carried me [Ezekiel] out *i-t-s* of the LORD

John 11:33 When Jesus...saw her [Mary] weeping...he groaned *i-t-s*

Acts 19:21 Paul purposed *i-t-s*... to go to Jerusalem

Acts 20:22 I [Paul] go bound *i-t-s* unto Jerusalem

Rom 8:9 But ye are not in the flesh, but *i-t-S*

Gal 5:16 Walk *i-t-S*...not fulfil the lust of the flesh

Gal 5:25 If we live *i-t-S,* let us also walk *i-t-S*

Rev 1:10 I [John] was *i-t-S* on the Lord's day

Rev 21:10 he [an angel] carried me [John] away *i-t-s* to a great...mountain

INCLINE [D, TH]

Ps 17:6 *i* thine [God's] ear unto me...hear my speech

Ps 40:1 I waited patiently... and he [God] *i'd* unto me, and heard my cry

Prov 2:18 her [the strange woman's] house *i'th* unto death

Prov 4:20 My son...*i* thine ear unto my sayings

INCORRUPTIBLE

1 Cor 9:25 they do it to obtain a corruptible crown...we an *i*

1 Cor 15:52 dead shall be raised *i,* and we shall all be changed

INCREASE [D, ING, TH]

Gen 7:18 the waters...were *i'd* greatly upon the earth

Ex 1:7 the children of Israel... *i'd* abundantly

Lev 26:4 and the land shall yield her *i*

Job 1:10 his [Job's] substance is *i'd* in the land

Ps 3:1 how are they *i'd* that trouble me [David]

Ps 67:6 Then shall the earth yield her *i*

Ps 73:12 these are the ungodly...they *i* in riches

Ps 105:24 And he [God] *i'd* his people greatly

Prov 1:5 A wise man will hear, and will *i* learning

Prov 24:5 a man of knowledge *i'th* strength

Eccl 1:18 he that *i'th* knowledge *i'th* sorrow

Eccl 5:10 not be satisfied with silver; nor he that loveth abundance with *i*

Isa 9:7 Of the *i* of his [Messiah's] government and peace there shall be no end

Luke 2:52 Jesus *i'd* in wisdom and stature

Luke 17:5 apostles said unto the Lord, *I* our faith

John 3:30 He [Jesus] must *i,* but I [John the Baptist] must decrease

Acts 6:7 word of God *i'd;* and the...disciples multiplied

1 Cor 3:7 neither is he that planteth any thing...but God that giveth the *i*

Col 1:10 being fruitful in every good work, and *i'ing* in the knowledge of God

1 Thes 3:12 the Lord make you to *i* and abound in love

INDIA (a region that served as the eastern limit of the Persian Empire). Esth 1:1; 8:9.

INFIRMITY [IES]

Ps 77:10 my *i:* but I will remember...the most High

Prov 18:14 The spirit of a man will sustain his *i*

Matt 8:17 might be fulfilled... Himself [Jesus] took our *i'ies*...bare our sicknesses

Rom 8:26 the Spirit also helpeth our *i'ies*

Rom 15:1 We...strong ought to bear the *i'ies* of the weak

2 Cor 12:9 gladly...will I [Paul] ...glory in my *i'ies*

Gal 4:13 through *i* of the flesh I [Paul] preached the gospel

Heb 4:15 not an high priest [Jesus] which cannot be touched with...our *i'ies*

INHERIT [ED]

Josh 14:1 countries which the children of Israel *i'ed*

Ps 37:9 those that wait upon the LORD...shall *i* the earth

Ps 37:29 The righteous shall *i* the land

Prov 11:29 He that troubleth his own house...*i* the wind

Matt 5:5 Blessed are the meek: for they shall *i* the earth

Matt 25:34 Come...*i* the kingdom prepared for you

Luke 18:18 Good Master, what shall I [rich young ruler] do to *i* eternal life

1 Cor 6:10 nor extortioners, shall *i* the kingdom of God

Gal 5:21 they which do such things shall not *i* the kingdom of God

Rev 21:7 He that overcometh shall *i* all things

INHERITANCE

Num 18:23 among...Israel they [Levites] have no *i*

Num 27:8 a man die, and have no son...cause his *i* to pass unto his daughter

Deut 32:9 Jacob is the lot of his [God's] *i*

Josh 11:23 Joshua gave it [Canaan] for an *i* unto Israel

Ps 2:8 I [God] shall give thee the heathen for thine *i*

Ps 33:12 Blessed is...the people whom he [God] hath chosen for his own *i*

Ps 94:14 neither will he [God] forsake his *i*

Prov 20:21 An *i* may be gotten hastily at the beginning

Mark 12:7 kill him [the heir], and the *i* shall be ours

Eph 1:11 In whom [Jesus] also we have obtained an *i*

Eph 5:5 no...idolater, hath...*i* in the kingdom of Christ

Heb 11:8 Abraham...called... into a place which he should after receive for an *i,* obeyed

INIQUITY [IES]

Ex 20:5 I the LORD...am a jealous God, visiting the *i* of the fathers upon the children

Num 14:18 The LORD is longsuffering...forgiving *i*

Job 13:23 How many are mine *i'ies* and sins

Job 15:16 filthy is man, which drinketh *i* like water

Job 34:22 There is no darkness...where the workers of *i* may hide

Ps 5:5 thou [God] hatest all workers of *i*

Ps 25:11 O LORD, pardon mine *i;* for it is great

Ps 31:10 my strength faileth because of mine *i*

Ps 51:2 Wash me throughly from mine *i*

Ps 51:5 I was shapen in *i;* and in sin did my mother conceive me

Ps 51:9 blot out all mine *i'ies*

Ps 85:2 Thou [God] hast forgiven the *i* of thy people

Ps 103:10 He [God] hath not dealt with us...nor rewarded us according to our *i'ies*

Prov 10:29 destruction shall be to the workers of *i*

Isa 6:7 thine [Isaiah's] *i* is taken away

Isa 40:2 her [Israel's] *i* is pardoned: for she hath received...double for all her sins

Isa 53:5 he [God's servant] was bruised for our *i'ies*

Isa 53:6 LORD...laid on him [God's servant]...*i* of us all

Isa 59:2 *i'ies* have separated... you and your God

Isa 64:6 our *i'ies,* like the wind, have taken us away

Jer 14:20 We acknowledge, O LORD...the *i* of our fathers

Jer 31:30 every one shall die for his own *i*

Lam 5:7 we have borne their [our fathers'] *i'ies*

Matt 23:28 ye [Pharisees] are full of hypocrisy and *i*

Luke 13:27 depart from me [Jesus], all ye workers of *i*

Rom 4:7 Blessed are they whose *i'ies* are forgiven

1 Cor 13:6 [charity] rejoiceth not in *i,* but...in the truth

2 Tim 2:19 every one that nameth the name of Christ depart from *i*

Heb 10:17 sins and *i'ies* will I [God] remember no more

Jas 3:6 the tongue is a fire, a world of *i*

INSTRUCT [ED]

Job 40:2 Shall he that contendeth with the Almighty *i* him

Ps 32:8 I [God] will *i* thee and teach thee...guide thee

Prov 21:11 when the wise is *i'ed,* he receiveth knowledge

Luke 1:4 certainty of those things, wherein thou hast been *i'ed*

1 Cor 2:16 who hath known the mind of the Lord, that he may *i* him

Phil 4:12 I [Paul] am *i'ed* both to be full and to be hungry

INTEGRITY

Job 2:9 Dost thou [Job] still retain thine *i*

Job 31:6 Let me [Job] be weighed...that God may know mine *i*

Ps 25:21 Let *i* and uprightness preserve me

Prov 19:1 Better is the poor that walketh in his *i,* than he that is perverse

Prov 20:7 The just man walketh in his *i*

INTERCESSION [S]

Rom 8:26 the Spirit itself maketh *i*...with groanings

Rom 8:34 who [Jesus]... maketh *i* for us

1 Tim 2:1 that...prayers, *i's,* and giving of thanks, be made for all men

Heb 7:25 he [Jesus] ever liveth to make *i* for them

INVISIBLE

Rom 1:20 i things of him [God]...are clearly seen

Col 1:15 Who [Jesus] is the image of the *i* God

1 Tim 1:17 unto the King eternal, immortal, *i*...be honour and glory

ISAAC (a son born to Abraham and Sarah in their old age and father of Jacob and Esau). Gen 17:19,21; **21:3–12;** 22:2–14; 24:4–67; **25:5–28;** 26:1–35; 27:1–46 • Heb 11:9,20.

ISAIAH (a major prophet of Judah and author of the book that bears his name; he warned that the nation would be destroyed by Assyria, but a righteous remnant would be saved). 2 Kgs 19:2–20; 20:1–19 • 2 Chr 26:22; 32:20,32 • **Isa 1:2–9; 11:11.** *Esaias:* Matt 4:14.

ISAIAH, BOOK OF. A major Old Testament prophetic book noted for its prediction of the coming Messiah (7:14; 9:7) and particularly its emphasis on the Messiah as God's "suffering servant" (42:1–9; 49:1–6; 50:4–9; 52:13–53:12). Many Bible students call Isaiah the "fifth Gospel" because it echoes the New Testament themes of salvation and redemption.

ISCARIOT, JUDAS (the disciple who betrayed Jesus). Matt 10:4; 26:14,25,47; 27:3 • Mark 3:19; 14:10,43 • Luke 22:3,

47–48 • John 6:71; 12:4; 13:2, 26,29; 18:2–5 • Acts 1:16,25.

ISH-BOSHETH (a son of King Saul who succeeded his father as king of Israel and served briefly until defeated by David). 2 Sam 2:8–15; 3:7–15; 4:5–12. *Esh-baal:* 1 Chr 8:33.

ISHMAEL (Abraham's son born to Sarah's maid Hagar; known as the father of the Arab peoples). **Gen 16:1–16;** 17:25; 21:8–21; 25:9–18 • 1 Chr 1:28–31.

ISRAEL
1. Another name for Jacob. Gen 32:28; 35:10. See *Jacob*.
2. The Northern Kingdom, formed when the ten northern tribes rebelled against the two southern tribes and established its own kingship under Rehoboam. 1 Kgs 12:1–33.

3. A general name for the entire nation of the Jewish people. Num 1:2.

ISSACHAR (a son of Jacob and ancestor of one of the twelve tribes of Israel). Gen 30:17–18; 35:23; 46:13; 49:14 • Ex 1:3 • Num 1:8,28–29 • Josh 17:10–11 • Judg 5:15 • 1 Chr 2:1; 7:1; 12:32,40 • Ezek 48:25–26,33. The tribe of Issachar settled in northern Canaan. Josh 19:17–23.

ITHAMAR (youngest son of Aaron who oversaw the tabernacle during the wilderness wanderings). Ex 6:23; 28:1; **38:21** • Lev 10:6–16 • 1 Chr 24:1–6.

ITUREA (a small province ruled by Herod Philip when John the Baptist began his ministry). Luke 3:1.

-J-

JABBOK (a small stream beside which Jacob wrestled with an angel). **Gen 32:22–31** • Num 21:24 • Deut 2:37; 3:16 • Josh 12:2 • Judg 11:13,22.

JACHIN AND BOAZ (two bronze pillars which stood in front of Solomon's temple at Jerusalem). 1 Kgs 7:13–22 • 2 Chr 3:17.

JACOB (father of several sons who became the ancestors of the twelve tribes of Israel). See **Gen 25:19–34; 27:1–35:29; 48:1–49:33** for a sketch of Jacob.

1. Born with twin brother Esau (Gen 25:21–26)
2. Secured Esau's birthright (Gen 25:28–34)
3. Secured his father's blessing (Gen 27:1–41)
4. Fled to Haran (Gen 27:42–28:10)
5. Saw vision of angels at Bethel (Gen 28:11–22)
6. Worked seven years for Leah (Gen 29:16–25)
7. Worked seven years for Rachel (Gen 29:26–30)
8. Birth of his sons (Gen 29:31–30:24)
9. Wrestled with an angel at Peniel (Gen 32:24–30)
10. Name changed from Jacob to *Israel* (Gen 32:28; 35:10)
11. Reconciled with Esau (Gen 33:1–16)
12. Blessed Joseph and Joseph's sons (Gen 48:1–22)
13. Blessed his other sons (Gen 49:1–28)
14. Died in Egypt (Gen 49: 29–33)
15. Buried in Canaan (Gen 50:1–14)

Jacob is also mentioned in Ex 1:1,5 • Lev 26:42 • Josh 24:4 • 1 Sam 12:8 • Mal 1:2 • Matt 1:2; 8:11 • Luke 1:33; 13:28 • John 4:5,12 • Acts 3:13; 7:8–46 • Rom 9:13; 11:26 • Heb 11:9,20–21.

JAEL (a woman who killed Sisera, a commander of the forces of King Jabin of Hazor). **Judg 4:17–22; 5:6,24.**

JAH. See *Jehovah.*

JAIR (a minor judge of Israel). Judg 10:3–5.

JAIRUS (a ruler of a synagogue whose daughter was raised from the dead by Jesus). Mark 5:22–23,36–43 • Luke 8:41–42,49–56.

JAMBRES (an Egyptian magician who opposed Moses). 2 Tim 3:8.

JAMES

1. A son of Zebedee and a disciple of Jesus. Matt 4:21; 10:2; 17:1 • Mark 1:19,29; 3:17; 5:37; 9:2; 10:35,41; 13:3; 14:33 • Luke 5:10; 6:14; 8:51; 9:28,54 • Acts 1:13; 12:2.

2. A son of Alphaeus and a disciple of Jesus. Matt 10:3 • Mark 3:18 • Luke 6:15 • Acts 1:13.

3. A half brother of Jesus who became a leader in the church at Jerusalem and probable author of the New Testament book that bears his name. Matt 13:55; 27:56 • Mark 6:3; 15:40; 16:1 • Acts 12:17; 15:13; 21:18 • 1 Cor 15:7 • Gal 1:19; 2:9,12 • Jas 1:1 • Jude 1.

JAMES, EPISTLE OF. A

short epistle written probably by James, the half brother of Jesus, and known for its plain language and practical application of the gospel to the believer's daily life.

JANNES (an Egyptian magician who opposed Moses). 2 Tim 3:8.

JAPHETH (a son of Noah considered the father of the Indo-European races). Gen 5:32; 6:10; 7:13; **9:18–27; 10:1–5** • 1 Chr 1:4–5.

JAPHO. See *Joppa.*

JASHOBEAM (chief of David's mighty men, or brave warriors). 1 Chr 11:10–11; 27:2.

JASON (a citizen of Thessalonica who provided lodging for Paul and Silas). Acts 17:5–9.

JAVAN (a son of Japheth considered the father of the Ionians, or Greeks). Gen 10:2,4 • 1 Chr 1:5–7 • Isa 66:19.

JEBUS. See *Jerusalem.*

JEBUSITES (tribal enemies of the Israelites from whom David took the city of Jebus, or Jerusalem). Gen 15:21 • Josh 15:63 • Judg 1:21; 3:5; 19:11 • **2 Sam 5:6–9** • 1 Kgs 9:20 • 1 Chr 11:4–6 • 2 Chr 8:7 • Ezra 9:1 • Neh 9:8.

JECONIAH. See *Jehoiachin.*

JEHOAHAZ

1. A king of the Northern Kingdom who led the nation into sin and idolatry. 2 Kgs 10:35; **13:1–8** • 2 Chr 25:17,25.

2. Son and successor of Josiah as king of Judah. Jehoahaz reigned only three months. 2 Kgs 23:31–34 • 2 Chr 36:2,4. *Shallum:* 1 Chr 3:15.

JEHOASH. See *Joash,* No. 1.

JEHOIACHIN (son and successor of Jehoiakim as king of Judah. Jehoiachin reigned only three months). **2 Kgs 24:8–16;** 25:27 • 2 Chr 36:8–9 • Jer 52:31. *Coniah:* Jer 22:24. *Jeconiah:* 1 Chr 3:16–17.

JEHOIAKIM (a king of Judah who was defeated and carried away as a captive by the Babylonians). 2 Kgs 24:1–6 • 1 Chr 3:15–16 • **2 Chr 36:4–8** • Jer 26:1–23; 36:1–32 • Dan 1:1–2. *Eliakim:* 2 Kgs 23:34.

JEHORAM
1. A king of Judah who murdered his own brothers in order to succeed his father Jehoshaphat. 1 Kgs 22:50 • **2 Chr 21:1–20.** *Joram:* 2 Kgs 8:21.
2. A king of Israel who was assassinated by Jehu. 2 Kgs 1:17; 3:1,6; **9:24.** *Joram:* 2 Kgs 8:16.

JEHOSHAPHAT (a king of Judah who implemented religious reforms). 1 Kgs 22:2–50 • **2 Chr 17:1–12;** 18:1–21:1. *Josaphat:* Matt 1:8.

JEHOSHUAH. See *Joshua.*

JEHOVAH (a name for God, rendered "LORD" in most translations of the Bible, which comes from a Hebrew verb meaning "to be," indicating His eternity and self-existence). Ex 6:3 • Ps 83:18 • Isa 12:2; 26:4. *JAH:* Ps 68:4.

JEHOVAH-JIREH (a name for God meaning "the LORD will provide"). Gen 22:14.

JEHOVAH-NISSI (a name for God meaning "the LORD is my banner"). Ex 17:15–16.

JEHOVAH-SHALOM (name of an altar built by Gideon, meaning "the LORD is peace"). Judg 6:24.

JEHU (a king of Israel who gained the throne by killing King Ahab's descendants). 2 Kgs 9:2–10:36.

JEMIMA (a daughter of Job born after his recovery from affliction). Job 42:14.

JEPHTHAE. See *Jephthah.*

JEPHTHAH (a judge of Israel who made a rash vow to sacrifice his only child as an offering to God). **Judg 11:1–40;** 12:1–7. *Jephthae:* Heb 11:32.

JEREMIAH (a major prophet who preached God's message of doom to the nation of Judah before it fell to the Babylonians and author of the book that bears his name). He is mentioned outside the Book of Jeremiah in 2 Chr 35:25; 36:12, 21–22 • Ezra 1:1 • Dan 9:2. *Jeremias:* Matt 16:14. *Jeremy:* Matt 2:17; 27:9.

JEREMIAH, BOOK OF. A major Old Testament prophetic book noted for its warnings that the nation of Judah would fall to the Babylonians unless the people repented and turned back to God. Jeremiah also expounded the concept of a new covenant (Jer 31). This new agreement between God and His people, based on grace and forgiveness, was needed because the old covenant of law had failed to keep the people on the path of righteousness.

JEREMIAS. See *Jeremiah.*

JEREMY. See *Jeremiah.*

JERICHO (a Canaanite city captured by Joshua and regarded as one of the world's oldest cities). Num 22:1; 31:12 • Deut 34:3 • **Josh 6:1–27** • 2 Kgs 2:4–18. The Jericho of the New Testament was built on a site near Old Testament Jericho. Matt 20:29 • Mark 10:46 • Luke 19:1.

JEROBOAM
1. Jeroboam I, first king of the Northern Kingdom after the kingdom of Solomon split into two separate nations following the death of Solomon. 1 Kgs 12:17–30 • 2 Chr 13:19–20.
2. Jeroboam II, king of Israel who was denounced for his encouragement of idol worship. 2 Kgs 14:16–29 • **Amos 7:7–9.**

JERUBBAAL. See *Gideon.*

JERUSALEM (the religious and political capital of the Jewish people and the city where Jesus was crucified).
1. Called *Salem* in Abraham's time (Gen 14:18)
2. Then known as *Jebus,* captured by David and made his capital (2 Sam 5:6–8 • 1 Chr 11:4)
3. Site of first temple built by Solomon (1 Kgs 5:5–8)
4. Captured by Babylonia (Jer 39:1–8)
5. Temple rebuilt under Zerubbabel (Ezra 1:1–4)
6. Walls rebuilt under Nehemiah (Neh 12:27–47)
7. Jesus predicted its destruction (Luke 19:41–44)
8. Jesus enters as the triumphant Messiah (Matt 21:9–10)

9. Jesus crucified outside the city (Luke 9:31; 23:33)

10. Church begins at Jerusalem (Acts 2:1–47)

11. Future heavenly city described as "new Jerusalem" (Rev 21:1–3)

JESHUA. See *Joshua.*

JESSE (father of David and an ancestor of Christ). **Ruth 4:17,22** • 1 Sam 16:1–22 • 1 Chr 2:13–15 • Isa 11:1–10 • **Matt 1:5–6** • Luke 3:32 • Acts 13:22 • Rom 15:12.

JESUS, APPEARANCES OF, AFTER HIS RESURRECTION

1. To Mary Magdalene at the empty tomb (Mark 16:9 • John 20:11–18)

2. To other women at the empty tomb (Matt 28:1–10)

3. To two followers on their way to Emmaus (Mark 16:12–13 • Luke 24:13–32)

4. To Peter, apparently in Jerusalem (Luke 24:33–35)

5. To ten of His disciples in Jerusalem, Thomas absent (Luke 24:36–43 • John 20:19–25)

6. To the eleven disciples in Jerusalem, Thomas present (John 20:26–29)

7. To His disciples at the Sea of Galilee (John 21:1–14)

8. To His disciples at His ascension near Jerusalem (Mark 16:19–20 • Luke 24:44–53)

9. To five hundred followers (1 Cor 15:6)

10. To James and all the apostles (1 Cor 15:7)

11. To the apostle Paul (1 Cor 15:8)

JESUS, LIFE AND MINISTRY OF

1. Genealogies of (Matt 1:1–17 • Luke 3:23–38)

2. Birth in Bethlehem (Luke 2:1–20)

3. Flight into Egypt and settlement in Nazareth (Matt 2:13–23 • Luke 2:39–40)

4. Found among esteemed teachers in Jerusalem (Luke 2:41–52)

5. Baptized by John the Baptist (Matt 3:13–17 • Mark 1:9–11)

6. Tempted in the wilderness (Matt 4:1–11 • Mark 1:12–13 • Luke 4:1–13)

7. Centered His early ministry around Capernaum in Galilee (Matt 4:13–16 • Luke 4:22–31)

8. Selected twelve disciples for special training (Matt 10:2–4 • Mark 3:13–19 • Luke 6:12–16)

9. Sermon on the Mount (Matt 5:1–7:29 • Luke 6:17–49)

10. Sent disciples out to preach and heal (Matt 10:1, 5–42 • Mark 6:7–13 • Luke 9:1–6)

11. Predicted His death, resurrection, and return (Luke 12:35–59)

12. Transfiguration (Matt 17:1–8 • Mark 9:2–8 • Luke 9:28–36)

13. Triumphal entry into Jerusalem (Matt 21:1–11 • Mark 11:1–11 • Luke 19:28–40 • John 12:12–19)

14. Instituted the Memorial Supper (Matt 26:26–30 • Mark 14:22–26 • Luke 22:14–20)

15. Agonized in prayer in Gethsemane (Matt 26:36–46 • Mark 14:26,32–42 • Luke 22:39–46)

16. Betrayed by Judas and arrested (Matt 26:47–56 • Mark 14:43–52 • Luke 22:47–53 • John 18:1–12)

17. Trial before the Jewish authorities (Matt 26:57–68; 27:1–2 • Mark 14:53–65; 15:1 • Luke 22:54–23:1 • John 18:24)

18. Trial before Pilate (Matt 27:2–26 • Mark 15:1–15 • Luke 23:2–25 • John 18:28–19:16)

19. Crucifixion by Roman soldiers (Matt 27:33–37 • Mark 15:22–26 • Luke 23:32–34 • John 19:17–24)

20. Death (Matt 27:45–54 • Mark 15:33–39 • Luke 23:44–48 • John 19:28–30)

21. Burial in Joseph's tomb (Matt 27:57–60 • Mark 15:42–46 • Luke 23:50–54 • John 19:38–42)

22. Resurrection (Matt 28:2–4 • 1 Cor 15:1–19)

23. Appearances to His followers. See *Jesus, Appearances of, After His Resurrection.*

24. Great Commission to His followers (Matt 28:16–20 • Mark 16:15–18 • Acts 1:7–8)

25. Ascension to His Father (Mark 16:19 • Luke 24:50–51 • Acts 1:9–11)

JESUS, MIRACLES OF

1. Blind Bartimaeus healed (Matt 20:29–34 • Mark 10:46–52 • Luke 18:35–43)

2. Blind man at Bethsaida healed (Mark 8:22–26)

3. Centurion's servant healed (Matt 8:5–13 • Luke 7:1–10)

4. Daughter of a Canaanite woman healed (Matt 15:21–28 • Mark 7:24–30)

5. Deaf man healed (Mark 7:31–37)

6. Demon-possessed blind man healed (Matt 12:22–24)

7. Demon-possessed boy healed (Matt 17:14–21 • Mark 9:14–29 • Luke 9:37–42)

8. Demon-possessed deaf man healed (Matt 9:32–34)

9. Demon-possessed man healed at Capernaum (Mark 1:21–26 • Luke 4:31–35)

10. Ear of Malchus healed (Luke 22:50–51 • John 18:10)

11. Feeding of the five thousand (Matt 14:13–23 • Mark 6:30–44 • Luke 9:10–17 • John 6:1–15)

12. Feeding of the four thousand (Matt 15:29–38 • Mark 8:1–10)

13. First miraculous catch of fish on the Sea of Galilee (Luke 5:4–10)

14. Jairus's daughter healed (Matt 9:23–26 • Mark 5:35–42 • Luke 8:49–56)

15. Lame man healed on the sabbath (John 5:1–15)

16. Lazarus raised from the dead (John 11:1–44)

17. A leper healed (Matt 8:1–4 • Mark 1:40–45 • Luke 5:12–16)

18. Man blind from birth healed (John 9:1–41)

19. Man with a paralyzed hand healed on the Sabbath (Matt 12:9–14 • Mark 3:1–6 • Luke 6:6–11)

20. Man with the dropsy healed (Luke 14:1–6)

21. Paralyzed man healed (Matt 9:1–8 • Mark 2:1–12 • Luke 5:17–26)

22. Peter's mother-in-law healed (Matt 8:14–15 • Mark 1:29–31 • Luke 4:38–39)

23. Production of a coin to pay the temple tax (Matt 17:24–27)

24. Royal official's son healed (John 4:46–54)

25. Second miraculous catch of fish at the Sea of Galilee (John 21:1–14)

26. Stilling of the storm (Matt 8:18,23–27 • Mark 4:35–41 • Luke 8:22–25)

27. Ten lepers healed (Luke 17:11–19)

28. Transfiguration before His disciples (Matt 17:1–8 • Mark 9:2–8 • Luke 9:28–36)

29. Two blind men healed (Matt 9:27–31)

30. Walking on the water (Matt 14:24–36 • Mark 6:45–56 • John 6:16–21)

31. Water turned into wine (John 2:1–11)

32. Widow's son raised from the dead (Luke 7:11–17)

33. Wild man among the tombs healed (Matt 8:28–34 • Mark 5:1–20 • Luke 8:26–39)

34. Withering of a fig tree (Matt 21:19–22 • Mark 11:20–26)

35. Woman with a crooked back healed (Luke 13:10–17)

36. Woman with a hemorrhage healed (Matt 9:20–22 • Mark 5:24–34 • Luke 8:43–48)

JESUS, PARABLES OF

1. The barren fig tree (Luke 13:1–9)

2. Building on sand and rock (Matt 7:24–27)

3. The dishonest manager (Luke 16:1–8)

4. The dragnet (Matt 13:47–51)

5. The good Samaritan (Luke 10:25–37)

6. The hidden treasure (Matt 13:44)

7. The lamp on a lampstand (Mark 4:21–25 • Luke 8:16–18)

8. The landowner (Matt 13:52)

9. The large banquet (Luke 14:15–24)

10. The lost coin (Luke 15:8–10)

11. The lost sheep (Matt 18:12–14 • Luke 15:1–7)

12. The minas (Luke 19:11–27)

13. The mustard seed (Matt 13:31–32 • Mark 4:30–32 • Luke 13:18–19)

14. The pearl of great price (Matt 13:45–46)

15. The persistent widow (Luke 18:1–8)

16. The prodigal son (Luke 15:11–32)

17. The proud Pharisee (Luke 18:9–14)

18. The rich fool (Luke 12:13–21)

19. The rich man and Lazarus (Luke 16:19–31)

20. The sower and the soils (Matt 13:1–9 • Mark 4:1–9 • Luke 8:4–8)

21. The talents (Matt 25:14–30)

22. The ten virgins (Matt 25:1–13)

23. The two vineyard workers (Matt 21:28–32)

24. The unforgiving servant (Matt 18:23–35)

25. The vineyard owner (Matt 21:33–46 • Mark 12:1–12 • Luke 20:9–19)

26. The vineyard workers (Matt 20:1–16)

27. The wedding banquet (Matt 22:1–14)

28. The wheat and the tares (Matt 13:24–30)

29. The yeast (Matt 13:33–35 • Luke 13:20–21)

JESUS, PROPHECIES ABOUT. See *Messianic Prophecies.*

JETHRO (Moses' father-in-law who advised Moses to delegate some of his leadership responsibilities). Ex 3:1; 4:18; **18:1–27.** *Hobab:* Num 10:29. *Reuel:* Ex 2:18.

JEZEBEL (a wife of King Ahab who promoted Baal worship in Israel). 1 Kgs 16:31; 18:4,13; 19:1–2; 21:5–25 • 2 Kgs 9:7–37 • Rev 2:20.

JEZREEL (a symbolic name, meaning "God scatters," given by the prophet Hosea to his son to show that King Jehu and his family would be punished). Hos 1:3–5.

JOAB (commander of King David's army during most of David's reign). 1 Sam 26:6 • 2 Sam 2:13–32; 3:22–31; 11:1–25; 14:1–33; 18:2–29; 20:9–23 • 1 Kgs 2:5–33 • 1 Chr 11:6–39; 19:8–15; 21:2–6; 27:7, 24,34.

JOANNA (a woman who prepared spices for Jesus' burial and proclaimed His resurrection). Luke 8:1–3; 23:55–56; **24:1–10.**

JOASH
1. A king of Judah who brought religious reforms to the nation but then turned to idol worship. 2 Kgs 12:4–20 • 2 Chr 24:1–22. *Jehoash:* 2 Kgs 11:21.
2. A king of Israel who led the nation into sin through his idolatry. 2 Kgs 13:10–25.

JOATHAM. See *Jotham.*

JOB (a godly man whose faith sustained him through fierce trials and sufferings). **Job 1:1–22; 42:1–17** • Ezek 14:14,20 • Jas 5:11.

JOB, BOOK OF. A wisdom book of the Old Testament that addresses the issue of human suffering. The book is written in the form of a poetic drama revolving around the discussion of this problem by Job and his three friends: Eliphaz, Bildad, and Zophar.

JOEL (a prophet of Judah in the days of King Uzziah and author of the book that bears his name). Joel 1:1 • Acts 2:16.

JOEL, BOOK OF. A brief prophetic book of the Old Testament that uses a devastating swarm of locusts (1:1–20) as an early warning sign of God's judgment in order to call His people to repentance. The prophet predicted the outpouring of God's spirit (2:28–32), an event that happened on the day of Pentecost (Acts 2:16–21).

JOHANAN (a supporter of Gedaliah, governor of Judah, who took a remnant of the Jews to Egypt). **2 Kgs 25:22–23** • Jer 40:8–16; **41:11–18**; 42:1,8; 43:2–6.

JOHN, FIRST, SECOND, AND THIRD EPISTLES OF. Three short epistles written by John, one of the twelve disciples of Jesus. First John focuses on such themes as the incarnation of Christ (1:1–5) and the meaning of love and fellowship

(2:15–5:3). Second John calls on believers to abide in the commandments of God (vv. 1–10). Third John commends two believers and condemns a third.

JOHN, GOSPEL OF. One of the four Gospels, written by the apostle John to show that "Jesus is the Christ, the Son of God" (20:31). John is unique among the Gospels in that it majors on the theological meaning of the events in Jesus' life rather than the events themselves. Also unique to John's Gospel are the "I am" sayings of Jesus, in which Jesus reveals characteristics of His divine nature.

JOHN THE APOSTLE (a fisherman from Galilee who became one of the twelve apostles of Jesus and author of the Gospel that bears his name as well as the books of 1, 2, 3 John and Revelation). Matt 4:21; 10:2; 17:1 • Mark 1:19,29; 3:17; 5:37; 9:2,38; 10:35,41; 13:3; 14:33 • Luke 5:10; 6:14; 8:51; 9:28,49,54; 22:8 • Acts 1:13; 3:1–11; 4:13,19; 8:14; 12:2 • Gal 2:9 • Rev 1:1,4,9; 21:2.

JOHN THE BAPTIST (a prophet who prepared the way for Christ). Matt 3:1–14; 4:12; 9:14; 11:2–18; 14:2–10; 16:14; 17:13; 21:25–32 • Mark 1:4–14;

2:18; 6:14–29; 8:28; 11:30–32 • Luke 1:13–63; 3:2–20; 5:33; 7:18–33; 9:7–9; 11:1; 16:16; 20:4,6 • John 1:6–40; 3:23–27; 4:1; 5:33–36; 10:40–41 • Acts 1:5,22; 10:37; 11:16; 13:24–25; 19:4.

JONAH (a prophet swallowed by a "great fish" while fleeing from God's call to preach at Nineveh in Assyria). 2 Kgs 14:25 • Jon 1:17. *Jonas:* Luke 11:30.

JONAH, BOOK OF. A short prophetic book of the Old Testament that emphasizes God's universal love. Through his experience of preaching to the pagan citizens of Nineveh, Jonah learned that God is concerned for all people, not just the citizens of his native land (4:1–11).

JONAS. See *Jonah.*

JONATHAN (a loyal friend of David). 1 Sam 13:2–22; 14:1–49; 18:1–4; 19:1–7; 20:1–42; 23:16–18; 31:2 • 2 Sam 1:4–26; 4:4; 9:3–7; 21:7–14 • 1 Chr 8:33–34; 9:39–40; 10:2.

JOPPA (a city where Peter had his vision on full acceptance of the Gentiles). 2 Chr 2:16 • Ezra 3:7 • Jon 1:3 • Acts

9:36–43; **10:5–32;** 11:5,13. *Japho:* Josh 19:46.

JORAM. See *Jehoram.*

JORDAN RIVER (the major river of Palestine in which Jesus was baptized). Gen 13:8–13; 32:10 • Num 34:12 • Deut 3:27 • Josh 3:17; 4:1–24 • 2 Sam 17:22–24 • 2 Kgs 2:5–14; 5:10–14 • **Matt 3:6–15.**

JOSAPHAT. See *Jehoshaphat.*

JOSEPH
1. A son of Jacob, sold into slavery by his brothers, who became a high official in the Egyptian government. See **Gen 37–50** for a sketch of Joseph. Ex 1:5–8; 13:19 • Num 27:1; 32:33; 34:23; 36:12 • Deut 27:12 • Josh 14:4; 16:1,4; 17:1–16; 24:32 • Ps 105:17 • John 4:5 • Acts 7:9–18 • Heb 11:21–22.
2. The husband of Mary, Jesus' mother. Matt 1:16–24; 2:13–23 • Luke 1:27; 2:4–43; 3:23 • John 1:45; 6:42.
3. A secret disciple of Jesus who buried Jesus in his own tomb. Matt 27:57–60 • **Mark 15:43–46** • **Luke 23:50–53** • John 19:38.

JOSES. See *Barnabas.*

JOSHUA (Moses' successor who led the Israelites into the Promised Land and rallied the people to victory over the Canaanites). Ex 17:9–14; 24: 13; 32:17; 33:11 • Num 11: 28; 14:6–38; 26:65; 27:18– 23; 32:12,28; 34:17 • Deut 1:38; 3:21,28; 31:3–23; 34:9 • **Josh 1:1–24:31** • Judg 2:6–23 • 1 Kgs 16:34. *Hoshea:* Deut 32:44. *Jehoshuah:* 1 Chr 7:27. *Jeshua:* Neh 8:17. *Oshea:* Num 13:8.

JOSHUA, BOOK OF. An Old Testament book that details the conquest and settlement of the land of Canaan by the Israelites under the leadership of Joshua.

JOSIAH (a king of Judah who led a reform movement to reestablish God's Law and abolish idolatry). 2 Kgs 22:3–9; **23:3–25.** *Josias:* Matt 1:10–11.

JOTHAM (a king of Judah who failed to destroy places of pagan worship). **2 Kgs 15:5–38;** 16:1 • 1 Chr 3:12; 5:17 • 2 Chr 26:21,23; 27:1–9 • Isa 1:1; 7:1 • Hos 1:1 • Mic 1:1. *Joatham:* Matt 1:9.

JOURNEY [ED, ING, INGS]
Gen 12:9 Abram *j'ed,* going on still toward the south
Ex 3:18 let us [Israelites] go... three days' *j*...that we may sacrifice to the LORD

Jon 3:3 Nineveh was...great city of three days' *j*

Luke 9:3 Take nothing for your *j,* neither staves

Luke 10:33 Samaritan, as he *j'ed,* came where he [the wounded traveler] was

Luke 13:22 he [Jesus] went through the cities...teaching, and *j'ing* toward Jerusalem

Luke 15:13 younger son...took his *j* into a far country

Acts 9:3 as he [Paul] *j'ed,* he came near Damascus

2 Cor 11:26 In *j'ings* often, in perils of waters

JOY

Ps 16:11 in thy [God's] presence is fulness of *j*

Ps 30:5 weeping may endure for a night, but *j* cometh in the morning

Ps 43:4 Then will I go...unto God my exceeding *j*

Ps 51:12 Restore...the *j* of thy [God's] salvation

Ps 126:5 They that sow in tears shall reap in *j*

Prov 15:21 Folly is *j* to him that is destitute of wisdom

Isa 12:3 with *j*...draw water out of the wells of salvation

Isa 52:9 Break forth into *j*...ye waste places of Jerusalem

Lam 5:15 *j* of our heart is ceased; our dance is turned into mourning

Hab 3:18 I will *j* in the God of my salvation

Matt 2:10 they [wise men]... rejoiced with...great *j*

Matt 28:8 And they [the women] departed quickly... with fear and great *j*

Luke 2:10 bring you [shepherds] good tidings of great *j*

Luke 15:10 *j*...over one sinner that repenteth

John 16:20 your sorrow shall be turned into *j*

Acts 20:24 I [Paul] might finish my course with *j*

Rom 14:17 kingdom of God is... peace, and *j*

Gal 5:22 fruit of the Spirit is love, *j,* peace

Heb 12:2 who [Jesus] for the *j* that was set before him endured the cross

Jas 1:2 count it all *j* when ye fall into divers temptations

3 John 4 no greater *j*...children walk in truth

JOYFUL [LY, NESS]

Ps 35:9 my soul shall be *j* in the LORD

Ps 66:1 Make a *j* noise unto God, all ye lands

Ps 95:1 make a *j* noise to the rock of our salvation

Ps 149:5 Let the saints be *j* in glory...sing aloud

Eccl 9:9 Live *j'ly* with the wife whom thou lovest

Isa 49:13 Sing, O heavens; and be *j,* O earth

Luke 19:6 he [Zacchaeus]... received him [Jesus] *j'ly*

Col 1:11 Strengthened...unto all patience...with *j'ness*

JUBAL (a musician regarded as the ancestor of those who play the harp and the flute). Gen 4:21.

JUDAEA (a district in southern Palestine in New Testament times). Matt 2:1,5,22 • Mark 1:5; 3:7 • Luke 6:17 • John 4:3,47,54 • Acts 10:37 • Rom 15:31 • 2 Cor 1:16 • Gal 1:22 • 1 Thes 2:14.

JUDAH
1. A son of Jacob and ancestor of one of the twelve tribes of Israel. Gen 29:35; 38:1–26; 43:3,8; 44:14–18; 46:12,28; 49:8–9 • Ex 1:2 • Num 26:19 • Ruth 4:12 • 1 Chr 2:1–10; 4:1,21,27; 5:2; 9:4 • Neh 11:24. The tribe of Judah settled in southern Canaan. Josh 15:1–12.
2. The Southern Kingdom, or nation of Judah, with Jerusalem as its capital that was overrun and taken into exile by the Babylonians. 2 Chr 36:4–20.

JUDAS (one of the twelve disciples of Jesus, called "brother of James" to set him apart from the disciple Judas [Iscariot] who betrayed Jesus). Luke 6:16 • John 14:22 • Acts 1:13.

Lebbaeus: Matt 10:3. *Thaddaeus:* Mark 3:18.

JUDAS ISCARIOT. See *Iscariot, Judas.*

JUDE (half brother of Jesus and author of the New Testament epistle that bears his name). Jude 1. *Judas:* Matt 13:55.

JUDE, EPISTLE OF. A short letter written like a brief essay or tract and addressed to the problem of false teachings in the early church.

JUDGE [S, ST, TH]
Gen 18:25 Shall not the *J* of all the earth do right
Ex 18:13 on the morrow... Moses sat to *j* the people
Judg 2:16 LORD raised up *j's*
1 Sam 2:10 the LORD shall *j* the ends of the earth
1 Sam 8:6 they [the people] said, Give us a king to *j* us
1 Kgs 3:9 Give...thy [God's] servant [Solomon] an understanding heart to *j* thy people
Job 22:13 can he [God] *j* through the dark cloud
Ps 7:8 j me, O LORD, according to my righteousness
Ps 7:11 God *j'th* the righteous
Ps 43:1 J me, O God, and plead my cause

Ps 72:2 He [God] shall *j* thy people with righteousness

Ps 75:7 God is the *j*...putteth down one...setteth up another

Prov 31:9 *j* righteously, and plead the cause of the poor

Lam 3:59 thou [God] hast seen my wrong: *j* thou my cause

Matt 7:1 *J* not, that ye be not judged

John 7:24 *J* not according to the appearance

John 12:48 word that I [Jesus] have spoken...shall *j* him in the last day

Rom 14:10 But why dost thou *j* thy brother

2 Tim 4:1 Jesus Christ, who shall *j* the quick and the dead

2 Tim 4:8 the righteous *j,* shall give me [Paul] at that day [a crown of righteousness]

Jas 2:4 ye...are become *j's* of evil thoughts

Jas 4:12 one lawgiver [God]... who art thou that *j'st* another

Rev 19:11 in righteousness he [Jesus] doth *j*

JUDGES, BOOK OF. A historical book of the Old Testament that records the exploits of several different judges, or military deliverers, in Israel's history.

JUDGES OF ISRAEL (popular military leaders or deliverers who led Israel between the time of Joshua's death and the beginning of the kingship). The judges of Israel were: Othniel (Judg 3:9–11), Ehud (Judg 3:15–30), Shamgar (Judg 3:31), Deborah and Barak (Judg 4:4–24), Gideon (Judg 6:11–8:32), Abimelech (Judg 9:1–54), Tola (Judg 10:1–2), Jair (Judg 10:3–5), Jephthah (Judg 11:1–12:7), Ibzan (Judg 12:8–10), Elon (Judg 12:11–12), Abdon (Judg 12:13–15), Samson (Judg 14:1–16:31), Eli (1 Sam 4:15–18), Samuel (1 Sam 7:15), and Samuel's sons (1 Sam 8:1–3).

JUDGMENT

Ex 12:12 against all the gods of Egypt I [God]...execute *j*

1 Chr 18:14 David reigned... and executed *j*

Job 8:3 Doth God pervert *j*

Job 32:9 neither do the aged understand *j*

Ps 1:5 the ungodly shall not stand in the *j*

Ps 72:2 He [God] shall judge... thy poor with *j*

Ps 101:1 I will sing of mercy and *j:* unto thee [God]

Ps 119:66 Teach me good *j* and knowledge

Prov 21:3 To do justice and *j* is more acceptable to the LORD than sacrifice

Prov 29:26 every man's *j* cometh from the LORD

Eccl 12:14 God shall bring every work into *j*

Isa 42:1 he [God's servant] shall bring forth *j* to the Gentiles

Jer 9:24 I am the LORD which exercise ... *j*

Jer 33:15 he [Messiah] shall execute *j* and righteousness

Amos 5:24 But let *j* run down as waters

Matt 5:22 whosoever is angry with his brother...shall be in danger of the *j*

John 5:30 as I [Jesus] hear, I judge: and my *j* is just

John 9:39 For *j* I [Jesus] am come into this world

Rom 14:10 we shall all stand before the *j* seat of Christ

2 Cor 5:10 we must all appear before the *j* seat of Christ

Heb 9:27 appointed unto men once to die, but after this the *j*

1 Pet 4:17 *j* must begin at the house of God

1 John 4:17 we may have boldness in the day of *j*

Rev 14:7 Fear God...for the hour of his *j* is come

JUDGMENT OF GOD

Rom 2:3 thinkest thou...that thou shalt escape the *j-o-G*

2 Thes 1:5 a manifest token of the righteous *j-o-G*

JUPITER (chief god of Roman mythology and a name applied to Barnabas by the citizens of Lystra). Acts 14:12.

JUST [LY]

Gen 6:9 Noah was a *j* man

Job 4:17 Shall mortal man be more *j* than God

Ps 37:12 The wicked plotteth against the *j*

Prov 4:18 path of the *j* is as the shining light

Prov 11:1 a *j* weight is his [God's] delight

Prov 20:7 The *j* man walketh in his integrity

Eccl 7:20 not a *j* man upon earth, that...sinneth not

Isa 45:21 no God...beside me; a *j* God and a Saviour

Mic 6:8 what doth the LORD require...but to do *j'ly*

Hab 2:4 but the *j* shall live by his faith

Matt 1:19 Joseph her [Mary's] husband, being a *j* man

Luke 2:25 Simeon...was *j* and devout

Rom 1:17 as it is written, The *j* shall live by faith

Col 4:1 give unto your servants that which is *j*

1 Pet 3:18 For Christ also hath once suffered for sins, the *j* for the unjust

1 John 1:9 he [Jesus] is faithful and *j* to forgive us our sins

545

JUSTICE

Job 8:3 or doth the Almighty pervert *j*

Ps 82:3 do *j* to the afflicted and needy

Prov 21:3 To do *j*...is more acceptable...than sacrifice

Jer 23:5 a King [Jesus] shall... execute judgment and *j*

JUSTIFICATION

Rom 4:25 Who [Jesus]...was raised again for our *j*

Rom 5:18 by the righteousness of one [Jesus] the free gift came...unto *j* of life

JUSTIFY [IED, IETH]

Job 9:20 If I *j* myself, mine own mouth...condemn me

Job 25:4 How then can man be *j'ied* with God

Matt 12:37 by thy words thou shalt be *j'ied*

Rom 3:24 *j'ied* freely by his [God's] grace through... Christ Jesus

Rom 3:28 *j'ied* by faith without the deeds of the law

Rom 5:1 being *j'ied* by faith, we have peace with God

Rom 8:33 It is God that *j'ieth*

1 Cor 6:11 ye are *j'ied* in the name of the Lord

Gal 2:16 a man is not *j'ied* by the works of the law

Titus 3:7 *j'ied* by his [God's] grace, we should be made heirs...of eternal life

Jas 2:21 Was not Abraham our father *j'ied* by works

-K-

KADESH (a wilderness region where the Israelites camped before entering Canaan). Gen 14:7; 16:14; 20:1 • Num 20:1,14, 16–22; **33:36–37** • Deut 1:46 • Judg 11:16–17 • Ps 29:8. *Kadesh-barnea:* **Num 32:8** • Josh 14:7.

KEDAR (a son of Ishmael and founder of an Arabic tribe). Gen 25:12–13 • Isa 21:17 • Jer 49:28–29.

KEDESH (one of the six cities of refuge, situated in the territory of Naphtali). Josh 20:1–7 • Judg 4:10–11 • 1 Chr 6:76.

KEEP [ETH, ING]

Gen 2:15 God...put him [Adam] into the garden of Eden...to *k* it

Ex 12:14 *k* it [the Passover] a feast to the LORD

Ex 19:5 *k* my [God's] covenant, then ye shall be a peculiar treasure

Ex 20:8 Remember the sabbath day, to *k* it holy

Ex 31:14 *k* the sabbath...it is holy unto you

Deut 5:10 showing mercy unto...them that...*k* my [God's] commandments

Ps 17:8 *K* me as the apple of the eye...hide me

Ps 34:13 *K* thy tongue from evil...thy lips from...guile

Ps 91:11 he [God] shall...*k* thee in all thy ways

Ps 119:4 Thou [God] hast commanded us to *k* thy precepts

Ps 119:34 Give me understanding, and I shall *k* thy [God's] law

Ps 119:146 save me...I shall *k* thy [God's] testimonies

Ps 121:4 he [God] that *k'eth* Israel...neither slumber nor sleep

Ps 127:1 except the LORD *k* the city, the watchman waketh but in vain

Ps 141:3 Set a watch, O LORD... *k* the door of my lips

Prov 3:1 let thine heart *k* my [God's] commandments

Prov 4:23 *K* thy heart with all diligence

Prov 13:3 He that *k'eth* his mouth *k'eth* his life

Prov 21:23 *k'eth* his...tongue *k'eth* his soul from troubles

Prov 29:11 fool uttereth all his mind...wise man *k'eth* it in

Eccl 3:7 time to *k* silence, and a time to speak

Isa 26:3 wilt *k* him...whose mind is stayed on thee [God]

Ezek 20:19 walk in my [God's] statutes, and *k* my judgments

Hab 2:20 let all the earth *k* silence before him [God]

Mark 7:9 reject the command-ment...that ye [Pharisees] may *k* your own tradition

Luke 2:8 shepherds...*k'ing* watch over their flock

Luke 11:28 Yea rather, blessed are they that hear the word of God, and *k* it

John 9:16 This man [Jesus] is not of God, because he *k'eth* not the sabbath

John 14:15 If ye love me [Jesus], *k* my commandments

John 15:10 If ye *k* my [Jesus'] commandments, ye shall abide in my love

1 Cor 7:19 Circumcision is nothing...but the *k'ing* of the commandments

1 Cor 9:27 But I [Paul] *k* under my body, and bring it into subjection

1 Cor 14:28 no interpreter, let him *k* silence in the church

Eph 4:3 *k* the unity of the Spirit in the bond of peace

Phil 4:7 peace of God...*k* your hearts...through Christ

2 Thes 3:3 Lord...shall stablish you...*k* you from evil

2 Tim 1:12 he [Jesus] is able to *k* that...I have committed

Jas 1:27 Pure religion...is this... to *k* himself unspotted

Jas 2:10 *k* the whole law, and yet offend in one point, he is guilty of all

1 John 5:3 this is the love of God...*k* his commandments

1 John 5:21 Little children, *k* yourselves from idols

Jude 24 unto him [Jesus] that is able to *k* you from falling

Rev 2:26 he that...*k'eth* my [Jesus'] works...to him will I give power

KEEP HIS COMMANDMENTS

Deut 13:4 Ye shall walk after the LORD...and *k-h-c*

Ps 78:7 That they might...not forget the works of God, but *k-h-c*

Eccl 12:13 *k-h-c:* for this is the whole duty of man

1 John 2:3 we do know that we know him, if we *k-h-c*

KENAN (a son of Enoch and great-grandson of Adam). 1 Chr 1:1–2. *Cainan:* Gen 5:9.

KENITES (a nomadic Midian-ite tribe that was friendly toward the Israelites). Gen 15:19 • Num 24:20–22 • Judg 4:11,17–22 • 1 Sam 15:6; 30:29 • 1 Chr 2:55.

KENIZZITES (a Canaanite tribe whose land was promised to Abraham's descendants). Gen 15:18–19.

KEPT
Ex 3:1 Moses *k* the flock of Jethro

Ps 18:21 For I have *k* the ways of the LORD

Ps 32:3 When I *k* silence, my bones waxed old

Ps 78:56 they...provoked... God...*k* not his testimonies

Ps 119:55 I have remembered thy [God's] name...and have *k* thy law

Matt 19:20 these things have I *k* from my youth

Luke 2:19 But Mary *k* all these things...in her heart

John 17:12 I [Jesus] *k* them [the disciples] in thy [God's] name...none...is lost

Gal 3:23 before faith came, we were *k* under the law

2 Tim 4:7 I [Paul]...have fought a good fight...*k* the faith

1 Pet 1:5 *k* by the power of God through faith

KETURAH (a wife of Abraham whose sons were ancestors of Arabian tribes). Gen 25:1,4 • 1 Chr 1:32–33.

KEY [S]

Matt 16:19 give unto thee the *k's* of the kingdom

Rev 9:1 to him [angel] was given...*k* of...bottomless pit

KIDRON (a valley or ravine that David crossed while fleeing from his son Absalom). **2 Sam 15:23–30** • 2 Kgs 23:4–6,12 • 2 Chr 15:16; 29:16; 30:14 • Jer 31:40. *Cedron:* John 18:1.

KILL [ED, EST, ETH]

Gen 37:31 they [Joseph's brothers]...*k'ed* a kid of the goats

Ex 2:14 intendest thou [Moses] to *k* me [Hebrew slave], as thou *k'est* the Egyptian

Ex 20:13 Thou shalt not *k*

Num 35:15 every one that *k'eth* any person unawares may flee

Deut 5:17 Thou shalt not *k*

1 Sam 2:6 The LORD *k'eth,* and maketh alive

2 Sam 12:9 thou [David] hast *k'ed* Uriah the Hittite

Ps 44:22 for thy [God's] sake are we *k'ed* all the day long

Prov 21:25 The desire of the slothful *k'eth* him

Eccl 3:3 A time to *k,* and a time to heal

Matt 5:21 whosoever shall *k*... in danger of the judgment

Matt 23:37 O Jerusalem...thou that *k'est* the prophets

Mark 3:4 Is it lawful...on the sabbath...save life, or to *k*

Mark 8:31 Son of man must suffer...and be *k'ed*

Mark 9:31 after...he [Jesus] is *k'ed,* he shall rise

Mark 12:7 *k* him [the heir]... inheritance shall be ours

Luke 12:4 Be not afraid of them that *k* the body

Luke 12:5 after he hath *k'ed* hath power to cast into hell

Luke 15:23 bring hither the fatted calf, and *k* it

Luke 22:2 chief priests and scribes sought how they might *k* him [Jesus]

John 10:10 thief cometh...to *k,* and to destroy

John 16:2 whosoever *k'eth* you will think that he doeth God service

Acts 10:13 Peter; *k,* and eat

Acts 12:2 he [Herod] *k'ed* James the brother of John

Rom 8:36 For thy sake we are *k'ed* all the day long

2 Cor 3:6 letter *k'eth,* but the spirit giveth life

Jas 4:2 ye *k,* and desire to have, and cannot obtain

Rev 11:7 beast...shall overcome them [two witnesses], and *k* them

KINGDOM [S]

Ex 19:6 unto me [God] a *k* of priests, and an holy nation

1 Sam 15:28 The LORD hath rent the *k* of Israel from thee [Saul] this day

2 Sam 7:16 thine [David's] house and thy *k* shall be established for ever

1 Kgs 4:21 And Solomon reigned over all *k's*

1 Chr 29:11 thine is the *k,* O LORD...thou art exalted

Ps 22:28 the *k* is the LORD's

Ps 68:32 Sing unto God, ye *k's* of the earth

Ps 145:13 Thy [God's] *k* is an everlasting *k*

Dan 2:39 after thee [Nebuchadnezzar] shall arise another *k*

Dan 4:3 his [God's] *k* is an everlasting kingdom

Dan 4:31 The *k* is departed from thee [Nebuchadnezzar]

Dan 5:28 Thy [Belshazzar's] *k* is divided...given to...Medes

Matt 6:10 Thy [God's] *k* come. Thy will be done

Matt 8:12 children of the *k*... cast...into outer darkness

Matt 24:7 nation shall rise against nation...*k* against *k*

Mark 3:24 *k* be divided against itself, that *k* cannot stand

Luke 1:33 of his [Jesus'] *k* there shall be no end

Luke 4:5 the devil...showed unto him [Jesus] all the *k's* of the world

Luke 12:32 your Father's good pleasure to give you the *k*

Luke 23:42 remember me [thief] when thou [Jesus] comest into thy *k*

John 18:36 My [Jesus'] *k* is not of this world

1 Thes 2:12 God, who hath called you unto his *k*

Rev 11:15 *k's* of this world are become the *k's* of our Lord

KINGDOM OF GOD

Matt 6:33 seek ye first the *k-o-G,* and his righteousness

Mark 1:15 time is fulfilled, and the *k-o-G* is at hand

Mark 9:47 better...to enter into the *k-o-G* with one eye

Mark 10:14 forbid them [children] not...such is the *k-o-G*

Mark 10:25 eye of a needle, than for a rich man to enter into the *k-o-G*

Luke 9:2 he [Jesus] sent them [the disciples]...to preach... *k-o-G*

Luke 9:62 No man...looking back, is fit for the *k-o-G*

John 3:3 Except a man be born again...cannot see the *k-o-G*

Rom 14:17 *k-o-G* is not meat and drink; but righteousness

1 Cor 6:9 the unrighteous shall not inherit the *k-o-G*

1 Cor 15:50 flesh and blood cannot inherit the *k-o-G*

KINGDOM OF HEAVEN

Matt 5:10 Blessed are they which are persecuted... their's is the *k-o-h*

Matt 5:20 ye shall in no case enter into the *k-o-h*

Matt 7:21 Not every one that saith unto me, Lord, Lord, shall enter into the *k-o-h*

Matt 16:19 I [Jesus] will give... thee...keys of the *k-o-h*

Matt 18:4 humble himself as this little child, the same is greatest in the *k-o-h*

Matt 23:13 ye [scribes and Pharisees] shut up the *k-o-h* against men

KINGS, BOOKS OF FIRST AND SECOND. Two historical books of the Old Testament that cover a period of roughly four centuries in Jewish history—from about 970 to 587 B.C. First Kings begins with the reign of Solomon as successor to David (1 Kgs 1:1–11:43). The closing chapters of 2 Kings cover the final years of the nation of Judah before it fell to the Babylonians.

KING'S HIGHWAY (an important road linking Damascus and Egypt that ran through Israel). Num 20:17–21.

KIRJATH-ARBA. See *Hebron.*

KIRJATH-JEARIM (a fortified city of the Gibeonites where the ark of the covenant was kept for a time). Josh 9:17; 15:60; 18:28 • **1 Chr 13–16.** *Baalah:* Josh 15:9.

KISHON (a river in northern Palestine where Elijah killed the prophets of Baal). Judg 4:13 • **1 Kgs 18:40.** *Kison:* Ps 83:9.

KISON. See *Kishon.*

KISS [ED]

Gen 50:1 Joseph...wept upon him [Jacob], and *k'ed* him

Ps 85:10 righteousness and peace have *k'ed* each other

Matt 26:49 he [Judas]...said, Hail...and *k'ed* him [Jesus]

Luke 15:20 his [prodigal son's] father...fell on his neck, and *k'ed* him

Luke 22:48 Judas, betrayest thou the Son of man with a *k*

2 Cor 13:12 Greet one another with an holy *k*

1 Pet 5:14 Greet ye one another with a *k* of charity

KITTIM. See *Cyprus.*

KNOCK [ED]

Luke 11:9 k, and it shall be opened unto you

Acts 12:13 as Peter *k'ed* at the door...a damsel came

Rev 3:20 I [Jesus] stand at the door, and *k*

KNOW THAT I AM THE LORD

Ex 7:5 Egyptians shall *k-t-I-a-t-L,* when I stretch forth mine hand upon Egypt

Ezek 6:7 slain shall fall...and ye shall *k-t-I-a-t-L*

Ezek 16:62 will establish my covenant with thee; and thou shalt *k-t-I-a-t-L*

Ezek 30:19 will I execute judgments in Egypt: and they shall *k-t-I-a-t-L*

KNOW THE LORD

Jer 31:34 they shall teach no more...*K-t-L:* for they shall all know me

Heb 8:11 not teach...his brother, saying, *K-t-L:* for all shall know me

KNOWLEDGE

Gen 2:17 tree of the *k* of good and evil, thou shalt not eat

1 Sam 2:3 for the LORD is a God of *k,* and by him actions are weighed

Job 21:22 Shall any teach God *k?* seeing he judgeth

Job 35:16 he [Job] multiplieth words without *k*

Ps 19:2 night unto night showeth *k*

Ps 139:6 Such *k* is too wonderful for me

Ps 144:3 what is man, that thou [God] takest *k* of him

Prov 1:7 fear of the LORD is the beginning of *k*

Prov 10:14 Wise men lay up *k:* but the mouth of the foolish is near destruction

Prov 20:15 the lips of *k* are a precious jewel

Prov 24:5 a man of *k* increaseth strength

Eccl 1:18 he that increaseth *k* increaseth sorrow

Hos 6:6 I [God] desired...*k* of God more than...offerings

Hab 2:14 earth...filled with the *k* of the glory of the LORD

Rom 11:33 depth of the riches... wisdom and *k* of God

1 Cor 12:8 to one is given...
word of wisdom: to another...
word of *k*

1 Cor 13:2 though I [Paul]...
understand...all *k*

Eph 3:19 know the love of
Christ, which passeth *k*

Phil 1:9 love may abound...in *k*
and in all judgment

1 Tim 2:4 all men...to come
unto the *k* of the truth

2 Tim 3:7 never able to come to
the *k* of the truth

2 Pet 1:5 add to your faith virtue; and to virtue *k*

2 Pet 3:18 grow in grace, and in
the *k* of our Lord

KOHATH (a son of Levi and
founder of the Kohathites,
priests who cared for the tabernacle accessories). Gen 46:11 •
Ex 6:18–19 • Num 3:30–31.

KORAH (leader of a rebellion
against Moses in the wilderness). Ex 6:21,24 • Num
16:30–33. *Core:* Jude 11.

-L-

LABAN (father of Leah and Rachel, who were given in marriage to Jacob). Gen 24:29, 50; 29:5–29; 30:25–40; 31:2–55.

LABOUR [ED, ETH, S]
Ex 20:9 Six days shalt thou *l*, and do all thy work
Ps 104:23 Man goeth forth...to his *l* until the evening
Ps 127:1 Except the LORD build the house, they *l* in vain that build it
Prov 23:4 *L* not to be rich
Eccl 3:9 What profit hath he... wherein he *l'eth*
Eccl 3:13 man should...enjoy the good of all his *l*
Matt 11:28 Come unto me [Jesus], all ye that *l* and are heavy laden
1 Cor 3:8 his own reward according to his own *l*
1 Cor 15:58 your *l* is not in vain in the Lord
2 Cor 11:23 in *l's*...abundant, in stripes above measure
Phil 2:16 I [Paul] have not... *l'ed* in vain
Heb 4:11 Let us *l* therefore to enter into that rest

LABOURER [S]
Matt 9:37 The harvest...is plenteous, but the *l's* are few
Luke 10:7 for the *l* is worthy of his hire

1 Cor 3:9 For we are *l's* together with God

LACHISH (an Amorite city captured by Joshua). **Josh 10:3–35;** 12:11; 15:39 • 2 Kgs 14:19; 18:14–17 • 2 Chr 25:27 • Neh 11:30 • Isa 36:1–2 • Jer 34:1,7.

LACK [ED, EST]
Gen 18:28 wilt thou [God] destroy all the city for *l* of five
Hos 4:6 people are destroyed for *l* of knowledge
Matt 19:20 these things have I kept...what *l* I yet
Luke 18:22 *l'est* thou one thing: sell all...distribute unto the poor
Luke 22:35 When I [Jesus] sent you [the disciples] without purse...*l'ed* ye any thing
Jas 1:5 any of you *l* wisdom, let him ask of God

LAISH. See *Dan,* No. 2.

LAMB OF GOD
John 1:29 the *L-o-G*...taketh away the sin of the world
John 1:36 he [John the Baptist] saith, Behold the *L-o-G*

LAME
Prov 26:7 The legs of the *l* are not equal
Luke 7:22 tell John...how that the blind see, the *l* walk

Luke 14:13 call the poor...the *l,* the blind

LAMECH (father of Noah). **Gen 5:25–31** • 1 Chr 1:3 • Luke 3:36.

LAMENTATIONS, BOOK OF. A short book of the Old Testament that expresses the prophet Jeremiah's grief at the destruction of Jerusalem and the temple by the pagan Babylonians.

LAMP [S]
Judg 7:20 brake the pitchers... held the *l's* in their...hands
2 Sam 22:29 For thou art my *l,* O LORD
Job 41:19 Out of his [God's] mouth go burning *l's*
Ps 119:105 Thy [God's] word is a *l* unto my feet
Matt 25:3 foolish took their *l's,* and took no oil

LAODICEA (a major city in Asia Minor where one of the seven churches addressed in the Book of Revelation was located). Col 2:1; 4:13–16 • **Rev 3:14–18.**

LASCIVIOUSNESS
Gal 5:19 works of the flesh are...Adultery...*l*
Jude 4 certain men...turning the grace of our God into *l*

LAST
Prov 23:32 At the *l* it [wine] biteth like a serpent
Isa 2:2 in the *l* days...LORD's house shall be established
Isa 44:6 I [God] am the first, and I am the *l*
Matt 20:8 give them [the laborers] their hire...from the *l* unto the first
Mark 9:35 desire to be first, the same shall be *l*
Mark 10:31 many that are first shall be *l*
1 Cor 15:26 The *l* enemy... destroyed is death
1 Cor 15:45 the *l* Adam was made a quickening spirit
2 Tim 3:1 in the *l* days perilous times shall come
Heb 1:2 Hath in these *l* days spoken...by his [God's] Son
Rev 1:11 I [Jesus] am Alpha and Omega, the first and the *l*
Rev 22:13 I [Jesus] am...the first and the *l*

LAWFUL [LY]
Matt 12:2 thy [Jesus'] disciples do that which is not *l*... upon the sabbath day
Matt 19:3 Is it *l* for a man to put away his wife
Mark 3:4 Is it *l* to do good on the sabbath...or...evil
Mark 12:14 Is it *l* to give tribute to Caesar
1 Cor 6:12 All things are *l* unto me [Paul], but all things are not expedient

1 Tim 1:8 the law is good, if a man use it *l'ly*

LAWLESS
1 Tim 1:9 law is...made...for the *l* and disobedient

LAY [ETH, ING]
Ps 71:10 they that *l* wait for my soul take counsel
Prov 10:14 Wise men *l* up knowledge
Isa 28:16 I [God] *l* in Zion for a foundation...a tried stone
Jer 6:21 Behold, I [God] will *l* stumblingblocks before this people
Ezek 25:17 know that I am the LORD, when I shall *l* my vengeance upon them
Matt 6:20 *l* up for yourselves treasures in heaven
Matt 28:6 Come, see the place where the Lord *l*
Luke 9:58 Son of man hath not where to *l* his head
Luke 12:21 he that *l'eth* up treasure...not rich toward God
Luke 21:12 *l* their hands on you [the disciples], and persecute you
John 10:15 I [Jesus] *l* down my life for the sheep
John 13:37 Peter said...Lord... I will *l* down my life for thy [Jesus'] sake
John 15:13 that a man *l* down his life for his friends

1 Cor 3:11 can no man *l* than that is laid...Jesus Christ
1 Cor 16:2 *l* by him in store, as God hath prospered
1 Tim 4:14 with the *l'ing* on of the hands of the presbytery
1 Tim 5:22 *L* hands suddenly on no man
Heb 12:1 *l* aside...the sin which doth...beset us
1 Pet 2:1 *l'ing* aside all malice, and all guile

LAZARUS (the brother of Mary and Martha whom Jesus raised from the dead). **John 11:1–44;** 12:1–11.

LEAD [ETH]
Ex 13:21 LORD went before them [Israelites]...to *l* them
Ps 23:2 he [God] *l'eth* me beside the still waters
Ps 25:5 *L* me in thy [God's] truth, and teach me
Ps 61:2 *l* me to the rock that is higher than I
Ps 139:10 Even there shall thy [God's] hand *l* me
Isa 11:6 and a little child shall *l* them
Isa 40:11 He [God]...shall gently *l* those...with young
Matt 6:13 *l* us not into temptation...deliver us from evil
Matt 7:14 narrow is the way, which *l'eth* unto life
Luke 6:39 he [Jesus] spake a parable...Can...blind *l*... blind

Rev 7:17 Lamb...shall *l* them unto living...waters

LEAH (a wife of Jacob who gave birth to several of his children). **Gen 29:16–35; 30:9–20; 31:4,14; 33:1–7; 34:1; 35:23; 46:15,18; 49:31.**

LEARN [ED, ING]
Ps 119:73 understanding, that I may *l* thy [God's] commandments
Prov 1:5 A wise man...will increase *l'ing*
Isa 1:17 **L** to do well...relieve the oppressed
Jer 10:2 Thus saith the LORD, **L** not the way of the heathen
Dan 1:17 God gave them [Daniel and his friends]...skill in all *l'ing* and wisdom
Matt 11:29 Take my [Jesus'] yoke...and *l* of me
Phil 4:11 I [Paul] have *l'ed,* in whatsoever state I am, therewith to be content
2 Tim 3:7 *l'ing,* and never able to come to the...truth
Heb 5:8 Though he [Jesus] were a Son, yet *l'ed* he obedience

LEAST
Matt 2:6 Bethlehem, in the land of Juda, art not the *l* among the princes of Juda
Matt 25:40 as ye have done it unto one of the *l* of these my [Jesus'] brethren

Luke 7:28 he that is *l* in the kingdom...is greater than he [John the Baptist]
Luke 9:48 *l* among you all, the same shall be great
Eph 3:8 Unto me [Paul], who am less than the *l* of all saints

LEAVEN
Matt 13:33 kingdom of heaven is like unto *l*
Luke 12:1 Beware ye of the *l* of the Pharisees
1 Cor 5:6 a little *l* leaveneth the whole lump

LEBANON (a rugged mountainous region in northern Palestine). Deut 1:7; 3:25 • Josh 11:16–17; 12:7; 13:5–7 • Judg 3:1–3 • 1 Kgs 5:5–18 • Isa 29:17; 37:24 • Ezek 17:3 • Hos 14:5–7.

LEBBAEUS. See *Judas.*

LED
Ps 68:18 Thou hast ascended on high...*l* captivity captive
Prov 4:11 I have taught thee... *l* thee in right paths
Isa 55:12 go out with joy, and be *l* forth with peace
Luke 4:1 Jesus...was *l* by the Spirit into the wilderness
Luke 24:50 he [Jesus] *l* them out as far as to Bethany
Acts 8:32 He [Jesus] was *l* as a sheep to the slaughter

Acts 9:8 l him [Paul] by the hand...into Damascus

Rom 8:14 l by the Spirit of God...are the sons of God

Gal 5:18 if ye be *l* of the Spirit...not under the law

2 Pet 3:17 lest ye also, being *l* away with the error of the wicked, fall

LEHI (a site where Samson killed one thousand Philistines). Judg 15:9–15.

LEMUEL (an unknown king mentioned in the Book of Proverbs). Prov 31:1–31.

LEPER [S]

2 Kgs 5:1 Naaman...was also a mighty man...but he was a *l*

2 Kgs 15:5 the king [Azariah]... was a *l* unto...his death

Matt 8:2 there came a *l* and worshipped him [Jesus]

Matt 11:5 l's are cleansed, and the deaf hear

Mark 14:3 in...house of Simon the *l,* as he [Jesus] sat at meat

Luke 17:12 there met him [Jesus] ten men that were *l's*

LEVI

1. A son of Jacob and ancestor of the Levites. Gen 29:34; 34:25,30; 35:23; 49:5 • Ex 1:2; 6:16 • Num 3:17; 16:1; 26:59 • 1 Chr 6:38,43,47 • Ezra 8:18.

The tribe of Levi, known as the Levites, were responsible for taking care of the tabernacle and temple and assisting the priests in their ceremonial duties. Num 3:5–8.

2. Another name for Matthew. See *Matthew*.

LEVITICUS, BOOK OF. An Old Testament book filled with instructions about sanctification of the priests, regulations for worship and ceremonial offerings, and personal purification and dietary laws. The theme of the book is holiness.

LIAR [S]

Ps 116:11 I said in my haste, All men are *l's*

Prov 19:22 a poor man is better than a *l*

Rom 3:4 let God be true, but every man a *l*

Titus 1:12 The Cretians are alway *l's,* evil beasts

1 John 1:10 that we have not sinned...make him [God] a *l*

1 John 4:20 say, I love God... hateth his brother, he is a *l*

LIBERTY

Lev 25:10 hallow the fiftieth year, and proclaim *l*

Ps 119:45 walk at *l:* for I seek thy [God's] precepts

Isa 61:1 sent me [God's servant]...to proclaim *l* to the captives

Luke 4:18 to set at *l* them that are bruised

Acts 26:32 This man [Paul] might have been set at *l*

1 Cor 8:9 lest...this *l* of yours become a stumblingblock

2 Cor 3:17 where the Spirit of the Lord is, there is *l*

Gal 5:1 Stand fast therefore in the *l* wherewith Christ hath made us free

2 Pet 2:19 While they promise them *l,* they...are the servants of corruption

LIBYA (Greek name for Africa). Jer 46:9 • Ezek 30:5; 38:5 • Dan 11:43 • Acts 2:10. *Lubim:* Nah 3:9. *Phut:* Ezek 27:10.

LIE [S, ST, TH]

Lev 19:11 not steal...neither *l* one to another

Num 23:19 God is not a man, that he should *l*

Job 13:4 forgers of *l's*...physicians of no value

Ps 23:2 He [God] maketh me to *l* down in green pastures

Ps 58:3 the wicked...go astray ...speaking *l's*

Ps 62:9 men of high degree are a *l:* to be laid in the balance

Prov 3:24 When thou *l'st* down, thou shalt not be afraid... sleep shall be sweet

Prov 14:5 A faithful witness will not *l*

Prov 14:25 but a deceitful witness speaketh *l's*

Isa 11:6 and the leopard shall *l* down with the kid

Ezek 34:15 I [God] will feed my flock, and I will cause them to *l* down

Nah 3:1 Woe to the bloody city... full of *l's* and robbery

Zeph 3:13 remnant of Israel shall not...speak *l's*

Mark 5:23 My [Jairus's]... daughter *l'th* at the point of death

Acts 5:3 Ananias, why hath Satan filled thine heart to *l*

Rom 1:25 changed the truth of God into a *l*

Rom 12:18 as much as *l'th* in you, live peaceably

1 John 1:6 say that we have fellowship with him [God], and walk in darkness, we *l*

LIFE

Gen 2:7 And the LORD God... breathed into his [man's] nostrils the breath of *l*

Deut 19:21 *l* shall go for *l,* eye for eye, tooth for tooth

Josh 1:5 not any man...stand before thee [Joshua] all the days of thy *l*

Job 2:6 he [Job] is in thine [Satan's] hand; but save his *l*

Job 36:6 He [God] preserveth not the *l* of the wicked

Ps 23:6 mercy shall follow me all the days of my *l*

Ps 27:1 LORD is the strength of my *l;* of whom...be afraid

Ps 31:10 *l* is spent with grief, and my years with sighing

Ps 38:12 They...that seek after my *l* lay snares for me

Prov 4:23 Keep thy heart...for out of it are the issues of *l*

Prov 8:35 For whoso findeth me findeth *l*

Prov 18:21 Death and *l* are in the...tongue

Jer 21:8 I [God] set before you... *l,* and...death

Matt 6:25 no thought for your *l,* what ye shall eat

Matt 19:16 what good thing shall I do...have eternal *l*

Matt 20:28 Even as the Son of man came...to give his *l* a ransom for many

Mark 8:35 whosoever will save his *l* shall lose it

Luke 12:15 man's *l* consisteth not in the abundance of the things...he possesseth

John 1:4 In him [Jesus] was *l*... the light of men

John 3:15 whosoever believeth ...have eternal *l*

John 3:36 He that believeth on the Son hath everlasting *l*

John 6:35 I [Jesus] am the bread of *l*

John 6:47 He that believeth on me [Jesus] hath everlasting *l*

John 10:10 I [Jesus] am come that they might have *l*

John 10:15 and I [Jesus] lay down my *l* for the sheep

John 11:25 I [Jesus] am the resurrection, and the *l*

John 14:6 I [Jesus] am the way, the truth, and the *l*

John 15:13 that a man lay down his *l* for his friends

Rom 6:23 gift of God is eternal *l* through Jesus Christ

Rom 8:38 death, nor *l,* nor angels, nor principalities

1 Cor 15:19 in this *l* only we have hope in Christ, we are...most miserable

Phil 2:16 Holding forth the word of *l*

Jas 4:14 what is your *l?* It is even a vapour, that... vanisheth away

1 John 2:25 this is the promise ...even eternal *l*

1 John 3:14 passed from death unto *l*...we love the brethren

1 John 5:12 He that hath the Son hath *l*

Rev 20:15 not found written in the book of *l* was cast into the lake of fire

Rev 22:17 let him take the water of *l* freely

LIGHT [S]

Gen 1:3 God said, Let there be *l:* and there was *l*

Gen 1:16 two great *l's;* the greater *l* to rule the day

Ps 27:1 The LORD is my *l* and my salvation

Ps 119:105 Thy [God's] word is...a *l* unto my path

Prov 4:18 path of the just is as the shining *l*

Isa 2:5 come ye, and let us walk in the *l* of the LORD

Isa 9:2 people...in darkness have seen a great *l*

Isa 60:1 Arise, shine; for thy *l* is come

Isa 60:3 Gentiles shall come to thy [God's] *l*

Amos 5:18 day of the LORD is darkness, and not *l*

Matt 5:14 Ye are the *l* of the world

Matt 11:30 my [Jesus'] yoke is easy, and my burden is *l*

Luke 2:32 A *l* to lighten the Gentiles...glory of...Israel

Luke 16:8 children of this world are...wiser than the children of *l*

John 1:4 In him [Jesus] was life...life was the *l* of men

John 1:9 That was the true *L* [Jesus]

John 8:12 I [Jesus] am the *l* of the world

Acts 9:3 shined round about him [Paul] a *l* from heaven

Acts 13:47 set thee [Paul] to be a *l* of the Gentiles

Acts 26:18 turn them from darkness to *l*

Rom 13:12 and let us put on the armour of *l*

Phil 2:15 midst of...perverse nation...ye shine as *l's*

Jas 1:17 Every good gift...is... from the Father of *l's*

1 Pet 2:9 who [Jesus] hath called you...into his marvellous *l*

1 John 1:5 God is *l,* and in him is no darkness

1 John 2:10 He that loveth his brother abideth in the *l*

LIGHT OF THE WORLD, JESUS AS. See *"I Am" Statements of Jesus.*

LIKENESS

Gen 1:26 make man in our image, after our *l*

Ezek 10:10 four had one *l,* as if a wheel had been in the midst of a wheel

Phil 2:7 took upon him [Jesus] ...form of a servant...made in the *l* of men

LIVE [ING, S, TH]

Gen 2:7 and man became a *l'ing* soul

Gen 45:7 God sent me [Joseph] ...to save your *l's*

Deut 8:3 that man doth not *l* by bread only

Job 14:14 If a man die, shall he *l* again

Job 19:25 I [Job] know that my redeemer *l'th*

Ps 63:4 Thus will I bless thee [God] while I *l*

Ps 142:5 Thou [God] art my refuge and my portion in the land of the *l'ing*

Jer 2:13 forsaken me [God] the fountain of *l'ing* waters

Ezek 37:3 Son of man, can these bones *l*

Dan 6:26 men tremble and fear before the God of Daniel...the *l'ing* God

Jon 4:3 better for me [Jonah] to die than to *l*

Hab 2:4 but the just shall *l* by his faith

Matt 4:4 Man shall not *l* by bread alone

Mark 12:27 not the God of the dead, but...of the *l'ing*

Mark 12:44 she [a widow]... cast in...all her *l'ing*

Luke 9:56 Son of man is not come to destroy men's *l's,* but to save them

Luke 15:13 younger son... wasted his substance with riotous *l'ing*

Luke 24:5 Why seek...the *l'ing* among the dead

John 4:10 he [Jesus] would have given...*l'ing* water

John 6:51 I [Jesus] am the *l'ing* bread

John 11:25 believeth in me [Jesus], though he were dead, yet shall he *l*

John 11:26 *l'th*...in me [Jesus] shall never die

Acts 17:28 in him [Jesus] we *l,* and move...have our being

Rom 12:1 present your bodies a *l'ing* sacrifice

Rom 12:18 If it be possible...*l* peaceably with all men

Rom 14:7 none...*l'th* to himself ...no man dieth to himself

Rom 14:8 whether we *l*...or die, we are the Lord's

1 Cor 9:14 preach the gospel should *l* of the gospel

Gal 2:14 why compellest thou [Peter] the Gentiles to *l* as do the Jews

Gal 2:19 I [Paul]...am dead to the law...might *l* unto God

Gal 2:20 I [Paul] *l;* yet not I, but Christ *l'th* in me

Gal 5:25 *l* in the Spirit, let us also walk in the Spirit

Phil 1:21 to me [Paul] to *l* is Christ, and to die is gain

1 John 3:16 we ought to lay down our *l's* for the brethren

1 John 4:9 God sent his...Son... we might *l* through him

Rev 1:18 I am he [Jesus] that *l'th,* and was dead

LIVELY

Ps 38:19 mine enemies are *l,* and they are strong

1 Pet 1:3 a *l* hope by the resurrection of Jesus Christ

1 Pet 2:5 Ye also, as *l* stones, are built up a spiritual house

LIVING GOD

Josh 3:10 ye shall know that the *l-G* is among you

Ps 42:2 My soul thirsteth for God, for the *l-G*

Jer 10:10 he [God] is the *l-G,* and an everlasting king

Dan 6:20 O Daniel, servant of the *l-G*

Matt 16:16 Peter...said, Thou
art the Christ...Son of the
l-G
John 6:69 we [the disciples]
believe and are sure...thou
art...the Son of the *l-G*
2 Cor 6:16 for ye are the temple
of the *l-G*
1 Tim 3:15 church of the *l-G,*
the...ground of the truth
Heb 10:31 a fearful thing to fall
into the hands of the *l-G*

LO-AMMI (a symbolic name
for Hosea's son, meaning "not
my people," and signifying
God's rejection of Israel). Hos
1:8–9.

LOD. See *Lydda.*

LONGSUFFERING
Ps 86:15 But thou, O Lord,
art...gracious, *l*
Gal 5:22 fruit of the Spirit is
love...*l*, gentleness
2 Pet 3:9 Lord is...*l* to us-ward,
not willing that any should
perish

LORD IS GOOD
Ps 34:8 O taste and see that
the *L-i-g*
Ps 100:5 the *L-i-g;* his mercy is
everlasting
Lam 3:25 The *L-i-g* unto them
that wait for him
Nah 1:7 The *L-i-g,* a strong
hold in the day of trouble

LORD WAS WITH HIM
Gen 39:3 his [Joseph's] master
saw that the *L-w-w-h*
1 Sam 3:19 Samuel grew, and
the *L-w-w-h*
1 Sam 18:12 Saul was afraid of
David, because the *L-w-w-h*
1 Sam 18:14 David behaved
himself wisely...the *L-w-w-h*
2 Kgs 18:7 the *L-w-w-h;* and
he [Hezekiah] prospered
1 Chr 9:20 Phinehas...was the
ruler...and the *L-w-w-h*
Luke 1:66 hand of the *L-w-w-h*
[John the Baptist]

LORD'S PRAYER. Matt
6:9–13 • Luke 11:1–4.

LORD'S SUPPER. Matt 26:
26–30 • Mark 14:22–26 • Luke
22:14–20 • 1 Cor 11:17–34.

LO-RUHAMAH (a symbolic
name for Hosea's daughter,
meaning "unloved," and expressing God's displeasure
with Israel). Hos 1:6.

LOSE [TH]
Eccl 3:6 A time to get, and a
time to *l*
Matt 10:39 *l'th* his life for my
[Jesus'] sake shall find it
Mark 8:36 gain the whole
world, and *l* his own soul
Luke 17:33 Whosoever shall...
save his life shall *l* it

LOSS
Acts 27:22 no *l* of any man's life...but of the ship
1 Cor 3:15 man's work shall be burned, he shall suffer *l*
Phil 3:7 what things were gain to me [Paul]...I counted *l*

LOST
Ps 119:176 I have gone astray like a *l* sheep
Matt 15:24 I [Jesus] am not sent but unto the *l* sheep of the house of Israel
Luke 15:6 I have found my sheep which was *l*
Luke 19:10 For the Son of man is come to seek and to save that which was *l*
John 17:12 I [Jesus] have kept, and none of them [the disciples] is *l*

LOT (Abraham's nephew who escaped the destruction of Sodom). Gen 11:27,31; 12:4–5; 13:1–14; 14:12–16; **19:1–29** • Deut 2:9,19 • Ps 83:8 • Luke 17:28–29 • 2 Pet 2:7.

LOT'S WIFE TURNED INTO A PILLAR OF SALT. Gen 19:26.

LOVE [D, ING, LY, ST, TH]
Gen 29:20 unto him [Jacob] but a few days, for the *l* he had to her [Rachel]
Gen 37:3 Israel *l'd* Joseph more than all his children

Lev 19:18 *l* thy neighbour as thyself: I am the LORD
Deut 6:5 *l* the LORD thy God with all thine heart
Josh 23:11 Take good heed... that ye *l* the LORD your God
Job 19:19 they whom I [Job] *l'd* are turned against me
Ps 87:2 The LORD *l'th* the gates of Zion
Ps 116:1 I *l* the LORD, because he hath heard my voice
Ps 119:97 O how *l* I thy [God's] law
Prov 3:12 whom the LORD *l'th* he correcteth
Prov 7:18 take our fill of *l* until the morning
Prov 10:12 Hatred stirreth up strifes: but *l* covereth all sins
Prov 17:17 A friend *l'th* at all times
Prov 22:1 good name...to be chosen than great riches... *l'ing* favour rather than silver
Eccl 3:8 A time to *l,* and a time to hate
Eccl 9:9 Live joyfully with the wife whom thou *l'st*
Song 2:4 his [God's] banner over me was *l*
Song 8:7 Many waters cannot quench *l*
Jer 31:3 I [God] have *l'd* thee with an everlasting *l*
Hos 11:4 I [God] drew them with...bands of *l*
Mic 6:8 what doth the LORD require...but to...*l* mercy

Matt 5:44 **L** your enemies, bless them that curse you

Matt 10:37 **l'th** father or mother more than me [Jesus] is not worthy of me

Matt 22:39 Thou shalt *l* thy neighbour as thyself

Luke 16:13 he will hate the one, and *l* the other

John 3:16 God so *l'd* the world... gave his only...Son

John 13:34 *l* one another; as I [Jesus] have *l'd* you

John 14:15 If ye *l* me [Jesus], keep my commandments

John 15:9 Father hath *l'd* me [Jesus], so have I *l'd* you

John 21:15 Simon...*l'st* thou me [Jesus] more than these

Rom 5:8 God commendeth his *l* toward us

Rom 8:28 we know that all things work together for good to them that *l* God

Rom 8:37 we are more than conquerors through him [Jesus] that *l'd* us

1 Cor 2:9 the things which God hath prepared for them that *l* him

2 Cor 5:14 the *l* of Christ constraineth us

2 Cor 9:7 for God *l'th* a cheerful giver

Gal 2:20 live by...faith of...Son of God, who *l'd* me [Paul]

Gal 5:22 But the fruit of the Spirit is *l,* joy, peace

Eph 3:19 *l* of Christ, which passeth knowledge

Eph 4:15 speaking the truth in *l*...grow up into him [Jesus]

Eph 5:2 walk in *l,* as Christ also hath *l'd* us

Eph 5:25 Husbands, *l* your wives, even as Christ also *l'd* the church

Phil 1:9 that your *l* may abound yet more and more

Phil 4:8 whatsoever things are *l'ly*...of good report

1 Tim 6:10 *l* of money is the root of all evil

2 Tim 1:7 God hath not given us the spirit of fear; but...*l*

Heb 12:6 whom the Lord *l'th* he chasteneth

Jas 1:12 receive the crown of life...promised to them that *l* him [Jesus]

1 John 2:10 He that *l'th* his brother abideth in the light

1 John 2:15 any man *l* the world, the *l* of the Father is not in him

1 John 3:14 He that *l'th* not his brother abideth in death

1 John 4:7 every one that *l'th* is born of God

1 John 4:10 not that we *l'd* God, but that he *l'd* us

1 John 4:16 he that dwelleth in *l* dwelleth in God

1 John 4:19 We *l* him [Jesus], because he first *l'd* us

1 John 4:20 how can he *l* God whom he hath not seen

1 John 5:3 this is the *l* of God ...keep his commandments

Rev 2:4 thou [the church at Ephesus] hast left thy first *l*

LOVE CHAPTER OF THE BIBLE. 1 Cor 13.

LOVE OF GOD

Rom 5:5 the *l-o-G* is shed abroad in our hearts

Rom 8:39 height, nor depth... shall...separate us from the *l-o-G*...in Christ

1 John 3:16 perceive we the *l-o-G*, because he [Jesus] laid down his life for us

1 John 4:9 In this [God's Son] was manifested the *l-o-G* toward us

LOVE ONE ANOTHER

John 13:34 That ye *l-o-a;* as I [Jesus] have loved you

Rom 13:8 Owe no man any thing, but to *l-o-a*

1 John 3:11 the message...ye heard...we should *l-o-a*

1 John 4:7 Beloved, let us *l-o-a:* for love is of God

LOVE THY NEIGHBOUR

Matt 5:43 it hath been said, Thou shalt *l-t-n,* and hate thine enemy

Matt 19:19 Thou shalt *l-t-n* as thyself

Matt 22:39 second is like unto it, Thou shalt *l-t-n* as thyself

Mark 12:31 *l-t-n* as thyself. There is none other commandment greater

Rom 13:9 any other commandment...namely, Thou shalt *l-t-n* as thyself

Gal 5:14 all the law is fulfilled in one word...*l-t-n* as thyself

Jas 2:8 fulfil the royal law... Thou shalt *l-t-n* as thyself

LOVINGKINDNESS

Ps 36:7 How excellent is thy *l,* O God

Ps 63:3 thy [God's] *l* is better than life, my lips...praise thee

Ps 92:2 To show forth thy [God's] *l* in the morning

Jer 9:24 I am the LORD which exercise *l,* judgment

LUBIM. See *Libya.*

LUCAS. See *Luke.*

LUCIFER. See *Satan.*

LUDIM (a people descended from Mizraim, a son of Ham). Gen 10:13 • 1 Chr 1:11.

LUKE (a believer of Gentile descent, apparently a physician, who accompanied Paul on some of his missionary journeys and author of the Gospel that bears his name, as well as the Book of Acts). Col 4:14 • 2 Tim 4:11. *Lucas:* Phlm 24.

LUKE, GOSPEL OF. One of the four Gospels which portrays Jesus as the Savior of all people, Gentiles as well as Jews. Luke shows that Jesus associated with all types of people, including sinners (5:30; 15:2), the poor and outcasts (6:20–23; 16:19–31), and the Samaritans (17:11–19).

LUST [S]
Matt 5:28 whosoever looketh on a woman to *l* after her
Mark 4:19 the *l's*...entering in, choke the word
Rom 1:24 God...gave them up to uncleanness through the *l's* of their own hearts
Gal 5:16 Walk in the Spirit... not fulfil the *l* of the flesh
Jas 4:3 that ye may consume it upon your *l's*
1 John 2:16 the *l* of the eyes, and the pride of life

LUZ. See *Bethel.*

LYCAONIA (a Roman province of Asia Minor visited by Paul). Acts 14:1–6,11.

LYCIA (a province of Asia Minor visited by Paul). Acts 27:5.

LYDDA (a town where Peter healed a lame man). Acts 9:32–35. *Lod:* 1 Chr 8:12 • Ezra 2:33 • Neh 7:37; 11:35.

LYDIA (a businesswoman converted under Paul's ministry at Philippi). Acts 16:14–15,40.

LYSANIAS (governor of Abilene, a region in Syria, when John the Baptist began his ministry). Luke 3:1.

LYSTRA (a city in Asia Minor where Paul was stoned by unbelieving Jews). **Acts 14: 6–20;** 16:1–2 • 2 Tim 3:11.

-M-

MACEDONIA (a mountainous country north of Greece and the first European territory visited by the apostle Paul). **Acts 16:9–12;** 18:5; 19:21–29; 20:1–3; 27:2 • Rom 15:26 • 1 Cor 16:5 • 2 Cor 1:16; 2:13; 7:5; 8:1; 9:2–4; 11:9 • Phil 4:15 • 1 Thes 1:7–8; 4:10 • 1 Tim 1:3.

MACHIR (son of Manasseh and ancestor of the Machirites). Gen 50:23 • Num 26:29; 32:39–40 • Judg 5:14.

MACHPELAH (a field with a cave that Abraham bought as a burial ground). **Gen 23:7–19;** 25:9; 49:29–31; 50:13.

MAD [NESS]
1 Sam 21:13 he [David]... feigned himself *m* in their hands
Luke 6:11 they [scribes and Pharisees] were filled with *m'ness*...what they might do to Jesus
John 10:20 He [Jesus] hath a devil, and is *m*
Acts 26:24 Paul...much learning doth make thee *m*

MADIAN. See *Midian,* No. 2.

MAGDALA (a city near the Sea of Galilee and probably the home of Mary Magdalene). Matt 15:39; 27:56.

MAGNIFY [IED]
Josh 4:14 LORD *m'ied* Joshua in the sight of all Israel
Job 7:17 What is man, that thou [God] shouldest *m* him
Ps 34:3 m the LORD with me
Ps 40:16 The LORD be *m'ied*
Ps 69:30 I will...*m* him [God] with thanksgiving
Luke 1:46 Mary said, My soul doth *m* the Lord
Phil 1:20 Christ shall be *m'ied* in my [Paul's] body

MAHANAIM (a sacred site where Jacob was visited by angels). **Gen 32:1–2** • Josh 13:26–30; 21:38 • 2 Sam 2:8–29; 17:24,27 • 1 Kgs 4:14 • 1 Chr 6:80.

MAHER-SHALAL-HASH-BAZ (a symbolic name for Isaiah's son, meaning "hasten the booty," signifying that Assyria would conquer Israel and Syria). Isa 8:1–4.

MALACHI (a prophet after the Exile and author of the book that bears his name). Mal 1:1.

MALACHI, BOOK OF. A short prophetic book of the Old Testament written after the Exile and directed against the shallow worship practices of the Jewish people.

MALCHI-SHUA (a son of King Saul who was killed by the Philistines at Gilboa). 1 Chr 10:2. *Melchi-shua:* 1 Sam 14:49.

MALCHUS (a servant whose ear was cut off by Peter). John 18:10–11.

MALE
Gen 1:27 m and female created he [God] them
Mark 10:6 from the beginning of the creation God made them *m* and female
Luke 2:23 Every *m*...shall be called holy to the Lord
Gal 3:28 neither *m* nor female... all one in Christ Jesus

MALICE
Eph 4:31 Let all bitterness, and wrath, and anger...be put away from you, with all *m*
Titus 3:3 living in *m* and envy
1 Pet 2:1 Wherefore laying aside all *m,* and all guile

MAMRE
1. A town or district near Hebron where Abraham lived. Gen 13:18; 18:1–4; 23:17–19; 25:9; 35:27; 49:30; 50:13.
2. An Amorite supporter of Abraham. Gen 14:13,24.

MANASSEH
1. A son of Joseph and ancestor of one of the twelve tribes of Israel. Gen 41:51; 46:20; 48:1–20; 50:23 • Num 26:28–29; 27:1; 32:39–41; 36:1 • Deut 3:12–15 • Josh 13:31; 17:1–3 • 1 Kgs 4:13 • 1 Chr 7:14,17. *Manasses:* Rev 7:6. The tribe of Manasseh settled in central and northern Canaan on both sides of the Jordan River. Josh 17:1–17.
2. A king of Judah who encouraged pagan worship among the people. **2 Kgs 21:1–16** • 2 Chr 33:1–20.

MANASSES. See *Manasseh.*

MANIFEST [ED]
Mark 4:22 nothing hid, which shall not be *m'ed*
Luke 8:17 nothing is secret, that shall not be made *m*
John 9:3 that the works of God should be made *m* in him
1 Cor 3:13 Every man's work shall be made *m*
2 Cor 4:10 life also of Jesus might be made *m* in our body
1 Tim 3:16 God was *m* in the flesh, justified in the Spirit
1 John 3:8 For this purpose the Son of God was *m'ed*
1 John 4:9 In this [Jesus' death]...*m'ed* the love of God
Rev 15:4 thy [God's] judgments are made *m*

MANKIND
1 Cor 6:9 unrighteous shall not inherit...nor abusers of themselves with *m*
Jas 3:7 every kind of beasts... hath been tamed of *m*

MANNA PROVIDED FOR ISRAEL IN THE WILDERNESS. Ex 16:13–31.

MARA (a name, meaning "bitter," which signified Naomi's sorrow). Ruth 1:3–21.

MARAN-ATHA (an Aramaic phrase, meaning "come, O Lord," which expresses hope for the second coming of Jesus). 1 Cor 16:22.

MARCUS. See *Mark*.

MARK (a believer and author of the Gospel that bears his name who accompanied Paul and Barnabas on the first missionary journey as far as Perga and then returned to Jerusalem). Acts 12:12; **13:13;** 15:36–41 • 2 Tim 4:11. *Marcus:* 1 Pet 5:13.

MARK, GOSPEL OF. One of the four Gospels and probably the first to be written. Mark portrays Jesus as a person of action. He also emphasizes the humanity of Jesus, including incidents which reveal His

disappointment (8:12), anger (11:15–17), sorrow (14:34), and fatigue (4:38).

MARRIAGE
Matt 22:2 a certain king, which made a *m* for his son
Mark 12:25 neither marry, nor are given in *m*
John 2:1 there was a *m* in Cana of Galilee
Heb 13:4 M is honourable in all...the bed undefiled
Rev 19:9 called unto the *m* supper of the Lamb

MARRY [IED, IETH]
Jer 3:14 Turn...for I [God] am *m'ied* unto you
Matt 5:32 shall *m* her that is divorced committeth adultery
Mark 10:11 Whosoever...put away his wife, and *m* another, committeth adultery
Luke 14:20 m'ied a wife, and therefore I cannot come
Luke 16:18 putteth away his wife, and *m'ieth* another, committeth adultery
1 Cor 7:9 let them *m*...it is better to *m* than to burn
1 Cor 7:33 he that is *m'ied* careth for...things...of... world
1 Tim 5:14 that the younger women *m,* bear children, guide the house

MARTHA (the sister of Mary and Lazarus whom Jesus

rebuked because of her excessive worry about domestic duties). **Luke 10:38–42** • John 11:1–39; 12:2.

MARVEL [LED]
Matt 8:10 he [Jesus] *m'led*...I have not found so great faith

Matt 8:27 *m'led,* saying, What manner of man [Jesus] is this

Matt 21:20 they [the disciples] *m'led,* saying, How soon is the fig tree withered

Mark 6:6 he [Jesus] *m'led* because of their unbelief

Mark 15:44 Pilate *m'led* if he [Jesus] were already dead

Luke 2:33 Joseph and his mother *m'led* at those things...spoken of him [Jesus]

John 3:7 *M* not that I [Jesus] said...Ye [Nicodemus] must be born again

John 7:15 Jews *m'led*...How knoweth this man [Jesus] letters

Acts 4:13 they [religious leaders] *m'led*...they [Peter and John] had been with Jesus

Gal 1:6 I [Paul] *m* that ye are...removed from him [Jesus] that called you

1 John 3:13 *M* not, my brethren, if the world hate you

MARVELLOUS
1 Chr 16:24 Declare his [God's] glory...his *m* works among all nations

Ps 31:21 he [God] hath showed me his *m* kindness

Ps 98:1 for he [God] hath done *m* things

Ps 139:14 I will praise thee [God]...*m* are thy works

1 Pet 2:9 him [Jesus] who hath called you out of darkness into his *m* light

Rev 15:3 Great and *m* are thy works, Lord...Almighty

MARY
1. Earthly mother of Jesus. Matt 1:16,18,20; 2:11 • Mark 6:3 • **Luke 1:26–56;** 2:5,16,19, 34 • Acts 1:14.

2. A woman, called Mary Magdalene, who witnessed the crucifixion of Jesus and visited the empty tomb. **Matt 27:56,61;** 28:1 • Mark 15:40,47; 16:9 • Luke 8:2; 24:10 • John 19:25; **20:1–18.**

3. Sister of Martha and Lazarus. Luke 10:39,42 • John 11:1–45; 12:3.

MATHUSALA. See *Methuselah.*

MATTANIAH. See *Zedekiah.*

MATTHEW (a tax collector who became a disciple of Jesus and author of the Gospel that bears his name). Matt 9:9; 10:3 • Mark 3:18 • Luke 6:15 • Acts 1:13. *Levi:* Mark 2:13–17 • Luke 5:27–32.

MATTHEW, GOSPEL OF.
One of the four Gospels written to show the Jewish people that Jesus was the Messiah promised in the Old Testament. Matthew's Gospel also emphasizes the teaching ministry of Jesus, particularly His instructions to His disciples in the Sermon on the Mount (5:1–7:29).

MATTHIAS (the person who replaced Judas as an apostle). Acts 1:15–26.

MEASURE [D, ING, S]
Deut 25:14 not have...divers *m's,* a great and a small
Deut 25:15 a perfect and just *m* shalt thou have
Job 38:5 Who hath laid the *m's* thereof, if thou knowest
Ps 39:4 LORD, make me to know...the *m* of my days
Isa 40:12 Who [God]...*m'd* the waters...hollow of his hand
Ezek 40:3 a man...with a line of flax...and a *m'ing* reed
Hos 1:10 Israel shall be as the sand of the sea...cannot be *m'd*
Mark 4:24 with what *m* ye mete, it shall be *m'd* to you
Luke 13:21 like leaven, which a woman took and hid in three *m's* of meal
2 Cor 11:23 in stripes above *m,* in prisons more frequent

Gal 1:13 beyond *m* I [Paul] persecuted the church
Eph 4:7 grace according to the *m* of the gift of Christ
Eph 4:13 all come...unto the *m*... of the fulness of Christ
Rev 6:6 I [John] heard a voice... *m* of wheat for a penny

MEDES (descendants of Japheth who founded an ancient kingdom between the Tigris River and the Caspian Sea). Gen 10:2 • 2 Kgs 17:6 • Esth 1:3,19 • Isa 13:17 • Dan 5:30–31; 6:1–28 • Acts 2:9.

MEDIATOR
1 Tim 2:5 one God, and one *m* between God and men
Heb 8:6 he [Jesus] is the *m* of a better covenant
Heb 9:15 he [Jesus] is the *m* of the new testament

MEDITATE
Ps 1:2 in his [God's] law doth he *m* day and night
Ps 119:15 I will *m* in thy [God's] precepts
Ps 143:5 I *m* on all thy [God's] works
Luke 21:14 not to *m* before what ye shall answer
1 Tim 4:15 M upon these things; give thyself...to them

MEDITERRANEAN SEA.
See *Great Sea.*

MEEK [NESS]

Num 12:3 the man Moses was very *m,* above all the men

Ps 37:11 But the *m* shall inherit the earth

Ps 147:6 LORD lifteth up the *m*...casteth...wicked down

Isa 61:1 to preach good tidings unto the *m*

Matt 5:5 Blessed are the *m*... they shall inherit the earth

Matt 11:29 I [Jesus] am *m* and lowly in heart

Gal 5:23 *M'ness,* temperance: against such there is no law

Gal 6:1 restore...spirit of *m'ness*...lest thou...be tempted

Col 3:12 Put on...kindness... *m'ness,* longsuffering

1 Pet 3:15 be ready always to give an answer...with *m'ness* and fear

MEGIDDO (a fortified city in the plain of Jezreel associated with the great battle in the end-time). Josh 12:21; 17:11 • Judg 1:27–28; 5:19–21 • 1 Kgs 4:12; 9:15–27 • 2 Kgs 23:29–30 • Rev 16:16. *Megiddon:* Zech 12:11.

MEGIDDON. See *Megiddo.*

MELCHISEDEC. See *Melchizedek.*

MELCHI-SHUA. See *Malchishua.*

MELCHIZEDEK (king of Salem who received tithes from Abraham). **Gen 14:18–20** • Ps 110:4. *Melchisedec:* Heb 7:11.

MELITA (an island where Paul was shipwrecked while sailing to Rome). Acts 28:1–8.

MEMBER [S]

Job 17:7 eye...is dim...all my *m's* are as a shadow

Rom 12:5 So we...are one body in Christ, and every one *m's* one of another

1 Cor 6:15 your bodies are the *m's* of Christ

1 Cor 12:19 all one *m,* where were the body

1 Cor 12:26 one *m* suffer, all the *m's* suffer

Jas 3:5 tongue is a little *m,* and boasteth great things

MEMORIAL SUPPER. See *Jesus, Life and Ministry of; Lord's Supper.*

MENAHEM (a king of Israel who killed Shallum to assume the throne). 2 Kgs 15:14–22.

MEPHIBOSHETH (a son of Jonathan who was honored by King David). 2 Sam 4:4; **9:1–13;** 16:1–4; 19:24–30; 21:7. *Meribbaal:* 1 Chr 8:34.

MERCIFUL

Deut 21:8 Be *m,* O LORD, unto thy people Israel

Ps 41:4 I said, LORD, be *m* unto me: heal my soul

Ps 67:1 God be *m* unto us, and bless us

Ps 103:8 LORD is *m* and gracious, slow to anger

Matt 5:7 Blessed are the *m:* for they shall obtain mercy

MERCURIUS (Roman name for the pagan god Mercury and the name applied to Paul by the people of Lystra). Acts 14:12.

MERCY [IES]

Gen 39:21 LORD was with Joseph, and showed him *m*

Ex 20:6 showing *m* unto... them that love me [God]

1 Chr 16:34 he [God] is good; for his *m* endureth for ever

Ps 6:2 Have *m* upon me, O LORD; for I am weak

Ps 13:5 But I have trusted in thy [God's] *m*

Ps 23:6 *m* shall follow me all the days of my life

Ps 25:6 Remember, O LORD, thy tender *m'ies*

Ps 40:11 Withhold not thou thy [God's] tender *m'ies*

Ps 85:7 Show us thy *m,* O LORD...grant us thy salvation

Ps 94:18 My foot slippeth; thy *m,* O LORD, held me up

Ps 103:8 LORD is...slow to anger, and plenteous in *m*

Ps 103:17 *m* of the LORD is from everlasting

Ps 119:77 Let thy [God's] tender *m'ies* come unto me

Ps 136:1 give thanks unto the LORD...*m* endureth for ever

Isa 49:13 the LORD...will have *m* upon his afflicted

Hos 6:6 For I [God] desired *m,* and not sacrifice

Mic 6:8 LORD require of thee, but to...love *m*

Matt 23:23 you [Pharisees]... have omitted the weightier matters of the law...*m,* and faith

Luke 16:24 Abraham, have *m*...and send Lazarus

Rom 12:1 *m'ies* of God...present your bodies a living sacrifice

2 Cor 1:3 Father of *m'ies,* and the God of all comfort

Eph 2:4 God, who is rich in *m*...loved us

Col 3:12 Put on...bowels of *m'ies,* kindness

Titus 3:5 according to his [God's] *m* he saved us

Heb 4:16 obtain *m,* and find grace to help

1 Pet 2:10 had not obtained *m,* but now have obtained *m*

Jude 21 *m* of our Lord Jesus Christ unto eternal life

MERIB-BAAL. See *Mephibosheth.*

MERODACH (a pagan Babylonian god of war). Jer 50:2.

MERODACH-BALADAN. See *Berodach-baladan.*

MERRY
Prov 15:13 A *m* heart maketh a cheerful countenance
Prov 17:22 A *m* heart doeth good like a medicine
Luke 15:23 bring...the fatted calf...let us eat, and be *m*
Jas 5:13 Is any *m?* let him sing psalms

MESHACH (Daniel's friend who was thrown into the fiery furnace for refusing to worship an idol). Dan 1:7; 2:49; **3:13–30.**

MESOPOTAMIA (the territory between the Tigris and Euphrates rivers). Gen 24:10 • Deut 23:4 • Judg 3:8,10 • 1 Chr 19:6 • Acts 2:9; 7:2. *Padan-aram:* Gen 25:20.

MESSENGER
Prov 13:17 A wicked *m* falleth into mischief
Mal 3:1 I [God] will send my *m*...he shall prepare the way
Luke 7:27 I send my [God's] *m* before thy face

MESSIANIC PROPHECIES OF THE OLD TESTAMENT AND THEIR FULFILLMENT IN JESUS CHRIST
1. Star out of Jacob (Num 24:17 • Luke 3:34)
2. Of the house of David (Isa 11:1–10 • Matt 1:1)
3. Son of man (Dan 7:13 • Mark 8:38)
4. Named Immanuel (Isa 7:14 • Matt 1:22–23)
5. Chief cornerstone (Ps 118:22 • 1 Pet 2:4,7)
6. A prophet like Moses (Deut 18:15–19 • Mark 6:14–15)
7. Bring in the new covenant (Jer 31:31–34 • Heb 12:24)
8. Call the Gentiles (Isa 11:10 • Rom 15:9–12)
9. Die for mankind's sin (Isa 53:4–6 • 1 Pet 1:18–20)
10. Born of a virgin (Isa 7:14 • Matt 1:18–25)
11. Born at Bethlehem (Mic 5:2 • Luke 2:4–7)
12. Flight into Egypt (Hos 11:1 • Matt 2:13–15)
13. Preceeded by a forerunner (Mal 3:1–2 • Mark 1:1–8)
14. Ministry of miracles (Isa 35:5–6 • Matt 11:4–5)
15. Meek and gentle (Isa 42:1–4 • Matt 12:15–21)
16. Full of wisdom and power (Isa 11:2 • Matt 3:16–17)
17. Anointed to preach God's good news (Isa 61:2–3 • Luke 4:43)

MIDNIGHT

18. Triumphal entry into Jerusalem (Zech 9:9–10 • Matt 21:1–11)

19. Betrayed for thirty pieces of silver (Zech 11:12–13 • Matt 26:14–15)

20. Rejected by His own people (Isa 53:3 • John 1:11)

21. Crucified with criminals (Isa 53:12 • Matt 27:38)

22. Silent before His accusers (Isa 53:7 • Mark 15:4–5)

23. Mocked on the cross (Ps 22:6–8 • Matt 27:39–44)

24. No bones broken (Ps 34:20 • John 19:32–33,36)

25. Died for others (Isa 53:1–12 • 1 Pet 3:18)

26. Buried with the rich (Isa 53:9 • Matt 27:57–60)

27. Ascended to His Father (Ps 68:18 • Eph 4:8–10)

28. Makes intercession for believers (Zech 6:13 • Rom 8:34)

29. Serves as a heavenly high priest (Zech 6:12–13 • Heb 8:1–2)

30. Exalted above all (Ps 2:6–12 • Phil 2:9–11)

METHUSELAH (a son of Enoch who lived to the age of 969, the oldest recorded age in the Bible). **Gen 5:21–27** • 1 Chr 1:3. *Mathusala:* Luke 3:37.

MICAH (a prophet who denounced social injustices and author of the book that bears his name). Jer 26:18 • Mic 1:1.

MICAH, BOOK OF. A short prophetic book of the Old Testament known for its prediction that the Messiah would be born in Bethlehem (5:2).

MICAIAH (a prophet who predicted that King Ahab would be killed). **1 Kgs 22:8–28** • 2 Chr 18:7–27.

MICHAEL (an archangel who was thought to serve as a guardian over Israel). Dan 10:13,21; 12:1 • Jude 9 • Rev 12:7.

MICHAL (a daughter of King Saul and a wife of David). 1 Sam 14:49; 18:20–28; 19:9–17; 25:44 • 2 Sam 3:13–16; 6:16–23.

MIDIAN
1. A son of Abraham and founder of the Midianites. Gen 25:1–4 • 1 Chr 1:32–33.
2. A region in the Arabian desert occupied by the Midianites. Ex 2:15 • Judg 7:8–25; 8:3–28. *Madian:* Acts 7:29.

MIDIANITES (nomadic traders who occupied the land of Midian). Gen 37:28,36 • Num 31:2–7 • Judg 6:2–33; 7:1–25 • Ps 83:9.

MIDNIGHT
Ps 119:62 At *m* I will rise to give thanks unto thee [God]

Mark 13:35 know not when the master...cometh, at even, or at *m*

Acts 16:25 at *m* Paul and Silas prayed, and sang praises

MIGHT

Gen 43:32 *m* not eat bread with the Hebrews...abomination unto the Egyptians

Deut 6:5 love the LORD thy God...with all thy *m*

Judg 6:14 Go in this thy [Gideon's] *m,* and thou shalt save Israel

2 Sam 6:14 David danced... with all his *m*

2 Chr 20:6 in thine [God's] hand is...power and *m*

Job 23:3 Oh that I knew where I *m* find him [God]

Ps 119:11 Thy [God's] word have I hid in mine heart, that I *m* not sin against thee

Ps 145:6 the *m* of thy [God's] terrible acts

Eccl 9:10 hand findeth to do, do it with thy *m*

Jer 9:1 I [Jeremiah] *m* weep day and night for...my people

Jer 9:23 neither let the mighty man glory in his *m*

Zech 4:6 Not by *m*...but by my [God's] spirit

Mark 14:35 if...possible, the hour *m* pass from him [Jesus]

John 3:17 the world through him [Jesus] *m* be saved

John 10:10 I [Jesus] am come that they *m* have life

John 20:31 that ye *m* believe that Jesus is the Christ

Rom 10:1 my [Paul's]... prayer...for Israel is, that they *m* be saved

1 Cor 9:22 all things to all men...I [Paul] *m*...save some

2 Cor 4:10 life...of Jesus *m* be... manifest in our body

2 Cor 8:9 he [Jesus] became poor, that ye through his poverty *m* be rich

Gal 4:5 we *m* receive the adoption of sons

Eph 6:10 be strong in the Lord, and in the power of his *m*

1 John 4:9 God sent his...Son... that we *m* live through him

MIGHTY

Ex 1:7 children of Israel... waxed exceeding *m*

Deut 6:21 LORD brought us [Israelites] out...*m* hand

2 Sam 1:27 How are the *m* fallen

1 Chr 11:11 number of the *m* men whom David had

Job 12:19 He [God]...overthroweth the *m*

Job 34:24 He [God] shall break in pieces *m* men

Job 36:5 Behold, God...is *m* in strength and wisdom

Ps 24:8 LORD strong and *m,* the LORD *m* in battle

Ps 50:1 The *m* God, even the LORD, hath spoken

Ps 89:6 who among the...*m* can be likened unto the LORD

Ps 150:2 Praise him [God] for his *m* acts...his...greatness

Isa 9:6 his [Jesus'] name shall be called...The *m* God

Ezek 20:34 I [God]...will gather you...with a *m* hand

Amos 5:24 let judgment run down as waters, and righteousness as a *m* stream

Matt 13:58 And he [Jesus] did not many *m* works... because of their unbelief

Acts 2:2 a sound from heaven as of a rushing *m* wind

1 Cor 1:26 not many *m,* not many noble, are called

1 Cor 1:27 weak things of the world to confound the...*m*

1 Pet 5:6 Humble yourselves... under the *m* hand of God

MILCOM (supreme god of the Ammonites). 1 Kgs 11:5,33 • 2 Kgs 23:13. *Molech:* Lev 20:2. *Moloch:* Acts 7:43.

MILETUS (a city where Paul met the leaders of the Ephesian church). Acts 20:15–38. *Miletum:* 2 Tim 4:20.

MILLO

1. A fortress at Shechem whose occupants proclaimed Abimelech as their king. Judg 9:6,20.

2. A defensive fortress tower built by David near Jerusalem and improved by Solomon. **2 Sam 5:9** • **1 Kgs 9:15,24;** 11:27 • 2 Kgs 12:20 • 1 Chr 11:8 • 2 Chr 32:5.

MIND [S]

Neh 4:6 the people had a *m* to work

Prov 29:11 A fool uttereth all his *m*

Isa 26:3 keep him in perfect peace...*m* is stayed on thee

Mark 12:30 love the Lord... with all thy *m*

Luke 8:35 the man [demoniac]... clothed...in his right *m*

Rom 1:28 God gave them over to a reprobate *m*

Rom 8:5 they...after the flesh do *m* the things of the flesh

Rom 11:34 who hath known the *m* of the Lord

Rom 12:2 transformed by the renewing of your *m*

Eph 4:17 walk not as other Gentiles...vanity of their *m*

Phil 2:2 the same love, being of one accord, of one *m*

Phil 2:3 but in lowliness of *m* let each esteem other better than themselves

Phil 2:5 this *m* be in you, which was also in Christ

Phil 4:7 peace of God...shall keep your hearts and *m's*

2 Tim 1:7 God hath not given us the spirit of fear; but...of a sound *m*

Heb 8:10 I [God] will put my laws into their *m*

1 Pet 1:13 Wherefore gird up the loins of your *m*

MINDFUL

1 Chr 16:15 Be ye *m*...of his [God's] covenant

Ps 8:4 What is man, that thou [God] art *m* of him

Ps 115:12 LORD hath been *m* of us: he will bless us

MINISTER [ED, S]

Ps 9:8 he [God] shall *m* judgment to the people

Ps 103:21 Bless ye the LORD... ye *m's* of his

Matt 20:28 Son of man came not to be *m'ed* unto, but to *m*

Mark 10:43 great among you, shall be your *m*

Rom 15:16 I [Paul] should be... *m* of Jesus...to the Gentiles

1 Cor 3:5 Who then is Paul... Apollos, but *m's* by whom ye believed

2 Cor 11:23 Are they *m's* of Christ...I [Paul] am more

Eph 3:7 I [Paul] was made a *m*, according to...grace

1 Pet 4:10 even so *m* the same one to another

MINISTRY

Acts 6:4 we [the apostles] will give ourselves continually... to the *m* of the word

2 Cor 5:18 God...hath given to us the *m* of reconciliation

Eph 4:12 perfecting of the saints, for the work of the *m*

2 Tim 4:5 work of an evangelist, make full proof of thy *m*

Heb 8:6 now hath he [Jesus] obtained a more excellent *m*

MIRACLE [S]

Mark 6:52 they [the disciples] considered not the *m* of the loaves

John 2:11 This beginning of *m's* did Jesus in Cana

John 3:2 no man can do these *m's* that thou [Jesus] doest, except God be with him

John 9:16 How can a man that is a sinner do such *m's*

John 12:37 though he [Jesus] had done so many *m's*...yet they believed not

Acts 6:8 Stephen...did great wonders and *m's*

1 Cor 12:10 To another the working of *m's*

MIRACLES OF JESUS. See *Jesus, Miracles of.*

MIRIAM (a sister of Moses who arranged for their mother Jochebed to care for him). **Ex 2:4–10; 15:20–21** • Num 12:1–16; 20:1; 26:59 • Deut 24:9 • 1 Chr 6:3 • Mic 6:4.

MIZPAH (a place where Jacob and Laban made a covenant

and agreed to a friendly sepa-ration). Gen 31:44–53.

MIZRAIM (a son of Ham whose descendants settled in Egypt). Gen 10:6,13 • 1 Chr 1:8,11.

MNASON (a believer who accompanied Paul on his last visit to Jerusalem). Acts 21:16.

MOAB (a son of Lot and the name of the land inhabited by him and his descendants). Gen 19:33–37 • Num 21:11–29 • Judg 11:15–25 • Ruth 1:1–22 • Jer 48:1–47.

MOABITES (inhabitants of Moab who were pagan wor-shipers and enemies of the Israelites). Gen 19:37 • Num 22:4 • Deut 2:9,11,29 • Judg 3:28 • 2 Sam 8:2 • 1 Kgs 11:1, 33 • 2 Kgs 3:18,21–24; 23:13; 24:2 • 1 Chr 18:2 • Ezra 9:1.

MOCK [ED, ETH, ING]
1 Kgs 18:27 Elijah *m'ed* them [prophets of Baal]...Cry aloud...he is a god
Job 12:4 I [Job] am as one *m'ed* of his neighbour
Prov 14:9 Fools...*m* at sin
Prov 17:5 Whoso *m'eth* the poor reproacheth his Maker
Jer 20:7 I am in derision daily, every one *m'eth* me

Mark 10:34 they shall *m* him [Jesus]...scourge him
Mark 15:31 chief priests *m'ing* said...himself he [Jesus] cannot save
Luke 18:32 he [Jesus] shall be delivered unto the Gentiles, and shall be *m'ed*
Luke 23:36 the soldiers also *m'ed* him [Jesus]
Acts 2:13 *m'ing* said, These men [converts at Pentecost] are full of new wine
Gal 6:7 Be not deceived; God is not *m'ed*

MODEL PRAYER OF JESUS. See *Lord's Prayer.*

MOLECH. See *Milcom.*

MOLOCH. See *Milcom.*

MORDECAI (a Jewish exile in Persia and a kinsman of Esther). Esth 2:5–23; 3:2–6; 4:1–17; 5:9–14; 6:2–13; 7:9–10; 8:1–15; 9:3–31; 10:2–3.

MOREH (a place near Shechem where Abraham built an altar after entering Canaan). **Gen 12:6–7** • Deut 11:30.

MORESHETH-GATH (birth-place of the prophet Micah). Mic 1:14.

MORIAH (a mountainous area near Jerusalem where Abraham was directed to sacrifice his son Isaac). **Gen 22:1–13** • 2 Chr 3:1.

MOSES (the great lawgiver and prophet who led the Israelites out of Egypt and guided their formative years as a nation). Moses is the central personality in the books of Exodus, Leviticus, Numbers, and Deuteronomy.

1. Hidden on the Nile River as a baby (Ex 2:1–5)

2. Reared in the house of Pharaoh (Ex 2:6–10)

3. Fled to the land of Midian (Ex 2:11–22)

4. Called to deliver the Hebrews from slavery (Ex 2:23–4:17)

5. Led Israelites out of Egypt (Ex 13:17–22)

6. Brought water out of a rock (Ex 17:3–6)

7. Received the Ten Commandments (Ex 19:3; 20:1–17)

8. Struck a rock in sin (Num 20:11–12)

9. Raised up a brass serpent (Num 21:8–9)

10. Joshua chosen as his successor (Num 27:18–23)

11. Death of Moses (Deut 34:1–8)

Moses is also mentioned in Josh 1:1–17; 8:31–35; 11:12–23; 13:8–33; 14:2–11; 22:4–9 •

2 Kgs 18:4–12 • 1 Chr 23:13–15 • Ps 106:16–32 • Isa 63:11–12 • Dan 9:11,13 • Matt 17:3–4 • Mark 9:4–5 • Luke 16:29–31 • John 7:19–23 • Acts 7:20–44 • Rom 10:5,19 • Heb 3:2–16; 11:23–24 • Rev 15:3.

MOURN [ETH, ING]
Job 2:11 Job's three friends... came...to *m* with him
Ps 38:6 I am troubled...I go *m'ing* all the day long
Ps 88:9 Mine eye *m'eth* by reason of affliction
Eccl 3:4 a time to *m,* and a time to dance
Isa 60:20 the days of thy *m'ing* shall be ended
Isa 61:2 to comfort all that *m*
Amos 8:10 And I [God] will turn your feasts into *m'ing*
Matt 5:4 Blessed are they that *m*...shall be comforted
Matt 9:15 children...*m,* as long as the bridegroom [Jesus] is with them
Jas 4:9 Be afflicted, and *m*

MOVE [D, ING, TH]
Gen 1:2 Spirit of God *m'd* upon the...waters
Gen 9:3 Every *m'ing* thing that liveth shall be meat
Ps 16:8 he [God] is at my right hand, I shall not be *m'd*
Ps 46:5 God is in the midst of her [Jerusalem]...not be *m'd*
Ps 62:2 he [God] is my defence; I shall not be greatly *m'd*

Ps 69:34 praise him [God], the seas, and every thing that *m'th* therein

Ps 96:10 the LORD reigneth: the world...shall not be *m'd*

Isa 6:4 posts of the door *m'd* at the voice of him [God]

Mark 6:34 Jesus...was *m'd* with compassion toward them [the crowds]

John 5:3 multitude...waiting for the *m'ing* of the water

Acts 17:28 in him [God] we live... *m*...have our being

Heb 12:28 a kingdom which cannot be *m'd*

2 Pet 1:21 holy men...spake as...*m'd* by the Holy Ghost

MULTITUDE [S]

Gen 32:12 thy [Jacob's] seed as the sand...which cannot be numbered for *m*

Ex 12:38 mixed *m* went up... with them [Israelites]

Ps 69:13 O God, in the *m* of thy mercy hear me

Ps 109:30 I will praise him [God] among the *m*

Joel 3:14 *M's, m's* in the valley of decision

Matt 5:1 seeing...*m's,* he [Jesus] went...into a mountain

Matt 15:33 should we have... bread...fill so great a *m*

Matt 22:33 *m* heard this, they were astonished

Mark 4:1 whole *m* was by the sea on the land

Mark 5:31 seest the *m* thronging thee [Jesus], and sayest... Who touched me

Luke 2:13 with the angel a *m* of the heavenly host

Luke 23:1 *m*...arose, and led him [Jesus] unto Pilate

John 6:2 great *m* followed him [Jesus]...they saw his miracles

1 Pet 4:8 charity shall cover the *m* of sins

Rev 7:9 a great *m,* which no man could number

MURMUR [ED, ING, INGS]

Ex 15:24 the people *m'ed* against Moses

Num 14:27 I [God]...heard... *m'ings* of the children of Israel

Luke 5:30 Pharisees *m'ed* against his [Jesus'] disciples

John 6:41 *m'ed*...because he [Jesus] said, I am the bread... from heaven

John 7:12 there was much *m'ing* among the people concerning him [Jesus]

Phil 2:14 Do all things without *m'ings* and disputings

MYSTERY [IES]

Mark 4:11 Unto you [the disciples] it is given to know the *m* of the kingdom

Luke 8:10 it is given to know the *m'ies* of the kingdom... but to others in parables

1 Cor 2:7 we speak the wisdom of God in a *m*

1 Cor 4:1 ministers of Christ... stewards of the *m'ies* of God

1 Cor 13:2 though I [Paul]... understand all *m'ies,* and all knowledge

1 Cor 15:51 I show you a *m;* We shall not all sleep

Eph 5:32 a great *m*...I [Paul] speak concerning Christ

1 Tim 3:9 Holding the *m* of the faith in a pure conscience

-N-

NAAMAN (a captain in the Syrian army who was healed of leprosy by the prophet Elisha). **2 Kgs 5:1–14** • Luke 4:27.

NABAL (a wealthy herdsman who refused to provide food for David and his army). **1 Sam 25:2–42** • 2 Sam 3:3.

NABOTH (an Israelite who was framed and killed by Jezebel so Ahab could take possession of his vineyard). **1 Kgs 21:1–23** • 2 Kgs 9:21–26.

NADAB
1. Aaron's son who was destroyed for offering "strange fire" to God. Ex 24:1,9–12; 28:1 • **Lev 10:1–7.**
2. A king of Israel who was assassinated and succeeded by Baasha. 1 Kgs 14:20; **15:25–31.**

NAHASH (a king of Ammon who befriended David). 2 Sam 10:1–2.

NAHUM (a prophet of Judah and author of the book that bears his name). Nah 1:1. *Naum:* Luke 3:25.

NAHUM, BOOK OF. A short prophetic book of the Old Testament that predicted the downfall of the pagan nation of Assyria because of the atrocities which it committed against God's people (3:7–19).

NAIN (a village near the Sea of Galilee where Jesus raised a widow's son from the dead). Luke 7:11–17.

NAIOTH (a place where David fled to escape from King Saul). 1 Sam 19:18–23; 20:1.

NAOMI (mother-in-law of Ruth). Ruth 1–4.

NAPHTALI (a son of Jacob and ancestor of one of the twelve tribes of Israel). Gen 30:8; 35:25; 46:24; 49:21 • Ex 1:4 • 1 Chr 2:2; 7:13 • Ezek 48:34. The tribe of Naphtali settled in northern Canaan. Josh 19:32–39.

NAPHTUHIM (inhabitants of central Egypt who were descendants of Mizraim, son of Ham). Gen 10:13.

NATHAN (a prophet who rebuked King David for his sin with Bathsheba). 2 Sam 7:2–17; **12:1–25** • 1 Kgs 1:8–45 • 1 Chr 17:1–15; 29:29 • 2 Chr 9:29; 29:25 • Ps 51:1.

NATHANAEL.
See *Bartholomew.*

NATION [S]

Gen 12:2 make of thee [Abraham] a great *n*

Gen 17:5 a father of many *n's* have I [God] made thee [Abraham]

Gen 25:23 Two *n's* are in thy [Rebekah's] womb

Ex 19:6 ye [Israel] shall be unto me [God]...an holy *n*

Deut 9:1 possess *n's* greater and mightier than thyself

Deut 28:1 God will set thee... above all *n's* of the earth

1 Sam 8:5 make us a king to judge us like all the *n's*

2 Sam 7:23 what one *n*...is like thy [God's] people

1 Chr 16:24 Declare...his [God's] marvellous works among all *n's*

Ps 22:28 and he [God] is the governor among the *n's*

Ps 33:12 Blessed is the *n* whose God is the LORD

Ps 67:2 thy [God's] way may be known...thy saving health among all *n's*

Ps 72:11 all kings...all *n's* shall serve him [God]

Ps 82:8 judge the earth...thou [God]...inherit all *n's*

Ps 96:5 For all the gods of the *n's* are idols

Ps 113:4 The LORD is high above all *n's*

Prov 14:34 Righteousness exalteth a *n*

Isa 2:4 n shall not lift up sword against *n*

Isa 40:15 Behold, the *n's* are as a drop of a bucket

Isa 52:10 LORD hath made bare his...arm in...all the *n's*

Isa 60:12 n...that will not serve thee [God] shall perish

Jer 1:5 ordained thee [Jeremiah] a prophet unto the *n's*

Jer 2:11 Hath a *n* changed their gods

Jer 50:41 a people shall come from the north, and a great *n*

Ezek 12:15 I [God] shall scatter them among the *n's*

Mic 4:3 n shall not lift up a sword against *n*

Zeph 3:6 I [God] have cut off the *n's*...towers are desolate

Hag 2:7 and the desire of all *n's* shall come

Zech 8:22 strong *n's* shall come to seek the LORD

Mal 3:9 ye have robbed me [God], even this whole *n*

Matt 24:7 n shall rise against *n*...kingdom against kingdom

Matt 24:14 gospel of the kingdom...preached...unto all *n's*

Matt 25:32 before him [Jesus] shall be gathered all *n's*

Matt 28:19 teach all *n's,* baptizing them

Luke 24:47 repentance... preached...among all *n's*

John 11:50 one man should die...that the whole *n* perish not

Acts 2:5 devout men, out of every *n* under heaven

Acts 10:35 in every *n* he that feareth him [God]...is accepted with him

Acts 17:26 And [God] hath made of one blood all *n's*

Phil 2:15 in the midst of a crooked and perverse *n*

1 Pet 2:9 ye are a chosen generation...an holy *n*

Rev 7:9 multitude, which no man could number, of all *n's*

NATURAL
Deut 34:7 his [Moses'] eye...not dim, nor...*n* force abated

1 Cor 2:14 n man receiveth not the things of the Spirit

1 Cor 15:44 It is sown a *n* body... raised a spiritual body

NATURE
Rom 1:26 women did change the natural use into that... against *n*

Rom 2:14 Gentiles...do by *n*... things contained in the law

2 Pet 1:4 ye might be partakers of the divine *n*

NAUM. See *Nahum.*

NAZARETH (hometown of Jesus in the province of Galilee). Matt 2:20–23 • Luke 4:16–30.

NAZARITE (a person especially consecrated to God whose vows included abstaining from strong drink and not cutting his hair). Num 6:2–21 • Judg 13:5–7 • Lam 4:7 • Amos 2:11–12.

NEAPOLIS (a seaport where Paul landed during the second missionary journey). Acts 16:11.

NEBO
1. The highest point of Mount Pisgah where Moses died. Deut 32:49; 34:5–6.
2. Babylonian god of science and knowledge. Isa 46:1.

NEBUCHADNEZZAR (a king of Babylonia who captured Jerusalem and carried Judah into exile). **2 Kgs 25:1–26** • 2 Chr 36:7–13 • Jer 28:11–14 • Dan 1–4. *Nebuchadrezzar:* Jer 51:34.

NEBUCHADREZZAR. See *Nebuchadnezzar.*

NEBUZAR-ADAN (an officer in Nebuchadnezzar's army during the Babylonian siege of Jerusalem). 2 Kgs 25:8–20 • Jer 39:11–14.

NECHO, NECHOH. See *Pharaoh.*

NEED [ED, ETH, S]
Matt 3:14 I [John the Baptist] have *n* to be baptized of thee [Jesus]...comest...to me

Matt 6:8 Father knoweth what things ye have *n* of

Luke 5:31 They that are whole *n* not a physician

Luke 15:7 joy...over one sinner ...than over...just persons, which *n* no repentance

John 4:4 he [Jesus] must *n's* go through Samaria

Acts 2:45 sold...and parted them [possessions] to all men, as every man had *n*

Acts 17:25 though he [God] *n'ed* any thing, seeing he... giveth...life

1 Cor 12:21 eye cannot say unto the hand...no *n* of thee

Phil 4:19 But my God shall supply all your *n*

2 Tim 2:15 a workman that *n'eth* not to be ashamed

Heb 4:16 and find grace to help in time of *n*

Heb 7:27 Who [Jesus] *n'eth* not daily...to offer up sacrifice, first for his own sins

NEEDY

Deut 15:11 open thine hand... to thy *n,* in thy land

Job 24:14 The murderer...killeth the poor and *n*

Ps 37:14 The wicked have... bent their bow, to cast down the poor and *n*

Ps 40:17 I am poor and *n;* yet the Lord thinketh upon me

Ps 82:3 do justice to the afflicted and *n*

Ps 86:1 O LORD, hear me: for I am poor and *n*

Prov 31:9 and plead the cause of the poor and *n*

Amos 8:6 buy the poor for silver...*n* for a pair of shoes

NEGLECT [ED]

Matt 18:17 if he shall *n* to hear them, tell it unto the church

Acts 6:1 widows were *n'ed* in the daily ministration

1 Tim 4:14 N not the gift that is in thee [Timothy]

Heb 2:3 How shall we escape, if we *n* so great salvation

NEHEMIAH (governor of Jerusalem who helped rebuild the city wall after the Exile and author of the book that bears his name). Neh 1:11; 2:1–6; 8:1–13.

NEHEMIAH, BOOK OF. An Old Testament historical book that records the rebuilding of Jerusalem's defensive wall after the Exile under the leadership of Nehemiah (1:1–7:73). The book also recounts the religious reforms undertaken by Nehemiah and Ezra.

NEIGHBOUR [S]

Ex 20:16 not bear false witness against thy *n*

Lev 19:13 not defraud thy *n,* neither rob him

Lev 19:18 but thou shalt love thy *n* as thyself

Ps 79:4 We are become a reproach to our *n's*

Prov 11:12 He that is void of wisdom despiseth his *n*

Prov 14:20 The poor is hated even of his own *n:* but the rich hath many friends

Prov 24:28 Be not a witness against thy *n* without cause

Prov 27:10 better is a *n* that is near than a brother far off

Jer 31:34 they shall teach no more every man his *n*

Zech 8:17 let none of you imagine evil...against his *n*

Matt 22:39 Thou shalt love thy *n* as thyself

Luke 10:36 Which...of these three...was *n* unto him that fell among the thieves

Luke 15:6 he calleth...*n's,* saying...Rejoice with me...I have found my sheep

Rom 13:10 Love worketh no ill to his *n*

Gal 5:14 Thou shalt love thy *n* as thyself

Eph 4:25 speak every man truth with his *n*

Jas 2:8 fulfil the royal law... love thy *n* as thyself

NERGAL (a Babylonian god of war). 2 Kgs 17:30.

NERGAL-SHAREZER (a Babylonian prince who released Jeremiah from prison). Jer 39:3–14.

NEW

Ex 1:8 there arose up a *n* king ...which knew not Joseph

Ps 40:3 And he [God] hath put a *n* song in my mouth

Ps 96:1 sing unto the LORD a *n* song...all the earth

Eccl 1:9 there is no *n* thing under the sun

Isa 1:14 Your *n* moons...my [God's] soul hateth

Isa 42:10 Sing unto the LORD a *n* song

Isa 65:17 I [God] create *n* heavens and a new earth

Lam 3:23 they [God's mercies] are *n* every morning: great is thy faithfulness

Ezek 36:26 a *n* spirit will I [God] put within you

Amos 8:5 *n* moon be gone, that we may sell corn

Matt 27:60 laid it [Jesus' body] in his [Joseph's] own *n* tomb

Mark 2:22 no man putteth *n* wine into old bottles

Luke 22:20 cup is the *n* testament in my [Jesus'] blood

John 13:34 A *n* commandment I [Jesus] give unto you

Acts 2:13 men [converts at Pentecost] are full of *n* wine

1 Cor 5:7 Purge out...the old leaven...may be a *n* lump

2 Cor 3:6 Who [Jesus]...made us able ministers of the *n* testament...of the spirit

2 Cor 5:17 any man be in Christ, he is a *n* creature
Eph 4:24 put on the *n* man
2 Pet 3:13 we...look for *n* heavens and a *n* earth
Rev 21:1 I [John] saw a *n* heaven and a *n* earth
Rev 21:5 Behold, I [Jesus] make all things *n*

NEW BIRTH DISCUSSION OF JESUS WITH NICODEMUS. John 3:1–21.

NEW COVENANT
Jer 31:31 I [God] will make a *n-c* with the house of Israel
Heb 8:8 I [God] will make a *n-c* with the house of Israel
Heb 8:13 he [God] saith, A *n-c,* he hath made the first old
Heb 12:24 And to Jesus the mediator of the *n-c*

NEW JERUSALEM
Rev 3:12 the city of my God, which is *n-J*
Rev 21:2 I John saw the...*n-J,* coming down from God

NEWNESS
Rom 6:4 even so we also should walk in *n* of life
Rom 7:6 serve in *n* of spirit... not in...oldness of the letter

NIBHAZ (an idol worshiped by the Avites, who settled in Samaria). 2 Kgs 17:31.

NICANOR (one of the seven men chosen as "deacons" in the church at Jerusalem). Acts 6:1–5.

NICODEMUS (a Pharisee who talked with Jesus about the new birth and helped prepare Jesus' body for burial). **John 3:1–21;** 7:50–52; **19:39–40.**

NICOLAITANES (an early Christian sect condemned for its false beliefs). Rev 2:6,15.

NICOLAS (one of the seven men chosen as "deacons" in the church at Jerusalem). Acts 6:1–5.

NIMROD (a son of Cush who became a powerful king and empire builder in Babylonia, or Shinar). Gen 10:8–12 • 1 Chr 1:8–10 • Mic 5:6.

NINEVE. See *Nineveh.*

NINEVEH (capital of Assyria where the prophet Jonah preached God's message of judgment). Gen 10:11–12 • 2 Kgs 19:36 • Isa 37:37 • **Jon 1–4** • Nah 1:1; 2:8; 3:7 • Zeph 2:13 • Matt 12:41. *Nineve:* Luke 11:32.

NISROCH (a false god worshiped by King Sennacherib of Assyria). **2 Kgs 19:36–37** • Isa 37:38.

NO (capital of upper Egypt). Jer 46:25 • Ezek 30:14–16 • Nah 3:8.

NOAH (a righteous man who was chosen by God to preserve life on earth by building an ark to escape the great flood). Gen 5:29–32; 6:8–22; **7:1–8:22;** 9:1–29; 10:1,32 • 1 Chr 1:4 • Isa 54:9 • Ezek 14:14,20 • Heb 11:7 • 1 Pet 3:20 • 2 Pet 2:5. *Noe:* Luke 17:26.

NOB (a city where David fled to escape King Saul's wrath). **1 Sam 21:1–9;** 22:9–23 • Neh 11:32 • Isa 10:32.

NOD (a region where Cain lived after murdering his brother Abel). Gen 4:16–17.

NOE. See *Noah.*

NOPH (an ancient royal city of the Egyptians). Isa 19:13 • Jer 2:16; 44:1; 46:14,19 • Ezek 30:13,16.

NORTHERN KINGDOM (ISRAEL) FALLS TO ASSYRIA. 2 Kgs 17.

NORTHERN TRIBES OF ISRAEL REVOLT. 1 Kgs 12:6–24.

NOTHING
Deut 2:7 forty years...God hath been with thee; thou hast lacked *n*
Josh 11:15 he [Joshua] left *n* undone of all that the LORD commanded Moses
2 Sam 12:3 poor man had *n,* save one little ewe lamb
Job 8:9 we...know *n,* because our days...are a shadow
Ps 49:17 when he dieth he shall carry *n* away
Prov 13:7 There is that maketh himself rich, yet hath *n*
Eccl 2:24 n better for a man, than that...his soul enjoy good in his labour
Isa 40:17 All nations before him [God] are as *n*
Isa 44:10 a graven image that is profitable for *n*
Jer 32:17 there is *n* too hard for thee [God]
Dan 4:35 inhabitants of the earth are reputed as *n*
Matt 5:13 salt...is...good for *n,* but to be cast out
Matt 17:20 n shall be impossible unto you
Mark 6:8 they [the disciples']... take *n* for their journey
Mark 7:15 n from without a man...can defile him

Mark 9:29 This kind can come forth by *n,* but by prayer

Luke 5:5 toiled all the night, and have taken *n*

Luke 23:9 but he [Jesus] answered him [Pilate] *n*

John 3:27 receive *n,* except it be given him from heaven

John 5:19 The Son [Jesus] can do *n* of himself

John 15:5 for without me [Jesus] ye can do *n*

Acts 11:8 *n*...unclean...entered into my [Peter's] mouth

Rom 14:14 I [Peter] know... there is *n* unclean of itself

1 Cor 1:19 I [God]...will bring to *n* the understanding of the prudent

1 Cor 7:19 Circumcision is *n,* and uncircumcision is *n*

1 Cor 13:2 though I [Paul]... have not charity, I am *n*

Phil 2:3 Let *n* be done through strife or vainglory

1 Tim 6:7 For we brought *n* into this world

Heb 7:19 For the law made *n* perfect

NUMBERS, BOOK OF. An Old Testament book that focuses on the Israelites in the wilderness of Sinai—a period of more than forty years between their departure from Egypt and their occupation of Canaan.

-O-

OATH [S]
Matt 5:33 perform unto the Lord thine *o's*

Matt 26:72 And again he [Peter] denied with an *o,* I do not know the man [Jesus]

Heb 7:20 not without an *o* he [Jesus] was made priest

Jas 5:12 neither by any other *o:* but let your yea be yea

OBADIAH (a prophet of Judah and author of the book that bears his name). Obad 1.

OBADIAH, BOOK OF. A short prophetic book of the Old Testament that pronounces judgment against the Edomites because of their mistreatment of God's people, the Israelites.

OBED-EDOM (a Philistine in whose house the ark of the covenant was kept before its removal to Jerusalem). 2 Sam 6:10–12 • 1 Chr 13:13–14; 15:24–25.

OBEDIENCE
Rom 5:19 so by the *o* of one [Jesus] shall many be made righteous

2 Cor 10:5 bringing into captivity every thought to the *o* of Christ

Heb 5:8 Though he [Jesus] were a Son, yet learned he *o*

OBEDIENT
Isa 1:19 willing and *o,* ye shall eat the good of the land

Acts 6:7 company of the priests were *o* to the faith

Phil 2:8 he [Jesus] humbled himself...became *o* unto death

1 Pet 1:14 As *o* children, not... according to the former lusts

OBEY [ED, ETH, ING]
Gen 22:18 thou [Abraham] hast *o'ed* my [God's] voice

Ex 5:2 Who is the LORD, that I [Pharaoh] should *o* his voice

Deut 27:10 Thou shalt...*o* the voice of the LORD

Josh 24:24 our God will we serve...his voice will we *o*

1 Sam 15:22 Behold, to *o* is better than sacrifice

Jer 11:3 Cursed be the man... *o'eth* not...this covenant

Jer 26:13 amend your ways... and *o* the voice of the LORD

Mark 4:41 even the wind and the sea *o* him [Jesus]

Acts 5:29 We [the apostles]...*o* God rather than men

Gal 3:1 bewitched you [Galatians]...not *o* the truth

Eph 6:1 Children, *o* your parents in the Lord

Col 3:20 Children, *o* your parents in all things

Heb 5:9 he [Jesus] became the author of...salvation unto all them that *o* him

Heb 11:8 he [Abraham]... *o'ed*...not knowing whither he went

Jas 3:3 bits in the horses' mouths, that they may *o* us

1 Pet 1:22 purified your souls in *o'ing* the truth

OFFER [ED, ETH, ING, INGS]

Gen 4:4 LORD had respect unto Abel and to his *o'ing*

Gen 22:2 *o* him [Isaac] there for a burnt *o'ing*

Lev 10:1 And Nadab and Abihu ...*o'ed* strange fire before the LORD

Ps 50:23 Whoso *o'eth* praise glorifieth me [God]

Ps 51:16 thou [God] delightest not in burnt *o'ing*

Ps 96:8 bring an *o'ing,* and come into his [God's] courts

Ps 119:108 Accept...the freewill *o'ings* of my mouth

Hos 6:6 I [God] desired...the knowledge of God more than burnt *o'ings*

Amos 5:22 neither will I [God] regard the peace *o'ings*

Mal 3:8 have we robbed thee [God]? In tithes and *o'ings*

Matt 5:24 be reconciled to thy brother, and then...*o* thy gift

Mark 12:33 to love him [God] with all the heart...is more than...*o'ings* and sacrifices

Luke 6:29 smiteth thee on the one cheek *o* also the other

Luke 11:12 if he shall ask an egg, will he *o* him a scorpion

Luke 21:4 all these have of their abundance cast in unto the *o'ings* of God

Luke 23:36 the soldiers also mocked him [Jesus]...*o'ing* him vinegar

1 Cor 8:1 Now as touching things *o'ed* unto idols

Eph 5:2 Christ...hath given himself for us an *o'ing*

2 Tim 4:6 I [Paul] am now ready to be *o'ed*

Heb 7:27 he [Jesus] did once, when he *o'ed* up himself

Heb 9:28 Christ was once *o'ed* to bear the sins of many

Heb 10:10 sanctified through the *o'ing*...of Jesus Christ

Heb 10:12 he [Jesus] had *o'ed* one sacrifice for sins for ever

Heb 11:4 Abel *o'ed* unto God a more excellent sacrifice

Heb 11:17 Abraham, when he was tried, *o'ed* up Isaac

Heb 13:15 let us *o* the sacrifice of praise to God

Jas 2:21 Was not Abraham our father justified...when he had *o'ed* Isaac his son

OFFSPRING

Job 5:25 seed...great, and thine [Job's] *o* as the grass

Acts 17:28 For we are also his [God's] *o*

Acts 17:29 we are the *o* of God

Rev 22:16 I [Jesus] am the root and the *o* of David

OG (an Amorite king defeated by the Israelites at Edrei). **Num 21:32–35** • Deut 3:1,8, 10–13 • Josh 12:4 • Ps 135:11.

OLD MAN / NEW MAN. Eph 4:17–29.

OLIVES, MOUNT OF (a hill near Jerusalem where Jesus was betrayed on the night before His crucifixion). Zech 14:4 • Matt 21:1; 24:3; **26:30** • Mark 11:1; 13:3; 14:26 • Luke 19:29,37; 21:37; 22:39 • John 8:1. *Mount Olivet:* 2 Sam 15:30 • Acts 1:12.

OLIVET, MOUNT. See *Olives, Mount of.*

OMRI (a king of Israel who built Samaria as the capital city of the Northern Kingdom). **1 Kgs 16:23–28** • 2 Kgs 8:26 • 2 Chr 22:2 • Mic 6:16.

ON
1. A leader who rebelled against Moses in the wilderness. Num 16:1–35.
2. A city of lower Egypt noted as a center of sun worship. Gen 41:45,50. *Aven:* Amos 1:5.

ONAN (a son of Judah who failed to consummate a marriage union with Tamar). **Gen 38:8–10;** 46:12 • Num 26:19 • 1 Chr 2:3.

ONESIMUS (a slave who was converted under Paul's ministry). Col 4:7–9 • Phlm 10.

ONESIPHORUS (a believer who befriended Paul when he was a prisoner in Rome). 2 Tim 1:16–18; 4:19.

OPEN [ED, EST, ETH]
Gen 3:7 eyes of them [Adam and Eve] both were *o'ed*
Job 11:5 that God would...*o* his lips against thee
Ps 51:15 O Lord, *o* thou my lips
Ps 119:131 I *o'ed* my mouth, and...longed for thy [God's] commandments
Ps 145:16 Thou [God] *o'est* thine hand, and satisfiest the desire of every living thing
Ps 146:8 The LORD *o'eth* the eyes of the blind
Prov 13:3 he that *o'eth* wide his lips shall have destruction
Prov 27:5 *O* rebuke is better than secret love
Isa 35:5 Then the eyes of the blind shall be *o'ed*
Isa 42:7 To *o* the blind eyes, to bring out the prisoners
Isa 53:7 he [God's servant]... *o'ed* not his mouth

Lam 3:46 enemies have *o'ed* their mouths against us

Ezek 3:2 I [Ezekiel] *o'ed* my mouth, and he [God] caused me to eat that roll

Mal 3:10 prove me [God]...herewith...if I will not *o* you the windows of heaven

Matt 3:16 heavens were *o'ed* unto him [Jesus]

Matt 7:7 knock, and it shall be *o'ed* unto you

Matt 27:52 graves were *o'ed;* and many bodies...arose

Mark 7:34 he [Jesus]...saith... Ephphatha, that is, Be *o'ed*

Luke 24:31 eyes were *o'ed,* and they [Emmaus travelers] knew him [Jesus]

John 9:30 know not from whence he [Jesus] is, and yet he hath *o'ed* mine eyes

John 10:21 Can a devil *o* the eyes of the blind

Acts 9:8 when his [Saul's] eyes were *o'ed,* he saw no man

Acts 14:27 he [God] had *o'ed* the door of faith unto...Gentiles

Acts 26:18 To *o* their eyes, and to turn them from darkness

Rom 3:13 Their throat is an *o* sepulchre

1 Cor 16:9 a great door...is *o'ed* unto me [Paul]

1 Pet 3:12 the eyes of the Lord are over the righteous, and his ears are *o*

Rev 3:7 write...he that *o'eth,* and no man shutteth

Rev 3:8 I [Jesus] have set before thee an *o* door

Rev 3:20 any man...*o* the door, I [Jesus] will come in

Rev 4:1 door...*o'ed* in heaven

Rev 5:9 worthy to take the book, and to *o* the seals

OPENLY

Matt 6:4 Father which seeth in secret...shall reward thee *o*

Mark 8:32 he [Jesus] spake that saying [about his death] *o*

John 11:54 Jesus...walked no more *o* among the Jews

OPHIR (a gold-producing region visited by the ships of Solomon and the Phoenicians). **1 Kgs 9:26–28;** 10:11; 22:48 • 1 Chr 29:4 • 2 Chr 8:18; 9:10 • Job 22:24; 28:16 • Ps 45:9 • Isa 13:12.

OPHRAH (Gideon's hometown where an angel assured him of God's guidance and protection). **Judg 6:11–14,24;** 8:27,32; 9:5.

ORDAIN [ED]

1 Chr 17:9 I [God] will *o* a place for my people Israel

Ps 8:3 moon and the stars, which thou [God] hast *o'ed*

Jer 1:5 I [God] *o'ed* thee [Jeremiah] a prophet unto the nations

Mark 3:14 he [Jesus] *o'ed* twelve...they should be with him

John 15:16 I [Jesus] have chosen you, and *o'ed* you

Rom 13:1 the powers that be are *o'ed* of God

1 Cor 9:14 the Lord *o'ed*... they...should live of the gospel

ORDINANCE [S]

Ex 12:43 LORD said...This is the *o* of the passover

Lev 18:4 Ye shall...keep mine [God's] *o's*

1 Pet 2:13 Submit yourselves to every *o* of man

ORNAN. See *Araunah*.

OSEE. See *Hosea*.

OSHEA. See *Joshua*.

OTHNIEL (the first judge of Israel who defeated the king of Mesopotamia). Judg 3:9–11.

OUGHT

Matt 5:23 rememberest...thy brother hath *o* against thee

Luke 11:42 these *o* ye [Pharisees] to have done

Luke 12:12 Holy Ghost shall teach you...what ye *o* to say

Luke 18:1 men *o* always to pray, and not to faint

John 13:14 ye also *o* to wash one another's feet

John 19:7 and by our law he [Jesus] *o* to die

Acts 5:29 We [the apostles] *o* to obey God rather than men

Rom 12:3 think of himself more highly...he *o* to think

Rom 15:1 strong *o* to bear the infirmities of the weak

Eph 5:28 So *o* men to love... wives as their own bodies

Col 4:6 ye may know how ye *o* to answer every man

Heb 2:1 *o* to give...heed to... things...we have heard

Jas 3:10 My brethren, these things *o* not so to be

2 Pet 3:11 what manner of persons *o* ye to be

1 John 4:11 Beloved...we *o* also to love one another

OVERCOME [TH]

Num 13:30 for we are well able to *o* it [Canaan]

John 16:33 be of good cheer; I [Jesus] have *o* the world

Rom 12:21 Be not *o* of evil, but *o* evil with good

1 John 2:13 young men...ye have *o* the wicked one

1 John 5:4 and this is the victory that *o'th* the world

Rev 17:14 Lamb shall *o* them: for he is Lord of lords

Rev 21:7 He that *o'th* shall inherit all things

OWE [ST, TH]

Matt 18:28 he [servant] laid hands on him...saying, Pay me that thou *o'st*

Luke 16:5 How much *o'st* thou unto my lord

Rom 13:8 **O** no man any thing, but to love one another

Phlm 18 he [Onesimus]...**o'th** thee ought, put that on mine [Paul's] account

OZIAS. See *Uzziah*.

-P-

PADAN-ARAM.
See *Mesopotamia.*

PALESTINE (the territory of the Canaanites that became known as the land of the people of Israel). Joel 3:4. *Palestina:* Ex 15:14 • Isa 14:29,31.

PAMPHYLIA (a coastal region in Asia Minor visited by Paul). Acts 2:10; **13:13; 14: 24–25;** 15:38; 27:5.

PAPHOS (a city on the island of Cyprus where Paul blinded the magician Elymas). Acts 13:6–12.

PARABLES OF JESUS. See *Jesus, Parables of.*

PARDON [ED, ETH]
1 Sam 15:25 p my [Saul's] sin, and turn again with me
Neh 9:17 a God ready to *p,* gracious and merciful
Ps 25:11 O LORD, *p* mine iniquity; for it is great
Isa 40:2 her [Jerusalem's] iniquity is *p'ed*
Jer 33:8 I [God] will *p* all their iniquities
Mic 7:18 Who is a God like unto thee, that *p'eth* iniquity

PARMENAS (one of the seven men chosen as "deacons" in the church at Jerusalem). Acts 6:1–5.

PARTHIANS (inhabitants of Parthia, a country north of Media and Persia). Acts 2:1,9.

PASHUR (a priest who had the prophet Jeremiah imprisoned). **Jer 20:3–6;** 38:1.

PASSOVER (a festival that commemorated the Exodus of Israel from Egypt). **Ex 12:11–48** • Num 9:2–14 • 2 Chr 30:1–18; 35:1–19 • Matt 26:2–19 • Mark 14:1–16 • Luke 22:1–15 • 1 Cor 5:7 • Heb 11:28.

PASTOR [S]
Jer 3:15 I [God] will give you *p's* according to mine heart
Jer 17:16 I [Jeremiah] have not hastened from being a *p*
Jer 23:1 Woe be unto the *p's* that...scatter the sheep
Eph 4:11 he [God] gave some, apostles...and some, *p's*

PATHROS (a name for upper Egypt). Isa 11:11 • Jer 44:1,15 • Ezek 29:14; 30:14.

PATIENCE
Rom 5:3 tribulation worketh *p*
Rom 15:5 the God of *p*...grant you to be likeminded
1 Thes 1:3 Remembering... your work of faith...and *p* of hope

1 Tim 6:11 follow after...faith, love, *p,* meekness

Heb 12:1 run with *p* the race that is set before us

Jas 1:3 that the trying of your faith worketh *p*

Jas 5:7 husbandman waiteth for the...fruit of the earth, and hath long *p* for it

PATIENT [LY]

Ps 40:1 I waited *p'ly* for the LORD; and he inclined unto me

Eccl 7:8 the *p* in spirit is better than the proud in spirit

Rom 12:12 Rejoicing in hope; *p* in tribulation

1 Thes 5:14 support the weak, be *p* toward all men

Heb 6:15 And so, after he [Abraham] had *p'ly* endured, he obtained the promise

Jas 5:7 *p* therefore, brethren, unto the coming of the Lord

PATMOS (a desolate island where the apostle John was exiled and where he wrote the Book of Revelation). Rev 1:9.

PAUL (an apostle to the Gentiles who was converted from persecuting the Christian faith to proclaiming its truths). Also known as *Saul* (Acts 8:1), Paul is the central personality of the second half of the Book of Acts. Recognized as the author of thirteen epistles of the New Testament: Romans, 1 and 2 Corinthians, Galatians, Ephesians, Philippians, Colossians, 1 and 2 Thessalonians, 1 and 2 Timothy, Titus, and Philemon. See **Acts 13–28** for a sketch of Paul's life.

1. Consented to Stephen's death (Acts 7:59–8:1)

2. Converted on road to Damascus (Acts 9:1–9)

3. Ministered with Barnabas at Antioch (Acts 11:25–26)

4. First missionary journey (Acts 13:1–14:28)

5. Second missionary journey (Acts 15:36–18:23)

6. Third missionary journey (Acts 19:1–21:16)

7. Arrested in Jerusalem and detained in Caesarea (Acts 21:27–26:32)

8. Journey to Rome and shipwrecked (Acts 27:1–28:10)

9. Preached while under house arrest at Rome (Acts 28:16–31)

PAULUS, SERGIUS (Roman proconsul of Cyprus who was converted under Paul's ministry). Acts 13:4–12.

PAY [ED, ETH]

Ps 37:21 The wicked borroweth, and *p'eth* not again

Ps 66:13 I will *p* thee [God] my vows

Prov 7:14 this day have I *p'ed* my vows

Eccl 5:4 thou vowest a vow unto God, defer not to *p* it

Matt 18:34 his lord...delivered him to the tormentors, till he should *p* all

Matt 23:23 ye [scribes and Pharisees] *p* tithe of mint and anise and cummin

Rom 13:6 for this cause *p* ye tribute...are God's ministers

PEACE

Job 33:31 hold thy [Job's] *p,* and I [God] will speak

Ps 4:8 I will both lay me down in *p,* and sleep

Ps 34:14 seek *p,* and pursue it

Ps 55:18 He [God] hath delivered my soul in *p*

Ps 83:1 hold not thy *p,* and be not still, O God

Ps 119:165 Great *p* have they which love thy [God's] law

Ps 122:7 P be within thy walls

Prov 17:28 a fool, when he holdeth his *p,* is counted wise

Eccl 3:8 a time of war, and a time of *p*

Isa 9:6 his [Messiah's] name shall be called...Prince of *P*

Isa 26:3 keep him in perfect *p*...mind is stayed on thee [God]

Isa 48:22 no *p,* saith the LORD, unto the wicked

Isa 52:7 beautiful...the feet of him...that publisheth *p*

Isa 53:5 chastisement of our *p*...upon him [God's servant]

Jer 29:7 And seek the *p* of the city...for in the *p* thereof shall ye have *p*

Matt 10:34 I [Jesus] came not to send *p,* but a sword

Mark 4:39 he [Jesus]...said unto the sea, *P,* be still

Luke 2:14 Glory to God...on earth *p,* good will toward men

Luke 10:5 whatsoever house ye enter...*P* be to this house

John 14:27 my [Jesus'] *p* I give unto you

John 16:33 that in me [Jesus] ye might have *p*

Rom 2:10 honour, and *p,* to every man that worketh good

Rom 5:1 we have *p* with God through...Jesus Christ

Rom 10:15 beautiful are the feet of them that preach the gospel of *p*

Rom 14:19 follow after the things which make for *p*

1 Cor 14:33 God is not the author of confusion, but of *p*

Gal 5:22 fruit of the Spirit is love, joy, *p,* longsuffering

Eph 2:14 he [Jesus] is our *p,* who hath made both one

Eph 4:3 unity of the Spirit in the bond of *p*

Phil 4:7 p of God, which passeth all understanding

Col 3:15 let the *p* of God rule in your hearts

2 Thes 3:16 Now the Lord of *p* himself give you *p*

PECULIAR PEOPLE

Deut 14:2 LORD hath chosen thee [Israel] to be a *p-p*

Titus 2:14 he [Jesus] might... purify unto himself a *p-p*

1 Pet 2:9 ye [Christians] are... an holy nation, a *p-p*

PEKAH (a king of Israel who assassinated Pekahiah to gain the throne). **2 Kgs 15:23–31** • 2 Chr 28:6 • Isa 7:1–9.

PEKAHIAH (a king of Israel who was assassinated and succeeded by Pekah, one of his military officers). 2 Kgs 15:23–26.

PELETHITES (a loyal unit of David's soldiers). 2 Sam 8:18; 15:14–18; 20:7,23 • 1 Kgs 1:38,44 • 1 Chr 18:17.

PENIEL (a place near the Jabbok River where Jacob wrestled with an angel). Gen 32:24–32. *Penuel:* Judg 8:8.

PENTECOST (a harvest festival being observed in Jerusalem when the Holy Spirit came in power upon the early believers). **Acts 2:1–47;** 20:16 • 1 Cor 16:8. *Feast of Harvest* or *Ingathering:* Ex 23:16. *Feast of Weeks:* Ex 34:22.

PENUEL. See *Peniel.*

PEOPLE OF GOD

Heb 4:9 There remaineth...a rest to the *p-o-G*

Heb 11:25 Choosing...to suffer affliction with the *p-o-G*

1 Pet 2:10 in time past were not a people...now the *p-o-G*

PEOR. See *Baal-peor.*

PERCEIVE [D, ING, ST, TH]

Job 33:14 God speaketh... twice, yet man *p'th* it not

Job 38:18 Hast thou [Job] *p'd* the breadth of the earth

Isa 6:9 see ye indeed, but *p* not

Mark 7:18 not *p,* that whatsoever...entereth into the man...cannot defile

Luke 6:41 *p'st* not the beam that is in thine own eye

Luke 8:46 I [Jesus] *p* that virtue is gone out of me

Luke 9:47 Jesus, *p'ing*...their heart, took a child

Acts 4:13 they [the Sanhedrin] ...*p'd* that they [Peter and John] were unlearned ...men

Acts 10:34 I [Peter] *p* that God is no respecter of persons

1 John 3:16 *p* we the love of God, because he [Jesus] laid down his life

PERFECT [ED, ING, LY]

Gen 6:9 Noah was a just man and *p* in his generations

Job 1:1 that man [Job] was *p* and upright

Ps 18:30 his [God's] way is *p*...
word...is tried

Ps 18:32 It is God that...
maketh my way *p*

Ps 19:7 law of the LORD is *p,*
converting the soul

Prov 4:18 path of the just...
shineth...unto the *p* day

Matt 5:48 even as your Father
which is in heaven is *p*

Rom 12:2 prove what is that
good...and *p,* will of God

1 Cor 1:10 *p'ly* joined together
in the same mind

1 Cor 13:10 But when that
which is *p* is come

2 Cor 12:9 My [Jesus'] grace is
sufficient...strength is made
p in weakness

Eph 4:12 *p'ing* of the saints,
for the work of the ministry

2 Tim 3:17 That the man of
God may be *p*

Heb 5:9 And being made *p,* he
[Jesus] became the author
of eternal salvation

Heb 10:14 he [Jesus] hath
p'ed...them that are sanctified

Jas 1:17 good gift and every *p*
gift is from above

1 John 4:12 If we love one
another...his [God's] love is
p'ed in us

1 John 4:18 but *p* love casteth
out fear

PERFECTION

Ps 50:2 Out of Zion, the *p* of
beauty, God hath shined

2 Cor 13:9 this also we wish,
even your *p*

Heb 6:1 let us go on unto *p*

Heb 7:11 If...*p* were by the
Levitical priesthood

PERGA (capital of Pamphylia
and a city visited by the apostle Paul). Acts 13:13–14; 14:25.

PERGAMOS (a city where one
of the seven churches addressed
by John in the Book of Revelation was located). Rev 2:12–17.

PERISH [ED, ETH, ING]

2 Sam 1:27 How are the mighty
fallen, and the weapons of
war *p'ed*

Job 3:3 Let the day *p* wherein
I [Job] was born

Job 33:18 He keepeth...his life
from *p'ing* by the sword

Job 34:15 All flesh shall *p*
together...man...unto dust

Ps 1:6 but the way of the
ungodly shall *p*

Ps 68:2 the wicked *p* at the
presence of God

Prov 19:9 and he that speaketh
lies shall *p*

Prov 29:18 Where there is no
vision, the people *p*

Matt 18:14 that one of these
little ones should *p*

Mark 4:38 Master [Jesus], car-
est thou not that we [the
disciples] *p*

Luke 15:17 father's [servants] have bread...and I [prodigal son] *p* with hunger

John 3:16 whosoever believeth in him [Jesus] should not *p*

John 6:27 Labour not for the meat which *p'eth*

1 Cor 1:18 For the preaching of the cross is to them that *p* foolishness

2 Cor 4:16 outward man *p,* yet the inward man is renewed

2 Pet 3:9 The Lord...is longsuffering to us-ward, not willing that any should *p*

PERIZZITES (descendants of Perez who were conquered by Joshua's forces). Gen 15:20; 34:30 • Ex 3:8,17; 23:23 • Deut 7:1; 20:17 • **Josh 3:10;** 12:8; 17:15; 24:11 • Judg 1:4–5; 3:5 • 1 Kgs 9:20 • 2 Chr 8:7 • Ezra 9:1 • Neh 9:8.

PERSECUTE [D, ING, ST]

Ps 7:1 O LORD...save me from all them that *p* me

Ps 31:15 deliver me...from them that *p* me

Ps 119:161 Princes have *p'd* me without a cause

Matt 5:10 Blessed are they... *p'd* for righteousness' sake

Matt 5:11 Blessed are ye, when men shall...*p* you

Matt 5:44 Love...enemies... pray for them which...*p* you

John 15:20 If they have *p'd* me [Jesus]...also *p* you

Acts 9:4 Saul, Saul, why *p'st* thou me [Jesus]

Rom 12:14 Bless them which *p* you: bless...curse not

1 Cor 15:9 I [Paul] *p'd* the church of God

2 Cor 4:9 *P'd,* but not forsaken; cast down, but not destroyed

Phil 3:6 Concerning zeal, *p'ing* the church

PERSECUTION

Lam 5:5 Our necks are under *p:* we...have no rest

Acts 8:1 a great *p* against the church...at Jerusalem

Rom 8:35 Who shall separate us from the love of Christ? shall...distress, or *p*

2 Tim 3:12 all that will live... in Christ Jesus shall suffer *p*

PERSIA (a great empire that conquered Babylonia and allowed the Israelites to return to their native land). **2 Chr 36:20–23** • Ezra 1:1–8; 3:7; 4:3–24; 6:14; 7:1; 9:9 • Esth 1:3–18; 10:2 • Ezek 27:10; 38:5 • Dan 8:20; 10:1–20; 11:2.

PERSUADE [D, ST, TH]

Luke 16:31 neither will they be *p'd,* though one rose from the dead

Acts 18:13 This fellow [Paul] *p'th* men to worship God contrary to the law

Acts 26:28 Almost thou [Paul] *p'st* me [Agrippa] to be a Christian

Rom 8:38 I [Paul] am *p'd,* that neither death, nor life

Rom 14:14 I [Paul]...am *p'd*... that there is nothing unclean of itself

2 Cor 5:11 Knowing...the terror of the Lord, we *p* men

2 Tim 1:12 know whom I [Paul] have believed, and am *p'd* that he [Jesus] is able

PETER. See *Simon,* No. 1.

PETER, FIRST AND SECOND EPISTLES OF. Two short epistles, probably from the apostle Peter, written to encourage Christians who were experiencing persecution and discouragement (1 Peter) and to warn them against false teachers (2 Peter).

PHARAOH (title of the king of Egypt). The named pharaohs of the Bible are Shishak (1 Kgs 14:25–26), So (2 Kgs 17:4), Tirhakah (2 Kgs 19:9), Nechoh (2 Kgs 23:29; *Necho:* Jer 46:2) and Hophra (Jer 44:30).

PHARISEES (a Jewish sect whose traditional religious views brought them into conflict with Jesus and the apostles). Matt 12:14–34; 15:12–14; 16:1; 19:3; 22:15; 23:13–33 •

Luke 7:36–50; 11:53–54 • Acts 5:34; 15:5; 23:5–8; 26:5 • Phil 3:5.

PHARPAR (a river of Damascus). 2 Kgs 5:9–12.

PHEBE (a believer commended by Paul for her support). Rom 16:1–2.

PHENICE (a Mediterranean coastal region north of Israel). Acts 11:19; 15:3. *Phenicia:* Acts 21:2.

PHENICIA. See *Phenice.*

PHILADELPHIA (a city where one of the seven churches addressed by John in the Book of Revelation was located). Rev 3:7–13.

PHILEMON (a believer to whom Paul wrote on behalf of Philemon's slave). Phlm 1,9–21.

PHILEMON, EPISTLE TO. A short book written by Paul to help Onesimus, a runaway slave. Paul encouraged Philemon to welcome Onesimus back as a Christian brother (v. 16).

PHILIP
1. One of the twelve apostles of Jesus. Matt 10:3 • Mark 3:18 • Luke 6:14 • John

1:43–48; 6:5–7; 12:20–22; 14:8–12 • Acts 1:13.

2. One of the seven men chosen as "deacons" in the church at Jerusalem and an evangelist in the early church. Acts 6:5; 8:5–40; 21:8.

3. A Roman ruler in northern Palestine. Luke 3:1. See also *Herod,* No. 4.

PHILIPPI (a city where Paul and Silas were miraculously released from prison). **Acts 16:12–34;** 20:6 • Phil 1:1 • 1 Thes 2:2.

PHILIPPIANS, EPISTLE TO THE. A short epistle written by Paul to the church at Philippi—a group for whom he expressed great appreciation and thanksgiving (1:1–11). Philippians has been called Paul's "epistle of joy" (4:4).

PHILISTIA (a coastal region beside the Mediterranean Sea that served as the land of the Philistines). Gen 21:32–34 • Ps 60:8; 87:4; 108:9.

PHILISTIM. See *Philistines.*

PHILISTINES (inhabitants of Philistia who were enemies of the Israelites, especially during the days of Saul and David). Gen 26:1–18 • Ex 13:17 • Josh 13:2–3 • Judg 14:1–4; 15:3–20;

16:5–31 • 1 Sam 17:8–57 • 2 Sam 21:15–19 • 1 Chr 10:1–12 • Jer 47:1–4 • Amos 6:2; 9:7. *Philistim:* Gen 10:14.

PHILISTINES, SEA OF THE. See *Great Sea.*

PHINEHAS

1. Aaron's grandson who became a high priest of Israel. 1 Chr 9:19–20.

2. A son of Levi and priest who corrupted his office through immoral behavior. 1 Sam 2:22–24.

PHRYGIA (a region of Asia Minor visited by Paul). Acts 2:10; **16:6.**

PHUT. See *Libya.*

PHYSICIAN [S]

Jer 8:22 Is there no balm in Gilead...no *p* there

Mark 5:26 [a certain woman] had suffered many things of many *p's*

Luke 5:31 They that are whole need not a *p*

Col 4:14 Luke, the beloved *p,* and Demas, greet you

PIERCE [D, ING, INGS]

Job 30:17 My [Job's] bones are *p'd*...in the night

Prov 12:18 There is that speaketh like the *p'ings* of a sword

Zech 12:10 they shall look upon me [the Messiah] whom they have *p'd*

Luke 2:35 sword shall *p* through thy [Mary's]... soul

John 19:34 one of the soldiers... *p'd* his [Jesus'] side

Heb 4:12 word of God is... sharper...twoedged sword, *p'ing*...soul and spirit

Rev 1:7 he [Jesus] cometh... every eye shall see him, and they also which *p'd* him

PILATE (the Roman governor of Judea who presided at Jesus' trial). **Matt 27:2–65 • Mark 15:1–44** • Luke 3:1; 13:1; **23:1–52 • John 18:29–38; 19:1–38** • Acts 3:13; 4:27; 13:28 • 1 Tim 6:13.

PILLAR OF CLOUD AND FIRE LEAD ISRAEL. Ex 13:17–22.

PISGAH, MOUNT (a mountain peak in Moab from which Moses viewed Canaan before his death). Num 21:20; 23:14 • Deut 3:27; **34:1–6.**

PISIDIA (a mountainous district in Asia Minor visited by Paul). Acts 13:14; 14:24.

PISON (one of four rivers which flowed out of the Garden of Eden). Gen 2:10–14.

PITHOM (an Egyptian city built by Hebrew slaves). Ex 1:11.

PLAGUES AGAINST EGYPT
1. Water turned into blood (Ex 7:20–25)
2. Frogs (Ex 8:1–7)
3. Lice (Ex 8:16–19)
4. Flies (Ex 8:20–24)
5. Diseased livestock (Ex 9:3–7)
6. Boils (Ex 9:8–12)
7. Hail (Ex 9:13–25)
8. Locusts (Ex 10:1–15)
9. Darkness (Ex 10:21–23)
10. Death of Egyptian firstborn (Ex 12:1–36)

PLAIN, SEA OF THE. See *Salt Sea.*

PLEASE [D, ING]
1 Sam 12:22 p'd the LORD to make you his people

Ps 40:13 Be *p'd,* O LORD, to deliver me

Ps 69:31 This also shall *p* the LORD better than an ox

Isa 53:10 it *p'd* the LORD to bruise him [God's servant]

Mic 6:7 LORD be *p'd* with thousands of rams

Matt 17:5 my [God's] beloved Son, in whom I am well *p'd*

Luke 3:22 my [God's] beloved Son; in thee I am well *p'd*

John 8:29 I [Jesus] do always those things that *p* him [God]

Rom 8:8 they that are in the flesh cannot *p* God

1 Cor 1:21 it *p'd* God by the foolishness of preaching

Col 1:19 it *p'd* the Father that in him [Jesus] should all fulness dwell

Col 3:20 obey your parents... well *p'ing* unto the Lord

Heb 11:6 without faith it is impossible to *p* him [God]

1 John 3:22 do those things... *p'ing* in his [God's] sight

PLEASURE [S]

Job 22:3 any *p* to the Almighty, that thou art righteous

Job 36:11 If they obey...him [God], they shall spend their...years in *p's*

Ps 147:11 The Lord taketh *p* in them that fear him

Ps 149:4 For the Lord taketh *p* in his people

Prov 21:17 He that loveth *p* shall be a poor man

Isa 44:28 He [Cyrus]...shall perform all my [God's] *p*

Ezek 33:11 I [God] have no *p* in the death of the wicked

Mal 1:10 I have no *p* in you, saith the Lord of hosts

Luke 12:32 your Father's good *p* to give you the kingdom

Eph 1:9 his [Jesus'] good *p*... he hath purposed in himself

2 Tim 3:4 lovers of *p's* more than lovers of God

Heb 11:25 Choosing rather to suffer affliction...than to enjoy the *p's* of sin

Rev 4:11 thou [God] hast created all things...for thy *p* they...were created

PONTUS (a coastal region along the Black Sea where Priscilla and Aquila settled). Acts 2:5,9; **18:2** • 1 Pet 1:1.

POOR

Lev 19:10 thou shalt leave them [grapes] for the *p*

Deut 15:11 the *p* shall never cease out of the land

2 Sam 12:3 *p* man had nothing, save one little ewe lamb

Job 5:15 He [God] saveth the *p* from the sword

Job 30:25 was not my [Job's] soul grieved for the *p*

Job 36:6 He [God]...giveth right to the *p*

Ps 34:6 This *p* man cried, and the Lord heard him

Ps 40:17 I am *p* and needy; yet the Lord thinketh upon me

Ps 72:13 He [God] shall spare the *p* and needy

Ps 109:22 I am *p* and needy, and my heart is wounded

Prov 14:20 The *p* is hated even of his own neighbour

Prov 21:17 He that loveth pleasure shall be a *p* man

Prov 22:2 rich and *p*...Lord is the maker of them all

Prov 22:22 Rob not the *p,* because he is *p*

Eccl 4:13 Better is a *p* and a wise child than an old and foolish king

Isa 25:4 thou [God] hast been a strength to the *p*

Amos 2:6 they [Israel] sold... the *p* for a pair of shoes

Matt 5:3 Blessed are the *p* in spirit

Mark 10:21 sell whatsoever thou [rich young ruler] hast, and give to the *p*

Mark 14:7 For ye have the *p* with you always

Luke 4:18 anointed me [Jesus] to preach the gospel to the *p*

Luke 14:13 makest a feast, call the *p,* the maimed

Luke 19:8 Behold, Lord, the half of my [Zacchaeus's] goods I give to the *p*

1 Cor 13:3 though I [Paul] bestow...goods to feed the *p*

2 Cor 8:9 he [Jesus] was rich, yet...he became *p*

Jas 2:5 God chosen the *p* of this world rich in faith

POSSESSION [S]

Gen 17:8 I [God] will give... Canaan, for an everlasting *p*

Gen 47:27 they [Israel] had *p's* therein [in Egypt], and grew, and multiplied

Ps 2:8 I [God] shall give thee [his Son]...the uttermost parts of the earth for thy *p*

Mark 10:22 he [rich young ruler]...went away grieved: for he had great *p's*

Acts 5:1 Ananias, with Sapphira his wife, sold a *p*

POSSIBLE

Matt 19:26 but with God all things are *p*

Matt 26:39 if it be *p,* let this cup pass from me [Jesus]

Mark 9:23 all things are *p* to him that believeth

Luke 18:27 things...impossible with men are *p* with God

Rom 12:18 If it be *p*...live peaceably with all men

Heb 10:4 not *p*...blood of bulls... should take away sins

POTIPHAR (an Egyptian official who had Joseph imprisoned). Gen 37:36; **39:1–20.**

POWER [S]

Ex 15:6 Thy right hand, O LORD, is...glorious in *p*

1 Chr 29:11 Thine, O LORD, is the greatness, and the *p*

Job 37:23 he [God] is excellent in *p,* and in judgment

Ps 49:15 redeem my soul from the *p* of the grave

Ps 68:35 he [God]...giveth strength and *p* unto his people

Ps 111:6 He [God] hath showed...the *p* of his works

Prov 18:21 Death and life are in the *p* of the tongue

Jer 32:17 thou [God] hast made...the earth by thy great *p*

Nah 1:3 LORD is slow to anger, and great in *p*

Zech 4:6 Not by might, nor by *p,* but by my [God's] spirit

Matt 6:13 thine [God's] is the kingdom, and the *p*

Matt 24:30 Son of man coming in the clouds...with *p*

Matt 28:18 All *p* is given unto me [Jesus]

Mark 13:25 the *p's* that are in heaven shall be shaken

Luke 4:32 his [Jesus'] word was with *p*

Luke 9:1 he [Jesus]...gave them [disciples] *p*...over... devils

Luke 24:49 tarry ye [the disciples]...until...endued with *p*

John 1:12 gave he [Jesus] *p* to become the sons of God

John 19:11 no *p* at all against me [Jesus], except it were given thee [Pilate] from above

Acts 6:8 Stephen, full of faith and *p,* did great wonders

Rom 8:38 neither death, nor life...nor *p's*

Rom 13:1 every soul be subject unto the higher *p's*

1 Cor 4:20 kingdom of God is not in word, but in *p*

Eph 6:10 be strong in the Lord, and in the *p* of his might

Eph 6:12 we wrestle...against principalities, against *p's*

2 Tim 1:7 God hath not given us the spirit of fear; but of *p*

Rev 4:11 Thou [God] art worthy...to receive glory...*p*

POWER OF GOD

Matt 22:29 not knowing the scriptures, nor the *p-o-G*

Luke 22:69 Son of man sit on the right hand of the *p-o-G*

Rom 1:16 it [the gospel] is the *p-o-G* unto salvation

1 Cor 1:18 the preaching of the cross...is the *p-o-G*

1 Cor 2:5 your faith should... stand...in the *p-o-G*

POWERFUL

Ps 29:4 voice of the LORD is *p*

Heb 4:12 For the word of God is quick, and *p*

PRAISE [D, ING, S]

1 Chr 16:25 great is the LORD, and greatly to be *p'd*

1 Chr 29:13 we thank thee [God]...*p* thy glorious name

Ps 18:3 call upon the LORD, who is worthy to be *p'd*

Ps 21:13 so will we sing and *p* thy [God's] power

Ps 44:8 In God we boast...and *p* thy name for ever

Ps 47:7 sing ye [God's] *p's* with understanding

Ps 51:15 my mouth shall show forth thy [God's] *p*

Ps 67:3 Let the people *p* thee, O God...all...*p* thee

Ps 79:13 show forth thy [God's] *p* to all generations

Ps 84:4 they will be still *p'ing* thee [God]

Ps 92:1 a good thing...to sing *p's* unto thy [God's] name

Ps 100:4 Enter into his [God's] ...courts with *p*

Ps 145:3 Great is the LORD, and greatly to be *p'd*

Isa 42:10 Sing unto the LORD... his *p*...the end of the earth

Luke 2:20 shepherds returned, glorifying and *p'ing* God

John 12:43 loved the *p* of men more than the *p* of God

Acts 16:25 Paul and Silas... sang *p's* unto God

1 Pet 2:9 show forth the *p's* of him [God] who hath called you out of darkness

Rev 19:5 *P* our God, all ye his servants...ye that fear him

PRAISE THE LORD

Ps 7:17 I will *p-t-L* according to his righteousness

Ps 107:15 Oh that men would *p-t-L* for his goodness

Ps 117:1 O *P-t-L,* all ye nations...all ye people

Ps 150:6 Let every thing that hath breath *p-t-L*

PRAY [EST, ETH, ING]

2 Chr 7:14 my [God's] people... humble themselves, and *p*

Ps 5:2 unto thee [God] will I *p*

Ps 55:17 Evening, and morning, and at noon, will I *p*

Jer 14:11 said the LORD unto me [Jeremiah], *P* not for this people for their good

Dan 6:11 these men...found Daniel *p'ing*...before...God

Matt 6:6 when thou *p'est,* enter into thy closet

Matt 6:9 *p* ye: Our Father which art in heaven

Mark 6:46 he [Jesus] departed into a mountain to *p*

Mark 11:25 when ye stand *p'ing,* forgive

Mark 13:33 watch and *p:* for ye know not when the time is

Luke 6:28 *p* for them which despitefully use you

Luke 11:1 Lord, teach us to *p*

John 14:16 I [Jesus] will *p* the Father, and he shall give you another Comforter

John 17:9 I [Jesus] *p*...for them [the disciples] which thou [God] hast given me

Acts 10:9 Peter went up upon the housetop to *p*

Rom 8:26 we know not what we should *p* for as we ought

1 Cor 14:14 if I [Paul] *p*... unknown tongue...spirit *p'eth*

2 Cor 5:20 we *p* you...be ye reconciled to God

1 Thes 5:17 *P* without ceasing

Jas 5:13 Is any among you afflicted? let him *p*

Jas 5:16 *p* one for another, that ye may be healed

PRAYER

2 Chr 7:12 I [God] have heard thy [Solomon's] *p*

Ps 6:9 LORD will receive my *p*

Ps 66:20 God...hath not turned away my *p*

Ps 102:17 He [God] will regard the *p* of the destitute

Prov 15:29 The LORD...heareth the *p* of the righteous

Matt 21:22 whatsoever ye shall ask in *p,* believing, ye shall receive

Luke 19:46 My [God's] house is the house of *p*

Acts 6:4 we [the apostles] will give ourselves...to *p*

Rom 10:1 my [Paul's]...*p* to God for Israel...they might be saved

Jas 5:15 the *p* of faith shall save the sick

Jas 5:16 fervent *p* of a righteous man availeth much

PREACH [ED, ING]

Isa 61:1 the LORD hath anointed me [God's servant] to *p* good tidings

Matt 3:1 John the Baptist, *p'ing* in the wilderness

Matt 4:17 Jesus began to *p,* and to say, Repent

Matt 24:14 gospel...shall be *p'ed* in all the world

Mark 1:4 John did baptize... and *p*...repentance

Mark 3:14 that he [Jesus] might send them [the disciples] forth to *p*

Luke 24:47 remission of sins... be *p'ed* in his [Jesus'] name

Acts 5:42 they [the apostles] ceased not to...*p* Jesus Christ

Acts 8:4 they [believers]...went every where *p'ing* the word

Acts 8:5 Philip went down to... Samaria, and *p'ed* Christ

1 Cor 1:18 For the *p'ing* of the cross is to them that perish foolishness

1 Cor 1:21 it pleased God by the foolishness of *p'ing* to save them that believe

1 Cor 1:23 But we *p* Christ crucified

1 Cor 9:27 lest...when I [Paul] have *p'ed* to others, I myself should be a castaway

1 Cor 15:14 if Christ be not risen, then is our *p'ing* vain

2 Cor 4:5 we *p* not ourselves, but Christ Jesus

Eph 3:8 I [Paul] should *p* among the Gentiles

Phil 1:18 Christ is *p'ed;* and I [Paul]...do rejoice

2 Tim 4:2 *P* the word; be instant in season

1 Pet 3:19 he [Jesus] went and *p'ed* unto the spirits in prison

PREACH THE GOSPEL

Mark 16:15 Go ye into all the world, and *p-t-g* to every creature

Luke 4:18 he [God]...anointed me [Jesus] to *p-t-g* to... poor

Rom 1:15 I [Paul] am ready to **p-t-g** to you that are at Rome

Rom 10:15 beautiful are the feet of them that **p-t-g**

1 Cor 1:17 For Christ sent me [Paul] not to baptize, but to **p-t-g**

1 Cor 9:14 they which **p-t-g** should live of the gospel

PREACHER
Eccl 1:2 Vanity of vanities, saith the **P**...all is vanity

Rom 10:14 and how shall they hear without a **p**

2 Tim 1:11 I [Paul] am appointed a **p**...of the Gentiles

PRECEPT [S]
Ps 119:27 me to understand the way of thy [God's] **p's**

Ps 119:100 I understand... because I keep thy [God's] **p's**

Isa 28:10 **p** upon **p;** line upon line...here a little

Dan 9:5 We have sinned... rebelled, even by departing from thy [God's] **p's**

Mark 10:5 Jesus...said...For the hardness of your heart he [Moses] wrote you this **p**

PRECIOUS
Ps 116:15 **P** in the sight of the LORD is...death of his saints

Ps 139:17 How **p** also are thy thoughts...O God

Prov 17:8 A gift is as a **p** stone in the eyes of him that hath it

Eccl 7:1 A good name is better than **p** ointment

Isa 28:16 a tried stone, a **p** corner stone

Matt 26:7 came...a woman having an alabaster box of very **p** ointment

1 Cor 3:12 if any man build upon this foundation gold, silver, **p** stones

Rev 21:19 foundations...were garnished with...**p** stones

PREDESTINATE [D]
Rom 8:29 whom he [God] did foreknow, he also did **p**

Eph 1:5 Having **p'd** us unto the adoption of children by Jesus Christ

Eph 1:11 **p'd** according to the purpose of him [God] who worketh all things

PRESENCE OF THE LORD
Gen 3:8 Adam and his wife hid...from the **p-o-t-L**

Ps 114:7 Tremble, thou earth, at the **p-o-t-L**

Jon 1:3 Jonah rose up to flee... from the **p-o-t-L**

2 Thes 1:9 punished with... destruction from the **p-o-t-L**

PRICE
1 Chr 21:24 I [David] will verily buy it [a threshingfloor] for the full **p**

Job 28:18 the **p** of wisdom is above rubies

Prov 31:10 find a virtuous woman...*p*...above rubies

Isa 55:1 buy wine and milk without money and without *p*

Matt 13:46 when he had found one pearl of great *p*

Acts 5:2 [Ananias] kept back part of the *p*

1 Cor 6:20 ye are bought with a *p:* therefore glorify God

PRIDE

Lev 26:19 I [God] will break the *p* of your power

Ps 10:2 wicked in his *p* doth persecute the poor

Ps 73:6 *p* compasseth them about as a chain

Prov 8:13 The fear of the LORD is to hate...*p*

Prov 16:18 *P* goeth before destruction

1 John 2:16 the lust of the eyes, and the *p* of life

PRINCIPALITY [IES]

Rom 8:38 neither death, nor life, nor angels, nor *p'ies*

Eph 1:21 Far above all *p,* and power, and might

Eph 6:12 we wrestle...against *p'ies,* against powers

Col 2:15 having spoiled *p'ies* and powers, he [Jesus] made a show of them openly

PROCHORUS (one of the seven men chosen as "deacons" in the church at Jerusalem). Acts 6:1–5.

PROCLAIM [ED]

Lev 23:4 holy convocations, which ye shall *p*

Prov 20:6 Most men will *p* every one his own goodness

Isa 61:1 the LORD...hath sent me [God's servant]...to *p* liberty to the captives

Jon 3:5 people of Nineveh believed God, and *p'ed* a fast

Luke 12:3 spoken in the ear in closets shall be *p'ed* upon the housetops

PROFANE [D]

Ezek 23:38 they have...*p'd* my [God's] sabbaths

Ezek 44:23 teach...the difference between the holy and *p*

Mal 2:11 Judah hath *p'd* the holiness of the LORD

1 Tim 4:7 refuse *p* and old wives' fables

2 Tim 2:16 But shun *p* and vain babblings

PROFESS [ING]

Matt 7:23 will I [Jesus] *p*...I never knew you

Rom 1:22 *P'ing* themselves... wise, they became fools

Titus 1:16 *p* that they know God; but in works...deny him

PROFESSION

1 Tim 6:12 thou...hast professed a good *p*

Heb 3:1 consider the...High Priest of our *p,* Christ Jesus

Heb 10:23 Let us hold fast the **p** of our faith

PROFIT [ETH]
Ps 30:9 **p** is there in my blood, when I go down to the pit
Eccl 1:3 What **p** hath a man of all his labour
Jer 2:11 changed their glory for that which doth not **p**
Mark 8:36 **p** a man, if he... gain the whole world, and lose his own soul
John 6:63 spirit that quickeneth; the flesh **p'eth** nothing
Rom 3:1 or what **p** is there of circumcision
1 Cor 13:3 have not charity, it **p'eth** me nothing
Jas 2:14 doth it **p**...though a man...have not works

PROMISE [D, S]
Josh 23:10 he [God]...fighteth for you, as he hath **p'd**
2 Chr 1:9 thy [God's] **p** unto David...be established
Jer 33:14 I [God] will perform that...which I have **p'd**
Luke 24:49 behold, I [Jesus] send the **p** of my Father
Rom 15:8 Jesus Christ was a minister...truth of God, to confirm the **p's** made
Gal 3:21 the law then against the **p's** of God
Gal 3:29 Abraham's seed, and heirs according to the **p**

Gal 4:28 we, brethren...are the children of **p**
Eph 3:6 Gentiles should be... partakers of his [God's] **p**
Eph 6:2 Honour thy father... first commandment with **p**
Titus 1:2 eternal life, which God, that cannot lie, **p'd**
Heb 11:9 he [Abraham] sojourned in the land of **p**
Jas 1:12 crown of life, which the Lord hath **p'd**
2 Pet 3:4 Where is the **p** of his [Jesus'] coming
1 John 2:25 **p** that he [Jesus] hath **p'd** us, even eternal life

PROPHECIES ABOUT JESUS. See *Messianic Prophecies.*

PROPHECY [IES]
1 Cor 12:10 to another **p;** to another discerning of spirits
1 Cor 13:2 though I [Paul] have the gift of **p**
1 Cor 13:8 whether there be **p'ies,** they shall fail
2 Pet 1:20 no **p** of the scripture is of...private interpretation

PROPHESY [IED, IETH]
Ezek 37:4 he [God] said...**P** upon these bones...hear the word
Joel 2:28 your sons and your daughters shall **p**
Amos 7:15 LORD said...Go, **p** unto my people Israel

Matt 7:22 have we not *p'ied* in thy [Jesus'] name

Mark 7:6 Well hath Esaias *p'ied* of you hypocrites

Acts 2:18 pour out...my [God's] Spirit...they shall *p*

Rom 12:6 let us *p* according to the proportion of faith

1 Cor 13:9 we know in part, and we *p* in part

1 Cor 14:5 greater is he that *p'ieth* than he that speaketh with tongues

PROPITIATION

Rom 3:25 Whom [Jesus] God hath set forth...a *p* through faith

1 John 2:2 he [Jesus] is the *p* for our sins...not for ours only

1 John 4:10 God...sent his Son to be the *p* for our sins

PROUD

Job 40:12 Look on every one that is *p,* and bring him low

Ps 94:2 thou [God]...render a reward to the *p*

Ps 119:69 The *p* have forged a lie against me

Prov 6:17 A *p* look, a lying tongue

Prov 16:5 one that is *p* in heart is an abomination

Eccl 7:8 the patient in spirit is better than the *p* in spirit

2 Tim 3:2 men shall be... covetous, boasters, *p*

Jas 4:6 God resisteth the *p,* but giveth grace unto the humble

PROVE [D, TH]

Deut 13:3 God *p'th* you... whether ye love the LORD

Ps 26:2 Examine me, O LORD, and *p* me; try...my heart

Mal 3:10 *p* me now...saith the LORD of hosts

Rom 12:2 *p* what is that good, and...perfect, will of God

Gal 6:4 But let every man *p* his own work

1 Thes 5:21 *P* all things; hold fast that which is good

1 Tim 3:10 be *p'd;* then let them use the office of a deacon

PROVERBS, BOOK OF. A wisdom book of the Old Testament filled with pithy sayings on how to live with maturity and integrity under the watchful eye of God—the source of all wisdom.

PROVOKE [D, ING]

Deut 32:16 They *p'd* him [God]...with strange gods

Ps 78:17 sinned...against him [God] by *p'ing*...most High

Ps 78:58 *p'd* him [God] to anger with their high places

1 Cor 10:22 Do we *p* the Lord to jealousy

1 Cor 13:5 [charity] is not easily *p'd,* thinketh no evil

Gal 5:26 not be desirous of vain glory, *p'ing* one another
Eph 6:4 fathers, *p* not your children to wrath
Heb 10:24 consider one another to *p*...to good works

PSALMS, BOOK OF. A poetic book of the Old Testament filled with hymns of praise and prayers that probably were meant to be sung to the accompaniment of a musical instrument. King David of Judah wrote many of these psalms (see, for example, Pss 54; 59; 65).

PUBLIUS (a Roman official who entertained Paul on the island of Miletus after a shipwreck). Acts 28:7–8.

PUL. See *Tiglath-Pileser III.*

PUNISH [ED]
Isa 13:11 And I [God] will *p* the world for their evil
Jer 21:14 I [God] will *p* you according to...your doings
Jer 50:18 Behold, I [God] will *p* the king of Babylon

2 Thes 1:9 *p'ed* with everlasting destruction from the presence of the Lord

PURIFY [IED, IETH]
Titus 2:14 that he [Jesus] might...*p*...a peculiar people
Jas 4:8 and *p* your hearts, ye double minded
1 Pet 1:22 *p'ied* your souls in obeying the truth
1 John 3:3 every man that hath this hope...*p'ieth* himself

PURPOSE [D, TH]
Eccl 3:1 a time to every *p* under the heaven
Dan 1:8 Daniel *p'd*...that he would not defile himself
Rom 8:28 to them who are the called according to his *p*
2 Cor 9:7 as he *p'th* in his heart, so let him give
Eph 3:11 eternal *p* which he *p'd* in Christ Jesus
1 John 3:8 For this *p* the Son of God was manifested

-Q-

QUAIL PROVIDED FOR ISRAEL IN THE WILDERNESS. Ex 16:1–13.

QUENCH [ED]
2 Chr 34:25 my [God's] wrath... shall not be *q'ed*
Song 8:7 Many waters cannot *q* love
Jer 7:20 mine [God's] anger... shall not be *q'ed*
Matt 12:20 A bruised reed shall he [God's servant] not break, and smoking flax shall he not *q*
Mark 9:44 Where their worm dieth not...fire is not *q'ed*
Eph 6:16 ye shall...*q* all the fiery darts of the wicked
1 Thes 5:19 *Q* not the Spirit

QUICK [EN, ENED, ENETH, ENING]
Ps 71:20 Thou [God]...shalt *q'en* me

Ps 80:18 *q'en* us, and we will call upon thy [God's] name
Ps 119:88 *Q'en* me after thy [God's] lovingkindness
Ps 143:11 *Q'en* me, O Lord, for thy name's sake
Isa 11:3 make him [God's servant] of *q* understanding
John 5:21 Son *q'eneth* whom he will
John 6:63 the spirit that *q'eneth*...flesh profiteth nothing
Acts 10:42 he [Jesus]...was ordained...Judge of *q* and dead
1 Cor 15:45 the last Adam was made a *q'ening* spirit
Eph 2:1 And you hath he *q'ened,* who were dead in trespasses and sins
2 Tim 4:1 Jesus Christ...shall judge the *q* and the dead
Heb 4:12 For the word of God is *q,* and powerful

-R-

RABBAH (capital city of the Ammonites captured by David's army). Josh 13:25 • **2 Sam 12:26–31** • 1 Chr 20:1 • Jer 49:2–3 • Ezek 25:5 • Amos 1:14. *Rabbath:* Ezek 21:20.

RABBATH. See *Rabbah.*

RACE
Eccl 9:11 I...saw...that the *r* is not to the swift
1 Cor 9:24 in a *r* run all, but one receiveth the prize
Heb 12:1 run with patience the *r*...set before us

RACHAB. See *Rahab.*

RACHEL (Jacob's wife who died giving birth to Benjamin). Gen 29:6–31; 30:1–25; 31:4–34; 33:1–7; **35:16–24;** 46:19–25; 48:7 • Ruth 4:11 • Matt 2:18. *Rahel:* Jer 31:15–17.

RAHAB (a harlot who hid the spies sent by Joshua to scout the city of Jericho). **Josh 2:1–24;** 6:17–25 • Heb 11:31 • Jas 2:25. *Rachab:* Matt 1:5.

RAHEL. See *Rachel.*

RAINBOW AS GOD'S COVENANT SYMBOL. Gen 9:11–17.

RAISE [D, TH]
Judg 2:16 Nevertheless the LORD *r'd* up judges
Ps 41:10 LORD, be merciful unto me, and *r* me up
Ps 113:7 He [God] *r'th* up the poor out of the dust
Jer 23:5 I [God] will *r* unto David a righteous Branch
Amos 9:11 day will I [God] *r* up the tabernacle of David
Hab 1:6 I [God] *r* up the Chaldeans...bitter...nation
Matt 10:8 Heal the sick, cleanse the lepers, *r* the dead
Matt 16:21 he [Jesus] must... be killed, and be *r'd* again
John 2:19 Destroy this temple, and in three days I [Jesus] will *r* it up
John 5:21 as the Father *r'th* up the dead, and quickeneth them
Acts 10:40 Him [Jesus] God *r'd* up the third day
Rom 6:4 as Christ was *r'd*... we...walk in newness of life
Rom 10:9 believe...God hath *r'd* him [Jesus] from the dead
1 Cor 6:14 God...will also *r* up us
1 Cor 15:16 if the dead rise not, then is not Christ *r'd*
2 Tim 2:8 Jesus Christ...was *r'd* from the dead
Heb 11:19 God was able to *r* him [Jesus] up

RAMAH. See *Ramoth-gilead.*

621

RAMESES (a district of Egypt where Jacob and his descendants settled). **Gen 47:11** • Ex 12:37 • Num 33:3,5.

RAMOTH. See *Ramoth-gilead.*

RAMOTH-GILEAD (an Amorite city that became one of the six cities of refuge). Deut 4:43 • Josh 20:8 • 1 Chr 6:80. *Ramah:* 2 Kgs 8:29. *Ramoth:* 1 Kgs 22:3.

RANSOM
Prov 13:8 The *r* of a man's life are his riches
Hos 13:14 I [God] will *r* them from the power of the grave
Mark 10:45 the Son of man came...to give his life a *r*
1 Tim 2:6 Who [Jesus] gave himself a *r* for all

READY
Ex 17:4 they be almost *r* to stone me [Moses]
Job 17:1 My [Job's] days are extinct...graves are *r* for me
Ps 86:5 thou, Lord, art good, and *r* to forgive
Mark 14:38 The spirit truly is *r,* but the flesh is weak
Luke 12:40 Be ye...*r*...the Son of man cometh...when ye think not
Luke 22:33 Lord, I [Peter] am *r* to go with thee
Rom 1:15 I [Paul] am *r* to preach...at Rome also

2 Tim 4:6 For I [Paul] am now *r* to be offered
1 Pet 3:15 be *r* always to give an answer to every man

REAP [ETH, ING]
Lev 19:9 not wholly *r* the corners of thy field
Job 4:8 they that...sow wickedness, *r* the same
Ps 126:5 They that sow in tears shall *r* in joy
Prov 22:8 He that soweth iniquity shall *r* vanity
Hos 8:7 they have sown the wind...*r* the whirlwind
Matt 25:24 an hard man, *r'ing* where thou hast not sown
Luke 12:24 Consider...ravens: for they neither sow nor *r*
John 4:37 One soweth, and another *r'eth*
2 Cor 9:6 soweth bountifully shall *r* also bountifully
Gal 6:7 whatsoever a man soweth, that shall he also *r*
Gal 6:9 shall *r,* if we faint not

REASON [ING]
Ps 90:10 if by *r* of strength they [days of our years] be fourscore years
Isa 1:18 Come now, and let us *r* together, saith the LORD
Luke 9:46 *r'ing* among them [the disciples], which... should be greatest
Acts 6:2 not *r* that we [the apostles] should leave... word of God...serve tables

1 Pet 3:15 asketh you a *r* of the hope that is in you

REBECCA. See *Rebekah.*

REBEKAH (wife of Isaac and mother of Jacob and Esau). Gen 22:23; 24:15–67; 26:7–8,35; 27:5–46; 28:5; 49:31. *Rebecca:* Rom 9:10.

REBUKE [D, S, TH]
Ps 6:1 O LORD, *r* me not in thine anger
Ps 119:21 Thou [God] hast *r'd* the proud that are cursed
Prov 27:5 Open *r* is better than secret love
Eccl 7:5 It is better to hear the *r* of the wise
Ezek 25:17 I [God] will execute... vengeance...furious *r's*
Nah 1:4 He [God] *r'th* the sea, and maketh it dry
Matt 16:22 Peter took him [Jesus], and began to *r* him
Mark 8:33 he [Jesus] *r'd* Peter... Get...behind me, Satan
Luke 8:24 Then he [Jesus] arose, and *r'd* the wind
Titus 2:15 These things speak... and *r* with all authority
Rev 3:19 As many as I [Jesus] love, I *r* and chasten

RECEIVE [D, ING, TH]
Job 2:10 *r* good at the hand of God, and...not *r* evil
Prov 19:20 Hear counsel, and *r* instruction

Isa 40:2 Jerusalem...hath *r'd* of the LORD'S hand double
Mal 3:10 not be room enough to *r* it [God's blessing]
Matt 7:8 For every one that asketh *r'th*
Matt 10:8 freely ye have *r'd,* freely give
Matt 11:5 blind *r* their sight, and the lame walk
Matt 18:5 whoso...*r* one such little child...*r'th* me [Jesus]
Matt 21:22 ask in prayer, believing, ye shall *r*
Mark 10:15 Whosoever shall not *r* the kingdom of God as a little child
Luke 23:41 we [two thieves] *r* the due reward of our deeds
John 1:11 came unto his [Jesus'] own...own *r'd* him not
John 3:27 *r* nothing, except it be given him from heaven
John 14:3 come again, and *r* you unto myself [Jesus]
John 20:22 he [Jesus] breathed on them [the disciples]...*R* ye the Holy Ghost
Acts 1:8 But ye [the apostles] shall *r* power
Acts 8:17 they [the Samaritans] *r'd* the Holy Ghost
Acts 17:11 they [the Bereans] *r'd* the word with...readiness
Acts 20:35 It is more blessed to give than to *r*
Rom 8:15 ye have *r'd* the Spirit of adoption
1 Cor 2:14 natural man *r'th* not the things of the Spirit

1 Cor 3:14 If any man's work abide...he shall *r* a reward

Heb 11:8 called to...a place which he [Abraham] should after *r* for an inheritance

Heb 11:13 died in faith, not having *r'd* the promises

Jas 1:12 man...endureth temptation...*r* the crown of life

Jas 4:3 Ye ask, and *r* not, because ye ask amiss

1 Pet 1:9 **R'ing** the end of your faith, even...salvation

1 Pet 5:4 ye shall *r* a crown of glory that fadeth not

Rev 4:11 Thou art worthy, O Lord, to *r* glory and honour

RECHAB (father of Jehonadab and ancestor of the Rechabites). 2 Kgs 10:15–23 • Jer 35:6–19.

RECKON [ED, ETH]

Matt 25:19 lord of those servants...*r'eth* with them

Luke 22:37 he [Jesus] was *r'ed* among the transgressors

Rom 8:18 *r* that the sufferings... not worthy to be compared

RECONCILE [D, ING]

Matt 5:24 be *r'd* to thy brother...then...offer thy gift

2 Cor 5:19 God was in Christ, *r'ing* the world unto himself

2 Cor 5:20 in Christ's stead, be ye *r'd* to God

Eph 2:16 he [Jesus] might *r* both unto God...by the cross

RECONCILIATION

2 Chr 29:24 priests...made *r* with their [animals'] blood

2 Cor 5:18 God...hath given to us the ministry of *r*

Heb 2:17 he [Jesus] might... make *r*...sins of the people

RED SEA (a body of water that the Israelites crossed miraculously to escape the Egyptian army). Ex 10:19; **14:16–29; 15:4,22** • Num 33:10–11.

REDEEM [ED, ETH, ING]

Ps 26:11 *r* me, and be merciful unto me

Ps 34:22 The Lord *r'eth* the soul of his servants

Ps 49:15 But God will *r* my soul from...the grave

Ps 77:15 Thou [God] hast... *r'ed* thy people

Ps 107:2 Let the *r'ed* of the Lord say so

Isa 43:1 Fear not: for I [God] have *r'ed* thee [Israel]

Isa 50:2 Is my [God's] hand shortened...that it cannot *r*

Isa 52:9 for the Lord...hath *r'ed* Jerusalem

Luke 1:68 the Lord...hath visited and *r'ed* his people

Gal 3:13 Christ hath *r'ed* us from the curse of the law

Gal 4:5 To *r* them that were under the law

Eph 5:16 **R'ing** the time, because the days are evil

Col 4:5 Walk in wisdom...**r'ing** the time

Titus 2:14 he [Jesus] might **r** us from all iniquity

REDEMPTION

Ps 130:7 for with the LORD there is...plenteous **r**

Rom 3:24 justified...through the **r** that is in Christ Jesus

Eph 1:7 we have **r** through his [Jesus'] blood

Heb 9:12 by his [Jesus'] own blood he...obtained...**r**

REGENERATION

Matt 19:28 ye which...followed me [Jesus], in the **r**...sit upon twelve thrones

Titus 3:5 he [Jesus] saved us, by the washing of **r**

REHOBOAM (son and successor of Solomon as king of Judah who refused to implement the reform measures called for by northern leaders). 1 Kgs 11:43; **12:1–24;** 14:21–31; 15:6 • 1 Chr 3:10 • 2 Chr 9:31; 10:1–18; 11:1–22; 12:1–16; 13:7. *Roboam:* Matt 1:7.

REIGN [ED, ETH]

Gen 37:8 Shalt thou [Joseph] indeed **r** over us

Judg 9:8 The trees...said unto the olive tree, **R** thou over us

2 Sam 5:4 David was thirty years old when he began to **r**

1 Chr 29:26 David the son of Jesse **r'ed** over all Israel

Ps 47:8 God **r'eth** over the heathen

Ps 93:1 The LORD **r'eth,** he is clothed with majesty

Ps 146:10 LORD shall **r** for ever

Jer 23:5 a King shall **r** and prosper...execute judgment

Luke 1:33 he [Jesus] shall **r** over the house of Jacob for ever

Rom 5:14 death **r'ed** from Adam to Moses

Rom 6:12 Let not sin...**r** in your mortal body

1 Cor 15:25 he [Jesus] must **r,** till...all enemies under his feet

Rev 11:15 Christ...shall **r** for ever and ever

Rev 19:6 Alleluia...the Lord God omnipotent **r'eth**

REJECT [ED]

1 Sam 15:26 thou [Saul] hast **r'ed** the word of the LORD

Isa 53:3 he [God's servant] is despised and **r'ed** of men

Mark 7:9 ye [Pharisees] **r** the commandment of God

Mark 12:10 The stone which the builders **r'ed**

Luke 17:25 must he [Jesus] suffer many things, and be **r'ed** of this generation

REJOICE [D, ING, TH]

Deut 30:9 for the LORD will again *r* over thee

1 Sam 2:1 My [Hannah's] heart *r'th* in the LORD

1 Chr 16:10 let the heart of them *r* that seek the LORD

Job 8:21 Till he [God] fill...thy lips with *r'ing*

Ps 5:11 those that put their trust in thee [God] *r*

Ps 19:8 statutes of the LORD are right, *r'ing* the heart

Ps 32:11 Be glad in the LORD, and *r,* ye righteous

Ps 40:16 Let all those that seek thee [God] *r* and be glad

Ps 63:7 in the shadow of thy [God's] wings will I *r*

Ps 97:1 The LORD reigneth; let the earth *r*

Ps 108:7 God hath spoken in his holiness; I will *r*

Ps 118:24 day...LORD hath made; we will *r* and be glad

Ps 119:14 I have *r'd* in...thy [God's] testimonies

Ps 126:6 come again with *r'ing,* bringing his sheaves

Prov 5:18 and *r* with the wife of thy youth

Prov 15:30 The light of the eyes *r'th* the heart

Eccl 11:9 *R,* O young man, in thy youth

Isa 29:19 poor...shall *r* in the Holy One of Israel

Joel 2:21 be glad and *r:* for the LORD will do great things

Matt 2:10 they [the wise men] *r'd* with...great joy

Matt 5:12 *R*...for great is your reward in heaven

Luke 15:6 *R* with me; for I have found my sheep

John 8:56 Abraham *r'd* to see my [Jesus'] day

Rom 12:12 *R'ing* in hope; patient in tribulation

Rom 12:15 *R* with them that do *r*...weep with them that weep

Phil 1:18 Christ is preached; and I [Paul] therein do *r*

REJOICE IN THE LORD

Ps 33:1 *R-i-t-L,* O ye righteous

Ps 97:12 *R-i-t-L*...and give thanks at...his holiness

Hab 3:18 I will *r-i-t-L,* I will joy in...my salvation

Phil 3:1 Finally, my brethren, *r-i-t-L*

Phil 4:4 *R-i-t-L* alway: and again I say, Rejoice

REMEMBER [ED, EST, ETH, ING]

Gen 8:1 God *r'ed* Noah, and every living thing

Gen 9:16 that I [God] may *r* the everlasting covenant

Ex 2:24 God heard their [Israel's] groaning, and...*r'ed* his covenant

Ex 20:8 *R* the sabbath day, to keep it holy

Deut 8:18 thou shalt *r* the LORD thy God

Deut 15:15 **r** that thou [Israel] wast a bondman in...Egypt

Ps 20:7 we will **r** the name of the LORD our God

Ps 25:7 **R** not the sins of my youth, nor my transgressions

Ps 45:17 make thy [God's] name to be **r'ed**

Ps 77:10 **r** the years of the right hand of the most High

Ps 78:39 he [God] **r'ed** that they were but flesh

Ps 98:3 He [God] hath **r'ed** his mercy...toward...Israel

Ps 103:14 For...he [God] **r'eth** that we are dust

Ps 137:1 we [Israelites] wept, when we **r'ed** Zion

Ps 137:7 **R,** O LORD, the children of Edom

Eccl 12:1 **R** now thy Creator in the days of thy youth

Jer 31:34 I [God] will **r** their sin no more

Jon 2:7 my [Jonah's] soul fainted...I **r'ed** the LORD

Matt 5:23 there [at the altar] **r'est** that thy brother hath ought against thee

Luke 22:61 And Peter **r'ed** the word of the Lord

Luke 23:42 Lord, **r** me [thief] when thou comest into thy kingdom

Luke 24:8 they [the disciples] **r'ed** his [Jesus'] words

John 16:21 as soon as she is delivered of the child, she **r'eth** no more the anguish

1 Thes 1:3 **R'ing** without ceasing your work of faith

2 Tim 2:8 **R** that Jesus Christ... was raised from the dead

Heb 10:17 their sins...will I [God] **r** no more

REMEMBRANCE

Ps 30:4 give thanks at the **r** of his [God's] holiness

Ps 102:12 endure for ever; and thy [God's] **r** unto all generations

Luke 22:19 This is my [Jesus'] body...this do in **r** of me

John 14:26 the Comforter... bring all things to your **r**

REMISSION

Heb 9:22 without shedding of blood is no **r**

Heb 10:18 where **r**...is, there is no more offering for sin

REMISSION OF SINS

Matt 26:28 my [Jesus'] blood... is shed for many for the **r-o-s**

Mark 1:4 John did baptize... preach the baptism of repentance for the **r-o-s**

Luke 24:47 repentance and **r-o-s** should be preached...among all nations

Acts 2:38 be baptized...in the name of Jesus...for the **r-o-s**

Acts 10:43 whosoever believeth in him [Jesus] shall receive **r-o-s**

REMPHAN (a pagan Babylonian god worshiped by the Israelites). Acts 7:41–43.

RENDER [ED, ING]
Ps 38:20 They...that *r* evil for good are mine adversaries
Ps 116:12 r unto the LORD for all his benefits
Prov 12:14 and the recompence of a man's hands shall be *r'ed* unto him
Luke 20:25 R...unto Caesar
Rom 2:6 Who [God] will *r* to... man according to his deeds
1 Cor 7:3 husband *r* unto the wife due benevolence
1 Thes 5:15 See that none *r* evil for evil unto any man
1 Pet 3:9 Not *r'ing* evil for evil...railing for railing

RENEW [ED, EST, ING]
Ps 51:10 clean heart, O God... *r* a right spirit within me
Ps 104:30 thou [God] *r'est* the face of the earth
Isa 40:31 they that wait upon the LORD...*r* their strength
Rom 12:2 be ye transformed by the *r'ing* of your mind
2 Cor 4:16 yet the inward man is *r'ed* day by day

REPENT [ED, ETH]
Gen 6:6 it *r'ed* the LORD that he had made man
Job 42:6 I [Job] abhor myself... *r* in dust and ashes
Matt 4:17 Jesus began to preach, and to say, *R*
Luke 15:7 joy...in heaven over one sinner that *r'eth*
Luke 17:3 if he [your brother] *r,* forgive him
Acts 2:38 Peter said...*R,* and be baptized every one of you
Rev 3:19 I [Jesus] rebuke... chasten: be zealous...and *r*

REPENTANCE
Matt 9:13 I [Jesus] am...come to call...sinners to *r*
Luke 24:47 r...preached...among all nations
2 Cor 7:10 godly sorrow worketh *r* to salvation
2 Pet 3:9 all should come to *r*

REPHAIM (a valley near Jerusalem where David defeated the Philistines). **2 Sam 5:18–25;** 23:13 • 1 Chr 11:15; 14:9 • Isa 17:5.

REPROACH [ED, ETH]
Ps 31:11 I was a *r* among all mine enemies
Ps 55:12 For it was not an enemy that *r'ed* me
Ps 102:8 Mine enemies *r* me all the day
Prov 14:31 He that oppresseth the poor *r'eth* his Maker
Prov 14:34 but sin is a *r* to any people
Heb 11:26 Esteeming...*r* of Christ greater riches than... treasures in Egypt

Heb 13:13 go...unto him [Jesus]...bearing his *r*

1 Pet 4:14 ye be *r'ed* for the name of Christ, happy are ye

REPROBATE [S]

Rom 1:28 God gave them over to a *r* mind

2 Cor 13:6 I [Paul] trust that ye...know...we are not *r's*

2 Tim 3:8 men of corrupt minds, *r* concerning the faith

REPROVE [D, TH]

Ps 50:8 I [God] will not *r* thee for thy sacrifices

Prov 9:7 He that *r'th* a scorner getteth...shame

John 16:8 he [the Holy Spirit] will *r* the world of sin

Eph 5:13 all things that are *r'ed* are made manifest

2 Tim 4:2 *r,* rebuke, exhort with all longsuffering

REPUTATION

Phil 2:7 made himself [Jesus] of no *r*...took...form of a servant

Phil 2:29 Receive him [Epaphroditus]...and hold such in *r*

RESIST [ED, ETH]

Matt 5:39 I [Jesus] say unto you, That ye *r* not evil

Acts 7:51 ye do always *r* the Holy Ghost

Heb 12:4 Ye have not yet *r'ed* unto blood

Jas 4:6 God *r'eth*...proud... giveth grace unto the humble

Jas 4:7 *R* the devil, and he will flee from you

RESPECT [ETH]

Gen 4:4 the LORD had *r* unto Abel and to his offering

Ps 40:4 Blessed is that man that...*r'eth* not the proud

Ps 119:15 I will...have *r* unto thy [God's] ways

RESPECT OF PERSONS

Prov 24:23 not good to have *r-o-p* in judgment

Rom 2:11 For there is no *r-o-p* with God

Eph 6:9 neither is there *r-o-p* with him [Jesus]

1 Pet 1:17 who [God] without *r-o-p* judgeth...every man's work

RESTORE [TH]

Ps 23:3 He [God] *r'th* my soul

Ps 51:12 *R* unto me the joy of thy [God's] salvation

Luke 19:8 Behold, Lord...I [Zacchaeus] *r* him fourfold

Acts 1:6 Lord, wilt thou...*r* again the kingdom to Israel

Gal 6:1 *r* such an one in the spirit of meekness

RESURRECTION

Matt 27:53 [the saints] came out of the graves after his [Jesus'] *r*

Luke 20:33 Therefore in the *r* whose wife of them is she

John 11:25 I [Jesus] am the *r,* and the life

Acts 4:33 gave the apostles witness of the *r* of...Jesus

Acts 17:32 they [philosophers] heard of the *r*...mocked

1 Cor 15:13 no *r* of the dead, then is Christ not risen

Phil 3:10 I [Paul] may know him [Jesus]...power of his *r*

1 Pet 1:3 a lively hope by the *r* of Jesus Christ

Rev 20:6 Blessed...is he that hath part in the first *r*

RESURRECTION AND THE LIFE, JESUS AS. See *"I Am" Statements of Jesus.*

RESURRECTION OF JESUS. See *Jesus, Life and Ministry of.*

REUBEN (a son of Jacob and ancestor of one of the twelve tribes of Israel). Gen 29:32; 37:21–29; 42:22,37; 46:8–9; 48:5; 49:3. The tribe of Reuben settled east of the Jordan River along the Dead Sea. Num 32:1–25.

REUEL. See *Jethro.*

REVEAL [ED, ETH]
Job 20:27 heaven shall *r* his [man's] iniquity

Isa 40:5 glory of the LORD shall be *r'ed*

Dan 2:28 there is a God in heaven that *r'eth* secrets

Matt 16:17 flesh and blood... not *r'ed* it unto thee [Peter]

Luke 10:21 hid these things from the wise and...*r'ed* them unto babes

Luke 10:22 no man knoweth... who the Father is...and he to whom the Son will *r* him

Rom 1:17 righteousness of God *r'ed* from faith to faith

1 Cor 3:13 it [man's work] shall be *r'ed* by fire

Phil 3:15 God shall *r* even this

1 Pet 1:5 kept by the power of God through faith...ready to be *r'ed* in the last time

1 Pet 4:13 when his [Jesus'] glory shall be *r'ed*

REVELATION
Gal 1:12 neither was I [Paul] taught it, but by the *r* of Jesus Christ

Eph 3:3 by *r* he [God] made known...the mystery

Rev 1:1 **R** of Jesus Christ, which God gave

REVELATION OF JOHN, BOOK OF THE. The last book of the New Testament that consists of a series of visions revealed by the Lord to the apostle John. These visions are considered by some interpreters to portray the end of the present age and the coming of God's kingdom.

REVERENCE

Lev 26:2 keep my [God's] sabbaths, and *r* my sanctuary

Luke 20:13 it may be they will *r* him [vineyard owner's son]

Heb 12:28 we may serve God... with *r* and godly fear

REVILE [D]

Matt 5:11 Blessed are ye, when men shall *r* you

Mark 15:32 And they [two thieves] that were crucified with him [Jesus] *r'd* him

1 Pet 2:23 Who [Jesus], when he was *r'd*, *r'd* not again

REWARD [ED, ETH]

Gen 15:1 I [God] am thy [Abraham's]...great *r*

Ps 18:20 Lord *r'ed* me according to my righteousness

Ps 31:23 the Lord...plentifully *r'eth* the proud doer

Ps 58:11 Verily there is a *r* for the righteous

Ps 103:10 He [God] hath not... *r'ed* us according to our iniquities

Ps 127:3 and the fruit of the womb is his [God's] *r*

Prov 17:13 Whoso *r'eth* evil for good, evil shall not depart from his house

Matt 5:12 great is your *r* in heaven: for so persecuted they the prophets

Matt 5:46 love them which love you, what *r* have ye

Luke 23:41 we [two thieves] receive...due *r* of our deeds

1 Cor 3:8 every man shall receive his own *r*

Col 3:24 ye shall receive the *r* of the inheritance

1 Tim 5:18 The labourer is worthy of his *r*

REZIN (a king of Syria who was killed in the conquest by the Assyrians). **2 Kgs 15:37; 16:5–9** • Isa 7:4,8; 8:6; 9:11.

RHODES (a Greek island that Paul's ship passed). Acts 21:1.

RIGHT HAND OF GOD

Mark 16:19 he [Jesus] was received up...and sat on the *r-h-o-G*

Acts 7:55 he [Stephen]... saw...Jesus standing on the *r-h-o-G*

Col 3:1 seek those things... above, where Christ sitteth on the *r-h-o-G*

Heb 10:12 this man [Jesus]... sat down on the *r-h-o-G*

1 Pet 3:22 Who [Jesus] is gone into heaven...on the *r-h-o-G*

RIGHTEOUS [LY, NESS]

Gen 15:6 the Lord...counted it...for *r'ness*

Gen 18:23 Wilt thou [God]... destroy the *r* with the wicked

Job 15:14 What is man...that he should be *r*

Job 32:1 because he [Job] was *r* in his own eyes

Ps 1:6 For the LORD knoweth the way of the *r*

Ps 9:8 And he [God] shall judge the world in *r'ness*

Ps 19:9 judgments of the LORD are true and *r*

Ps 23:3 he [God] leadeth me in the paths of *r'ness*

Ps 35:28 my tongue shall speak of thy [God's] *r'ness*

Ps 37:16 A little that a *r* man hath is better than...riches

Ps 37:29 The *r* shall inherit the land...dwell therein

Ps 45:7 Thou [God] lovest *r'ness,* and hatest wickedness

Ps 97:6 The heavens declare his [God's] *r'ness*

Ps 119:137 **R** art thou, O LORD... upright...thy judgments

Ps 129:4 LORD is *r:* he hath cut...the cords of the wicked

Ps 145:17 The LORD is *r* in all his ways...holy in...works

Prov 10:11 The mouth of a *r* man is a well of life

Prov 14:34 **R'ness** exalteth a nation

Prov 15:29 The LORD...heareth the prayer of the *r*

Prov 16:8 Better is a little with *r'ness* than great revenues

Prov 31:9 judge *r'ly,* and plead the cause of the poor

Isa 62:2 the Gentiles shall see thy [God's] *r'ness*

Jer 23:5 I [God] will raise unto David a *r* Branch

Amos 5:24 let judgment run down as waters, and *r'ness* as a mighty stream

Mal 4:2 Sun of *r'ness* arise with healing in his wings

Matt 5:6 Blessed are they which...thirst after *r'ness*

Matt 5:20 except your *r'ness*... exceed...*r'ness* of the scribes

Matt 6:33 But seek ye first the kingdom of God, and his *r'ness*

Luke 5:32 I [Jesus] came not to call the *r*...to repentance

Luke 23:47 Certainly this [Jesus] was a *r* man

Rom 1:17 *r'ness* of God revealed from faith to faith

Rom 3:10 As it is written, There is none *r,* no, not one

Rom 4:3 Abraham believed God...counted...for *r'ness*

Rom 5:19 by the obedience of one [Jesus]...many be made *r*

Rom 10:10 with the heart man believeth unto *r'ness*

2 Cor 5:21 might be made... *r'ness* of God in him [Jesus]

2 Cor 6:14 what fellowship hath *r'ness* with unrighteousness

Eph 6:14 having on the breast-plate of *r'ness*

2 Tim 4:8 laid up for me [Paul] a crown of *r'ness*

Jas 5:16 fervent prayer of a *r* man availeth much

1 Pet 3:12 For the eyes of the Lord are over the *r*
1 Pet 3:14 if ye suffer for *r'ness'* sake, happy are ye

RIMMON (a pagan god worshiped by Naaman the leper). 2 Kgs 5:18.

ROBOAM. See *Rehoboam.*

ROMANS, EPISTLE TO THE. An epistle on the themes of righteousness and salvation, written by the apostle Paul to the Christians at Rome. The most systematic and theological of all of Paul's epistles, Romans expresses his conviction that the gospel is the power of salvation to all who believe (1:16–17).

ROME (capital city of the Roman Empire and the place where Paul was imprisoned during his final days). Acts 2:10; 18:2; 19:21; 23:11; **28:14–16** • Rom 1:7,15 • 2 Tim 1:17.

RUHAMAH (a symbolic name, meaning "having obtained favor," given by the prophet Hosea to his daughter to show that Israel would be forgiven). Hos 2:1.

RULE [ING, TH]
Gen 1:16 two great lights; the greater light to *r* the day
2 Sam 23:3 He that *r'th* over men must be just
Matt 2:6 a Governor, that shall *r* my people Israel
Col 3:15 let the peace of God *r* in your hearts
1 Tim 3:5 if a man know not how to *r* his own house
1 Tim 3:12 deacons...*r'ing*... their own houses well

RUN [NETH, NING]
Ps 23:5 my cup *r'neth* over
Eccl 1:7 All the rivers *r* into the sea...sea is not full
Isa 40:31 they shall *r,* and not be weary
Jer 5:1 **R** ye [Jeremiah] to and fro through...streets of Jerusalem
Amos 5:24 let judgment *r* down as waters
Hab 2:2 Write the vision...that he may *r* that readeth it
Matt 28:8 they [the women] departed...and did *r* to bring his [Jesus'] disciples word
Luke 6:38 pressed down... shaken together, and *r'ning* over
1 Cor 9:24 r all, but one receiveth the prize
Gal 5:7 Ye did *r* well; who did hinder you
Heb 12:1 let us *r* with patience the race...before us

RUTH (a Moabite woman who remained loyal to her Jewish mother-in-law Naomi after the death of their husbands). Ruth 1–4.

RUTH, BOOK OF. A short Old Testament book on the power of love in dismal circumstances. Love bound Ruth and her mother-in-law Naomi together, even after their husbands died (1:1–2:23).

-S-

SACKCLOTH AND ASHES
Esth 4:3 and many [Jews] lay in *s-a-a*

Dan 9:3 seek [God] by prayer... with fasting, and *s-a-a*

Matt 11:21 they [Tyre and Sidon] would have repented long ago in *s-a-a*

SACRIFICE [S]
1 Sam 15:22 Behold, to obey is better than *s*

Ps 4:5 Offer the *s's* of righteousness...trust in the LORD

Ps 51:17 The *s's* of God are a broken spirit

Ps 116:17 offer to thee [God] the *s* of thanksgiving

Prov 15:8 The *s* of the wicked is an abomination

Prov 17:1 Better is a dry morsel...than...*s's* with strife

Hos 6:6 For I [God] desired mercy, and not *s*

Jon 2:9 I will *s* unto thee [God] with...thanksgiving

Rom 12:1 present your bodies a living *s*

Heb 7:27 Who [Jesus] needeth not daily...to offer up *s*

Heb 11:4 Abel offered...a more excellent *s* than Cain

Heb 13:15 offer the *s* of praise to God continually

1 Pet 2:5 offer up spiritual *s's,* acceptable to God

SADDUCEES (a priestly aristocratic party of New Testament times that often opposed Jesus and His teachings). Matt 3:7; **16:1,6,11–12; 22:23–34** • **Mark 12:18** • **Luke 20:27** • Acts 4:1–3; 5:17–18; 23:6–8.

SAINTS
2 Chr 6:41 let thy [God's] *s* rejoice in goodness

Ps 30:4 Sing unto the LORD, O ye *s* of his

Ps 89:7 God is greatly to be feared in...assembly of the *s*

Ps 116:15 Precious in the sight of the LORD...death of his *s*

Matt 27:52 bodies of the *s* which slept arose

Rom 12:13 Distributing to the necessity of *s*

1 Cor 1:2 them...sanctified in Christ Jesus, called to be *s*

Eph 3:8 Unto me [Paul], who am less than the least of all *s*

Eph 4:12 perfecting of the *s,* for the work of the ministry

Rev 17:6 woman drunken with the blood of the *s*

SAKE [S]
Ps 23:3 paths of righteousness for his [God's] name's *s*

Matt 5:10 Blessed are they which are persecuted for righteousness' *s*

Mark 8:35 lose his life for my [Jesus'] *s* and the gospel's

Luke 21:17 ye shall be hated... for my [Jesus'] name's *s*

Acts 9:16 he [Paul] must suffer for my [Jesus'] name's *s*

Rom 8:36 For thy [God's] *s* we are killed all the day long

1 Cor 4:10 We are fools for Christ's *s*

2 Cor 8:9 for your *s's* he [Jesus] became poor

1 Tim 5:23 use a little wine for thy stomach's *s*

1 Pet 3:14 suffer for righteousness' *s,* happy are ye

SALAMIS (a town on the island of Cyprus where Paul and Barnabas preached during the first missionary journey). Acts 13:4–5.

SALEM. See *Jerusalem.*

SALIM (a place near the Jordan River where John the Baptist baptized). John 3:23.

SALOME (a woman who witnessed the crucifixion of Jesus and visited His tomb). Mark 15:40–41; 16:1.

SALT

Job 6:6 Can that which is unsavoury be eaten without *s*

Matt 5:13 Ye are the *s* of the earth

Col 4:6 Let your speech be... seasoned with *s*

SALT SEA (a salt-saturated body of water, referred to today as the *Dead Sea,* into which the Jordan River empties in southern Palestine). Gen 14:3 • Josh 3:16. *East Sea:* Joel 2:20. *Sea of the Plain:* Deut 3:17.

SAMARIA (capital city of Israel, or the Northern Kingdom, that was captured by the Assyrians). 1 Kgs 16:24–29; 20:1–22 • **2 Kgs 17:3–24** • Amos 3:11–12.

SAMARITANS (inhabitants of the district of Samaria who were considered inferior by the Jews because of their mixed-blood ancestry). 2 Kgs 17:29 • Matt 10:5 • Luke 9:52; 10:33; 17:16 • John 4:9–40; 8:48 • Acts 8:25.

SAMOS (an island of Greece visited by the apostle Paul). Acts 20:15.

SAMOTHRACIA (an island in the Aegean Sea visited by the apostle Paul). Acts 16:11.

SAMSON (a judge of Israel with great physical strength who died when he destroyed a pagan Philistine temple). Judg 13:24; 14:1–20; 15:1–16; **16:1–31** • Heb 11:32.

SAMUEL (a prophet and the last judge of Israel who anointed the first two kings of Judah—Saul and David). 1 Sam 1:20; 2:18–26; 3:1–21; 4:1; 7:3–15; 8:1–22; **9:14–27; 10:1–25;** 11:7–14; 12:1–25; 13: 8–15; 15:1–35; **16:1–23;** 25:1; 28:3,11–20 • 1 Chr 6:28; 9:22; 11:3; 26:28; 29:29 • 2 Chr 35:18 • Ps 99:6 • Jer 15:1 • Acts 3:24; 13:20 • Heb 11:32. *Shemuel:* 1 Chr 6:33.

SAMUEL, BOOKS OF FIRST AND SECOND. Two historical books of the Old Testament named for the prophet Samuel, who anointed Saul and David as the first two kings of Israel. Their anointing marked the transition of the nation from a loose confederacy of tribes to a united kingdom under the leadership of a king.

SANBALLAT (a Samaritan who plotted to kill Nehemiah to stop his rebuilding projects). Neh 2:10,19; 4:1,7; 6:1–14; 13:28.

SANCTIFICATION
1 Thes 4:3 this is the will of God, even your *s*
2 Thes 2:13 God hath...chosen you to salvation through *s* of the Spirit

1 Pet 1:2 Elect...through *s* of the Spirit

SANCTIFY [IED]
Gen 2:3 God blessed the seventh day, and *s'ied* it
Lev 20:7 *S* yourselves therefore, and be ye holy
Deut 5:12 Keep the sabbath day to *s* it
Josh 3:5 Joshua said unto the people, *S* yourselves
1 Chr 15:14 priests...*s'ied* themselves to bring...the ark
Joel 1:14 *S* ye a fast, call a solemn assembly
John 17:17 *S* them [the disciples] through thy [God's] truth: thy word is truth
1 Cor 6:11 ye are washed...ye are *s'ied*...ye are justified
1 Tim 4:5 it is *s'ied* by the word of God and prayer
1 Pet 3:15 But *s* the Lord God in your hearts

SAPPHIRA (a believer struck dead for lying and withholding money she had pledged to the church). Acts 5:1–11.

SARAH (wife of Abraham and mother of Isaac). Gen 17:15–21; 18:6–15; 20:2–18; 21:1–12; 23:1–19; 24:36; 25:10; 49:31 • Isa 51:2 • Rom 9:9 • *Sara:* Heb 11:11 • 1 Pet 3:6. *Sarai:* Gen 11:30; 12:5.

SARDIS (a city of Asia Minor and site of one of the seven churches addressed by John in the Book of Revelation). Rev 3:1–6.

SAREPTA. See *Zarephath.*

SARGON (a king of Assyria who captured Samaria and carried the Northern Kingdom into exile). Isa 20:1.

SARON. See *Sharon.*

SATAN (an evil being who opposes God; the devil). 1 Chr 21:1 • Job 1:6–12; 2:1–7 • Ps 109:6 • Zech 3:1–2 • Matt 4:10; 12:26; 16:23 • Mark 1:13; 3:23, 26; 4:15; 8:33 • Luke 4:8; 10:18; 11:18; 13:16; 22:3,31 • John 13:27 • Acts 5:3; 26:18 • Rom 16:20 • 1 Cor 5:5; 7:5 • 2 Cor 2:11; 11:14; 12:7 • 1 Thes 2:18 • 2 Thes 2:9 • 1 Tim 1:20; 5:15 • Rev 2:9,13,24; 3:9; 12:9; 20:2,7. *Belial:* 2 Cor 6:15. *Lucifer:* Isa 14:12.

SAUL
1. The first king of Israel who tried to kill David and was defeated by the Philistines. 1 Sam 9:1–31:12 • 1 Chr 10:2–13.
2. The original name of the apostle Paul. See *Paul.*

SAVE [D, ING, TH]
Ex 14:30 LORD *s'd* Israel...out of...hand of...Egyptians
Job 2:6 he [Job] is in thine [Satan's] hand; but *s* his life
Ps 7:1 *s* me from all them that persecute me
Ps 7:10 My defence is of God, which *s'th* the upright
Ps 44:6 not trust in my bow, neither shall my sword *s* me
Ps 55:16 I will call upon God; and the LORD shall *s* me
Ps 67:2 thy [God's] *s'ing* health among all nations
Ps 80:19 cause thy [God's] face to shine...we shall be *s'd*
Ps 107:13 he [God] *s'd* them out of their distresses
Prov 20:22 wait on the LORD, and he shall *s* thee
Isa 45:22 be ye *s'd,* all the ends of the earth
Isa 59:1 LORD'S hand is not shortened, that it cannot *s*
Jer 8:20 summer is ended, and we are not *s'd*
Matt 1:21 he [Jesus] shall *s* his people from their sins
Matt 10:22 he that endureth to the end shall be *s'd*
Mark 8:35 whosoever will *s* his life shall lose it
Mark 10:26 Who...can be *s'd*
Luke 19:10 Son of man is come to seek and to *s* that which was lost
Luke 23:35 He [Jesus] *s'd* others; let him save himself

John 3:17 the world through him [Jesus] might be *s'd*

John 12:47 I [Jesus] came not to judge...but to *s* the world

Acts 2:21 whosoever shall call on...the Lord shall be *s'd*

Acts 4:12 none other name... whereby we must be *s'd*

Rom 5:10 we shall be *s'd* by his [Jesus'] life

Rom 10:13 whosoever shall call upon the name of the Lord shall be *s'd*

1 Cor 1:21 it pleased God by the foolishness of preaching to *s* them that believe

1 Cor 9:22 I [Paul] am made all things to all men, that I might...*s* some

Eph 2:8 by grace are ye *s'd* through faith

1 Tim 1:15 Christ Jesus came into the world to *s* sinners

2 Tim 1:9 Who [Jesus]...*s'd*... called us with an holy calling

Heb 7:25 he [Jesus] is able also to *s* them to the uttermost

Jas 2:14 though a man...have not works? can faith *s* him

SAVIOUR

2 Sam 22:3 The God of my rock ...is...my high tower...*s*

Isa 43:11 beside me [God] there is no *s*

Luke 2:11 unto you is born...in the city of David a *S*

1 John 4:14 Father sent the Son to be the *S* of the world

SCEVA (a Jewish priest whose sons tried to cast out evil spirits as Paul did). Acts 19:11–16.

SCRIPTURE [S]

Luke 4:21 This day is this *s* fulfilled in your ears

Luke 24:45 they [the disciples] might understand the *s's*

John 5:39 Search the *s's;* for in them...ye have eternal life

John 20:9 as yet they [the disciples] knew not the *s,* that he [Jesus] must rise again

Acts 17:11 These [the Bereans]... searched the *s's* daily

Rom 4:3 what saith the *s?* Abraham believed God

1 Cor 15:3 Christ died for our sins according to the *s's*

2 Tim 3:16 All *s* is given by inspiration of God

2 Pet 1:20 Knowing this...no prophecy of the *s* is of any private interpretation

SECOND COMING OF JESUS. Matt 25:32–46 • Luke 12:35–48 • John 14:3 • 1 Thes 4:13–18.

SECRET [S]

Deut 29:29 *s* things belong unto the LORD

Ps 44:21 God...knoweth the *s's* of the heart

Ps 91:1 dwelleth in the *s* place of the most High

Ezek 28:3 no *s* that they can hide from thee [God]

Dan 2:28 a God in heaven that revealeth *s's*

Matt 6:6 pray to thy Father which is in *s*

Rom 2:16 God shall judge the *s's* of men by Jesus Christ

SECUNDUS (a believer who accompanied Paul on his third missionary journey). Acts 20:4.

SEEK [ETH, ING]

2 Chr 7:14 If my [God's] people... pray, and *s* my face

Ps 40:16 those that *s* thee [God] rejoice and be glad

Ps 63:1 thou art my God; early will I *s* thee

Ps 105:4 **S** the LORD, and his strength: seek his face

Ps 119:2 Blessed are they... that *s* him [God] with the whole heart

Isa 55:6 **S** ye the LORD while he may be found

Lam 3:25 LORD is good...to the soul that *s'eth* him

Matt 7:7 **s,** and ye shall find

Matt 7:8 he that *s'eth* findeth

Mark 8:12 Why doth this generation *s* after a sign

Luke 12:31 But rather *s* ye the kingdom of God

Luke 17:33 Whosoever shall *s* to save his life shall lose it

Luke 19:10 Son of man is come to *s* and to save that which was lost

John 5:30 because I [Jesus] *s*... the will of the Father

Rom 3:11 there is none that *s'eth* after God

1 Cor 1:22 and the Greeks *s* after wisdom

1 Cor 13:5 [charity] *s'eth* not her own

Col 3:1 *s* those things...above

1 Pet 5:8 devil...walketh... *s'ing* whom he may devour

SEEK THE LORD

1 Chr 16:11 **S-t-L** and his strength...continually

Ps 34:10 they that *s-t-L* shall not want any good thing

Prov 28:5 they that *s-t-L* understand all things

Amos 5:6 **S-t-L,** and ye shall live

Zech 8:22 nations shall come to *s-t-L* of hosts

SEM. See *Shem.*

SENIR. See *Hermon, Mount.*

SENNACHERIB (a king of Assyria who demanded tribute from King Hezekiah of Judah). **2 Kgs 18:13–16; 19:16–36** • 2 Chr 32:1–22 • Isa 36:1; 37:17,21,37.

SEPARATE [D]

Prov 19:4 Wealth maketh... friends; but the poor is *s'd* from his neighbour

Isa 59:2 iniquities have *s'd* between you and your God

Matt 25:32 he [Jesus] shall *s* them one from another

Acts 13:2 **S** me Barnabas and Saul for the work
Rom 8:39 Nor height...shall... **s** us from the love of God
2 Cor 6:17 come out...and be ye **s,** saith the Lord

SEPHARVAIM (a city whose residents colonized the Northern Kingdom after Samaria fell to the Assyrians). 2 Kgs 17:24–31.

SERAIAH (a leader who carried Jeremiah's prophecy of doom for Judah to the city of Babylon). Jer 51:59–61.

SERMON ON THE MOUNT. Matt 5–7.

SERVANT [S]
Gen 9:25 a **s** of **s's** shall he [Canaan] be
Job 1:8 Hast thou [Satan] considered my [God's] **s** Job
Ps 31:16 Make thy [God's] face to shine upon thy **s**
Ps 34:22 The LORD redeemeth the soul of his **s's**
Ps 113:1 Praise, O ye **s's** of the LORD
Ps 116:16 I am thy [God's] **s**... son of thine handmaid
Ps 119:125 I am thy [God's] **s;** give me understanding
Prov 14:35 The king's favour is toward a wise **s**
Isa 42:1 Behold my [God's] **s,** whom I uphold

Isa 52:13 my [God's] **s** shall deal prudently
Dan 9:17 hear the prayer of thy [God's] **s**
Mal 1:6 A son honoureth his father, and a **s** his master
Matt 10:24 disciple is not above his master, nor the **s** above his lord
Matt 23:11 he that is greatest... shall be your **s**
Matt 25:21 Well done, thou good and faithful **s**
Mark 9:35 the same shall be last of all, and **s** of all
Luke 12:37 Blessed are those **s's,** whom the lord...shall find watching
Luke 15:19 make me [the prodigal son] as one of thy hired **s's**
John 8:34 Whosoever committeth sin is the **s** of sin
Rom 6:18 ye became the **s's** of righteousness
1 Cor 9:19 I [Paul] made myself **s** unto all
Gal 4:7 Wherefore thou art no more a **s,** but a son
Phil 2:7 took upon him [Jesus] the form of a **s**

SERVANT SONGS OF ISAIAH. Isa 42:1–4; 49:1–6; 50:4–9; 52:13–53:12.

SERVE [D, ING, ST]
Gen 27:29 Let people **s** thee [God]...nations bow down
Gen 29:20 Jacob **s'd** seven years for Rachel

Deut 6:13 Thou shalt fear the LORD thy God, and *s* him

Ps 72:11 Yea...all nations shall *s* him [God]

Dan 3:17 our [Daniel's three friends'] God whom we *s* is able to deliver us

Dan 6:16 God whom thou [Daniel] *s'st*...deliver thee

Matt 4:10 worship the LORD... him only shalt thou *s*

Luke 16:13 No servant can *s* two masters

John 12:26 any man *s* me [Jesus], let him follow me

Acts 6:2 not reason that we [the apostles] should...*s* tables

Rom 1:25 Who...worshipped and *s'd* the creature more than the Creator

Rom 12:11 fervent in spirit; *s'ing* the Lord

Gal 5:13 by love *s* one another

SERVE THE LORD

Josh 24:15 as for me [Joshua] and my house, we will *s-t-L*

Ps 100:2 *S-t-L* with gladness

Jer 30:9 they [Israel and Judah] shall *s-t-L*...and David their king

SERVICE

John 16:2 the time cometh... whosoever killeth you will think that he doeth God *s*

Rom 12:1 present your bodies a living sacrifice...which is your reasonable *s*

Rev 2:19 I know thy works... and *s,* and faith

SEVEN CHURCHES, LETTERS TO

1. To Ephesus (Rev 2:1–7)
2. To Smyrna (Rev 2:8–11)
3. To Pergamos (Rev 2:12–17)
4. To Thyatira (Rev 2:18–29)
5. To Sardis (Rev 3:1–6)
6. To Philadelphia (Rev 3:7–13)
7. To Laodicea (Rev 3:14–22)

SEVEN LAST WORDS OF JESUS FROM THE CROSS

1. "Father, forgive them; for they know not what they do" (Luke 23:34)
2. "Verily I say unto thee, to day shalt thou be with me in paradise" (Luke 23:43)
3. "Woman, behold they son!...Behold thy mother!" (John 19:26–27)
4. "My God, my God, why hast thou forsaken me" (Matt 27:46 • Mark 15:34)
5. "I thirst" (John 19:28)
6. "It is finished" (John 19:30)
7. "Father, into thy hands I commend my spirit" (Luke 23:46)

SEVEN SIGNS OF JESUS IN JOHN'S GOSPEL

1. Turning of water into wine (John 2:1–11)

2. Healing of a nobleman's son (John 4:46–54)

3. Healing of a paralyzed man (John 5:1–9)

4. Feeding of the five thousand (John 6:5–14)

5. Walking on the water (John 6:15–21)

6. Healing of a man born blind (John 9:1–7)

7. Raising of Lazarus from the dead (John 11:38–44)

SEVENTY WEEKS VISION OF DANIEL. Dan 9:24–27.

SHADRACH (one of Daniel's friends who was miraculously delivered from the fiery furnace). Dan 1:7; 2:49; **3:1–28.**

SHALLUM. See *Jehoahaz,* No. 2.

SHALMANESER (an Assyrian king who defeated the Northern Kingdom and deported its people). **2 Kgs 17:3–6;** 18:9.

SHAME [D]
Ps 4:2 how long will ye turn my [God's] glory into *s*
Ps 14:6 Ye have *s'd* the counsel of the poor
Ps 35:4 Let them be...put to *s* that seek after my soul
Ps 83:16 Fill their faces with *s*... may seek thy [God's] name
Ps 119:31 O LORD, put me not to *s*

Prov 3:35 s shall be the promotion of fools
Prov 13:18 s shall be to him that refuseth instruction
Prov 29:15 a child left to himself bringeth his mother to *s*
1 Cor 14:35 it is a *s* for women to speak in the church
Phil 3:19 glory is in their *s*
Heb 12:2 Jesus...endured the cross, despising the *s*

SHAMEFULLY
Hos 2:5 she that conceived them hath done *s*
Mark 12:4 and...they [husbandmen]...sent him [servant] away *s* handled

SHAMGAR (a judge who delivered Israel from the Philistines). **Judg 3:31;** 5:6.

SHARON (a fertile coastal plain along the Mediterranean Sea). 1 Chr 27:29 • Song 2:1 • Isa 33:9; 35:2; 65:10. *Saron:* Acts 9:35.

SHEAR-JASHUB (a symbolic name, meaning "a remnant shall return," given by Isaiah to his son to show God's promise to His people after their period of exile). Isa 7:3–4.

SHECHEM
1. A tribal leader killed by Simeon and Levi for seducing their sister Dinah. Gen 34:1–29.

2. A city of refuge in the territory of Ephraim. Josh 20:7 •
Judg 9:1–57 • 1 Kgs 12:1,25.
Sichem: Gen 12:6. *Sychem:*
Acts 7:16.

SHEEP
1 Sam 15:14 What meaneth...
this bleating of the *s*
2 Sam 7:8 I [God] took thee
[David] from the sheepcote,
from following the *s*
Ps 44:22 we are counted as *s*
for the slaughter
Ps 74:1 why doth thine [God's]
anger smoke against the *s*
of thy pasture
Ps 95:7 people of his [God's]
pasture, and the *s* of his hand
Ps 119:176 I have gone astray
like a lost *s*
Isa 53:6 All we like *s* have gone
astray
Matt 10:16 send you forth as *s*
in the midst of wolves
Matt 15:24 I [Jesus] am not
sent but unto the lost *s* of
the house of Israel
Mark 6:34 Jesus...saw...
people...as *s* not having a
shepherd
Luke 15:6 I have found my *s*
which was lost
John 10:7 I [Jesus] am the door
of the *s*
John 10:11 good shepherd [Jesus]
giveth his life for the *s*
John 21:16 He [Jesus] saith
unto him [Peter]...Feed
my *s*

1 Pet 2:25 For ye were as *s*
going astray

SHEM (the oldest son of Noah
who was preserved in the ark).
Gen 5:32; 6:10; **7:13; 9:18–27;**
10:1–31; 11:10–11 • 1 Chr
1:4,17,24. *Sem:* Luke 3:36.

SHEMAIAH (a prophet of
Judah who warned King Rehoboam not to attack Israel).
1 Kgs 12:22–24 • 2 Chr 11:2.

SHEMER (a man who sold
King Omri of the Northern
Kingdom a hill on which the
city of Samaria was built).
1 Kgs 16:24.

SHEMUEL. See *Samuel.*

SHENIR. See *Hermon, Mount.*

SHEPHERD [S]
Gen 47:3 Thy servants [the
Hebrews] are *s's*
Ps 23:1 The LORD is my *s;* I
shall not want
Isa 40:11 He [God] shall feed
his flock like a *s*
Ezek 34:2 Son of man, prophesy against the *s's* of Israel
Matt 9:36 were scattered abroad,
as sheep having no *s*
Luke 2:8 in the same country
s's abiding in the field
John 10:11 I [Jesus] am the
good *s*...giveth his life

Heb 13:20 that great *s* [Jesus] of the sheep
1 Pet 5:4 when the chief *S* [Jesus] shall appear

SHESHACH. See *Babylonia.*

SHESH-BAZZAR. See *Zerubbabel.*

SHIELD
Gen 15:1 Fear not, Abram: I [God] am thy *s*
2 Sam 22:3 in him will I trust: he [God] is my *s*
Ps 5:12 wilt thou [God] compass him as with a *s*
Ps 33:20 the LORD...is...our *s*
Ps 84:11 For the LORD God is a sun and *s*
Ps 115:11 the LORD: he is their help and their *s*
Prov 30:5 he [God] is a *s* unto them...put their trust in him
Eph 6:16 Above all, taking the *s* of faith

SHILOAH. See *Siloam.*

SHILOH
1. A town in Ephraim where the Philistines captured the ark of the covenant. Josh 18:1–10 • Judg 21:12–23 • **1 Sam 4:3–11** • Jer 7:12,14.
2. A title of the coming Messiah that identified Him as a descendant of Judah. Gen 49:10.

SHIMEI (a man who insulted David when he was fleeing from Absalom). **2 Sam 16:5–13; 19:16–23** • 1 Kgs 2:8–44.

SHINAR. See *Babylonia.*

SHINE [D, ING, TH]
Num 6:25 The LORD make his face *s* upon thee
Ps 31:16 Make thy [God's] face to *s* upon thy servant
Ps 67:1 God...bless us; and cause his face to *s* upon us
Prov 4:18 But the path of the just is as the *s'ing* light
Eccl 8:1 a man's wisdom maketh his face to *s*
Isa 9:2 upon them [people in darkness] hath the light *s'd*
Isa 60:1 Arise, *s;* for thy light is come
Matt 5:16 Let your light so *s* before men
Matt 17:2 and his [Jesus'] face did *s* as the sun
John 1:5 light *s'th* in darkness
John 5:35 He [Jesus] was a burning and a *s'ing* light
Acts 9:3 there *s'd* round about him [Paul] a light
2 Cor 4:6 For God...hath *s'd* in our hearts
Rev 21:23 And the city had no need of the sun...to *s*

SHUSHAN (the wealthy and powerful capital city of Persia where Esther interceded for her people). Neh 1:1 • Esth

1:2,5; 2:3–8; 3:15; 4:8,16; 8:14–15; 9:6–19 • Dan 8:2.

SICHEM. See *Shechem,* No. 2.

SICKNESS [ES]
Matt 4:23 Jesus went about... healing all manner of *s*
Matt 8:17 spoken by Esaias... Himself [Jesus] took our infirmities, and bare our *s'es*
John 11:4 Jesus...said, This *s* is not unto death

SIDON (a Phoenician city founded by Sidon, oldest son of Canaan). **Gen 10:15,19** • Matt 11:21–22; 15:21 • Mark 3:8; 7:24,31 • Luke 4:26; 6:17; 10:13–14 • Acts 12:20; 27:3. *Zidon:* Josh 11:8.

SIGHT
Ex 3:3 I [Moses] will now turn aside, and see this great *s*
Num 13:33 we were in our own *s* as grasshoppers
Judg 2:11 children of Israel did evil in the *s* of the LORD
1 Chr 29:25 the LORD magnified Solomon exceedingly in the *s* of all Israel
Ps 9:19 let the heathen be judged in thy [God's] *s*
Ps 19:14 Let the words of my mouth...be acceptable in thy [God's] *s,* O LORD
Ps 78:12 Marvellous things did he [God] in the *s* of their fathers, in...Egypt

Ps 90:4 a thousand years in thy [God's] *s* are...as yesterday
Ps 116:15 Precious in the *s* of the LORD...death of his saints
Eccl 6:9 Better is the *s* of the eyes than the wandering of the desire
Matt 11:5 blind receive their *s,* and the lame walk
Luke 1:15 he [John the Baptist] shall be great...*s* of the Lord
Luke 15:21 I [prodigal son] have sinned...in thy *s*
Acts 9:9 And he [Paul] was three days without *s*
Jas 4:10 Humble yourselves in the *s* of the Lord

SIGN [S]
Gen 1:14 let them [lights] be for *s's,* and for seasons
Deut 6:8 bind them [Scriptures] for a *s* upon thine hand
Isa 7:14 the Lord himself shall give you a *s*
Dan 4:3 How great are his [God's] *s's*
Matt 12:39 An evil...generation seeketh after a *s*
Matt 24:3 what shall be the *s* of thy [Jesus'] coming
Luke 2:12 this shall be a *s* unto you...babe wrapped in swaddling clothes
1 Cor 1:22 the Jews require a *s*
Rev 15:1 I [John] saw another *s* in heaven, great... marvellous

SIGNS AND WONDERS
Deut 6:22 LORD showed *s-a-w*... upon Egypt
Mark 13:22 false prophets shall rise...show *s-a-w*
John 4:48 Except ye see *s-a-w*, ye will not believe
Acts 5:12 by the hands of the apostles were many *s-a-w* wrought among the people

SIHON (an Amorite king who refused to allow the Israelites to pass through his territory). Num 21:21–30.

SILAS (a church leader imprisoned with Paul at Philippi). Acts 15:40–41; 16:19,23. *Silvanus:* 2 Cor 1:19 • 2 Thes 1:1.

SILENCE
Ps 39:2 I was dumb with *s,* I held my peace
Eccl 3:7 a time to keep *s,* and a time to speak
Hab 2:20 let all the earth keep *s* before him [God]
1 Cor 14:28 no interpreter, let him keep *s* in the church
1 Cor 14:34 Let your women keep *s* in the churches

SILOAH. See *Siloam.*

SILOAM (a water reservoir supplied through King Hezekiah's underground tunnel from a spring outside Jerusalem). 2 Kgs 20:20 • Luke 13:4 • John 9:7–11. *Shiloah:* Isa 8:6. *Siloah:* Neh 3:15.

SILVANUS. See *Silas.*

SIMEON
1. A son of Jacob and ancestor of one of the twelve tribes of Israel. Gen 29:33; 34:25,30; 35:23; 42:24,36; 43:23; 46:10; 48:5; 49:5 • Ex 1:2; 6:15. The tribe of Simeon settled in southern Canaan. Josh 19:1–9.
2. A righteous man who blessed the child Jesus in the temple at Jerusalem. Luke 2:25–35.

SIMON
1. Simon Peter, one of the twelve apostles or disciples of Jesus and the leader of the church in Jerusalem after the resurrection and ascension of Jesus. Matt 4:18; 10:2; 16:16–17; 17:25 • Mark 1:16–36; 3:16; 14:37 • Luke 5:4–10; 6:14; 22:31; 24:34 • John 1:40–42; 6:8, 68; 13:6,9,24,36; 18:10,15,25; 20:2,6; 21:2–17 • Acts 10:5,18, 32 • 2 Pet 1:1.
    (1) A fisherman and brother of Andrew (Matt 4:18)
    (2) Called by Jesus (Matt 4:18–22)
    (3) Included among Jesus' twelve apostles (Matt 10:2–4)

(4) Walked on the water to meet Jesus (Matt 14:28–33)

(5) Confessed Jesus as the Son of God (Matt 16:13–19)

(6) Condemned by Jesus for refusing to believe that Jesus would die (Matt 16:21–23)

(7) Witnessed the transfiguration of Jesus (Matt 17:1–8 • 2 Pet 1:16–18)

(8) With Jesus in the Garden of Gethsemane (Mark 14:32–42)

(9) Denied Jesus three times (Matt 26:69–75)

(10) Cut off the ear of a slave when Jesus was arrested (John 18:10–11)

(11) Ran to inspect the empty tomb after Jesus was resurrected (John 20:1–8)

(12) Reinstated by Jesus and challenged to continue His work (John 21:15–22)

(13) Preached sermon on the day of Pentecost when three thousand people believed on Jesus (Acts 2:38–41)

(14) Became the key leader in the early church at Jerusalem (Acts 3:12–26)

(15) Preached the gospel to Gentiles (Acts 10:24–48)

2. Simon Zelotes or Simon the Canaanite, another of the twelve apostles or disciples of Jesus. Matt 10:4 • Mark 3:18 • Luke 6:15 • Acts 1:13.

SIMPLE

Ps 19:7 testimony of the LORD is sure, making wise the *s*

Prov 8:5 O ye *s,* understand wisdom

Prov 22:3 but the *s* pass on, and are punished

SIN [NED, NETH, S]

Gen 4:7 if thou [Cain] doest not well, *s* lieth at the door

Lev 16:34 make an atonement... for all their *s's* once a year

1 Sam 15:24 Saul said...I have *s'ned*

2 Chr 7:14 then will I [God] hear...forgive their *s*

Job 1:22 In all this Job *s'ned* not, nor charged God

Job 13:23 How many are mine iniquities and *s's*

Ps 32:1 Blessed is he...whose *s* is covered

Ps 41:4 for I have *s'ned* against thee [God]

Ps 51:2 cleanse me from my *s*

Ps 51:3 my *s* is ever before me

Ps 51:4 Against thee [God], thee only, have I *s'ned*

Ps 51:9 Hide thy [God's] face from my *s's*

Ps 103:10 He [God] hath not dealt with us after our *s's*

Ps 119:11 Thy [God's] word have I hid in mine heart, that I might not *s*

Prov 14:34 but *s* is a reproach to any people

Eccl 7:20 not a just man upon earth, that...*s'neth* not

Isa 1:18 though your *s's* be as scarlet...white as snow

Isa 6:7 touched thy [Isaiah's] lips...iniquity is taken away...*s* purged

Isa 40:2 she [Jerusalem] ...received...double for... her *s's*

Jer 14:20 we have *s'ned* against thee [God]

Jer 31:34 I [God] will remember their *s* no more

Ezek 18:20 The soul that *s'neth,* it shall die

Mic 7:19 thou [God] wilt cast all their *s's* into the...sea

Matt 1:21 he [Jesus] shall save his people from their *s's*

Matt 18:21 Lord, how oft shall my brother *s* against me, and I forgive him

Matt 26:28 my [Jesus'] blood... is shed for many for the remission of *s's*

Luke 15:21 I [the prodigal son] have *s'ned* against heaven, and in thy [his father's] sight

Luke 24:47 remission of *s's*... preached in his [Jesus'] name

John 1:29 Behold the Lamb of God, which taketh away the *s* of the world

John 8:7 He that is without *s*... let him first cast a stone

John 9:2 who did *s,* this man, or his parents

John 16:8 he [Jesus] will reprove the world of *s*

Rom 3:9 Jews and Gentiles... they are all under *s*

Rom 3:23 all...*s'ned,* and come short of the glory of God

Rom 4:7 Blessed are they... whose *s's* are covered

Rom 5:12 by one man [Adam] *s* entered into the world

Rom 6:1 continue in *s,* that grace may abound

Rom 6:12 Let not *s*...reign in your mortal body

Rom 6:23 wages of *s* is death

Rom 7:17 no more I [Paul] that do it, but *s*...in me

1 Cor 6:18 he...committeth fornication *s'neth* against his own body

1 Cor 15:17 Christ be not raised...yet in your *s's*

2 Cor 5:21 he [God] hath made him [Jesus] to be *s* for us

Heb 9:28 Christ was...offered to bear the *s's* of many

Heb 10:4 not possible that the blood of bulls...should take away *s's*

Heb 12:1 lay aside...the *s* which doth so easily beset us

Jas 4:17 knoweth to do good, and doeth it not, to him it is *s*

1 John 1:7 blood of Jesus... cleanseth us from all *s*

1 John 1:8 say that we have no **s,** we deceive ourselves

1 John 1:9 he [Jesus] is faithful...to forgive us our **s's**

1 John 1:10 If we say that we have not **s'ned,** we make him [Jesus] a liar

1 John 2:1 these things write I unto you, that ye **s** not

1 John 2:2 he [Jesus] is the propitiation for our **s's**

1 John 4:10 he [God]...sent his Son [Jesus] to be the propitiation for our **s's**

SIN, WILDERNESS OF (a desert region where manna and quail were miraculously provided for the Israelites). Ex 16:1–8.

SINAI (a mountain peak where Moses received the Ten Commandments and other parts of the Law from God). Ex **19–23;** 24:16; 31:18; 34:2–32 • Lev 7:38; 25:1; 26:46 • Num 1:1,19; 3:1–14; 9:1,5; 10:12; 26:64; 28:6; 33:15–16 • Deut 33:2 • Judg 5:5 • Neh 9:13 • Ps 68:8,17 • Gal 4:24–25. *Sina:* Acts 7:30.

SINCERITY

Josh 24:14 serve him [God] in **s** and in truth

1 Cor 5:8 keep the feast...with the...bread of **s**

2 Cor 8:8 I [Paul] speak...to prove the **s** of your love

SING [ING]

Ex 15:21 **S** ye to the LORD, for he hath triumphed

Ps 59:17 Unto thee...will I **s:** for God is my defence

Ps 67:4 let the nations be glad and **s** for joy

Ps 81:1 **S** aloud unto God our strength: make a joyful noise

Ps 92:1 It is a good thing...to **s** praises unto thy [God's] name

Ps 100:2 come before his [God's] presence with **s'ing**

Ps 137:4 How shall we **s** the LORD's song in a strange land

Song 2:12 the time of the **s'ing** of birds is come

Isa 49:13 break forth into **s'ing,** O mountains

Isa 52:9 **s** together, ye waste places of Jerusalem

Col 3:16 **s'ing** with grace in your hearts to the Lord

Jas 5:13 Is any merry? let him **s** psalms

SING UNTO THE LORD

1 Chr 16:23 **S-u-t-L,** all the earth

Ps 13:6 I will **s-u-t-L**...he... dealt bountifully with me

Ps 95:1 let us **s-u-t-L**...the rock of our salvation

Ps 96:1 **s-u-t-L,** all the earth

Ps 98:1 O **s-u-t-L** a new song

Ps 104:33 I will **s-u-t-L** as long as I live

Isa 12:5 **S-u-t-L;** for he hath done excellent things

SINNED AGAINST THE LORD

Ex 10:16 I [Pharaoh] have **s-a-t-L** your God

Josh 7:20 I [Achan] have **s-a-t-L** God of Israel

2 Sam 12:13 I [David] have **s-a-t-L**

SINNER [S]

Ps 1:1 Blessed is the man that walketh not...nor standeth in the way of **s's**

Eccl 9:18 but one **s** destroyeth much good

Mark 2:17 I [Jesus] came...to call...**s's** to repentance

Luke 5:30 Why do ye [Jesus] eat...with...**s's**

Luke 15:10 joy...over one **s** that repenteth

Luke 18:13 God be merciful to me [publican] a **s**

Rom 5:8 while we were yet **s's,** Christ died for us

1 Tim 1:15 Christ...came into the world to save **s's**

Jas 4:8 Cleanse your hands, ye **s's**...purify your hearts

SION. See *Zion.*

SIRION. See *Hermon, Mount.*

SISERA (a Canaanite commander killed by Jael). Judg 4:2–22.

SLEEP [EST, ETH, ING]

Ps 13:3 lighten mine eyes, lest I **s** the **s** of death

Ps 44:23 Awake, why **s'est** thou, O Lord

Prov 6:9 How long wilt thou **s,** O sluggard

Prov 20:13 Love not **s,** lest thou come to poverty

Mark 5:39 the damsel is not dead, but **s'eth**

Mark 13:36 coming suddenly he [Jesus] find you **s'ing**

Mark 14:41 **S** on now, and take your [the disciples'] rest

John 11:11 he [Jesus] saith... Our friend Lazarus **s'eth**

1 Cor 15:51 shall not all **s,** but we shall all be changed

SLEPT

Ps 3:5 I laid me down and **s**

Matt 28:13 Say ye, His [Jesus'] disciples...stole him away while we **s**

1 Cor 15:20 now is Christ...the firstfruits of them that **s**

SMYRNA (a city north of Ephesus where one of the seven churches addressed by John in the Book of Revelation was located). Rev 2:8–11.

SOBER [LY, NESS]

Acts 26:25 I [Paul]...speak... words of truth and **s'ness**

1 Thes 5:6 let us not sleep... but...watch and be **s**

1 Tim 3:2 A bishop...must be blameless...vigilant, *s*

Titus 2:12 we should live *s'ly,* righteously, and godly

1 Pet 5:8 Be *s,* be vigilant...the devil...walketh about

SODOM (a city destroyed by God because of its wickedness and often mentioned as a symbol of evil and as a warning to sinners). **Gen 19:1–28** • Isa 1:9 • Jer 49:18 • Ezek 16:46–49 • Amos 4:11 • Zeph 2:9 • Matt 11:23–24 • 2 Pet 2:6 • Jude 7 • Rev 11:8. *Sodoma:* Rom 9:29.

SODOMA. See *Sodom.*

SOLOMON (David's son and successor as king of Israel, known for his wisdom, wealth, and lavish lifestyle, and probable author of the books of Ecclesiastes and Song of Solomon). See **1 Kgs 1–11** • **2 Chr 1–9** for a sketch of Solomon's life.

1. Prayed for wisdom and insight (1 Kgs 3:1–28)

2. Governed efficiently and became wealthy (1 Kgs 4:1–30)

3. Encouraged trade and commerce (1 Kgs 10:14–29)

4. Built the temple in Jerusalem (1 Kgs 5–8)

5. Married pagan wives (1 Kgs 11:1–8)

6. Burdened his subjects with excessive taxes (1 Kgs 12:4)

7. Northern tribes rebelled against his policies (1 Kgs 11:14–40)

8. Death of Solomon (1 Kgs 11:41–43).

SON OF GOD

Matt 27:40 If thou [Jesus] be the *S-o-G,* come down from the cross

Matt 27:54 Truly this [Jesus] was the *S-o-G*

Luke 1:35 that holy thing... shall be called the *S-o-G*

Luke 4:3 If thou be the *S-o-G,* command this stone...be made bread

John 1:34 I [John the Baptist]... bare record that this [Jesus] is the *S-o-G*

John 20:31 believe that Jesus is the Christ, the *S-o-G*

1 John 4:15 Whosoever shall confess that Jesus is the *S-o-G,* God dwelleth in him

1 John 5:12 he that hath not the *S-o-G* hath not life

SON OF MAN

Ps 8:4 What is...the *s-o-m,* that thou [God] visitest him

Ezek 2:1 *S-o-m* [Ezekiel], stand upon thy feet

Matt 12:8 the *S-o-m* [Jesus] is Lord even of the sabbath day

Matt 16:13 Whom do men say that I [Jesus] the *S-o-m* am

Matt 24:44 an hour as ye think not...*S-o-m* [Jesus] cometh

Mark 10:45 **S-o-m** [Jesus] came not to be ministered unto, but to minister

Luke 9:58 **S-o-m** [Jesus] hath not where to lay his head

Luke 22:48 But Jesus said... Judas, betrayest thou the **S-o-m** with a kiss

John 3:14 even so must the **S-o-m** [Jesus] be lifted up

John 12:23 The hour is come, that the **S-o-m** [Jesus] should be glorified

SONG OF DEBORAH. Judg 5:1–31.

SONG OF MARY. Luke 1:46–55.

SONG OF MIRIAM. Ex 15:20–21.

SONG OF MOSES. Deut 32:1–44.

SONG OF SOLOMON, BOOK OF. A short Old Testament book, probably written by Solomon, that is filled with expressions of affection between two lovers (1:13; 4:1–11; 7:2–10). Some interpreters insist the song symbolizes God's love for His people Israel, while others believe the book is a healthy affirmation of the joys of physical love between husband and wife.

SONG OF ZACHARIAS. Luke 1:67–79.

SOPATER (a believer who accompanied Paul on the third missionary journey). Acts 20:4.

SORROW [FUL, S]

Ps 18:5 The **s's** of hell compassed me about

Ps 38:17 my **s** is continually before me

Eccl 1:18 he that increaseth knowledge increaseth **s**

Isa 53:3 man of **s's**...acquainted with grief

Jer 45:3 for the LORD hath added grief to my **s**

Matt 19:22 he [rich young ruler] went away **s'ful**

Matt 24:8 All these are the beginning of **s's**

Matt 26:38 My [Jesus'] soul is exceeding **s'ful**

John 16:20 your **s** shall be turned into joy

2 Cor 7:10 godly **s** worketh repentance to salvation

Rev 21:4 no more death, neither **s**, nor crying

SOSIPATER (a kinsman of Paul whose greetings were sent to the church at Rome). Rom 16:21.

SOSTHENES (a ruler of the synagogue at Corinth who was beaten by a mob). Acts 18:17.

SOUL [S]

Gen 2:7 man became a living *s*

Deut 6:5 thou shalt love the LORD thy God...with all thy *s*

1 Sam 18:1 *s* of Jonathan was knit with the *s* of David

Job 19:2 How long will ye vex my [Job's] *s*

Ps 19:7 law of the LORD is perfect, converting the *s*

Ps 23:3 He [God] restoreth my *s*

Ps 25:1 Unto thee, O LORD, do I lift up my *s*

Ps 33:20 Our *s* waiteth for the LORD; he is our help

Ps 35:9 And my *s* shall be joyful in the LORD

Ps 42:2 My *s* thirsteth for God

Ps 42:5 Why art thou cast down, O my *s*

Ps 56:13 thou [God] hast delivered my *s* from death

Ps 72:13 He [God]...shall save the *s's* of the needy

Ps 84:2 My *s*...fainteth for the courts of the LORD

Ps 103:1 Bless the LORD, O my *s*...bless his holy name

Ps 142:4 refuge failed me; no man cared for my *s*

Prov 11:30 and he that winneth *s's* is wise

Prov 18:7 A fool's...lips are the snare of his *s*

Lam 3:24 The LORD is my portion, saith my *s*

Ezek 18:20 The *s* that sinneth, it shall die

Mic 6:7 shall I give...fruit of my body for the sin of my *s*

Matt 10:28 but rather fear him which is able to destroy...*s* and body

Matt 11:29 ye shall find rest unto your *s's*

Matt 16:26 what shall a man give in exchange for his *s*

Mark 14:34 My [Jesus'] *s* is... sorrowful unto death

John 12:27 Now is my [Jesus'] *s* troubled

Rom 13:1 every *s* be subject unto the higher powers

1 Pet 2:11 abstain from fleshly lusts, which war against the *s*

1 Pet 2:25 returned unto the... Bishop of your *s's*

SOUND [ING]

John 3:8 The wind bloweth... thou hearest the *s*

Acts 2:2 *s* from heaven as of a... mighty wind

1 Cor 13:1 I [Paul] am become as *s'ing* brass

1 Cor 14:8 if the trumpet give an uncertain *s*

1 Cor 15:52 trumpet shall *s,* and the dead...raised

2 Tim 4:3 when they will not endure *s* doctrine

SOUTHERN KINGDOM (JUDAH) FALLS TO BABYLONIA. 2 Kgs 25.

SOW [ED, ETH]

Ps 126:5 They that *s* in tears shall reap in joy

Prov 22:8 He that *s'eth* iniquity shall reap vanity

Matt 13:24 kingdom...is likened unto a man which *s'ed* good seed

Luke 8:5 as he [a sower] *s'ed*, some fell by the way side

Luke 12:24 Consider the ravens...they neither *s* nor reap

John 4:37 One *s'eth*, and another reapeth

2 Cor 9:6 *s'eth* bountifully shall reap also bountifully

Gal 6:7 whatsoever a man *s'eth*, that shall he also reap

SOWN

Hos 8:7 they have *s* the wind, and...reap the whirlwind

Hag 1:6 Ye have *s* much, and bring in little

Mark 4:18 these are they which are *s* among thorns

1 Cor 15:42 It [the body] is *s* in corruption; it is raised in incorruption

SPAIN (a country in Europe that Paul expressed a desire to visit). Rom 15:24,28.

SPEECH

Gen 11:1 And the whole earth was...of one *s*

Ex 4:10 I [Moses] am slow of *s*

Prov 17:7 Excellent *s* becometh not a fool

Isa 28:23 Give ye ear...hearken, and hear my [God's] *s*

Mark 14:70 thou [Peter] art a Galilaean, and thy *s* agreeth

1 Cor 2:1 I [Paul]...came not with excellency of *s*

Col 4:6 Let your *s* be...seasoned with salt

SPIES SENT INTO CANAAN. Num 13:1–33.

SPIRIT [S]

1 Sam 28:7 Seek me [Saul] a woman that hath a familiar *s*

2 Kgs 2:9 let a double portion of thy [Elijah's] *s* be upon me [Elisha]

Job 32:8 there is a *s* in man

Ps 31:5 Into thine hand I commit my *s*

Ps 51:10 O God...renew a right *s* within me

Prov 16:18 Pride goeth before destruction...haughty *s* before a fall

Prov 25:28 He that hath no rule over his own *s*

Isa 32:15 Until the *s* be poured upon us from on high

Isa 42:1 I [God] have put my *s* upon him [God's servant]

Ezek 3:24 Then the *s* entered into me [Ezekiel]

Ezek 11:19 I [God] will put a new *s* within you

Dan 6:3 because an excellent *s* was in him [Daniel]

Joel 2:28 I [God] will pour out my *s* upon all flesh

Zech 4:6 Not by might...but by my [God's] *s*

Matt 5:3 Blessed are the poor in *s*

Matt 26:41 the *s*...is willing, but the flesh is weak

Mark 6:7 he [Jesus]...gave them [the disciples] power over unclean *s's*

Luke 23:46 Father, into thy hands I [Jesus] commend my *s*...gave up the ghost

John 3:5 Except a man be born of water and of the *S*

John 4:23 worship the Father in *s* and in truth

John 16:13 the *S* of truth [Holy Spirit], is come

Acts 17:16 his [Paul's] *s* was stirred in him

Rom 8:16 The *S* itself beareth witness with our *s*

1 Cor 12:4 diversities of gifts, but the same *S*

1 Cor 12:10 to another discerning of *s's*

2 Cor 3:6 letter killeth, but the *s* giveth life

Gal 5:16 Walk in the *S*

Gal 5:22 fruit of the *S* is love, joy, peace, longsuffering

Eph 4:3 unity of the *S* in the bond of peace

Eph 6:17 sword of the *S*...the word of God

2 Tim 1:7 God hath not given us the *s* of fear

1 John 4:1 try the *s's* whether they are of God

Rev 2:7 hear what the *S* saith unto the churches

SPIRIT, FILLING OF, AT PENTECOST. Acts 2:1–21.

SPIRIT OF GOD

Gen 1:2 *S-o-G* moved upon the face of the waters

1 Sam 11:6 And the *s-o-G* came upon Saul

Job 33:4 The *s-o-G* hath made me [Job]

Matt 3:16 Jesus...saw the *S-o-G* descending like a dove

Rom 8:14 led by the *S-o-G,* they are the sons of God

1 Cor 3:16 Know ye not...that the *S-o-G* dwelleth in you

Eph 4:30 And grieve not the holy *S-o-G*

SPIRIT OF THE LORD

Judg 6:34 the *s-o-t-L* came upon Gideon

1 Sam 16:13 the *s-o-t-L* came upon David

Isa 11:2 the *s-o-t-L* shall rest upon him [God's servant]

Isa 61:1 The *s-o-t-L* GOD is upon me [God's servant]

Luke 4:18 The *S-o-t-L* is upon me [Jesus]

Acts 8:39 the *S-o-t-L* caught away Philip

2 Cor 3:17 where the *S-o-t-L* is, there is liberty

SPIRITUAL [LY]
Rom 8:6 to be *s'ly* minded is life and peace
1 Cor 14:1 Follow after charity, and desire *s* gifts
1 Cor 15:44 It is sown a natural body...raised a *s* body
Eph 6:12 we wrestle...against *s* wickedness in high places
1 Pet 2:5 Ye also, as lively stones, are built up a *s* house

STAND [EST, ETH, ING]
Ex 3:5 the place...thou [Moses] *s'est* is holy ground
Ex 14:13 *s* still, and see the salvation of the LORD
Job 19:25 my [Job's] redeemer... shall *s* at the latter day
Ps 1:1 walketh not...nor *s'eth* in the way of sinners
Ps 24:3 who shall *s* in his [God's] holy place
Prov 12:7 the house of the righteous shall *s*
Isa 40:8 but the word of our God shall *s* for ever
Mal 3:2 who shall *s* when he [God] appeareth
Matt 12:25 house divided against itself shall not *s*
Acts 7:55 he [Stephen]...saw... Jesus *s'ing* on the right hand
Rom 14:10 all *s* before the judgment seat of Christ
1 Cor 10:12 thinketh he *s'eth* take heed lest he fall

1 Cor 16:13 Watch ye, *s* fast in the faith...be strong
Gal 5:1 *S* fast...in the liberty... Christ hath made us free
Eph 6:11 able to *s* against the wiles of the devil
2 Thes 2:15 Therefore, brethren, *s* fast
Rev 3:20 I [Jesus] *s* at the door, and knock

STATUTE [S]
Ex 27:21 a *s* for ever unto their generations
Lev 10:11 teach...Israel all the *s's*...the LORD hath spoken
Lev 16:34 this shall be an everlasting *s* unto you
Deut 5:31 I [God] will speak unto thee [Moses] all the commandments...*s's*... judgments
1 Kgs 3:3 Solomon loved the LORD, walking in the *s's* of David his father
Ps 19:8 The *s's* of the LORD are right, rejoicing the heart
Ps 119:12 Blessed art thou, O LORD: teach me thy *s's*
Ezek 20:19 walk in my [God's] *s's,* and keep my judgments

STEDFAST [LY, NESS]
Luke 9:51 he [Jesus] *s'ly* set his face to go to Jerusalem
1 Cor 15:58 Therefore...be ye *s,* unmoveable
Col 2:5 and the *s'ness* of your faith in Christ

Heb 3:14 hold the beginning of our confidence *s* unto the end

STEPHEN (a believer who became the first Christian martyr when he was stoned because of his testimony). Acts 6:5–9; **7:55–60;** 8:2; 11:19; 22:20.

STEWARD [S]
Matt 20:8 lord of the vineyard saith unto his *s,* Call the labourers...give them their hire
Luke 16:8 the lord commended the unjust *s*
1 Cor 4:2 required in *s's,* that a man be found faithful
Titus 1:7 a bishop must be blameless, as the *s* of God
1 Pet 4:10 good *s's* of the manifold grace of God

STEWARDSHIP
Luke 16:2 give an account of thy *s*...be no longer steward
Luke 16:3 my lord taketh away from me the *s*

STONE [D, S, ST]
Gen 31:45 Jacob took a *s,* and set it up for a pillar
Ex 17:4 this people...be almost ready to *s* me [Moses]
Ex 31:18 two...tables of *s,* written with...finger of God
Lev 26:1 neither shall ye set up any image of *s*
Josh 4:6 What mean ye by these *s's*

1 Sam 17:50 David prevailed... with a sling and...a *s*
Ps 118:22 *s* which the builders refused is become the head *s*
Eccl 3:5 and a time to gather *s's* together
Isa 28:16 I [God] lay in Zion for a foundation...a tried *s*
Matt 4:3 command that these *s's* be made bread
Matt 21:42 The *s* which the builders rejected
Matt 24:2 There shall not be left here one *s* upon another
Matt 27:66 they [soldiers]... made...sepulchre sure, sealing the *s*
Mark 16:4 they [the women] saw...the *s* was rolled away
Luke 13:34 O Jerusalem... which killest the prophets, and *s'st* them
John 1:42 called Cephas...by interpretation, A *s*
Acts 4:11 the *s* which was set at nought of you builders
Acts 7:59 they *s'd* Stephen
1 Pet 2:8 a *s* of stumbling, and a rock of offence
Rev 21:19 foundations...garnished with...precious *s's*

STRAIGHT
Isa 40:3 make *s* in the desert a highway for our God
Luke 3:4 Prepare ye the way of the Lord, make his paths *s*

Acts 9:11 go into the street which is called *S*

STRANGER [S]

Deut 10:19 Love ye...the *s*

Ps 54:3 For *s's* are risen up against me

Ps 69:8 I am become a *s* unto my brethren

Matt 25:35 I was a *s,* and ye took me in

Eph 2:19 therefore ye are no more *s's* and foreigners

Heb 13:2 Be not forgetful to entertain *s's*

STRENGTH

Ex 13:14 By *s* of hand the LORD brought us [Israel] out from Egypt

Ex 15:2 LORD is my *s* and song

Job 12:13 With him [God] is wisdom and *s*

Ps 18:2 my God, my *s,* in whom I will trust

Ps 19:14 words of my mouth... be acceptable...my *s,* and my redeemer

Ps 27:1 the LORD is the *s* of my life

Ps 43:2 For thou art the God of my *s*

Ps 46:1 God is our refuge and *s,* a...help in trouble

Ps 71:9 forsake me not when my *s* faileth

Ps 84:5 Blessed is the man whose *s* is in thee [God]

Ps 90:10 if by reason of *s* they [days of our years] be fourscore years

Ps 118:14 The LORD is my *s* and song...my salvation

Isa 12:2 LORD JEHOVAH is my *s* and my song

Isa 30:15 in quietness and in confidence shall be your *s*

Isa 40:31 they that wait upon the LORD shall renew their *s*

Hab 3:19 LORD God is my *s*

Mark 12:30 love the Lord thy God...with all thy *s*

2 Cor 12:9 my [Paul's] *s* is made perfect in weakness

STRENGTHEN [ED, ETH, ING]

Ps 27:14 he [God] shall *s* thine heart: wait...on the LORD

Luke 22:43 there appeared an angel...*s'ing* him [Jesus]

Phil 4:13 do all things through Christ which *s'eth* me [Paul]

2 Tim 4:17 the Lord stood with me [Paul], and *s'ed* me

STRIPES

Isa 53:5 with his [God's servant's] *s* we are healed

2 Cor 11:24 five times received I [Paul] forty *s*

1 Pet 2:24 by whose [Jesus'] *s* ye were healed

STRIVE [D, ING, TH]

Luke 13:24 *S* to enter in at the strait gate

Rom 15:20 so have I [Paul] *s'd* to preach the gospel

1 Cor 9:25 every man that *s'th* for the mastery is temperate in all things

Phil 1:27 one mind *s'ing* together for...the gospel

2 Tim 2:24 the servant of the Lord must not *s*

STRONG [ER]

Deut 31:6 Be *s* and of a good courage, fear not

Ps 24:8 The LORD *s* and mighty ...mighty in battle

Ps 71:7 but thou [God] art my *s* refuge

Ps 89:8 who is a *s* LORD like unto thee

Prov 18:10 The name of the LORD is a *s* tower

Eccl 9:11 the race is not to the swift, nor the battle to the *s*

Luke 2:40 child [Jesus] grew, and waxed *s* in spirit

Rom 15:1 *s* ought to bear the infirmities of the weak

1 Cor 1:25 the weakness of God is *s'er* than men

2 Cor 12:10 when I [Paul] am weak, then am I *s*

Eph 6:10 Finally, my brethren, be *s* in the Lord

STUMBLINGBLOCK [S]

Jer 6:21 I [God] will lay *s's* before this people

Rom 14:13 no man put a *s*...in his brother's way

1 Cor 1:23 Christ crucified, unto the Jews a *s*

1 Cor 8:9 liberty...become a *s* to them that are weak

SUBMISSION TO OTHERS IN THE LORD. 1 Pet 3:1–12.

SUBMIT [TING]

Eph 5:21 *S'ting* yourselves one to another...fear of God

Eph 5:22 Wives, *s* yourselves unto your own husbands

Jas 4:7 *S* yourselves therefore to God. Resist the devil

1 Pet 5:5 ye younger, *s* yourselves unto the elder

SUCCOTH-BENOTH (an idol set up in Samaria by the people who colonized the area after the Northern Kingdom fell to the Assyrians). 2 Kgs 17:29–30.

SUFFER [ED, ETH, INGS]

Ps 55:22 he [God] shall never *s* the righteous to be moved

Matt 16:21 Jesus...must go... and *s* many things

Matt 19:14 *S* little children, and forbid them not

Luke 24:26 Ought not Christ to have *s'ed* these things

Luke 24:46 thus it behoved Christ to *s*

Acts 9:16 he [Paul] must *s* for my [Jesus'] name's sake

Rom 8:18 **s'ings**...not worthy to be compared with the glory...revealed
1 Cor 10:13 God...will not **s** you to be tempted above that ye are able
1 Cor 13:4 Charity **s'eth** long, and is kind...envieth not
Phil 3:10 the fellowship of his [Jesus'] **s'ings**
2 Tim 2:12 If we **s**, we shall also reign with him [Jesus]
Heb 5:8 learned he [Jesus] obedience by the things which he **s'ed**
1 Pet 4:13 ye are partakers of Christ's **s'ings**

SUKKIIMS (an African or Ethiopian tribe allied with Pharaoh Shishak of Egypt when he invaded Judah). 2 Chr 12:3.

SUN STANDS STILL AT AJALON. Josh 10:12–14.

SUSANNA (a woman who provided food and lodging for Jesus). Luke 8:2–3.

SWEAR
Lev 19:12 ye shall not **s** by my [God's] name falsely
Matt 5:34 I [Jesus] say unto you, **S** not at all
Mark 14:71 he [Peter] began to curse and to **s**

SYCHAR (a city of Samaria where Jesus talked to the woman at Jacob's well). John 4:5–42.

SYCHEM. See *Shechem*, No. 2.

SYNAGOGUE [S]
Matt 4:23 Jesus went about all Galilee, teaching in their **s's**
Mark 5:22 one of the rulers of the **s,** Jairus by name
Mark 13:9 in the **s's** ye shall be beaten
Luke 4:16 he [Jesus] went into the **s**...stood up for to read

SYRACUSE (a city in Sicily visited by Paul). Acts 28:12.

SYRIA (a nation northeast of Israel which was a persistent enemy of the Jews across several centuries). Judg 10:6 • 2 Sam 8:11–13 • 1 Kgs 20:1–34 • 2 Kgs 13:3–24 • Isa 17:1–3 • Luke 2:2 • Acts 15:23,41. *Aram:* Num 23:7.

SYRIA-DAMASCUS. See *Damascus.*

-T-

TABERNACLE BUILT IN THE WILDERNESS. Ex 36:8–38:21.

TABITHA (a widow, also known as *Dorcas,* whom Peter restored to life). Acts 9:36–40.

TABOR, MOUNT (a mountain from which the judge Deborah sent Barak to defeat the Canaanites). Josh 19:22 • **Judg 4:6–14;** 8:18 • Ps 89:12 • Jer 46:18 • Hos 5:1.

TAMAR (Absalom's sister who was sexually assaulted by her half brother Amnon). **2 Sam 13:1–32** • 1 Chr 3:9.

TARPELITES (a tribe which colonized Samaria after the Northern Kingdom fell to Assyria). Ezra 4:9.

TARSUS (capital city of the Roman province of Silicia and the place where Paul was born). Acts 9:11,30; 11:25; 21:39; 22:3.

TARTAK (a pagan god worshiped by the Avites, a people who colonized Samaria after the Northern Kingdom fell to the Assyrians). 2 Kgs 17:31.

TATNAI (a Persian official who tried to stop the Jews from rebuilding the temple in Jerusalem). Ezra 5:3–17.

TAUGHT
Ps 119:102 thy [God's] judgments: for thou hast *t* me
Isa 54:13 all thy children shall be *t* of the LORD
Mark 1:22 he [Jesus] *t* them as one that had authority
Mark 4:2 he [Jesus] *t* them many things by parables
John 8:28 but as my Father hath *t* me [Jesus], I speak these things
2 Thes 2:15 hold the traditions which ye have been *t*

TEACH [EST, ETH, ING]
Deut 6:7 thou shalt *t* them [God's commands] diligently unto thy children
Job 21:22 Shall any *t* God knowledge
Job 36:22 God exalteth by his power: who *t'eth* like him
Ps 25:4 Show me thy ways, O LORD; *t* me thy paths
Ps 51:13 Then will I *t* transgressors thy [God's] ways
Ps 86:11 **T** me thy way, O LORD...walk in thy truth
Ps 90:12 So *t* us to number our days
Prov 16:23 heart of the wise *t'eth* his mouth
Jer 31:34 they shall *t* no more every man his neighbour

Matt 21:23 elders...came unto him [Jesus] as he was *t'ing*

Matt 28:19 Go ye therefore, and *t* all nations

Matt 28:20 **T'ing** them to observe all things

Mark 8:31 he [Jesus] began to *t*...Son of man must suffer

Luke 11:1 Lord, *t* us [the disciples] to pray

Luke 12:12 Holy Ghost shall *t* you...what ye ought to say

John 14:26 the Comforter...he shall *t* you all things

Rom 2:21 Thou therefore which *t'est* another, *t'est* thou not thyself

Col 3:16 *t'ing*...one another in psalms and hymns

1 Tim 3:2 A bishop...given to hospitality, apt to *t*

TEACHER [S]

Ps 119:99 I have more understanding than all my *t's*

John 3:2 know...thou [Jesus] art a *t* come from God

1 Cor 12:29 are all prophets? are all *t's*

Eph 4:11 he [God] gave some, apostles...some...pastors ...*t's*

TEARS

Ps 6:6 water...couch with my *t*

Ps 126:5 They that sow in *t* shall reap in joy

Jer 9:1 Oh that my [Jeremiah's] head were waters, and...eyes a fountain of *t*

Rev 21:4 God shall wipe away all *t* from their eyes

TEKOA (a fortress city near Bethlehem and hometown of the prophet Amos). 2 Chr 11:6; 20:20 • Jer 6:1 • Amos 1:1. *Tekoah:* 2 Sam 14:2,4,9.

TEKOAH. See *Tekoa.*

TEL-ABIB (a Babylonian city where the prophet Ezekiel lived with the other Jewish captives). Ezek 3:15.

TEMPERANCE

Gal 5:23 Meekness, *t:* against such there is no law

2 Pet 1:6 And to knowledge *t;* and to *t* patience

TEMPERATE

1 Cor 9:25 And every man that striveth for the mastery is *t* in all things

Titus 1:8 a lover of good men, sober, just, holy, *t*

Titus 2:2 That the aged men be sober, grave, *t*

TEMPT [ED, ING]

Deut 6:16 Ye shall not *t* the LORD your God

Ps 78:41 Yea, they turned back and *t'ed* God

Matt 4:1 was Jesus led...into the wilderness to be *t'ed*

Matt 4:7 Thou shalt not *t* the Lord thy God

664

Mark 8:11 seeking of him [Jesus] a sign...*t'ing* him

John 8:6 t'ing him [Jesus]...to accuse him

1 Cor 7:5 Satan *t* you not for your incontinency

1 Cor 10:13 God...will not suffer you to be *t'ed* above that ye are able

Heb 4:15 high priest [Jesus]...was...*t'ed* like as we are

Jas 1:13 Let no man say...I am *t'ed* of God

TEMPTATION [S]

Matt 6:13 lead us not into *t*

Luke 4:13 when the devil had ended all the *t,* he departed from him [Jesus] for a season

1 Cor 10:13 no *t* taken you but such as is common to man

Jas 1:2 count it all joy when ye fall into divers *t's*

Jas 1:12 Blessed is the man that endureth *t*

2 Pet 2:9 Lord knoweth how to deliver...out of *t's*

TEMPTATIONS OF JESUS.
See *Jesus, Life and Ministry of.*

TEN COMMANDMENTS.
Ex 20:1–17 • Deut 5:7–21.

TERAH (father of Abraham).
Gen 11:24–32 • Josh 24:2 • 1 Chr 1:26. *Thara:* Luke 3:34.

TERTULLUS (a Jewish lawyer who accused Paul of desecrating the temple). Acts 24:1–8.

TESTIFY [IED, IETH, ING]

Num 35:30 one witness shall not *t* against any person to cause him to die

Isa 59:12 our sins *t* against us

John 4:44 Jesus...*t'ied*...a prophet hath no honour in his own country

Acts 20:21 t'ing...to the Jews, and...Greeks, repentance

Acts 23:11 Paul...hast *t'ied* of me [Jesus] in Jerusalem

Heb 7:17 he [God] *t'ieth,* Thou art a priest for ever

1 John 4:14 we...do *t* that the Father sent the Son

1 John 5:9 the witness of God... hath *t'ied* of his Son

Rev 22:20 He [Jesus] which *t'ieth*...saith...I come quickly

TESTIMONY [IES]

Deut 6:20 What mean the *t'ies*...which...God hath commanded you

Ps 19:7 t of...LORD is sure, making wise the simple

Ps 119:24 Thy [God's] *t'ies* also are my delight

Mark 6:11 shake off the dust... for a *t* against them

John 21:24 and we know that his *t* is true

2 Tim 1:8 Be not...ashamed of the *t* of our Lord

THADDAEUS. See *Judas.*

THANK

Matt 11:25 I [Jesus] *t* thee... Lord of heaven and earth

Luke 18:11 Pharisee... prayed...God, I *t* thee, that I am not as other men

Phil 1:3 I [Paul] *t* my God upon...remembrance of you

THANKS

1 Chr 16:34 give *t* unto the LORD; for he is good

Ps 92:1 It is a good thing to give *t* unto the LORD

Ps 107:1 give *t* unto the LORD, for he is good

Luke 22:19 And he [Jesus] took bread, and gave *t*

1 Cor 11:24 he [Jesus] had given *t,* he brake it [bread]

1 Cor 15:57 t be to God, which giveth us the victory

2 Cor 9:15 T be unto God for his unspeakable gift

1 Thes 5:18 In every thing give *t*...this is...will of God

THARA. See *Terah.*

THEBEZ (a fortified city where Abimelech was killed). **Judg 9:50–55** • 2 Sam 11:21.

THEOPHILUS (a friend to whom Luke addressed the Gospel of Luke and the Book of Acts). Luke 1:3 • Acts 1:1.

THESSALONIANS, FIRST AND SECOND EPISTLES TO THE. Two epistles written by the apostle Paul to the believers in the church at Thessalonica. The theme of both letters is the second coming of Christ.

THESSALONICA (a city on the Macedonian coast where Paul preached and founded a church). Acts 17:1–13 • 1 Thes 1:1.

THIEF [VES]

Matt 6:20 where *t'ves* do not break through nor steal

Mark 14:48 Are ye come out, as against a *t*

Mark 15:27 with him [Jesus] they crucify two *t'ves*

Luke 10:30 A certain man... fell among *t'ves*

Luke 19:46 ye have made it [God's house] a den of *t'ves*

John 10:10 The *t* cometh not, but for to steal

John 12:6 This he [Judas] said...because he was a *t*

1 Thes 5:2 the day of the Lord so cometh as a *t* in the night

2 Pet 3:10 the day of the Lord will come as a *t* in the night

THINK [EST, ETH]

Prov 23:7 as he *t'eth* in his heart, so is he

Jer 29:11 I [God] know the thoughts that I *t* toward you

Matt 6:7 heathen...*t*...they shall be heard for...much speaking

Matt 24:44 such an hour as ye *t* not the Son of man cometh

Luke 10:36 Which...of these... *t'est* thou, was neighbour

John 16:2 that whosoever killeth you will *t* that he doeth God service

Rom 12:3 not to *t* of himself... highly than he ought to *t*

1 Cor 10:12 *t'eth* he standeth take heed lest he fall

1 Cor 13:5 [charity] is not easily provoked, *t'eth* no evil

Gal 6:3 For if a man *t* himself to be something, when he is nothing

Eph 3:20 unto him [Jesus] that is able to do...above all that we ask or *t*

Phil 4:8 if there be any praise, *t* on these things

THOMAS (a disciple of Jesus who insisted on indisputable proof that Jesus was alive). Matt 10:3 • Mark 3:18 • Luke 6:15 • John 11:16; 14:5; **20:24–29;** 21:2 • Acts 1:13.

THORN IN THE FLESH, PAUL'S. 2 Cor 12:7–10.

THOUGHT [S]

Gen 50:20 ye *t* evil against me [Joseph]; but God meant it unto good

Job 21:27 Behold, I [God] know your *t's*

Job 42:2 no *t* can be withholden from thee [God]

Ps 92:5 O Lord...thy *t's* are very deep

Prov 16:3 Commit thy works unto the Lord, and thy *t's* shall be established

Isa 55:8 For my [God's] *t's* are not your *t's*

Jer 29:11 I [God] know the *t's* that I think toward you

Matt 6:27 Which of you by taking *t* can add one cubit unto his stature

Mark 7:21 out of the heart of men, proceed evil *t's*

1 Cor 3:20 The Lord knoweth the *t's* of the wise

1 Cor 13:11 I [Paul] understood as a child, I *t* as a child

Phil 2:6 Who [Jesus]...*t* it not robbery to be equal with God

Heb 4:12 the word of God...is a discerner of the *t's* and intents of the heart

THRONE

Ps 45:6 Thy *t,* O God, is for ever and ever

Ps 97:2 righteousness and judgment are the habitation of his [God's] *t*

Prov 20:28 his [the king's] *t* is upholden by mercy

Isa 6:1 I [Isaiah] saw also the Lord...upon a *t*

Isa 66:1 Thus saith the Lord, The heaven is my [God's] *t*

Jer 33:17 David shall never want a man to sit upon the *t* of the house of Israel

Lam 5:19 thy [God's] *t* from generation to generation

Matt 19:28 Son of man shall sit in the *t* of his glory

Matt 25:31 shall he [Jesus] sit upon the *t* of his glory

Luke 1:32 God shall give unto him [Jesus] the *t* of...David

Heb 4:16 Let us...come boldly unto the *t* of grace

Rev 4:2 one [Jesus] sat on the *t*

THRONE OF GOD

Heb 12:2 Jesus...is set down at the right hand of the *t-o-G*

Rev 7:15 before the *t-o-G,* and serve him day and night

Rev 22:1 water of life...proceeding out of the *t-o-G*

THYATIRA (hometown of Lydia and site of one of the seven churches addressed by John in the Book of Revelation). Acts 16:14 • Rev 1:1; 2:18,24.

TIBERIAS

1 A city near the Sea of Galilee built by Herod Antipas and named for the Roman emperor Tiberius. John 6:1,23; 21:1.

2. Another name for the Sea of Galilee. See *Galilee, Sea of.*

TIGLATH-PILESER III (an Assyrian king who defeated the Northern Kingdom and carried Jewish captives to Assyria). 2 Kgs 15:29; 16:1–10. *Pul:* 1 Chr 5:26. *Tilgath-pilneser:* 2 Chr 28:20.

TILGATH-PILNESER. See *Tiglath-pileser III.*

TIMON (one of the seven men chosen as "deacons" in the church at Jerusalem). Acts 6:1–5.

TIMOTHEUS. See *Timothy.*

TIMOTHY (a young believer, also called *Timotheus,* who traveled with Paul and briefly shared his imprisonment at Rome). **Acts 16:1–3; 17:14–15; 18:1–5;** 19:22; 20:4 • Rom 16:21 • 1 Cor 4:17; 16:10 • 2 Cor 1:1,19 • **Phil 1:1; 2:19,23** • Col 1:1 • 1 Thes 1:1; 3:2,6 • 2 Thes 1:1 • 1 Tim 1:2,18; 6:20 • 2 Tim 1:2 • Phlm 1 • Heb 13:23.

TIMOTHY, FIRST AND SECOND EPISTLES TO. Two short epistles of the apostle Paul to his friend and fellow missionary, Timothy. The first epistle is practical in scope, instructing Timothy on how to lead a church. In 2 Timothy Paul expresses tender affection for the young minister (1:1–2:26) and speaks of the possibility of his own execution (4:6–22).

TIRZAH (capital of the Northern Kingdom before Samaria was built). 1 Kgs 14:17; 15:21,33; 16:6–23 • 2 Kgs 15:14–16 • Song 6:4.

TITHE [S]
Lev 27:30 all the *t* of the land... is the LORD'S
Deut 14:22 Thou shalt...*t* all the increase of thy seed
Neh 13:12 Then brought all Judah the *t* of the corn
Mal 3:8 have we robbed thee [God]? In *t's* and offerings
Mal 3:10 Bring ye all the *t's* into the storehouse
Luke 11:42 ye [Pharisees] *t* mint and rue and...herbs
Heb 7:6 he [Melchisedec]... received *t's* of Abraham

TITUS (a church leader and traveling companion of Paul). 2 Cor 2:13; 7:6–14; 8:6,16,23; 12:18 • Gal 2:1–3 • 2 Tim 4:10 • Titus 1:4–3:11.

TITUS, EPISTLE TO. A short epistle from the apostle Paul to Titus in which he deals with several practical church matters (1:5–16) and the behavior of Christians in an immoral world (3:1–11).

TOBIAH (an Ammonite who opposed Nehemiah's reconstruction of Jerusalem's wall). Neh 2:10,19; 4:3,7; 6:1–19; 13:4,7–8.

TOLA (a minor judge of Israel). Judg 10:1–2.

TONGUE, POWER OF. Jas 3:1–12.

TONGUES, SPEAKING IN. 1 Cor 14:7–40.

TOOTH FOR A TOOTH
Matt 5:38 An eye for an eye, and a *t-f-a-t*

TOPHET (a place of human sacrifice in the Valley of Hinnom near Jerusalem). Jer 7:31–32.

TOWER OF BABEL. Gen 11:1–9.

TRADITION [S]
Matt 15:6 commandment of God of none effect by your [Pharisees'] *t*
Mark 7:5 Why walk not thy [Jesus'] disciples according to the *t* of the elders
2 Thes 2:15 hold the *t's* which ye have been taught

TRANSFIGURATION OF JESUS. See *Jesus, Life and Ministry of.*

TRANSGRESS [ED, ETH]

Deut 26:13 I have not *t'ed* thy [God's] commandments

Jer 2:29 all have *t'ed* against me, saith the LORD

Matt 15:2 Why do thy [Jesus'] disciples *t* the tradition of the elders...wash not their hands

1 John 3:4 Whosoever committeth sin *t'eth* also the law

TRANSGRESSION [S]

1 Chr 10:13 Saul died for his *t*...against the LORD

Job 13:23 make me [Job] to know my *t* and my sin

Ps 32:1 Blessed is he whose *t* is forgiven

Ps 32:5 I will confess my *t's* unto the LORD

Ps 51:3 I acknowledge my *t's*

Prov 12:13 The wicked is snared by the *t* of his lips

Prov 29:6 In the *t* of an evil man there is a snare

Isa 53:5 he [God's servant] was wounded for our *t's*

Amos 1:3 For three *t's* of Damascus, and for four

TRANSGRESSOR [S]

Ps 51:13 Then will I teach *t's* thy [God's] ways

Prov 22:12 he [God] overthroweth the words of the *t*

Mark 15:28 he [Jesus] was numbered with the *t's*

TREASURE [S]

Ex 19:5 ye [Israel] shall be a peculiar *t* unto me [God]

Ps 135:4 LORD hath chosen... Israel for his peculiar *t*

Prov 10:2 *T's* of wickedness profit nothing

Prov 15:16 Better is little with the fear of the LORD than great *t* and trouble

Matt 2:11 they [the wise men] had opened their *t's*

Matt 6:20 lay up for yourselves *t's* in heaven

Matt 13:44 kingdom of heaven is like unto *t* hid in a field

Luke 12:34 where your *t* is, there will your heart be also

2 Cor 4:7 we have this *t* in earthen vessels

Col 2:3 In whom [Jesus] are hid all the *t's* of wisdom

TREE OF KNOWLEDGE OF GOOD AND EVIL (a tree in the Garden of Eden declared off-limits for Adam and Eve by the Lord). Gen 2:9–17.

TREE OF LIFE (a tree in the Garden of Eden whose fruit would bring eternal life). Gen 2:9 • Rev 22:2.

TRESPASS [ED, ES]

Ezra 9:15 we are before thee [God] in our *t'es*

Ezek 15:8 they have committed a *t,* saith the Lord GOD

Ezek 39:23 Israel went into captivity...because they *t'ed* against me [God]

Matt 6:14 if ye forgive men their *t'es,* your...Father will also forgive you

Mark 11:25 your Father...may forgive you your *t'es*

Luke 17:3 If thy brother *t* against thee, rebuke him

2 Cor 5:19 God was...not imputing their *t'es* unto them

Eph 2:1 hath he [Jesus] quickened, who were dead in *t'es*

TRIBULATION [S]

Matt 24:21 then shall be great *t*

John 16:33 In the world ye shall have *t*

Rom 5:3 knowing that *t* worketh patience

Rom 8:35 Who shall separate us...shall *t,* or distress

2 Cor 1:4 Who [Jesus] comforteth us in all our *t*

Eph 3:13 I [Paul] desire that ye faint not at my *t's* for you

TRIUMPHAL ENTRY OF JESUS. See *Jesus, Life and Ministry of.*

TROAS (a city on the coast of Mysia where Paul received a vision). **Acts 16:8–11;** 20:5–6 • 2 Cor 2:12 • 2 Tim 4:13.

TROPHIMUS (a believer who accompanied Paul on the third missionary journey). Acts 20:4; 21:29 • 2 Tim 4:20.

TROUBLE [D, TH]

1 Sam 16:14 an evil spirit from the LORD *t'd* him [Saul]

1 Kgs 18:17 Art thou [Elijah] he that *t'th* Israel

Job 14:1 Man...is of few days, and full of *t*

Ps 9:9 The LORD...will be a refuge...in times of *t*

Ps 31:9 Have mercy upon me, O LORD, for I am in *t*

Ps 38:6 I am *t'd;* I am bowed down greatly

Ps 46:1 God is...a very present help in *t*

Ps 77:2 In the day of my *t* I sought the Lord

Ps 90:7 by thy [God's] wrath are we *t'd*

Ps 108:12 Give us help from *t*

Prov 15:27 He that is greedy of gain *t'th* his own house

Jer 8:15 We looked for peace... and for a time of health, and behold *t*

Matt 2:3 he [Herod] was *t'd,* and all Jerusalem with him

Luke 1:29 she [Mary] was *t'd* at his [the angel's] saying

John 12:27 Now is my [Jesus'] soul *t'd*...what shall I say

John 14:1 Let not your heart be *t'd*...believe...in me

2 Cor 4:8 We are *t'd* on every side...not distressed

Gal 1:7 some that *t* you, and would pervert the gospel

2 Thes 1:6 recompense tribulation to them that *t* you

TRUE

Ps 19:9 judgments of the LORD are *t* and righteous

Zech 7:9 Execute *t* judgment, and show mercy

John 1:9 the *t* Light [Jesus]... lighteth every man

John 6:32 my [Jesus'] Father giveth you the *t* bread

John 15:1 I [Jesus] am the *t* vine...Father...the husbandman

John 21:24 we know that his [John's] testimony is *t*

Rom 3:4 let God be *t,* but every man a liar

TRUE VINE, JESUS AS. See *"I Am" Statements of Jesus.*

TRUST [ED, ETH, ING]

Deut 32:37 Where are their gods...in whom they *t'ed*

2 Sam 22:3 The God of my rock; in him will I *t*

Job 13:15 Though he [God] slay me [Job]...I *t* in him

Ps 13:5 I have *t'ed* in thy [God's] mercy

Ps 16:1 Preserve me...for in thee [God] do I put my *t*

Ps 26:1 I have *t'ed*...in the LORD...I shall not slide

Ps 34:8 blessed is the man that *t'eth* in him [God]

Ps 37:5 *t*...in him [God]...he shall bring it to pass

Ps 56:3 What time I am afraid, I will *t* in thee [God]

Ps 112:7 his heart is fixed, *t'ing* in the LORD

Ps 118:8 better to *t* in the LORD than...confidence in man

Prov 3:5 *T* in the LORD with all thine heart

Prov 11:28 He that *t'eth* in his riches shall fall

Mark 10:24 hard is it for them that *t* in riches to enter... the kingdom

1 Tim 1:11 According to the glorious gospel...which was committed to my [Paul's] *t*

TRUTH

1 Sam 12:24 serve him [God] in *t* with all your heart

Ps 25:5 Lead me in thy [God's] *t,* and teach me

Ps 33:4 all his [God's] works are done in *t*

Ps 86:11 Teach me...I will walk in thy [God's] *t*

Ps 100:5 his [God's] *t* endureth to all generations

Ps 119:30 I have chosen the way of *t*

John 1:17 grace and *t* came by Jesus Christ

John 4:24 must worship him [God] in spirit and in *t*

John 8:32 know the *t,* and the *t* shall make you free

John 14:6 I [Jesus] am the way, the *t,* and the life

John 16:13 the Spirit of *t*... will guide you into all *t*

John 18:38 Pilate saith unto him [Jesus], What is *t*
Acts 10:34 Of a *t* I [Peter] perceive that God is no respecter of persons
1 Cor 13:6 [charity] rejoiceth in the *t*
Gal 4:16 Am I [Paul]...enemy, because I tell you the *t*
Eph 4:15 speaking the *t* in love
1 Tim 2:4 Who [God] will have all men...come unto the knowledge of the *t*
1 Tim 3:15 the church...the pillar and ground of the *t*
2 Tim 2:15 workman...needeth not to be ashamed, rightly dividing the word of *t*

1 John 1:8 If we say that we have no sin...*t* is not in us
3 John 4 no greater joy than to hear that my [John's] children walk in *t*

TYRANNUS (a citizen of Ephesus who allowed Paul to use his lecture hall). Acts 19:8–10.

TYRE (an ancient Phoenician city and thriving trade center north of Palestine). Josh 19:29 • 1 Kgs 5:1–12 • Joel 3:4–6 • Matt 15:21–28. *Tyrus:* Ezek 26:1–21; 27:1–36 • Amos 1:10.

TYRUS. See *Tyre.*

-U-

UNBELIEF
Mark 9:24 Lord, I believe; help thou mine *u*
Heb 3:12 lest there be in any of you an evil heart of *u*
Heb 4:11 lest any man fall after the same example of *u*

UNBELIEVERS
1 Cor 6:6 brother goeth to law with brother...before the *u*
2 Cor 6:14 Be ye not unequally yoked together with *u*

UNBELIEVING
Acts 14:2 But the *u* Jews stirred up the Gentiles
1 Cor 7:14 the *u* husband is sanctified by the wife
Titus 1:15 unto them that are defiled and *u* is nothing pure

UNCIRCUMCISED
1 Sam 17:26 this *u* Philistine [Goliath], that he should defy...the living God
Ezek 44:9 No stranger, *u* in heart...shall enter into my [God's] sanctuary
Acts 7:51 stiffnecked and *u* in heart and ears

UNCIRCUMCISION
1 Cor 7:19 Circumcision is nothing, and *u* is nothing
Gal 5:6 neither circumcision availeth any thing, nor *u*

Col 3:11 neither Greek nor Jew, circumcision nor *u*

UNCLEAN [NESS]
Num 19:11 He that toucheth the dead body...*u* seven days
Isa 6:5 because I [Isaiah] am a man of *u* lips
Isa 64:6 But we are all as an *u* thing
Mark 6:7 And he [Jesus]...gave them [the disciples] power over *u* spirits
Acts 10:14 I [Peter] have never eaten any thing...*u*
Rom 1:24 God also gave them up to *u'ness*
Rom 14:14 persuaded...that there is nothing *u* of itself
Gal 5:19 works of the flesh are manifest...Adultery, fornication, *u'ness*
1 Thes 4:7 God hath not called us unto *u'ness*

UNDEFILED
Ps 119:1 Blessed are the *u*... walk in the law of the LORD
Heb 7:26 high priest [Jesus]... who is holy, harmless, *u*
Jas 1:27 Pure religion and *u* before God and the Father

UNDERSTAND [EST, ETH, ING]
1 Kgs 4:29 God gave Solomon wisdom and *u'ing*
Job 26:12 by his [God's] *u'ing* he smiteth...the proud

Job 28:28 and to depart from evil is *u'ing*

Job 32:9 neither do the aged *u* judgment

Ps 119:27 Make me to *u* the way of thy [God's] precepts

Ps 119:34 Give me *u'ing,* and I shall keep thy [God's] law

Ps 147:5 Great is our Lord... his *u'ing* is infinite

Prov 2:2 and apply thine heart to *u'ing*

Prov 2:5 Then shalt thou *u* the fear of the LORD

Prov 3:5 and lean not unto thine own *u'ing*

Prov 4:7 and with all thy getting get *u'ing*

Prov 10:13 a rod is for...him that is void of *u'ing*

Prov 14:6 knowledge is easy unto him that *u'eth*

Prov 17:28 he that shutteth his lips is...a man of *u'ing*

Isa 40:28 there is no searching of his [God's] *u'ing*

Isa 44:18 he [God] hath shut their eyes...and...hearts, that they cannot *u*

Dan 9:22 come forth to give thee [Daniel] skill and *u'ing*

Dan 10:14 make thee [Daniel] *u* what shall befall thy people

Matt 15:16 Are ye [the disciples] also yet without *u'ing*

Mark 8:21 How is it that ye [the disciples] do not *u*

Luke 24:45 opened he [Jesus] their [Emmaus travelers'] *u'ing*...might *u* the scriptures

Acts 8:30 Philip...said, *U'est* thou [Ethiopian eunuch] what thou readest

Rom 3:11 none that *u'eth*... none that seeketh after God

1 Cor 13:2 though I [Paul]...*u* all mysteries

1 Cor 14:19 I [Paul] had rather speak five words with my *u'ing*...than...unknown tongue

Phil 4:7 peace of God, which passeth all *u'ing*

Heb 11:3 we *u*...worlds were framed by the word of God

UNDERSTOOD

Job 13:1 mine [Job's] ear hath heard and *u* it

Job 42:3 I [Job] uttered that I *u* not; things too wonderful

Isa 40:21 have ye not *u* from the foundations of the earth

John 12:16 These things *u* not his [Jesus'] disciples

1 Cor 13:11 When I [Paul] was a child...I *u* as a child

UNGODLY [INESS]

Ps 1:1 man that walketh not in the counsel of the *u*

Prov 16:27 An *u* man diggeth up evil

Rom 1:18 wrath of God is revealed...against all *u'iness*

Rom 5:6 in due time Christ died for the *u*
Titus 2:12 denying *u'iness*... we should live soberly
Jude 18 mockers...should walk after their own *u* lusts

UNJUST
Matt 5:45 he [God]...sendeth rain on the just and...*u*
Luke 16:8 the lord commended the *u* steward
1 Pet 3:18 Christ...suffered for sins, the just for the *u*

UNKNOWN
Acts 17:23 altar with this inscription, TO THE *U* GOD
1 Cor 14:4 speaketh in an *u* tongue edifieth himself
1 Cor 14:19 I [Paul] had rather speak...with...understanding...than...in an *u* tongue

UNRIGHTEOUS [NESS]
Ps 92:15 and there is no *u'ness* in him [God]
Isa 55:7 Let the wicked forsake his way, and the *u* man his thoughts
Rom 1:18 wrath of God is revealed from heaven against all...*u'ness* of men
1 Cor 6:9 the *u* shall not inherit the kingdom of God
2 Cor 6:14 what fellowship... righteousness with *u'ness*
1 John 1:9 he [Jesus] is faithful...to cleanse us from all *u'ness*

UNSEARCHABLE
Ps 145:3 Great is the LORD... his greatness is *u*
Rom 11:33 how *u* are his [God's] judgments
Eph 3:8 I [Paul] should preach... the *u* riches of Christ

UR OF THE CHALDEES (a city in Mesopotamia where Abraham spent his early life before going to Canaan). **Gen 11:28,31;** 15:7 • Neh 9:7.

URIAH (a Hittite warrior whom David had killed after his affair with Uriah's wife). **2 Sam 11:1–26;** 12:9–10; 23:39 • 1 Kgs 15:5 • 1 Chr 11:41. *Urias:* Matt 1:6.

URIAS. See *Uriah.*

URIJAH (a prophet killed by King Jehoiakim for predicting God's judgment on Judah). Jer 26:20–23.

URIM AND THUMMIN (two objects in the breastplate of the high priest which were cast as lots to help determine God's will). Ex 28:30 • Lev 8:8 • Num 27:21 • Deut 33:8 • Ezra 2:63 • Neh 7:65.

UZ (a place west of the Arabian desert where Job lived). **Job 1:1** • Jer 25:20.

UZZA (an Israelite struck dead for touching the ark of the covenant). 1 Chr 13:7–11.

UZZIAH (a king of Judah who contracted leprosy as a divine punishment for assuming duties that belonged to the priesthood). 2 Kgs 15:13–34 • **2 Chr 26:1–23;** 27:2 • Isa 1:1; 6:1; 7:1 • Hos 1:1 • Amos 1:1 • Zech 14:5. *Azariah:* 2 Kgs 14:21. *Ozias:* Matt 1:8.

-V-

VAIN

Ex 20:7 not take the name of the LORD...in *v*

Ps 2:1 Why do...the people imagine a *v* thing

Ps 60:11 *v* is the help of man

Ps 127:1 Except the LORD build the house, they labour in *v* that build it

Prov 31:30 Favour is deceitful, and beauty is *v*

Matt 6:7 when ye pray, use not *v* repetitions

1 Cor 3:20 The Lord knoweth the thoughts of the wise, that they are *v*

1 Cor 15:14 if Christ be not risen, then is our preaching *v*

2 Tim 2:16 But shun profane and *v* babblings

VANITY [IES]

Job 35:13 God will not hear *v*, neither...regard it

Ps 31:6 I have hated them that regard lying *v'ies*

Ps 39:5 every man at his best state is altogether *v*

Ps 94:11 LORD knoweth the thoughts of man...they are *v*

Ps 144:4 Man is like to *v:* his days are as a shadow

Eccl 1:2 *v* of *v'ies;* all is *v*

Isa 41:29 they are all *v;* their works are nothing

Acts 14:15 Sirs [people of Lystra]...turn from these *v'ies*

Eph 4:17 walk not...in the *v* of their mind

VASHTI (the queen of Ahasuerus of Persia who was replaced by Esther). Esth 1:9–12; 2:1–4,15–17.

VENGEANCE

Ps 94:1 God, to whom *v* belongeth, show thyself

Isa 61:2 To proclaim...the day of *v* of our God

Luke 21:22 these be the days of *v*...things...may be fulfilled

Rom 12:19 *V* is mine; I will repay, saith the Lord

VICTORY

Isa 25:8 He [God] will swallow up death in *v*

1 Cor 15:55 O grave, where is thy *v*

1 Cor 15:57 God...giveth us the *v* through...Jesus Christ

1 John 5:4 this is the *v* that overcometh the world

VINE [S]

Judg 9:12 said the trees unto the *v*...reign over us

Song 2:15 the little foxes, that spoil the *v's*

Mic 4:4 sit every man under his *v* and under his fig tree

Luke 22:18 I [Jesus] will not drink of the fruit of the *v*

John 15:5 I [Jesus] am the *v,* ye are the branches

VINE OF SODOM (a plant which produced a beautiful fruit that was unfit to eat—a fitting description of Israel's idolatry). Deut 32:32.

VIRTUE
Mark 5:30 Jesus...knowing... that *v* had gone out of him
Phil 4:8 if there be any *v*... think on these things
2 Pet 1:5 add to your faith *v;* and to virtue knowledge

VIRTUOUS
Ruth 3:11 all the city...doth know...thou art a *v* woman
Prov 12:4 A *v* woman is a crown to her husband
Prov 31:10 Who can find a *v* woman...price...above rubies

VISION [S]
Prov 29:18 Where there is no *v,* the people perish
Ezek 1:1 heavens...opened, and I [Ezekiel] saw *v's*
Ezek 11:24 the spirit...brought me [Ezekiel] in a *v*...into Chaldea
Dan 2:19 Then was the secret revealed...in a night *v*
Joel 2:28 your young men shall see *v's*
Hab 2:2 Write the *v,* and make it plain upon tables

Luke 1:22 he [Zacharias] had seen a *v* in the temple
Acts 16:9 a *v* appeared to Paul in the night
Acts 26:19 I [Paul] was not disobedient unto the heavenly *v*

VOICE [S]
Gen 22:18 thou [Abraham] hast obeyed my [God's] *v*
Ex 5:2 Who is the LORD, that I [Pharaoh] should obey his *v*
Josh 24:24 our God will we serve...his *v* will we obey
1 Kgs 19:12 and after the fire a still small *v*
Job 40:9 canst thou thunder with a *v* like him [God]
Ps 27:7 Hear, O LORD, when I cry with my *v*
Ps 66:8 make the *v* of his [God's] praise to be heard
Ps 116:1 he [God] hath heard my *v* and my supplications
Isa 40:3 The *v* of him that crieth in the wilderness
Jon 2:2 and thou [God] heardest my [Jonah's] *v*
Matt 3:3 The *v* of one crying in the wilderness
Matt 3:17 a *v* from heaven... my [God's] beloved Son
Mark 9:7 a *v* came out of the cloud...This is my [God's] beloved Son
Luke 23:46 when Jesus had cried with a loud *v*
John 10:27 My [Jesus'] sheep hear my *v*...I know them

Acts 9:4 a *v* saying...Saul, why persecutest...me [Jesus]

1 Cor 14:10 There are...so many...*v's* in the world

Heb 3:15 To day if ye will hear his [God's] *v*

Rev 1:10 I [John]...heard behind me a great *v*

Rev 3:20 any man hear my [Jesus'] *v,* and open the door

VOICE OF THE LORD

Gen 3:8 they [Adam and Eve] heard the *v-o-t-L*

Deut 13:18 thou shalt hearken to the *v-o-t-L*

1 Sam 15:22 Hath the LORD as great delight in... sacrifices, as in obeying the *v-o-t-L*

Ps 29:4 the *v-o-t-L* is powerful... full of majesty

Isa 6:8 I [Isaiah] heard the *v-o-t-L*...Whom shall I send

VOW [ED, EST, S]

Judg 11:30 Jephthah *v'ed* a *v* unto the LORD

Ps 50:14 and pay thy *v's* unto the most High

Ps 116:14 I will pay my *v's* unto the LORD

Eccl 5:4 *v'est* a *v* unto God, defer not to pay it

Jon 1:16 the men...offered a sacrifice...and made *v's*

Jon 2:9 I will pay that that I have *v'ed*

-W-

WAGES
Lev 19:13 **w** of him...shall not abide with thee all night
Hag 1:6 earneth **w** to put it into a bag with holes
Rom 6:23 the **w** of sin is death

WAIT ON THE LORD
Ps 27:14 **W-o-t-L:** be of good courage...strengthen thine heart
Ps 37:34 **W-o-t-L,** and keep his way...he shall exalt thee
Prov 20:22 **w-o-t-L,** and he shall save thee

WALLS OF JERUSALEM REBUILT AFTER THE EXILE. Neh 6:15.

WANDERING IN THE WILDERNESS BY ISRAEL. Num 14:20–35.

WATCH [ED, ETH, ING]
Job 14:16 dost thou [God] not **w** over my sin
Ps 90:4 For a thousand years in thy [God's] sight are...as a **w** in the night
Ps 141:3 Set a **w,** O LORD, before my mouth
Matt 24:42 **W** therefore: for ye know not what hour
Mark 14:37 couldest not thou [Peter] **w** one hour

Luke 2:8 shepherds...keeping **w** over their flock
Luke 12:37 Blessed are those... the lord...find **w'ing**
Luke 12:39 goodman...had known...thief would come, he would have **w'ed**
1 Pet 4:7 be ye...sober, and **w** unto prayer
Rev 16:15 I [Jesus] come as a thief. Blessed is he that **w'eth**

WATER [EST, ETH, S]
Gen 1:2 the Spirit of God moved upon...the **w's**
Gen 7:24 the **w's** prevailed upon the earth
Gen 9:11 neither shall all flesh be cut off any more by the **w's** of a flood
Ex 7:18 Egyptians shall loathe to drink of the **w** of the river
Ex 14:22 **w's** were a wall unto [the Israelites]
Num 20:11 Moses...smote the rock...and...**w** came out
Josh 9:27 Joshua made them [Gibeonites]...drawers of **w**
1 Kgs 18:38 fire of the LORD fell...and licked up the **w**
Job 5:10 Who [God]...sendeth **w's** upon the fields
Ps 1:3 like a tree planted by the rivers of **w**
Ps 22:14 I am poured out like **w**...bones are out of joint
Ps 23:2 he [God] leadeth me beside the still **w's**

Ps 63:1 flesh longeth for thee [God] in a dry and thirsty land, where no *w* is

Ps 65:9 Thou [God] visitest the earth, and *w'est* it

Ps 69:14 let me be delivered... out of the deep *w's*

Ps 119:136 Rivers of *w's* run down mine eyes

Prov 5:15 Drink *w's* out of thine own cistern

Prov 25:21 if he [one's enemy] be thirsty, give him *w*

Eccl 11:1 Cast thy bread upon the *w's*

Song 8:7 Many *w's* cannot quench love

Isa 11:9 earth shall be full of the knowledge of the LORD, as the *w's* cover the sea

Isa 40:12 Who [God] hath measured the *w's* in...his hand

Isa 55:1 every one that thirsteth, come ye to the *w's*

Jer 2:13 forsaken me [God] the fountain of living *w's*

Jer 9:1 Oh that my [Jeremiah's] head were *w's*

Ezek 7:17 all knees shall be weak as *w*

Ezek 12:18 drink thy [Ezekiel's] *w* with trembling

Amos 5:24 let judgment run down as *w's*

Hab 2:14 earth...filled with... the glory of the LORD, as the *w's* cover the sea

Mark 1:8 I [John the Baptist]... have baptized you with *w*

Luke 8:24 he [Jesus]...rebuked... the raging of the *w*

John 3:5 Except a man be born of *w* and of the Spirit

John 4:14 drinketh of the *w* that I [Jesus] shall give him

Acts 1:5 John...baptized with *w;* but ye shall be baptized with the Holy Ghost

Acts 8:36 here is *w;* what doth hinder me [Ethiopian eunuch] to be baptized

1 Cor 3:7 neither he that *w'eth;* but God that giveth the increase

Rev 22:17 whosoever will, let him take the *w* of life freely

WAY [S] OF THE LORD

2 Sam 22:22 I have kept the *w's-o-t-L*

2 Kgs 21:22 he [Amon]...walked not in the *w-o-t-L*

Ps 18:21 For I have kept the *w's-o-t-L*

Ps 138:5 they shall sing in the *w's-o-t-L*

Isa 40:3 Prepare...the *w-o-t-L*

Jer 5:4 they are foolish: for they know not the *w-o-t-L*

Ezek 33:17 the...people say, The *w-o-t-L* is not equal

Hos 14:9 for the *w's-o-t-L* are right, and...just

Mark 1:3 Prepare...the *w-o-t-L,* make his paths straight

Acts 13:10 wilt thou [Elymas]... pervert the right *w's-o-t-L*

WAY OF THE SEA (a road that ran from Phoenicia to Egypt, passing through Palestine). Isa 9:1.

WAY, THE TRUTH, AND THE LIFE, JESUS AS. See *"I Am" Statements of Jesus.*

WAYS
Deut 10:12 what doth...God require...to walk in all his *w*
1 Sam 18:14 David behaved... wisely in all his *w*
2 Chr 7:14 If my [God's] people... shall...turn from their wicked *w;* then will I hear
Job 34:21 his [God's] eyes are upon the *w* of man
Ps 25:4 Show me thy *w,* O LORD, teach me thy paths
Ps 128:1 Blessed is every one... walketh in his [God's] *w*
Prov 3:6 In all thy *w* acknowledge him [God]
Prov 14:12 the end thereof are the *w* of death
Prov 28:18 he that is perverse in his *w* shall fall
Isa 55:8 neither are your *w* my *w,* saith the LORD
Lam 3:40 search and try our *w,* and turn...to the LORD
Rom 11:33 how unsearchable are his [God's] judgments... his *w* past finding out
Jas 1:8 A double minded man is unstable in all his *w*

WEAK [ENED]
Ps 6:2 Have mercy upon me, O LORD; for I am *w*
Ps 102:23 He [God] *w'ened* my strength in the way
Matt 26:41 the spirit...is willing, but the flesh is *w*
Acts 20:35 so labouring ye ought to support the *w*
1 Cor 1:27 God hath chosen... *w* things of the world to confound the...mighty
1 Cor 9:22 became...*w,* that I [Paul] might gain the *w*

WEAKNESS
1 Cor 1:25 the *w* of God is stronger than men
1 Cor 15:43 it [the body] is sown in *w*...raised in power
2 Cor 12:9 my [Jesus'] strength is made perfect in *w*

WICKED [LY, NESS]
Gen 6:5 God saw that the *w'ness* of man was great
Gen 18:23 Wilt thou [God]... destroy...righteous with the *w*
Job 4:8 they that...sow *w'ness,* reap the same
Job 18:5 Yea, the light of the *w* shall be put out
Job 27:4 My [Job's] lips shall not speak *w'ness*
Ps 10:2 *w* in his pride doth persecute the poor
Ps 34:21 Evil shall slay the *w*
Ps 58:3 The *w* are estranged from the womb

Ps 71:4 Deliver me, O my God, out of the hand of the *w*

Ps 84:10 rather be a door-keeper...than to dwell in the tents of *w'ness*

Ps 94:3 LORD...how long shall the *w* triumph

Ps 106:6 committed iniquity, we have done *w'ly*

Ps 129:4 he [God] hath cut asunder the cords of the *w*

Prov 4:17 they [evil men] eat the bread of *w'ness*

Prov 15:29 The LORD is far from the *w*

Isa 53:9 he [God's servant] made his grave with the *w*

Jer 4:14 O Jerusalem, wash thine heart from *w'ness*

Jer 17:9 The heart is...desperately *w:* who can know it

Hos 10:13 Ye have plowed *w'ness*...reaped iniquity

Jon 1:2 their [Ninevites'] *w'ness* is...before me [God]

Matt 16:4 A *w*...generation seeketh after a sign

Eph 6:12 we wrestle...against spiritual *w'ness*

Eph 6:16 able to quench all the fiery darts of the *w*

WICKED ONE

Matt 13:19 cometh the *w-o*... catcheth...which was sown

Matt 13:38 the tares are the children of the *w-o*

1 John 2:14 and ye have overcome the *w-o*

1 John 3:12 Cain...was of that *w-o,* and slew his brother

1 John 5:18 begotten of God... that *w-o* toucheth him not

WILL OF GOD

Mark 3:35 do the *w-o-G,* the same is my brother

Rom 12:2 what is that good... and perfect, *w-o-G*

1 Thes 4:3 this is the *w-o-G*... abstain from fornication

1 Thes 5:18 give thanks...this is the *w-o-G* in Christ Jesus

1 John 2:17 he that doeth the *w-o-G* abideth for ever

WINE

Job 32:19 my belly is as *w* which hath no vent

Prov 4:17 they...drink the *w* of violence

Prov 20:1 *W* is a mocker, strong drink is raging

Isa 5:22 Woe unto them that are mighty to drink *w*

Mark 2:22 no man putteth new *w* into old bottles

John 2:3 mother of Jesus saith...They have no *w*

Acts 2:13 men [believers at Pentecost] are full of new *w*

Eph 5:18 be not drunk with *w*

1 Tim 3:8 deacons be grave... not given to much *w*

1 Tim 5:23 use a little *w* for thy stomach's sake

WISDOM

1 Kgs 4:29 God gave Solomon *w* and understanding
Job 28:28 Behold, the fear of the Lord, that is *w*
Job 34:35 his [Job's] words were without *w*
Ps 90:12 number our days... apply our hearts unto *w*
Ps 111:10 fear of the LORD is the beginning of *w*
Prov 2:2 So that thou incline thine ear unto *w*
Prov 4:7 **W** is the principal thing; therefore get *w*
Prov 10:13 In the lips of him that hath understanding *w* is found
Prov 23:4 Labour not to be rich: cease from thine own *w*
Eccl 1:18 For in much *w* is much grief
Isa 11:2 the spirit of *w* and understanding
Jer 9:23 Let not the wise man glory in his *w*
Luke 2:52 And Jesus increased in *w* and stature
Acts 6:3 seven men...full of the Holy Ghost and *w*
1 Cor 1:20 hath not God made foolish the *w* of this world
1 Cor 1:22 Jews require a sign... Greeks seek after *w*
1 Cor 3:19 *w* of this world is foolishness with God
Col 3:16 word of Christ dwell in you richly in all *w*
Jas 1:5 If any of you lack *w,* let him ask of God

WISE

Ps 19:7 testimony of the LORD is sure, making *w* the simple
Prov 3:7 Be not *w* in thine own eyes: fear the LORD
Prov 6:6 consider her [the ant's] ways, and be *w*
Eccl 4:13 Better is a poor and a *w* child than an old and foolish king
Isa 5:21 Woe unto them that are *w* in their own eyes
Jer 9:23 Let not the *w* man glory in his wisdom
Matt 2:1 when Jesus was born... came *w* men from the east
Matt 7:24 a *w* man, which built his house upon a rock
Matt 10:16 *w* as serpents, and harmless as doves
Matt 11:25 thou [God] hast hid these things from the *w*
Matt 25:8 foolish said unto the *w,* Give us of your oil
Rom 12:16 Be not *w* in your own conceits
1 Cor 1:20 Where is the *w?* where is the scribe
1 Cor 1:26 not many *w* men after the flesh...are called

WISE MEN VISIT THE CHILD JESUS. Matt 2:1–12.

WITNESS [ES]

Ex 20:16 not bear false *w* against thy neighbour
Ps 35:11 False *w'es* did rise up
Prov 19:9 A false *w* shall not be unpunished

Matt 24:14 gospel...preached... for a *w* unto all nations

Mark 14:56 many bare false *w* against him [Jesus]

John 1:8 He [John the Baptist] ...was sent to bear *w* of that Light [Jesus]

Acts 1:8 and ye shall be *w'es* unto me [Jesus]

Acts 22:15 thou shalt be his [Jesus'] *w* unto all men

Rom 8:16 The Spirit itself beareth *w* with our spirit

Heb 12:1 compassed about with so great a cloud of *w'es*

WIVES

Matt 19:8 Moses...suffered you to put away your *w*

Eph 5:22 **W,** submit...unto your own husbands

Eph 5:25 Husbands, love your *w*...as Christ...loved the church

Col 3:18 **W,** submit...unto your own husbands

Col 3:19 Husbands, love your *w*...be not bitter

1 Tim 4:7 But refuse profane and old *w'* fables

1 Pet 3:1 *w,* be in subjection to your own husbands

WOMAN AT THE WELL TALKS WITH JESUS. John 4:5–42.

WONDERS

Ps 77:14 Thou art the God that doest *w*

Ps 96:3 Declare his [God's]...*w* among all people

John 4:48 Except ye see signs and *w,* ye will not believe

Acts 2:43 *w* and signs were done by the apostles

Acts 6:8 Stephen, full of faith and power, did great *w*

WORD [S]

Job 8:2 *w's* of thy [Job's] mouth be like a strong wind

Ps 12:6 The *w's* of the LORD are pure *w's:* as silver

Ps 19:14 Let the *w's* of my mouth...be acceptable in thy [God's] sight

Ps 119:11 Thy [God's] *w* have I hid in mine heart

Ps 119:81 I hope in thy [God's] *w*

Ps 119:105 Thy [God's] *w* is a lamp unto my feet

Prov 15:1 but grievous *w's* stir up anger

Prov 15:23 a *w* spoken in due season, how good is it

Isa 40:8 the *w* of our God shall stand for ever

Jer 1:9 I [God]...put my *w's* in thy [Jeremiah's] mouth

Dan 12:9 Go thy way, Daniel: for the *w's* are closed up

Mal 2:17 have wearied the LORD with your *w's*

Matt 12:36 That every idle *w* that men shall speak, they shall give account

Matt 24:35 my [Jesus'] *w's* shall not pass away

Luke 1:38 And Mary said...be it unto me according to thy [God's] *w*

Luke 4:32 his [Jesus'] *w* was with power

Luke 5:5 at thy [Jesus'] *w* I [Peter] will let down the net

John 1:1 In the beginning was the *W*...*W* was God

John 6:68 thou [Jesus] hast the *w's* of eternal life

John 17:17 Sanctify them... thy [God's] *w* is truth

Acts 8:4 they that...scattered abroad went every where preaching the *w*

1 Cor 2:4 my [Paul's] preaching was not with enticing *w's*

2 Cor 5:19 committed unto us the *w* of reconciliation

Col 3:17 And whatsoever ye do in *w* or deed

2 Tim 2:15 a workman...rightly dividing the *w* of truth

Jas 1:22 doers of the *w,* and not hearers only

1 John 3:18 let us not love in *w*...but in deed

WORD OF GOD

Prov 30:5 Every *w-o-G* is pure

Luke 4:4 not live by bread alone, but by every *w-o-G*

Luke 5:1 people pressed upon him [Jesus] to hear the *w-o-G*

Luke 8:21 my [Jesus'] brethren are these which hear the *w-o-G,* and do it

Acts 4:31 place was shaken... filled with the Holy Ghost... spake the *w-o-G*

Rom 10:17 faith cometh by hearing...hearing by the *w-o-G*

Eph 6:17 the sword of the Spirit, which is the *w-o-G*

Heb 4:12 the *w-o-G* is quick, and powerful

Heb 11:3 the worlds were framed by the *w-o-G*

WORD [S] OF THE LORD

Ps 33:6 By the *w-o-t-L* were the heavens made

Amos 8:11 not a famine of bread...but of hearing the *w's-o-t-L*

Acts 19:10 all...in Asia heard the *w-o-t-L*

1 Pet 1:25 the *w-o-t-L* endureth for ever

WORK [ETH, ING]

Gen 2:2 on the seventh day God ended his *w*

Ex 23:12 Six days thou shalt do thy *w*

Neh 4:6 for the people had a mind to *w*

Ps 8:3 consider thy [God's] heavens, the *w* of thy fingers

Ps 77:12 I will meditate also of all thy [God's] *w*

Ps 90:17 establish thou [God] the *w* of our hands

Ps 115:4 Their idols are...the *w* of men's hands

Eccl 12:14 God shall bring every *w* into judgment

John 4:34 My [Jesus'] meat is...to finish his [God's] *w*

John 5:17 My [Jesus'] Father *w'eth*...and I *w*

John 6:29 the *w* of God, that ye believe on him [Jesus]

John 9:4 night cometh, when no man can *w*

John 17:4 I [Jesus] have finished the *w* which thou [God] gavest me to do

Acts 13:2 Separate me Barnabas and Saul for the *w*

Rom 8:28 we know...all things *w* together for good

Rom 13:10 Love *w'eth* no ill to his neighbour

1 Cor 3:14 If any man's *w* abide...receive a reward

1 Cor 12:10 To another the *w'ing* of miracles

Eph 4:12 perfecting of the saints...*w* of the ministry

Phil 1:6 he [God] which hath begun a good *w* in you

Phil 2:13 God...*w'eth* in you... to do of his good pleasure

1 Tim 3:1 office of a bishop, he desireth a good *w*

Heb 13:21 *w'ing* in you that which is wellpleasing in his [God's] sight

WORK [S] OF GOD

Ps 64:9 all men...shall declare the *w-o-G*

Ps 66:5 Come and see the *w's-o-G*

Ps 78:7 not forget the *w's-o-G,* but keep his commandments

Eccl 7:13 Consider the *w-o-G*

Eccl 8:17 Then I beheld all the *w-o-G*

John 6:28 that we might work the *w's-o-G*

Acts 2:11 hear them speak... the wonderful *w's-o-G*

WORK [S] OF THE LORD

Ps 77:11 I will remember the *w's-o-t-L*...thy wonders

Ps 118:17 I shall...declare the *w's-o-t-L*

Jer 48:10 Cursed be he that doeth the *w-o-t-L* deceitfully

Jer 51:10 declare in Zion the *w-o-t-L* our God

1 Cor 15:58 stedfast, unmoveable, always abounding in the *w-o-t-L*

WORKERS

Ps 6:8 Depart from me, all ye *w* of iniquity

1 Cor 12:29 are all teachers? are all *w* of miracles

Phil 3:2 Beware of dogs, beware of evil *w*

WORKS

1 Chr 16:9 talk ye of all his [God's] wondrous *w*

1 Chr 16:24 Declare his [God's] glory...marvellous *w* among all nations

Job 37:14 consider the wondrous *w* of God

Ps 33:4 all his [God's] *w* are done in truth

Ps 40:5 Many, O LORD...are thy wonderful *w*

Ps 92:5 O LORD, how great are thy *w*

Ps 143:5 I meditate on all thy [God's] *w*

Ps 145:9 his [God's] tender mercies are over all his *w*

Matt 5:16 see your good *w,* and glorify your Father

Matt 13:58 he [Jesus] did not many mighty *w* there

John 6:28 that we might work the *w* of God

John 9:3 *w* of God should be made manifest in him [Jesus]

John 14:12 greater *w* than these shall he do

Gal 2:16 man is not justified by the *w* of the law

Eph 2:9 Not of *w,* lest any man should boast

2 Tim 3:17 That the man of God may be perfect... furnished unto all good *w*

Titus 3:5 Not by *w* of righteousness...we have done

Jas 2:17 faith, if it hath not *w,* is dead, being alone

Rev 3:8 I [Jesus] know thy [church at Philadelphia's] *w*

WORSHIP [PED, PETH]

Ps 95:6 w and bow down [before God]

Ps 99:5 w at his [God's] footstool; for he is holy

Jer 25:6 go not after other gods...to *w* them

Dan 3:6 whoso falleth not down and *w'peth* shall...be cast into the...furnace

Dan 3:18 we [Daniel's three friends] will not...*w* the golden image

Matt 2:2 we [the wise men]... are come to *w* him [Jesus]

John 4:24 they...must *w* him [God] in spirit and in truth

Acts 17:23 Whom...ye ignorantly *w,* him [God] declare I [Paul] unto you

Acts 17:25 Neither is [God] *w'ped* with men's hands

Rom 1:25 Who [ungodly people]...*w'ped*...served... creature more than... Creator

Rev 7:11 all the angels...fell before the throne on their faces, and *w'ped* God

WORSHIP THE LORD

1 Chr 16:29 w-t-L in the beauty of holiness

Ps 96:9 O *w-t-L* in the beauty of holiness

Luke 4:8 w-t-L thy God, and him only shalt thou serve

WRATH

Ex 32:11 why doth thy [God's] *w* wax hot

Job 5:2 For *w* killeth the foolish man

Ps 21:9 LORD shall swallow them up in his *w*

Ps 90:7 by thy [God's] *w* are we troubled

Prov 14:29 He that is slow to *w* is of great understanding

Matt 3:7 warned you [Pharisee] to flee from the *w*

Rom 5:9 we shall be saved from *w* through him [Jesus]

Eph 4:26 let not the sun go down upon your *w*

Eph 6:4 fathers, provoke not your children to *w*

Rev 6:17 the great day of his [God's] *w* is come

WRATH OF GOD

Ps 78:31 The *w-o-G*...slew the fattest of them

John 3:36 believeth not the Son...*w-o-G* abideth on him

Rom 1:18 *w-o-G* is revealed... against all ungodliness

Rev 16:1 pour out the vials of the *w-o-G* upon the earth

-Y-

YIELD [ED, ING]

Gen 1:11 earth bring forth grass, the herb *y'ing* seed

Num 17:8 rod of Aaron...budded...*y'ed* almonds

Ps 67:6 Then shall the earth *y* her increase

Matt 27:50 Jesus...*y'ed* up the ghost

Rom 6:13 but *y* yourselves unto God

Rev 22:2 the tree of life...*y'ed* her fruit every month

YOKE

Deut 28:48 he [God] shall put a *y* of iron upon thy neck

1 Kgs 19:19 Elisha...was plowing with twelve *y* of oxen

2 Chr 10:14 My [Rehoboam's] father made your *y* heavy

Jer 28:2 I [God] have broken the *y* of...Babylon

Matt 11:30 my [Jesus'] *y* is easy, and my burden is light

Gal 5:1 be not entangled again with the *y* of bondage

YOUTH

1 Sam 17:33 thou [David] art but a *y,* and he [Goliath] a man of war

Ps 25:7 Remember not the sins of my *y*

Ps 71:17 O God, thou hast taught me from my *y*

Prov 5:18 rejoice with the wife of thy *y*

Eccl 12:1 Remember now thy Creator in the days of thy *y*

Matt 19:20 All these things have I kept from my *y* up

1 Tim 4:12 Let no man despise thy *y*

-Z-

ZABULON. See *Zebulun*.

ZACCHAEUS (a tax collector who met Jesus and vowed to give half of his wealth to the poor and make restitution to those whom he had cheated). Luke 19:1–10.

ZACHARIAH (a king of Israel who ruled only about three months before being assassinated). 2 Kgs 14:29; 15:8–11.

ZACHARIAS (father of John the Baptist). Luke 1:5–79.

ZAMZUMMIMS (a race of giants who lived in the region later occupied by the Ammonites). Deut 2:20–21.

ZAREPHATH (a coastal town of Phoenicia where Elijah restored a widow's son to life). **1 Kgs 17:9–24** • Obad 20. *Sarepta:* Luke 4:26.

ZEAL
Ps 69:9 the *z* of thine house hath eaten me up
John 2:17 written, The *z* of thine house hath eaten me up
Phil 3:6 Concerning *z,* persecuting the church

ZEALOUS
Acts 21:20 Jews...which believe...are all *z* of the law
Acts 22:3 I [Paul]...was *z* toward God, as ye all are
Titus 2:14 purify unto himself [God] a peculiar people, *z* of good works

ZEBAH (a Midianite king killed by Gideon's army). Judg 8:4–28.

ZEBEDEE (father of James and John, disciples of Jesus). Matt 4:21–22; 10:2; 20:20; 26:37; 27:56 • Mark 1:19–20; 3:17; 10:35 • Luke 5:10 • John 21:2.

ZEBOIIM. See *Zeboim*.

ZEBOIM (a city destroyed along with Sodom and Gomorrah because of its sin). Gen 10:19 • **Deut 29:23** • Hos 11:8. *Zeboiim:* Gen 14:2,8.

ZEBULUN (a son of Jacob and ancestor of one of the twelve tribes of Israel). Gen 30:20; 35:23; 46:14; 49:13 • Ex 1:3 • 1 Chr 2:1. The tribe of Zebulun settled in northern Canaan. Josh 19:10–16. *Zabulon:* Matt 4:13.

ZECHARIAH (a prophet after the Exile and author of the book that bears his name). Ezra 5:1.

ZECHARIAH, BOOK OF. A prophetic book of the Old

Testament written to encourage the Jewish people during the difficult years after they returned from the Exile. Zechariah encouraged the people to complete the task of rebuilding the temple in Jerusalem.

ZEDEKIAH (the last king of Judah who ruled as a puppet king under King Nebuchadnezzar of Babylonia and who was often condemned by the prophet Jeremiah). **2 Kgs 24:15–20;** 25:2–7 • 1 Chr 3:15 • 2 Chr 36:10–11 • **Jer 21–52.** *Mattaniah:* 2 Kgs 24:17.

ZELOPHEHAD (an Israelite whose five daughters petitioned for the right to inherit his property because he had no sons). Num 26:33; **27:1–8.**

ZELOTES (a political-religious party of Jesus' time whose aim was to overthrow Roman rule and establish a Jewish theocracy). Luke 6:15.

ZEPHANIAH (a priest and friend of the prophet Jeremiah and author of the book that bears his name). 2 Kgs 25:18 • Jer 21:1; 29:25,29; 37:3; 52:24.

ZEPHANIAH, BOOK OF. A short prophetic book of the Old Testament known for its portrayal of the certainty of God's judgment against the nation of Judah (1:1–2:15). The prophet Zephaniah also declared that God would spare a faithful remnant (3:13), through which His promise of a future Messiah would be accomplished.

ZERUBBABEL (a Jewish leader who supervised the rebuilding of the temple in Jerusalem after the Exile). Hag 2:21–23 • **Zech 4:6–10.** *Sheshbazzar:* Ezra 5:14. *Zorobabel:* Matt 1:12–13.

ZIBA (a former servant of King Saul who helped David locate Jonathan's son Mephibosheth). 2 Sam 9:2–11.

ZIDON. See *Sidon.*

ZIKLAG (a city where David hid from King Saul). 1 Sam 27:5–6.

ZILPAH (Leah's maid who became a concubine of Jacob and bore two of his twelve sons, Gad and Asher). Gen 30:9–13.

ZIMRI (a chariot commander who assassinated King Elah of Israel and assumed the throne). 1 Kgs 16:8–20.

ZIN (a desert wilderness near the Dead Sea through which the Israelites passed). Num 13:21; 20:1; 27:14; 33:36; 34:3–4 • Deut 32:51 • Josh 15:1–3.

ZION (another name for the city of Jerusalem, particularly used in the Psalms). Pss 48:2, 11–12; 102:13–21; 137:1,3; 149:2 • Lam 2:1–18. *Sion:* Rev 14:1.

ZIPH (a city where David hid from King Saul). 1 Sam 23:14–18.

ZIPPORAH (wife of Moses). Ex 2:21–22; 4:25; 18:2.

ZOAR (a city destroyed along with Sodom and Gomorrah because of its sin). **Gen 19:20–25** • Deut 34:3 • Isa 15:5 • Jer 48:34. *Bela:* Gen 14:2.

ZOBAH (a Syrian kingdom that warred against King Saul). 1 Sam 14:47. *Hamath-zobah:* 2 Chr 8:3. *Zoba:* 2 Sam 10:6,8.

ZOPHAR (one of the three friends who comforted Job). His speeches appear in Job 11:1–20; 20:1–29.

ZOROBABEL.
See *Zerubbabel.*

NOTES

NOTES

NOTES

NOTES

NOTES

NOTES

NOTES